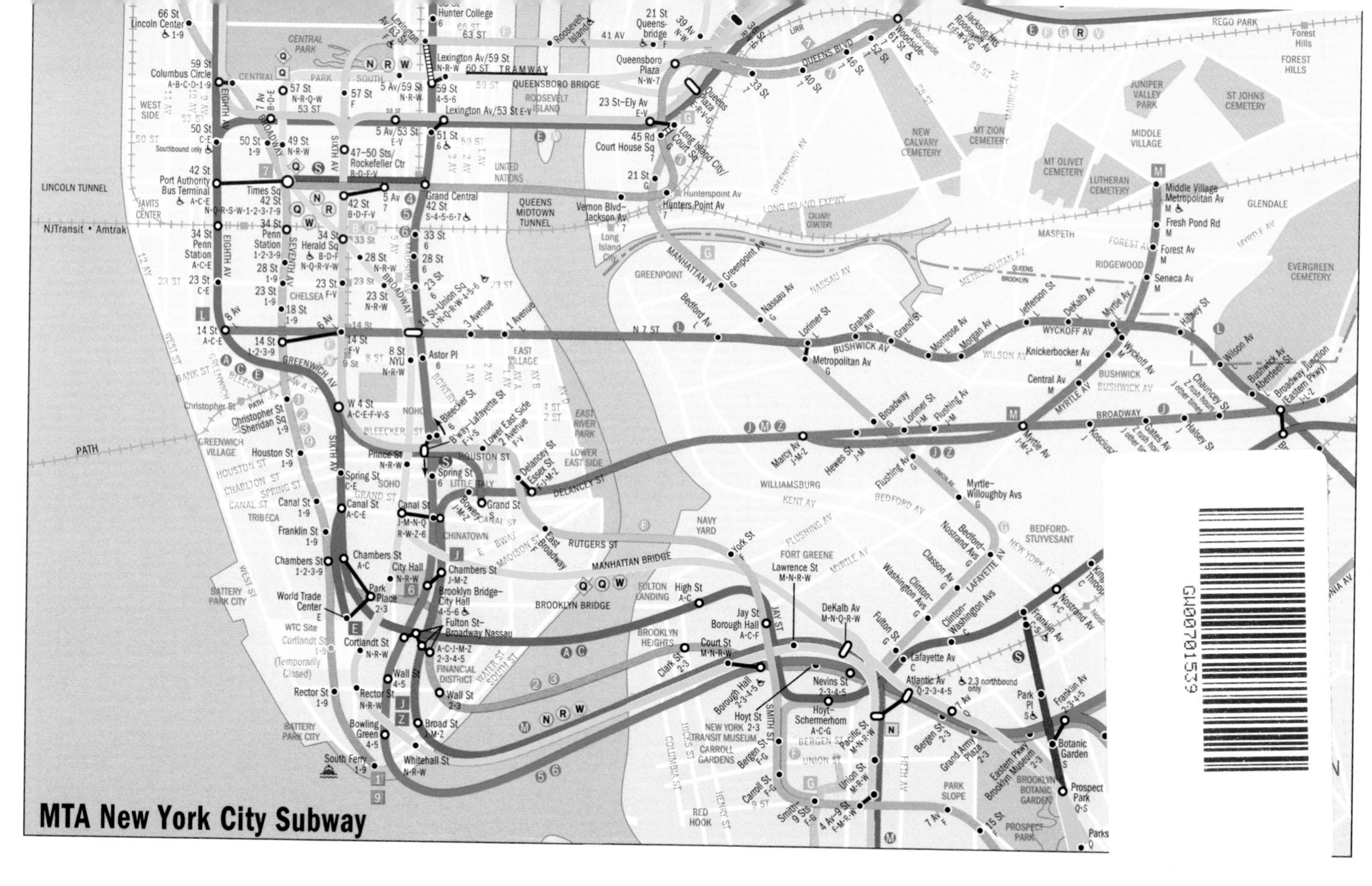
MTA New York City Subway
LINCOLN TUNNEL
NJTransit • Amtrak
PATH
CENTRAL PARK
WEST SIDE
66 St
Lincoln Center
59 St
Columbus Circle
A·B·C·D·1·9
50 St
42 St
Port Authority
Bus Terminal
34 St
Penn Station
14 St
Times Sq
42 St
Grand Central
42 St
Lexington Av/59 St
QUEENSBORO BRIDGE
ROOSEVELT ISLAND
UNITED NATIONS
QUEENS MIDTOWN TUNNEL
Queensboro Plaza
Queens Plaza
Long Island City/
Court Sq
Hunters Point Av
Vernon Blvd–
Jackson Av
GREENPOINT
WILLIAMSBURG
BEDFORD-STUYVESANT
NAVY YARD
FORT GREENE
MASPETH
RIDGEWOOD
MIDDLE VILLAGE
FOREST HILLS
REGO PARK
JUNIPER VALLEY PARK
ST JOHNS CEMETERY
NEW CALVARY CEMETERY
MT ZION CEMETERY
MT OLIVET CEMETERY
LUTHERAN CEMETERY
EVERGREEN CEMETERY
Middle Village
Metropolitan Av
Myrtle Av
Broadway Junction
(Eastern Pkwy)
14 St–Union Sq
Astor Pl
W 4 St
Christopher St
Sheridan Sq
Houston St
Canal St
Chambers St
World Trade Center
WTC Site
Cortlandt St
(Temporarily Closed)
Rector St
South Ferry
Bowling Green
Whitehall St
Wall St
Broad St
Fulton St–
Broadway Nassau
Brooklyn Bridge–
City Hall
City Hall
Park Place
GREENWICH VILLAGE
SOHO
TRIBECA
CHINATOWN
LITTLE ITALY
EAST VILLAGE
LOWER EAST SIDE
FINANCIAL DISTRICT
BATTERY PARK CITY
MANHATTAN BRIDGE
BROOKLYN BRIDGE
FULTON LANDING
BROOKLYN HEIGHTS
High St
Jay St
Borough Hall
Court St
Clark St
Lawrence St
DeKalb Av
Nevins St
Hoyt–Schermerhorn
Atlantic Av
Lafayette Av
Fulton St
NEW YORK TRANSIT MUSEUM
CARROLL GARDENS
RED HOOK
PARK SLOPE
PROSPECT PARK
BROOKLYN BOTANIC GARDEN
Botanic Garden
Prospect Park
Franklin Av
Nostrand Av
Eastern Pkwy
Brooklyn Museum
Grand Army Plaza
Bergen St
7 Av
Union St
4 Av–9 St
Smith–9 Sts
Carroll St
Marcy Av
Hewes St
Lorimer St
Flushing Av
Myrtle–
Willoughby Avs
Bedford–
Nostrand Avs
Classon Av
Clinton–
Washington Avs
Metropolitan Av
Bedford Av
Nassau Av
Greenpoint Av
Graham Av
Grand St
Montrose Av
Morgan Av
Jefferson St
DeKalb Av
Wyckoff Av
Halsey St
Wilson Av
Knickerbocker Av
Central Av
Chauncey St
Gates Av
Kosciuszko St
Seneca Av
Forest Av
Fresh Pond Rd
Woodside–
61 St
Jackson Hts
Roosevelt Av
52 St
46 St
40 St
33 St
21 St
Queensbridge
39 Av
23 St–Ely Av
45 Rd
Court House Sq
Delancey St
Essex St
East Broadway
Grand St
Bowery
Spring St
Prince St
Bleecker St
B'way–Lafayette St
Lower East Side
2 Avenue
1 Avenue
3 Avenue
TRAMWAY
Roosevelt Island
Hunter College

UNION SQUARE
W. 15th St.
E. 15th St.
W. 14th St.
E. 14th St.
10th Ave.
9th Ave.
8th Ave.
MEAT PACKING DISTRICT
Little W. 12th St.
Gansevoort St.
Horatio St.
Jane St.
W. 12th St.
Bethune St.
Bank St.
W. 11th St.
Perry St.
Charles St.
W. 10th St.
Christopher St.
Grove St.
West St.
Eighth Ave.
W. 4th St.
Greenwich Ave.
ABINGDON SQUARE
GREENWICH VILLAGE
Seventh Ave. S
W. 13th St.
(6th Ave.)
Milligan Pl.
Patchin Pl.
Avenue of the Americas
Gay St.
Waverly Pl.
SHERIDAN SQUARE
W. Washington Pl.
Jones St.
Cornelia St.
St. Luke's Chapel
Commerce St.
Bleecker St.
Bedford St.
Barrow St.
Greenwich St.
Morton St.
St. Lukes Pl.
Carmine St.
Downing St.
Leroy St.
Hudson St.
West St.
Clarkson St.
W. Houston St.
Washington St.
King St.
Charlton St.
Vandam St.
Spring St.
Dominick St.
Broome St.
Varick St.
Watts St.
Desbrosses St.
Vestry St.
Laight St.
Hubert St.
Beach St.
Ericsson Pl.
TRIBECA
Holland Tunnel
Joe Dimaggio Hwy. (West Side Hwy.)
W. 12th St.
Fifth Ave.
E. 11th St.
University Pl.
W. 10th St.
W. 9th St.
W. 8th St.
E. 8th St.
Macdougal Alley
Washington Mews
Waverly Pl.
Washington Square Park
Washington Sq. S
New York University
W. 3rd St.
Minetta La.
Ave. of the Americas (Sixth Ave.)
Macdougal St.
La Guardia Pl.
Bleecker St.
W. Houston St.
Sullivan St.
Thompson St.
West Broadway
New Museum of Contemporary Art
Museum for African Art
SOHO
Spring St.
Wooster St.
Greene St.
Mercer St.
Broadway
Crosby St.
Grand St.
Canal St.
Lispenard St.
Walker St.
White St.
Fourth Ave.
Grace Church
Astor Pl.
Broadway
Lafayette St.
Shinbone Al.
Jones Al.
Gt. Jones St.
Bond St.
NOHO
Prince St.
Cleveland Pl.
Centre St.
Howard St.
Baxter St.
LITTLE ITALY
CHINATOWN
Third Ave.
Second Ave.
St. Mark's in the Bowery
Stuyvesant St.
Cooper Union
COOPER SQUARE
First Ave.
St. Marks Pl.
E. 7th St.
E. 6th St.
E. 5th St.
E. 4th St.
E. 3rd St.
E. 2nd St.
E. 1st St.
Avenue A
E. 13th St.
E. 12th St.
E. 11th St.
E. 10th St.
E. 9th St.
E. 8th St.
Tompkins Square Park
EAST VILLAGE
Ave. B
Ave. C
Ave. D
FDR Drive
E. Houston St.
Clinton St.
Ridge St.
Pitt St.
Columbia St.
Stanton St.
Congregations Anshe Chesed
Rivington St.
Williamsburg Br.
Mulberry St.
Mott St.
The Bowery
Chrystie St.
Forsyth St.
Eldridge St.
Allen St.
Orchard St.
Ludlow St.
Essex St.
Norfolk St.
Suffolk St.
Willett St.
Lewis St.
Spring St.
Kenmare St.
Delancey St.
Broome St.
LES Tenement Museum
LOWER EAST SIDE
Elizabeth St.
The Bowery
Grand St.
Hester St.
Mahayana Buddhist Temple
Eldridge St. Synagogue
Canal St.
Division St.
Pike St.
Rutgers St.
East Broadway
Madison St.
Montgomery St.
Clinton St.
Cherry St.
South St.
Water St.
Jackson St.

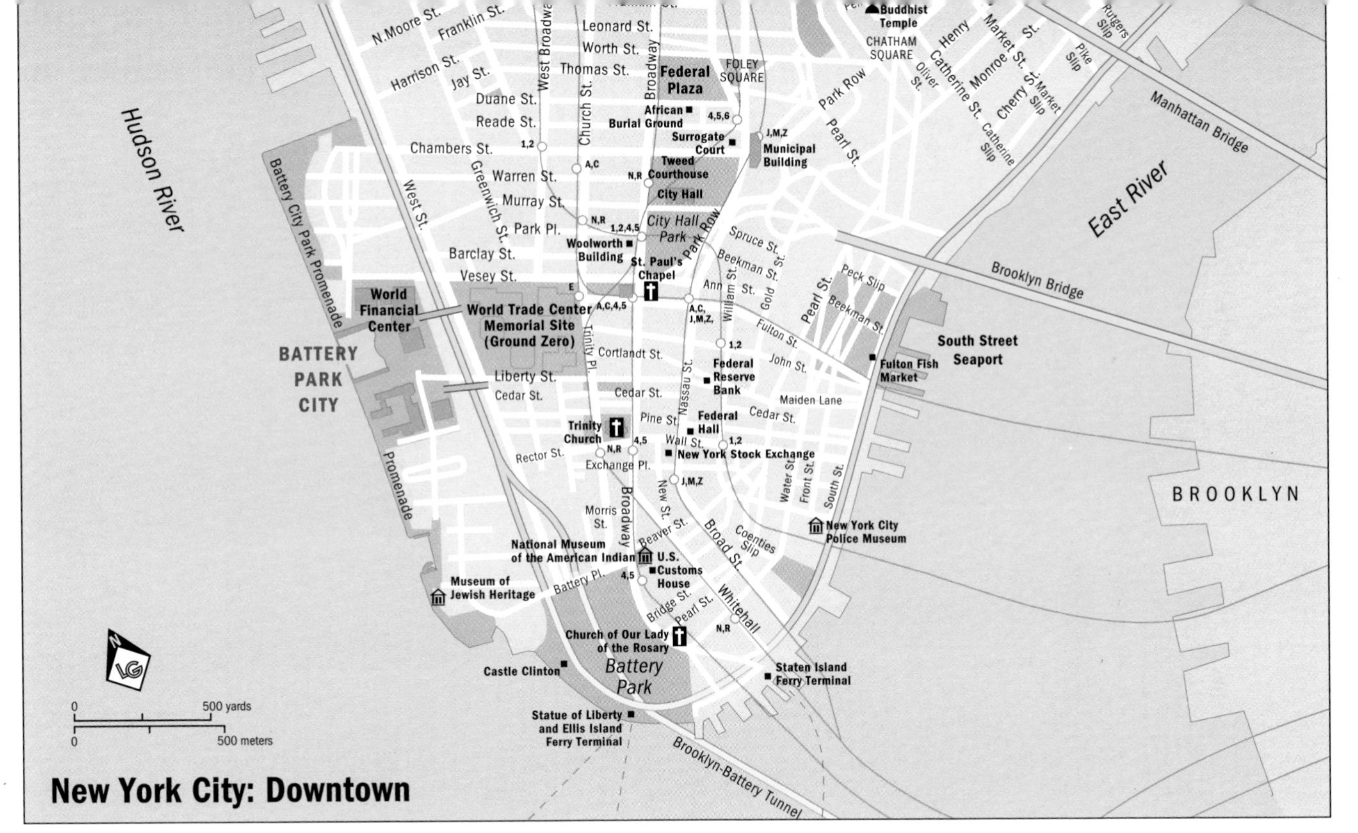
New York City: Downtown
Hudson River
East River
BROOKLYN
BATTERY PARK CITY
Battery City Park Promenade
Promenade
World Financial Center
World Trade Center Memorial Site (Ground Zero)
Federal Plaza
FOLEY SQUARE
CHATHAM SQUARE
Buddhist Temple
African Burial Ground
Surrogate Court
Municipal Building
Tweed Courthouse
City Hall
City Hall Park
Woolworth Building
St. Paul's Chapel
Federal Reserve Bank
Federal Hall
New York Stock Exchange
Trinity Church
South Street Seaport
Fulton Fish Market
New York City Police Museum
National Museum of the American Indian
U.S. Customs House
Museum of Jewish Heritage
Church of Our Lady of the Rosary
Battery Park
Castle Clinton
Statue of Liberty and Ellis Island Ferry Terminal
Staten Island Ferry Terminal
Brooklyn-Battery Tunnel
Brooklyn Bridge
Manhattan Bridge
N.Moore St.
Franklin St.
Harrison St.
Jay St.
Duane St.
Reade St.
Chambers St.
Warren St.
Murray St.
Park Pl.
Barclay St.
Vesey St.
Greenwich St.
West St.
West Broadway
Church St.
Broadway
Leonard St.
Worth St.
Thomas St.
Liberty St.
Cedar St.
Cortlandt St.
Trinity Pl.
Pine St.
Wall St.
Rector St.
Exchange Pl.
Morris St.
Battery Pl.
Beaver St.
New St.
Broad St.
Bridge St.
Pearl St.
Whitehall
Coenties Slip
Water St.
Front St.
South St.
Maiden Lane
John St.
Fulton St.
Nassau St.
William St.
Ann St.
Gold St.
Beekman St.
Spruce St.
Park Row
Peck Slip
Henry
Market St.
Monroe St.
Catherine St.
Oliver St.
Cherry St.
Market Slip
Catherine Slip
Pike Slip
Rutgers Slip
1,2
A,C
N,R
1,2,4,5
E
A,C,4,5
4,5,6
J,M,Z
A,C, J,M,Z,
4,5
J,M,Z
0
500 yards
500 meters

New York City: Midtown
W. 60th St.
W. 59th St.
W. 58th St.
W. 57th St.
W. 56th St.
W. 55th St.
W. 54th St.
W. 53rd St.
W. 52nd St.
W. 51st St.
W. 50th St.
W. 49th St.
W. 48th St.
W. 47th St.
W. 46th St.
W. 45th St.
W. 44th St.
W. 43rd St.
W. 42nd St.
W. 41st St.
W. 39th St.
W. 34th St.
W. 31st St.
W. 30th St.
W. 29th St.
W. 28th St.
W. 27th St.
W. 23rd St.
W. 14th St.
St. Paul the Apostle
COLUMBUS CIRCLE
Central Park S
Carnegie Hall
NYC & Company Convention & Visitors Bureau
Twelfth Ave.
Eleventh Ave.
Tenth Ave.
Ninth Ave.
Eighth Ave.
Seventh Ave.
Broadway
Dyer Ave.
Intrepid Sea-Air-Space Museum
Schubert Theater
New York Times Building
TIMES SQUARE
Tow Ha
Port Authority Bus Terminal
Lincoln Tunnel
Jacob K. Javits Convention Center
HELL'S KITCHEN
GARMENT DISTRICT
Macy'
General Post Office
Madison Square Garden
Penn Station
Hudson River
Joe Dimaggio Hwy.
General Theological Seminary
Chelsea Hotel
Cushman Row
CHELSEA
0 500 yards
0 500 meters
A,B,C,D,1,2
N,Q,R,W
B,D,E
C,E
1
N,R,W
1,2,3,N,Q,R,S
A,C,E
7
1,2,3
1,2
A,C,E,L
1,2,3,L

Grand Army Plaza
E. 60th St.
N,R,W
Roosevelt Island Tramway
Queensboro Bridge
E. 59th St.
4,5,6
Bloomingdale's
Plaza Hotel
F.A.O. Schwarz
E. 58th St.
Madison-Lexington Venture Building
E. 57th St.
Second Ave.
First Ave.
Third Ave.
Marlborough Gallery
Trump Tower
IBM Building
E. 56th St.
E. 55th St.
E. 54th St.
Museum of Modern Art
St. Thomas
Museum of Television & Radio
Central Synagogue
Citicorp Center
St. Peter's
Seagram Building
E. 53rd St.
CBS Building
E. 52nd St.
St. Patrick's Cathedral
Radio City Music Hall
E. 51st St.
B,D,F
St. Batholemew's
E. 50th St.
Rockefeller Center
Sak's Fifth Avenue
Waldorf-Astoria Hotel
E. 49th St.
TURTLE BAY
E. 48th St.
Fifth Ave.
Madison Ave.
Park Ave.
Lexington Ave.
E. 47th St.
United Nations
E. 46th St.
Met Life Building
E. 45th St.
Algonquin Hotel
E. 44th St.
Grand Central Terminal
4,5,6,S
Chrysler Building
E. 43rd St.
Ford Foundation
B,D,F,V
7
E. 42nd St.
Bryant Park
New York Public Library
Whitney Museum Branch
Daily News Building
E. 41st St.
Queens-Midtown Tunnel
W. 40th St.
E. 40th St.
American Standard Building
E. 39th St.
FDR Dr.
MURRAY HILL
W. 38th St.
E. 38th St.
East River
W. 37th St.
E. 37th St.
Pierpont Morgan Library
W. 36th St.
E. 36th St.
W. 35th St.
E. 35th St.
HERALD SQUARE
B,D,F,N, Q,R,V,W
Empire State Building
E. 34th St.
W. 33rd St.
E. 33rd St.
International Student Hospice
W. 32nd St.
E. 32nd St.
E. 31st St.
E. 30th St.
E. 29th St.
N,R
E. 28th St.
E. 27th St.
Avenue of the Americas (6th Ave.)
W. 26th St.
Madison Square Park
E. 26th St.
W. 25th St.
E. 25th St.
Metropolitan Life Insurance Buildings
W. 24th St.
E. 24th St.
Park Ave. S.
E. 23rd St.
Flatiron Building
Peter Cooper Rd.
W. 22nd St.
E. 22nd St.
Broadway
W. 21st St.
Gramercy Park
E. 21st St.
W. 20th St.
E. 20th St.
GRAMERCY PARK
W. 19th St.
Theodore Roosevelt Birthplace
E. 19th St.
Irving Pl.
W. 18th St.
E. 18th St.
W. 17th St.
E. 17th St.
Union Square Park
W. 16th St.
E. 16th St.
STUYVESANT SQUARE
W. 15th St.
E. 15th St.
F,L,V
N,R,Q,W
L,4,5,6
L
W. 14th St.
E. 14th St.
Ave. A
Ave. B
Ave. C

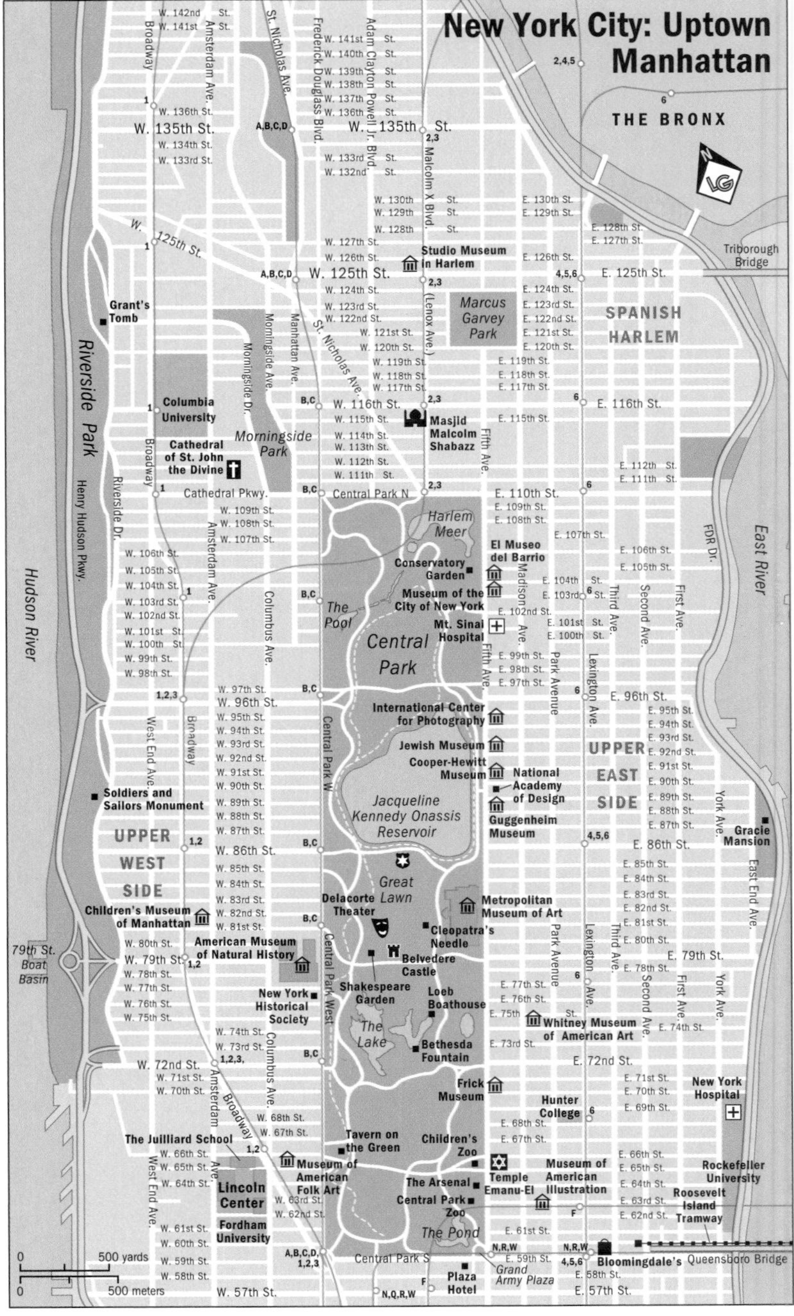
New York City: Uptown Manhattan
THE BRONX
SPANISH HARLEM
UPPER EAST SIDE
UPPER WEST SIDE
Hudson River
East River
Riverside Park
Central Park
Morningside Park
Marcus Garvey Park
Jacqueline Kennedy Onassis Reservoir
Great Lawn
Harlem Meer
The Pool
The Lake
The Pond
Grant's Tomb
Columbia University
Cathedral of St. John the Divine
Studio Museum in Harlem
Masjid Malcolm Shabazz
El Museo del Barrio
Conservatory Garden
Museum of the City of New York
Mt. Sinai Hospital
International Center for Photography
Jewish Museum
Cooper-Hewitt Museum
National Academy of Design
Guggenheim Museum
Soldiers and Sailors Monument
Children's Museum of Manhattan
American Museum of Natural History
New York Historical Society
Delacorte Theater
Metropolitan Museum of Art
Cleopatra's Needle
Belvedere Castle
Shakespeare Garden
Loeb Boathouse
Bethesda Fountain
Whitney Museum of American Art
Frick Museum
Hunter College
Gracie Mansion
New York Hospital
Rockefeller University
Roosevelt Island Tramway
Queensboro Bridge
Triborough Bridge
The Juilliard School
Lincoln Center
Fordham University
Museum of American Folk Art
Tavern on the Green
Children's Zoo
The Arsenal
Central Park Zoo
Temple Emanu-El
Museum of American Illustration
Bloomingdale's
Plaza Hotel
Grand Army Plaza
79th St. Boat Basin
Broadway
Amsterdam Ave.
Columbus Ave.
Central Park West
West End Ave.
Riverside Dr.
Henry Hudson Pkwy.
St. Nicholas Ave.
Frederick Douglass Blvd.
Adam Clayton Powell Jr. Blvd
Malcolm X Blvd. (Lenox Ave.)
Morningside Dr.
Morningside Ave.
Manhattan Ave.
Fifth Ave.
Madison Ave.
Park Avenue
Lexington Ave.
Third Ave.
Second Ave.
First Ave.
York Ave.
East End Ave.
FDR Dr.
W. 135th St.
W. 125th St.
W. 116th St.
Cathedral Pkwy.
Central Park N
E. 110th St.
W. 96th St.
E. 96th St.
W. 86th St.
E. 86th St.
W. 79th St.
E. 79th St.
W. 72nd St.
E. 72nd St.
E. 125th St.
E. 116th St.
Central Park S
W. 57th St.
E. 57th St.
0 500 yards
0 500 meters

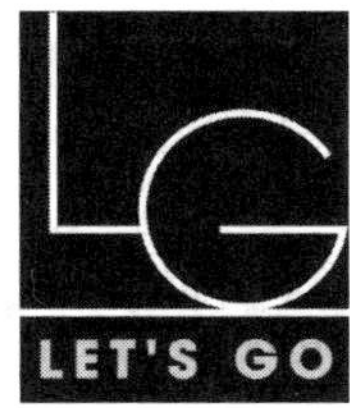

■ THE RESOURCE FOR THE INDEPENDENT TRAVELER

"The guides are aimed not only at young budget travelers but at the indepedent traveler; a sort of streetwise cookbook for traveling alone."

—The New York Times

"Unbeatable; good sight-seeing advice; up-to-date info on restaurants, hotels, and inns; a commitment to money-saving travel; and a wry style that brightens nearly every page."

—The Washington Post

"Lighthearted and sophisticated, informative and fun to read. [Let's Go] helps the novice traveler navigate like a knowledgeable old hand."

—Atlanta Journal-Constitution

"A world-wise traveling companion—always ready with friendly advice and helpful hints, all sprinkled with a bit of wit."

—The Philadelphia Inquirer

■ THE BEST TRAVEL BARGAINS IN YOUR PRICE RANGE

"All the dirt, dirt cheap."

—People

"Anything you need to know about budget traveling is detailed in this book."

—The Chicago Sun-Times

"Let's Go follows the creed that you don't have to toss your life's savings to the wind to travel—unless you want to."

—The Salt Lake Tribune

■ REAL ADVICE FOR REAL EXPERIENCES

"The writers seem to have experienced every rooster-packed bus and lunar-surfaced mattress about which they write."

—The New York Times

"A guide should tell you what to expect from a destination. Here Let's Go shines."

—The Chicago Tribune

"Let's Go's] devoted updaters really walk the walk (and thumb the ride, and trek the trail). Learn how to fish, haggle, find work—anywhere."

—Food & Wine

LET'S GO PUBLICATIONS

TRAVEL GUIDES

Alaska 1st edition **NEW TITLE**
Australia 2004
Austria & Switzerland 2004
Brazil 1st edition **NEW TITLE**
Britain & Ireland 2004
California 2004
Central America 8th edition
Chile 1st edition
China 4th edition
Costa Rica 1st edition
Eastern Europe 2004
Egypt 2nd edition
Europe 2004
France 2004
Germany 2004
Greece 2004
Hawaii 2004
India & Nepal 8th edition
Ireland 2004
Israel 4th edition
Italy 2004
Japan 1st edition **NEW TITLE**
Mexico 20th edition
Middle East 4th edition
New Zealand 6th edition
Pacific Northwest 1st edition **NEW TITLE**
Peru, Ecuador & Bolivia 3rd edition
Puerto Rico 1st edition **NEW TITLE**
South Africa 5th edition
Southeast Asia 8th edition
Southwest USA 3rd edition
Spain & Portugal 2004
Thailand 1st edition
Turkey 5th edition
USA 2004
Western Europe 2004

CITY GUIDES

Amsterdam 2004 3rd Edition
Barcelona 2004 3rd Edition
Boston 2004 4th Edition
London 2004
New York City 2004
Paris 2004
Rome 2004 12th Edition
San Francisco 2004 4th Edition
Washington, D.C. 2004 13th Edition

MAP GUIDES

Amsterdam
Berlin
Boston
Chicago
Dublin
Florence
Hong Kong
London
Los Angeles
Madrid
New Orleans
New York City
Paris
Prague
Rome
San Francisco
Seattle
Sydney
Venice
Washington, D.C.

COMING SOON:

Road Trip USA

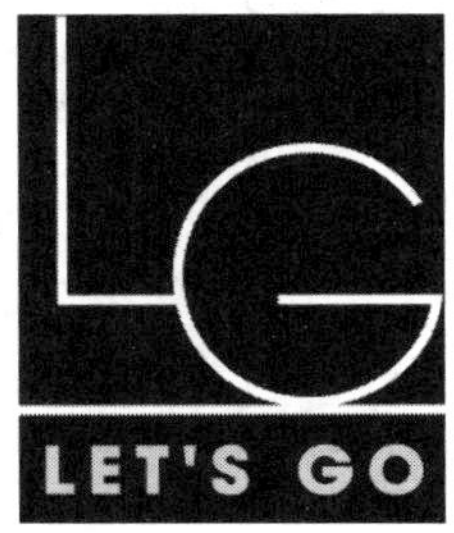

NEW YORK CITY 2004

DAVID A. PARKER EDITOR

MEGAN MORAN-GATES ASSOCIATE EDITOR

RESEARCHER-WRITERS
MONIQUE C. JAMES
ANGELA E. KIM
JAMES M. SCHAFFER

AMELIA AOS SHOWALTER MAP EDITOR
JOANNA SHAWN BRIGID O'LEARY MANAGING EDITOR

MACMILLAN

HELPING LET'S GO If you want to share your discoveries, suggestions, or corrections, please drop us a line. We read every piece of correspondence, whether a postcard, a 10-page email, or a coconut. **Address mail to:**

Let's Go: New York City
67 Mount Auburn Street
Cambridge, MA 02138
USA

Visit Let's Go at **http://www.letsgo.com,** or send email to:

feedback@letsgo.com
Subject: "Let's Go: New York City"

In addition to the invaluable travel advice our readers share with us, many are kind enough to offer their services as researchers or editors. Unfortunately, our charter enables us to employ only currently enrolled Harvard students.

Published in Great Britain 2004 by Macmillan, an imprint of Pan Macmillan Ltd.
20 New Wharf Road, London N1 9RR
Basingstoke and Oxford
Associated companies throughout the world
www.panmacmillan.com

Maps by David Lindroth copyright © 2004 by St. Martin's Press.

Published in the United States of America by St. Martin's Press.

ISBN: 1 4050 3327 4
First edition
10 9 8 7 6 5 4 3 2 1

Let's Go: New York City is written by Let's Go Publications, 67 Mount Auburn Street, Cambridge, MA 02138, USA.

ADVERTISING DISCLAIMER All advertisements appearing in Let's Go publications are sold by an independent agency not affiliated with the editorial production of the guides. Advertisers are never given preferential treatment, and the guides are researched, written, and published independent of advertising. Advertisements do not imply endorsement of products or services by Let's Go, and Let's Go does not vouch for the accuracy of information provided in advertisements.

If you are interested in purchasing advertising space in a Let's Go publication, contact: Let's Go Advertising Sales, 67 Mount Auburn St., Cambridge, MA 02138, USA.

HOW TO USE THIS BOOK

PRICE DIVERSITY AND RANKINGS. Our favorite palces are denoted by the Let's Go thumbs-up (☒). Since the best value does not always mean the cheapest, we have incorporated a system of price ranges in the guide. Each listing is followed by a price icon, from ❶ to ❺. You can find an explanation of these ranges for **Food** (see p. 149) and for **Accommodations** (see p. 255).

ORGANIZATION. The coverage in this book is divided into the five boroughs, which themselves are often broken down into smaller neighborhoods. Read **Discover NYC** to get acquainted with the specifc neighborhoods of New York City.

FEATURES AND ARTICLES. Throughout this book, you'll find sidebars in black boxes and longer articles—built-in reading material for the airplane, long lines, or afternoons at a cafe. Don't miss the book's longer article: a guided tour with NYC's former Parks Commissioner through some of Manhattan's unknown emerald gems.

WHEN TO USE IT

ONE-TWO MONTHS BEFORE YOU GO. **Planning Your Trip** (p. 295) has advice about passports, plane tickets, insurance, and more. **Accommodations** (p. 255) can help you with booking a room from home.

2 WEEKS BEFORE YOU GO. Start thinking about your ideal trip. **Discover NYC** (p. 1) lists 8 Things To Do In NYC, a few suggested itineraries, some maps to get you acquainted with the five boroughs, and the scoop on each of the city's neighborhoods. Read up on New York history in the **Life & Times** chapter (p. 41).

ON THE ROAD. **Once in NYC** (p. 27) will be your best friend once you've arrived, with all the practical information you'll need. When you feel like striking out of the city, the **Daytripping** (p. 279) chapter will help; it provides options for daytrips, weekend trips, and roadtrips in the Bay Area and beyond. The **Service Directory** (p. 323) contains a list of local services. Should you decide that you want to do something more than see the sights, turn to **Alternatives to Tourism** (p. 309) for information on volunteering, studying, and working in New York. Finally, just remember to put down this guide once in a while and explore on your own; you'll be glad you did.

A NOTE TO OUR READERS The information for this book was gathered by *Let's Go* researchers from May through August of 2003. Each listing is based on one researcher's opinion, formed during his or her visit at a particular time. Those traveling at other times may have different experiences since prices, dates, hours, and conditions are always subject to change. You are urged to check the facts presented in this book beforehand to avoid inconvenience and surprises.

Contents

discover nyc 1

the five boroughs 1
8 things to do in nyc 21
suggested itineraries 22
sightseeing tours 24

once in nyc 27

getting into new york 27
getting around new york 29
keeping in touch 32
getting money from home 35
safety and security 36
local life in new york 37

life & times 41

traders and traitors 41
worms in the big apple 42
the new metropolis 43
the world's capital 43
new york today 45

sights 47

manhattan 47
brooklyn 103
queens 112
the bronx 118
staten island 123

museums & galleries 127

museums by neighborhood 128
museum directory 128
galleries 142

food & drink 149

listings by type of food 150
listings by neighborhood 153
financial district and civic center 153 chinatown 154
little italy 156 nolita 157
lower east side 158 tribeca 160
soho 160 greenwich village 161
east village 164
chelsea and herald square 169
union square, gramercy, and murray hill 171
the theater district and hell's kitchen 173 midtown 174
upper east side 175
upper west side 176
morningside heights 178
harlem and washington heights 179
brooklyn 181 queens 187
the bronx 189 staten island 191

nightlife 193

bars and lounges 193
dance clubs 208

entertainment 211

dance 211
film 214
music 216
theater 223
sports 231

shopping 239

shopping by type 239
shopping by neighborhood 241
financial district and civic center 241
chinatown and little italy 241
lower east side 242
soho 243 greenwich village 244
east village 246 chelsea and the flatiron district 248
herald square 249
midtown 250
upper east side 251
upper west side 251
brooklyn 252

accommodations 255

hostels 257
bed and breakfasts 257
hotels 259
accommodations by price 259
accommodations by neighborhood 261
little italy 261
greenwich village 261
east village 261
union square, gramercy, and murray hill 263
chelsea 264
herald square 265
midtown 267
times square and theater district 267
upper east side 269
upper west side 270
harlem 271
brooklyn 273
queens 275
long-term accommodations 275

daytripping 279

long island 279
hudson valley 287
the catskills 289
new jersey 289
connecticut 292

planning your trip 295

embassies and consulates 295
documents and formalities 295
money 297
health 298
insurance 299
packing 299
getting to new york 300
specific concerns 303
public holidays in 2004 307

alternatives to tourism 309

volunteering 312
studying 315
working 317

service directory 323

index 329

map appendix 352

greater new york 2 - 3
brooklyn 4 - 5
the bronx 8 - 9
manhattan 16
staten island 17
queens 18 - 19
long island 281
atlantic city 291
new york metropolitan area 354 - 355
greater new york 356 - 357
manhattan 358 - 359
lower manhattan 360 - 361
chinatown & little italy 362 - 363
soho & tribeca 364 - 365
greenwich village 366 - 368
lower east side 369
east village 370 - 371
lower midtown 372 - 374
midtown 375 - 377
upper east side 378 - 379
central park north 380 - 381
upper west side 382 - 383
washington heights 384
harlem & morningside heights 384 - 385
brooklyn 386 - 387
williamsburg & greenpoint 388
brooklyn heights & downtown brooklyn 389
park slope & prospect park 390
carroll gardens & red hook 391
queens 392 - 393
astoria & long island city 394
flushing & corona 395
the bronx 396 - 397
staten island 398
downtown bus routes 399
uptown bus routes 400

PRICE RANGES>>NEW YORK

Our researchers list establishments in order of value from best to worst; our favorites are denoted by the Let's Go thumbs-up (☒). Since the best value is not always the cheapest price, we have incorporated a system of price ranges for quick reference. Our price ranges are based on a rough expectation of what you will spend. For **accommodations,** we base our price range off the cheapest price for which a single traveler can stay for one night. For **restaurants** and other dining establishments, we estimate the average amount that you will spend in that restaurant. The table below tells you what you will *typically* find in New York at the corresponding price range; keep in mind that a particularly expensive ice cream stand may still only be marked a ❷, depending on what you will spend.

ACCOMMODATIONS	RANGE	WHAT YOU'RE *LIKELY* TO FIND
❶	under $40	Dorm rooms or dorm-style rooms. Expect bunk beds and a communal bath; you may have to provide or rent towels and sheets.
❷	$40-80	Upper-end hostels or small hotels. You may have a private bathroom, or there may be a sink in your room and communal shower in the hall.
❸	$81-100	A small room with a private bath. Should have decent amenities, such as phone and TV. Breakfast may be included in the price of the room.
❹	$101-120	Similar to 3, but may have more amenities or be in a more touristed area.
❺	$121+	Large hotels or upscale chains. If it's a 5 and it doesn't have the perks you want, you've paid too much.
FOOD		
❶	under $7	Mostly street-corner stands, pizza places, or fast-food joints. Rarely ever a sit-down meal.
❷	$7-12	Some sandwiches and take-out options, but also quite a few ethnic restaurants or options outside of Manhattan.
❸	$13-18	Entrees are more expensive, but chances are, you're paying for decor and ambience.
❹	$19-30	As in 3, the higher prices are probably related to better service, but in these restaurants, the food will tend to be a little fancier or more elaborate.
❺	$31+	If you're not getting delicious food with great service in a well-appointed space, you're paying for nothing more than hype.

RESEARCHER-WRITERS

Monique C. James

Brooklyn wasn't enough for Monique. After fully conquering the fullest of the boroughs (and coming to the conclusion that it might be a pretty nice place to live), this Miami native worked her way through Manhattan's biggest neighborhood and Harlem might never be the same. Even with all of this, she still had time to visit every spot on the Museum Mile and fit in some shopping in SoHo.

Angela E. Kim

Hailing from Los Angeles, Angela quickly picked up the New York hustle and with her quick-witted savvy, it wouldn't be surprising to find her on the winning end of some three-card monte in Times Square. The galleries of Chelsea and diners of Queens will have to do without her visits: she's off to law school.

James M. Schaffer

Raised in Manhattan and educated in Brooklyn, James has since added Queens, Staten Island, and the Bronx to his repertoire of boroughs. A peace-loving philosopher of sorts, James knows more about the East Village than should be allowed. As true a New Yorker as can be found, James could always be counted on for a frank assessment, an extended metaphor, or a big hug. Hurray for James!

Jennifer Jue-Steuck *Atlantic City*

Heather Schofield *Foxwoods and Mohegan Sun*

CONTRIBUTING WRITERS

Henry J. Stern *"New York Parks"*

Currently the president of NYCivic, Henry Stern has served the City of New York as a member of the City Council and as Commissioner of Parks and Recreation, a position he held for fifteen years.

Eric Goldwyn *"Bubblin' Up"*

A graduate of Bowdoin College, Eric is currently a successful magazine publisher, T-shirt designer for Mel Hagopian Clothing, and producer of beats for underground rapper Sassafrass McJazz. He was born and raised in Manhattan, where he still lives. He loves tapioca pearls and the New York Mets.

ACKNOWLEDGMENTS

DAVID THANKS: Shawn Badlani, John Barkett, Sara Barnett, Fritz Behr, Michael Bloomberg, Camelback, Zebra Chime, James Crawford, Dunia Dickey, Danny Garcia, Suzanne Gershowitz, Sarah Heyward, Joe Hickey, Monique James, Abigail Joseph, Colin Jost, Angela Kim, Sandy Koufax, Talib Kweli, Miranda Lash, Foghorn Leghorn, Sarah Levine-Gronningsater, Stef Levner, Dusty Lewis, Todd Liu, Matt Mahan, Sassafrass McJazz, Steve Mott, Mike Murphy, Apurva Patel, Rebecca Podolsky, Jose Reyes, Eliah Seton, Megan Smith, Kuzzi Smooth, Andrew Sodroski, Henry Stern (StarQuest), The Man With The White Beard, Mookie Wilson, and Tim and Nina Zagat.

Special thanks to Rob Cacace, Eric Goldwyn, Eve Marson, Megan Moran-Gates, Joanna O'Leary, Sarah Robinson, James Schaffer, and the Delta Shuttle.

Love and gratitude to Diane, Emily, and Mel Parker.

This goes out to Manhattan, the Island of Staten, Brooklyn and Queens is living phat, and the Boogie Down, enough props enough clout…dedicated to the eight million.

MEGAN THANKS: Dave, for being your unique self, playing with the zebra chime, and putting together a book in your spare time. Scrobins, thanks for the unrelenting support, cookies, and laughs. To the rest of the pod: the absurd discussions, constant distractions, and tomfoolery were much appreciated. Special thanks to Chez Renard for good times and a rent-free summer. As always, Mom, Dad, Taylor, Adri, and Rob: thanks for your love and friendship.

AMELIA THANKS: Joanna for everything, Mapland for laughter and late nights, my family for love and the Ford Explorer, and Amanda for being the best partner in crime around.

Editor
David A. Parker
Associate Editor
Megan Moran-Gates
Managing Editor
Joanna Shawn Brigid O'Leary
Map Editor Amelia Aos Showalter
Photographer Luke Marion
Typesetter Jeffrey Hoffman Yip

INSIDE

the five boroughs **1**

the bronx **6** brooklyn **6**

manhattan **11** queens **20**

staten island **21**

8 things to do in nyc **21**

suggested itineraries **22**

sightseeing tours **24**

Discover NYC

There's no one truth about New York. It can be anything to anybody, and often is. Don't trust anybody who begins a sentence with the words "you know you're a real New Yorker when..." New York belongs to nobody, but even more than that, it belongs to everybody (i.e. you). *Let's Go* is a guide, nothing more. We'll help you find a place to stay, suggest a good choice for lunch, even give our opinions about a museum or two. But there's only one way to 'discover' New York: on your own. We'll do our best to make it easy for you.

THE FIVE BOROUGHS

New York City is made up of **five boroughs:** the Bronx, Brooklyn, Manhattan, Queens, and Staten Island. For quick reference, Manhattan is the one everyone's heard of, Queens is the biggest in size (and the most diverse), Brooklyn has the most people (by itself, it would be the fourth-largest city in America), the Bronx is the only part of New York City physically connected to the United States, and Staten Island is the most residential.

Totowa
80
46
46
4
Hackensack
46
Passaic
80
95
95
3
17
46
Caldwell
Garden State Pkwy.
21
3
Montclair
280
1
9
Secaucus
Hudson River
95
Passaic River
Hackensack River
(East)
Weehawken
9A
Ninth Ave.
East Orange
Kearny
(West)
95
495
Union City
Tenth Ave.
57th St.
Lincoln Tunnel
Newark
280
West Side Hwy.
Second Ave.
Pulaski Skyway
1
9
Hoboken
14th St.
E. River Dr.
Houston St.
Holland Tunnel
East R.
78
Jersey City
World Trade Center Site
22
78
Brooklyn Bridge
Ellis Is.
Newark Internat'l Airport
95
N.J. Tnpk. Ext.
278
Bayonne
Liberty Is.
Newark Bay
Brooklyn-Battery Tunnel
81
440
Elizabeth
FERRY
Upper New York Bay
Ocean Pkwy.
Bayonne Br.
Kill Van Kull
Gowanus Expwy.
Goethals Bridge
Ft. Hamilton Pkwy.
1
9
440
278
Staten Island Expwy.
STATEN ISLAND
Verrazano-Narrows Bridge
New Jersey Tnpk.
Belt Pkwy.
95
Lower New York Bay
West Shore Expwy.
Arthur Kill
Outerbridge Crossing

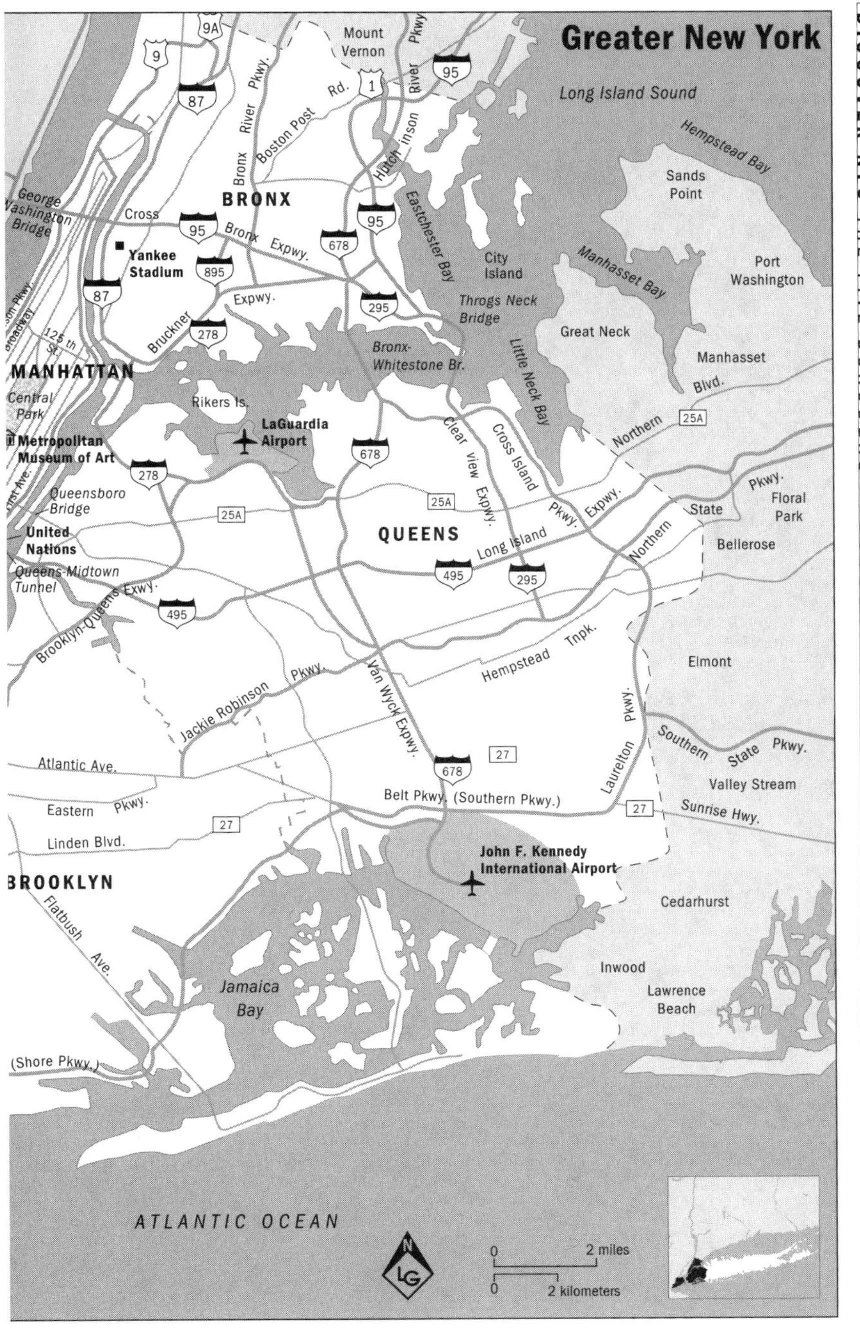
Greater New York
Long Island Sound
Hempstead Bay
Sands Point
Port Washington
Manhasset Bay
Great Neck
Manhasset
Mount Vernon
City Island
Throgs Neck Bridge
Bronx-Whitestone Br.
Eastchester Bay
Little Neck Bay
BRONX
Yankee Stadium
George Washington Bridge
MANHATTAN
Central Park
Metropolitan Museum of Art
United Nations
Queensboro Bridge
Queens-Midtown Tunnel
Rikers Is.
LaGuardia Airport
QUEENS
Floral Park
Bellerose
Elmont
Valley Stream
BROOKLYN
John F. Kennedy International Airport
Cedarhurst
Inwood
Lawrence Beach
Jamaica Bay
ATLANTIC OCEAN
Cross Bronx Expwy.
Bruckner Expwy.
Bronx River Pkwy.
Boston Post Rd.
Hutchinson River Pkwy.
Clearview Expwy.
Cross Island Pkwy.
Long Island Expwy.
Northern Blvd.
Northern State Pkwy.
Brooklyn-Queens Exwy.
Jackie Robinson Pkwy.
Hempstead Tnpk.
Van Wyck Expwy.
Laurelton Pkwy.
Southern State Pkwy.
Belt Pkwy. (Southern Pkwy.)
Sunrise Hwy.
Atlantic Ave.
Eastern Pkwy.
Linden Blvd.
Flatbush Ave.
(Shore Pkwy.)
125th St.
Broadway
9A
9
87
1
95
678
895
295
278
25A
495
27
0
2 miles
2 kilometers
N
LG

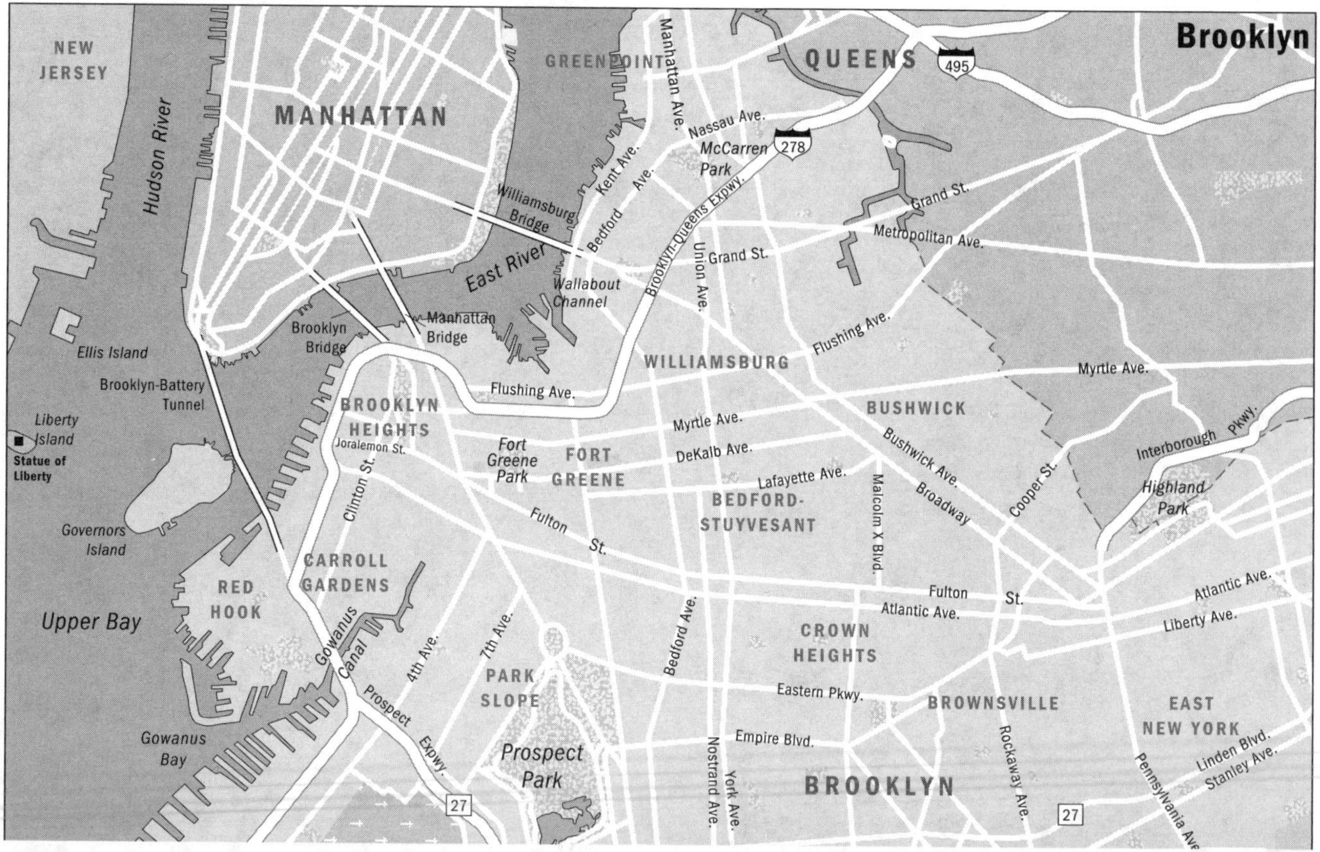

Brooklyn

NEW JERSEY
MANHATTAN
GREENPOINT
QUEENS
495
Hudson River
Manhattan Ave.
Nassau Ave.
McCarren Park
278
Kent Ave.
Bedford Ave.
Williamsburg Bridge
Brooklyn-Queens Expwy.
Grand St.
Metropolitan Ave.
Union Ave.
East River
Wallabout Channel
Brooklyn Bridge
Manhattan Bridge
Ellis Island
Flushing Ave.
WILLIAMSBURG
Myrtle Ave.
Brooklyn-Battery Tunnel
BROOKLYN HEIGHTS
BUSHWICK
Liberty Island
Statue of Liberty
Joralemon St.
Fort Greene Park
FORT GREENE
DeKalb Ave.
Bushwick Ave.
Interborough Pkwy.
Lafayette Ave.
Malcolm X Blvd.
Highland Park
BEDFORD-STUYVESANT
Broadway
Cooper St.
Clinton St.
Governors Island
Fulton St.
CARROLL GARDENS
RED HOOK
Atlantic Ave.
Liberty Ave.
Upper Bay
Bedford Ave.
CROWN HEIGHTS
Gowanus Canal
4th Ave.
7th Ave.
PARK SLOPE
Eastern Pkwy.
BROWNSVILLE
EAST NEW YORK
Prospect Expwy.
Empire Blvd.
Gowanus Bay
Prospect Park
Nostrand Ave.
York Ave.
BROOKLYN
Rockaway Ave.
Linden Blvd.
Stanley Ave.
Pennsylvania Ave.
27

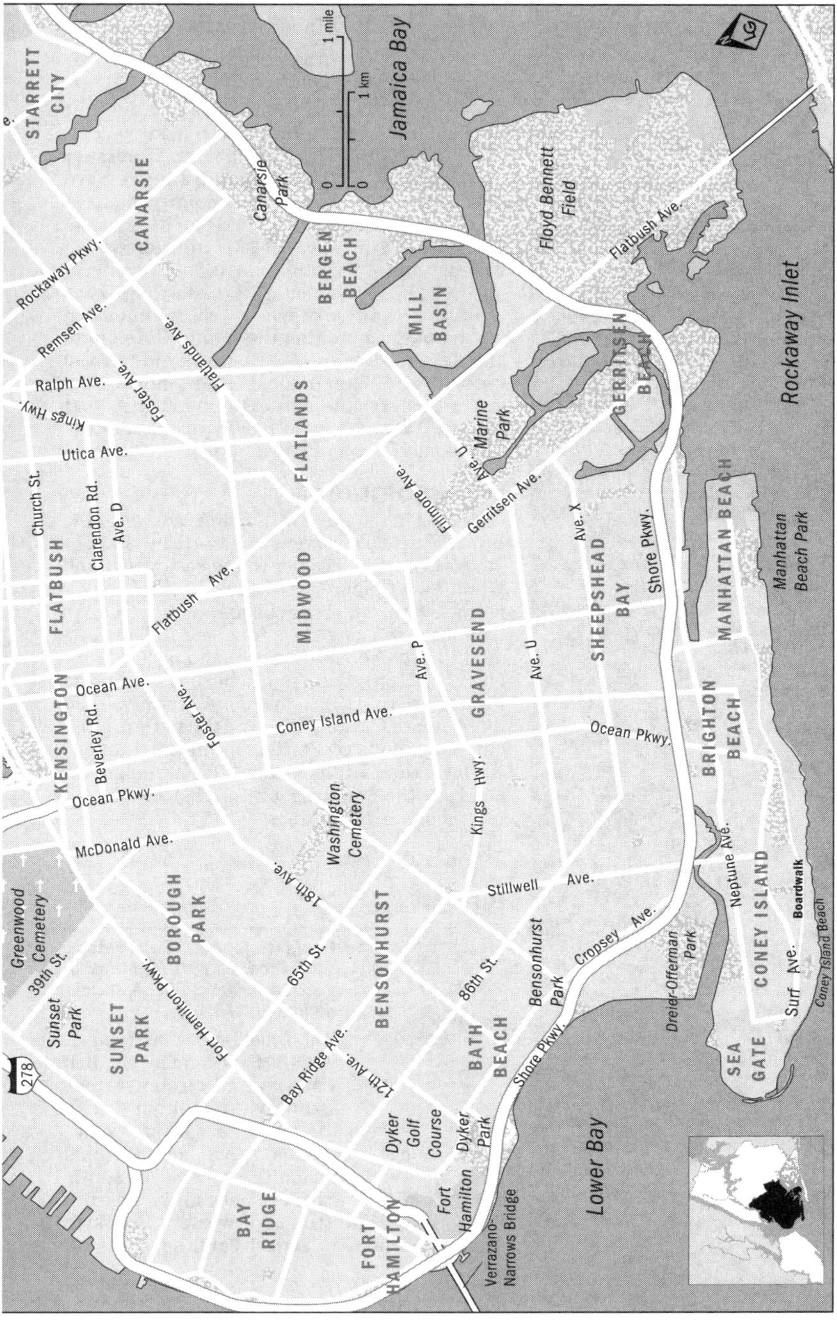

STARRETT CITY
CANARSIE
Canarsie Park
BERGEN BEACH
MILL BASIN
Jamaica Bay
0 1 mile
0 1 km
Floyd Bennett Field
Flatbush Ave.
Rockaway Inlet
GERRITSEN BEACH
Marine Park
FLATLANDS
FLATBUSH
KENSINGTON
MIDWOOD
GRAVESEND
SHEEPSHEAD BAY
MANHATTAN BEACH
Manhattan Beach Park
BRIGHTON BEACH
CONEY ISLAND
SEA GATE
Boardwalk
Coney Island Beach
Surf Ave.
Neptune Ave.
Dreier-Offerman Park
Rockaway Pkwy.
Remsen Ave.
Ralph Ave.
Kings Hwy.
Utica Ave.
Church St.
Clarendon Rd.
Ave. D
Foster Ave.
Flatlands Ave.
Flatbush Ave.
Ocean Ave.
Beverley Rd.
Ocean Pkwy.
McDonald Ave.
Coney Island Ave.
Fillmore Ave.
Ave. U
Gerritsen Ave.
Ave. X
Shore Pkwy.
Ave. P
Kings Hwy.
Ave. U
Ocean Pkwy.
Stillwell Ave.
Cropsey Ave.
Washington Cemetery
18th Ave.
65th St.
86th St.
Bay Ridge Ave.
12th Ave.
Fort Hamilton Pkwy.
Greenwood Cemetery
39th St.
Sunset Park
SUNSET PARK
BOROUGH PARK
BENSONHURST
Bensonhurst Park
BATH BEACH
Dyker Park
Dyker Golf Course
Fort Hamilton
Verrazano-Narrows Bridge
Lower Bay
BAY RIDGE
FORT HAMILTON
278

The Big Apple's Seed

Every time a New York Met hits a home run in Flushing's **Shea Stadium** (p. 115), an oversized plastic apple rises from behind the outfield wall in celebration, a physical manifestation of the city's nickname: the Big Apple.

According to scholars Barry Popik and Gerald Cohen, the nickname got its start in the 1920s, when John G. FitzGerald named his horse-racing column "Around the Big Apple." FitzGerald apparently heard New York so dubbed by African-American stable-hands in New Orleans who looked upon Gotham as the big time—the big reward for years on the minor tracks.

A less plausible, but sexier explanation comes from Peter Salwen, who claims that the Big Apple derives from Gotham's long history of prostitution. Salwen writes that Evelyn de Saint-Evremond ran a first-class bordello in the early 19th century. When Evelyn was shortened to Eve, the "young men-about-town soon got into the habit of referring to their amorous adventures as 'having a taste of Eve's Apples.'" Hence the Big Apple. Popik disagrees with Salwen, telling *Let's Go,* "Big Apple doesn't come from whores."

In either case, Big Apple didn't become prevalent until Charles Gillett, former president of the **NY Convention and Visitors Bureau** (p. 327), popularized the name with his Big Apple Campaign in 1971. His P.R. ploy hit onto something inexplicably catchy.

THE BRONX

see map pp. 396-397

Sights: p. 118. Food: p. 189. Nightlife: p. 207.

Major highways have cut the Bronx into many pieces. The **Major Deegan Expressway (I-87)** runs up the western border of the borough, next to the Harlem River. **The Cross-Bronx Expressway (I-95)** runs across the borough before turning north on its eastern-most edge. Up the center of the borough runs the **Bronx River Parkway.** Several avenues run north-south, including the Grand Concourse and Jerome Ave. on the western side of the borough and White Plains Rd. and Boston Rd. on the eastern side. Streets running east-west include Tremont Ave., Fordham Rd. and the Bronx and Pelham Pkwy.

NEIGHBORHOODS

High on a hill in the northwestern corner of the Bronx, Riverdale surveys Van Cortlandt Park to the east (p. 121). Farther to the east, you'll find Woodlawn Cemetery (p. 123). In the Bronx's northeastern corner is Pelham Bay Park (p. 123), flanking a working-class Irish and Italian community. To the southeast of the park is City Island (p. 123). Back in the borough center is Bronx Park (p. 119), home of the Bronx Zoo and the Botanic Garden. West of the park are the neighborhoods of Fordham and Belmont (p. 120). Farther south lie the different neighborhoods of the South Bronx (p. 118), one of the city's most destitute areas.

BROOKLYN

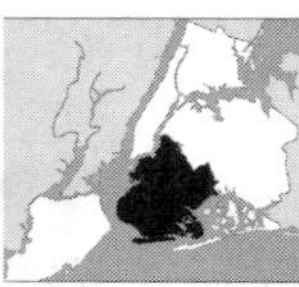

see map p. 386-387

***Sights:** p. 102. **Galleries:** p. 146. **Food:** p. 181. **Nightlife:** p. 205. **Shopping:** p. 252. **Accommodations:** p. 273.*

The **Brooklyn-Queens Expressway (BQE)** pours into the **Belt Parkway** and circumscribes Brooklyn. Brooklyn's main avenues dissect the borough. Ocean Pkwy., Ocean Ave., Coney Island Ave., and diagonal Flatbush Ave. run from the beaches of southern Brooklyn to Prospect Park in the heart of the borough. The streets of western Brooklyn (including those in **Sunset Park, Bensonhurst,**

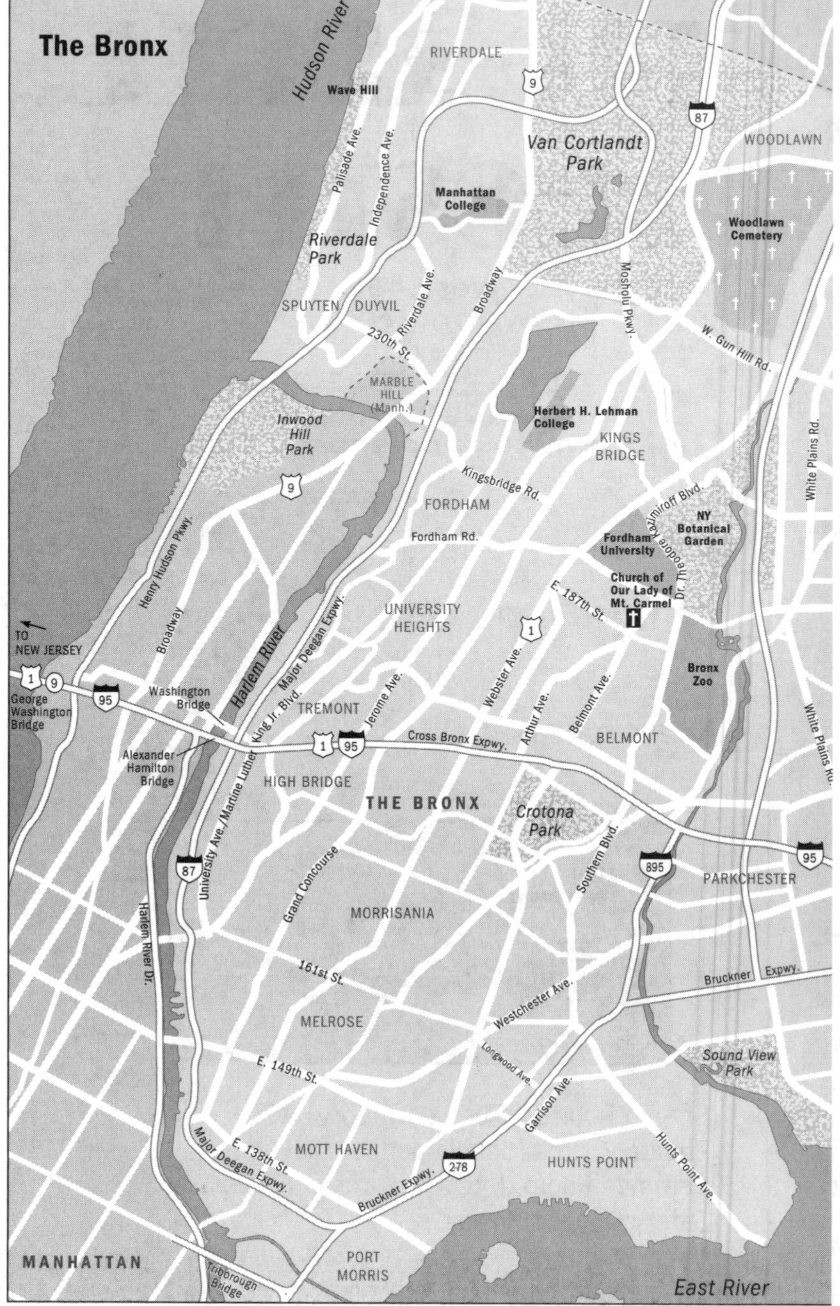
The Bronx
Hudson River
RIVERDALE
Wave Hill
Palisade Ave.
Independence Ave.
Van Cortlandt Park
WOODLAWN
Manhattan College
Woodlawn Cemetery
Riverdale Park
Mosholu Pkwy.
Riverdale Ave.
Broadway
SPUYTEN DUYVIL
230th St.
W. Gun Hill Rd.
MARBLE HILL (Manh.)
Inwood Hill Park
Herbert H. Lehman College
KINGS BRIDGE
White Plains Rd.
Kingsbridge Rd.
FORDHAM
Dr. Theodore Kazimiroff Blvd.
NY Botanical Garden
Fordham Rd.
Fordham University
Henry Hudson Pkwy.
Church of Our Lady of Mt. Carmel
E. 187th St.
Major Deegan Expwy.
UNIVERSITY HEIGHTS
TO NEW JERSEY
Broadway
Webster Ave.
Bronx Zoo
Harlem River
Washington Bridge
Arthur Ave.
Belmont Ave.
George Washington Bridge
TREMONT
Jerome Ave.
King Jr. Blvd.
White Plains Rd.
Cross Bronx Expwy.
BELMONT
Alexander Hamilton Bridge
HIGH BRIDGE
University Ave./Martine Luther
THE BRONX
Crotona Park
Southern Blvd.
PARKCHESTER
Grand Concourse
Harlem River Dr.
MORRISANIA
161st St.
Bruckner Expwy.
Westchester Ave.
MELROSE
Longwood Ave.
Sound View Park
E. 149th St.
Garrison Ave.
Hunts Point Ave.
E. 138th St.
MOTT HAVEN
Major Deegan Expwy.
HUNTS POINT
Bruckner Expwy.
MANHATTAN
PORT MORRIS
Triborough Bridge
East River

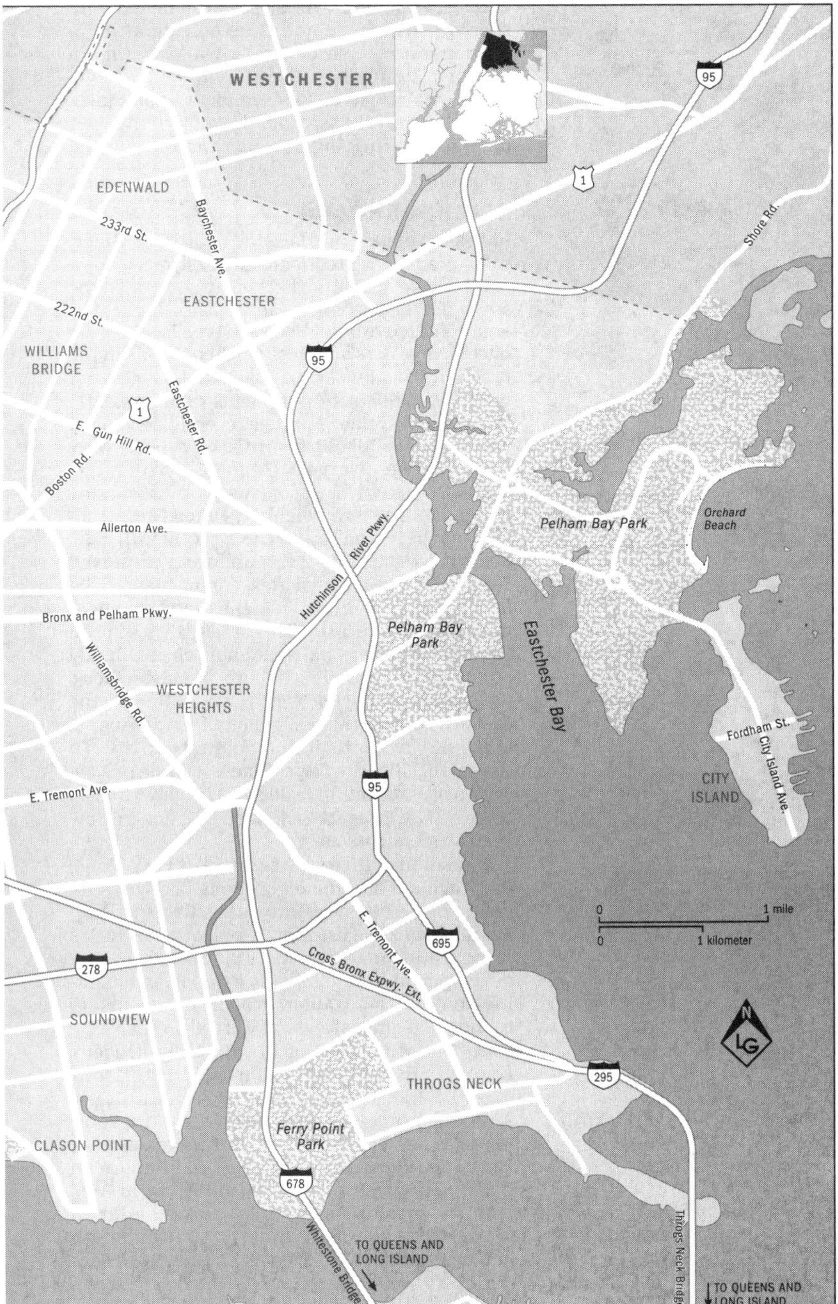

WESTCHESTER
95
1
EDENWALD
233rd St.
Baychester Ave.
Shore Rd.
EASTCHESTER
222nd St.
WILLIAMS BRIDGE
95
1
Eastchester Rd.
E. Gun Hill Rd.
Boston Rd.
Allerton Ave.
Hutchinson River Pkwy.
Pelham Bay Park
Orchard Beach
Bronx and Pelham Pkwy.
Pelham Bay Park
Eastchester Bay
Williamsbridge Rd.
WESTCHESTER HEIGHTS
Fordham St.
City Island Ave.
CITY ISLAND
95
E. Tremont Ave.
0 1 mile
0 1 kilometer
E. Tremont Ave.
695
278
Cross Bronx Expwy. Ext.
SOUNDVIEW
295
THROGS NECK
Ferry Point Park
CLASON POINT
678
Whitestone Bridge
TO QUEENS AND LONG ISLAND
Throgs Neck Bridge
TO QUEENS AND LONG ISLAND

Joggers in Central Park

Little Asia, Flushing

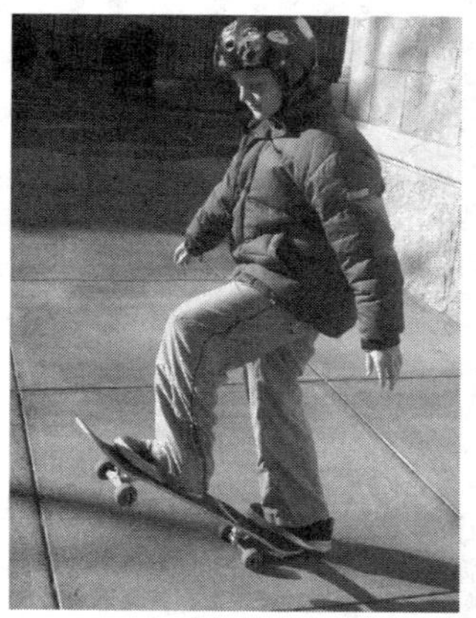
Skateboarder

Borough Park, and **Park Slope**) are aligned with the western shore and thus collide at a 45-degree angle with central Brooklyn's main arteries. In northern Brooklyn, several avenues—Atlantic Ave., Eastern Pkwy., and Flushing Ave.—travel east from downtown the ever diverse and thriving borough that is Queens.

NEIGHBORHOODS

In the borough's northeastern corner is **Greenpoint** (Map 21), a predominantly Polish neighborhood whose main drag is Manhattan Ave. To the south is **Williamsburg** (Map 21). Northside, the area centered around Bedford Ave., has become one of New York's hottest neighborhoods in the past ten years. Further to the south and closer to the BQE, Williamsburg remains predominantly Hasidic and Latino. Another recently developed community is **DUMBO,** short for **Down Under Manhattan Bridge Overpass** (Map 22), which has begun to expand far beyond its roots as an artist colony. Its western neighbor, **Fulton Ferry** (Map 22), is where you'll find the Brooklyn Bridge. **Brooklyn Heights** (Map 22), a uniformly preserved 19th-century residential area, sprang up with the development of Brooklyn-Manhattan steamboat transportation in 1814. This area's rows of posh Greek Revival and Italianate houses essentially created New York's first suburb. **Downtown Brooklyn** (Map 22) is the borough's civic center. To the east, **Fort Greene** (Map 22), along DeKalb Ave., is a hub of black artistic and cultural activity. To the south, hilly **Park Slope** (Map 23) is one of New York's most beautiful residential neighborhoods, bordered by **Prospect Park** (Map 23), one of New York's emerald gems.

Just south of Atlantic Ave., west of Park Slope, lies **Cobble Hill,** whose gorgeous brownstone-lined sidestreets segue into **Carroll Gardens** (Map 20, B3; Map 24). Historically one of New York's most traditional Italian neighborhoods, the development of Smith St. as a dining and nightlife center has attracted crowds of trendsters to the once-quiet streets of Carroll Gardens.

On the other side of the Brooklyn-Queens Expwy. (BQE) is the industrial waterfront area of **Red Hook** (Map 20, A3; Map 24). Although not as accessible by public transportation as its neighbors, Red Hook is yet another Brooklyn neighborhood that has begun to boom. Cobblestone streets and Atlantic Ave. lead to warehouses, docks, and wonderful views of the Statue of Liberty. Farther south is **Sunset Park** (Map 20, B4), home to Greenwood Cemetery, the largest in Brooklyn. The nearby Shore Rd. of **Bay Ridge** (Map 20, A4) is lined with mansions overlooking the Verrazano-Narrows Bridge and New York Harbor. **Bensonhurst** (Map 20, B5) to the southeast, is centered around Stillwell and Park Ave. Neighboring **Borough Park** (Map 20, B4) is the largest Hasidic Jewish neighborhood in Brooklyn, and quite possibly, the world. Just southeast of Prospect Park and east of Borough Park is **Flatbush** (Map 20, D4), where Manhattan's turn-of-the-century aristocracy maintained summer homes; you can wander around Argyle St. and Ditmars Ave. to see some of the old mansions.

Two seaside communities lie in southern Brooklyn. **Brighton Beach** (Map 20, C6), or "Little Odessa by the Sea," is populated heavily by Eastern European immigrants. To the west, **Coney Island** (Map 20, B6) will take you back to a New York of years past.

MANHATTAN

see maps pp. 358

Above 14th Street, Manhattan is an organized grid of avenues running north-south and streets east-west, the result of an expansion scheme adopted in 1811. Street numbers increase as one travels north. Avenues are slightly less predictable: some are numbered while others are named. The numbers of the avenues increase as one goes west. **Broadway,** which follows an old Algonquin trail, bravely defies the rectangular pattern and cuts diagonally across the island, veering east of Fifth Ave. at 23rd St.; Central Park and Fifth Ave. (south of 59th St. and north of 110th St.) separate the city into the East Side and West Side.

Below 14th Street, the city dissolves into a charming but complicated tangle of old, narrow streets. The confusion intensifies south of Houston St., where streets are not numbered. The **Financial District/Wall Street area,** set over the original Dutch layout, is full of narrow, winding, one-way streets. **Greenwich Village,** only slightly less Byzantine in design, is especially complicated west of Sixth Ave. The **East Village and Alphabet City** are grid-like, with alphabetized avenues from Ave. A to Ave. D east of First Ave.

When setting off to find something, make sure you have not only its address (i.e., 180 East End Ave.), but also the cross-streets (in this case, 88th and 89th St.). Note that some streets have two names: **Sixth Avenue,** for example, is also known as **Avenue of the Americas.**

FINANCIAL DISTRICT

see map p. 358

Subway: 1, 2, to Wall St./William St.; 4, 5 to Bowling Green, Wall St./Broadway; N, R, W to Rector St., Whitehall St.; 1, 2, 4, 5, A, C, J, M, Z to Fulton St./Broadway-Nassau St.; J, M, Z to Broad St.; 1, 9 to South Ferry. ***Sights:*** *p. 49.* ***Food:*** *p. 153.* ***Shopping:*** *p. 241.*

For those who see in New York the seeds of American financial imperium, it's fitting that the oldest part of the city is also its historical financial center. Although the Financial District now lags behind Midtown in office space, it still serves as a worldwide Mecca of capitalism. Bounded roughly by Battery Park on the south and Fulton St. on the north, the Financial District extends from the Hudson River and the East River. Broadway runs uptown-downtown and slices through the neighborhood's center. The main thoroughfare is Wall St., which runs east-west. **Trinity Church** (p. 51) and **the New York Stock Exchange** (p. 50) are located here, as is Ground Zero, the **World Trade Center Memorial** (p. 52).

THE CIVIC CENTER

see map pp. 360-361

Subway: 1, 2 to Park Pl.; N, R to City Hall; 4, 5, 6 to Brooklyn Bridge-City Hall; J, M, Z to Chambers St./Centre St. ***Sights:*** *p. 52.* ***Food:*** *p. 153.* ***Shopping:*** *p. 241.*

The grandiose architecture and palpable authority of the Civic Center are a testament to New York's 19th-century reinvention of itself as the Empire City. The sobriety of the seat of government rests in the imposing limestone of the Beaux-Arts landmarks that fill the area. Nothing reflects New York's ascent to dominance like the Brooklyn Bridge, the greatest engineering feat of its time and still one of New York's most impressive sights. Just north of the Financial District, the neighborhood centers around City Hall. Most government buildings cluster around Broadway, Park Row, and Centre St. The Civic Center becomes Chinatown at Worth St., at the intersection once known as the Five Points.

SOUTH STREET SEAPORT

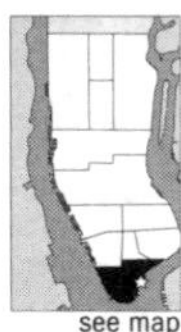

see map pp. 360-361

Subway: 1, 2, 4, 5, A, C, J, M, Z to Fulton St./Broadway-Nassau St. ***Sights:*** *p. 54.*

Bounded by Fulton St. on the south, Dover St. on the north, Pearl St. on the west, and the East River on the east, the South Street Seaport is one of New York's most heavily touristed locales. Don't miss the **Fulton Fish Market** (p. 55).

CHINATOWN

see map pp. 362-363

Subway: J, M, Z to Canal St./Centre St.; N, Q, R, W to Canal St./Broadway; 4, 6 to Canal St./Lafayette St. Walk east on Canal St. to get to Mott St. Follow the curved street to get to the Bowery, Confucius Plaza, and E. Broadway. ***Sights:*** *p. 56.* ***Food:*** *p. 154.* ***Shopping:*** *p. 241.*

Sitting atop the former site of the Five Points, New York's first slum, Chinatown is loosely bounded by Worth St. on the south, Canal St. on the north, Broadway on the west, and the Bowery on the east, although this area has colonized much of Little Italy and parts of the Lower East Side. Despite the creeping gentrification and homogenization of much of Lower Manhattan, Chinatown has retained its unique personality. The community that maintains seven Chinese newspapers, over 300 garment factories, and innumerable food shops, New York's Chinatown contains the largest Asian community in the US outside San Francisco.

LITTLE ITALY

see map pp. 362-363

Subway: 6 to Spring St./Lafayette St.; J, M, Z to Canal St./Centre St.; N, Q, R, W to Canal St./Broadway; 4, 6 to Canal St./Lafayette St.; S to Grand St.; F to E. Broadway; F, V, S to Broadway-Lafayette St. ***Sights:*** *p. 56.* ***Food:*** *p. 156.* ***Shopping:*** *p. 241.* ***Accommodations:*** *p. 258.*

There's not much of Little Italy left in New York. Immigration giveth, and immigration taketh away. What remains of the neighborhood is mostly located on Mulberry St., east of SoHo and west of the Lower East Side. Perhaps worth walking through for a sense of the old atmosphere, but the food here is not budget by any means. Super-trendy **NoLIta (North of Little Italy)** and **Noho (North of Houston St.)** are short on sights but long on unique designer goodies and hip eats.

LOWER EAST SIDE

Subway: F, V to Lower East Side-Second Ave.; F to E. Broadway; F, J, M, Z to Delancey St.-Essex St. ***Sights:*** *p. 58.* ***Food:*** *p. 158.* ***Nightlife:*** *p. 194.* ***Shopping:*** *p. 242.*

see map pp. 369

Down below E. Houston and east of the Bowery lurks the trendily seedy Lower East Side, where old-timers rub shoulders with heroin dealers and twenty-somethings emulate *la vie bohème*. A traditional destination for immigrants, the neighborhood retains its multicultural flavor but is slowly evolving from working-class to young, hip, and chic. Highlights include the **Lower East Side Tenement Museum** (p. 137) and **Katz's Delicatessen** (p. 158).

TRIBECA

Subway: 1, 9 to Canal St./Varick St.; C, E to Canal St./Ave. of the Americas (Sixth Ave.); 1, 9 to Franklin St.; 1, 2, 3, 9 to Chambers St./W. Broadway; A, C to Chambers St./Church St. ***Sights:*** *p. 58.* ***Food:*** *p. 160.* ***Nightlife:*** *p. 198.*

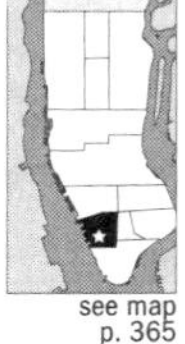
see map p. 365

Bounded by Canal St. on the north, the Hudson River on the west, Vesey St. on the south, and E. Broadway on the east, **Triangle Below Canal Street** is a primarily residential neighborhood populated with bars and expensive restaurants.

SOHO

Subway: C, E to Spring St./Ave. of the Americas (Sixth Ave.); 6 to Spring St./Lafayette St.; N, R to Prince St.; 1, 2 to W. Houston St.; F, S, V to Broadway-Lafayette St. ***Sights:*** *p. 59.* ***Galleries:*** *p. 143.* ***Food:*** *p. 160.* ***Nightlife:*** *p. 198.* ***Shopping:*** *p. 243.*

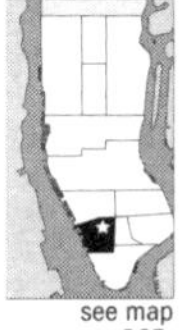
see map p. 365

SoHo, the district **South of Houston Street** (say "HOW-ston"), sits between TriBeCa and Greenwich Village. It is bounded by Crosby St. on the east, Sullivan St. to the west, and Canal St. to the south. New Yorkers visit the neighborhood for its art galleries and shopping.

GREENWICH VILLAGE

Subway: A, C, E, F, V, S to W. 4th St.; A, C, E, L to 14th St./Eighth Ave.; 1, 2, 3 to 14th St./Seventh Ave.; F, L, V to 14th St./Ave. of the Americas (Sixth Ave.); 4, 5, 6, L, N, Q, R, W to 14th St.-Union Sq.; 1, 9 to Houston St., Christopher St.; N, R to 8th St.-NYU; L to Sixth Ave., Eighth Ave.; 6 to Bleecker St. ***Sights:*** *p. 59.* ***Food:*** *p. 161.* ***Nightlife:*** *p. 199.* ***Shopping:*** *p. 244.* ***Accommodations:*** *p. 258.*

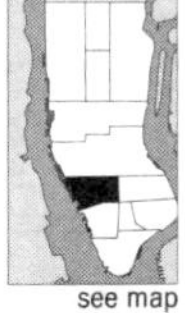
see map pp. 366-367

The Village is located west of Broadway, between Houston and 14th St. Between Broadway and Sixth Ave., the streets are organized in grid-like fashion; west of Sixth Ave., however, they dissolve into a confusing, tangled web. While rent is no longer low in the Village, the area is still a center for the rebellious and the intellectual. Highlights include **Washington Square Park** (p. 60) and the neighborhood's jazz clubs.

EAST VILLAGE AND ALPHABET CITY

see map pp. 370-371

Subway: 6 to Astor Pl., Bleecker St.; L to First Ave., Third Ave.; F, V to Lower East Side-Second Ave. ***Sights:*** *p. 65.* ***Food:*** *p. 164.* ***Nightlife:*** *p. 197.* ***Shopping:*** *p. 246.* ***Accommodations:*** *p. 259.*

The East Village—east of Broadway, north of E. Houston, and south of 14th St.—was carved out of the Bowery and the Lower East Side in the early 1960s, as artists and writers moved here to escape high rents in the West Village. **St. Mark's Place** (p. 65) is the center of the East Village scene. **East 6th Street** is often called "Little India" for the door-to-door South Asian eateries that line the street east of Second Ave. **Alphabet City** lies to the east of First Ave., south of 14th St., and north of Houston St. Here, the avenues give up on numbers and adopt letters. The area is generally safe during the day, but use caution east of Ave. B after dark. The nightlife in the East Village is among the city's best.

GRAMERCY PARK, UNION SQUARE, AND MURRAY HILL

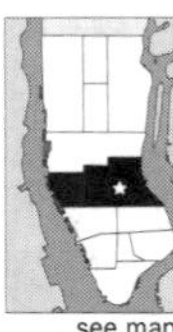
see map pp. 372-373

Subway: 4, 5, 6, L, N, Q, R, W to 14th St.-Union Sq.; 6 to 23rd St./Park Ave. S; N, R to 23rd St./Broadway; 6 to 28th St., 33rd St./Park Ave. S. ***Sights:*** *p. 68, p. 72.* ***Food:*** *p. 171.* ***Nightlife:*** *p. 201.* ***Accommodations:*** *p. 261.*

At 14th St., between Broadway and Park Ave. S, you'll find Union Square. Gramercy Park is located to the northeast, at the southern end of Lexington Ave., between 20th and 21st St. The surrounding neighborhood is called Gramercy, after the park. Murray Hill is in the 30s on the East Side.

CHELSEA

see map pp. 372-373

Subway: 1, 2, 3 to 14th St./Seventh Ave.; A, C, E, L to 14th St./Eighth Ave.; C, E to 23rd St./Eighth Ave.; 1, 9 to 23rd St./Seventh Ave.; 1, 9 to 28th St./Seventh Ave. ***Sights:*** *p. 72.* ***Galleries:*** *p. 144.* ***Food:*** *p. 169.* ***Nightlife:*** *p. 201.* ***Shopping:*** *p. 248.* ***Accommodations:*** *p. 263.*

Extending west from Sixth Ave. to the Hudson River, between 14th and 28th St., Chelsea is home to some of the city's best galleries and clubs. Chelsea has supplanted the West Village as New York's gay capital.

HERALD SQUARE AND THE GARMENT DISTRICT

see map pp. 372-373

Subway: B, D, F, N, Q, R, W to Herald Sq. ***Sights:*** *p. 74.* ***Food:*** *p. 169.* ***Shopping:*** *p. 249.* ***Accommodations:*** *p. 265.*

Herald Square is located between 34th and 35th St., between Broadway and Sixth Ave. The area is a center for shopping. One block to the east is the **Empire State Building** (p. 74).

HELL'S KITCHEN (OR CLINTON)

Subway: 1, 2, 3, 9 to 34th St.-Penn Station/Seventh Ave.; A, C, E to 34th-Penn Station/Eighth Ave.; B, D, F, N, Q, R, V, W to 34th St.-Herald Sq. for Herald Sq. and Garment District. ***Sights:*** *p. 77.* ***Food:*** *p. 173.*

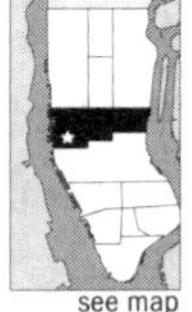
see map pp. 376-377

Between Eighth Ave. and the Hudson River, 34th and 59th St., is **Hell's Kitchen,** a one-time breeding ground of gang violence that has been gentrified. Dance fights still occasionally break out on Ninth Ave.

MIDTOWN

Subway: 4, 5, 6, 7, S to 42nd St.-Grand Central; E, V, 6 to 51st St.; 4, 5, 6, N, R, W to 59th St.-Lexington Ave.; F to Lexington Ave./63rd St.; B, D, F, V, 7 to 42nd St.-Bryant Park; B, D, F, V to 47th-50th St.-Rockefeller Center; 1, 2, 3, 7, 9, N, Q, R, S, W to 42nd St.-Times Sq.; A, C, E to 42nd St.-Port Authority; E, V to Fifth Ave./53rd St.; 1, 9 to 50th St./Broadway. 1, 2, 3, 7, 9, N, Q, R, S, W to 42nd St.-Times Sq. for Times Sq. and Theater District. ***Sights:*** *p. 77.* ***Galleries:*** *p. 145.* ***Food:*** *p. 174.* ***Shopping:*** *p. 250.* ***Accommodations:*** *p. 265.*

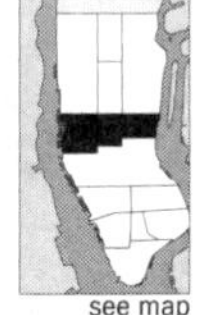
see map pp. 376-377

East of Eighth Ave., from about 42nd St. to 59th St., lies Midtown. Mammoth office buildings and posh hotels dominate the skies, and the streets are lined with high-brow stores. On Midtown's East Side are luxurious **Fifth Avenue** (p. 77), more solemn Park Ave. (p. 81), and the United Nations (p. 81). On the West Side are Times Square (p. 84), the Theater District (p. 84), and Central Park S. (p. 85).

UPPER EAST SIDE

Subway: N, R, W to Fifth Ave./59th St. 4, 5, 6, N, R, W to 59th St.-Lexington Ave.; F to Lexington Ave./63rd St.; 6 to 68th St., 77th St., 96th St.; 4, 5, 6 to 86th St./Lexington Ave. ***Sights:*** *p. 91.* ***Galleries:*** *p. 145.* ***Food:*** *p. 175.* ***Nightlife:*** *p. 203.* ***Shopping:*** *p. 251.* ***Accommodations:*** *p. 269.*

see map pp. 378-379

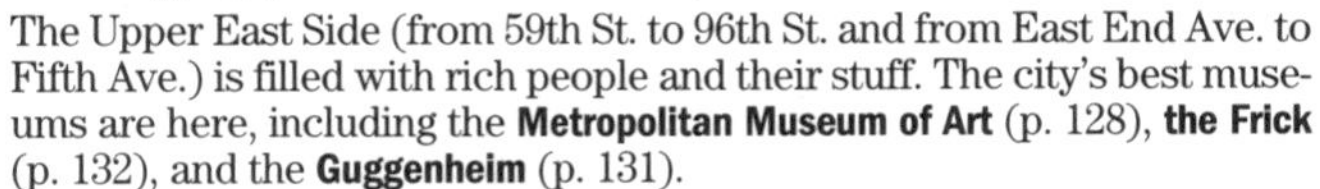

The Upper East Side (from 59th St. to 96th St. and from East End Ave. to Fifth Ave.) is filled with rich people and their stuff. The city's best museums are here, including the **Metropolitan Museum of Art** (p. 128), **the Frick** (p. 132), and the **Guggenheim** (p. 131).

UPPER WEST SIDE

Subway: 1, 9, A, B, C, D to 59th St.-Columbus Circle; 1, 9 to 66th St., 79th St., 86th St./Broadway; 1, 2, 3, 9 to 72nd St./Broadway; B, C to 72nd St./Central Park W., 81st St.; B, C to 86th St./Central Park W., 96th St./Central Park W.; 1, 2, 3, 9 to 96th St./Broadway. ***Sights:*** *p. 94.* ***Food:*** *p. 176.* ***Nightlife:*** *p. 204.* ***Shopping:*** *p. 251.* ***Accommodations:*** *p. 269.*

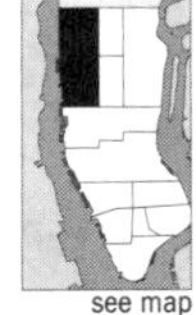
see map pp. 382-383

Located between 59th and 110th St. west of Central Park, the Upper West Side is home to exciting dining, shopping, and cultural activity. The neighborhood's biggest attractions are **Lincoln Center** (p. 95; p. 216) and the **American Museum of Natural History** (p. 130).

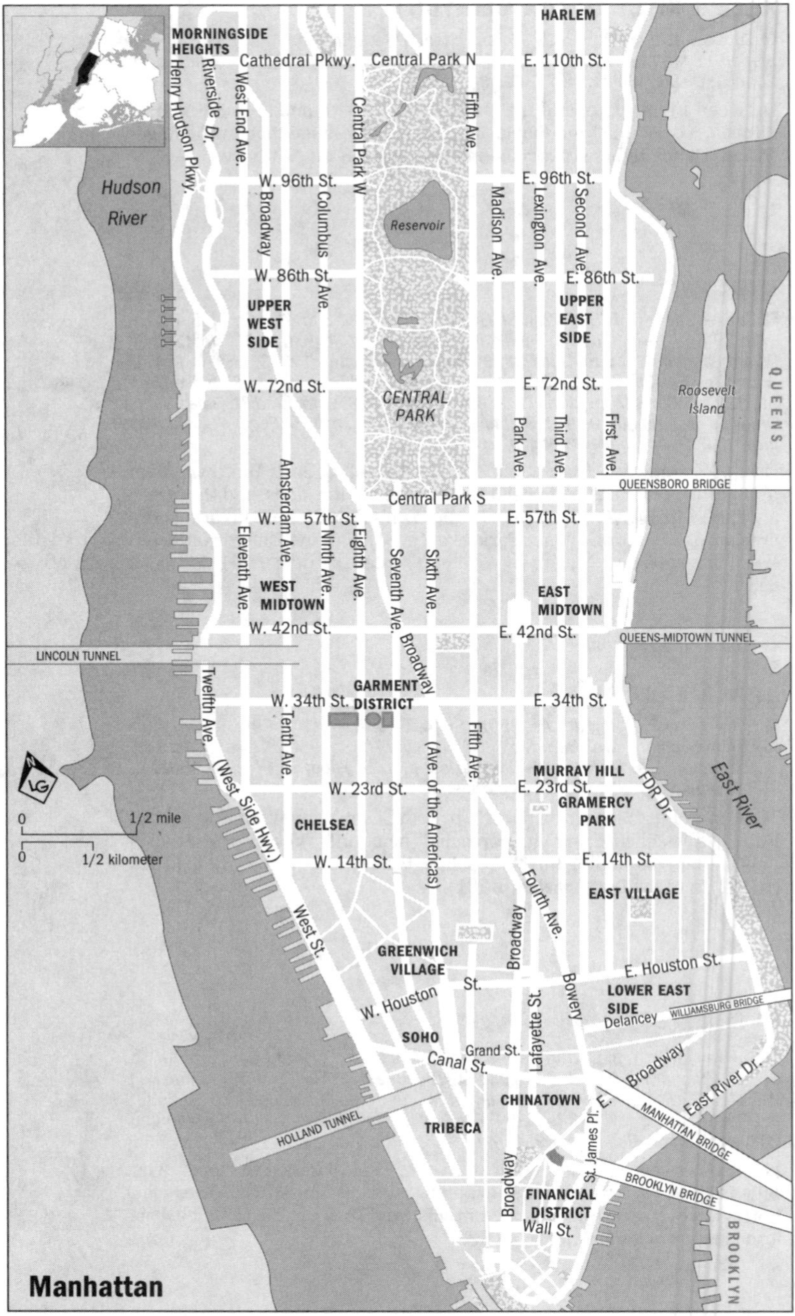
HARLEM
MORNINGSIDE HEIGHTS
Cathedral Pkwy.
Central Park N
E. 110th St.
Henry Hudson Pkwy.
Riverside Dr.
West End Ave.
Central Park W
Fifth Ave.
Hudson River
W. 96th St.
E. 96th St.
Broadway
Columbus Ave.
Reservoir
Madison Ave.
Lexington Ave.
Second Ave.
W. 86th St.
E. 86th St.
UPPER WEST SIDE
UPPER EAST SIDE
W. 72nd St.
E. 72nd St.
CENTRAL PARK
Park Ave.
Third Ave.
First Ave.
Roosevelt Island
QUEENS
QUEENSBORO BRIDGE
Central Park S
W. 57th St.
E. 57th St.
Amsterdam Ave.
Eleventh Ave.
Ninth Ave.
Eighth Ave.
Seventh Ave.
Sixth Ave.
WEST MIDTOWN
EAST MIDTOWN
W. 42nd St.
E. 42nd St.
QUEENS-MIDTOWN TUNNEL
LINCOLN TUNNEL
Broadway
Twelfth Ave.
GARMENT DISTRICT
W. 34th St.
E. 34th St.
Tenth Ave.
(Ave. of the Americas)
Fifth Ave.
MURRAY HILL
FDR Dr.
East River
(West Side Hwy.)
W. 23rd St.
E. 23rd St.
GRAMERCY PARK
0
1/2 mile
0
1/2 kilometer
CHELSEA
W. 14th St.
E. 14th St.
Fourth Ave.
EAST VILLAGE
West St.
Broadway
GREENWICH VILLAGE
E. Houston St.
St.
Bowery
W. Houston
LOWER EAST SIDE
Delancey
WILLIAMSBURG BRIDGE
SOHO
Grand St.
Lafayette St.
Canal St.
Broadway
East River Dr.
E. Broadway
CHINATOWN
HOLLAND TUNNEL
TRIBECA
MANHATTAN BRIDGE
St. James Pl.
Broadway
BROOKLYN BRIDGE
FINANCIAL DISTRICT
Wall St.
BROOKLYN
Manhattan

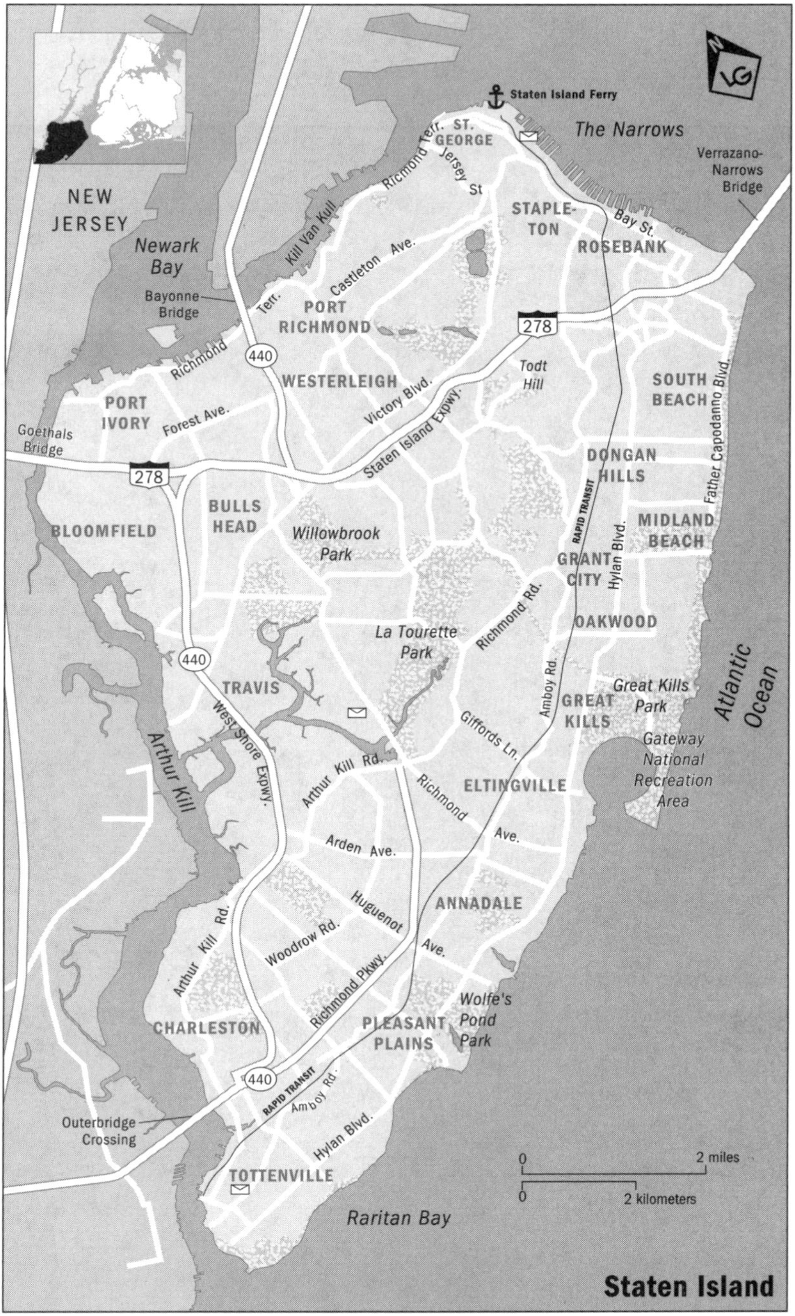

Staten Island Ferry
The Narrows
Verrazano-Narrows Bridge
ST. GEORGE
Richmond Terr.
Jersey St
Kill Van Kull
NEW JERSEY
Newark Bay
Bayonne Bridge
STAPLETON
Bay St.
ROSEBANK
Castleton Ave.
PORT RICHMOND
Richmond Terr.
278
440
Todt Hill
WESTERLEIGH
Victory Blvd.
SOUTH BEACH
Father Capodanno Blvd.
PORT IVORY
Forest Ave.
Goethals Bridge
Staten Island Expwy.
278
DONGAN HILLS
RAPID TRANSIT
BULLS HEAD
BLOOMFIELD
Willowbrook Park
MIDLAND BEACH
Hylan Blvd.
GRANT CITY
Richmond Rd.
OAKWOOD
La Tourette Park
440
Atlantic Ocean
Great Kills Park
Amboy Rd.
TRAVIS
GREAT KILLS
Gifford Ln.
West Shore Expwy.
Gateway National Recreation Area
Arthur Kill
Arthur Kill Rd.
ELTINGVILLE
Richmond Ave.
Arden Ave.
Huguenot Ave.
ANNADALE
Arthur Kill Rd.
Woodrow Rd.
Richmond Pkwy.
Wolfe's Pond Park
CHARLESTON
PLEASANT PLAINS
440
RAPID TRANSIT
Amboy Rd.
Hylan Blvd.
Outerbridge Crossing
TOTTENVILLE
0 2 miles
0 2 kilometers
Raritan Bay

Staten Island

MANHATTAN
East River
Triboro Bridge
Rikers Island
Flushing Bay
Bronx-Whitestone Bridge
WHITESTONE
Throgs Neck Bridge
Little Neck Bay
COLLEGE POINT
Cross Island Pkwy.
BAY TERRACE
FDR Dr.
LaGuardia Airport
Ditmars Blvd.
ASTORIA
M N, W
Bell Blvd.
FLUSHING
BAYSIDE
21st St.
31st St.
Grand Central Pkwy.
EAST ELMHURST
Astoria Blvd.
Queensboro Bridge
LONG ISLAND CITY
M 7
AUBURNDALE
Northern Blvd.
Northern Blvd.
CORONA
JACKSON HEIGHTS
46th Ave.
Francis Lewis Blvd.
Clearview Expwy.
Flushing Meadows Corona Park
WOODSIDE
Roosevelt Ave.
Kissena Park
HUNTER POINT
Queens Blvd.
Broadway
Junction Blvd.
Alley Park
SUNNYSIDE
FRESH MEADOWS
ELMHURST
Queens Expwy.
UTOPIA
Cunningham Park
Long Island Expwy.
Queens Blvd.
Queens-Midtown Tunnel
REGO PARK
MASPETH
HILL-CREST
164th St.
Union Tnpk.
Main St.
Grand Central Pkwy.
JAMAICA ESTATES
Brooklyn-
MIDDLE VILLAGE
FOREST HILLS
Hillside Ave.
Metropolitan Ave.
Manhattan Bridge
RIDGEWOOD
Woodhaven Blvd.
Jamaica Ave.
HOLLIS
Forest Park
KEW GARDENS
Pkwy.
Myrtle Ave.
GLENDALE
Jackie Robinson Pkwy./Interborough
Lefferts Blvd.
Van Wyck Expwy.
JAMAICA
Guy Brewer Ave.
ST. ALBANS
Linden Blvd.
WOODHAVEN
RICHMOND HILL
Jamaica Ave.
Merrick Blvd.
SOUTH JAMAICA
Conduit Ave.
OZONE PARK
Atlantic Ave.
Rockaway Blvd.
A B C D E
1 2 3
295 678 278 495 25 25A

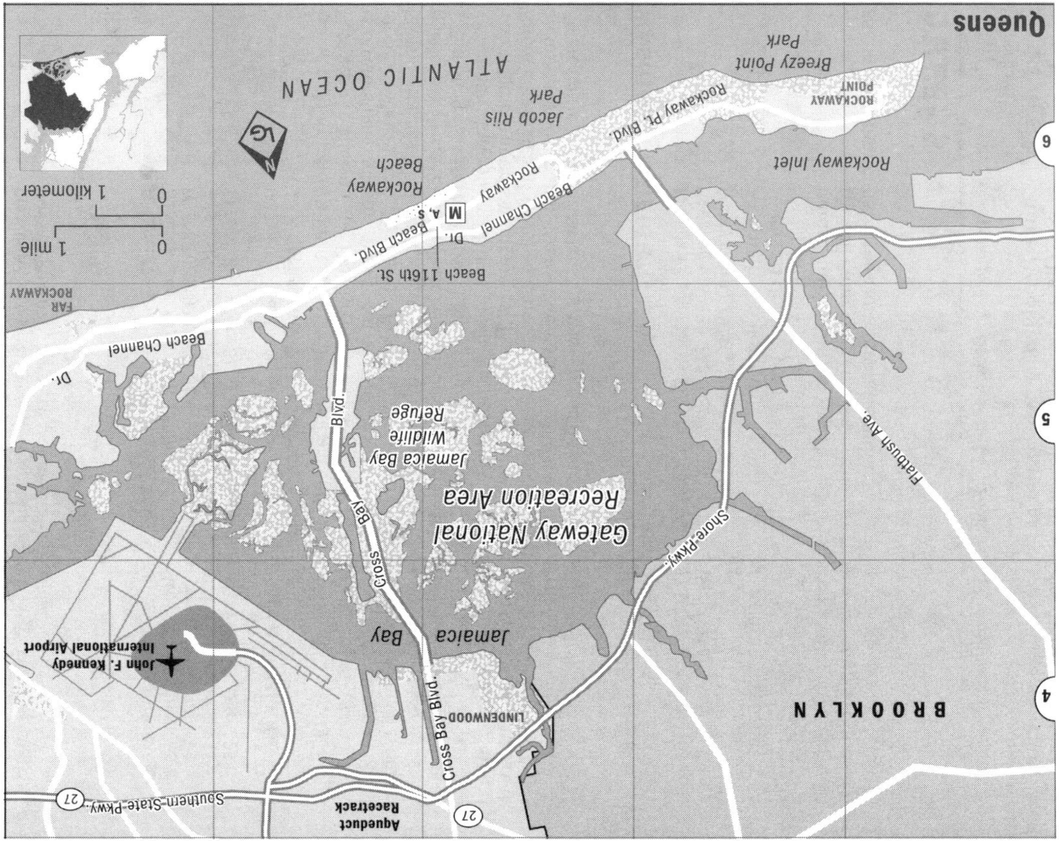

Queens

BROOKLYN

ATLANTIC OCEAN

Gateway National Recreation Area

Jamaica Bay Wildlife Refuge

Jamaica Bay

John F. Kennedy International Airport

Aqueduct Racetrack

LINDENWOOD

Cross Bay Blvd.

Southern State Pkwy.

Shore Pkwy.

Flatbush Ave.

Rockaway Inlet

Breezy Point Park

ROCKAWAY POINT

Rockaway Pt. Blvd.

Jacob Riis Park

Rockaway Beach

Beach Channel Dr.

Rockaway Beach Blvd.

Beach 116th St.

A, S

FAR ROCKAWAY

0 1 mile

0 1 kilometer

4

5

6

MORNINGSIDE HEIGHTS

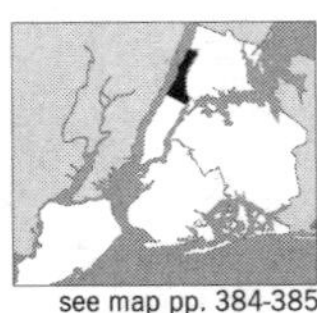
see map pp. 384-385

Subway: 1 to Cathedral Pkwy. (110th St.), 116th St.-Columbia University, 125th St./Broadway. ***Sights:*** *p. 96.* ***Food:*** *p. 178.*

Above 110th St. and below 125th St., between Amsterdam Ave. and the Hudson River, Morningside Heights, the neighborhood between the Upper West Side and Harlem, is New York's own little college town, home to Columbia University.

HARLEM

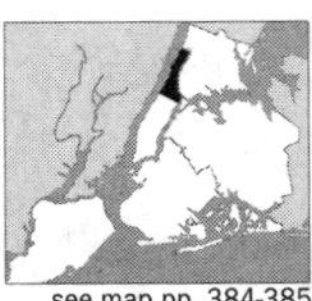
see map pp. 384-385

Subway: 6 to 103rd St., Central Park N. (110th St.), 116th St. at Lexington Ave.; 4, 5, 6 to 125th St./Lexington Ave.; 2, 3 to Central Park N. (110th St.), 116th St., 125th St., 135th St. at Lenox (Sixth) Ave.; 3 to 145th St./Lenox (Sixth) Ave., 148th St.; B, C to Cathedral Pkwy. (110th St.), 116th St., 135th St. at Central Park W.; A, B, C, D to 125th St./Central Park W.; A, B, C, D to 145th St./St. Nicholas Ave.; 1 to 137th St., 145th St. at Broadway. Map 19. ***Sights:*** *p. 98.* ***Food:*** *p. 179.* ***Shopping:*** *p. 252.* ***Accommodations:*** *p. 272.*

Harlem, Manhattan's largest neighborhood, extends from 110th St. to the 150s, between the Hudson and East Rivers. The poor and dangerous Harlem of urban legend refers mainly to the area south of 125th St. in the Manhattan Valley, particularly along Frederick Douglass and Adam Clayton Powell Blvd. Central Harlem's main thoroughfare is 125th St. Many of this neighborhood's streets have been renamed for past black leaders: Sixth (Lenox Ave.) is also referred to as Malcolm X Blvd., and 125th St. is also Martin Luther King Jr. Blvd.

Spanish Harlem, or El Barrio, sits between 96th and 125th St. on the East Side. The neighborhood's main artery, E. 116th St., overflows with fruit stands, Puerto Rican eateries, and flavored crushed-ice vendors on scorching summer days. The anarchic chaos that the area experienced during the height of the late-80s crack epidemic has waned somewhat, but widespread poverty remains.

WASHINGTON HEIGHTS

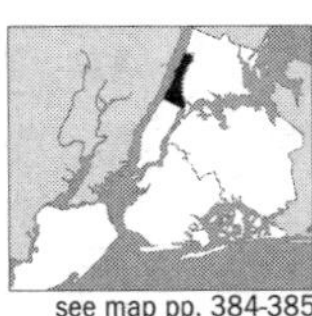
see map pp. 384-385

Subway: C to 155th St./St. Nicholas Ave., 163rd St.; 1, A, C to 168th St.-Broadway; A to 175th St., 181st St., 190th St.; 1, 9 to 181st St./St. Nicholas Ave., 191st St. ***Sights:*** *p. 100.*

Although the demolishing hand of the corporate contractor rendered downtown neighborhoods so many clusters of flattened blocks, Manhattan Island's curves north of 155th St. eluded the leveling eye of the postmodern architect. Head for the hills and visit an area of New York that is home to almost as many Dominicans as the Dominican Republic.

QUEENS

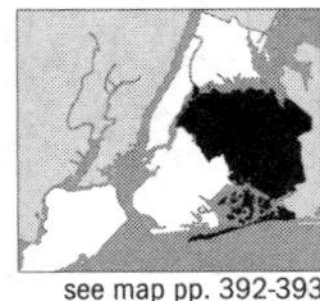
see map pp. 392-393

Sights: *p. 112.* ***Galleries:*** *p. 147.* ***Food:*** *p. 187.* ***Accommodations:*** *p. 273.*

Unlike Brooklyn, in which the parts make up a cohesive whole, Queens is full of relatively self-contained neighborhoods, a vestige of the borough's past as a collection of unincorporated villages. Although Queens has been a single body

for most of the past century, it remains postally balkanized. Don't try to send a letter to Queens, NY or it will never get farther than a magical land of undelivered mail. Address all your correspondence with the borough by neighborhood: Astoria, NY; Jackson Heights, NY; and so on.

On the borough's western edge are **Astoria** and **Long Island City** (p. 112). As you move to the east, you'll find **Jackson Heights, Elmhurst,** and **Corona** (p. 113). To the south of Corona are **Forest Hills** and **Forest Park** (p. 114). **Flushing Meadows-Corona Park** (p. 114) sits, not surprisingly, between **Flushing** (p. 116) and Corona. **Jamaica** (p. 117) is south of Flushing, and **the Rockaways** (p. 117) are in the southwest. Use a map; the very useful Queens Bus Map (free) is available on most Queens buses.

Unisphere, Flushing Meadows Park

STATEN ISLAND

Sights: *p. 123.* ***Food:*** *p. 191.*

see map p. 398

Unlike the rest of the city, Staten Island is quite spread out. Pick up much-needed maps of Staten Island's bus routes as well as other pamphlets at the Staten Island Chamber of Commerce, 130 Bay St. To reach it, bear left from the ferry station onto Bay St. (☎718-727-1900. Open M-F 9am-5pm.)

Bronx Zoo

8 THINGS TO DO IN NYC

8. Feed a marmoset. Actually, this is probably a bad idea. But go to the Bronx Zoo and find out what a marmoset is. Then tell us, because we don't know. What we do know is that the Bronx Zoo is the only place in New York where leopards and zebras outnumber squirrels and pigeons.

7. Take the 7. Forget Epcot Center. You want to see a little piece of every part of the world? Take the 7 train through Queens, the most diverse community in the United States.

6. Pay your respects at the World Trade Center Site.

5. Get a free cruise. Need a reason to go to Staten Island at 6 AM? The sunset from the Ferry is one of New York's most unknown (and breathtaking) pleasures.

All Lit Up

4. Look at pretty pictures. From the Met to the Frick to the galleries of Williamsburg, you can enjoy the works of a lot of good painters, sculptors, drawers, and innovative multimedia-ers.

3. Walk on water. The greatest engineering spectacle of the 19th century is still the greatest symbol of a city of interconnected boroughs. It should be required for every person who sets foot in New York to take the 1.2-mile stroll across the Brooklyn Bridge.

2. Visit Central Park. 150 years ago, the greatest urban park in the world. Some things never change.

1. Hit the sidewalk. Forget the museums and monuments, diners and dance clubs. From Flatbush to Flushing, Mott Street to Mott Haven, down to Tottenville and back again, if you want to experience New York, keep your eyes on the prize and ear to the street.

SUGGESTED ITINERARIES

WHEN TO GO. Always. Spring is joyous, the summer is steamingly, stickily, and intensely New York, Central Park in the fall is painfully beautiful, and the holiday season in the city is as enchanting as the movies make it out to be. Tourists flock to New York at all times of the year, but if you can't decide which season suits your fancy, you'll get smart, pack your bags, and move here. Hey, eight million people can't be wrong, right?

DAY 1: WALK INTO NYC

Begin your day among the serene brownstones of Brooklyn Heights and ask yourself "is this really New York?" Walk down to the Promenade and take in the stunning landscape of downtown Manhattan. Stop for lunch at **Grimaldi's,** get on the **Brooklyn Bridge** and walk right into the skyline you were just admiring. When you get off the Bridge, explore New York's **Civic Center** and **Financial District.** Do some shopping at **Century 21,** buy some music and electronics at **J&R,** and swing east for dinner in **Chinatown.**

DAY 2: TOURIST'S DELIGHT

Wake up early and do all the things that you think you're supposed to do in New York. Check out the **Statue of Liberty** and **Ellis Island** in the morning, have lunch at **a mediocre and overpriced restaurant,** take a ride to the top of the **Empire State Building** and then spend the afternoon aimlessly wandering around **Midtown,** cooing at the tall buildings. Go see *Cats* and have dinner in **Times Square,** where you can sate your homesick belly with the neighborhood's bevy of delightful 'casual dining' chains. If you still have any will to live, squeeze into your black pants and get grooving with a bunch of Jersey kids at a sweaty nightclub on the **West Side.**

DAY 3: PRETEND YOU'RE RICH AND/OR CLASSY

Skulk into the **Plaza** or the **Pierre** and then stroll out like you just spent a night in the Presidential suite. Go into **Bergdorf-Goodman** and ask for a shopping bag, and then fill it with leaves (this will make it look like you bought something). Take a carriage ride around **Central Park,** and if the weather permits, stop for a picnic. Exit the park on the **Upper East Side** and attempt to gain entrance to one of the palatial apartment buildings on **Fifth and Park Avenues** by telling the doorman you're there to see "Uncle Moneybags." If this fails, head over to Madison Avenue and collect some more swanky shopping bags. Fill these with rocks. Now that you have some money, buy yourself some culture at any of the fine museums that line **Fifth Avenue.**

DAY 4: DO NOT PASS 14TH STREET

This should be pretty self-explanatory. We've spent a lifetime wandering the streets that make up the neighborhoods of downtown Manhattan. If you can't amuse yourself for a day, we can't help you.

DAYS 5 AND 6: CHOOSE YOUR OWN BOROUGH

Many people treat the four 'outer-boroughs' as a single, monolithic entity. These people are idiots. In fact, almost all of the public transportation that connects Brooklyn, Queens, the Bronx, and Staten Island goes through Manhattan. So if you want to spend some time outside of Manhattan (and you should), you'll need to do it one borough at a time.

A day in **Brooklyn** should begin with a visit to the **Brooklyn Museum of Art** and the neighboring **Brooklyn Botanic Gardens,** followed by lunch in **Park Slope** and a peek at **Prospect Park.** Take the **F** train to the ocean, eat at **Nathan's,** walk on the beach, and ride the **Cyclone.** Head to **Fort Greene** or **Carroll Gardens** for dinner and walk over to see an opera at **BAM.** Hail a cab to **Williamsburg** and the city's best nightlife.

When in **Queens,** eat your way along the **7** train. Check the art at **MoMA** in **Long Island City,** and then head east through a culinary tour of India (**Jackson Heights**), Latin America (**Corona**), Greece (**Astoria**), and Asia (**Flushing**). If it happens to be the summer, root for the hometown Mets at **Shea Stadium.**

By itself, the **Bronx Zoo** can take a full day to explore. After a full afternoon of lions, tigers, and ice-cream bars shaped like bears, walk a few blocks to **Arthur Avenue.** Stuff yourself silly on New York's best Italian food before you leave the Bronx.

Even if you don't want to spend a day in **Staten Island,** no visit to New York should be complete without a trip across the **Staten Island Ferry.** Why spend money on an expensive boat tour when you can get one for free? Once in SI, check out historic **Richmond Town,** New York's answer to Colonial Williamsburg.

DAY 7: WEST SIDE STORY AND BEYOND

The **Upper West Side** is one of Manhattan's most pleasant neighborhoods, and you should make sure to visit before your trip is over. Have

125th St., Harlem

Brooklyn brownstones

Apollo Theater

brunch on **Columbus Avenue,** visit the apartment houses of **Central Park West,** and walk north along **Broadway** until you hit **Columbia.** Visit the world's largest cathedral (**St. John the Divine,** still unfinished) and work your way up to **Harlem**. You'll find plenty to do here, but your day won't be done until you sit down to a full Dominican dinner in **Washington Heights.**

SIGHTSEEING TOURS

WALKING TOURS

Joyce Gold's Tours (☎212-242-5762; www.nyctours.com). Ms. Gold has read over 900 books on the history of Manhattan, the subject that she teaches at NYU and at the New School. On 45 days a year, she and a company of adventurers give tours focusing on architecture, history, and ethnic groups within the city. Approx. 2-2½hr., depending on the subject. $12.

Radical Walking Tours (☎718-492-0069; http://www.he.net/~radtours/). Historian/activist Bruce Kayton leads tours that cover the alternative history of NYC. For example, tours of Greenwich Village highlight radicals and revolutionaries John Reed and Emma Goldman, and the artistic and theatrical movements that flourished around them. Trips to Harlem, the Lower East Side, and Central Park also available. Even locals will learn fascinating details about the city's history. Call for schedule and departure sites. 2-3hr. All tours $10.

Big Onion Walking Tours (☎212-439-1090; www.bigonion.com). Grad students in American history from Columbia and NYU lead tours of historic districts and ethnic neighborhoods. Themed excursions include "Brooklyn Bridge to Brooklyn Heights," "Before Stonewall: A Gay and Lesbian History Tour," "Immigrant New York," "Historic Harlem," and the "Multi-Ethnic

Eating Tour," which explores the gastronomical delights of places such as Chinatown and Little Italy. Tours average 2hr. Group tours and bus tours also available. $12-18, students and seniors $10-16. "Show-up" tours June-Aug. Th-Su; Sept.-May Sa-Su.

Municipal Art Society (☎212-439-1049; www.mas.org). Guided walking tours. Destinations vary but include most major Manhattan districts, such as SoHo and Times Square. **Free tour** of Grand Central Station W 12:30pm, at info booth on the main concourse. Other tours $12-15. Call in advance.

92nd Street Y, 1395 Lexington Ave., at 92nd St. (☎212-415-5628; www.92ndsty.org/tours/tours.asp). The Y leads an astounding variety of walking tours covering all boroughs. Learn about the Garment District, SoHo artists, and the brownstones of Brooklyn through literary tours, museum visits, and even an all-night candlelight tour. Tours vary in length. Admission $20-60. Call for the latest tours.

BOAT TOURS

Circle Line Tours, W. 42nd St., at the Hudson River, Pier 83 (☎212-563-3200; www.circleline.com). 3hr. full-circle boat tour around Manhattan island $26, seniors $20, children $13; 2hr. semi-circle tour $21, seniors $17, children $10. No reservations necessary; arrive 30-45min. before tour starts. Call for schedule.

BUS TOURS

Brooklyn Attitude, 224 W. 35th St., between Seventh and Eighth Ave. (☎718-398-0939; www.brooklynx.org/tourism/brooklynattitude). Bus tour with several walking excursions through ethnic and historic neighborhoods in Brooklyn. Departure points in both mid-Manhattan and Brooklyn. $15-35.

Gray Line Sight-Seeing, 42nd St. and Eighth Ave., at the Port Authority Terminal (☎212-445-0848 or 800-669-0051; www.graylinenewyork.com). Huge bus tour company offers many trips, including jaunts through Manhattan and gambling junkets to Atlantic City. The Downtown tour (frequent departures daily beginning at 8:20am; $35, ages 5-11 $25) and Uptown tour (frequent departures daily 8:30am-5pm; $35, ages 5-11 $25) allow you to get on and off the bus at points to explore on your own. The 6hr. night tour (daily every 15min. 6-9pm; $35, children $20) covers many sights. Reservations aren't required for in-city tours, but arrive at the terminal 30min. early.

Harlem Spirituals, 690 Eighth Ave., between 43rd and 44th St. (☎212-391-0900; www.harlemspirituals.com). Offers tours of Manhattan, Brooklyn, and the Bronx. Tours of upper Manhattan, such as "Harlem on Sunday" (4hr.; Su 9:15am; $45) and "Gospel on a Weekday" (4hr.; W 8:45am; $45), include trips to historic homes and Baptist services. "Soul Food and Jazz" (M, Th, Sa 7pm-midnight; $99) features a tour of Harlem, a filling meal at a Harlem restaurant (usually **Sylvia's,** p. 180), and an evening at a jazz club. Reserve in advance.

Heart of Brooklyn Trolley (☎718-282-7789). This trolley system connects major sights around Prospect Park such as the **Brooklyn Museum of Art** (p. 131), the **Botanic Garden** (p. 107), and the **9th St. Bandshell** (p. 107). Wheelchair-accessible. Sa-Su noon-6pm. Free.

Lower East Side Tenement Museum Walking Tours (☎212-431-0233; www.tenement.org). See p. 137 for museum info and directions. Neighborhood heritage tour strolls through the Lower East Side and examines how different immigrant groups have shaped the area. Call for tour dates and times. Apr.-Dec. $9, students and seniors $7; combination tickets available for walking tours and tenement tours.

INSIDE

getting into new york **27**
getting around new york **29**
keeping in touch **32**
by mail **32** by phone **33**
by email and internet **34**
getting money from home **35**
safety and security **36**
personal safety **36** financial security **36**
drugs and alcohol **37**
local life in new york **37**
newspapers and magazines **37** radio **38**
taxes and tipping **38** etiquette **38**

Once in NYC

GETTING INTO NEW YORK

TO AND FROM THE AIRPORT

Travel between the airports and Manhattan is a choice between inconvenience and money. **Public transportation** is cheap, but you will almost definitely have to transfer from bus to subway, subway to bus, or subway to subway at least twice. **Private bus** companies (shuttles) charge slightly more, but will take you directly from the airport to any one of many Manhattan destinations: Grand Central Terminal (42nd St. and Park Ave.), the Port Authority Bus Terminal (41st St. and Eighth Ave.), or several prominent hotels. Most private services peter out or vanish entirely between midnight and 6am. If you're willing to pay, a **taxi** is the most comfortable way of getting to the city. Heavy traffic will make the trip slightly more expensive; traveling during rush hour (7:30-10am and 4-7:30pm) can be hard on your wallet. Passengers are responsible for paying bridge and tunnel tolls, but there are **no extra fees for luggage or additional passengers.**

The best resource for ground transportation to the airports is the Port Authority of NJ and NY's website, **www.panynj.gov.** If you make lodging reservations ahead of time, be sure to ask about **limousine services**—some hostels offer transportation from the airports for reasonable fares. **All time estimates below are for getting to Midtown Manhattan.**

JFK AIRPORT

30-60min. drive from Midtown. ***Taxis:*** *$35 flat rate from JFK to Manhattan, plus tolls and tip.*

BY SUBWAY. Catch a free yellow-and-blue JFK Long-Term Parking and Subway bus from any airport terminal to the **Howard Beach-JFK Airport subway station.** You can take the **A train** from there to several points in the city. (Entire trip 60-75min; bus runs every 15-20min; $2, exact change only.) Heading from Manhattan to JFK, take the Far Rockaway A train.

BY BUS. The local **Green Line Q10 bus** stops at the airport and connects to the A, E, J, Z, F, and R subway lines, which in turn go to Manhattan. Tell the driver what line you want, and ask him to tell you where to get off. (Entire trip 60-75min.; bus runs every 20-25min, 24hr.; $2 for both bus and subway transfer, exact change only.) Although these routes are safe during the day, nighttime travelers should check with the information desk to find the safest way into the city.

BY SHUTTLE. The **New York Airport Service** express bus (☎718-875-8200) is a private line that runs between JFK and Grand Central Terminal, Penn Station, and Port Authority. (45-60min.; departs JFK every 20-25min. 6:15am-11:10pm, $13-15.) Transfer service to Midtown hotels is available at extra charge. The **Super-Shuttle** (☎212-258-3826) will drop you anywhere in Manhattan between Battery Park and 227th St. (45-60min.; 24hr.; $13-22.) Inquire about all three at JFK's Ground Transportation Center.

LAGUARDIA AIRPORT (LGA)

20-25min. drive from Midtown. ***Taxis:*** *$16-26, plus tolls and tip.*

BY BUS AND SUBWAY. The **M60 bus** connects to Manhattan subway lines 1 at 110th St./Broadway; A, B, C, D at 125th St./St. Nicholas Ave.; 2, 3 at 125th St./Lenox (Sixth) Ave.; 4, 5, 6 at 125th St./Lexington Ave. In Queens, catch the N or W at Astoria Blvd./31st St. For 24hr. bus service between LGA and Queens subways, look for "Q33" and "Q48" stops in front of each terminal. The **Q33 bus** goes to Jackson Heights/Roosevelt Ave. in Queens for E, F, G, R, V, 7; the **Q48 bus** goes to 74th St.-Broadway in Queens for E, F, G, R, V, 7. (Allow at least 90min. for all routes; M60 runs daily 5am-1am, Q33 and Q488 24hr.; all buses $2.) Be especially careful traveling these routes at night.

BY SHUTTLE. See above information for JFK.

NEWARK LIBERTY INTERNATIONAL AIRPORT (EWR)

40-50min. drive from Midtown. ***Taxis:*** *$34-55, plus tolls and tip. NYC taxis are not required to go to Newark, but if they do, the fare will be what is shown on the meter PLUS $10 PLUS round-trip tolls to AND from the airport.*

BY BUS. Bus #107 by the New Jersey Transit Authority (NJTA ☎973-762-5100) covers Newark, Newark International Airport (North Terminal) and Port Authority. (25min.; every 30-45min. 6am-midnight; $3.60.)

BY TRAIN. AirTrain (☎800-626-7433) now provides direct service between EWR's Newark International Airport Rail Link Station and Penn Station. (20min.; 5 AM-2AM; $11.55 to New York's Penn Station) Look for signs marked "Monorail/AirTrain Link" (do *not* follow signs for "Ground Transportation"). The airport's Rail Link station is accessible by Amtrak and NJTA.

BY SHUTTLE. Olympia Airport Express (☎212-964-6233, 877-894-9155) runs from the airport to Port Authority, Grand Central Terminal, and Penn Station. (40-50min.; every 5-10min., 24hr.; $12) **SuperShuttle** (☎800-258-3826) runs from Newark to anywhere between Battery Park and 227th St. (40-50min.; 24hr.; $13-22).

GETTING AROUND NEW YORK

BY FOOT

If you really want to study, appreciate, and love New York, you have to experience the city on foot. Skip the museums and sights, restaurants and bars. Save your money and turn your entire visit to New York into one extended stroll. Although having a destination is totally optional (and sometimes not even that desirable), you can often get from one place to the next faster on foot than you would in gridlock traffic or waiting for the local on a sweaty subway platform.

Because Manhattan is on a simple grid with streets with increasing numbers, spending five minutes with a street map (many of which can be found in the back of this book) and knowing what a compass looks like will make it hard for you to get too lost. And if you are totally unable to differentiate between north and south and simple maps make you sad, you might get lost, which is in many ways far more fun than knowing where you're going.

In case your the type of person who likes to know this sort of thing, one mile equals about 20 avenue (north-south) or 10 street (east-west) blocks.

BY SUBWAY

The subway is the lifeblood of New York. In fact, the train (as most New Yorkers call it) is so important to the city's residents that the current Mayor made a campaign promise to forgo his official limousine for a ride on the Lexington Avenue line. Each day, six million people move through the city's 468 stations. And like the city itself, the subway never sleeps: with only minor service changes, the subway covers its 685 miles of tracks 24 hours a day, 365 days a year.

The subway is not without its frustrations, but on the whole, it remains one of the most reliable and cost-effective methods of transportation in New York. Long distances are best traveled by subway because a passenger, once inside, may transfer onto any of the other trains without restrictions. Free, extremely useful subway maps are available at any subway token booth; additional copies are posted in all stations and subway cars. Service advisories are posted throughout stations. Since trains and riders decrease at night, it's advisable—and often quicker—to take a cab after 11pm.

In Manhattan, the biggest **subway hubs** are 42nd St.-Grand Central on the East Side and 42nd St.-Times Square on the West Side; these two stops are connected by the 7 and S trains. **The subways are much more useful for traveling north-south than east-west,** but crosstown shuttle buses run on several streets, including 14th, 23rd, 34th, 42nd, 57th, 79th, and 86th St. **Express trains** stop only at certain major stations; **locals** stop everywhere. Be sure to **check the letter or number and the destination of each train,** since trains with different destinations often use the same track. When in doubt, ask the conductor, who usually sits near the middle of the train.

You'll see lit glass globes outside most subway entrances. Green means that the entrance is staffed 24hr. while red indicates that the entrance is closed or restricted in some way, usually during off (night) hours. Sometimes the light is neither red nor green. We don't know what this means, but it's probably not a good thing. Read the sign posted above the stairs.

FARES. In 2003, the City of New York bid a fond farewell to the subway token. Although some buses continue to accept exact change, you won't be able to get on the subway without a **MetroCard**. The magnetic-strip card, first introduced in 1995, is sold in all subway stations and at many newsstands, pharmacies, and grocery stores with MetroCard stickers in the storefront windows. Subway and bus fare is $2 per ride with the MetroCard, but the **Pay-Per-Ride MetroCard** gets you 20% credit automatically added after you spend $10—for example, 12 rides for the price of 10. Even more importantly, MetroCards can be used for subway-bus, bus-subway, and bus-bus transfers. When you swipe the card on the initial ride, a free transfer is electronically stored on your MetroCard and is good for up to 2hr. **Without the MetroCard, bus-subway and subway-bus transfers are not free.**

UNLIMITED METROCARDS. **"Unlimited Rides" MetroCards** (as opposed to "Pay-Per-Ride" cards) are sold in one-day ($7 **Fun Pass**), seven-day ($21 **7-Day Unlimited Ride**) and 30-day ($70 **30-Day Unlimited Ride**) denominations and are good for unlimited use of the subway and bus systems during the specified period. **The Unlimited Rides Card is highly recommended for tourists who plan on visiting many sights.** Those with disabilities or over 65 qualify for a Reduced Fare card; call ☎ 718-243-4999 for information.

SAFETY. Though some New Yorkers wax nostalgic for the rough-and-tumble days of graffiti-covered subway cars and hoppable turnstiles, most residents and visitors have been pleased to see the underground world become cleaner and safer in recent years. Even so, the subway is not always the safest place. Central Manhattan is generally considered safe at all hours, but exercise caution when traveling in other parts of the city. Stay away from the platform's edge, and board the train during non-rush hours from the off-peak waiting area, marked at the center of every platform (this area is monitored by cameras, and the conductor's car stops here). Once you board, stay near the middle to be close to the conductor. During rush hour and in crowded stations, hold your bag with the opening facing you to discourage pickpockets.

BY BUS

Because buses are often mired in traffic, they can take twice as long as subways, but they are almost always safer, cleaner, and quieter. They'll also get you closer to your destination, since most buses stop every two blocks or so and run crosstown (east-west), as well as uptown and downtown (north-south). Buses can be a nightmare for long-distance travel over 40 north-south blocks (except late at night, when traffic is manageable), but for shorter—and especially crosstown—trips, they are often as quick as, and more convenient than, trains. The MTA transfer system provides north-south travelers with a paper slip, valid for a free ride east-west, or vice versa, but you must ask the driver for a transfer when you board and pay your fare. Make sure you ring when you want to get off. If you use a MetroCard, you can transfer within 2hr., free of charge, from bus to subway or from bus to bus.

Bus stops are indicated by a blue sign post announcing the bus number or a glass-walled shelter displaying a map of the bus's route and a pretty unreliable schedule of arrival times. From 10pm-5am, you can request any stop along the bus's route. A flat fare of $2 is charged at all times when you board; either a MetroCard (see above for more information), exact change, or a subway token is required. Dollar bills are not accepted. Ask for outer borough bus maps at any outer borough subway station; different restrictions apply to them as many are operated by private companies.

BY TAXI

Only government-licensed yellow taxis are permitted by law to pick up without prearrangement; you will likely be overcharged if you use a non-yellow "gypsy cab." When hailing a cab: if the center light on the cab's roof is lit, then the cabbie is picking up fares; if it is dark, the cab is already taken. If you can't find anything on the street, commandeer a radio-dispatched cab (see **Service Directory,** p. 324, for phone numbers). Keep in mind that you can't cram more than four people into a cab. The meter starts at $2 and clicks 30¢ for the first 1/3 mi. (about every four street blocks), then 30¢ each 1/5 of a mi. thereafter and 20¢ per mi. when the cab is not moving; a 50¢ night surcharge is in effect between 8pm and 6am. Any bridge or tunnel tolls will be added to the total charge, and drivers might ask that you pay the tolls as you go through them. Cabbies also expect a 15-20% overall tip. Some drivers may illegally try to show the naïve visitor the "scenic route"; glance at a street map before embarking to avoid being taken for a ride. Furthermore, a cab driver **must take you to any destination within the five boroughs of New York City,** no matter how far afield it might be.

Before you leave the cab, ask for a receipt, which will have the taxi's identification number (either its meter number or its medallion). You need this number to trace lost articles or to make a complaint to the **Taxi Commission** (☎212-692-8294).

BY CAR

If you can, avoid driving in the city. When behind the wheel in New York, you are locked in combat with aggressive taxis, careless pedestrians, and lunatic bicycle couriers. If you do choose to drive in Manhattan, you must **stay alert** and **know where you are going.** Amber lights last only about four seconds; **both right and left turns on red lights are prohibited;** many vehicles (illegally) change lanes without signalling. During rush hours, certain lanes—particularly roads leading to bridges and tunnels—are **closed or reversed.** Save sightseeing for later: never take your eyes off the road.

Most avenues and streets run one-way. Streets usually run east if they're even-numbered and west if they're odd-numbered. Wide transverse streets (125th, 116th, 106th, 96th, 86th, 79th, 72nd, 57th, 42nd, 34th, 23rd and 14th St.) are two-way. When traveling uptown or downtown, you are generally better served by taking an avenue on which traffic travels one-way. On these avenues, traffic lights are synchronized so that lights turn from red to green in succession. Consult road maps for details.

Although driving in Manhattan can be incredibly frustrating, its reasonably simple grid makes navigating the streets pretty intuitive, even for a first-time visitor. When traveling to Brooklyn, Queens, the Bronx, or Staten Island, however, be sure to know exactly where you're going: even the most experienced New York driver will have a story about the wrong turn off of Astoria Blvd., the missed exit on the Bruckner Expressway, or just simply getting lost on Bedford Ave.

The hassle of parking, however, truly makes having a car nothing but a nuisance. Don't be surprised if you have to park many blocks from your destination. Read the signs carefully; a space is usually legal only on certain days of the week. The city has never been squeamish about towing, and recovering a towed car will cost $100 or more. Some streets have parking meters that cost 25¢ per 15min., with a limit of 1-2hr. **Parking lots** are the easiest but the most expensive option. Depending on where you park (Midtown being most expensive), garage rates may range from $6 to $15 for the first hr. to $40 per day. The cheapest parking lots are downtown—try the far west end of Houston St. Many garages have lower weekend rates.

Break-ins and car theft happen often, particularly if you have a radio. The wailing of a car alarm is such a familiar tune to New Yorkers that you may hear them sing along. Never leave anything visible inside your car. **You may want to use a steering wheel locking device.** Children under 40 lb. should ride only in a specially-designed car seat, available for a small fee from most car rental agencies.

You must have a New York State license to drive in New York unless you are a resident of another state or Canadian province and have a valid drivers license from there. New York's minimum driving age is 16. New York State honors all valid foreign licenses; see www.nydmv.state.ny.us/license.htm or call the **New York State Department of Motor Vehicles** (☎212-645-5550; see p. 327 for locations) for details.

CAR RENTAL. All agencies maintain varying minimum-age requirements and require proof of age as well as a security deposit. Agencies in Queens and Yonkers are often less expensive than their Manhattan counterparts, especially for one-day rentals. Most auto insurance policies will cover rented cars, and some credit cards take care of your rental insurance costs if you've charged the vehicle to their card (but be sure to ask about all the particulars from the companies themselves). For car rental agencies, refer to the **Service Directory,** p. 323.

You may also consider getting a membership at **Zipcar** (www.zipcar.com). The company, launched in 2002, provides members with temporary cars at $10-14 per hr. You can reserve online (1hr. min., up to 2 months ahead) after getting a membership through the website. The cars are located off-street throughout the city and are available for use by members for any length of time. The service pays for gas, insurance, maintenance, and off-street parking. Zipcar stations are scattered throughout Manhattan, Brooklyn, and Hoboken; check online for details.

EMBASSIES AND CONSULATES

CONSULAR SERVICES IN NEW YORK

AUSTRALIA. Embassy and Consulate: Moonah Pl., Yarralumla **(Canberra),** ACT 2600 (☎02 6214 5600; fax 6214 5970; http://usembassy-australia.state.gov/consular). **Other Consulates:** MLC Centre, Level 59, 19-29 Martin Pl., **Sydney,** NSW 2000 (☎02 9373 9200; fax 9373 9184); 553 St. Kilda Rd., **Melbourne,** VIC 3004 (☎03 9526 5900; fax 9510 4646); 16 St. George's Terr., 13th fl., **Perth,** WA 6000 (☎08 9202 1224; fax 9231 9444).

CANADA. Embassy and Consulate: Consular Section, 490 Sussex Dr., **Ottawa,** P.O. Box 866, Station B, Ottowa, Ontario K1P 5T1 (☎613-238-5335; fax 613-688-3081; www.usembassycanada.gov). **Other Consulates** (☎1-900-451-2778 or www.amcits.com): 615 Macleod Trail SE, Room 1000, **Calgary,** AB T2G 4T8 (☎403-266-8962; fax 264-6630); 1969 Upper Water St., Purdy's Wharf Tower II, ste. 904, **Halifax,** NS B3J 3R7 (☎902-429-2480; fax 423-6861); 1155 St. Alexandre, **Montréal,** QC H3B 1Z1 (mailing address: P.O. Box 65, Postal Station Desjardins, Montréal, QC H5B 1G1 (☎514-398-9695; fax 981-5059); 2 Place Terrasse Dufferin, behind Château Frontenac, B.P. 939, **Québec City,** QC G1R 4T9; 360 University Ave., **Toronto,** ON M5G 1S4 (☎418-692-2095; fax 692-2096); 1075 W. Pender St., Mezzanine (mailing address: 1095 W. Pender St., 21st fl., **Vancouver,** BC V6E 2M6 (☎604-685-4311; fax 685-7175).

IRELAND. Embassy and Consulate: 42 Elgin Rd., Ballsbridge, **Dublin** 4 (☎01 668 8777 or 668 7122; fax 668 9946; www.usembassy.ie).

NEW ZEALAND. Embassy and Consulate: 29 Fitzherbert Terr. (or P.O. Box 1190), Thorndon, **Wellington** (☎04 462 6000; fax 478 0490; http://usembassy.org.nz). **Other Consulate:** 23 Customs St., Citibank Building, 3rd fl., **Auckland** (☎09 303 2724; fax 366 0870).

SOUTH AFRICA. Embassy and Consulate: 877 Pretorius St., **Pretoria,** P.O. Box 9536, Pretoria 0001 (☎012 342 1048; fax 342 2244; http://usembassy.state.gov/pretoria). **Other Consulates:** Broadway Industries Center, Heerengracht, Foreshore, **Cape Town** (mailing address: P.O. Box 6773, Roggebaai, 8012; ☎021 342 1048; fax 342 2244); 303 West St., Old Mutual Building, 31st fl., **Durban** (☎031 305 7600; fax 305 7691); No. 1 River St., Killarney, **Johannesburg,** P.O. Box 1762, Houghton, 2041 (☎011 644 8000; fax 646 6916).

UK. Embassy and Consulate: 24 Grosvenor Sq., **London** W1A 1AE (☎020 7499 9000; fax 7495 5012; www.usembassy.org.uk). **Other Consulates**: Queen's House, 14 Queen St., Belfast, **N. Ireland** BT1 6EQ (☎028 9032 8239; fax 9024 8482); 3 Regent Terr., Edinburgh, **Scotland** EH7 5BW (☎0131 556 8315; fax 557 6023).

KEEPING IN TOUCH

BY MAIL

US Postal Service: *☎800-275-8777; www.usps.com. Hours vary widely according to the branch, although many are open M-F 9am-5pm; call for details. For postal services, see the* ***Service Directory,*** *p. 327.*

SENDING MAIL FROM NEW YORK

The **postal rate** for letters under 1 oz. headed anywhere in the **US** is 37¢; postcards and aerogrammes cost 23¢. Letters and aerogrammes to Canada cost 60¢, postcards 50¢. For Australia, Ireland, New Zealand, South Africa, and the UK, rates are 80¢ for letters, 70¢ for postcards or aerogrammes. All international mail should be marked "AIR MAIL" or "PAR AVION" on the front, and will arrive by air at their destination in about four to seven days. A post office clerk (or the official online rate calculator at http://postcalc.usps.gov) will give you rates on anything else.

Postage **stamps** for domestic and international letters and postcards can be purchased at all post offices as well as at most convenience stores, drugstores and pharmacies, and even at some ATMs. Note that these stamps will most likely come in 37¢ or 23¢ increments (the amount of domestic postage rates), meaning those sending mail abroad will have to affix more postage than needed to their letters.

All domestic and international mail with proper postage weighing under 15 oz. (that includes letters and postcards) can be dropped in round-topped, dark blue mailboxes found on street corners. Postmen usually collect from these Mondays to Saturdays, at 5pm.

For a **24hr. post office,** go to the General Post Office/James A. Farley Station (☎212-330-3002), 421 Eighth Ave., between 30th and 31st St.

RECEIVING MAIL IN NEW YORK

If you don't have a mailing address in New York, you can still receive mail via **General Delivery** (known as *Poste Restante* in most other parts of the world). Mail addressed to you at the following address will be held for pick-up for up to 30 days: General Delivery, General Post Office/James A. Farley Station, 421 Eighth Ave., New York, NY 10001 (Map 14, B6). A photo ID is required for pick-up (for US General Delivery, go to 390 Ninth Ave., at W. 30th St.).

BY PHONE

TIME DIFFERENCES

New York is 4hr. behind **Greenwich Mean Time (GMT),** 3hr. ahead of Vancouver and San Francisco, 6hr. behind Johannesburg, 14hr. behind Sydney, and 16hr. behind Auckland (NZ). The US observes **daylight savings time,** and fall and spring switchover times vary.

4AM	7AM	10AM	NOON	2PM	10PM
Vancouver	Toronto	London	Hanoi	China	Sydney
Seattle	Ottawa	(GMT)	Bangkok	Hong Kong	Canberra
San Francisco	New York		Jakarta	Manila	Melbourne
Los Angeles	Boston		Phnom Penh	Singapore	

CALLING ABROAD FROM NEW YORK

To place an international call from New York, dial: 011 (the international dialing prefix for calls out of the US) + country code of where you're calling (Australia 61; Ireland 353; New Zealand 64; South Africa 27; UK 44) + area code + local number. The country code for the United States is 1. When calling Canada, simply dial the appropriate area code and the local number. To have an operator assist you, dial "0" and ask for the overseas operator.

International calls are cheapest using **prepaid phone cards,** which are available at most convenience stores, drugstores, and pharmacies (chemists). These cards range from $5 to $100 and charge a certain per-minute list price (from about 12¢ up) for a set amount of minutes; instructions on the card tell you how to place a call. Make sure any card you buy is issued by a reputable national phone service carrier, or phone service may be spotty. The street vendor-hawked prepaid cards with too-good-to-be-true rates usually are: many have unreliable service, and may have hidden hardware and dial-up charges that make the prices no better than the more "reputable" cards sold at convenience stores and pharmacies.

No matter how you place a call, national and international phone rates tend to be highest in the morning, lower in the evening, and lowest on Sunday and at night.

CALLING WITHIN NEW YORK

Operator ☎0 (free). Collect/reverse-charge calls ☎0. Directory assistance ☎411. All 24hr.

The three-digit telephone (or city) codes in the USA are called "area codes." The area codes for Manhattan are ☎212, 347, 646 and 917. For Brooklyn, Queens, the Bronx, and Staten Island, the area codes are 718 and 347. The 917 area code is also used for many cellular phones and pagers in all five boroughs. **All New York City calls made within and between all five area codes must be dialed using 1 + the area code + the 7-digit telephone number.**

Toll-free numbers (no charge or coins necessary) are used by businesses to encourage requests for information, and usually accessible only within the US. The numbers are preceded by the area codes ☎800, 888, 866, and 877.

To get a local or national telephone number, dial ☎411. If you want to charge a long-distance call to the person you're calling, call collect by dialing "0" instead of "1" before the 10-digit number, and an operator will come on the line to assist you (the person you're calling, however, has the right to refuse the call). For **emergency** services, **dial ☎911.**

The cheapest way to place a call to anywhere in the Greater New York area is to use a coin-operated **pay phone,** available on street corners and in hotel lobbies, bars, restaurants, and subway stations. Many phones also accept credit cards; no pennies accepted. Cost per local call on most phones is 50¢ for an unlimited amount of time. Don't be surprised, however, if you pick up a receiver and hear no dial tone: New York's pay phones are famously unreliable. A good alternative is to use a prepaid phone card (see below), which can be used for local, long-distance, and international calls.

CELL PHONES

If your cell phone plan isn't based in the US, it probably won't work in New York. European GSM phones, for example, are not compatible with the American GSM network. You can rent a New York cell phone for a hefty price. Rental fees usually range between $15-100 per week, but can go even higher; delivery charges are around $10-15. International calls can cost as much as $3 per min.—read the rental contracts carefully, so that you won't get any nasty surprises on your bill. The following companies provide cell phones for rent:

Europe-USA Cellular Phone Rentals, 150 E. 69th St.(☎800-964-2468 or 212-734-6344; www.europe-usa-mobile-cellular-phone-rental.com). Mobile phone rentals cover European networks. $1.45 per min. plus $5 per day or $20 per week. Most international calls $2.45 per min.

TravellCell.com, (☎877-235-5746; www.travelcell.com). Phone rental $3 per day. $25 gets you 38min., not including long-distance charges. $50 min. prepaid purchase required with every rental.

RentCell.com, (☎800-404-3093 or 404-467-4508; www.rentcell.com). $40-60 per wk. or $100-180 per month, depending on phone selected. Call for international calling rates.

BY EMAIL AND INTERNET

There are plenty of places to check your email or surf the web in New York City. Go to www.letsgo.com for a listing of them. Or just visit one of the following wired establishments.

Easy Internet Cafe, 234 W. 42nd St., between Seventh and Eighth Ave., next to Madame Tussaud's wax museum (www.easyeverything.com). Absolutely mammoth cybercafe with over 800 computers. At $1 for 21min. of access, it's one of the city's better deals. Beware the machine where you buy your access code: it doesn't give change. Open 24hr.

NY Computer Cafe, 274 E. 57th St., between Second and Third Av

e. (☎212-872-1704). $12 per hr. Printing, scanning, CD-recording, and faxing services also available. Lessons offered from $50 per hr. PCs and Macs available. Coffee $1.25-3. Open M-F 8am-11pm, Sa 10am-11pm, Su 11am-11pm.

CyberCafe, 250 West 49th St., between Broadway and Eighth Ave. (☎212-333-4109; www.cyber-cafe.com). Small, quiet cafe with big-screen TV and astronomical prices. It's $6.40 for the first 30min., $3.20 for each subsequent 15min. you're online. Open M-W 8am-11pm, Th-Sa 24hr., Su 11am-11pm.

Bryant Park, Sixth Ave., between 40th and 42nd St., behind the library (park management ☎212-768-4242; www.bryantpark.org/html/wirelesspark.htm). Subway: B, D, F, V to 42nd St./Ave. of the Americas (Sixth Ave.); 7 to Fifth Ave./42nd St. Map 13, D1. Free wireless computing available anytime the park is open. However, the service is available only to laptops and handheld devices with 802.11b ethernet cards. How-to guides to get started are available at the park entrances. Open daily 7am-9pm.

Burger King, 182 Broadway, at John St. Subway: 1, 2, 4, 5, A, C, J, M, Z to Fulton St./Broadway-Nassau St. Who would've thought? 10 terminals available for your use, luxuriously appointed in one of America's largest fast-food establishments. Deeply inhale the sweet aroma of french fries. 20min. free with purchase of a value combo ($3.29-6.19). Open M-Sa 7am-11pm, Su 8am-10pm.

Inka Travel and Internet Cafe, 349 5th Ave., between 4th and 5th St., Brooklyn. (☎718-788-5604) Subway F, M, N, R to Fourth Ave./9th St. Map 23, A2, 8. Inka's Internet Cafe may be a little bit pricey for regular World Wide Web exploring ($8 per hour, $5 per 1/2 hour, and $3 per 15 min.), but it's perfect for your quick email needs: Inka will let you check for free. Open daily 9am-10pm.

GETTING MONEY FROM HOME

If you run out of money while traveling, the easiest and cheapest solution is to have someone back home make a deposit to your credit card or cash (ATM) card. Failing that, consider one of the following options.

WIRING MONEY. It is possible to arrange a **bank money transfer,** which means asking a bank back home to wire money to a bank in the US. This is the cheapest way to transfer cash, but it's also the slowest, usually taking several days or more. Note that some banks may only release your funds in local currency, potentially sticking you with a poor exchange rate; inquire about this in advance. Money transfer services like **Western Union** are faster and more convenient than bank transfers—but also much pricier. Western Union has many locations worldwide. To find one, visit www.westernunion.com, or call in the US ☎800-325-6000; in Australia ☎800 501 500; in Canada ☎800-235-0000; in New Zealand ☎800 27 0000; in South Africa ☎0860 100031; in the UK ☎0800 83 38 33. Money transfer services are also available at **American Express** and **Thomas Cook** offices.

US STATE DEPARTMENT (US CITIZENS ONLY). In dire emergencies only, the US State Department will forward money within hours to the nearest consular office, which will then disburse it according to instructions for a US$15 fee. If you wish to use this service, you must contact the Overseas Citizens Service division of the US State Department (☎202-647-5225; nights, Sundays, and holidays ☎202-647-4000).

SAFETY AND SECURITY

PERSONAL SAFETY

New York is a remarkably safe city, far safer than any other American town of its size. In fact, a visitor to New York is far less likely to encounter personal danger than a visitor to almost any other large metropolis in the world. Still, don't be stupid. Be discreet with street maps and cameras; address requests for directions to police officers or store-owners. New York has very few public bathrooms, but stay out of the ones you see; the decor ranges from very dirty to reprehensibly filthy, and the ambience is either vaguely or oppressively threatening. Instead, try department stores, hotels, or restaurants. If you suspect you're being followed, duck into a nearby store or restaurant.

EXPLORING BY DAY AND BY NIGHT. New York is a big city and occasionally bad things happen to good people. These misfortunes can occur in both the safest and most threatening of neighborhoods, which themselves can sometimes be separated by only a single block. No matter where you are, always **be alert** and conscious of your surroundings. Nighttime requires extra precautions—stay out of large public parks and less-traversed, secluded areas.

There is no sure-fire way to avoid all the threatening situations you might encounter when you travel, but a good self-defense course will give you concrete ways to react to unwanted advances. **Impact, Prepare, and Model Mugging** can refer you to local self-defense courses in the US (☎800-345-5425). Visit the website at www.impactsafety.org for a list of nearby chapters. Workshops (2-3hr.) start at US$50; full courses run US$350-500.

TERRORISM. Following the September 11, 2001 terrorist attacks on New York and Washington, D.C., there is an elevated threat of further terrorist activities in the United States. Terrorists often target landmarks popular with tourists; however, the threat of an attack is generally not specific or great enough to warrant avoiding certain places or modes of transportation. Stay aware of developments in the news and watch for alerts from federal, state, and local law enforcement officials. Also, allow extra time for airport security and do not pack sharp objects in your carry-on luggage, as these things will be confiscated. Contact your home country's foreign affairs office for travel information and advisories.

FINANCIAL SECURITY

Rip-off artists seek the wealthy as well as the unwary, so hide your riches, especially in neighborhoods where you feel uncomfortable. Carrying a shoulder bag is better than having a backpack. In the midst of a crowd, it is easy for pickpockets to unzip backpack pockets and remove items. Tourists make especially juicy prey because they tend to carry large quantities of cash. Don't count your money in public or use large bills. Tuck your wallet into a less accessible pocket and keep an extra $10 or so in a more obvious one (this is "Mugging Money," a NYC tradition—it appeases the criminals and you aren't left destitute). If you must say your calling card number in a telephone booth, do so very quietly; if you punch it in, make sure no one can look over your shoulder.

Con artists run rampant on New York's streets. Beware of hustlers working in groups. Be distrustful of sob stories that require a donation from you. Remember that no one ever wins at three-card monte. If you take a car into the city, do not leave *anything* visible inside the car—put it all in the trunk, and if your tape deck/radio is removable, remove it and put it in the trunk also. You should never sleep in your car, no matter how low on cash you are.

If someone tries to hand you a baby, they might rifle through your pockets while you hold it and then leave you with the child. This is one of the oldest tricks in the book, and while we've never heard of it happening in New York, you never know, right?

PROTECTING YOUR VALUABLES. There are a few steps you can take to minimize the financial risk associated with traveling. First, **bring as little with you as possible.** Second, buy a few combination **padlocks** to secure your belongings either in your pack or in a hostel or train station locker. Third, **carry as little cash as possible.** Keep your traveler's checks and ATM/credit cards in a **money belt**—not a "fanny pack"—along with your passport and ID cards. Fourth, **keep a small cash reserve separate from your primary stash**—about $50 sewn into or stored in the depths of your pack, along with your traveler's check numbers and important photocopies.

DRUGS AND ALCOHOL

You must be 21 years old to purchase alcoholic beverages legally in New York State. The more popular drinking spots, as well as more upscale liquor stores, are likely to card. Smaller convenience stores and liquor stores in poorer neighborhoods will usually accept any type of ID, but few stores will let you get away with no proof of age whatsoever.

Possession of marijuana, cocaine, crack, heroin, methamphetamine, MDMA ("ecstasy"), hallucinogens, and most opiate derivatives (among many other chemicals) is punishable by stiff fines and imprisonment. Not that we should have to tell you this, but attempting to purchase illegal drugs of any sort is a **very bad idea.** Out-of-towners seeking (or on) a high are walking targets—not just for cops, but for thieves, as well.

If you carry **prescription drugs** when you travel, it is vital to have a copy of the prescriptions themselves readily accessible at US Customs. Check with the US Customs Service before your trip for more information.

LOCAL LIFE IN NEW YORK

NEWSPAPERS AND MAGAZINES

New York supports over 100 different newspapers, reflecting the diversity of its urban landscape. Weekly ethnic papers cater to the black, Hispanic, Irish, Japanese, Chinese, Indian, Korean, and Greek communities, among others. The city has three major dailies: ***The New York Times*** (www.nytimes.com) is the most respected; ***The Daily News*** (www.nydailynews.com) is the most popular; and ***The New York Post*** (www.nypost.com) is the most outrageous (except for their bizarrely accurate horoscopes).

FREE STUFF

GOURMET FOOD

Who needs money to eat well? At **Zabar's** (p. 178), you can gorge yourselves on free samples. Don't be embarrassed about doing this: we've eaten many a free meal of cheese, crackers, and the occasional slice of meat.

BASKETBALL

Frequented by streetball legends and professionals alike, **Rucker Park** (155th St. and Eighth Ave.) features NYC's best basketball. Five to one that a squad from the Ruck could beat the Knicks.

LANGUAGE LESSONS

Experts say that the best way to pick up another language is through immersion. Head to **Borough Park** for **Yiddish, Brighton Beach** for **Russian** and **Queens** for **languages you didn't even know existed.**

LAP DANCES

Here at *Let's Go*, we pride ourselves on being judgmental about restaurants, stores, and hotels—but never about people. If you want a lap dance, be our guest. And if you're too cheap to pay for your thrills, try the **6 train during rush hour.** Get on in the Bronx, get a seat and prepare yourself for the ride of your life.

MATTRESSES

At **1-800-Mattres,** the phone call is free and the mattresses are so affordable they might as well be. Leave off the last 'S' for **savings!**

The Village Voice (www.villagevoice.com), the country's largest alternative weekly newspaper, captures a spirit of the city each Wednesday that you won't find in the dailies. The left-leaning *Voice* stages lively political debates and prints quirky reflections on New York life. It also sponsors some excellent investigative city reporting—and the city's most intriguing set of personal ads. The real estate and nightlife listings are legendary and indispensable to visitors and natives alike. Best of all, it can be picked up **free** at many street corners and at almost all newsstands and bookstores.

New York is the magazine publishing capital of the country; most national periodicals have their headquarters somewhere in the city. The respected ***New Yorker*** (www.newyorker.com) contains invaluable museum, concert, theater, and movie listings for the tourist. ***Time Out New York*** (www.timeoutny.com) also contains helpful entertainment listings and colorful, well-written articles.

RADIO

New York City's radio spectrum has everything from soulless elevator instrumentals to pirate radio broadcasts of underground sounds and community activism. The lower on the dial, the less commercial the sounds will be.

TYPE	DIAL POSITION
Classical	WNYC 93.9, WQXR 96.3
Jazz	WBGO 88.3, WQCD 101.9
College/Indie/Alternative/Popular	WCWP 88.1, WPSC 88.7, WNYU 89.1, WKCR 89.9, WSOU 89.5, WFMU 91.1, WDRE 92.7, WXRK 92.3
Classic Rock	WQXR 104.3, WNEW 102.7
Top 40	WRKS 98.7, WPLJ 95.5, WHTZ 100.3, WRCN 103.9, WMXV 105.1
Hip-Hop/R&B/Soul	WQHT 97.1, WBLS 107.5, WWPR 105.1, WWRL 1600AM
Oldies	WCBS 101.1
Foreign-Language	WADO 1280AM, WWRV 1330AM, WKDM 1380AM, WZRC 1480AM
News	WABC 770AM, WCBS 880AM, WINS 1010AM, WBBR 1130AM
Public Radio	WNYC 93.9, WNYC 820AM, WBAI 99.5
Sports	WFAN 660AM, WABC 770AM
Pirate	88.7 Steal This Radio (Lower East Side)

TAXES AND TIPPING

The prices quoted throughout *Let's Go* do not include New York 8.625% sales tax, which applies to hotel rooms (plus a 5% hotel tax and $2 hotel fee per room per night).

Tipping is more or less compulsory in the US. Remember that service is never included on a New York bill, unless you're in a large party at a restaurant (six or more people), in which case it is noted. You can always give more or less based on the service you receive, but as a general rule, tip cab drivers and waiters 15-20%, coat-checkers $1, bellhops around $1 per bag, hotel maids $1 a day, and bartenders $1 per drink.

ETIQUETTE

SMOKING. There are basically two places in New York City where smoking is legal: your home and the street. You can smoke in some outdoor public places, but be prepared for dirty looks and ostentatious coughing. When it comes to smoking in New York, if you have to ask, you probably can't.

SUBWAYS. Try to read the subway maps before asking for help, and have your money ready when buying MetroCards. Wait for people to get off the train before you try to get on; give up your seat to people who need it more. Hold doors at your own risk, and never for more than a few seconds.

FRIENDLINESS. Of the many urban legends about New York, there is no greater myth than the belief that New Yorkers are unfriendly. We're sure that some people reading this book are really nice and some are kind of terrible people; the same variety exists among the eight million residents of New York. Don't be afraid to be friendly; most New Yorkers don't bite, although we will admit that the ones that do are pretty freaky.

"You Wanna

INSIDE

traders and traitors: 1624-1811 **41**
worms in the big apple: 1812-1897 **42**
the new metropolis: 1898-1929 **43**
the world's capital: 1930-2001 **43**
new york today **45**

Life & Times

TRADERS AND TRAITORS: 1624-1811

In 1624 the Dutch West Indies Company founded New Amsterdam, on the southernmost tip of Manhattan, as a trading post. Dutch governor Peter Minuit bought Manhattan Island in 1626 for 60 guilders ($25 today)—ironically, from Indians who didn't even come from the place. Diverse old New Amsterdam's artisans, sailors, trappers, and slaves all mingled together, speaking no fewer than 18 languages. Dictatorial Calvinist Peter Stuyvesant, one of Minuit's successors, lost the Dutch settlement to the British in 1664. New York schools, businesses, and neighborhoods now bear this unlikely folk hero's name.

The city grew into a major port with a population of 20,000—only to be captured for seven years by the Brits during the Revolutionary War. A 1776 fire destroyed a quarter of the pillaged and deserted city. When the defeated British finally left in 1783, New York's buildings were in ruins and one-third of its population in Canadian exile. Making a valiant comeback, New York served briefly as the nation's capital and established the first stock exchange, which met under a buttonwood tree on Wall St. (p. 50).

PLACES. For a taste of Old New York, check out Federal-style buildings such as **St. Paul's Chapel** (p. 52), houses on Charlton St., Vandam St., and the **South St. Seaport** area (p. 54), and **old City Hall,** built in 1802 (p. 53).

Literary Legacies

Since **William Bradford** founded the country's first newspaper (the *New York Gazette*) in 1725, New York City has been America's literary capital. **Herman Melville** and **Washington Irving** were both born in Lower Manhattan; Irving gave New York its ever-enduring pen- (and movie-) name, **Gotham. Walt Whitman,** born in South Huntington, Long Island, edited the controversial **Brooklyn Eagle** newspaper. **Edgar Allen Poe** lived in uptown poverty in the rural Bronx (p. 121). Starving **Greenwich Village** novelists such as **Willa Cather, John Reed,** and **Theodore Dreiser** helped establish the city's literary center; **e.e. cummings** and **Djuna Barnes** both lived off 10th St. at **Patchin Place** (p. 64). **Edna St. Vincent Millay** lived at Bedford St., where she founded the **Cherry Lane Theatre.** Midtown's legendary **Algonquin Hotel** (see p. 78) witnessed the 1919 **Round Table** weekly lunch meetings attended by such noted wits such as **Robert Benchley, Dorothy Parker, Alexander Woollcott,** and **Edna Ferber. Harold Ross** dreamed up *The New Yorker* here.

The area surrounding Columbia University witnessed the 1920s flowering of the **Harlem Renaissance:** novelists **George Schuyler, Claude McKay** and **Zora Neale Hurston,** as well as poet **Langston Hughes** and his circle, set the stage for next-generation black writers like **Ralph Ellison** and **James Baldwin.**

WORMS IN THE BIG APPLE: 1812-1897

By the early 19th century, the nation's largest metropolis was plagued by fires, riots, wild farmyard animals, widespread political corruption and a foul water supply that caused a **cholera epidemic.** Many citizens, eager to protect trade with the South, initially opposed the **Civil War (1861-65);** the attack on South Carolina's Fort Sumter rallied New York to the Northern side, but a class-biased conscription act in July 1863 led to the infamous **New York City Draft Riots,** which erupted throughout Manhattan at the cost of over a thousand lives. After the war, a half-century of prosperity helped New York to evolve into its recognizable modern self. **The 1898 incorporation of New York City** merged New York with Brooklyn (and parts of what is now Queens and the Bronx) brought the population to a worldwide high of three million. Emigration from western and northern Europe rose dramatically. Germans and Irish came over in droves between 1840 and 1860; in 1855, European-born immigrants constituted nearly half of New York's population. When the **1811 Commissioner's Plan** established Manhattan's rectilinear street grid, merchants built mansions for themselves on the new streets and tenements for the increasing numbers of immigrants from western and northern Europe. With 2000 farms still in New York, the city began to expand both horizontally and vertically. "It'll be a great place if they ever finish it," O. Henry quipped.

New York's political corruption peaked in the 1850s under **"Boss" William Tweed,** who bribed voters—often immigrants—with money and jobs. An embezzler *par excellence*, Boss Tweed robbed the city of somewhere between 100 and 200 million dollars. When citizens complained, Tweed asked defiantly, "Well, what are you going to do about it?" Tweed was busted in 1875, but his **Tammany Hall** machine influenced New York City politics well into the 20th century. **Teddy Roosevelt** headed the police department in the 1890s, reforming New York in time for the new century. He sallied forth at night dressed in a cape, searching for policemen who were sleeping on the job or consorting with prostitutes. He befriended New York's most famed photographer of the era, social reformer and journalist **Jacob Riis.**

THE NEW METROPOLIS: 1898-1929

On January 1, 1898, modern New York was born when the independent cities of Manhattan and Brooklyn merged. Sometimes wistfully referred to in Brooklyn as "The Great Mistake," the union cemented New York's role as the country's most powerful urban center. The world-renowned **subway** system opened in 1904, heralding an era of rapid change and the booming business world of the **Roaring Twenties. Mayor Fiorello LaGuardia's** leadership engendered fierce civic pride that saw New Yorkers through the **Great Depression**.

Between 1890-1930, thousands of Italians, Lithuanians, Russians, Poles, and Greeks fled famine, religious persecution, and political unrest for New York. The US didn't always live up to expectations. Immigrants often worked long hours in detestable and unsafe conditions for meager wages; Tammany Hall-based "ward bosses" helped confused new arrivals find jobs and housing—in exchange for votes. Nonetheless, many immigrants rose from being employees to employers and moved from downtown (particularly the **Lower East Side,** see p. 58) to parts north.

It was also during this time that Harlem renters opened their tenements to the many southern blacks who had rushed north to New York. Within the span of a few years, Harlem was transformed from a predominantly Jewish neighborhood into a bustling black city within a city. In the 1920s, the cultural vitality of Harlem's 80,000 blacks sparked the **Harlem Renaissance.** Even so, there was not always strength in numbers. People of color were charged more than their white counterparts for the unhealthy tenement rooms, and the **Cotton Club,** Harlem's famous jazz club, didn't allow blacks inside unless they were performing (p. 219).

PLACES. Urban planner **Robert Moses** became New York's most powerful official, creating 36 parks; a network of roads to make them accessible to the public (every expressway and parkway in Greater New York was constructed under Moses); 12 bridges and tunnels; **Lincoln Center** (p. 95); **Shea Stadium** (p. 115); and numerous housing projects.

Made possible by combining such new technologies as the elevator and the steel frame, skyscrapers allowed the city to explode upward in tandem with New York's spectacular commercial and human growth. The first skyscraper, the **Flatiron Building,** sprouted up on 23rd St. in 1902 (p. 71). In 1913, **Cass Gilbert** gilded the 55-story **Woolworth Building** with Gothic flourishes, piling on antique "W"s and dubbing it the "Cathedral of Commerce" (p. 53). The Art Deco **Empire State Building** (p. 74) and the **Chrysler Building** (p. 84) were fashioned from stone and steel.

THE WORLD'S CAPITAL: 1930-2001

Post-World War II prosperity brought more immigrants and businesses to the city. But even as the world celebrated New York as the new century's capital, cracks in the city's foundations appeared. By the 1960s, crises in public transportation, education, and housing exacerbated racial tensions and fostered heightened criminal activity. By 1975, the city was pleading unsuccessfully with President Gerald Ford and the federal government to rescue it from impending bankruptcy. One headline from the period reads, "Ford to City: Drop Dead."

Resilient NYC rebounded with an attitude of streetwise hope. The state's massive (if goofy) **"I Love New York" campaign** spread cheer via bumper stickers. Large manufacturing, which had gone south and west of New York, was supplanted by fresh money from high finance and infotech. Booming **Wall Street** (p. 50) was hip again in the 1980s, and the city's upper-middle class face recovered some of its lost vitality. In poorer areas, meanwhile, discontent pervaded and manifested itself in waves of crime and vandalism that scared off potential tourists. With a New Yorker's armor of

The Big Apple in Flux

Ethnicities of all kinds thrive in the five boroughs. Dominicans are heavily represented in Washington Heights (see p. 98), the Lower East Side (see p. 58), and Bushwick in Brooklyn. Russian immigrants have settled in Brooklyn's Brighton Beach (see p. 111) and Central Queens. Sunset Park (p. 110) and Bensonhurst (p. 110) are becoming increasingly Chinese, while Flatbush (p. 109) and the northern Bronx are Jamaican enclaves. Flushing's Main St. (p. 116) recalls Korea; Israeli eateries pepper Queens Blvd. in Forest Hills (p. 114); Jackson Heights bustles with large Indian and South American populations. In Brooklyn, an Arab community centers around Atlantic Ave. in Brooklyn Heights.

Immigration can change a neighborhood's personality quickly. Traditionally Greek Astoria, Queens (p. 112) is now making room for Egyptians and Croatians. In the Bronx, Belmont's Italian community is now also a home for Albanians. And Mexicans may currently outnumber Puerto Ricans in Spanish Harlem. The city is a revolving door. As people leave Ghana and Nigeria for New York City, Italians move out of Little Italy. The only constant is flux.

curmudgeonly humor, **Ed Koch** defended his city's declining reputation and became America's most visible mayor. Koch appeared on Saturday Night Live, providing an endless stream of quotables, most notably his catchphrase, "How'm I doing?"

As 1980s excess faded into early-1990s recession, racial conflict reached an all-time high. Bigoted beatings erupted in the boroughs. **David Dinkins,** the city's first black mayor, fought hard to encourage unity between the city's ethnic groups and dismantle bureaucratic corruption. Mounting fiscal crises and a persistent crime rate, however, led to Dinkins's 1993 defeat at the hands of liberal Republican **Rudolph Giuliani,** who successfully aimed to deter major crime by cracking down on vandalism. Giuliani cleaned up such formerly murky areas as **Times Square** (p. 84), but was criticized for "gentrifying" tourist-heavy Manhattan at the expense of the outer boroughs. Others asserted that Giuliani's war on crime encouraged an overzealous police force. Accusations of police brutality heightened with the 1997-8 sexual assault of **Abner Louima** and the February 1999 death of **Amadou Diallo.** Although the policemen involved were brought to trial, New Yorkers condemned Giuliani for his immoderate police strategies and his "no-apologies" stance.

PLACES. The capricious city has always warmed to the latest trends in architecture, hastily demolishing old buildings to make room for trendier edifices. New York's first curtain of pure glass was the 1950 **United Nations Secretariat Building,** a nightmare to air-condition (p. 83). Then, in 1958, Ludwig Mies Van der Rohe and Philip Johnson created the **Seagram Building** (p. 82), a glass tower set behind a plaza on Park Ave. As crowds mingled in the public space, the city's planning commission began offering perks to those who built plazas next to their towering office complexes. By the late 70s, plazas were replaced by high-tech atriums with gurgling fountains and pricey cafes. The leaner skyscrapers date from the early 1980s, when shrewd developers realized they could bypass zoning regulations *and* receive a bonus from the commission if they hoisted up much-condemned "sliver" buildings. Zoning policy in 1983 encouraged more room for air and sun. Whether environmental, overcrowding, and post-Sept. 11 security issues will dampen New Yorkers' enthusiasm for brutalist slabs of concrete, however, is anyone's guess.

NEW YORK TODAY

On September 11, 2001, New York was the site of the worst terrorist attack ever to take place in the United States. Over 3000 people died when two airplanes hijacked by Islamist terrorists flew into the World Trade Center. Among those who lost their lives in the tragedy were 343 firefighters, who quickly became a symbol of the heroism and courage of the New Yorker. The gaping pit that had once been filled by New York 's largest buildings became known as Ground Zero and was soon serving as a pilgrimage site for mourners from around the world.

New York is now taking the slow road back to recovery. A design by Daniel Libeskind has been selected as a replacement for the World Trade Center, and the future of Downtown New York remains a hot topic. Unfortunately, the attacks, along with some disastrous fiscal decisions made by the administration of Mayor Rudolph Giuliani and the refusals of Governor George Pataki and President George W. Bush to aid New York 's fragile economy, have left the city in a precarious financial situation. Consequently, New York's billionaire Mayor, Michael Bloomberg, has been forced to raise taxes and cut spending.

Still, New York plods along, surmounting any adversity that comes its way. Indeed, just recently New York took yet another hard hit, when on August 14 the lights went out in the Blackout of 2003. Affecting parts of Canada, Michigan, Ohio, Connecticut, Pennsylvania, and New Jersey, in New York City alone, the day-long outage cost business owners millions of dollars in revenue. But, unlike the last noteworthy New York blackout of 1977, which sparked extensive looting and arson, New Yorkers in 2003 earned praise for their level-headedness and sense of community throughout the crisis.

Although the events of the recent past may have given the Big Apple a little bit of a limp, the city that never sleeps is not without the swagger befitting the capital of the world.

INSIDE

manhattan **47**

the statue of liberty **47** ellis island **49**
financial district **49** the civic center **52**
south street seaport museum **54**
chinatown and little italy **56** lower east side **58**
tribeca **58** soho **59**
greenwich village **59** the east village and alphabet city **65**
lower midtown **68** hell's kitchen **77**
midtown **77** central park **86**
upper east side **91** upper west side **94**
harlem **98** washington heights **100**
roosevelt island **102**

brooklyn **102**
queens **112**
the bronx **118**
staten island **123**

Sights

MANHATTAN

THE STATUE OF LIBERTY

...Give me your tired, your poor,
Your huddled masses yearning to breathe free,
The wretched refuse of your teeming shore;
Send these, the homeless, tempest-tost to me,
I lift my lamp beside the golden door!
—Emma Lazarus, 1883

Stands on Liberty Island in New York Harbor, about 1 mi. southwest of Manhattan. Subway: 4, 5 to Bowling Green; N, R to Whitehall St.; 1, 9 to South Ferry. Map 7, C6. ☎212-363-3200. Ferries leave for Liberty Island from the piers at Battery Park (daily every 30min., 9am-3:50pm). Ferry hours may be extended slightly during the summer and on certain holidays. Ferry information ☎212-269-5755. Tickets for ferry, access to Liberty Island and Ellis Island $10, seniors $8, ages 4-12 $4, under 4 free. Buy tickets in Castle Clinton's central courtyard, just to the right of the ferry dock as one faces the harbor. Liberty Island open daily 9am-5pm, with extended summer hours. Gift shop near cafeteria, with novelty kitsch such as $2 foam Liberty crowns. ***As of August 2002, only the grounds of Liberty Island are open to the public; the statue, museum, pedestal and crown are closed indefinitely.***

on the cheap

Sailing to Staten Island

Completely free, the **Staten Island ferry** may very well offer the world's premier sightseeing bargain. Wave Manhattan goodbye as you pass Ellis Island, the Statue of Liberty, and Governor's Island en route to Staten Island. The ferry began shuttling commuters in 1810, thanks to the entrepreneurial Cornelius Vanderbilt and his mother's money. It turned public in 1905, but the city charged varying fares (up to 25¢) for the scenic view until 1997. Postcard photographers flock here for some of the most marketable shots of the city. The ride is particularly exhilarating at sunset or nighttime.

(Subway: N, R to Whitehall St. ☎718-815-2628. Approx. 25min.; daily 24hr., M-F 1-4 trips per day, Sa-Su 4-6 trips per day; free.)

Located in New York Harbor, about a mile away from the southern tip of Manhattan, the Statue of Liberty has welcomed many immigrants to the New World. Lady Liberty's symbolic cachet has drawn tourists from all over the globe: in 2000, the last time that it was open for a full year, the Statue attracted more than six million visitors.

Despite serving as one of the most recognizable emblems of the United States, this quintessentially American statue has roots in the Old World. In 1865, French leftist intellectual Edouard-René de Laboulaye dreamt up the monument as a way of celebrating the Franco-American friendship established during the US Revolutionary War against the British. Frederic-Auguste Bartholdi constructed the actual statue in Paris with the aid of Gustave Eiffel (yes, that Eiffel). Once finished in 1884, the Statue was presented to the American ambassador on July 4. She was then disassembled and sent across the Atlantic in 220 crates.

Had it not been for Joseph Pulitzer, the tycoon publisher of the New York *World*, however, Lady Liberty might have remained in pieces. Funding was slow to come, and only after Pulitzer took control of the financing of the construction of the pedestal did the Statue literally get off the ground. (Pulitzer cleverly promised to publish the name of every single contributor in the pages of the *World*, no matter how small the contribution.) Once structurally complete in 1886, the pedestal received its finishing touch: the now-famous words of welcome by poet Emma Lazarus.

Since then, the world's beacon of freedom has served as a magnet for stupid stunts of dubious legality. In 1986, an Australian stuntman parachuted off the torch and landed safely. (Charged with parachuting without a license, he said: "I just couldn't help myself.") A New Yorker, protesting the conviction of Indian activist Leonard Peltier in the slaying of two FBI agents, used a mountain climbing rope to descend from the observation deck in 1990. In summer 2001, a daredevil Frenchman named Thierry Devaux tried to use a motorized parachute to land on the Statue of Liberty's torch; he got snagged on the gilded flame and clung to Lady Liberty's arm for a tense 30min. before police pulled him to safety and slapped on handcuffs.

Visitors to the monument are encouraged to board an early ferry, ideally the first one out of Battery Park, to avoid the despair-inducing lines that build up over the course of the day. Ferries run in a Battery Park-Liberty Island-Ellis Island loop. The ticket costs the same no matter how long you stay and regardless of whether you want to see only the statue or the immigration station, so you might as well do both. The ferry ride is one long, tourist-pleasing photo-op, with jaw-dropping views of the Lower Manhattan skyline, the Brooklyn Bridge, and, of course, the Statue itself.

Until 2001, visitors could ascend to the observation deck atop **Richard Morris Hunt's pedestal,** the pedestal's second-floor museum, and the crown. Since then, heightened security precautions have closed the monument off to the public indefinitely. Perhaps this is fitting: Bartholdi initially wanted people to view his work from the *outside*, and that the original plan was to fill up the inside of the statue with sand for added stability. The Liberty Island view of the statue is still superb. If you plan to make a day of it, bring a bag lunch: otherwise, you will be at the culinary mercy of the Liberty Island cafeteria.

ELLIS ISLAND

For instructions on how to get to Ellis Island, see the Statue of Liberty, above. Map 7, C6. ☎212-363-3200. Video documentary: Island of Hope, Island of Tears. 30min. Shown in 2 theaters, one with a preceding 15min. talk by a ranger. Film free, but you must get tickets at the info desk near the entrance in advance of the showing. Play: Embracing Freedom: America is My Home, based on oral histories of those who passed through Ellis Island. 30min. Performed daily Mar.-Oct.; nominal fee (for info call ☎212-561-4500). Audio tour 1¼hr. $5, seniors, students, and under 17 $4. Main Building Tour: Ranger-guided tours offered throughout the day. 45min. Free. Library ☎212-363-3200, ext. 158 or 161. American Family Immigration History Center ☎212-561-4500; www.ellisisland.org.

Ellis Island is the practical representation of the theoretical promise of the Statue of Liberty. Over 40% of all living Americans can trace their roots to an ancestor who came through Ellis Island. During the height of immigration (1892-1920), Ellis Island ushered over 22 million people into the US. The island's three floors of exhibits commemorate the site and its history, as well as the immigrant experience in America.

Ellis Island opened as a museum in 1990 after multimillion-dollar renovations. The museum is housed in a grand red brick and stone building, restored as it stood early in the 20th century. The building's stones are heavily rusticated, and four copper-domed towers give the former immigration depot the air of a military fortress. Two bald eagles, symbols of the US, perch over the building's central arch and entrance.

Since 2001, visitors have had access to the **American Family Immigration History Center's** thorough, user-friendly computerized database of immigrants who passed through Ellis Island. Would-be genealogists pay for 35min. of computer time ($5) to track ship records and arrival papers until 1924. Other highlights include the overwhelming Registry Room (where most of the processing took place); an exhibit on the *Peopling of America; Treasures from Home*, which displays a collection of artifacts and clothing that immigrants brought from the Old World; and various tours and dramatic displays (listed above). A research library, open to the public, is on the third floor.

FINANCIAL DISTRICT

Once a dock where men shucked their daily oyster catch, Pearl St. is now one of the richest streets in the whole world. Wall St. is the cornerstone of both the district and the entire financial universe. Once the northern border to the New Amsterdam settlement, the street takes its name from the wall built in 1653 to shield the Dutch from the invasion-happy British.

To ensure that sights are open and to get a true sense of the area's bustling atmosphere (Map 7), explore lower Manhattan during the week. Be prepared for heavy security—metal detectors and tightly guarded buildings are the norm here. **Sights are listed from south to north.**

the BIG $plurge

Sea-ing NYC

Tired of being the thousandth sardine in a subway, elbows in your groin, tattered map in hand? Sick of fighting for sidewalk space with the thousand rushing, crazed people beside you? If so, choose this refreshing, unique alternative to sightseeing in New York: kayaking down the Hudson River. With New York Kayak Company, beginners can "practice paddle" down the Hudson with a private instructor (2 hours, $80). After learning the fundamentals, embark on one of their more advanced tours, including the "Statue of Liberty". Paddle down the Hudson, pass the landmark Ellis Island and continue straight to the Statue of Liberty. Your instructor will take you as close to the big lady as allowed by the US Coast Guard (3 hours, $120). Other options include the "Boat Basin," a paddling tour 4 miles up the west side of Manhattan, offering a golden opportunity to view the bustling city skyline from the serenity of the sea (3 hours, $120).

New York Kayak Company, Pier 40, South Side, between W. Houston St. and West St. (☎800-529-2599). M 12pm-6pm, Tu-Th 10am-6pm, F-Sa 10am-5pm.

BATTERY PARK

Located on the southern tip of Manhattan. Subway: 4, 5 to Bowling Green; N, R to Whitehall St. Map 7, C6. ***Castle Clinton:*** *Map 7, B6, 22. Open M-F 8am-5pm. Tours of the Castle by request. Free.* ***New York Unearthed:*** *19 State St. Map 7, C5, 23. ☎212-748-8628. Open M-F noon-5pm. Free.*

At the very bottom of Manhattan rests Battery Park, thanks to landfills that replaced New York Harbor between State St. and the offshore **Castle Clinton.** Today, Castle Clinton acts as the ticket booth for the ferry to the Statue of Liberty and Ellis Island. Along its promenade, the park features beautiful views of Brooklyn and the Statue of Liberty. On the northern border of the park is **New York Unearthed,** an urban archaeology museum. Informative public exhibits are limited, since the museum keeps most of its two million excavated shards and trinkets in storage. Call ahead to check availability of the museum's free exhibitions.

BOWLING GREEN

Intersection of Battery Pl., Broadway, and Whitehall St. Subway: 4, 5 to Bowling Green. Map 7, C5.

The **National Museum of the American Indian** (p. 140) overlooks this tiny, triangular piece of land, a perfect perch for Peregrine falcons (say that 10 times fast). With a fence erected in 1771, Bowling Green is Manhattan's oldest park. At present, the governing statue in the park is that of a large charging bull, a shrine to the god of strong stock markets.

US CUSTOM HOUSE

1 Bowling Green. Subway: 4, 5 to Bowling Green. Map 7, C5.

Completed in 1907, when the city still derived most of its revenue from customs, the Custom House has been transformed into the Smithsonian's **National Museum of the American Indian** (p. 140). The magnificent Beaux Arts building, designed by Cass Gilbert, is fronted by exquisite sculptures of four women representing America, Europe, Africa, and Asia. The face of Mercury, the Roman god of commerce, crowns each of the building's 44 columns, paying homage to the most successful city-states in history.

NEW YORK STOCK EXCHANGE

18 Broad St., between Wall St. and Exchange Pl. Subway: 1, 2, to Wall St./William St.; 4, 5 to Wall St./ Broadway; N, R, W to Rector St.; J, M, Z to Broad St. Map 7, C4. ☎212-656-5165 or 656-5168. ***Closed indefinitely to the public.***

In 1792, 24 stockbrokers met beneath a buttonwood tree outside **68 Wall Street** and signed an agreement to trade with one another. From these humble beginnings sprang the 1903 Exchange building, a temple to capitalism designed by George B. Post in the Classical Revival style. A new addition at 20 Broad St. was opened in 1956. Over two billion shares routinely change hands per day in this high-security sanctum. The trading floor has been enclosed in glass ever since the 1960s, when activist Abbie Hoffman and his merry band of Yippies threw dollar bills on the floor. The traders stopped their work to chase frantically after the money, just as the protestors had anticipated. Today, the Exchange is closed to the public, with some exceptions made for large organized groups.

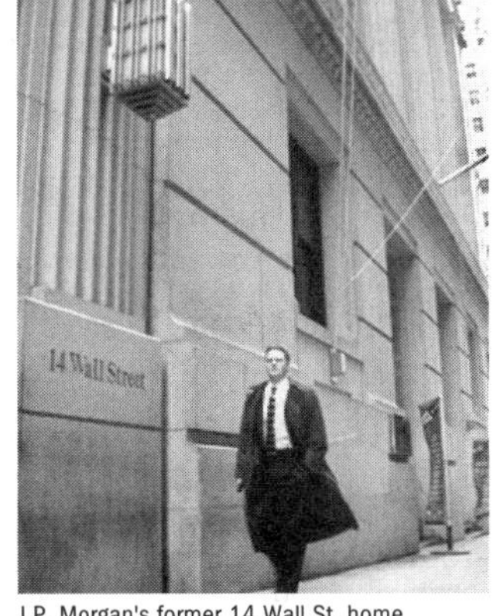

J.P. Morgan's former 14 Wall St. home

TRINITY CHURCH

Broadway, at Wall St. Subway: 4, 5 to Wall St./Broadway; N, R, W to Rector St. Map 7, C4, 15. Open M-F 7am-6pm, Sa-Su 8am-4pm. Museum open M-F 9am-11:45am and 1pm-3:45pm, Sa 10am-3:45pm, Su 1pm-3:45pm. Welcome Center open M-F 10-noon and 1-2:30pm. Su Eucharist 9, 11:15am.

Around the corner from the NYSE, this Gothic Revival Episcopal church has the last laugh over its towering, billion-dollar neighbors: Trinity Church owns much of the land on which these shrines to commerce sit. Its steeple and cemetery, which houses the grave of Alexander Hamilton, are delicately crafted amid the canyons of the Financial District. Since its construction in 1846, the Gothic spire of Trinity Church as served as a peaceful oasis in the midst of the biggest rat race in the world. Once inside, check out the modest museum behind the altar and the welcome center and gift shop to the left of the entrance.

Trinity Church, Financial District

FEDERAL HALL NATIONAL MEMORIAL

26 Wall St., at Nassau St. Disabled entrance at 15 Pine St. Subway: N, R, W to Rector St.; 1, 2, to Wall St./William St.; 4, 5 to Wall St./Broadway; J, M, Z to Broad St. Map 7, D4. ☎ 212-825-6888. Open M-F 9am-5pm. Call for tour times.

A fully-knickered George Washington stands guard in front of this Parthenon look-alike, which housed the original City Hall from 1703. It was renamed "Federal Hall" in 1789, when George Washington took his Oath of Office here. It served as the fledgling nation's first seat of government, and James Madison first presented the Bill of Rights to Congress here. The original structure was demolished in 1812 and later rebuilt to house numerous federal agencies.

Esplanade sculpture, Battery Park City

THE FEDERAL RESERVE BANK OF NEW YORK

33 Liberty St., between Nassau and William St. Subway: 1, 2, 4, 5, A, C, J, M, Z to Fulton St./Broadway-Nassau St. Map 7, C3. ☎212-720-6130; www.ny.frb.org. Free 1hr. tours M-F 9:30, 10:30, 11:30am, 1:30, and 2:30pm, but at least 1 wk. advance notice required. Must be 16+. 30 people per group max.

This 1924 mammoth neo-Renaissance building occupies an entire city block. Modeled after the Palazzo Strozzi, the home of a 15th-century Florentine banking family, the grave facade is designed to keep you away from one-fourth of the world's gold bullion. The gold, much of it foreign, is protected by 121 triple-locked compartments in a vault five stories below ground. If you love cold, hard cash, take a tour of the vaults.

WORLD TRADE CENTER SITE (GROUND ZERO)

On the corner of Liberty and West St. Subway: E to World Trade Center; N, R, to Cortlandt St.; 1, 2, 4, 5, A, C, J, M, Z to Fulton St./Broadway-Nassau St. Map 7, B3.

Words cannot describe the sadness of the empty lot where the World Trade Center once stood. One day, the space will be filled: with a memorial, a revitalized transit hub, even a new skyscraper or two. Today, however, the poignancy of the landscape lies in the profound sense of loss reflected in its physical vacancy. It must be seen to be understood.

BATTERY PARK CITY

Subway: E to World Trade Center; 1, 2, to Wall St./William St.; 4, 5 to Wall St./Broadway; N, R, W to Rector St.; 1, 2, 4, 5, A, C, J, M, Z to Fulton St./Broadway-Nassau St.; J, M, Z to Broad St.; 1, 2, 3, 9 to Chambers St./W. Broadway; A, C to Chambers St./Church St.; N, R to City Hall; 4, 5, 6 to Brooklyn Bridge-City Hall; 1, 2 to Park Pl. Map 7, A4.

When the World Trade Center was being constructed in the 1970s, the millions of tons of soil dug up were deposited west of West St. Along with large apartment complexes in Battery Park City, the **World Financial Center,** West St. between the World Trade Center and Hudson River (☎212-945-0505), was built upon the landfill. The 45,000 sq. ft. Winter Garden, opened in October 1988, is the centerpiece of the World Financial Center. The grand public space suffered severe damage on its east side during Sept. 11, and subsequently underwent extensive renovation to replace 2000 glass panes of the arched ceiling, half of the grand staircase and the marble flooring, and all 16 of the 40 ft. high Washingtonia robusta palm trees. The garden, which faces the river esplanade, hosts year-round festivals and performances open to the public. The most well-known of these is the spectacular New York International Orchid Show, held in mid-spring each year. The reopened Liberty Street Bridge, formerly known as South Bridge, connects Battery Park City to the rest of Lower Manhattan and provides a viewing site for Ground Zero.

THE CIVIC CENTER

Subway: 1, 2 to Park Pl.; N, R to City Hall; 4, 5, 6 to Brooklyn Bridge-City Hall; J, M, Z to Chambers St./Centre St.

The city's center of government is located immediately north of its financial district. City Hall is the neighborhood's center, and around it revolve courthouses, civic buildings, and federal buildings. **Sights are listed roughly from south to north.**

ST. PAUL'S CHAPEL

Broadway, between Fulton and Vesey St. Map 7, C2, 5. ☎212-602-0773. Chapel open M-F 9am-3pm, Su 7am-3pm. Su Eucharist 8am.

Inspired by the design of London's St. Martin-in-the-Fields, this chapel was built between 1764 and 1766, with the clock tower and spire added in 1794. Since then, St. Paul's has required little renovation. It is Manhattan's oldest church; George

Washington regularly prayed here in his personal pew. Until the winter of 2002, the gates surrounding the chapel served as a de facto memorial for the victims of the Sept. 11 attacks, with mourners leaving mementos and messages of both grief and hope. The many cards, photographs, and other items left at the Chapel have been stored for display in a museum that is to be built near the former site of the World Trade Center. Today, the **Out of the Dust** exhibit chronicles the Chapel's year-long ministry to WTC recovery workers. Pictures of Ground Zero, messages to those that died in the collapse, and tributes to the hundreds of men and women who risked their lives to rescue others can be seen in the sanctuary.

Street musicians

WOOLWORTH BUILDING

233 Broadway, between Barclay St. and Park Pl. Map 7, C2.

F.W. Woolworth supposedly paid $15.5 million to house the headquarters of his five-and-dime store empire in this elegant 1913 skyscraper, once known as the "Cathedral of Commerce." Fast-paced construction added an average of one and a half stories per week; once finished, the 792 ft. skyscraper was the tallest in the world. Its spectacular lobby is replete with Gothic arches and flourishes, glittering mosaics, gold painted mailboxes, imported marble designs, and carved caricatures. Note the depictions of Woolworth himself counting change and architect Cass Gilbert holding a model of the building. The murals on either end of the lobby's north-south hallway at the mezzanine level depict Labor and Commerce, respectively.

World Trade Center, c. 2000

CITY HALL

Broadway at Murray St., off Park Row. Map 7, D2. ☎212-788-6879. ***Closed to the public.***

The mayor of New York City keeps his offices in this elegant Neoclassical building. Press conferences are often held on its steps, and demonstrations (with permission, of course) may be coordinated to disrupt the mayoral train of thought. In 1865, thousands of mourners paid their respects to the body of Abraham Lincoln under the hall's vaulted rotunda. Winding stairs lead to the Governor's Room, in which portraits of American political heroes adorn the walls. City Hall sits in City Hall Park, which once held a jail, a public execution ground, and barracks for British soldiers. The area along Park Row, now graced

Woolworth Building, Civic Center

with a statue of journalist Horace Greeley, was formerly known as "Newspaper Row," because most of New York's papers were published near the one place in which they were guaranteed to find scandal.

TWEED COURTHOUSE

Chambers St., between Center St. and Broadway, north of City Hall. Map 7, D2.

Named after the infamous Boss Tweed of the Tammany Hall corruption scandals (p. 69), this courthouse took 10 years and $14 million—or the equivalent of $166 million today—to build. Rumor has it that $10 million went to Tweed himself, setting off a public outcry that marked the beginning of the end for Boss Tweed and his embezzling ways. In 2002, Mayor Michael Bloomberg moved the city's new Department of Education into the building.

SURROGATE'S COURT

31 Chambers St., near Center St. Map 7, D1, 3. ☎ 212-374-8244. Closed to the public.

Two sculpture groups—*New York in Its Infancy* and *New York in Revolutionary Times*—grace the Beaux Arts exterior of this overwhelming former Hall of Records. In front of the building's Mansard roof stand eight statues of notable New Yorkers (visitors may want to go across the street for a better view). Inside, Egyptian mosaics and the 12 signs of the Zodiac cover the foyer ceiling.

FEDERAL OFFICE BUILDING

290 Broadway, off Reade St., 1 block north of City Hall. Map 7, C1, 1.

The lobby has powerful public art installations—check out Clyde Lynds' stone piece depicting the discovery of the **African Burial Ground** (see below). On the floor of the central rotunda, a 40 ft. wide work of terrazzo and polished brass (entitled *The New Ring Shout* after a historical dance of celebration) commemorates the same site.

AFRICAN BURIAL GROUND

Corner of Duane and Elk St. Map 7, D1, 2.

In 1991, archaeologists found the remains of over 20,000 slaves buried only 20 ft. underground—making the site the largest known excavated African cemetery in the world. Congress declared it a national landmark in response to protests against a new Federal Court building slated to be built over the burial ground. The unassuming space now stands undisturbed, with plans in the works for an elaborate memorial. Some designs have suggested erecting a libation chamber, while others have proposed building a wall of faces (fashioned from members of New York's African-American community) to commemorate the African men, women, and children who are buried there and also the countless others who died during the Middle Passage.

BROOKLYN BRIDGE

Off Park Row, east of City Hall Park. Map 7, F2.

See p. 104 for information.

SOUTH STREET SEAPORT MUSEUM

Between FDR Dr. and Water St., and between Beekman and John St. Subway: 1, 2, 4, 5, A, C, J, M, Z to Fulton St./Broadway-Nassau St. Map 7, E3.

The shipping industry thrived here for most of the 19th century, when New York was the most important port city in the US. Bars, brothels, and crime flourished in the South St. Seaport for much of the 20th century. In the mid-1980s, the South Street Seaport Museum teamed up with the Rouse Corporation, which built Boston's Quincy Market, the St. Louis Union Station, and Baltimore's Harborplace, to redesign the 12-block "museum without walls."

SEAPORT MUSEUM VISITORS CENTER

209 Water St., at Fulton St. Map 7, E3, 12. ☎212-748-8600. Open Apr.-Sept. daily 10am-6pm; Oct.-Mar. M and W-Su 10am-5pm. Admission to ships, shops and tours $5, under 12 free. Walking around the museum is free.

The Visitors Center, your first stop at the Seaport Museum, provides information about the seaport and sells passes to any of the galleries, ships, or shops under the museum's auspices.

FULTON FISH MARKET

End of Fulton St., at South St. Seaport. Map 7, F3. ☎212-748-8786. Museum tours May-Oct. daily 6am. 1hr. $12. Reserve 1 week ahead. Walking around the fish market free.

The largest fresh fish market in the country, the Fulton Market's repeated clashes with the city haven't stopped it from opening at 4am—as it has for over 160 years. Many of New York's store and restaurant owners buy their fresh fish here (they've done so since the Dutch colonial period in the 1600s). Between midnight and 8am, you can see buyers surveying the still-gasping catch of the day. The Market is currently planning to move to a new state-of-the-art facility in Hunts Point in the Bronx, although it appears that it will stay in its current location until at least 2005.

PEKING

On the East River, off Fulton St. and next to Pier 16. Map 7, F3, 13. Open during museum hours. For a sample of this ship's rich history, catch the 15min. 1929 film of the ship's passage around Cape Horn, shown daily 10am-6pm. Free with museum admission (see above).

Built in 1911 by a Hamburg-based company, the *Peking* is the second-largest sailing ship ever launched. It spent most of its career on the "nitrate run" to Chile, a route that passes around Cape Horn, one of the world's most dangerous stretches of water.

OTHER SEAPORT MUSEUM SIGHTS

In addition to the *Peking*, there are five other ships open to the public. Some are stationary, such as the 325 ft. iron-hulled, full-rigged *Wavertree* (1885) which is currently undergoing a major restoration, and the *Ambrose*, a floating lighthouse built in 1907 to mark the entrance to New York Harbor. Others take to the open seas: the *Pioneer* (1885) offers wonderful 2hr. and 3hr. tours on board ship. Back on land, the museum occupies a number of the area's early 19th-century buildings. **Bowne & Co.,** 211 Water St. (Map 7, E3, 7), a re-creation of a 19th-century printing shop, offers demonstrations of letterpress printing. On Fulton St., between South and

Brooklyn Bridge

City Hall

Peking ship, South St. Seaport

life's green

Caged Birds Sing

Early-rising bird-watchers should take a sunrise stroll to **Sara Delano Roosevelt Park,** west of the Bowery, at the corner of Chrystie and Broome St. (Map 8, D1-D4). There, between about 7am-9am, a group of older Chinese men gather each morning from spring to fall to give sun to songbirds.

The men arrive at the small garden at the park's northern edge with beautiful wooden bird cages, covered in cloth so that their occupants don't wake too early. After positioning the cages, the owners gingerly remove the coverings and bid their songbirds good morning. They do some stretching exercises as they wait for their birds to wake up and warm to the sun. Once sufficiently bathed in light, the birds emit amazingly loud and melodic songs that are easily heard over the roar of early-morning traffic. This ritual is an old Chinese tradition intended as a distraction from vice, but as one of the men remarked, it's more "like walking your dog."

Yoga groups also practice to the morning birdsong: one such group is Falun Xiulian Dafa, the globally famous semi-religious Chinese sect that endures much political oppression from the Chinese government. Visit http://falun-ny.net for more info.

Front St., is **Schermerhorn Row.** Constructed between 1811 and 1812, these Georgian-Federal buildings once housed shops that served the throngs exiting the Fulton Ferry.

CHINATOWN AND LITTLE ITALY

Subway: 1, 9 to Canal St./Varick St.; A, C, E to Canal St./Sixth Ave.; J, M, Z to Canal St./Centre St.; N, Q, R, W to Canal St./Broadway; 4, 6 to Canal St./Lafayette St.; S to Grand St.; F to E. Broadway; 6 to Spring St./Lafayette St.; F, V, S to Broadway-Lafayette St.

Mott and Pell St., the unofficial centers of Chinatown, boil over with Chinese restaurants and commercial activity. Every inch of the old red and green awnings lining the storefronts is decorated with Chinese-style baby jackets, bamboo hats, stuffed Hello Kittys, and miniature Buddhas. If it's labels you're into, Canal is the street for you: every inch of the sidewalk is used for commercial space, and weekend afternoons can draw suffocating crowds. Don't let the low-priced merchandise snooker you, though—creative labeling abounds in several stores, and those are *not* Rolexes. During the Chinese New Year in February, the area's frenetic pace accelerates to fever pitch.

Immigration has propelled Chinatown into what was once Italian territory. Since the 1960s, Little Italy's borders have receded in the face of an aggressively expanding Chinatown, and the temptation of tourism has vanquished much of the neighborhood's authenticity. Mulberry St. remains the heart of the neighborhood. **Sights are listed from south to north.**

FIRST SHEARITH ISRAEL GRAVEYARD

South side of Chatham Sq., on St. James Pl., between James and Oliver St. Subway: J, M, Z to Canal St./Centre St. Map 8, D6, 41.

This historical site illustrates Chinatown's heritage as part of the Jewish Lower East Side. The cemetery served NYC's first Jewish congregation, the Spanish-Portuguese Shearith Israel Synagogue. Gravestones date from as early as 1656.

CHATHAM SQUARE AND KIMLAU SQUARE

At the intersection of Bowery and Doyers St., 3 blocks south of Canal St. Subway: 4, 5, 6 to Brooklyn Bridge-City Hall. Map 8, D6.

In the center of Chatham Sq. stands the granite ceremonial gateway of Kimlau Sq., a plaza named after a Chinese-American bomber pilot who died while serving in WWII. Also occupying the square is the 12 ft. **statue of Lin Ze Xu** (Map 8, D6, 46); the inscription on the base tersely describes him as a "pioneer" in the "war on drugs." Lin, a 19th-century Chinese commissioner in Canton, was exiled for his efforts to end China's socially destructive importation of opium from Great Britain and the Netherlands. His actions are believed to have precipitated the 1839-42 Opium Wars. Today, Chatham Sq. is often filled with an eclectic assortment of elderly Chinese people and young skateboarders.

Mahayana Buddhist Temple

MAHAYANA BUDDHIST TEMPLE

133 Canal St., near the Manhattan Bridge, between the Bowery and Chrystie St. Subway: J, M, Z to Canal St./Centre St. Map 8, D5, 22.

Brush up on your Chinese, because nothing in the Temple is in English. This modern space, with its large television, spotlights, and state-of-the-art sound system, might be surprising for those who think of Buddhism as a religion practiced in musty old monasteries in ancient Tibet. Here, the path to *satori* is strewn with *tchotchkes*. A 20 ft. golden Buddha fills up the stage in the auditorium. Visitors are asked to wear "decent clothes." Walk outside and you'll probably find a long line of travelers waiting for one of the many incarnations of the 'Chinatown bus' that stops here.

Chinese lanterns

MANHATTAN BRIDGE

Between Canal St. and the Bowery. Subway: J, M, Z to Canal St./Centre St. Map 8, F6.

Walking northeast toward where the Bowery and E. Broadway meet will bring you past the grand arch and flanking colonnades that mark the entrance to the Manhattan Bridge. These were designed by Carrère and Hastings, the same firm that designed the New York Public Library (p. 78) and the Frick Mansion (p. 132). Though far less popular than the walkway on the Brooklyn Bridge, the south side's bike and pedestrian path affords incredible views of Lower Manhattan, not to mention of the Brooklyn Bridge itself (p. 104).

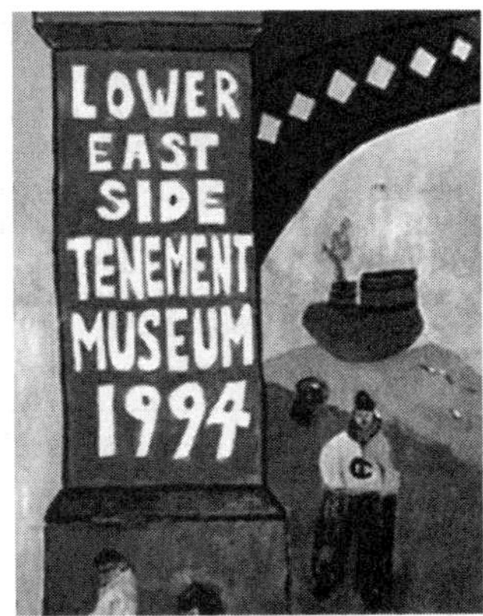

Lower East Side Tenement Museum

POLICE HEADQUARTERS

240 Centre St., between Broome St. and Centre St. Subway: J, M, Z to Canal St./Centre St. Map 8, B3, 12.

Actually, former police headquarters: this domed Beaux Arts giant became a luxury co-op apartment building in the 1970s. Gazing at the elegantly refurbished lobby, complete with marble columns and massive chandelier, makes it hard to imagine a more pleasant place to get booked.

LOWER EAST SIDE

Subway: F, V to Lower East Side-Second Ave.; F to E. Broadway; F, J, M, Z to Delancey St.-Essex St.

With 240,000 immigrants in one square mile, the Lower East Side was once the most densely settled area in New York. Initially populated by Irish immigrants in the mid-1800s, the area saw an influx of Eastern Europeans in the 50 years preceding WWI. Post-WWII migrants to the area were mostly African-Americans and Puerto Ricans, but Latin Americans and Asians have moved into the area over the last two decades. The Lower East Side is a world capital of indie-rock and underground music movements, both nurturing local talent and welcoming internationally touring bands. Hipsters patrol the streets and community gardens mingle with some of NYC's best graffiti. New bars, music venues and alluring little cafes spring up often. Don't miss the **Lower East Side Tenement Museum** (p. 137). **Sights are listed from north to south.**

CONGREGATION ANSHE CHESED

172-176 Norfolk St., between E. Houston and Stanton St. Subway: F, J, M, Z to Delancey St.-Essex St. Map 11, E1, 14. ☎212-780-0175.

New York's oldest reform synagogue was built in 1849 to seat 1500. While the impressive red Gothic Revival building is worth a peek, the synagogue—now a private space owned by the Angel Orensanz Association—is only open for services twice a month (on the 1st and 3rd F of the month).

LOWER EAST SIDE VISITORS CENTER

261 Broome St., between Orchard and Allen St. Subway: F, J, M, Z to Delancey St.-Essex St. Map 11, D3, 33. ☎212-226-9010. Free shopping tours meet in front of ***Katz's Deli*** *(p. 158) Su 11am. Open daily 10am-4pm.*

This helpful jumping-off point, full of maps and brochures, organizes a free shopping tour of the area for those who just want to be led to the best buys (instead of sniffing them out).

SUNG TAK BUDDHIST ASSOCIATION

15 Pike St., between E. Broadway and Henry St. Subway: F to E. Broadway. Map 11, F4, 41. ☎212-587-5936. Open daily 9:30am-6pm. Free.

Formerly the Congregation Sons of Israel Kalvarie, this dilapidated and graffiti-covered building stood abandoned for years until the Buddhist Association moved in. The newly renovated house of worship reflects its multicultural past in its juxtaposition of Middle Eastern and Asian architectural styles.

THE ELDRIDGE ST. SYNAGOGUE

12 Eldridge St., south of Canal St. Subway: J, M, Z to Canal St./Centre St. Map 11, D4, 39. ☎212-219-0903. Open Su and Tu-Th noon-4pm. Tours Tu and Th 11:30am and 2:30pm, Su on the hr. 11am-3pm. Tour tickets $5; children, students, and seniors $3.

This Moorish-style edifice, built in 1886 as the first synagogue for New York's Eastern Europeans, majestically presides over a crowded, noisy block. The synagogue, embarking on the second leg of its multimillion-dollar renovation project, is now a national historic sight open to the public.

TRIBECA

Bounded by Canal St. on the north, the Hudson River on the west, Vesey St. on the south and E. Broadway on the east. Subway: 1, 9 to Canal St./Varick St.; C, E to Canal St./Ave. of the Americas (Sixth Ave.); 1, 9 to Franklin St.; 1, 2, 3, 9 to Chambers St./W. Broadway; A, C to Chambers St./Church St.

Once an industrial wasteland, TriBeCa (Triangle Below Canal St.) has steadily evolved into a hip, mostly residential neighborhood full of confusing streets. One of the neighborhood's highlights is **Washington Market Park,** located in the triangle bounded by Greenwich, Chambers, and West St. This surprisingly large park hosts Thursday-evening concerts each week from late June to early August in its charming blue-and-white gazebo. Those hungry for a brush with the movies can pass by the **TriBeCa Grill,** 375 Greenwich St., owned by Robert DeNiro. The restaurant is on the ground floor of the **TriBeCa Films** building, in which Miramax and several other production companies work their cinematic magic. The actor/entrepreneur has also opened the **TriBeCa Bakery** in the middle of the block, and the chic, expensive, and surprisingly friendly **Nobu** on the corner of Franklin and Hudson St.

SOHO

Bounded in the north by Houston St., south by Canal St., west by W. Broadway, and east by Crosby St. Subway: C, E to Spring St./Ave. of the Americas (Sixth Ave.); 6 to Spring St./Lafayette St.; N, R to Prince St.; 1, 2 to W. Houston St.; F, S, V to Broadway-Lafayette St.

The story of SoHo's evolution is similar to that of many New York neighborhoods. In the earlier part of the century, SoHo was a dark industrial zone with factories and warehouses operating between its alleyways. In the mid-1940s, however, artists charmed by low rents and airy lofts moved in, and the trickle had swelled into a full-scale waterfall of migration by the 1960s. Led by Jean-Michel Basquiat, Keith Haring, and Kenny Scharf, SoHo's scene blossomed until the mid-1980s as the hotbed of NYC artistic innovation. The 90s brought a number of high-end designer boutiques, and SoHo quickly began recasting itself as a downtown Madison Ave. SoHo, like all of Lower Manhattan, suffered greatly after Sept. 11; only now are SoHo's businesses beginning to recover. Although it may no longer cradle the truly avant-garde, SoHo still boasts pockets of off-beat culture, high fashion, and meticulous design.

Designated a historic district in 1973 by the Landmarks Preservation Commission, SoHo is filled with cast-iron buildings—the result of a construction boom in the latter half of the 19th century, when the neighborhood was home to warehouses and factories. Especially notable is the **Haughwout Building,** with its delicate facade of arched windows set between Corinthian columns. Built in 1857, the five-story Haughwout boasts the first passenger elevator. Although the entire ground floor has been conquered by a Staples, the building is still definitely worth a stroll-by.

Don't concentrate on just one building: each narrow street is rich in architectural significance. Artwork abounds on West Broadway, and street vendors rival the many boutiques on Houston, Spring, and Prince St. on the weekends. Walk west away from Broadway to see smaller, lesser-known shops and colorful restaurants.

GREENWICH VILLAGE

Subway: A, C, E, F, V, S to W. 4th St.; A, C, E, L to 14th St./Eighth Ave.; 1, 2, 3 to 14th St./Seventh Ave.; F, L, V to 14th St./Ave. of the Americas (Sixth Ave.); 4, 5, 6, L, N, Q, R, W to 14th St.-Union Sq.; 1, 9 to Houston St., 1, 9 to Christopher St.; N, R to 8th St.-NYU; L to Sixth Ave., Eighth Ave.; 6 to Bleecker St.

Greenwich Village's relentless process of cultural ferment has layered grime, activism, and artistry atop a tangle of quaint, meandering streets. The area, once covered in farms and hills, developed in the mid-19th century into a staid high-society playground that fostered literary creativity (see **Walking Tour,** p. 62). Henry James captured the Village's debonair spirit in his 1880 novel, *Washington Square.*

Real-estate values plummeted at the turn of the century as German, Irish, and Italian immigrants found work in the industries along the Hudson River and in pockets of the Village. The Beat movement crystallized in the area some 50 years later, and the 60s saw the growth of a homosexual community around Christopher St.—along with growing tension between the Village's nonconformist ethos and the city government's aims. Violent clashes between police and homosexuals resulted in the **Stonewall Riots** of 1969, a powerful moment of awakening in the gay-rights movement. The punk scene exploded in the 1970s, adding mohawked and be-spiked rockers to the Village's diverse cast of characters. The 80s saw the beginnings of a gentrification process that has continued into the 21st century, making the Village a fashionable and comfortable settlement for those wealthier New Yorkers with a bit more spunk than their uptown counterparts.

The Village comes out in all of its (non)traditional glory for the wild **Village Halloween Parade.** This is your chance to see people dressed as toilets or condoms. Slap on your own wig, strap on your appendage of choice, and join the crowd—no one will blink a rhinestoned eyelash.

WASHINGTON SQUARE PARK AREA

Washington Sq. Park between 4th St. and Washington Sq. Park N., Macdougal St. and Greene St. Subway: A, C, E, F, V, S to W. 4th St. Map 10, E3.

Washington Sq. Park (see **Walking Tour,** p. 62) has stood at the center of Village life for most of this century. Native Americans once inhabited the marshland here, but by the mid-17th century it had become home to black slaves freed by the Dutch. The latter half of the 18th century saw the area converted into a potter's field for the burial of some 15,000 bodies of the poor and unknown, and then as a hanging-grounds during the Revolutionary War. As the area metamorphosed into a park and parade ground in the 1820s, high-toned residences made the area the center of New York's social scene. On the north side of the park lies **the Row** (Map 10, D3). Built largely in the 1830s, this stretch of stately Federal-style brick residences soon became an urban center populated by professionals, dandies, and novelists.

Washington Square Park became a base for low-level drug dealers in the late 1970s and early 80s; a noisy clean-up campaign in the mid-80s has made the park fairly safe, although its drug traffic has not altogether vanished (If you saw Larry Clark's film *Kids*, you'll recognize the area from the scene where said kids smoke blunts and beat the crap out of each other). Having undergone $900,000 worth of renovations in 1995, the park today hosts musicians, misunderstood teenagers, homeless people, and romping children.

At the north end of the Park stands the Washington Memorial Arch, built in 1889 to commemorate the centennial of George Washington's inauguration. Until 1964, Fifth Ave. actually ran through the arch; residents, however, complained of the noisy traffic and the city truncated this most esteemed of avenues.

NEW YORK UNIVERSITY

Campus map posted throughout the Village. NYU Information: 50 W. 4th St. Subway: 6 to Astor Pl.; N, R to 8th St.-NYU; A, C, E, F, V, S to W. 4th St.; 1, 9 to Christopher St. Map 10, E4. ☎212-998-4636. Free maps.

The country's largest private university, NYU is most notable for its stellar communications and film departments, as well as some of the Village's least appealing contemporary architecture. Many desperately functional-looking buildings around Washington Sq. proudly display the purple NYU flag.

Although NYU now sprawls throughout the city, the heart of the university is Washington Sq. Park. When it was founded in 1831, NYU considered using the Park as its central quad, but ultimately opted to do otherwise. For one day out of the year, however, NYU does take control of the Park: every Commencement since 1976 has been held in Washington Sq.

On the southeast side of the park, where Washington Sq. S. meets LaGuardia Pl., NYU's Loeb Student Center stands garnished with pieces of scrap metal that purportedly represent birds in flight. Mere steps away sits Gould Plaza, in front of NYU's Stern School of Business, and the Courant Institute of Mathematical Sciences. The plaza houses a shiny aluminum Dadaist sculpture by Jean Arp.

At Green St. and Waverly Pl. lies NYU's Brown Building, the former site of the Triangle Shirtwaist Company where a 1911 fire killed most of the primarily female staff—the doors had been chained shut to prevent the workers from taking too many breaks. The ensuing uproar led to new workplace regulations and a rejuvenated worker safety movement. Across the street looms another rust-colored giant, the Elmer Holmes Bobst Library, part of a bid to unify the severely disjointed campus with red sandstone facades. Unfortunately, money ran out before the project was complete, so NYU opted for the purple flags instead.

Washington Square Park

PICASSO

On Bleecker St., between LaGuardia Pl. and Mercer St., in the courtyard of the building complex on the south side of the street. Subway: A, C, E, F, V, S to W. 4th St. Map 10, E5, 86.

Proclaimed by the *New York Times* to be the city's ugliest piece of public art, this 36 ft., 60-ton structure of Norwegian black stone and sandblasted concrete is an adaptation of a 24 in. sheet metal sculpture by Pablo Picasso entitled *Bust of Sylvette*. Sitting in the center of NYU's Silver Towers (erstwhile home of noted literary couple Mel and Diane Parker), the massive reinterpretation was executed in the 60s by Norwegian sculptor Carl Nesjär. It stands in the midst of three 30-story residential towers designed by I. M. Pei. The tall concrete monolith's aura of disastrous aesthetics has created one of the only quiet spaces in a frantic neighborhood.

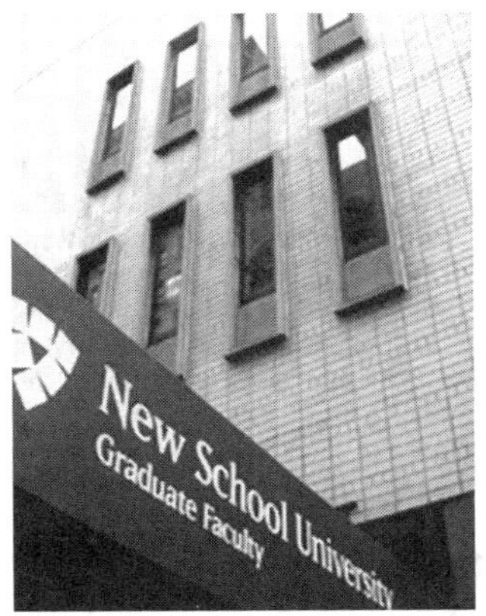

New School University

THE NEW SCHOOL

66 W. 12th St., between Sixth and Fifth Ave. Subway: F, L, V to 14th St./Sixth Ave/Ave. of the Americas. Map 10, D2, 8.

Formerly the New School for Social Research, this school's past faculty include John Dewey and W.E.B. DuBois. During WWII, the New School made itself famous by offering positions to European intellectuals fleeing the Nazis; it continues its tradition of progressive-minded thinking today. Former politician Bob Kerrey is the university's president.

Chess, Washington Square Park

GRACE CHURCH

802 Broadway, between 10th and 11th St. Subway: N, R to 8th St.-NYU. Map 10, F3, 36. ☎212-254-2000. Morning prayer M-F 7:30am; evening prayer M, Tu, Th, F 6pm; Su service 10am.

This church with the creepy Gothic exterior was constructed in 1845 using white marble mined by prisoners of the notorious New York State

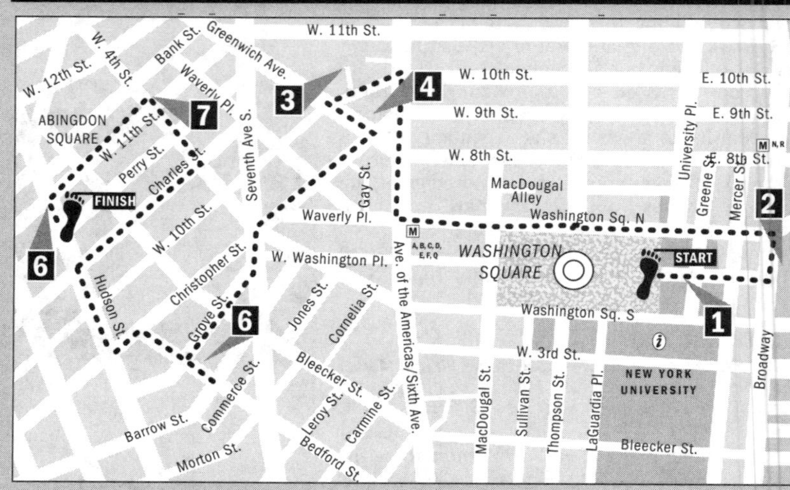

TIME: 1hr. 40min.

DISTANCE: 5 mi.

Now a high-rent location populated by professionals, Greenwich Village still retains fascinating traces of its vibrant, bohemian, and highly literary roots.

1 WASHINGTON SQUARE (P. 60). Writer Henry James (1843-1916) was born at 20 Washington Pl., just east of the Square; he later transformed his birthplace into the setting for *Washington Square*. Willa Cather lived at 60 Washington Sq. S. near the turn of the century. 1960s Beatniks Bob Dylan, Alan Ginsberg, and Jack Kerouac also hung out in the Square (it was conveniently close to NYU and the neighborhood cafes).

2 SHAKESPEARE AND CO. BOOKSTORE (P. 245). Browse high-brow journals, literature and vintage volumes as this Greenwich Village institution.

3 PATCHIN PLACE (P. 64). These three-story terraced houses, built in 1848, have sheltered such writers as Theodore Dreiser and the reclusive Djuna Barnes (the latter lived at Patchin Place from 1940 until her 1982 death). Poet e.e. cummings moved into a top-floor studio here after returning from Europe in 1923; he and his third wife, Marion Morehouse, eventually bought the entire house. He lived there until his death in 1962.

4 JEFFERSON MARKET LIBRARY (P. 64). This lovely library was once a prison and a courthouse. Mae West had to appear here for obscenity charges for her Broadway play *Sex*, which was the target of the Society for the Suppression of Vice.

5 75½ BEDFORD STREET (P. 63). Early 20th-century poet and bohemian "new woman" Edna St. Vincent Millay lived with her lover Eugen Boissevain in this three-story, 9½ ft. wide "dollhouse," otherwise known as Millay House. The couple only resided here for a year before moving upstate to escape the crowds drawn by Millay's celebrity status.

6 CHUMLEY'S (P. 63). This former Prohibition-era speakeasy has served F. Scott Fitzgerald, Edna St. Vincent Millay (see above), John Steinbeck, Ernest Hemingway, and countless other writers. It's now populated by college students, locals, and the odd bohemian survivor.

6 WHITE HORSE TAVERN (P. 200). Poet Dylan Thomas not only lived above this very Irish bar: he also drank himself to death here (with 18 shots of whiskey).

prison Sing Sing. Philanthropist Catharine Lorillard Wolfe is responsible for many of the additions to the church, including the beautiful East Window. The extremely dark and beautifully ornate interior, which used to be *the* place for weddings, still hosts a lovely St. Matthew Passion at Easter.

WEST OF SIXTH AVENUE (WEST VILLAGE)

The West Village (Map 10) is one of the city's nerve centers for gay and lesbian life. **Sights are listed roughly from south to north.**

75½ BEDFORD STREET

Near the corner of Commerce St. Subway: 1, 9 to Christopher St. Map 10, B5, 71.

75½ Bedford St. (see **Walking Tour,** p. 62) is the Village's narrowest building, measuring 9½ ft. across. The writer Edna St. Vincent Millay lived here from 1923-4; during this time she founded the **Cherry Lane Theater,** 38 Commerce St. (p. 225; Map 10, B5, 70), which has showcased off-Broadway theater ever since. Sandwiched between other complexes, these red-bricked quarters are easy to miss. Actors Lionel Barrymore and Cary Grant, who apparently also liked cramped quarters, each lived at 75½ Bedford after her departure.

CHUMLEY'S

86 Bedford St., between Grove and Barrow St. Subway: 1, 9 to Christopher St. Map 10, B4, 52. ☎212-675-4449. Open Su-Th 4pm-midnight, F-Sa 4pm-2am.

Once the center of the Greenwich Village literary movement, this bar and restaurant (see **Walking Tour,** p. 62) became a speakeasy in Prohibition days. Hundreds of authors, including the literary Johns (Dos Passos and Steinbeck), Ernest Hemingway, William Faulkner, and J.D. Salinger have raised a glass here—and now jackets from their books adorn the walls. The fascinating building—complete with original trap doors, secret elevators, and hidden escape routes—has survived four fires; it's open to explore even if you're not drinking here. Partly in homage to its clandestine history, no sign indicates that this cream-colored building with a brown door might be a bar. Legend has it that the term "to eighty-six," i.e., to refuse to serve an unwelcome customer, was coined here. If you manage to find the place, pick up a brochure written by Leland Chumley himself, and explore the site's amazing history.

CHURCH OF ST. LUKE'S IN THE FIELDS

479-485 Hudson St., between Barrow and Grove St. Subway: 1, 9 to Christopher St. Map 10, A5, 68.

At the western end of Grove St. is the Episcopalian Church of St. Luke's in the Fields. The third-oldest church in Manhattan, this severe brick building was named for the once-remote location at which it was built in 1821. The church is not open to the public for sightseeing, but welcomes all for Sunday Eucharists at 8 and 10:30am.

SHERIDAN SQUARE

Intersection of Seventh Ave., Christopher St., and W. 4th St. Subway: 1, 9 to Christopher St. Map 10, B4, 43.

Rioters against the Civil War draft gathered here in 1863 for some of the darkest days in NYC's history; protesters brutally murdered hundreds of free blacks. Since then, the area's vastly increased tolerance has become evident in the diversity of Christopher St.

The vicinity of the street near Sheridan Sq. has been renamed Stonewall Place after the **Stonewall Inn,** site of the 60s police raid that sparked the gay rights movement (p. 201; Map 10, B4, 41). In 1960s New York City, it was illegal for bars to serve liquor to homosexuals or suspected homosexuals. Like the few other gay bars in the area at the time, the Stonewall Inn operated without a liquor license. The police would enter a bar, force the patrons outside, arrest most or all of them, and fine the bar owners. Often the arrested men and women had their

The Cage, W. 4th and Sixth Ave.

Bleecker and MacDougal St.

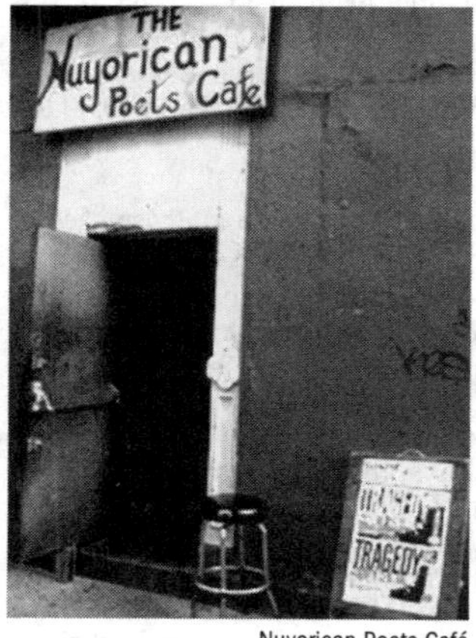

Nuyorican Poets Café

names published in the papers the next day, which meant that they were in constant danger of losing jobs and homes. One night in June 1969, however, the patrons fought back when the police raided the establishment. The Stonewall Riots are now regarded as the beginning of the modern gay rights movement. Each year, at the end of June, marches are held in many cities to commemorate the historic event.

Within Sheridan Sq., a small green park, two sculptures of same-sex couples stand locked in embrace as a tribute to the neighborhood's history. Rest your tired legs on one of the Square's benches after strolling through the Village, and pay homage to the warriors of the past who paved the way for modern day civil rights. An unhitched and stoic General Sheridan stands nearby.

JEFFERSON MARKET LIBRARY

425 Sixth Ave., at the intersection of W. 10th St. and Greenwich Ave. Subway: 1, 9 to Christopher St. Map 10, C3, 28. ☎ 212-243-4334. Open M and Th 10am-6pm, Tu and F noon-6pm, W noon-8pm, Sa 10am-5pm.

Built as a courthouse in 1876, this remarkable edifice (see **Walking Tour,** p. 62) served as a female detention facility before facing, and beating, a demolition plot in the early 60s. Once voted the fifth most beautiful building in the country, the building was carefully restored in 1967; it is now a public library. The library was scheduled to close on November 18. 1974, but the Greenwich Village community fought desperately to keep their beloved site open and won. The Victorian Gothic design, with its detailed brickwork, stained-glass windows, and turreted clock tower, suggests a cross between a castle and a church. The structure occupies the triangle formed by the intersection of W. 10th St., Sixth Ave., and Greenwich Ave. Just behind the former courthouse, a small but beautifully lush garden lies open to the public.

PATCHIN PLACE

10th St. and Sixth Ave. Subway: 1, 9 to Christopher St. Map 10, C3, 26.

Across from Jefferson Market Library are an iron gate and a street sign reading "Patchin Place." The modest, 145-year-old buildings lining the unassuming path (see **Walking Tour,** p. 62) were initially built as a boarding house for employees of a posh Fifth Ave. hotel, but have since housed writers e. e. cummings, Theodore Dreiser, and Djuna Barnes. cummings and Barnes, in fact, were neighbors; the latter was so reclusive that cummings would call her "just to see if she was still alive." Patchin Place has also housed Marlon Brando, John Masefield, Eugene O'Neill, and John Reed (who wrote the Russian Revolution chronicle *Ten Days that Shook the World* here).

MEAT-PACKING DISTRICT

South of West Chelsea, roughly from 17th St. to Little W. 12th St. Subway: A, C, E, L to 14th St./Eighth Ave. Map 10, A2 .

Walking up Hudson St. will lead you to the meat-packing district. In the past few years, lofts have sprung up in old factories, cafes in old garages, and clubs in old stockyards. Top-rate fashion designers such as Stella McCartney and Alexander McQueen have also trendified the neighborhood by opening shops here. This urban renewal, however, has had little effect on the shady weekend late-night scene.

THE EAST VILLAGE AND ALPHABET CITY

Subway: 6 to Astor Pl., Bleecker St.; L to First Ave., Third Ave.; F, V to Lower East Side-Second Ave.

The East Village—the section east of Broadway and north of E. Houston St.—was carved out of the Bowery and the Lower East Side in the early 1960s, as artists and writers moved here to escape high rents in Greenwich Village. Today, the East Village population represents greater diversity than its western neighbor; older Eastern European immigrants live alongside newer Hispanic and Asian arrivals. Punks, hippies, ravers, rastas, guppies, goths, beatniks, and virtually every other imaginable group also share the scene. This multicultural coexistence has not come easily; many poorer residents of the East Village feel that wealthier newcomers are pushing them out by raising rents. Those tensions, however, have forged the East Village's identity as one of the most overtly politicized regions of New York City.

East of First Ave., south of 14th St., and north of Houston St., the avenues give up on numbers and adopt letters. In its 60s heyday, Jimi Hendrix and the Fugs would play open-air shows to bright-eyed love children. You'll still find East Village "deadbeatniks" and hard-core anarchists, as well as artists and students, hanging out in local cafes and shops. However, the area has also found itself squarely in the growing path of New York's wave of gentrification, manifested in the increasing numbers of boutiques and chic eateries. The area is generally safe during the day. Addictive nightlife on Ave. A and B ensure some protection, but use caution east of Ave. B after dark. For information on current issues and events in Alphabet City, check free local papers at **St. Mark's Bookshop** (p. 247) and other stores in the area. Neighborhood posters also advertise current happenings. **Sights are listed from west to east.**

ST. MARK'S PLACE

Where E. 8th St. would be, between Cooper Sq. E. and Ave. A. Subway: 6 to Astor Pl. Map 12, C2, 19.

Full of pot-smoking flower children and musicians in the 1960s, this street gave Haight-Ashbury a run for its hashish. It also taught London's Kings Road how to do punk in the late 1970s, as mohawked youths hassled passersby from the brownstone steps off Astor Pl. Nowadays, those 60s and 70s youths still line the street—in their aged (but still tattooed) incarnations.

Present-day St. Mark's Pl. is a drag full of tiny ethnic eateries, street level shops, sidewalk vendors selling trinkets of all kinds (from plastic bug-eye sunglasses to PVC fetish wear), music shops, and, of course, tattoo shops. In a way, St. Mark's resembles a small-town Main Street—a small town with a bad-ass history. Unlike most other areas of the city, people here know one another; sometimes they even talk to and look after one another. Although many more-obscure-than-thou types now shun the commercialized (there's even a Gap) and crowded areas of the street, St. Mark's remains the hub of East Village life and a good place to start your tour of the neighborhood.

the hidden deal

Green Guerrillas

In 1973, Liz Christy and the "Green Guerrillas" began planting neighborhood window boxes and tree pits and throwing water balloons filled with seeds into the East Village and Alphabet City's abandoned lots. By 1986 they had transformed the northeast corner of Bowery and Houston into a flowering oasis named the **Liz Christy Bowery-Houston Garden,** 110 E. Houston St., between Bowery and Second Ave. (Map 12, C4. Open Sa noon-4pm; May- Sept. also open Tu 6pm-dusk.) The trend caught on, and community gardens blossomed across the East Village–a manifestation of residents' combined love of nature and social activism. One example is the **De Colores Community Yard and Garden,** E. 8th St., between Ave. B and C. (Map 12, F2, 54). Work on De Colores began in May of 1996. The group of East Village and Lower East Side community members decided to clear out a rubble-filled, city-owned lot and create a garden. This was partially a response to the City's destruction of a large, long-standing garden across the street in order to create a residence for the elderly. The community members, left to their own devices by the city, cut down trees, cleared building rubble and

ASTOR PLACE

At the junction of Lafayette Ave., Fourth Ave., and E. 8th St. Subway: 6 to Astor Pl. Map 12, C2, 31.

Simultaneously a small road and a large cultural intersection, this western border of the East Village simmers with street life. Check out the ever-popular **Beaver Murals** at the Astor Pl. subway stop—they pay homage to John Jacob Astor's prolific fur trade. Upstairs from the murals, the subway kiosk—a cast-iron Beaux Arts beauty—was built in 1985 as part of the station's reconstruction. A **large black cube** balanced on its corner distinguishes Astor Pl.'s position. The cube rotates if you and your friends push hard enough, but you may disturb Astor Pl.'s various denizens sitting (or sleeping) underneath it. "The Cube" (officially *The Alamo*, by Bernard Rosenthal) is a meeting point for countless rallies, marches, demonstrations, and impromptu performances (Map 12, B2, 18). It also provides asphalt for hordes of prepubescent skaters.

THE COOPER UNION FOUNDATION BUILDING

7 E. 7th St., at Cooper Sq., off Astor Pl. Subway: 6 to Astor Pl. Map 12, C3, 32. ☎212-353-4199. Gallery open M-Th 11am-7pm.

Peter Cooper, a self-educated industrialist, founded the Cooper Union for the Advancement of Science and Art in 1859 as a tuition-free technical and design school. Both the American Red Cross and the NAACP got their starts here. Cooper Union also stands as the oldest building in the US to incorporate steel beams (made of old railroad rails). The second-floor **Houghton Gallery** hosts changing exhibits on design and American history, as well as displays by the talented and stylish student body (but not during the summer). Find Cooper's statue in Cooper Sq., in front of the building.

ST. MARK'S CHURCH IN-THE-BOWERY

131 E. 10th St., between Second and Third Ave. Subway: 6 to Astor Pl. Map 12, C2, 19. ☎212-674-6377. West Yard open Su 11:30am-1pm, Tu 3-5pm, W 3-6pm, Sa 10:30am-12:30pm.

Erected in 1799, St. Mark's Church stands on the site of Peter Stuyvesant's estate chapel (the Dutch governor lies buried in its small cobblestone graveyard). St. Mark's has a long history of political activism, involvement in the arts, and innovative community programs. In the 19th century, it built a church to serve the immigrant communities around Tompkins Sq. Park. In the 1960s, the church organized neighborhood teenagers and young adults to rebuild the church after a devastating fire. St. Mark's was also the center for civil rights and antiwar organizing on the Lower East Side. Today, the church has an Hispanic ministry and offers weekly Eucharist (Su 1pm) and special feast day services conducted in Spanish. Sunday collections of food are delivered to the Catholic Worker Food Pantry on 3rd St. *The Catholic Worker* was founded by Dorothy Day, pacifist and social activist, who is now being considered for sainthood. The Direct Action Network, an anti-globalization group, meets weekly in the Parish Hall.

The church also hosts several community companies including the **Ontological Theater,** which continues to produce some of the better off-Broadway plays, the **Danspace Project,** and the **Poetry Project** (for overview of all three projects, see p. 230).

COLONNADE ROW

428-434 Lafayette Ave., at 4th St. Subway: 6 to Bleecker St. Map 12, B2, 17.

New York's most famous 19th-century millionaires—John Jacob Astor, Cornelius "Commodore" Vanderbilt, and members of the Roosevelt family—inhabited three of these four-columned houses built in 1833. There used to be nine of these houses; the four remaining are, sadly, the worse for wear.

THE SECOND AVENUE DELI

156 Second Ave., at E. 10th St. Subway: 6 to Astor Pl. Map 12, C2, 21.

This famous Jewish landmark, founded by Abe Lebewohl, is all that remains of the "Yiddish Rialto"—the stretch of Second Ave. between Houston and 14th St. that contained the Yiddish theater district in the early part of the 20th century. Stars of David in the sidewalk out front contain the names of actors and actresses who spent their lives entertaining Jewish immigrants. While this community is no longer the Jewish enclave that it once was, the historic deli remains a local mainstay with the meanest pastrami sandwich in town (see p. 164). Across the street is **Abe Lebewohl Park** (Map 12, C2, 20), built to commemorate the deli's founder, who was murdered in 1996.

NEW YORK MARBLE CEMETERIES

Second Ave., between E. 2nd and 3rd St. and 52-74 E. 2nd St., between First and Second Ave. Subway: F, V to Lower East Side-Second Ave. Map 12, C/D4, 90, 98. Open F 1-5pm and Sa 10am-2pm.

The New York Marble Cemeteries (so named for their below-ground vaults made of solid white Tuckahoe marble) were the city's first

even removed junkie's needles in order to create the De Colores garden. Once the lot was cleared, garden plots with wood and rocks were created along the perimeter and grass seed planted in the center. People design their own plots, and the common plots and grass are tended to communally. De Colores flowers have brightened this formerly dark and dangerous place. A flea market takes place every Saturday at 10am near the spacious garden. Another notable community garden is the **6th Street and Avenue B Garden** (Map 12, E3, 85): the mother of all community gardens, this fantasy jungle contains a towering sculpture by Edward Boros. (Open in summer daily 8am-8pm; other times Sa-Su 1-6pm.) The **Campos Plaza,** E. 12th St., between Ave. B and C (Map 12, F1, 16), contains a plethora of fruits and veggies. (Open Mar.-Oct. Su 3-5pm and intermittently during the week.) For more about garden activists, see our interview on p. 93 or visit www.greenguerillas.org.

Other spectacular East Village community gardens include:

El Sol Brillante, E. 12th St., between Ave. A and B. Map 12, E1, 12.

Gilbert's Sculpture Garden, E. 8th St., between Ave. C and D. Map 12, F2, 56.

Miracle Garden, E. 3rd St., at Ave. B. (entrance on E. 2nd St.) Map 12, E4, 105. Small but tall and lush.

Union Square

Walking the Dog

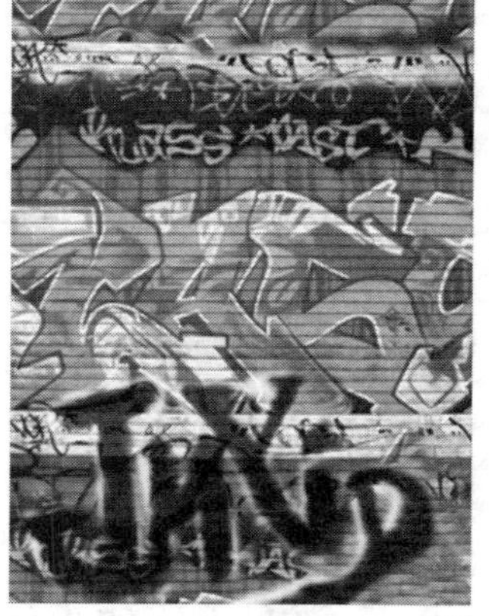
Graf

two non-sectarian graveyards. Both cemeteries can be viewed through the iron fences that surround them.

ST. GEORGE UKRAINIAN CATHOLIC CHURCH

On Taras Shevchenko Pl., near Cooper Sq. E. and E. 7th St. Subway: 6 to Astor Pl. Map 12, C3, 66. Mass Su 1pm.

Ukrainian-American life centers on E. 7th St., with cafes and several churches. Most remarkable of the latter is St. George Ukrainian Catholic Church. The present-day building dates from 1978, when St. George's parishioners gave generously to build the new church structure in classical Ukrainian Byzantine style architecture. The artwork inside, viewable only if you stop by Sunday after Mass, eclipses even the haunting icons that ornament the outer doors.

TOMPKINS SQUARE PARK

Between Ave. A and B and E. 7th and 10th St. Subway: L to First Ave. Map 12, D2. Open daily 6am-midnight.

Tompkins Sq. Park's history is one of clashes, protests, and marches, although the area has calmed down significantly in recent years. In 1988, police officers precipitated a riot when they attempted to forcibly evict a band of homeless people and their supporters from the park. An aspiring video artist recorded scenes of police brutality, sparking a public outcry and further police-inspired violence. "East Side Anarchists"—who hoofed down to Tompkins Sq. after tearing through St. Mark's Pl.—incited one of many riots that erupted in NYC following the Rodney King verdict in 1992. The park's designated **dog run** affords marvelous opportunities for canine-watching. In the summer, you're bound to stumble upon **impromptu concerts** here.

LOWER MIDTOWN

Between 14th and 42nd St., stretching all the way across Manhattan.

UNION SQUARE

Between Broadway and Park Ave. S., between 14th and 17th St. Subway: 4, 5, 6, L, N, Q, R, W to 14th St.-Union Sq. Map 13, E6. Greenmarket open M, W, F-Sa 7am-6pm.

So named because it was a "union" of two main roads (the Bowery and Bloomingdale Rd., now Fourth Ave. and Broadway), Union Sq. and the surrounding area was populated by high-society aristocrats before the Civil War. The square's name became doubly significant early in the 20th century, when the neighborhood became a center of New York's Socialist movement: the masses held their popular May Day celebrations in the park. The 1970s were unkind to all of New York's parks, and Union Sq. was no exception; by the middle of the 1980s, Union Sq. was on the 'Do Not Visit' list of both tourists and residents alike. Despite the danger and disrepair of the park, the surrounding neighborhood became the lightning rod for Manhattan's late entrance to New York's burgeoning hip-hop scene. After almost a decade of renovations and shifting demographics in the neighborhood, however, today's Union Sq. bears almost no resemblance to its earlier incarnations: drug dealers have been replaced by bond traders and aspiring MCs have given way to grinning NYU undergrads. In case you might worry that Union Square has lost its personality, fear not: many of the chain stores lining the perimieter of the park are more than happy to sell you cool urban swagger in the deep pockets of their $100 jeans.

As Manhattan's best transit hub and its location at the nexus of a number of different neighborhoods, Union Sq. has become the crossroads of downtown. In the Square itself, the scent of herbs and fresh bread wafts through the air, courtesy of the **Union Square Greenmarket** (p. 171). Farmers, fisherman, and bakers from all over the region come to sell fresh produce, jellies, and baked goods.

UNION SQUARE THEATRE (TAMMANY HALL)

100 E. 17th St., at Union Sq. E. Subway: 4, 5, 6, L, N, Q, R, W to 14th St.-Union Sq. Map 13, E5, 96.

Beginning with the election of Mayor Fernando Wood in 1854, the Democratic machine of Tammany Hall dominated New York's political scenes for almost a century. The group first began its ascent under William 'Boss' Tweed, one of the patron saints of municipal corruption. The Tweed Ring ultimately fell apart, but the Tammany Tiger came roaring back; the City would remain both overwhelmingly Democratic and corrupt until the election of 1932. The organization declined greatly during the mayoralty of Fiorello LaGuardia (1933-45), considered New York's best mayor by most and New York's only successful mayor by many. The decline was accelerated by woman's suffrage, immigration restrictions, and the social programs of the New Deal, which weakened voters' dependence on the machine. Tammany made a comeback after WWII under the leadership of Carmine De Sapio, but eventually collapsed during Mayor John Lindsay's time in office (1966-73).

Tammany Hall is now home to the Union Sq. Theater, and a small inscription on top of the door is one of the only reminders of the building's past. The theater recently housed the popular off-off-Broadway hits "Bat Boy" and "Our Lady of 121st Street," and currently shares the building with the NY Film Academy.

UNION SQUARE SAVINGS BANK

20 Union Sq. E. Subway: 4, 5, 6, L, N, Q, R, W to 14th St.-Union Sq. Map 13, E6, 118.

Although designed by Henry Bacon, architect of the Lincoln Memorial in Washington, D.C., this Neoclassical building was never declared a historic landmark. The bank, with its intimidating, towering white columns, is now the site of the **Daryl Roth Theatre,** currently home of the much talked-about dance/rock/funk/circus **De La Guarda** (for ticket information, see p. 212).

STUYVESANT SQUARE

Second Ave., between 15th and 17th St. Subway: L to Third Ave. or First Ave. Map 13, F6.

A park divided by Second Ave., Stuyvesant Sq. is named after Governor Peter Stuyvesant (p. 41), who owned farm property here in the 17th century. The Governor's statue (including his infamous peg leg) in the park's west side was created by Gertrude Vanderbilt Whitney, later the founder of the **Whitney Museum** (p. 133). On Rutherford Pl. is **St. George's Episcopal Church,** built in 1856 in the style of Romanesque Revival, as well as a Quaker **Friends Meeting House,** built in Greek Revival style in 1860.

GRAMERCY PARK

At the south end of Lexington Ave., between 20th and 21st St. Subway: 6 to 23rd St./Park Ave. S. Map 13, E5. Closed to the public.

In 1831 Samuel Ruggles, a developer fond of greenery, drained a marsh to create Gramercy Park and laid out 66 building lots around its perimeter. Buyers of Ruggles' lots received keys to enter the park; for many years, the keys were made of solid gold. Over 150 years later, little has changed. Gramercy, with its wide gravel paths, remains the only private park in New York, immaculately kept by its owners. You can stare longingly through the wrought iron gates at the manicured garden to see what you're missing. The surrounding real estate—a charming mix of Greek Revival and Victorian Gothic-style townhouses—includes the National Arts Club, the Players Club, the School of Visual Arts and some of the city's choicest residences.

NATIONAL ARTS CLUB

15 Gramercy Park S., at Irving Pl. Subway: 6 to 23rd St./Park Ave. S. Map 13, E5, 92. ☎212-475-3424. Gallery open M-F 10am-5pm, Sa-Su noon-5pm. Free.

Founded in 1893 by art critic Charles de Kay in an effort to create an American art scene independent of European inspiration, the National Arts Club boasts members such as Martin Scorcese, Robert Redford, and Uma Thurman. Its presidential alumni include Teddy Roosevelt, Woodrow Wilson and Dwight D. Eisenhower. The club occupies the former mansion of Samuel Tilden (a would-be American president who won the popular vote and lost the Electoral College). Some of the rooms are used as gallery space for temporary exhibitions.

PLAYERS CLUB

16 Gramercy Park S., at Irving Pl. Subway: 6 to 23rd St./Park Ave. S. Map 13, E5, 93. ☎212-228-7611. Tours for groups of 10 or more; call ahead. Suggested donation $5, students and seniors $3.

Actor Edwin Booth (brother of Lincoln's assassin) established the Players Club in 1888 as an exclusive social club for actors. Booth's portrait hangs over the club's fireplace. Members have included Mark Twain, Sir Laurence Olivier, Frank Sinatra, Walter Cronkite, and Richard Gere. The building, built in 1845, is one of the oldest brownstones in New York.

THE THEODORE ROOSEVELT BIRTHPLACE

28 E. 20th St. between Broadway and Park Ave. S. Subway: N, R to 23rd St./Broadway. Map 13, E5, 89. ☎212-260-1616; www.nps.gov/thrb. Open Tu-F 10am-5pm. Guided tours 30min., 10am-4pm. $3, under 18 free.

Teddy Roosevelt lived in this brownstone from birth until age 15. In 1923, the building was restored and transformed into a museum, which now consists of five elegant period rooms, decorated as they would have appeared in Teddy's childhood. The free exhibit downstairs highlights events in the 26th president's life, displaying the uniform TR wore as a Rough Rider during the Spanish-American War.

MADISON SQUARE PARK

Southern end of Madison Ave., between 23rd and 26th St. Subway: N, R to 23rd St./Broadway; 6 to 23rd St./Park Ave. S. Map 13, D4.

Less manic than the fast-moving Midtown commerce surrounding it, Madison Sq. Park allows for wonderful views of such surrounding skyscrapers as the Flatiron Building (p. 71) and the New York Life Insurance Building (p. 72). Before the park's opening, this public space hosted a game played by a group called the Knickerbockers: formerly known as "New York ball," it evolved into America's favorite pastime—baseball. At the park's Broadway entrance, the statue of William Seward (former NY Governor and US

Secretary of State) welcomes visitors. Statues of famous 19th-century generals, as well as occasional exhibits of contemporary art, stand around the park today.

FLATIRON BUILDING

175 Fifth Ave., off the southwest corner of Madison Sq. Park. Subway: N, R to 23rd St./Broadway; 6 to 23rd St./ Park Ave. S. Map 13, D4, 39.

New York's first skyscraper over 20 stories high, as well as one of the first buildings in which exterior walls were hung on a steel frame, this photogenic building (originally the Fuller Building) was named for its resemblance to the clothes-pressing device. The intersection of Broadway, Fifth Ave., and 23rd St. necessitated its dramatic wedge shape (only 6 ft. wide at its point). Constructed in 1902, its triangular shape produced wind currents that made women's skirts billow; police coined the term "23 skiddoo" to shoo gapers from the area. Among the many commercial tenants of the building is **St. Martin's Press,** the company that publishes this book.

METROPOLITAN LIFE INSURANCE TOWER

1 Madison Ave., at 23rd St. Subway: N, R to 23rd St./ Broadway; 6 to 23rd St./Park Ave. S. Map 13, E4, 43.

Surveying Madison Sq. Park from 700 ft. above ground, the white tower—a 1909 addition to the 1893 edifice inspired by the famed bell-tower of San Marco in Venice—was once the world's tallest building. The minute hands of the clocks (one on each of the building's four faces) weigh 1000 lb. each. The annex on 24th St., connected by a walkway, features an eye-catching neo-Gothic facade.

69TH REGIMENT ARMORY

68 Lexington Ave., at 26th St. Subway: 6 to 28th St./ Park Ave. S. Map 13, E4, 42. ☎212-532-6013. Closed to the public.

A large structure in the Beaux Arts style, the armory is notable for having hosted the infamous 1913 International Exhibition of Modern Art that brought Picasso, Matisse, and Duchamp—whom Teddy Roosevelt called "a bunch of lunatics"—to America's shores. Perhaps in homage to this history, temporary installations can sometimes still be found in

Murrary Hill

Sonnabend Gallery, Chelsea

This Guy

its old basketball courts. Now a recruiting facility for the Army National Guard, the Armory was thrown back into the spotlight after Sept. 11, when it became the city's command center for family and friends seeking missing persons.

NEW YORK LIFE INSURANCE BUILDING

51 Madison Ave., between 26th and 27th St. Subway: N, R to 28th St./Broadway; 6 to 28th St./ Park Ave. S. Map 13, E4, 41.

Built by Cass Gilbert (of **Woolworth Building** fame; see p. 53) in 1928, this multi-tiered structure is topped by a golden pyramid-shaped roof, and an old mechanical clock tower. The building is located on the former site of circusmeister P.T. Barnum's "Hippodrome," which was rebuilt by Stanford White and served as the original Madison Square Garden from 1890 to 1925. It soon became the premier spot for New York's trademark entertainment spectacles. Star architect and man-about-town White was fatally shot here in 1906 by the unstable husband of a former mistress; the story was later fictionalized in E.L. Doctorow's *Ragtime*.

CHURCH OF THE TRANSFIGURATION

1 E. 29th St., between Fifth and Madison Ave. Subway: N, R to 28th St./Broadway; 6 to 28th St./ Park Ave. S. Map 13, D3, 19. ☎212-684-6770; www.littlechurch.org. Open daily 8am-6pm.

Better known as "The Little Church Around the Corner," this church has been the home parish of New York's theater world ever since 1870, when a pastor agreed to bury Shakespearean actor George Holland here (actors then were considered low-lives). Today, the charming neo-Gothic cottage serves as the home for the Episcopal Actors' Guild and features the beautiful Lich Gate, peculiar green roofs, and a manicured garden with a bubbling fountain. Check out the stained-glass windows: they may look like a scene from the Bible, but the vignette is from *Hamlet*.

MURRAY HILL

Subway: 6 to 33rd St. Map 13, E1-2, F1-2.

Murray Hill is so named because Robert Murray, a rich man in revolutionary times, made his country home close to the present-day intersection of 37th St. and Park Ave. The upper crust of the late 19th and early 20th centuries lived in warm brownstones and apartments on these sedate residential streets.

On the neighborhood's southern border is one of America's premier acting schools—**American Academy of Dramatic Arts,** 120 Madison Ave., between 30th and 31st St. (Map 13, E3, 21). A peek at the class photos hanging in the lobby reveals the fresh faces of Kirk Douglas, Class of 1941; Grace Kelly, Class of 1948-49; and Robert Redford, Class of 1958-59. (For more info on studying here, see p. 317.) The highlight of Murray Hill, however, is the **Pierpont Morgan Library,** 29 E. 36th St., at Madison Ave. (Map 13, E2). The original library building was completed in 1906 and designed by Charles McKim. Built in the style of a Renaissance *palazzo*, the understated and elegant library is definitely worth a visit—both for architectural beauty and for its printed-word collection (for details about library, see p. 141). Unfortunately, the library is closed to the public for renovations until 2006.

CHELSEA

Subway: 1, 2, 3 to 14th St./Seventh Ave.; A, C, E, L to 14th St./Eighth Ave.; C, E to 23rd St./ Eighth Ave.; 1, 9 to 23rd St./Seventh Ave.; 1, 9 to 28th St./Seventh Ave. Map 13, B4-5, C4-5.

Chelsea is probably best known today for its visible and vocal gay community, which is most apparent during **Pride Weekend.** (Generally held between last 2 Sundays in June. ☎212-807-7433; www.nycpride.org.) The neighborhood is also legendary for its art, and the waterfront factories and warehouses from a bygone industrial era now house artistic spaces and underground hangouts.

While Chelsea retains some of its former grit, the superb galleries around **10th** and **11th Avenue** and **22nd Street** house some of the most cutting-edge art in the city. **Sights are listed from east to west.**

HOTEL CHELSEA

222 W. 23rd St., between Seventh and Eighth Ave. Subway: 1, 9 to 23rd St./Seventh Ave.; C, E to 23rd St./ Eighth Ave. Map 13, C4, 33. ☎212-243-3700.

This is hallowed ground for literati. Some 150 books have been penned in this maze-like 400-room complex, including works by Arthur Miller, Mark Twain, Vladimir Nabokov, and Dylan Thomas. The Chelsea also has rock-and-roll credibility: Joni Mitchell wrote the song *Chelsea Morning* here. Despite the hype, though, the hotel maintains a discreet atmosphere of institutional anonymity (for prices, see p. 259).

ST. PETER'S EPISCOPAL CHURCH

346 W. 20th St., between Eighth and Ninth Ave. Subway: C, E to 23rd St./Eighth Ave. Map 13, B5, 65. ☎212-929-2390.

A Greek Revival rectory and a Gothic Review main church building provide an interesting architectural mix. St. Peter's shares space with the non-denominational Chelsea Community Church. Episcopal services every Sunday at 10am.

GENERAL THEOLOGICAL SEMINARY

175 Ninth Ave., between 20th and 21st St. Subway: C, E to 23rd St./Eighth Ave. Map 13, B5, 62. Open M-F noon-3pm, Sa 11am-3pm.

The oldest Episcopal seminary in America (founded in 1817), the Chelsea Square complex stands on land donated by former teacher Clement Clarke Moore, who wrote *T'was the Night Before Christmas*. The calming grounds are open to the public: go through the regrettable 1960 exterior to find a serene, peaceful oasis punctuated by a 161 ft. bell tower. If you're lucky, you may catch some aspiring priests playing tennis.

CHELSEA MARKET

75 Ninth Ave., between W. 15th and W. 16th St. Subway: A, C, E, L to 14th St.-Eighth Ave. Map 13, B6, 102. www.chelseamarket.com. Open M-F 8am-7pm, Sa-Su 10am-6pm.

An intricate Nabisco factory complex, converted with industrial-themed decor (an indoor waterfall that comes out of a pipe; exposed

Chelsea Piers

Joyce Theater

Queer Apple

brick). Watch bakers work at the sprawling building's several bakeries. The market also houses a number of high-quality wholesalers, including a florist and a soup stand. The **Chelsea Wine Vault** offers free tastings every Friday 4-7pm and Saturday 1-5pm.

CUSHMAN ROW

406-418 W. 20th St., between Ninth and 10th Ave. Subway: C, E to 23rd St./Eighth Ave. Map 13, A5, 55.

Named for Don Alonzo Cushman, a 19th-century dry-goods mogul, this terrace of brownstones is one of the city's finest examples of the Greek Revival architectural style. Admire the wrought-iron railings while enjoying the shade of gingko trees lining one of the most bucolic walkways in otherwise frenetic Chelsea.

CHELSEA PIERS

On the Hudson River, at the far west end of 20th St. Subway: C, E to 23rd St./Eighth Ave. ☎ 212-336-6666; www.chelseapiers.com. Map 13, A5, 56. Hours vary according to activity. Call ahead.

This massive space eschews urban grit in favor of ludicrously bright colors and scrubbed-clean surfaces. Ocean liners once docked here—the *Carpathia* landed in Chelsea after rescuing survivors from the *Titanic*—but after years of disuse, the Piers were reincarnated in the 90s as a sports-entertainment complex with ice-skating rinks, bowling alleys, and even a golf driving range from which four stories of lunch-breaking yuppies thwack golf balls toward Jersey.

HERALD SQUARE AREA AND THE GARMENT DISTRICT

The *New York Herald* used to publish its daily newspaper in a building at the intersection of Broadway and Sixth Ave., between 34th and 35th St. The newspaper is long gone, but the (triangular) square survives. **Sights are arranged from east to west.**

THE EMPIRE STATE BUILDING

350 Fifth Ave., at 34th St. Subway: B, D, F, N, Q, R, V, W to 34th St.-Herald Sq. Map 13, D2. Observatory ☎ 212-736-3100. Open daily 9:30am-midnight (last elevator up at 11:30pm); tickets sold until 11:30pm. $9, seniors $7, under 12 $4. Skyride ☎ 212-279-9777. Open daily 10am-10pm. $11.50, ages 4-12 and seniors $8.50. Combination Pass $17, seniors $13, children $10.

Ever since King Kong first climbed the Empire State Building with his main squeeze in 1933, the skyscraper has attracted scores of tourists: the

Gay New York

New York has been a major center for American gay life since the 19th century. Poet "I sing the body electric" Walt Whitman enjoyed watching Brooklyn youths swim naked in the East River. Around lower Broadway and the Bowery, male hustlers wore red bowties to announce their profession to interested passersby. With the arrival of a more tolerant bohemian artistic culture, Greenwich Village also became a magnet for gays and lesbians.

Cherry Grove on Fire Island (p. 285), the first gay resort, was founded in the 1930s. The Oak Room at the Plaza Hotel (p. 86) had such a strong drag queen presence that real female customers were often mistaken for impersonators.

In spite of all this activity, however, gay life throughout the mid-20th century was nonetheless an underground affair. Gay establishments were routinely raided and their patrons harassed or arrested. It was during one such police raid of the Stonewall Inn in Greenwich Village, on June 27, 1969, that the bar's transsexual, gay, and hustler patrons spontaneously resisted arrest. Hundreds of New York's gay men and lesbians took to the streets in protest, and the

observatories welcome nearly four million visitors each year. Built on the site of the original Waldorf-Astoria hotel and completed in 1931, the limestone, granite, and stainless-steel-sheathed structure pioneered Art Deco design. The Empire State was among the first of the truly spectacular skyscrapers, stretching 1454 ft. into the sky and containing 2 mi. of shafts for its 73 elevators. Although not a reason for celebration, the building has reclaimed the distinction of being New York's tallest building after the attacks on the World Trade Center towers destroyed the previous record-holders.

The lobby stands as a gleaming shrine to Art Deco interior decorating, right down to its mail drops and elevator doors. It contains eight vaulted panels on The Seven Wonders of the Ancient World—the Eighth Wonder of the Modern World, of course, is the building itself. Follow arrows on the wall to find the escalator to the concourse level, where you can purchase tickets to the observatory. Note the sign indicating visibility level—a day with perfect visibility offers views for 80 mi. in any direction. Although the elevator shoots you up to the observation deck in less than 1min., prepare to wait up to an hour during peak visiting times in the summer. If the view isn't exciting enough, the Empire State offers the **New York Skyride,** a simulation of a spaceship journey through the city.

Since Sept. 11, security measures have been beefed up: all visitors and their bags must pass through metal detectors. Be prepared to show ID (passport, driver's license, or student ID).

MACY'S

151 W. 34th St., Herald Sq., between Broadway and Seventh Ave. Map 13, C2, 3. Subway: B, D, F, N, Q, R, V, W to 34th St.-Herald Sq.; 1, 2, 3, 9 to 34th St.-Penn Station/Seventh Ave. ☎212-695-4400. Open M-Sa 10am-8:30pm, Su 11am-7pm.

Stretching 10 floors up and housing two million sq. ft. of merchandise ranging from designer clothes to housewares, Macy's has come a long way from its first day of business in 1858, when it grossed $11.06. Although the oldest and largest Macy's in the world is no longer in top form, the store retains some antique touches: check out the wooden escalators on the upper floors. Modern additions include a number of in-store eateries, such as McDonald's in the children's department, Emack & Bolio's ice cream in the Juniors' department, and the Cellar Bar & Grill in the basement. The store sponsors the **Macy's Thanksgiving Day Parade,** a New York tradition buoyed by helium-filled, 10-story Snoopys and

incident—immortalized as the Stonewall Riot—is often credited as the inspiration for the modern gay rights movement. (The bar still exists today; see p. 59 and p. 201.) In the ensuing decades, the gay community of New York has grown into a vital and varied network that celebrates itself while responding to adversity.

Gay and lesbian neighborhoods still thrive in New York today. An established and well-heeled contingent still clusters around Christopher St. in the West Village (see p. 15), while the center of gay life has shifted uptown a few blocks to Chelsea (see p. 16). Buff men waltz from gym to juice-bar here, and rainbow flags fly over dry cleaners and taxi dispatch centers.

An edgier, often younger group rocks out in the East Village on First and Second Ave., south of E. 12th St. (p. 15). A large lesbian community in Park Slope has lent the neighborhood the moniker "Dyke Slope" (p. 178).

Hundreds of thousands turn out in late June for the annual **Pride Weekend** (p. 72), which wends its way down Fifth Ave. and into Greenwich Village. This ecstatic gay-pride event is jam-packed with juggling drag queens, jubilant confetti-tossers, and cheering throngs toting the banners of such gay organizations as the gay volleyball league and **Dykes on Bikes.**

Bullwinkles, as well as marching bands, floats, and general hoopla. Other annual Macy-sponsored events (☎212-494-4455) include the **Fourth of July fireworks** extravaganza on the East River, and late-August "Tap-A-Mania," when hundreds of tap-dancers cut loose on the sidewalks of 34th St.

PENNSYLVANIA STATION

Between 31st and 34th St., and between Seventh and Eighth Ave. Subway: 1, 2, 3, 9 to 34th St.-Penn Station/Seventh Ave.; A, C, E to 34th St.-Penn Station/Eighth Ave. Map 13, C3, 11.

The original Penn Station was built in 1910. Modeled on the Roman baths of Caracalla, it featured a grand waiting room with a 150 ft. high glass ceiling. In an act Lewis Mumford deemed "irresponsible public vandalism," that building was demolished in the 1960s in favor of a more practical space 50 ft. below ground. This massive utilitarian underground station now greets visitors coming into New York from all around the country with a shopping mall of franchise restaurants and bookstores.

MADISON SQUARE GARDEN

Between 31st and 34th St., Seventh and Eighth Ave. Subway: 1, 2, 3, 9 to 34th St.-Penn Station/Seventh Ave.; A, C, E to 34th St.-Penn Station/Eighth Ave. Map 13, C3, 10. ☎212-465-5800; www.thegarden.com. Tours every hr. on the hr. M-Sa 10am-3pm, Su and holidays 11am-3pm. $14, under 12 $12.

"The World's Most Famous Arena" sits atop Penn Station. The Garden is home to the NBA's New York Knicks, the WNBA's New York Liberty, and the NHL's New York Rangers. Other sporting highlights include figure skating, boxing and the annual Westminster Dog Show. MSG doubles as an entertainment complex, hosting a wide array of shows and concerts. A visit behind the scenes includes glimpses of the locker rooms, the arena and concert stage, backstage areas, and luxury boxes.

JAMES A. FARLEY BUILDING

421 Eighth Ave., between 31st and 33rd St. Subway: A, C, E to 34th St.-Penn Station/Eighth Ave. Map 13, B3, 7. Open M-Sa 7:30am-6pm.

New York's immense main post office confronts Madison Square Garden with 53 ft. high Corinthian columns. The broad portico of this Neoclassical building (completed in 1913 and later named for a Postmaster-General of the U.S.) bears a quotation from Herodotus, now the hopeful adopted motto of the US Postal Service: "Neither snow nor rain nor heat nor gloom of night stays these couriers from the swift completion of their appointed rounds." Climb up the grandiose steps and send a postcard home.

The city is now in early stages of converting the Post Office Building into a new Pennsylvania Station. Slated to open by 2008, the new terminus will bear the name of the late Senator Daniel Patrick Moynihan, one of the great statesmen in American history.

GARMENT DISTRICT

West 30s between Broadway and Eighth Ave. Subway: 1, 2, 3, 9 to 34th St.-Penn Station/Seventh Ave.; A, C, E to 34th St.-Penn Station/Eighth Ave. Map 13, C2.

The Garment District was once a redlight district known as the Tenderloin. By the 1930s, it had the largest concentration of apparel manufacturers in the world. Today, a small statue named *The Garment Worker*, depicting an aged man huddled over a sewing machine and an enormous button with a needle, sits near the corner of 39th St. and Seventh Ave. to commemorate the neighborhood's formative era. Walk along Broadway from the upper 20s to the lower 30s, checking out the latest fashions in wholesale and retail fabric, jewelry, clothing, perfume, accessories, and leather stores. Keep your eyes and hands open for signs and handouts advertising the day's sample sales, found almost exclusively in this district. The **Fashion Institute of Tech-**

nology is on the corner of Seventh Ave. and 27th St. One block uptown blooms the **Flower District,** 28th St., between Sixth and Seventh Ave. (Map 13, C3, 12). No garments here—wholesale distributors and buyers of flora congregate each morning to stock the city's florists and garden centers.

HELL'S KITCHEN (OR CLINTON)

Between 30th and 59th St., and between Eighth Ave. and the Hudson River. Subway: 4, 5, 6, N, R, W to 59th St.-Lexington Ave.; F to Lexington Ave./63rd St.; 6 to 68th St., 77th St., 96th St.; 4, 5, 6 to 86th St. Map 13, A4.

Hell's Kitchen purportedly got its name from a policemen fed-up with his beat. Once a breeding-ground for violence, this formerly gang-ridden neighborhood inspired Leonard Bernstein's 1957 *West Side Story* and Marvel Comics crime-fighter Daredevil. A slow wave of gentrification has painted urban renewal over a gritty core. Hell's Kitchen is mostly residential, but new restaurants and bars (especially along Ninth Avenue) make this rapidly changing neighborhood a great area to explore.

JACOB K. JAVITS CONVENTION CENTER

Along 12th Ave., between 34th and 38th St. Subway: A, C, E to 34th St.-Penn Station/Eighth Ave. Map 14, A5, 86. ☎212-216-2000; www.javitscenter.com.

This black glass monstrosity covers five blocks and hosts some of the largest events in the world, including international boat, car, and motorcycle shows. Check the website for the latest convivium (www.javitscenter.com). The April **International Auto Show** (☎718-746-5300; www.autoshowny.com) draws the biggest crowds, but the events are not limited to transportation—a toy fair, stationery expo, and fashion boutique are just some of the Center's other offerings.

JOHN JAY COLLEGE OF CRIMINAL JUSTICE

899 10th Ave. at 58th St. Subway: 1, 9, A, B, C, D to 59th St.-Columbus Circle. Map 14, A2, 2.

The school was initially the College of Police Science in 1965, but today John Jay trains civil servants of all kinds. Renovations have given the 1903 neo-Victorian central building (formerly the DeWitt Clinton High School) a postmodern glass atrium and extension.

A FIREFIGHTER'S PRAYER

On the corner of 8th Avenue and W. 44th St.

Originally commissioned by the Firefighters Association of Missouri, this bronze statue of a kneeling fireman was on its way to its final destination when it made a stopover in New York on September 9, 2001. The statue remained in its crate at JFK International Airport as the Twin Towers came crashing down two days later. It was immediately donated to the city as a reminder of the heroics of civil servants, especially firefighters. On Sept. 17, the New York *Post* ran a front page photograph with a fireman in an identical pose. Both New Yorkers and visitors alike seem to drift away from the midtown bustle as they stand, stare and contemplate the emotion here engraved.

MIDTOWN

From 42nd St. to 59th St., stretching all the way across Manhattan.

FIFTH AVENUE AREA

This is New York's glamour avenue and, along with Times Square, possibly the most heavily touristed area of the city. You can buy a big sapphire or an teddy bear two stories tall. St. Patrick's and Rockefeller Center, respective icons of world-governing doctrines (religion and money, duh), perpetually stare at each other with the statue of Atlas holding up the globe right in the middle. A late-night taxicab ride down this central artery, when the granite and marble are floodlit, is simply grand. **Sights are listed from south to north.**

NEW YORK PUBLIC LIBRARY

42nd St. and Fifth Ave. Subway: B, D, F, V to 42nd St./Ave. of the Americas (Sixth Ave.); 7 to Fifth Ave./42nd St. Map 14, D5, 91. ☎212-869-8089. Open Tu-W 11am-7:30pm, Th-Sa 10am-6pm. Tours of Humanities and Sciences Library Tu-Sa at 11am and 2pm. Free. Tours of the exhibition Tu-Sa 12:30 and 2pm. Free.

The main branch of the New York Public Library is a breath of fresh air from the skyscrapers lining Fifth Ave. With stairs leading to the entrance and the pediment pushed back behind the frieze, the library's Beaux Arts facade—loosely modeled after the Louvre— announces awesomely this house of knowledge and learning. Featured in the film *Ghostbusters*, two marble lions representing Patience and Fortitude dutifully guard the library against both ghosts and illiteracy. Inside, the main reading room is located on the third floor. It's not the most comfortable place to read, but the room is built on a grand scale and has been restored to its original greatness. The stacks at the library can be accessed with a library card.

BRYANT PARK

Sixth Ave., between 40th and 42nd St., behind the New York Public Library. Subway: B, D, F, V to 42nd St./Ave. of the Americas; 7 to Fifth Ave./42nd St. Map 14, D4. ☎212-768-4242. Open daily 7am-9pm. Film festival M during the summer.

Bryant Park has undergone several major transformations. Prior to its existence as a public park, the site served as a 1776 battleground for George Washington's troops as they fled British forces. Later it was a graveyard for paupers. In 1842, when the Croton Reservoir was constructed on the land now occupied by the New York Public Library (p. 78), the site behind the reservoir was designated "Reservoir Square" and used as a public space. The Crystal Palace, a glass and steel hall built for the first World's Fair, was erected here in 1853; it burned to the ground in 1858. During the Civil War, Union troops drilled and camped in the square. The area was renamed "Bryant Park" in 1884 to honor the memory of William Cullen Bryant (1794-1878), editor, poet, and leading advocate of the creation of New York's Central Park (p. 86). Until WWII, the park was sometimes used as an open-air reading room of the New York Public Library.

A century and a half after the glory days of the 1853 World's Fair, still-busy Bryant Park now boasts **free wireless Internet** access. The stage at the head of the park's open field features various free cultural events throughout the summer, including jazz concerts, classic film screenings, and amateur comedy.

THE ALGONQUIN HOTEL

44th St., between Fifth and Sixth Ave. Subway: B, D, F, V to 42nd St./Ave. of the Americas (Sixth Ave.); 7 to Fifth Ave./42nd St. Map 14, D4, 79.

Alexander Woollcott's "Round Table," a regular gathering of the 1920s' brightest theatrical and literary luminaries, made this hotel famous. The Algonquin's proximity to the offices of *The New Yorker* attracted the "vicious circle" of such barbed tongues as Robert Benchley, Dorothy Parker, and Harold Ross. The Oak Room still serves tea every afternoon, and folks say that—for better or for worse—the restaurant's menu and decor has changed little in 50 years.

ROCKEFELLER CENTER

Between 48th and 51st St., Fifth and Sixth Ave. Subway: B, D, F, V to 47th-50th St.-Rockefeller Center/Ave. of the Americas (Sixth Ave.). Map 14, D3. ☎212-332-6868, tours ☎664-3700; www.rockefellercenter.com. ***NBC Tour:*** *Reservations recommended by phone or online. Departs every 15min. from NBC Sweet Shop in the GE Building. M-Sa 8:30am-5:30pm, Su 9:30am-4:30pm. No* *children under 6. $17.75, seniors $15.25, ages 6-16 $15.25; groups over 4 or more $15.25.* ***Rockefeller Center Tour:*** *From the GE Building. ☎212-664-3700. Departs every hr. M-Sa 10am-5pm, Su 10am-4pm. Hours may be expanded during summer or Christmas season. No children under 6. $10, ages 6-16 $8; groups over 3 $8. Combo rate for NBC and Rockefeller Center Tours $21.* ***Radio City Music Hall Stage Door Tour:*** *www.radiocity.com. Map 14, D3, 36. Departs every 30min. M-Su 11am-3pm. $17, Seniors $14, under 12 $10, group discounts available.* *See p. 229 for Radio City Music Hall box office, p. 230 for ticket info about live television shows taped at the Rockefeller Center.*

Rockefeller Center got its start in the Roaring 1920s, when tycoon John D. Rockefeller, Jr. wanted to move the Metropolitan Opera to Midtown. Plans to bring culture to the area fell through when the Depression struck in 1929, so Rockefeller—still desiring to use the space for good—invited in the media instead. The Center, built during the 30s, became home to such radio companies as RKO, RCA, and NBC. Rockefeller's dream is now considered one of New York City's most impressive architectural feats.

The **Rockefeller Center Tour** introduces tourists to the highlights in and around the Center. The main entrance to Rockefeller Center is on Fifth Ave., between 49th and 50th St. The **Channel Gardens,** so named because they sit between the **Maison Française** on the left and the **British Empire Building** on the right, usher pedestrians toward **Tower Plaza.** This sunken space, topped by the gold-leafed statue of **Prometheus,** is surrounded by the flags of over 100 countries. During spring and summer, an **ice-skating rink** lies dormant beneath an overpriced cafe. The rink, better for people-watching than skating, reopens in winter in time for the **annual Christmas tree lighting,** one of New York's greatest traditions. (Tree lighting Dec. 3, 2003; call ☎212-332-6868 for info.)

Behind Tower Plaza is the **General Electric Building,** 30 Rockefeller Plaza (Map 14, D3, 42). This 70-story tower, once home to RCA, is the jewel of the complex. The GE Building is notable not only for its scale but also for its extensive artwork. Outside the building's main entrance is Lee Lawrie's limestone and glass frieze of Wisdom. On the inside, Jose Maria Sert's *American Progress* adorns the lobby's walls. NBC, which makes its home here, offers a 1hr. **NBC Studio Tour** that traces the network's history, from its first radio broadcast in 1926 through the heyday of TV programming in the 1950s and 60s to today's sitcoms (Map 14, D3, 41). The tour visits six studios including the infamous 8H studio, home of *Saturday Night Live.*

Herald Square

New York Public Library

View from Empire State Building

Rockefeller Center

Bryant Park

Swing 46, Midtown

A block north, on the corner of Sixth Ave. and 51st St., is **Radio City Music Hall** (Map 14, D3, 36). Narrowly escaping demolition in 1979, this Art Deco landmark received a complete interior restoration shortly thereafter. Built in 1932, the 5874-seat theater remains the largest in the world. It functioned as a movie theater between 1933 and 1975, premiering films like *King Kong* and *Breakfast at Tiffany's*. Now it is used mostly for its original purpose: live performance. Radio City's main attraction is the Rockettes, a high-stepping, long-legged dance troupe. The Music Hall's **Stage Door Tour** takes the visitor through the Great Stage and various rehearsal halls.

Back on Fifth Ave., in front of the **International Building** between 50th and 51st St., sits a bronze sculpture of **Atlas** holding up the weight of the world. Originally, the statue was not welcomed because of its purported resemblance to Italian dictator Benito Mussolini. For some lovely American consumerism, survey the many shops and restaurants of Rockefeller Center's underground concourse.

ST. PATRICK'S CATHEDRAL

Southeast corner of Fifth Ave. and 51st St. Subway: E, V to Fifth Ave./53rd St. Map 14, D3, 40. ☎212-753-2261. Open daily 7am-10pm. Mass Su 7, 8, 9, 10:15am, noon, 1, 4, 5:30pm.

New York's most famous church and America's largest Catholic cathedral opened in 1879, 21 years after work on it had begun: the American Civil War had put construction on hold in the 1860s, and the cathedral's famed steeples had yet to be erected even after its functional opening. Those twin spires, flanking the Fifth Ave. facade, are 330 ft. high and have been captured in countless photos and postcards. The cathedral's Gothic exterior recalls similar European structures, but the interior's majestic nave is closely related to those of Westminster, Exeter, and other English cathedrals. Once inside, it is hard to miss the Great Organ (especially when it's being played). It commands attention with its nearly 8000 pipes, some of which are as many as 32 ft. long; it even has a mechanism to simulate the sound of a 64 ft. pipe by joining two of these smaller ones. The South Transept's titular window, on the 50th St. side, presents a stained-glass portrayal of the life of Saint Patrick.

UNIVERSITY CLUB

1 W. 54th St., at Fifth Ave. Subway: E, V to Fifth Ave./53rd St. Map 14, D2, 24.

As its name indicates, this organization was among the first men's clubs to require its members to hold college degrees. Twenty prestigious university crests adorn its facade, which is as close as you'll get to the interior: entrance to the club is for members and guests only. If you're willing to pay through the nose, however, you can host events here: with a $3000 space fee, plus a starting price of $200-250 per person for catering for 175-350 guests, this big splurge should make a big splash.

SONY PLAZA

550 Madison Ave., between 55th and 56th St. Subway: N, R, W to Fifth Ave./59th St. ☎212-833-8830. Map 14, D2, 23. Lab open Tu-Sa 10am-6pm, Su noon-6pm.

The Sony Corporation recently bought and renamed Philip Johnson's postmodern masterpiece, the erstwhile AT&T Building. It now features two superstores offering interaction with state-of-the-art products. The stereo and television section downstairs shows releases by Sony-owned Columbia Pictures. Try the latest video games at the new Sony Wonder technology lab.

CROWN BUILDING

730 Fifth Ave., between 56th and 57th St. Subway: N, R, W to Fifth Ave./59th St. Map 14, D2, 20.

Completed in 1919, the Crown Building was originally topped by a 6 ft. copper goddess, who was later melted down for the WWII effort. In 1978, when the building was owned by Ferdinand and Imelda Marcos, the upper tier was overlaid with 24½-carat gold leaf and embedded with colored glass. As the sun sets, the reflected light creates a magnificent crown. Among other businesses, the building houses Playboy Enterprises.

TRUMP TOWER

725 Fifth Ave., at 56th St. Subway: N, R, W to Fifth Ave./59th St. Map 14, D2, 21.

Finally, a building to match Donald Trump's ego. Inside, stores such as Cartier, Salvatore Ferragamo, and an Avon Spa cater to expensive, if not refined, tastes. The 80 ft. indoor waterfall and sitting area provide free respite for weary Fifth Ave. shoppers.

PARK AVENUE

A luxurious boulevard with greenery running down its center, Park Ave. is lined with office buildings and hotels until around 59th St., when apartment building begin to dominate the thoroughfare. **Sights are listed from south to north.**

GRAND CENTRAL TERMINAL

E. 42nd St., between Madison and Lexington Ave., where Park Ave. should be. Subway: 4, 5, 6, 7, S to 42nd St.-Grand Central. Map 14, E4, 80. Tours W 12:30pm from information booth, run by Municipal Arts Society (☎212-935-3960); F 12:30pm from Philip Morris/Whitney Museum, on 42nd St. across the street from Grand Central, run by the Grand Central Partnership (☎212-697-1245). Free.

Completed in 1913, Grand Central is a train station of monumental proportions. On top of the richly classical main facade on 42nd St. stands a beautiful sculpture of Mercury, Roman god of transportation. Inside, the Main Concourse is the terminal's central space. A four-year renovation restored this area to mint condition, with zodiac constellations lining the newly cleaned ceiling. The information booth, in the middle of the Concourse, may be the most popular meeting place in New York. In the past, the whirring masses departed from Grand Central to take voyages across the continent; today, trains from the station only travel to Westchester and points north. Some

Trump Tower

Grand Central Terminal

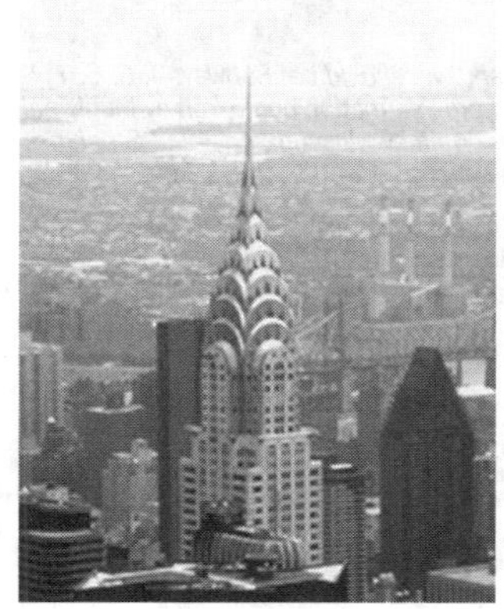
Empire State Building

trains leave from the station's lower level, which also contains the **Dining Concourse**—a larger version of the food court found in most malls.

MET LIFE BUILDING

200 Park Ave., at E. 45th St. Subway: 4, 5, 6, 7, S to 42nd St.-Grand Central. Map 14, E4, 80.

Resembling an oversized knife unsheathed beside Grand Central Terminal, this building punctuates Park Ave. Visible from anywhere on the avenue, the building accommodates 2.4 million sq. ft. of corporate cubicles and all the marble any person could possibly desire.

THE WALDORF-ASTORIA HOTEL

301 Park Ave., between 49th and 50th St. Subway: 6 to 51st St.; E, V to Lexington Ave./53rd St. Map 14, E3, 53. ☎ 212-355-3000.

Ritzier than the Ritz, the Waldorf-Astoria is the *crème de la crème* of Park Ave. hotels. Originally on the site of the Empire State Building, the hotel was relocated farther uptown in 1931. Cole Porter's piano sits in the front lounge, and a huge 9 ft., 8-sided clock—decorated with pictures of Washington, Lincoln, Franklin, Queen Victoria, Cleveland, Harrison, Grant, and Jackson—dominates the lobby. Every US President since Hoover has spent a night or two here while away from the White House. Bask in the luxury that you've been missing in your hostel ($205-$495 for guest rooms, $265-670 for suites).

ST. BARTHOLOMEW'S CHURCH

109 E. 50th St., at Park Ave. Subway: 6 to 51st St.; E, V to Lexington Ave./53rd St. ☎ 212-378-0200. Map 14, E3, 52. Su services 8, 9, 11am, 7pm. Wheelchair-accessible.

This Byzantine church, completed in 1919, relies heavily upon medieval European architectural styles. Look for the large mosaic of the Resurrection and life-sized marble angel in the devotional area left of the altar. St. Bart's hosts a summer festival of classical music on Sundays at 11am as part of its weekly service. Just outside is **Cafe St. Bart's,** a lovely but expensive outdoor cafe with a beautiful little garden attached.

SEAGRAM BUILDING

375 Park Ave., between 52nd and 53rd St. Subway: 6 to 51st St.; E, V to Lexington Ave./53rd St. Map 14, E3, 51.

This bronze and black skyscraper, built in 1958, is the only building in the city designed by the architect Ludwig Mies van der Rohe. The barren plaza in front evokes a sense of grandeur that is out of place along elegantly understated Park Ave.

CITIGROUP CENTER

The corner of 53rd St. and Lexington Ave. Subway: 6 to 51st St.; E, V to Lexington Ave./53rd St. Map 14, E2, 28.

With its 10-story stilts hovering over a church, this aluminum and glass skyscraper is one of the tallest buildings in New York and in the world—as well as one of Midtown's more distinctive buildings. The overhanging corners were designed after neighboring St. Peter's Lutheran Church insisted on keeping both its lot and its separate identity. A new church was, however, built in place of the old one.

The tower's base is cut away at the four corners, leaving it standing dramatically on a cross-shaped foundation which extends from the core to the center of each side. The atrium, open-air concourse and office tower lobby were renovated in 1997. The 45-degree angled roof was intended to be a solar collector; today, the roof supports a high-tech gadget, the TMD (Tuned Mass Damper), which senses and records the earth's tremors and warns of earthquakes.

TURTLE BAY AND UNITED NATIONS

Named after an 18th-century farm and located in the east 40s, this neighborhood now hosts the United Nations and the diplomats who work there. **Sights are listed from east to west.**

THE UNITED NATIONS BUILDING

First Ave., between 42nd and 48th St. Subway: 4, 5, 6, 7, S to 42nd St.-Grand Central. Map 14, F4, 84. ☎212-963-4475; General Assembly ☎212-963-7713. Tours depart from the UN visitor's entrance at First Ave. and 46th St. 1hr. Held every 15min. in 20 languages. M-F 9:15am-4:45pm, Sa-Su 9:30am-4:45pm. $10, over 62 $7.50, students $6.50, ages 4-14 $5.50; disabled 20% discount. Under 5 not admitted on tour.

Founded in 1945 just after WWII to serve as "a center for harmonizing the actions of nations," the United Nations fittingly makes its home in the world's most diverse city. Though located along what would be First Ave., the UN is international territory and not under US jurisdiction—as displayed by the member nations' 191 flags flying outside at equal height, in flagrant violation of American custom. The site consists of four main buildings: the General Assembly building, the Conference Building, the 39-floor Secretariat building, and the Dag Hammarskjöld Library, a gift from the Ford Foundation which was added in 1961. The complex was designed by an international team of 11 architects, led by Wallace K. Harrison from the US.

United Nations

Times Square

Broadway

A prominent feature of the General Assembly Lobby is the **Foucault pendulum,** given by the Netherlands to the UN in 1955. In the Eastern side of the lobby is a stained-glass window designed by the French artist Marc Chagall. The **Norman Rockwell mosaic,** the **Japanese Peace Bell,** and the **Chinese Ivory Carving** are also exhibited in the building. The only way to view the expansive General Assembly and the council rooms is by guided tour. Outside, a rose garden and statuary park provide a lovely view of the multi-hued East River and the industrial wastelands of western Queens. The United Nations garden contains several sculptures and statues that have been donated by different countries. Note the Evgeniy Vuchetich statue called *Let Us Beat Swords into Plowshares*, a gift from the former USSR in 1959.

DAILY NEWS BUILDING

220 E. 42nd St., between Second and Third Ave. Subway: 4, 5, 6, 7, S to 42nd St.-Grand Central. Map 14, F4, 85.

When this extremely expensive building project began in 1930, the *Daily News* had the largest circulation of all the newspapers in New York. At a time when other developers shunned the area east of Third Ave., the *Daily News* selected this site so that it could house its noisy printing presses in the same facility as its editorial offices. The structure contained the newspaper's offices in a tower set back above a 10-story base with larger floors to accommodate the presses. An addition designed by Harrison and Abramowitz was added to the east side of the tower in 1958. A large, revolving globe, set against a backdrop of black glass and aluminum in the center of the lobby, symbolizes the paper's global perspective; it was a popular tourist attraction when the building first opened. Although no longer occupied by the *Daily News*, the building is still one of New York's best known skyscrapers; the paper is still New York's most widely-read. Inside the lobby, you will find a massive globe and the mileages to many major cities worldwide.

THE CHRYSLER BUILDING

405 Lexington Ave., at E. 42nd St. Subway: 4, 5, 6, 7, S to 42nd St.-Grand Central. Map 14, E4, 81.

A spire influenced by radiator-grille design tops this Art Deco palace of industry—one of many details meant to evoke the romance of the automobile in the Chrysler's "Golden Age." Other monuments to motoring include stylized lightning-bolts symbolizing the energy of the new machine and flared gargoyles styled after 1929 hood ornaments and hubcaps. While many consider it to be the most aesthetically pleasing building in New York, it ruined architect William Van Alen's career: Walter Chrysler, unsatisfied with the final product, accused Van Alen of embezzlement and refused to pay him. Chrysler no longer has offices in the building. The stunning lobby was recently featured in celebrated artist Matthew Barney's avant-garde film *Cremaster III*.

TIMES SQUARE AND THE THEATER DISTRICT

At the intersection of 42nd St., Seventh Ave., and Broadway, the city offers up one of the world's largest electronic extravaganzas. Times Square may have given New York its reputation as a dark metropolis covered with strip clubs, neon, and filth, but today the smut has been replaced by teeming masses of smiling people with fanny packs, 30 ft. tall flatscreens announcing the conquests of reality TV, and a creepy homogeneity totally unbecoming to New York's true spirit. But it doesn't really matter what we think: at some point, whether you like it or not, you'll probably be one of the nearly 40 million people who pass through Times Square every year. Good luck.

ONE TIMES SQUARE

At 42nd St., Seventh Ave., and Broadway. Subway: 1, 2, 3, 7, 9, N, Q, R, S, W to 42nd St.-Times Square; A, C, E to 42nd St.-Port Authority; B, D, F, V, 7 to 42nd St.-Bryant Park. Map 14, C4.

The New York Times publisher Adolph Ochs moved the paper's offices here in 1904. Today, however, the *Times* tackles "all the news that's fit to print" at **229 West 43rd Street** (Map 14, C4, 74), and One Times Square is no more than a giant billboard. On New Year's Eve, millions gravitate to the building to see the ball drop—arrive before 8pm to get within a half-mile of the place. Expect to be a little bit squished.

THEATER DISTRICT

From 41st to 57th St., Broadway to Eighth Ave. Subway: 1, 2, 3, 7, A, C, E, N, Q, R, S, W. Map 14, B3, C3. *For info on specific theaters, see **Entertainment,** p. 223.*

While some theaters have been converted into movie houses or simply left to rot as the cost of live productions has skyrocketed, approximately 40 theaters remain active (most of them grouped around 45th St.), 22 of which have been declared historical landmarks. One highlight of the Theater District is **Shubert Alley,** half a block west of Broadway, between 44th and 45th St. Originally built as a fire exit between the Booth and Shubert Theaters, the alley now serves as a private street for pedestrians. After shows, fans often hover at stage doors to get their playbills signed.

CENTRAL PARK SOUTH, 57TH ST., AND VICINITY

Luxury hotels like the **Essex House,** the **St. Moritz,** and the **Plaza** overlook Central Park from Central Park S., between Fifth and Eighth Ave., where 59th St. should be. Two blocks south, on 57th St., galleries and stores surround New York's musical center, **Carnegie Hall. Sights are located from west to east.**

CARNEGIE HALL

*881 Seventh Ave., at W. 57th St. Subway: N, R, Q, W to 57th St.; B, D, E to Seventh Ave./53rd St. Map 14, C2, 8. ☎212-247-7800 or 903-9765 for tours; www.carnegiehall.org. Tours M–F 11:30am, 2pm, and 3pm. 1hr. Tickets may be purchased at box office on tour days. $6, students and seniors $5, under 12 $3. Group tours available. **Rose Museum:** 154 W. 57th St., 2nd fl. Open daily 11:30am-4pm and to concert ticketholders in the evenings. Museum, gift shop, and tours closed July–early Sept. Free.* *See **Entertainment,** p. 217, for concert information.*

Since hosting the American debut of Tchaikovsky, Carnegie Hall has continued its eclectic and illustrious career by drawing such artists as Caruso, Toscanini, and Bernstein; jazz greats Dizzy Gillespie, Ella Fitzgerald, and Billie Holiday; and rock-and-rollers The Beatles and The Rolling Stones. In the late 1950s, when an enormous red skyscraper threatened to replace Carnegie Hall, violinist Isaac Stern led a city-wide campaign to save the building; the City of New York eventually purchased the building for $5 million in 1960, and it was declared an historic landmark in 1962. Decades of patchwork maintenance and periodic face-lifts left the venue in various stages of disrepair until 1985 when a $60 million restoration and repair program returned the building to its earlier splendor. The small **Rose Museum** provides an exhibit on Carnegie Hall's history, as well as temporary displays.

CITY CENTER THEATER

130 W. 55th St., between Sixth and Seventh Ave. Subway: N, R, Q, W to 57th St./Seventh Ave.; B, D, E to Seventh Ave./53rd St.; 57th St./Ave. of the Americas (Sixth Ave.). Map 14, C2, 9. ☎212-581-1212 or 877-581-1212; www.citycenter.org. *See p. 213 for box office info.*

City Center's unique neo-Moorish facade recalls the building's Masonic origins: it was built in 1923 as a meeting hall for the members of the Ancient Arabic Order of the Nobles of the Mystic Shrine. After reverting to city ownership in 1943, the building became Manhattan's first performing arts center and the birthplace of both the New York City Opera and the New York City Ballet. Legendary artists Leonard Bernstein, Paul Robeson, and Tallulah Bankhead have all performed here. Sickles and crescents still adorn each doorway and four tiny windows face Mecca (or at least the East Side) from the limestone upper stories. The 60th anniversary season ('03-'04) features performances by the Alvin Ailey Dance Company, Martha Graham Dance Company, the American Ballet Theatre, and the New York Gilbert and Sullivan Players.

PLAZA HOTEL

758 Fifth Ave., at 59th St./Central Park S. Subway: N, R, W to Fifth Ave./59th St. Map 14, D1, 17.

Designed by famous architect Henry J. Hardenbergh in 1907, this French Renaissance-style luxury hotel and historic landmark also houses four world-renowned restaurants (including the Oak Room and the Oak Bar). The 16 Specialty Suites, with such names as the Louis XVI and the Vanderbilt, cost up to $18,000 per night. The hotel's splendid carved marble fireplaces, gold leaf, and crystal chandeliers have served as movie backdrops for *North by Northwest*, *The Way We Were*, *The Great Gatsby*, *Plaza Suite*, and *Barefoot in the Park*. Past guests have included Frank Lloyd Wright, The Beatles, Mark Twain, F. Scott Fitzgerald, and Kay Thompson's fictional characters in *Eloise*. Look for the **Pulitzer Fountain** next door.

GRAND ARMY PLAZA

59th St. and Fifth Ave. Subway: N, R, W to Fifth Ave./59th St. Map 14, D1.

Inspired by the Parisian style, Grand Army Plaza sits in front of the Plaza Hotel and doubles as an entrance to Central Park. Karl Bitter's bronze statue of Pomona, the goddess of abundance, graces the plaza's southern half. On the other side of Central Park S. sits Saint-Gaudens' gilt equestrian statue of Union General William Tecumseh Sherman.

CENTRAL PARK

Between 59th St. and 110th St., Fifth Ave., and between and Central Park W. Map 16-17. ***General Information:*** *☎212-360-3444; for parks and recreation info: ☎212-360-8111 (M-F 9am-5pm); www.centralparknyc.org. The Central Park Conservancy, which runs the park and offers public programs, has 4 visitor centers with brochures, calendars of events, and* ***free park maps,*** *at* ***Belvedere Castle*** *(☎212-772-0210), located mid-park at 79th St.; the* ***Charles A. Dana Discovery Center*** *(☎212-860-1370), at 110th St. near Fifth Ave.; the* ***North Meadow Recreation Center*** *(☎212-348-4867), mid-park at 97th St.; and the* ***Dairy,*** *mid-park near 65th St. (☎212-794-6564). The Dairy also showcases exhibits, books, and other collectibles reflecting the history of the park. Open Apr.-Oct. Tu-Su 10am-5pm; Nov.-Mar. Tu-Su 10am-4pm.* ***Trolley tours:*** *From Grand Army Plaza. ☎212-397-3809. May 1-Nov. M-F 10:30am, 1, 3pm.* ***Carriage tours:*** *From Central Park S. ☎212-246-0520. $34 for 30min. $10 each additional 15min.* ***Central Park Bicycle Tour:*** *From 2 Columbus Circle. ☎212-541-8759. 10am, 1, 4pm. $35 for 2hr., under 15 $20.* ***New York Skateout:*** *From 72nd St. and Central Park W. ☎212-486-1919. Tours daily 9am and 5pm. $25 for 1½hr.*

Until the mid-1800s, the 843 acres that are now Central Park were considered a social and geographical wasteland. There, the city's poorest residents, including Irish pig farmers, German gardeners, and the black Seneca Village population, squatted in shantytowns, huts, and caves. Some of New York's wealthiest citizens began to advocate the creation of a park around 1850, having long envied the public grounds of London and Paris. In 1853 Frederick Law Olmsted collaborated with Calvert Vaux to design the park. Their Greensward Plan, inspired by the English

Romantic tradition, took 15 years and over 20,000 workers to implement. Olmsted and Vaux's masterpiece is a delicate piece of man-made nature and a must-see for visitors. **Sights are listed from south to north.**

THE CHILDREN'S DISTRICT

Between 59th and 65th St. Map 17. ***The Dairy:*** *65th St., mid-park. Open Tu-Su Apr.-Oct. 10am-5pm; Nov.-Mar. 10am-4pm.* ***Carousel:*** *65th St., west of Center Dr. Open mid-Mar. to Thanksgiving daily 10am-dusk; Thanksgiving to mid-Mar., weather-permitting Sa-Su 10am-4pm. $1.* ***Wollman Memorial Rink:*** *Between 62nd and 63rd St., mid-park. For skating info, see p. 236.* ***Central Park Wildlife Center:*** *Between 63rd and 65th St., off Fifth Ave. ☎212-861-6030. Open Apr.-Oct. M-F 10am-5pm, Sa-Su 10:30am-5:30pm; Nov.-Mar. daily 10am-4:30pm. Last entry 30min. before closing.* ***Tisch Children's Zoo:*** *Between 65th and 66th St. Combined admission to both zoos $6 seniors $1.25, ages 3-12 50¢, under 2 free.*

Vaux and Olmsted designated this area as a place in which the young could frolic and receive affordable nourishment. At that time, the **Dairy** distributed food and purity-tested milk to poor families at risk for food poisoning. Today, it is one of the park's information centers. With valid picture ID, children and adults can borrow equipment at the Dairy and square off at the nearby **Chess and Checkers House.** East of the Dairy stand the 58 hand-carved horses of the Friedsam Memorial **Carousel,** brought from Coney Island and restored in 1893. To the south is **Wollman Memorial Rink,** where New Yorkers ice-skate in the winter. To the east is the **Central Park Wildlife Center,** a.k.a. **The Zoo,** which features polar bears and other mammals from different climates. North of the zoo is the **Tisch Children's Zoo,** a petting zoo.

SHEEP MEADOW AND THE MALL

Sheep Meadow: *From about 66th to 69th St., on the western side of Central Park, directly north of the Hecksher Ballfields.* ***Tavern on the Green:*** *West of Sheep Meadow, between 66th and 67th St. ☎212-873-3200; www.tavernonthe green.com. Open M-F noon-3pm and 5-10pm, Sa-Su 10am-3:30pm and 5-11pm. On average, lunch $11-26, dinner $15-37.* ***The Mall:*** *Runs roughly on a north-south line, between 66th St. to 71st St.* ***Bethesda Terrace and Fountain:*** *At the end of the mall, about 72nd St., mid-park. All locations Map 17.*

Named for the sheep who grazed there until lawnmowers put the flock out of work in 1934, the **Sheep Meadow** was a popular spot for love-ins and drug-fests in the 60s and 70s. On summer days, many tanning bodies cover its acres. The **Tavern on the Green** restaurant is located just west of the Sheep Meadow. Built in 1870, this rural Victorian Gothic structure originally housed the sheep who grazed there; it was only launched as a restaurant in 1934. Drop by to stare at the chandeliers, antique prints, paintings, and stained glass.

The Mall lies to the east of the Sheep Meadow and is lined with statues of famous authors and artists, especially towards its southern end. Towards the northern part of the walk are the **Naumberg Bandshell** and **Rumsey Playfield,** the home of SummerStage (☎212-360-2777; www.summerstage.org).

THE LAKE AND STRAWBERRY FIELDS

Following locations on Map 17. ***The Lake:*** *On the west side of the park, from approx. 72nd to 77th St.* ***Strawberry Fields:*** *West of the Lake at 72nd St. and West Dr.* ***Conservatory Water:*** *At 74th St., off Fifth Ave. Boat rental (☎212-517-2233) $10 per hr. with $20 deposit.* ***The Ramble:*** *74th to 79th St., mid-park. Bike rental (☎212-861-4127). Rates vary depending on bike. All locations Map 17.*

Would-be romantics awkwardly maneuver row-boats around the Lake. You, too, can woo your loved one by renting a boat at the **Loeb Boathouse,** mid-park at 75th St. (p. 236). To the west is **Strawberry Fields,** a memorial to John Lennon standing directly across from the Dakota, the apartment building in front of which he was shot. Yoko Ono battled for this space against city-council members who had planned a Bing Crosby memorial on the same spot. On John Lennon's birthday, October 9th, thousands gather around the **"Imagine" mosaic** to remember the legend.

Why Everyone LIkes Grass in the Big Apple

When one thinks of parks and New York City, Central Park leaps to mind. This great urban park, whose creation was authorized by the New York State Legislature 150 years ago, has set a national standard for open space within cities. Yet New York City has 1700 other parks, playgrounds, and landscaped areas (247 in the borough of Manhattan). Many of these green spaces offer scenery, history, athletic fields, and other opportunities to refresh the body and spirit. I would like to take you on a tour of the cliffside and waterfront parks of Manhattan, which are easily accessible by foot, bicycle, or public transportation.

Indeed, Central Park itself, busy as it is in summer, has neglected areas where park-goers rarely venture. The northern portion of the park, from 96th to 110th St., is its wildest and most natural as well as least traveled section. You can find the North Woods, an antebellum blockhouse, outlines of former forts and gun batteries, and a new island (Duck Island) in an old (but resuscitated) Meer. We begin with a freshly revived pool, fed by city water, near Central Park West and 102nd Street whose overflow empties into a fast-running, quickly descending stream that Olmsted called the Loch, whose waters gather in small pools and drop off doll's house waterfalls on their way to a straight channel under a large stone bridge called Huddlestone Arch. From there the water goes by an underground tube below the Lasker Swimming and Ice Skating Rink into Harlem Meer, which occupies the northeastern corner of the park.

North of Central Park, we find a chain of three Olmsted parks built around a sharp escarpment which forms a natural boundary between Harlem on the east and Morningside Heights and Hamilton Heights on the west. Morningside Park was assailed by Columbia University in the 1960s when the school tried to build a large gymnasium that would have bisected the natural area. The plan was abandoned after the 1968 riots but Columbia had already blasted away a substantial portion of the rockface, turning a steep slope into a cliff; the City built a pool at its base.

Proceeding north across the valley of 125th Street, which once severed Manhattan Island, we reach St. Nicholas Park, which stretches from 12th to 141st St. The topography is similar to Morningside, and the school on the hill is not Columbia but the City College of New York. The campus was built at the turn of the last century with stone excavated from the construction of New York City's first subway; however, that is not why the school is referred to as a subway college. In the 1930s, CCNY was known as the Harvard of the proletariat—seventy years later it is pursuing a comeback. The northern part of St. Nicholas Park will be the third site of Alexander Hamilton's home. The historic house was moved once and is now wedged between an apartment house on Covent Avenue and a church. The National Park Service plans to move it to a more suitable location in the park, which will look much more like its original setting.

Four blocks to the north Jackie Robinson (formerly Colonial Park) continues to separate Harlem from higher ground, in this case Sugar Hill. The name was changed almost thirty years ago to protest Anti-Colonial Park, but that did not meet the sponsor's second goal, honoring a great athlete and baseball pioneer. Sugar Hill was the home of wealthy blacks since the 1930s, including Walter While, longtime head of the NAACP.

Continuing north, we reach the 188-acre Highbridge Park. At this point, the cliff divides Washington Heights from the Harlem River. The park runs north to Dyckman St., and formerly contained the ruins of a blockhouse named Fort George (named for the King, not the President).

On the Hudson River side of Manhattan, there is a string of parks, starting with historic Battery Park, which contains Castle Clinton, where immigrants arrived before Ellis Island was built. It is also the site where the singer Jenny Lind (the Swedish nightingale) made her American debut in 1850. After its concert hall days, it become the New York City Aquarium, until it was unceremoniously demolished by Robert Moses to clear a path for the Brooklyn Battery Tunnel.

North of Battery Park is Robert F. Wagner, Jr. Park, named for the Senator's grandson and the Mayor's son, who was himself a remarkable public servant. Wagner Park has the best view of the Statue of Liberty. Then, on to Nelson A. Rockefeller Park, which honors the former Governor and Vice President. This park has remarkable animal sculptures by Thomas Otterness, and a walkway to the Hudson's edge continued from Wagner Park. To the east, one can see the excavation that was the World Trade Center.

The State and City have combined forces to build a new Hudson River Park, which stretches five miles north to 55th St. A number of recreational piers have been built, as well as a bikeway/pedestrian path that runs west of the former West Side Highway, but most of the construction of the linear park lies ahead.

Green space resumes at 68th St. with Riverside Park South and its 700 ft. long recreational pier, which is built on a southwest-northeast axis. The park was built by Donald Trump to city specifications, in exchange for city approval of Trump's construction of thousands of riverview apartments facing the new park. Riverside Park, the eastern part (sloping down from Riverside Drive) was designed by Olmsted in the 19th century, and the western part (along the river, including landfill and the Henry Hudson Parkway) was designed under Robert Moses' direction in the 20th century. At 323 acres, Riverside is the second largest park in Manhattan (Central Park has 843). You can walk yourself and your dog, play softball or handball (little Leaguers get preference), try your hand at tennis, or eat at the Boat Basin Cafe, an informal restaurant at 79th Street. The park ends at Tiemann Place and resumes eight blocks to the north.

On the Hudson riverfront between 138th and 145th St., a billion dollar sewage treatment plant was built about 20 years ago. To win community support, or at least acquiescence, for this project, the State built a park over the plant, called Riverbank. The park, which costs over $110 million, has a soccer field, gymnasium, swimming pool and ice skating rink. Enough soil was deposited so that trees can grow there. And, of course, river views are everywhere. Although it is the least natural park in the city, this park is worth seeing because it is widely used by the community and considered an important local amenity. North of it, Riverside Park resumes, becoming Fort Washington Park (158 acres) 160th St., and stretching north past the George Washington Bridge (179th St.). There is a little red lighthouse under the great gray bridge, made famous in a 1942 children's book by Geraldine Swift. The lighthouse is open to the public and has historical drawings and photographs surrounding its circular stairway.

The riverfront walk is broken until Dyckman St., but Fort Tryon park (named for the last British colonial governor, Lord Tryon), east of the highway (66 acres), contains the Cloisters (the medieval branch of the Metropolitan Museum of Art) built with stones brought over from Italy. This park is a gift from John D. Rockefeller, Jr. (father of Nelson, David, et al., and son of the founder the Standard Oil Company). It has spectacular views of the Palisades in New Jersey (another Rockefeller gift) and on the east it overlooks Inwood and the Bronx. The Heather Garden is a remarkable landscape feature, it is maintained by Parks with important help from the community (Henry Kissinger and Dr. Ruth Westheimer are major contributors). This park was used since the 1930s by refugees from Nazi Germany whose custom was to *spaziergehen*—to take a walk with the family on a on a weekend afternoon. In recent years, newer immigrants and their children have enjoyed the garden.

The next park on the Hudson, Inwood Hill (196 acres) is Manhattan's wilderness park. When you are in the midst of Inwood Hill Park, you cannot believe that you are on the island of Manhattan. It is relatively undeveloped, the few houses that were on the property having burned to the ground. In the park stand large tulip trees, some hundreds of years old. One such tree, still alive in 1936, supposedly grew on the site where the Dutch purchased land from the Leni-Lenape Indians, but the tree died in this century and only a marker remains. The Henry Hudson Parkway snakes its way along the west side of the park, moving toward the eponymous bridge that takes it, and its traffic, to Riverdale in the Bronx. The toll was 10¢ in December 1936 when Moses opened the first deck; it is now $2, matching the subway fare.

The waterfront parks of Manhattan do not surround the borough, but they cover most of the riverfronts, on way or another. They have scenic, historical, and recreational value. and also provide a circuit for visitors to hike or bike. Unless you are a marathoner, leave two days for the 32-mile walk.

Henry J. Stern was New York City's Commissioner of Parks and Recreation for 15 years, serving under Mayors Ed Koch and Rudolph Guiliani. He can be reached at StarQuest@nycivic.org.

the BIG $plurge

RIDE IN LUXURY

A stroll through Central Park on a sunny day is mesmerizing, but for those who would like to spare the wear and tear on that favorite pair of sneakers, there's another option. Allow yourself to be transported back to the times of the Park's opening with a horse-drawn carriage ride. You and three of your loved ones can be whisked away in style to visit all of Central Park's famous nooks and crannies.

There are a multitude of options when considering which tour and carriage are right for you. While the twenty-minute ($34-40) carriage rides can be negotiated on site along Central Park South, there are a number of other itineraries (most requiring reservations) that can be scheduled ahead of time so that no one will miss out on the ride.

On a typical twenty-minute, one-mile ride, you will see views of the Wollman Skating Rink, Carousel, Pond, Zoo, Sheep's Meadow, and the Mall and its literary walk statues, the Dairy and the Dakota, where ex-Beatle John Lennon lived.

The longer forty-minute ($100) ride, which again sits up to four people, includes

To the east of the Terrace and the Lake, competitive model-yachters gather to race at the **Conservatory Water.** Less serious yachters can rent remote-control sailboats. **Alice in Wonderland** and her friends live at 74th St. off Fifth Ave., at the north end of Conservatory Water. A statue of **Hans Christian Andersen,** a gift from Copenhagen in 1956, depicts him with the Ugly Duckling. The NY Public Library sponsors summer storytelling at the Andersen statue. (Usually Sa 11am; call ☎212-340-0849 for info.) North of the Lake is the **Ramble,** full of narrow trails that will make you forget you're in New York.

THE GREAT LAWN AND TURTLE POND

Great Lawn: *80th to 85th St., mid-park.* ***Turtle Pond:*** *Between 79th and 80th St., mid-park.* ***Belvedere Castle:*** *Just off the 79th St. Transverse. Observatory open Tu-Su10am-5pm.* ***Delacorte Theater:*** *80th St., mid-park (☎212-539-8650).* ***Swedish Cottage Marionette Theater:*** *☎212-988-9093. Reservations required. Shows usually Tu-F 10:30am and noon, Sa 1pm; summer M-Sa 10:30am, noon, 1pm. $6, children $5. All locations located on Map 17.*

The Great Lawn dominates the park in the lower 80s. The New York Philharmonic and the Metropolitan Opera Company hold summer performances here (p. 221). Overlooking the lawn and neighboring **Turtle Pond** is **Belvedere Castle,** designed by Calvert Vaux in 1869. The castle, rising from Vista Rock, was for many years only a weather station; it has been reincarnated to include a nature observatory and conservation center. Fieldpacks containing binoculars and bird guide books can be borrowed here with picture ID.

The **Delacorte Theater,** home to **Shakespeare in the Park** (p. 231), sits adjacent to Turtle Pond. The **Shakespeare Garden,** said to contain every plant, flower, and herb mentioned in the Bard's works, sits near the **Swedish Cottage Marionette Theater** at 81st St. mid-park. The former Swedish 19th-century schoolhouse, placed in the park in 1876, hosts regular puppet shows.

THE RESERVOIR AND POINTS NORTH

Reservoir: *From 86th to 95th St.* ***Conservatory Garden:*** *105th St., near Fifth Ave. ☎212-860-1382. Free tours of the Garden summer Sa at 11am. Gates open spring-fall daily 8am–dusk.* ***Harlem Meer:*** *110th St., near Fifth Ave., at the northeast corner of the park. ☎212-860-1370. Open Tu-Su Apr.-Oct. 10am-5pm; Nov.-Mar. 10am-4pm.* ***Lasker Pool and Rink:*** *Summer pool 11-2:30pm, 4-6:30pm. Free, bring your own lock. Oct.-Mar. skating rink with a fee. All locations Map 16.*

New Yorkers who jog around the **Reservoir** are treated to wonderful views of the Central Park W. skyline. This 11 acre lake holds the **Harlem Meer Performance Festival** on Sundays from late May to early September. To the north is **Conservatory Garden,** a romantic haven whose ordered paths and colorful flowers recall the European tradition of formal landscaping. The **Burnett Fountain,** located in the center of the south (English) section, depicts Mary and Dickon from Frances Hodgson Burnett's classic novel *The Secret Garden.* The **Charles A. Dana Discovery Center's** exhibitions and activities present Central Park as an environmental space to be explored by amateur and professional biologists alike. The Center, which also leads tours, loans out free fishing rods and provides bait for use in the Meer; carp, largemouth bass, and chain pickerel abound, but a catch-and-release policy is in effect.

UPPER EAST SIDE

Since the late 19th and early 20th centuries, when some of New York's wealthiest citizens built elaborate mansions along **Fifth Avenue,** the Upper East Side (Map 15) has been home to the city's richest residents. Today, some of these parkside mansions have been turned into museums, such as the **Frick Collection** (p. 132) and the **Cooper-Hewitt Museum** (p. 135). They are just two of the world-famous museums—including the **Metropolitan** (p. 128), the **Guggenheim** (p. 131), and the **Museum of the City of New York** (p. 139)—that line **Museum Mile,** from 82nd to 104th St. on Fifth Ave.

Madison Avenue, where most ordinary folk are content merely to window shop, is a fashion mecca. High-end designer boutiques, including Ralph Lauren, Louis Vuitton, and Prada, line this expensive walkway (see **Shopping,** p. 251). **Park Avenue,** from 59th to 96th St., is lined with dignified apartment buildings. North of 96th St., where the Metro-North train emerges from underground, the avenue becomes far less glamourous.

Lexington and **Third Avenues** are largely commercial, but the neighborhood becomes more and more residential as you go east. **Sights are listed from south to north.**

OLD BOYS CLUBS

Metropolitan Club: *1 E. 60th St., at Fifth Ave. Subway: N, R, W to Fifth Ave. Map 15, A6, 60.* ***Union Club:*** *101 E. 69th St., between Park Ave. and Lexington Ave. Subway: 6 to 68th St. Map 15, A6, 48.* ***Knickerbocker Club:*** *2 E. 62nd St. Subway: N, R, W to Fifth Ave. Map 15, A6, 55.*

all of the aforementioned places plus the Balto, Summerstage at Rumsey Playfield, the Lake, Strawberry Field's, Tavern on the Green, Columbus Circle, and the Trump International Hotel and Tower. This trip covers over 2.5 miles and reservations are mandatory.

From there, the duration of the tours increases in increments of 20 minutes and the prices vary. The longer tour will cover 6.5 miles and could last well over 80 minutes. The one-hour tour includes both of the tours above, and also exits the Park in front of the Dakota, goes up Central Park West, past the New York Historical Society, re-enters the park passing the Museum of Natural History, then continues with a beautiful excursion along the lake and ends by the Plaza Hotel. The total length is about 3 miles, again reservations are mandatory.

Also ask about evening tours for that extra romantic flair.

For tours, try ***Manhattan Carriage Company,*** *200 Central Park S. (☎212-664-1149. Office open daily 9am-8pm.)*

Sotheby's

Designed by Stanford White and built by David H. King Jr. in the Beaux-Arts style favored by White's famed architectural firm McKim, Mead, and White, the **Metropolitan Club** (first president: J. P. Morgan) was founded in 1891 by a group of distinguished gentlemen who were disgruntled with the rejection of some of their friends from the very exclusive **Union Club.** Inversely, the **Knickerbocker Club** was founded in 1871 by Union men who believed that the club's admissions policies had become *too* lax and liberal. Member names include Hamilton, Eisenhower, Roosevelt.

ARTS CLUBS

Grolier Club: 47 E. 60th St., between Madison and Park Ave. Subway: N, R, W to Fifth Ave. Map 15, B6, 62. ☎212-838-6690; www.grolierclub.org. ***Lotos Club:*** *5 E. 66th St., between Madison and Fifth Ave. Subway: 6 to 68th St. Map 15, B5, 45.*

The **Grolier Club,** an organization of book collectors founded in 1884, is named for prominent Renaissance bibliophile Jean Grolier. Completed in 1917, this Georgian structure houses a collection of fine bookbindings, quarterly exhibitions, and a specialized research library open by appointment. The **Lotos Club,** a private organization of actors, musicians, and journalists, was founded in 1870 as an institution to nurture and promote the arts. Early members included Samuel L. Clemens (Mark Twain) and George M. Cohan. The building was designed by Richard Howland Hunt in the French Renaissance style.

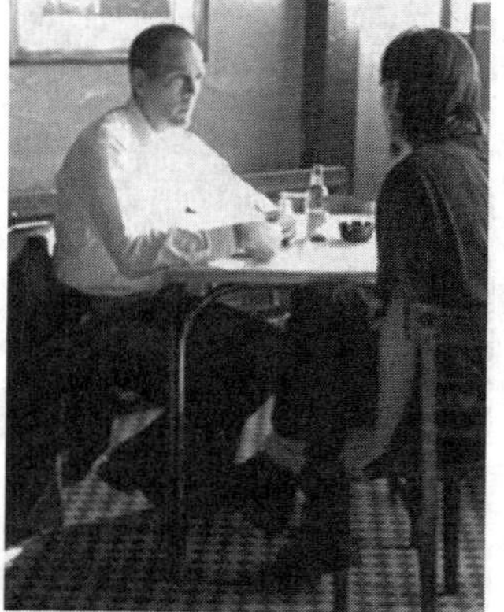

Fine Dining

TEMPLE EMANU-EL

1 E. 65th St., at Fifth Ave. Subway: N, R, W to Fifth Ave. Map 15, A6, 49. ☎212-744-1400. Open to the public daily 10am-5pm. Services Su-Th 5:30pm, F 5pm, Sa 10am.

The largest synagogue in the world, Temple Emanu-El was completed in 1929 for a primarily German-American congregation. A Romanesque facade, trimmed with archways representing the twelve tribes of Israel, greets visitors at the 65th St. entrance. Tours can be arranged after morning services and on Saturdays beginning at noon.

CHURCH OF ST. JEAN BAPTISTE

Corner of Lexington Ave. and 76th St. Subway: 6 to 77th St. Map 15, B5, 30. ☎212-472-2853. Weekday service 7:30am, 12:15, 5:30pm, Sunday 9, 10:30am, noon, 5:30pm, 7:30pm.

Strawberry Fileds

This massive, multi-domed Catholic church seems to have been placed specifically to watch over the hustle and bustle of lengthy Lexington Ave. To get a better view of its splendid paired towers and Corinthian porticoes, cross over to the other side of Lexington Ave. The building's interior is rich with paintings of biblical figures covering its high domes, intricate gold carvings, and the lively acoustics make it a wonderful place to hear music.

CARL SCHURZ PARK AND GRACIE MANSION

Between 84th and 90th St., along East End Ave. Subway: 4, 5, 6 to 86th St. Map 15, D4. Open dawn-1am. ***Gracie Mansion:*** *Map 15, D3, 19. ☎212-570-4751. Tours of Gracie Mansion Mar. to mid-Nov. W starting at 10 am, and Th from 12pm. 50min. By reservation only. $7, seniors $4.*

Named for the German immigrant who served as a Missouri senator and editor of the *New York Tribune*, the park overlooks the turbulent waters of the East River. **John Finley Walk,** which begins at E. 82nd St., forms a border on the eastern side of the park and is perfect for an afternoon run or a romantic evening stroll.

Gracie Mansion, at the northern end of the park (E. 88th St.), has been the official home of the mayor of New York City since 1942. Almost all of the objects in the recently restored mansion were made in New York, and many of the paintings and prints depict scenes of the City. The privately-funded Gracie Mansion Conservancy was established in 1981 to preserve, maintain, and enhance the mansion and its surroundings. Gracie Mansion's tradition of opening its doors to both tour and school groups is still honored. Although Mayor Michael Bloomberg hosts numerous official meetings, receptions, press conferences, luncheons and dinners at the house, he doesn't actually live in his official residence: billionaire Bloomberg resides at 17 E. 79th St., between Madison and Fifth Ave., in a five-story, 7500 sq. ft. limestone Beaux Arts mansion. He bought it in 1986 for $3.5 million.

HENDERSON PLACE HISTORIC DISTRICT

Between York and East End Ave., 86th and 87th St. Subway: 4, 5, 6, to 86th St. Map 15, C4, 18.

Of the original 32 connected houses of the Henderson Place Historic District, only 24 remain. Completed in 1882, inspired by the Queen Anne style and intended for "persons of moderate means," these private residences flaunt beautiful gables, dormers, mansards, and, some say, ghosts.

THE CHURCH OF THE HOLY TRINITY

316 E. 88th St., between First and Second Ave. Subway: 4, 5, 6 to 86th St. Map 15, C3, 16. ☎212-289-4100. Open to public M-F 9am-7pm, Su 8am-3pm. Services mid-Sept. to June 8, 9:15, 11am, 6pm; July to early Sept. 8, 10am, noon, 6pm.

This French Gothic-influenced Episcopal church was originally built to administer social services to the poorer residents of Yorkville. The interior contains 17 spectacular stained-glass windows, all designed by Henry Holiday (1839-1927). Holy Trinity is one of the few churches in the world in which all the windows were designed by one man, giving the building a unique stylistic homogeneity.

Holiday had an eye for beautifully rendered details and made lovingly crafted studies of human figures in opulent costumes. The stained-glass narratives provide a vivid tour of biblical scenes from both the Old and the New Testaments. Set back from the street, the building nicely complements the neighborhood and graces it with a small garden in front. There is also a bookstore where Christian literature can be purchased; open daily 11am-6pm.

ST. NICHOLAS RUSSIAN ORTHODOX CATHEDRAL

15 E. 97th St., between Fifth and Madison Ave. Subway: 6 to 96th St. Map 15, A2, 4. ☎212-289-1915.

Columbus Circle

Dakota Apartments

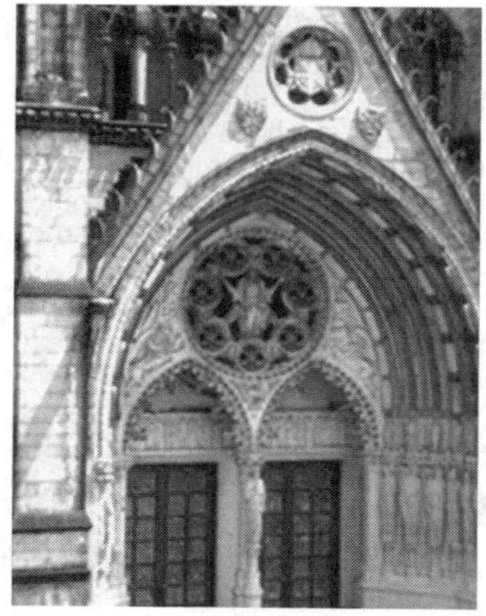
Cathedral of St. John the Divine

Five onion domes exuberantly top this Russian Baroque-style cathedral with a colorful history. Czar Nicholas II made the first donation to the building fund. The building was designed by John Bergesen according to the characteristic Russian model, with seven domes above a dark red brick facade trimmed with limestone and glazed tile in green, blue, and yellow. The church still attracts Russian immigrants, among many other visitors. Unfortunately, there is no exterior sign announcing the days and times of services and the gates on the front steps are often locked.

UPPER WEST SIDE

Subway: 1, 9, A, B, C, D to 59th St.-Columbus Circle; 1, 9 to 66th St.; 1, 2, 3, 9 to 72nd St./Broadway; B, C to 72nd St./Central Park W.; 1, 2 to 79th St.; B, C to 81st St.; 1, 2 to 86th St./Broadway; B, C to 86th St./Central Park W.; 1, 2, 3, 9 to 96th St./Broadway; B, C to 96th St./Central Park W. Map 18.

While **Central Park West** and **Riverside Drive** flank the Upper West Side with residential quietude, **Columbus Avenue, Amsterdam Avenue,** and **Broadway** are abuzz with action. The Upper West Side is one of the few neighborhoods in Manhattan that can legitimately be called a neighborhood; despite the troubling proliferation of chain stores in the area, the Upper West Side has maintained a pleasant cohesive sense of community that has eluded much of Manhattan in recent years. **Sights are listed from south to north.**

COLUMBUS CIRCLE

Intersection of Broadway, Eighth Ave., and Central Park S. Subway: 1, 9, A, B, C, D to 59th St.-Columbus Circle. Map 18, D6.

Midtown ends and the Upper West Side begins at this bustling nexus of pedestrian and automobile traffic. The circle takes its name from the memorial to Columbus that stands in its center. At the entrance to Central Park, a gold-domed monument commemorates those who died on the *USS Maine*. The black glass facade of Donald Trump's gargantuan **Trump International Hotel and Towers** (Map 18, D6), with its shiny silver globe, stands at 1 Central Park W.

THE GALLERY AT THE AMERICAN BIBLE SOCIETY

1865 Broadway, at 61st St. Subway: 1, 9, A, B, C, D, to 59th St.-Columbus Circle. Map 18, D6, 70. ☎ 212-408-1500; www.americanbible.org. Gallery open M-W and F 10am-6pm, Th 10am-7pm, Sa 10am-5pm. Library open M-F 9am-5pm. Wheelchair-accessible. Free.

The American Bible Society distributes the Good Book in nearly every tongue. Its gallery showcases rotating exhibitions of Judeo-Christian art, as well as rare and unorthodox

Bibles and four Gutenberg pages. If you ask, knowledgeable attendants will guide you through the holy gallery and into the exclusive library, which contains an extensive collection of Bibles and other Scriptures. 2004 exhibitions include *Art that Heals: Words and Images to Move the Spirit and Awaken the Soul* (May 14-July 31, 2004) and *Rites of Passage: Art and Religion in Romanian Life* (August 20-November 16, 2004).

LINCOLN CENTER

Columbus Ave., between 62nd and 66th St. Subway: 1, 9 to 66th St. Map 18, C6. ☎ 212-546-2656 or 875-5350; www.lincolncenter.org. Info booth near the Avery Hall entrance. Tours of theaters and galleries meet at the concourse, under the Met Opera House. 1hr. Daily 10am, 4:30pm; call for tour schedule. $10, students and seniors $8.50, children $5. Backstage tours of the Opera House M-F 3:45pm, Sa 10am; ☎ 212-769-7020 to reserve. See p. 216 for box office info.

Inspired by John D. Rockefeller's belief that "the arts are not for the privileged few, but for the many," New York's 16-acre center for all performing arts provides 11 facilities accommodating over 17,000 spectators. City planner Robert Moses masterminded Lincoln Center when Carnegie Hall (see p. 85) and the Metropolitan Opera House near Times Square seemed fated for destruction in 1955. The ensuing construction forced the eviction of thousands and erased a major part of the Hell's Kitchen area (see p. 77), including the neighborhood that was the setting for Leonard Bernstein's *West Side Story*. The complex, a reinterpretation of the public plazas in Rome and Venice, was initially dismissed by the *Times* as "a hulking disgrace," but the spacious, uncluttered architecture—as well as the performances that take place here—have made it one of New York's most admired locales.

The buildings of Lincoln Center are set around the **Josie Robertson Plaza,** where the cast of *Fame* danced at the beginning of each show. Straight ahead is the Mondrian-inspired glass facade of Lincoln Center's 1966 centerpiece, the **Metropolitan Opera House** (Map 18, C6, 65), designed by Wallace K. Harrison. Chagall murals grace the plaza and lobby, where a grand, multi-tiered staircase awaits the humble opera buff (p. 221).

To the left side of the plaza as you face the Opera House is the **New York State Theater** (Map 18, C6, 67), home of the New York City Ballet (p. 212) and the New York City Opera (p. 221). **Damrosch Park** (Map 18, C6), behind the theater, hosts frequent outdoor concerts and the perennially popular **Big Apple Circus** in the **Guggenheim Bandshell.** (Call for tour dates. Big Apple Circus can be reached at 505 Eighth Ave., 19th fl., New York, NY 10018-6505. ☎ 212-268-2500, ext. 163; www.bigapplecircus.org.)

On the right side of the plaza is **Avery Fisher Hall** (Map 18, C6, 66), designed in 1962 by Max Abramovitz and home to the New York Philharmonic (p. 216). To the right of the opera house are the **Vivian Beaumont Theater** and **Mitzi E. Newhouse Theater,** both housed in an Eero Saarinen-designed glass box (Map 18, C6, 63).

A footbridge across 65th St. leads to the prestigious **Juilliard School** (Map 18, C6), where Itzhak Perlman and Pinchas Zukerman honed their skills, and Robin Williams tried out his first comedy routines. Within the Juilliard building complex you'll find the intimate **Alice Tully Hall** (Map 18, C6, 62), home to the Chamber Music Society of Lincoln Center (p. 216). Behind Juilliard, in the Samuel B. and David Rose Building, the **Walter E. Reade Theater** (Map 18, C6, 61) features foreign films and special festivals (p. 215).

DAKOTA APARTMENTS

1 W. 72nd St., at the corner of Central Park W. Subway: B, C to 72nd St./Central Park W. Map 18, D5, 59.

Perhaps Manhattan's most famous apartment building, the Dakota counts Lauren Bacall, Leonard Bernstein, Roberta Flack, and Boris Karloff as its former residents. The complex, surrounded by open land and shanties right after its 1884 construction, was so far removed from the city that someone remarked, "It might as well be in the Dakota Territory." The name stuck, and architect Henry Hardenbergh (later architect of the Plaza Hotel) even gave the elegant building a frontier flair—look for the bas-relief Native American head and the stone garnish of corn and arrowheads that adorn the 'territory.' Beyond its history, the Dakota's claims to fame are rather macabre: *Rosemary's Baby* was filmed here, and resident John Lennon was assassinated outside on December 8, 1980.

ANSONIA HOTEL

2109 Broadway, between 73rd and 74th St. Subway: 1, 2, 3, 9 to 72nd St./Broadway. Map 17, C5, 45.

The *grande dame* of Beaux Arts apartments bristles with ornaments, curved Veronese balconies, and towers. Constructed in 1904, the Ansonia has 2500 apartments as well as various cafes, tea rooms, writing rooms, and a dining room seating 550. Its soundproof walls and thick floors enticed illustrious musically inclined tenants like Enrico Caruso, Arturo Toscanini, and Igor Stravinsky. Ansonia developer William Stokes raised chickens, ducks, and a pet bear on the building's roof. Worth strolling by, but you can't venture inside.

APTHORP APARTMENTS

2211 Broadway, at 79th St. Subway: 1, 2 to 79th St. Map 18, C4, 28.

The Apthorp's ornate iron gates, vaulted carriageways, and spacious interior courtyard have starred in such New York-based films as *The Cotton Club* and *Network*. Its simple marble facade features bas-relief vestal virgins. The apartments were built in 1908 on commission from William Waldorf Astor, who named them after the 1763 site owner.

RIVERSIDE PARK

West of Riverside Dr., from 72nd St. to the George Washington Bridge/175th St. Map 18, A1–5.

Along the Hudson River lies Riverside Park, where Upper West Siders walk their pooches, jog, play basketball, and enjoy wonderful views of the river and the Palisades in New Jersey. Although it's never wise to wander aimlessly in any urban park at night, Riverside Park can become exceptionally desolate.

MORNINGSIDE HEIGHTS

Subway: 1 to Cathedral Pkwy. (110th St.), 116th St.-Columbia University, 125th St./ Broadway. Map 19.

Above 110th St. and below 125th, this area straddling Harlem and the Upper West Side is dominated by Barnard College and Columbia University. Broadway is the neighborhood's main thoroughfare. **Sights are listed from south to north.**

CATHEDRAL OF ST. JOHN THE DIVINE

Amsterdam Ave., between 110th and 113th St. Subway: 1 to Cathedral Pkwy. (110th St.)/ Broadway. Map 19, B7, 39; Map 18, C1, 3. ☎212-316-7540; tours ☎212-932-7347. Open M-Sa 7:30am-6pm, Su 7:30am-6pm. Vertical tours (you go up 124 ft.) noon and 2pm on 1st and 3rd Sa of month. $10; reservations necessary. Regular horizontal tours Tu-Sa 11am, Su 1pm. $3. Suggested donation $2, students and seniors $1.

The largest cathedral in the world, unfinished St. John's has been under construction since 1892. This perpetual updating is reflected by its up-to-date altars and bays, which are dedicated not only to the sufferings of Christ, but also to the most touching experiences of the victims in this world. One memorial focuses on those that have died because of the AIDS epidemic, another remembers those that have died at the hands of genocide in Armenia, during the Holocaust, and in Bosnia, and another honors the members of the FDNY who lost their lives during Sept. 11. The central nave contains a 100-million-year-old nautilus fossil; the world's second largest organ stop, which consists of some 8035 pipes; and a "Poet's Corner" honoring writers such as Nathaniel Hawthorne and Edith Wharton. With a poet and two dance companies in residence, the Cathedral's extensive secular schedule complements Episcopal services with concerts, art exhibitions, poetry readings, lectures, theater, and dance events. The complex also contains a Greek amphitheater (still under construction), a peace fountain, and a beautiful Biblical Garden.

COLUMBIA UNIVERSITY

Morningside Dr. and Broadway, from 114th to 120th St. Subway: 1 to 116th St.-Columbia University. Map 19, A6. Group tours for prospective students late fall through spring, but no regularly scheduled public tours.

Chartered in 1754 as King's College, the university lost its original name in the American Revolution. In 1897 President Seth Low, seeking a healthy academic environment for students and professors, moved the school from 49th St. and Madison Ave. to its current location. The campus, designed by prominent New York architects McKim, Mead & White, is urban (don't come looking for grass), yet removed from surrounding Morningside Heights. Its centerpiece, the majestic Roman Classical **Low Library,** looms over **College Walk,** the school's central promenade that bustles with academics, students, and quacks. The **Alma Mater** statue in front of the building was a rallying point during the riots of 1968. Just to the east of Low Library stands **St. Paul's Chapel,** a small but beautiful space with magnificent acoustics. **Morningside Park,** where Meg Ryan discusses her sexual fantasies in *When Harry Met Sally*, is right to the east of campus along Morningside Dr. (between 110th and 123rd St).

RIVERSIDE CHURCH

490 Riverside Dr., at 120th St. Subway: 1 to 116th St.-Columbia University. Map 19, A6, 26. ☎212-870-6792. Open M-F 9am-4:30pm. Bell tower open Tu-Sa 10:30am-5pm, Su 9:45-10:45am and noon-4pm. Admission to observation deck Tu-Sa $2, students and seniors $1. Tours Su 12:30pm after services and upon request. Free.

Inspired by the Chartres Cathedral and supported by John D. Rockefeller Jr.'s philanthropy, this steel-framed church was constructed in only two years. The church has remained interdenominational since its first service in 1930. The tower observation deck, which looms 362 ft. above Riverside Dr., commands an amazing view both of the bells within and the expanse of the Hudson River and Riverside Park below. Best heard from the parks around the church, The Laura Spelman Rockefeller Memorial Carillon contains 74 bronze bells given in memory of John's mother. Concerts on this, the world's largest carillon resonate on Sundays at 10:30am, 12:30, and 3pm. Interdenomination, interracial, and international services and activities.

GENERAL GRANT NATIONAL MEMORIAL (GRANT'S TOMB)

Near the intersection of Riverside Dr. and 122nd St. Subway: 1 to 125th St./Broadway. Map 19, A6, 25. ☎212-666-1640. Open daily 9am-5pm. Free. Informal ranger-guided tours by request.

This granite mausoleum is the largest of its kind in America and rises to 150 ft. while resting atop a hill overlooking the Hudson River. Once covered with graffiti, the monument to Civil War general and 18th US President Ulysses S. Grant is now pristine. Bronze casts of other Union generals surround the tomb where Grant and his wife Julia lie. Grant's Civil War victories in the Battles of Vicksburg and Chattanooga, as well as Robert E. Lee's surrender at Appomattox, are depicted by mosaics in the tomb. Also highlights the effort involved in building the mausoleum by Richard T. Greener, the first black graduate of Harvard and secretary of the Grant monument Association. Across the street, **Sakura Park** in Riverside Park features a statue of General Daniel Butterfield (best known for composing "Taps"). Japanese for "cherry blossoms," the *sakura* were a gift to the city in 1912.

Belvedere Castle

Columbia University

Fort Tryon Park

HARLEM

Harlem is a place where I like to eat, sleep, drink, and be in love.
—Langston Hughes

Subway: 6 to 103rd St., Central Park N. (110th St.), 116th St. at Lexington Ave.; 4, 5, 6 to 125th St./Lexington Ave.; 2, 3 to Central Park N. (110th St.), 116th St., 125th St., 135th St. at Lenox (Sixth) Ave.; 3 to 145th St./Lenox (Sixth) Ave., 148th St.; B, C to Cathedral Pkwy. (110th St.), 116th St., 135th St. at Central Park W.; A, B, C, D to 125th St./Central Park W.; A, B, C, D to 145th St./St. Nicholas Ave.; 1, 9 to 137th St., 145th St. at Broadway. Map 19.

As the largest neighborhood in all of Manhattan, Harlem extends from 110th St. to the 150s, between the Hudson and East Rivers. Between 1910 and 1920, Harlem began its transformation into a largely African-American neighborhood. With Harlem's 1920s prosperity came an artistic and literary movement known as the Harlem Renaissance.

The 1960s radical Black Power movement, riding the civil rights tidal wave, thrived here. LeRoi Jones's Revolutionary Theater performed one-act plays in the streets; Malcolm X, Stokely Carmichael, and H. Rap Brown spoke against racism and injustice. In spite of the activism, however, Harlem's economic welfare declined rapidly. In the 1970s and 80s, members of the community recognized the need for economic revitalization as a route to empowerment. Today, thanks to the economic boom of the 1990s, pockets of Harlem are thriving again.

Spanish Harlem, or El Barrio, sits on the East Side, between 96th and 125th St., and supports a large Mexican and Puerto Rican population. The neighborhood's main artery is E. 116th St. Up Park Ave., on the East Side, stark examples of social and cultural stratification emerge. Pockets of brilliance survive this poverty, however; see the **Graffiti Wall of Fame** at 106th St. and Park Ave. El Barrio is at its best on **Puerto Rican Constitution Day**, July 25, when streets close off for serious festivity. Harlem's parks can also provide some relief from Manhattan's asphalt: 12.8 acre **Jackie Robinson Park** (145th-152nd St., between Edgecombe and Bradhurst Ave.) includes a bronze statue of the baseball player and a public pool, while **Marcus Garvey Park** (120th-124th St., between Fifth and Madison Ave.)—named after the "Back-to-Africa" movement advocate—features huge canopy trees, sloping rocks, and unsurpassed views of the city.

Some major streets are known in the Harlem area by more than one name: note Frederick Douglass Blvd. (Eighth Ave.); Adam Clayton Powell Jr. Blvd. (Seventh Ave.); and Lenox Ave. (Sixth Ave. or Malcolm X Blvd.). In the Harlem coverage, *Let's Go* generally uses the first choices mentioned above. **Sights are listed from south to north.**

TERESA HOTEL

Southwest corner of 125th St. and Powell Ave. Subway: 2, 3 to 125th St./Lenox (Sixth) Ave. Map 18, C5, 22.

After its segregation policy was dropped in 1940, the Teresa reigned for some years as the Waldorf of Harlem. Built and opened in 1913, the hotel was frequented by local celebrities. The Teresa made history in 1960, when it welcomed Fidel Castro after his eviction from the Shelburne Hotel; it was also the headquarters of such community and national organizations as the March on Washington led by A. Philip Randolph, and Malcolm X's Organization for African Unity. This historic building, that once served an integral role as a center for civil rights activists, has been reduced to a corporate space and can now only be appreciated from the outside.

CITY COLLEGE

Convent Ave., from 130th to 140th St. Enter at 138th St. Subway: 1 to 137th St. Map 19, B4, 10. ☎212-650-7000; www.ccny.cuny.edu.

Collegiate Gothic-style buildings and sprawling green lawns greet you as you face the campus of the City College of New York. Founded in 1847 by Townsend Harris to provide immigrants and the poor a chance to receive a higher education, City College is the nation's first public college and the alma mater of Woody Allen, Colin Powell, Edward Koch, Jonas Salk, and Walter Mosley.

THE SCHOMBURG CENTER FOR RESEARCH IN BLACK CULTURE

515 Lenox (Sixth) Ave., at 135th St. Subway: 2, 3 to 135th St./Lenox (Sixth) Ave. Map 19, C4, 12. ☎212-491-2265 or 491-2200; www.schomburgcenter.org. General Reference and Research open Tu-W 12pm-8pm, Th-F 12pm-6pm, Sa 10am-6pm. Wheelchair-accessible.

This research branch of the **New York Public Library** (p. 78) houses the city's vast archives, manuscripts, and rare books on black history and culture. Center namesake and avid black history scholar Arturo Schomburg amassed photographs, oral histories, and artwork, all of which are incorporated into the center's collection of some five million items. Check out the Latimer/Edison Art Gallery with rotating exhibits like 'The Art of African Women: Empowering Traditions.' The large and impressive research library contains a year-round exhibit featuring brief biographies of 100 notable black New Yorkers. Marcus Garvey was a frequent soapbox orator on this street corner from 1916-1917. The center also houses the **American Negro Theater,** famous during the 1940s, and **The Langston Hughes Auditorium,** a venue for a wide range of entertainment including concerts and plays featuring both local talent and celebrities.

THE ABYSSINIAN BAPTIST CHURCH

132 W. 138th St., between Lenox (Sixth) Ave. and Powell Blvd. Subway: 2, 3 to 135th St./Lenox (Sixth) Ave. Map 19, C4, 11. ☎212-862-7474; www.abyssinian.org. Su services 9 and 11am.

Abyssinian, established in 1808, is as known for its indispensable contributions to the community as it is for its famous pastors. Adam Clayton Powell Sr., a legendary figure credited with catalyzing the black migration to Harlem, presided over the pulpit; his son, Adam Clayton Powell Jr., succeeded his father in 1937 before becoming NYC's first black congressman. Today, the eloquent Calvin Butts preaches to the 5000-strong congregation each Sunday. Special rows are set aside each week for tourists and visitors. Services are at 9am and 11am

HAMILTON HEIGHTS

Between St. Nicholas and Amsterdam Ave., and between 140th and 145th St. ***Hamilton Grange:*** *287 Convent Ave., between 141st and 142nd. Subway: 1, 9 to 145th St./Broadway. Map 19, B4, 9. Open F-Su 9am-5pm. Free.*

Between Convent and St. Nicholas Ave. rests a residential neighborhood full of intricately designed brownstones. Surprisingly clean **Riverbank State Park** along the Hudson River, built over a controversial sewage plant in 1993, features ice and roller rinks, pool, tennis, tracks, baseball diamonds, and picnic fields. (Off the West Side Hwy., enter at 135th St. Map 19, A4. ☎212-693-3654.) The two-story, colonial-style **Hamilton Grange** was built by Alexander Hamilton, founding father and co-author of the *Federalist Papers*. The first floor documents Hamilton's life, while the upper two floors retain sparse colonial furnishings. Although it was just renovated in 1997, the house will be relocated to St. Nicholas Park within the next five years, where it will be designated a national landmark.

STRIVER'S ROW

138th and 139th St., between Powell and Frederick Douglass Blvd. (Eighth Ave.). Subway: B, C to 135th St./St. Nicholas Ave. Map 19, B4.

Perhaps Harlem's most prized possessions are its historic buildings. Originally envisioned as a "model housing project" for middle-class whites, Striver's Row reputedly acquired its nickname from Harlemites who felt their neighbors were striving too hard to attain middle-class status. Now part of the St. Nicholas Historic District, the impressive 1891 brownstones are featured in Spike Lee's *Jungle Fever*. The beautiful tan-bricked buildings, ranging in style from neocolonial to Italian Renaissance, sport wrought-iron railings and inviting stoops.

SUGAR HILL

143rd to 155th St., between St. Nicholas and Edgecombe Ave. Subway: A, B, C, D to 145th St./St. Nicholas Ave. Map 19, B3.

African-Americans with "sugar" (a.k.a. money) moved here in the 1920s and 30s; musical legends Duke Ellington and W.C. Handy lived in the neighborhood, while leaders W.E.B. DuBois and Thurgood Marshall both inhabited 409 Edgecombe. Some of the city's most notable gangsters operated here—Wesley Snipes starred as one in the film *Sugar Hill*. The area is also the birthplace of Sugarhill Records, the rap label that created the Sugarhill Gang; their 1979 *Rapper's Delight* became the first hip-hop song to reach the Top 40.

WASHINGTON HEIGHTS

Subway: C to 155th St./St. Nicholas Ave., 163rd St.; 1, A, C to 168th St.-Broadway; A to 175th St., 181st St., 190th St.; 1, 9 to 181st St./St. Nicholas Ave., 191st St. Map 19.

Even hillier than Park Slope, Washington Heights and its several parks make it one of the greenest neighborhoods in the five boroughs. Buildings perched atop high ridges peer down hundreds of feet at their next-door neighbors. Once predominantly Irish, Washington Heights' merging of large Latino, black, Greek, Armenian, and Jewish communities has brought its share of culture clashes. **Sights are listed from south to north.**

MORRIS-JUMEL MANSION

65 Jumel Terr., between 160th and 162nd St. Subway: C to 163rd St. Map 18, B2, 2. ☎212-923-8008. Open Su and W-Sa 10am-4pm. $3, seniors and students $2. Accompanied children under 12 free. Guided tours by appointment. Add 50¢ to admission, under 12 $1.50.

Built in 1765, the Georgian Morris-Jumel Mansion is Manhattan's oldest free-standing house. Loyalist Roger Morris abandoned the whitewashed stone brick house for England when the Revolutionary War started brewing; George Washington lived here while devising his battle plan for the successful (but little-known) Battle of Harlem Heights in 1776. Stephen and Eliza Jumel purchased the house in 1810, and Eliza married Aaron Burr in the front room a year after Stephen died in 1832. Famous bedchambers, purported Napoleonic gift ornaments, and some brilliant furniture wait for you look at them. A mossy brick path winds around the gardens, which afford a great view of the Harlem River. Don't be afraid to knock if the house seems closed. Across the street on **Sylvan Terrace,** French colonial houses stretch down the narrow, cobbled street.

AUDUBON BALLROOM

3940 Broadway, between 165th St and 166th St. Subway: C to 163rd St. Map 19, A2, 1.

During a rally on February 21, 1965, black leader Malcolm X was assassinated on the grounds of this building. The Audubon, partly rededicated in 1997 as a memorial to Malcolm X, also houses a medical research center. While most of the ballroom has been swallowed by commercial space (a bank and a restaurant), a memorial statue of Malcolm X—who eventually changed his name to El-Hajj Malik El-Shabazz (hence the inscription on the door)—stands in the main lobby.

GEORGE WASHINGTON BRIDGE

Best view from the corner of 181st St. and Riverside Dr. Also from Fort Tyron Park. Subway: A to 181st St./Washington Ave. Map 19 (inset), B3. Great views of Manhattan from the walking path on the bridge itself. Toll $6 from NJ to NY, free from NY to NJ.

The construction of this 14-lane, 3500 ft. suspension bridge coincided with the beginning of the Great Depression, and the ensuing purse-tightening left the bridge's two towers without the granite sheathing designer Othmar Amman had intended. During the long construction, neighborhood children (including the late philosopher-poet Jerry Goldberg) would use the structural supports of the George Washington Bridge as diving boards into the Hudson River. Le Corbusier, who proclaimed it "the most beautiful bridge in the world," was struck by the naked steelwork's precociously postmodern, erector-set look. Bikes and pedestrians are allowed on the wide walkway.

LITTLE RED LIGHTHOUSE

Fort Washington Park, 178th St. and Hudson River. Subway: A to 181st St./Washington Ave. From the intersection of Riverside Dr. and 181st St., go west across the suspended walkway. From there, follow the sloping, switchbacking path to the edge of the water. Map 19 (inset), A3, 5. ☎212-304-2365. Tours available if you call ahead.

Originally constructed in 1921 to steer barges away from Jeffrey's Hook, the lighthouse is perhaps best known from Hildegarde Hoyt Swift's book *The Little Red Lighthouse and the Great Grey Bridge.* When the lighthouse was decommissioned in 1947, Swift's book played a major role in saving it: millions of children who loved the *Little Red Lighthouse* story spoke out when the US Coast Guard wanted to sell and dismantle the structure. The trail there is a tad confusing, but manageable. To the south of the lighthouse are tennis courts and some lovely grass areas with picnic tables. At some places you can get down to the water's edge.

YESHIVA UNIVERSITY

Amsterdam Ave., from 182nd to 186th St. Subway: 1, 9 to 181st St./St. Nicholas Ave. Administrative offices at 500 185th St. Map 19 (inset), B3, 3. ☎212-960-5400.

Started in the Lower East Side in 1886, the university has since moved its main campus to these pallid university buildings in the middle of a bustling Hispanic neighborhood. The rabbinical and men's undergraduate programs are conducted here. The recently renamed David H. Zysman Hall is the campus' Gothic centerpiece, featuring Romanesque windows and colorful minarets amid the surrounding drab, institutional architecture.

FORT TRYON PARK

Bounded by Broadway on the east, the Hudson River on the west, Riverside Dr. on the north, and Overlook Terr. to the south. Subway: 1, 9 to 191st St./St. Nicholas Ave.; A to 190th St./Fort Washington Ave. Map 19 (inset), A2. ☎212-342-4865. Conservancy instructors take people climbing about twice a month.

Central Park designer Frederick Law Olmsted lovingly landscaped this park, which was donated to the city by John D. Rockefeller Jr. in 1935 in exchange for permission to construct Rockefeller University. This is one of the most majestic and wholly beautiful landscapes in the city. You can still see the crumbling remains of Fort Tryon, a Revolutionary War bulwark captured by the British in 1776. **Heather Garden** blossoms in the spring and fills the air with the beautiful scent of its flowers. The park also presents sensational views of the George Washington Bridge and the Palisades. Don't miss **the Cloisters,** the Met's palatial sanctuary for medieval art (p. 132). Experienced climbers can register to climb up and rappel down the 50 ft. face of the cliff on the eastern side of the park.

ROOSEVELT ISLAND

Subway: F to Roosevelt Island; 4, 5, 6, F, N, R, W to 59th St./Lexington Ave. Walk 2 blocks east from 59th St. and Lexington to Second Ave. and hop onto the tram. Map 15, D3-6. ☎718-832-4555. Tram every 15min. Su-Th 6am-2am, F-Sa 6am-3:30am; twice as frequently at rush hr. One-way $1.50; no Metrocards accepted. 4min. each way.

Just off the east coast of Manhattan, this 147-acre island in the East River is home to 9500 residents lucky enough to participate in this unlikely, semi-urban community. In 1969, during Mayor John Lindsay's mayoralty, the New York State Urban Development Corporation signed a 99-year lease with New York City to develop the island into mixed-income residential community with a largely traffic-free environment. The island was renamed Roosevelt Island in 1973, and the first residential complex opened in 1975.

Don't miss the bright red tram shuttle to the East River, one of the few publicly operated commuter cable cars in the world. The ride grants a grand view of the East Side as you rise to 250 ft. above the United Nations complex. The tram operates at an annual loss of $1 million, and its future has become uncertain since the subway opened to the island about 10 years ago. Once on the island, walk north or take the mini-bus (25¢) up **Main Street** and roam around a bit. A **walking/skating path** encircles the island. Gardens and playgrounds abound on the northern half, but the southern tip of the island is currently off-limits while the city restores the ruins of an old asylum and hospital. **Lighthouse Park,** at the northernmost tip of the island, is a pleasant retreat offering views of the swirling East River.

BROOKLYN

Until 1898, Brooklyn was its own city; with a population reaching one million, only neighboring New York and Chicago could boast more residents. Rather than test its luck as an independent entity, Brooklyn decided to cast its lot with the people of Manhattan Island. Although often erroneously depicted as annexation by New York, it was Brooklyn's decision (in the closest of votes) to unite with New York that created the foundation of modern New York City and its system of boroughs. Fiercely independent, Brooklyn has been the most populous section of New York for almost the entire twentieth-century. With a citizenry diverse in economic class, race, and religion, Brooklyn is the city within the City. **In the coverage below, neighborhoods are arranged from north to south.**

WILLIAMSBURG AND GREENPOINT

In the last 15 years, **Williamsburg** (Map 21) has gone from decaying reminder of industrial yesteryear to happening colony for the avant-garde to the present-day mecca of New York hipsters. The streets are brimming with bars, restaurants, galleries, theaters, movie-houses and establishments that combine properties of all the above. The neighborhood's flare for the funky centers around **Bedford Avenue** and **Berry Street,** though each year sees the increased sprawling of artistic liveliness. Three free community publications, *11211*, *Block*, and *The Brooklyn Rail* report on arts, local news and events. A Hasidic Jewish community thrives on the south side of town, along Broadway, Heyward St., Wythe St., and Bedford Ave. North of Broadway is predominantly Latino. **Greenpoint,** bounded by Java St. on the north, Meserole St. on the south, and Franklin St. on the west, is Brooklyn's northernmost region and borders Queens. Home to a large Polish population, it is also the birthplace of Mae West, Brooklynese, and the Union's Civil War ironclad **Monitor.** Italianate and Grecian houses, built during the 1850s shipbuilding boom, grace the neighborhood.

NEW YORK TRANSIT SYSTEM N. 7TH STREET FAN PLANT

Enter at westernmost end of N. 7th Street. Subway: L to Bedford Ave.

There are a few hidden gems among the cowering remains of Brooklyn's prior industrial splendor, and this abandoned lot (actually land owned by New York State) is one of the most spectacular. Clamber through a gate that local residents say has been open for over two years, and you can stroll out along the closest thing to an East River beach in Brooklyn. Bricks and discarded stuff abound, but there is an undeniable urban beauty as seaweed and old pylons mingle among the lapping waves. Aficionados of Brooklyn's waterfront assert that this vista affords one of the most breathtaking views of Manhattan's skyline.

RUSSIAN ORTHODOX CATHEDRAL OF THE TRANSFIGURATION

228 N. 12th St., at Driggs Ave. Subway: L to Bedford Ave.; G to Nassau Ave. Map 21.

Five striking, copper-covered, onion-shaped domes carry you off to Mother Russia. Built between 1916 and 1921, the cathedral's gorgeous stained-glass windows and triple-slashed crosses are just a hint of the beauty within.

ST. ANTHONY AND ALPHONSIUS CHURCH

862 Manhattan Ave., at Noble St. Subway: G to Greenpoint Ave. ☎ 718-383-3339.

Built in 1873 by Brooklynite Patrick Keeley, the Church features spectacular stained glass windows, among the best in New York. The "flamboyant gothic" work includes a clock in the steeple and a Columbus organ from 1892. Older nautical maps of the area use the steeple, once the highest point in Brooklyn, as a landmark. The lower chapel is open daily, but the main church opens its doors only for mass, held on Saturday and Sunday in both English and Spanish.

BROOKLYN BREWERY

79 N. 11th St., at Wythe Ave. Subway: L to Bedford Ave.; G to Nassau Ave. Map 21. ☎ 718-486-7422. Tap room open F 6-10pm, Sa noon-5pm. Tours and tastings Sa noon-4:30pm.

In the days when beer was an alternative to an unsanitary water supply, enterprising immigrants with brewing know-how began a century-long Brooklyn legacy. Poor business in the 1960s brought the beer boom to an end, but not the tradition: the Brooklyn Brewery, established in 1987, still makes Brooklyn Lager and Brooklyn Brown Ale (both found in the borough's bars). The brewery is a busy factory during the week and a lively spot on the weekend for the curious or thirsty.

FULTON LANDING AND DUMBO

Brooklyn owes most of its development to one man. When Robert Fulton invented the steamboat, he immediately chartered a ferry route across the East River. Brooklyn quickly become an attractive residential alternative to commercial Manhattan; it grew from a village of 2000 in 1816 to a city of half-a-million in less than forty years, growth almost entirely attributable to the Fulton Ferry. Fulton Landing recalls the days when the ferry, not the subway or the car, was the primary means of transportation between Fulton St. in Brooklyn and Fulton St. in Manhattan. DUMBO, which stands for Down Under Manhattan Bridge Overpass, hosts a thriving arts scene and a growing residential community.

BROOKLYN BRIDGE

From Brooklyn: entrance at the end of Adams St., at Tillary St. Subway: A, C to High St./Cadman Plaza E. From Manhattan: entrance at Park Row. Subway: J, M, Z, 4, 5, 6 to Brooklyn Bridge-City Hall. Map 22.

A walk across the Brooklyn Bridge at sunrise or sunset is one of the most exhilarating strolls New York City has to offer—especially when you're dodging the cyclists on the pedestrian path. The bridge gracefully spans the gap between Lower Manhattan's dense cluster of skyscrapers and Brooklyn's less intimidating shore. Georgia O'Keeffe and Joseph Stella acknowledged this technological and aesthetic triumph on canvas; Hart Crane paid tribute in verse.

Completed in 1883, the bridge is the product of elegant calculation, careful design, and human exertion. After chief architect John Augustus Roebling crushed his foot in a surveying accident and died of gangrene, his son Washington took over. When Washington himself succumbed to the bends, Washington's wife Emily Warren inherited the project. Plaques at either end of the walkway commemorate the Roeblings and the 20 workers who died in the bridge's underwater chambers during construction. A **gallery and performance space** is housed within the bridge's cavernous suspension cable storage chambers (p. 146).

FULTON FERRY

At the East River end of Old Fulton St. Subway: A, C to High St./Cadman Plaza E. Map 22.

One of Brooklyn's major centers of trade during the 19th century, this section of faded buildings is named for the ferry that ran services from here to Manhattan from 1642 until 1924. Enjoy the beautiful view of Lower Manhattan and the Brooklyn bridge from the pier or take a ride on the new water taxi which covers the old route of the Fulton Ferry.

THE EAGLE WAREHOUSE AND STORAGE CO.

28 Old Fulton St., between Columbia Heights and Hicks St. Subway: A, C to High St./Cadman Plaza E. Map 22, 8.

The *Brooklyn Eagle* newspaper was once printed in a building on this site. Its editor, Brooklyn poet-laureate Walt Whitman, was fired due either to laziness or to his bold anti-slavery views, depending upon the slant of your source. The current structure, an impressive 1894 warehouse, has been converted into apartments.

DOWN UNDER MANHATTAN BRIDGE OVERPASS (DUMBO)

The area between the Brooklyn Bridge and the Manhattan Bridge. Subway: F to York St.; A, C to High St./ Cadman Plaza E. Map 22.

New apartments, restaurants and stores mark the growing residency of this area surrounding the Manhattan Bridge. Some of the old warehouses have been transformed into galleries and theatres in this growing artistic area. the numerous tacked-on buzzers on the door of 135 Plymouth St., at Anchorage Pl. (Map 22, 5), indicate the building's several makeshift galleries (p. 146).

Mix Tapes

BROOKLYN HEIGHTS AND DOWNTOWN

Subway: M, N, R, 1, 2, 4, 5 to Court St.-Borough Hall. Map 22.

Brooklyn Heights, a well-preserved 19th-century residential area, sprang up with the development of steamboat transportation between Brooklyn and Manhattan in 1814. Rows of posh Greek Revival and Italianate houses in this area essentially created New York's first suburb. **Montague Street,** the neighborhood's main drag, has the stores, cafes, and mid-priced restaurants of a cute college town. Arthur Miller and W.H. Auden called this area home in the 1940s and 50s. Young and upwardly mobile types live here now, while **Atlantic Avenue** has a thriving Middle Eastern community. **Downtown** is the location of Brooklyn's **Civic Center**, and contains several grand municipal buildings. **Sights are listed from north to south.**

The Promenade

 PROMENADE

By the East River, between Remsen and Orange St. Subway: 1, 2 to Clark St. Map 22.

The view of the lower Manhattan skyline and the Brooklyn Bridge from this waterfront walkway is one of *the* New York sights to see—even if it doubles as the roof of the toxic Brooklyn-Queens Expwy. (BQE). To the left, Lady Liberty peeps from behind Staten Island; in fair weather, Ellis Island appears in full view.

PLYMOUTH CHURCH OF PILGRIMS

75 Hicks St., between Orange and Cranberry St. ☎718-624-4743. Subway: 1, 2 to Clark St. Map 22, 10.

Brooklyn brownstones, winter

NO WORK ALL PLAY

CELEBRATE BROOKLYN

If you're a Brooklynite, born and bred, then you probably already know the ins and outs of this 25-year-old summer festival. For the average traveler, however, it is a wonderful way to get acquainted with the City's most popolous borough, and also see some of the finest arts, dance music, and film the City has to offer.

Celebrate Brooklyn was founded in 1979 and is one of New York's longest-running free, summer outdoor performing arts festivals. In that time, over 200,000 people have enjoyed its offerings.

The festival runs from mid-June to mid-August and takes place at the Bandshell in Brooklyn's Prospect Park. Admission except for the benefit concerts and receptions (where tickets can go anywhere from $50 to upwards of $250 and more), is **free.** Organizers only request a $3 donation so that Celebrate Brooklyn can still offer top-name acts free of charge to residents and visitors.

(For more information call ☎718-855-7882 or check www.celebratebrooklyn.org.)

Before the Civil War, this simple red-brick church was part of the Underground Railroad and the center of New York abolitionist sentiments. Founded in 1847 and built in 1849, its courageous first minister and head abolitionist was Henry Ward Beecher, brother of *Uncle Tom's Cabin* author Harriet Beecher Stowe. He served from 1847 to 1887, and saw the likes of anti-slavery heroes, such as Abraham Lincoln, come to worship on several occasions over his years. A section of the actual Plymouth Rock was added to the adjoining arcade in 1934.

WILLOW STREET

Willow St., between Clark and Pierrepont St. Subway: 2, 3 to Clark St. Map 22, 11.

To see the Heights' potpourri of 19th-century styles ranging from Italianate to Classical Revival, explore Willow St. 155-159 are the oldest preserved Federal-Style Row Houses of the early nineteenth century (c. 1830) with dormer windows punctuating the sloping roofs.

BROOKLYN HISTORICAL SOCIETY

128 Pierrepont St., off Clinton St. Subway: M, N, R, 1, 2, 4, 5 to Court St.-Borough Hall. Map 22, 13. ☎718-222-4111; www.brooklynhistory.org. Open M and Th-Sa noon-5pm.

This striking building, lined with gargoyle-busts of Shakespeare, Beethoven, and others, houses both the very informative historical society and a museum devoted to appreciation of Brooklyn's past and present. Library and education center also open for study.

ST. ANN'S AND THE HOLY TRINITY EPISCOPAL CHURCH

Montague St., on the corner of Clinton St. Subway: 1, 2, 4, 5, M, N, R to Court St.-Borough Hall. Map 22. ☎718-834-8794. ***Arts at St. Ann's:*** *☎718-858-2424. Closed for renovations.*

One of the more impressive landmarks on Montague St., St. Ann's contains over 4000 sq. ft. of stained glass. **Saint Ann's**, an illustrious private school (noted alums include Jennifer Connelly, Mike D of the Beastie Boys, and Emily Parker) was founded on the church grounds and today resides in the old Crescent Athletic Club up the block on Pierrepont St. Before closing in 2001 for extensive repairs, the church was home to **Arts at St. Ann's,** a superb cultural center that has attracted such performers as Lou Reed and Marianne Faithfull.

BOROUGH HALL

209 Joralemon St., at the southern end of Fulton St. Mall. Subway: 1, 2, 4, 5, M, N, R to Court St.-Borough Hall. Map 22, 14. Tours Tu 1pm. Free.

Completed in 1851, this beautiful Greek temple-inspired edifice topped by a cupola once was the city hall of an independent Brooklyn. It now houses the Borough President's office.

PARK SLOPE AND PROSPECT PARK

Considered by many to be New York's nicest neighborhood, **Park Slope** is a residential oasis with charming brownstones, great dining, and beautiful people. Restaurants and stores line the north-south avenues; **Prospect Park West** is Brooklyn's own Central Park West, **Seventh Avenue** has long been the neighborhood's main drag, and **Fifth Avenue's** budding scene of restaurants, bars, and cute boutiques give it a hipper edge. Politically progressive, extremely tolerant, and with a strong sense of community, there are few better places to raise a family in New York. Neighboring **Prospect Park** is the borough's answer to Manhattan's Central Park (p. 86).

PROSPECT PARK

Bounded by Prospect Park W., Flatbush Ave., Ocean Ave., Parkside Ave., and Prospect Park SW. Subway: 1, 2 to Grand Army Plaza; F to 15 St.-Prospect Park; Q, S to Prospect Park. Map 23. ☎718-965-8951, events hotline ☎718-965-8999; www.prospectpark.org. Paddle boat and horse rental ☎718-282-7789. Th-F 11am-4pm, Sa-Su noon-6pm. Paddle boat $10 per hr., $10 deposit; horses $25-30 per hr. ***Memorial Arch:*** *Map 23, C2. Open to climbers Sa-Su 1-5pm. Free.* ***Leffert's Homestead:*** *Flatbush Ave. and Empire Blvd. Map 23, D3, 19. ☎718-965-6505. Open Th-F 1-4pm, Sa-Su and holidays 12pm-5pm July-Aug. also open W 1-4pm. Free.* ***Zoo:*** *Flatbush Ave., at Empire Blvd. Map 23, C3, 18. ☎718-399-7339. Open M-F 10am-5pm, Sa-Su 10am-5:30pm. $2.50, seniors $1.25, children 50¢. No bikes or in-line skates. Handicapped accessible.*

Frederick Law Olmsted and Calvert Vaux designed this 526-acre park in the mid-1800s and supposedly liked it better than their Manhattan project, Central Park. Today, sunbathers and ballplayers alike congregate on **Long Meadow** (Map 23, C3). **Prospect Lake** (Map 23, C5), south of the meadow, and **Lookout Hill** (Map 23, C4) both offer peaceful views of glacial pools. The 80 ft. high **Soldiers and Sailors Arch** in the middle of Grand Army Plaza, built in the 1890s to commemorate the North's Civil War victory, marks one of the site entrances. Those who climb to its top are rewarded with stunning views of the park. The bronze Victory Quadriga atop the arch, sporting a central female flanked by two winged figures, symbolizes the victorious Union. **Celebrate Brooklyn** summer concerts are held at the **Bandshell** (Map 23, B3, 17) in the northwestern corner of the park—enter at Prospect Park W and 9th St.

Prospect Park also contains a children's museum and a zoo. **Leffert's Homestead,** a preserved Dutch-style farmhouse built between 1777 and 1783 and moved from its original location on Flatbush Ave. and Maple St. in 1918, houses the **Children's Historic House Museum** and gives children the chance to play with toys from various cultures (Dutch, African-American, Native American). Nearby is a **Carousel** (Map 23, D3, 20). The **Prospect Park Wildlife Center/Zoo's** exotic fauna include a pair of capybaras, a red panda, and a cotton-top tamarin. The sea lions get fed at 11:30am, 2, and 4pm.

BROOKLYN BOTANIC GARDEN

1000 Washington Ave.; other entrances on Eastern Pkwy. and on Flatbush Ave. Subway: Q, S to Prospect Park; 1, 2 to Eastern Pkwy. Map 23, D3. ☎718-623-7000; Events Hotline ☎718-623-7333; www.bbg.org. Open Apr.-Sept. Tu-F 8am-6pm, Sa-Su 10am-6pm; Oct.-Mar. Tu-F 8am-4:30pm, Sa-Su 10am-4:30pm. $5, students and seniors $3, under 16 free, groups free. Tu free all day and Sa 10am-noon; seniors free every F.

from the road

I Believe I Can Bike

When I worked in Union Square last fall, my commute was a 50min., 10 mi. ride each way from my apartment in South Bronx. It was a simple matter of economics. My environmentally friendly daily ride saved me from the slow $1.50 burn of the subway.

Bike commuters know that each city offers unique challenges (San Francisco has the hills, Vancouver has the weather). In NYC, a city of eight million inhabitants, thousands of additional commuters converge on one tiny, horn-honking, brake-slamming traffic hell of an island. Bikes are vehicles, and New York state law requires that we share the road. Along with the city's 100,000 daily bike commuters, I join the freewheelin', mad-dashin' bicycle couriers and the regular food delivery guys. The latter can often be found lackadaisically biking the wrong way on Manhattan's busiest avenues, restaurant aprons flapping in the breeze.

I've stopped seeing the ordinary sights of the city. Now they're all just obstacles. And there are so many, and they are so varied. An Upper East Sider climbing out of her cab flings the door open and becomes a potentially lethal

This 52-acre fairyland was founded in 1910 by the Brooklyn Institute of Art and Sciences on a reclaimed waste dump. The artificial scenery seems so convincingly authentic that many water birds flock to the site. Favorite spots for children include the Discovery Garden, the discovery center in the Steinhardt Conservatory, the Fragran Garden with mint, lemon, violet, and other aromas, and the Japanese Hill-and-Pond Garden that ducks, turtles, koi, and heron call home for most of the year. The more formal **Cranford Rose Garden** crams in over 150 blooming varieties of roses into archways, bushes, and shrubbery. Every spring, visitors can take part in the **Sakura Matsuri** (Japanese cherry blossom festival) at the Cherry Walk and Cherry Esplanade. The **Shakespeare Garden** displays 80 plants mentioned in the Bard's works. The various pavilions of the **Steinhardt Conservatory** are climate-controlled to show desert, tropical, and other flora. Just outside of the conservatory, 100 varieties of tropical water-lilies and the sacred lotus grace the **Lily Pool Terrace** in summer; the **Annual Border's** rainbow assortment of flowering annuals blooms nearby.

BROOKLYN PUBLIC LIBRARY

Corner of Eastern Pkwy. and Flatbush Ave. Subway: F, M, N, R to Fourth Ave./9th St. ☎ 718-230-2100; www.brooklynpubliclibrary.org. Map 23, C2. Open M-Th 9am-8pm, F-Sa 9am-6pm, Su 1-5pm; closed Su mid-June to mid-Sept.

The striking Art Deco main branch of the Brooklyn Public Library stands majestically on Grand Army Plaza. Its front doors are flanked by two great pillars with gold engravings and the words 'Here are enshrined the longing of great hearts.' The library has spawned 53 branches and contains 1,600,000 volumes. Changing exhibitions are on the second floor.

BEDFORD-STUYVESANT

Bounded by Bedford Ave. on the west, Atlantic Ave. on the south, Broadway on the east, and Flushing Ave. on the north. Subway: C, S to Franklin Ave.; A, C to Nostrand Ave.; C to Kingston-Throop Ave. Map 20.

Although less well-known than Harlem, Bed-Stuy is New York City's oldest and largest African-American community. It's not a heavily touristed part of town, in part because it is not always a very safe neighborhood after dark. If you walk its streets during the day, however, you will be treated to some of the city's finest brownstones, especially in the southernmost part of the neighborhood, on Macon, MacDonough, Decatur, Bainbridge, and Chauncey St.

WEEKSVILLE

1968 Bergen St., between Buffalo and Rochester Ave. Subway: A, C to Utica Ave., walk 4 blocks south to Bergen St. and make left; 3, 4 to Utica Ave./Eastern Pkwy., walk 8 blocks north to Bergen St. and make a right. ☎ 718-756-5250; www.weeksvillesociety.org. Open Tu-Sa 10am-4:30pm, Su noon-6pm. $5, seniors and children under 18 $3.

A 19th-century African-American community, Weeksville dates back to the 1830s. Home to the first African-American female physician in the state and the first African-American police officer in the city, Weeksville was the center of African-American life in New York. Today, four buildings remain from its heyday and are the centerpiece of one of New York's most interesting cultural artifacts. Check out the excellent website for history, information, and a listing of educational programs held at Weeksville.

COBBLE HILL, CARROLL GARDENS, AND RED HOOK

Bounded together by the water, on the south and west, Hoyt St. on the east, and Atlantic Ave. on the north. Subway: F, G to Bergen St./Smith St., Carroll Gardens, Smith St.-9th St. Map 24.

Just south of Atlantic Avenue lies **Cobble Hill,** whose gorgeous brownstone-lined sidestreets segue into **Carroll Gardens. Smith Street** has recently become packed with some of the city's best new restaurants and bars. **Red Hook,** on the waterfront, was separated from the other two neighborhoods by the construction of the Brooklyn-Queens Expressway. After some shaky years, Red Hook is now NYC's hottest new neighborhood.

FLATBUSH

Bounded by Coney Island Ave. on the west, Ave. H on the south, Nostrand Ave. on the east, and Parkside Ave. on the north. Subway: Q to Church Ave./E. 18th St., Newkirk Ave.; 2, 5 to Church Ave./Nostrand Ave., Flatbush Ave.-Brooklyn College. Map 20.

Transformed by the introduction of the trolley in the late 19th century, Flatbush grew from a small town into a stomping ground for the well-to-do. You can wander around Argyle St. and Ditmas Ave. to see some of their old mansions and go on the annual house tour in April

block; MTA buses leave brown fogs of exhaust hanging in the air for me to accidentally suck in; potholes sneak up on my front wheel and swell into small canyons.

Every 10 blocks, I have to stop and wait for the light to change. Central Park is no better. There's something humbling about being passed by rows of aerodynamically crouched in-line speedskaters and spandexed bike racers, and then contending with weekend hordes of kids leisurely blocking the path with their scooters.

On my bike, still, I'm free—flying down Ocean Pkwy. toward Coney Island, musing about mausoleums in Woodlawn cemetery, or making the George Washington Bridge from Battery Park City in 45min. on the West Side Hwy. At 7pm on the last Friday night of every month, the international phenomenon of Critical Mass occurs in Union Square. From there, the joyful anarchy of hundreds of congregated bikers will take the group anywhere from the Brooklyn Bridge to Columbus Circle and back.

For more info about biking in NYC, try contacting Transportation Alternatives (www.transalt.org) for its collection of bike path maps of all the boroughs; Times Up (www.timesup.org) for its bike events, including Critical Mass; Recycle-a-bike (www.recycleabicycle.org) for free bike-fixing clinics and cheap used bikes; or Five Borough Bicycle Club (www.5bbc.org)—if you're itching to pull on the spandex shorts.

—Mandy Hu, 2003

(☎718-859-4868). In the first half of the 20th century, the neighborhood was home to the beloved Brooklyn Dodgers, who played in Ebbets Field. The stadium was demolished when owner Walter O'Malley moved the club to Los Angeles; a housing complex now stands in its stead. The neighborhood's extant highlight is Erasmus Hall Academy, 911 Flatbush Ave., at Church Ave., the second-oldest high school in North America (Map 20, C4, 3). Alumni include Neil Diamond, Barbara Streisand, and Barry Manilow. It was constructed in 1787 with the participation of Aaron Burr, John Jay, and Alexander Hamilton. No brick can be moved from the school's central building or, according to an antiquated charter, a neighboring Dutch Reform Church will repossess it. Once a predominantly Jewish immigrant neighborhood, Flatbush is now home to significant Jamaican and West Indian populations. On summer days, reggae music and exotic fruit stands fill major thoroughfares like Nostrand and Church Ave. At the south of the neighborhood lies Brooklyn College, the first public co-ed liberal arts college in NYC, and the Brooklyn Center for the Performing Arts (☎718-951-4000).

SUNSET PARK AND GREENWOOD CEMETERY

Bounded by the water on the west, 65th St. on the south, Eighth Ave. and Greenwood Cemetery on the east, and the Prospect Expwy. on the north. Subway: M, N, R to 25th St.; M, N, R, W to 36th St.; N, R to 45th St., 53rd St., 59th St.

Home to a melange of ethnic groups, most notably Latinos and Chinese, Sunset Park is the embodiment of the melting pot; lunch trucks sell Mexican food in the heart of Brooklyn's Chinatown. Avid consumers flock to the area's Fifth Ave., which is lined with discount stores and hybrid restaurants. Just to the northeast of the neighborhood is **Greenwood Cemetery,** Fifth Ave. and 25th St. Laid out over various hills (some of which offer views all the way to Manhattan and beyond), and with lakes and a chapel, Greenwood is as peaceful as the name suggests. On a clear day, Lady Liberty is visible from the elaborate Gothic Revival entrance on 25th St. This vast (478-acre), hilly kingdom of ornate mausoleums and tombstones makes for a pleasant, if morbid, walk. Samuel Morse, Horace Greeley, and William "Boss" Tweed slumber at this Victorian Necropolis, as do Leonard Bernstein and Mae West: come up and see her sometime. (Open daily 8am-4pm. 2hr. tours Su 1pm. $6.)

BENSONHURST AND BOROUGH PARK

Bensonhurst bounded by 26th St. on the southeast, 61st St. on the northeast, 14th Ave. on the northwest, and Gravesend Bay on the southwest. Subway: N to 18th Ave./64th St. Borough Park is north of Bensonhurst. Map 20.

Home to the *Honeymooners*, *Jungle Fever*, and *Welcome Back, Kotter*, Bensonhurst is one of the most famous neighborhoods of Brooklyn, thanks to the silver screen. 18th Ave., Cristofor Colombo Blvd., in southern Brooklyn, is the authentic Italian neighborhood that you couldn't find in Manhattan's Little Italy. Avid shoppers will find extremely cheap clothes here. The neighborhood centered around Stillwell and Park Ave., has recently seen an influx of Russians from Brighton Beach. Borough Park is the largest Hasidic Jewish neighborhood in Brooklyn. In contrast to the more visible Crown Heights Lubavitchers, the Bobovers of Borough Park prefer to maintain an insular community. As in the other Hasidic neighborhoods of Brooklyn, visitors will feel more welcome if they are dressed conservatively.

BAY RIDGE

**Bounded by Belt Pkwy. on the west, 101st St. on the south, Fort Hamilton Pkwy. on the east, 65th St. on the north. Subway: R to Bay Ridge Ave., 77th St., 86th St., Bay Ridge-95th St. Map 20.*

Predominantly Italian **Bay Ridge,** scene of John Travolta's strutting in the classic *Saturday Night Fever*, is chock full of Italian bakeries, pizza joints, rowdy youths, and discount stores, especially around 17th Ave. (Sadly, the 2001 Odyssey disco is no longer operational.) The neighborhood centers around 86th St.; nearby Shore Rd. is lined with mansions overlooking New York Harbor. The majestic, 4260 ft. long **Verrazano-Narrows Bridge,** Staten Island's only connection by automobile to the other boroughs, was the world's longest suspension bridge when it opened in 1964. It is still greatly admired as a feat of engineering.

CONEY ISLAND AND BRIGHTON BEACH

Subway: F, W to Coney Island-Stillwell Ave.; F, Q to W. 8th St.-NY Aquarium; Q to Ocean Pkwy., Brighton Beach. Map 20, B6-7.

Coney Island is Brooklyn straight out of the 1940s and 50s. Rides such as the Parachute Jump, the Wonder Wheel, and the Cyclone are legendary in these parts. Tourists beware: Coney Island is not a very safe place after dark.

Beyond Ocean Pkwy., east of Coney Island, lies **Brighton Beach,** or "Little Odessa by the Sea," an area populated heavily by Eastern European immigrants and written about in Neil Simon's *Brighton Beach Memoirs*. By day it is home to Eastern-European delis, grocery stores, and shops; at night, Russian music, from disco to folk, livens up the neighborhood. Manhattan Beach lies on the island's east coast.

CONEY ISLAND

Entrance: 834 Surf Ave., at W. 10th St. Map 20, B6, 10. ☎ 718-372-5159; www.coneyisland-usa.com. Open daily mid-June to Sept. noon-midnight; Easter weekend to mid-June F-Su noon-midnight. Park Admission $21.99 with rides on the Cyclone and $17.99 without the Cyclone. Weekends free F shuttle from Coney Island subway stop.

Coney Island is half theme park, half immersion in American nostalgia. Coney Island has adorned Brooklyn's south shore for over a century, undergoing several transformations. Hoping to make the somewhat shady resort into a "family place," George Tilyou built an amusement park (Steeplechase Park) that charged an entrance fee and offered exciting mechanical rides. Attendance at Coney Island in 1904 averaged 90,000 people per day. Coney Island barely survived the Depression and began a serious decline in the 1940s. The amusement park is still alive and well but holds on to its image from the early twentieth century.

This is a good place for kids if they're bored of brownstones. Take a 100-second-long, rickety, screaming whirl on the legendary **Cyclone,** built in 1927. The National Register has designated it a historic place, and couples have been married on it. The **Wonder Wheel,** at 150 ft., was the world's tallest when it was built. (In Deno's, on Surf Ave. $3.50.) **The Ghost Hall** is as scary as the *Munsters*, but it's pure Coney Island camp. (12th St., off Bowery. $3.50.) For the extra small, **Deno's,** right next to Astroland, has kiddie-sized rides like the Sea Serpent roller coaster ($2 per ride, $15 for 10). The real spirit of Coney Island, however, is at the **Coney Island Circus Sideshow,** which has sword swallowers, snake charmers, jugglers, and "freaks." (1208 Surf Ave., at 12th St. Open F 2-10pm, Sa-Su 1pm-midnight. $3, children $2.) Don't miss the **Mermaid Parade** in June, complete with floats and antique cars.

KEYSPAN PARK

On the south side of Surf Ave., between W. 17th and W. 19th St. Map 20, B4, 11. Subway: F, Q, W to Coney Island-Stillwell Ave. ☎ 718-449-TIXS/8497. Tickets $6-10.

After 43 years, baseball is back in Brooklyn. The newly erected stadium for the minor league Brooklyn Cyclones (the Class A affiliate of the Mets), Keyspan Park connects with other relics of yesteryear: ruins of Coney Island rides recall the days when the carnival grounds extended farther west. One may still see some half-sunk rusted cars from the deceased Thunderbolt coaster and the tall, worn skeleton of the Parachute Jump.

NEW YORK AQUARIUM

At Surf and W. 8th St. Subway: F, Q to W. 8th St.-NY Aquarium. Map 20, C6, 12. ☎ 718-265-3474. Open M-F 10am-6pm, Sa-Su and holidays 10am-7pm. $11, seniors and ages 2-12 $7. No bikes, in-line skates or pets allowed. Handicapped-accessible.

Home to the first beluga whale born in captivity, the aquarium has all the expected marine inhabitants from penguins and piranhas to sharks and jellyfish—and then some. Check out the coneys, the fish that gave Coney Island its name. An outdoor theater features wonderful performances by California sea lions. You can also participate in guided feedings of sharks, sea otters, walruses, and penguins.

QUEENS

Less a borough of famous sights or museums, Queens is notable primarily for its ethnic communities. Unlike Brooklyn, which contains many distinctive neighborhoods but remains united as a whole, Queens is more a collection of independent towns. According to the 2000 Census, Queens County is the most ethnically diverse county in the United States.

Resembling neither the orderly grid of Upper Manhattan nor the haphazard angles of Greenwich Village, Queens' streets originated from a mixed bag of urban planning techniques and therefore follow a logical—but extremely complicated—system. Streets generally run north-south and are numbered from west to east, from 1st St. in Astoria to 271st St. in Glen Oaks. Avenues run perpendicular to streets and are numbered from north to south, from Second Ave. to 165th Ave. The address of an establishment or residence often tells you the closest cross-street (for example, 45-07 32nd Ave. is near the intersection with 45th St.). The challenging parts of Queens's geography are its numbered drives, roads, and places set randomly amid the streets and avenues. Those exploring Queens in detail should pick up the large foldout Queens **bus map,** available at any subway station or on any bus within the borough. **Neighborhoods are listed from west to east.**

ASTORIA AND LONG ISLAND CITY

Astoria is located in the northwestern corner of Queens, across the river from Manhattan. Long Island City is located southwest of Astoria. Subway: All N and W stops between 36th Ave. and Astoria Ditmars Blvd. G, R, V to 36th St. or Steinway St. Map 26.

Astoria is New York's largest Greek neighborhood. **30th Avenue** is the major thoroughfare, while the blocks surrounding the **Ditmars Boulevard** subway stop are known as "Little Athens." Avid shoppers head east on **Broadway** to **Steinway Street.**

Mostly industrial **Long Island City,** at almost the same latitude as Roosevelt Island, has experienced a resurgence as Queens's artistic center—a revival anchored by **P.S.1** (p. 142) and the temporary coming of the **MoMA** (p. 130). Stretches on **Vernon Blvd.** have pleasant boardwalk sections along the water that end near the **Socrates Sculpture Park** (see below).

THE STEINWAY PIANO FACTORY

1 Steinway Pl., at 19th Rd. and 77th St. Subway: N, W to Ditmars Blvd. Walk 15 blocks south on Ditmars Blvd., 3 blocks east on Hazen St., turn south onto 19th Rd. Map 26, 8. ☎ 718-721-2600. Tours every other Th; call for info.

The Steinway company has manufactured its world-famous pianos here ever since it moved from its original Varick St. location in the Village during the 1860s. The area became a company town, complete with parks and post offices for employees. The 12,000 parts of a typical Steinway include a 340 lb. plate of cast iron, 40,000 lb. of string tension, and tiny bits of Brazilian deer skin. Over 95% of piano performances in the US are played on Steinway grands. The tour takes you through the process of building one of Steinway's grand pianos, weighing anywhere from 750-1365 lb.

THE SOCRATES SCULPTURE PARK

At the end of Broadway, across the Vernon Blvd. intersection. Subway: N, W to Broadway. Map 26, 1. ☎ 718-956-1819. Open daily 10am-dusk. Free.

Socrates Sculpture Park was an abandoned riverside landfill and illegal dumpsite until 1986 when a coalition of artists and community members, led by Mark di Suvero, transformed it into an open studio and exhibition space for artists and a neighborhood park for local residents. Participate in the artistic greatness by taking a free creative workshop or stopping by the annual Summer Solstice Celebration. Enjoy the great view of the Midtown skyline from the adjacent waterfront.

KAUFMAN-ASTORIA STUDIOS

34-12 36th St., corner of 35th St. and 35th Ave. Subway: G, R, V to 36th St. Map 26, 16.

The US's largest studio outside of Los Angeles sits on a 13-acre plot with eight sound stages. Paramount Pictures used these facilities to make such films as *Scent of a Woman* and *The Secret of My Success*. Television's *The Cosby Show* and *Sesame Street* were taped here as well. The studios are also home to Lifetime Television for Women and a 14-screen movie theater. To get to Sesame Street, exit the 36th Ave. station, walk one block to 35th Ave. and down to 35th St. The studios are closed to the public, but the **American Museum of the Moving Image** (p. 134) is next door.

CITICORP BUILDING

One Court Sq., at Jackson Ave. Subway: E, V to 23 St.-Ely Ave.; G to 21 St. Map 26, 19.

This 48-story structure in blue glass is the tallest New York building outside of Manhattan. Bankers and other office workers mill around the plaza at lunchtime, an incongruous companion to its industrial/artsy neighbors.

ELMHURST AND CORONA

Elmhurst: Subway: G, R, V to Elmhurst Ave. or Grand Ave./Newtown. Corona: Subway: 7 to 103rd St.-Corona Plaza, 111th St. Map 26.

Elmhurst is arguably the most ethnically diverse section of the most multicultural borough, with immigrants from more than 100 countries calling it home. The corner of Broadway and Whitney Ave. holds a plethora of great ethnic restaurants (see **Food,** p. 187). Now a largely Hispanic part of town, Corona was the site of Archie Bunker's house in *All in the Family*. Besides nearby **Flushing Meadows-Corona Park,** the main attraction of the area is the **Lemon Ice King of Corona** (p. 189). Jazz fans can visit **Louis Armstrong's House,** 34-56 107th St. (☎ 212-997-3670). **Malcolm X** lived at 23-11 97th St., in nearby East Elmhurst, from 1954 until his death in 1965.

Long Island City Art

Long before major galleries relocated here, a few quirky galleries and outdoor art spaces blazed the trail to Long Island City. Take the 7 train to 45 Rd.-Courthouse Sq., or the E, V to 23 St.-Ely Ave., and take a look around.

1. **P.S.1.** (p. 142) houses cutting-edge art in a converted high school.
2. Watch NYC's best graffiti artists at work, legally, on the outside of the **Phun Phactory** garments factory (☎718-204-7088).
3. See rotating installations of multimedia art at the **New York Center for Media Arts** (☎718-472-9414).
4. Tired of art? Watch bankers emerge from the **CitiCorp Building** (p. 113).
5. Holograms by appointment at the **Holocenter** (p. 147).
6. **The MoMA** (p. 130) lures with its big-name collection.

FOREST HILLS AND FOREST PARK

Subway: E, F, G, R, V to Forest Hills-71st Ave. Map 25, C2. ***Forest Park*** *☎718-235-4100, events info ☎718-520-5941, golf ☎718-296-0999. Subway: J, Z to Woodhaven Blvd. Map 25, C3. Open daily 6am-9pm.*

Forest Hills is an upscale, residential part of town, with many private streets and suburban-style houses (two-car garages!). It's pleasant to walk around, although there aren't too many specific attractions. To the south stands **Forest Park,** a densely wooded area with miles of park trails, a bandshell, a golf course, a carousel ($1), baseball diamonds, tennis courts, and horseback riding (p. 235).

FLUSHING MEADOWS-CORONA PARK

Subway: 7 to 111th St. or Willets Point-Shea Stadium. Map 27, D3.

From the Van Wyck Expwy., motorists gaze upon the ruins of a more glamorous past. Rusting towers and dilapidated buildings punctuate the serene trees of Flushing Meadows-Corona Park, home to the 1939 and 1964 World's Fairs. The 1255-acre swamp, nestled between Corona and Flushing, was a huge rubbish dump until city planners decided to turn the area into fairgrounds. The remnants from the first fair are long gone, and the monuments from the second are fast deteriorating. Behind the trees, however, lie several excellent attractions, sculptured gardens, and one or two well-kept monuments. The grounds are worth a visit, not only for these hidden gems, but for the old steel and concrete dinosaurs from the 1964 festivities. The park also has 17 baseball diamonds and vast stretches of open grass, attracting many visitors on sunny weekends.

NEW YORK HALL OF SCIENCE

47-01 111th St., at 48th Ave. Subway: 7 to 111th St. Map 27, C3, 18. ☎718-699-0005; www.nyscience.org. Open July-Aug. Tu-Su 9:30am-5pm; Sept.-June Tu-W 9:30am-2pm, Th-Su 9:30am-5pm. $7.50, seniors and under 17 $5, under 4 free. Free Sept.-June Tu and F 2-5pm.

This aging concrete hall, built in 1964, is currently getting a city-sponsored face-lift that will eventually create a 5500 sq. ft. addition and will refurbish the two rusty rockets flanking the museum. Although largely oriented toward children, this museum's 225 hands-on displays will keep visitors of all ages occupied. 2003 exhibits included displays on "Marvelous Molecules" and AIDS.

THE UNISPHERE

In front of the Arthur Ashe Stadium. Subway: 7 to Willets Point-Shea Stadium. Map 27, D3, 19.

One of the iconic centerpieces of the World's Fair, this huge, stainless-steel globe tilts in retro-futuristic glory over a fountain. Constructed by the steel industry for the 1964 World's Fair, the 700-ton Unisphere dramatically illustrates "man's aspirations toward Peace through mutual understanding and symboliz[es] his achievements in an expanding universe." The globe's three rings represent the orbits of the first communications satellite and the first American and Russian astronauts to orbit Earth.

NEW YORK STATE PAVILION

In Flushing Meadows Park. Subway: 7 to Willets Point-Shea Stadium. Map 27, D4, 23.

A true eyesore, with a stadium encircled by a mass of concrete fins and stringy wire. The two adjacent towers by architect Philip Johnson formed the original center of the 1964 World's Fair. Part of the pavilion is now the **Queens Theater in the Park** (p. 231). South of the Pavilion, across the expressway overpass and behind the Planet of the Apes Fountain, a restored **Coney Island carousel** pipes out manic chipmunk tunes. Remnants of the Pavilion's World's Fair heyday include a huge map of New York on the ground (now overgrown with weeds). Proposals for the Pavilion's future include a possible Air & Space Museum.

SHEA STADIUM

Subway: 7 to Willets Point-Shea Stadium. Map 27, C1, 4. ☎718-507-8499.

When the Brooklyn Dodgers were looking for new digs, Robert Moses offered team owner Walter O'Malley a chance to build a new stadium on some marshland in northeastern Queens. O'Malley held out for a new home in Brooklyn that never came and eventually moved the team to Los Angeles in 1957. When Manhattan's New York Giants left for the West Coast in that same year, New York was stuck with only the inaccessible and boringly successful Yankees. Five years later, William Shea united the blue of the Dodgers and the orange of the Giants and brought the New York Metropolitan Baseball Club to Queens. Although the 1962 Mets set new standards for futility, the team captured the hearts of New Yorkers from all five boroughs. In 1964, the Mets moved to Shea Stadium, which in later years would host Jets games, Beatles concerts, and papal masses. In 1969, the 'Amazin' Mets' captured their first world championship.

OTHER SIGHTS

While in the park, you can try your hand at a full course of par 3 **pitch 'n' putt golf.** (Map 27, C3. ☎718-271-8182. Open daily 8am-10pm. Greens fee Sa-Su $11-13.50, M-F $10-12.50. Club rental $1 each.) In the southern part of the park, **Meadow Lake** (Map 27, C3) offers paddle- and row-boating, while **Willow Lake Nature Area** (Map 27, D2) hosts free tours. Nearby, the **USTA National Tennis Center** (Map 27, D2, 17) and **Arthur Ashe Stadium** (☎718-760-6200) host the US Open.

The Queens Wildlife Center/Zoo, 53-51 111th St., near 53rd Ave., features animals from North America and beyond. Don't miss the bison and sea lions. Sheep, goats, cows, and other cuddly creatures frolic in the petting zoo. (☎718-271-1500. Open Apr.-Oct. M-F 10am-5pm, Sa-Su 10am-5:30pm; Nov.-Mar. daily 10am-4:30pm. $2.50, seniors $1.25, under 12 50¢). The **Queens Museum of Art** (☎718-592-9700) is located in the north wing of the New York City Building, next to the Unisphere. It contains the *Panorama of the City of New York*, the world's largest scale model of an urban area; one inch corresponds to 100 ft. of New York. The 1hr. tour gives an interesting history of the city and its major landmarks (Open W-F 10am-5pm, Sa-Su noon-5pm. Suggested donation: $5, students $2.50, seniors and children $2).

FLUSHING

Subway: 7 to Flushing-Main St. Map 27.

Flushing—whose name is a corruption of Vlissingen, the Dutch name for the village—was founded in 1654. **Main Street** and **Roosevelt Avenue** form the commercial hub of the neighborhood. Today, many signs around those streets are in Korean or Chinese characters, and ducks and dumplings adorn shop windows.

THE KINGSLAND HOMESTEAD

143-35 37th Ave. Subway: 7 to Flushing-Main St. Map 27, G1, 3. ☎718-939-0647; www.preserve.org/queens. Open Tu and Sa-Su 2:30-4:30pm. Historical Society open by appointment M-F 9:30am-5pm.

Built in 1775 and moved to its current location in 1968, the Homestead was designed in the Long Island half-house form. It holds a permanent collection of antique china and memorabilia that belonged to early trader Captain Joseph King, as well as a collection of antique dolls. A fully furnished "Victorian Room" depicts the typical middle-class furnishings of the time. As home of the **Queens Historical Society,** the Homestead annually displays three or four temporary exhibits focusing on aspects of the borough's history.

QUEENS BOTANICAL GARDEN

43-50 Main St., between Cherry Ave. and Dahlia Ave. Subway: 7 to Flushing-Main St. Walk 10min. south from the Flushing-Main St. 7 station or take the Q44 bus toward Jamaica. Map 27, F3, 20. ☎718-886-3800. Open Apr.-Oct. Tu-F 8am-6pm, Sa-Su 8am-7pm; Nov.-Mar. 8am-4:30pm. Free. Wheelchair-accessible.

An exhibition for the 1939 World's Fair in nearby Flushing Meadows-Corona Park (see p. 114), the garden had to move when the park was redesigned for the 1964 World's Fair. At its present site it boasts a 5000-bush rose garden, a 23 acre arboretum, more than nine acres of "theme gardens," and a new home compost demonstration site. Weekend wedding parties compete for gazebos and fountains as backdrops for commemorative photos. Check out their plant shop and subscribe to the "Garden Helper," a monthly newsletter on gardening.

FLUSHING TOWN HALL

137-35 Northern Blvd. Subway: 7 to Flushing-Main St. Map 27, F1. ☎718-463-7700; www.flushingtownhall.org. Concert tickets $20, students and seniors $15. Free.

The 1862 building now functions as a gallery and a performing space, as well as housing the **Flushing Council of Culture and the Arts.** Local art and historical exhibitions await inside. A small permanent exhibit on jazz in Queens includes original postcards and letters written by Louis Armstrong. Pick up the free **Queens Jazz Trail** map for details of how to get to the former homes of Dizzy Gillespie, Ella Fitzgerald, and ol' Satchmo himself, or try the tour (select Saturdays at 10 am). Live jazz and classical concerts take place on occasional Friday nights and Sunday afternoons—call for a schedule.

BOWNE HOUSE

37-01 Bowne St. Subway: 7 to Flushing-Main St. Map 27, G1, 2. ☎718-359-0528. Open Tu and Sa-Su 2:30-4:30pm. $2, seniors and under 14 $1.The house is currently undergoing major renovations, so call on F 9am-5pm if you want to go inside.

This 1661 two-story house filled with interesting antiques is New York City's oldest remaining residence. John Bowne defied Dutch governor Peter Stuyvesant's 1657 ban on Quaker meetings here, and was exiled for his efforts.

JAMAICA

Subway: E, J, Z to Jamaica Center. Map 25, D3.

Jamaica's main strip is the section of **Jamaica Avenue** stretching from 150th to 168th St. Restaurants selling succulent Jamaican beef patties, stores peddling African clothing and braids, and mobs of local bargain-hunters crowd the brick-lined **pedestrian mall** (Map 25, D3) on 165th St. Saint Albans is best explored by a walk down **Linden Boulevard.** West Indian culture proliferates on both sides of **Hillside Avenue** in the area's eastern part.

KING MANOR MUSEUM

At Jamaica Ave. and 153rd St. Map 25, D3, 6.

Built in 1750, **King Manor Museum** was from 1805 to 1827 the residence of Rufus King—early abolitionist, framer and signer of the Constitution, senator for New York, Presidential candidate, and ambassador to Great Britain. The house, set in 11-acre **King Park,** combines Georgian and Federal architectural styles. The period rooms downstairs give a glimpse of 19th-century life. (☎ 718-206-0545. Open Mar.-Dec. Th-F noon-1:30pm, Sa-Su 1-4:30pm. Admission, with guided tours only: $5, students and seniors $2, families $12.)

OTHER SIGHTS

The Gothic Revival **Grace Church,** 155-03 Jamaica Ave. is one of Queens' oldest churches (Map 25, D3, 9; Open daily 11am-1pm). Rufus King is buried in the graveyard. The elaborate Moorish facade of the **Tabernacle of Prayer,** 165-11 Jamaica Ave., recalls the building's past as the Loews Valencia movie theater (Map 25, D3, 7).

THE ROCKAWAYS

Subway: Take the A train to the end of the line. Map 25, A6-E6.

THE JAMAICA BAY WILDLIFE REFUGE

On Broad Channel, Jamaica Bay. Subway: A, S to Broad Channel. You can also take the Triboro Q53 bus (☎ 718-335-1000) or the Green Bus Lines Q21 (☎ 718-995-4700) from Rockaway Park-Beach 116 St. to the refuge entrance; $1-1.50, Metrocards accepted. Map 25, D5. ☎ 718-318-4340. Park open daily dawn to dusk. Visitors/Nature Center open daily 8:30am-5pm. Free, but pick up map and permit at Visitors Center.

At 9000 acres, the Jamaica Bay Wildlife Refuge is roughly the size of Manhattan and 10 times larger than Flushing Meadows-Corona Park. Nationally acclaimed, the Refuge harbors more than 325 species of birds and small animals, including the American oyster-catcher and the black-bellied plover. Apparently, it's one of the most popular resting spots for birds on their way down South during migration. Environmental slide shows and ranger-led walks are held on weekends.

ROCKAWAY BEACH

From Beach 3rd St. in Far Rockaway to Beach 149th St. in the west. Subway: A (marked "Far Rockaway") to all stops between Beach 36th St. and Beach 67th St. or A (marked "Rockaways") or A, S to all stops between Beach 90 St. and Rockaway Park-Beach 116 St. Map 25, D6. ☎ 718-318-4000. Lifeguards Memorial Day to Labor Day.

Immortalized by the Ramones in one of their pop-punk tributes, the 10 mi. long public beach is lined by a **boardwalk.** It's often pleasantly free of crowds, and there are no tacky souvenir stalls.

FIRST PRESBYTERIAN CHURCH

1324 Beach 12th St., at Central Ave. Subway: A to Far Rockaway-Mott Ave. ☎ 718-327-2440.

Railroad tycoon Russell Sage donated the money to build this church, noted for its magnificently enormous Louis Tiffany stained glass window and huge cemetery.

JACOB RIIS PARK

Just west of Rockaway Beach, separated from it by a huge chain-link fence. Subway: A (marked "Rockaways") or S; stop at Rockaway Park-Beach 116th St., then transfer to Green Bus Lines Q22 (☎718-995-4700) westward; $1-1.50, Metrocards accepted. Map 25, C6. ☎718-318-4300. Open 6am-midnight.

Part of the 26,000 acre Gateway National Recreation Area that extends into Brooklyn, Staten Island, and New Jersey, the park was named for Jacob Riis, a photojournalist and activist. In the early 1900s, he persuaded the city to turn this overgrown beach into a public park. Today, the area is lined with its own gorgeous beach and boardwalk, as well as basketball and handball courts and a golf course. West of the entrance, nature trails run through the remnants of Fort Tilden, a former U.S. Army base. A former nude beach is at the eastern end; in the 1980s the beach decided to "clean up its act" and now only allows topless sunbathing.

THE BRONX

The borough takes its name from Jonas Bronck, the European who settled in the area with his family in 1639. Until the turn of the 19th century, the area consisted largely of cottages, farmlands, and wild marshes. In the 1840s, the swelling tide of immigration brought scores of Italian and Irish settlers to the borough. Today, half of the borough's residents identify themselves as Hispanic; the Bronx is the geographical heart of New York's large Dominican community. The Bronx will give any visitor insight into the dynamics of burgeoning urban life, as well as a peek at numerous attractions. **In the coverage below, neighborhoods are arranged from south to north.**

SOUTH BRONX

Thirty fires a night raged here during the 1970s. Landlords torched buildings to collect insurance, and tenants burned down their own houses to collect welfare. When Ronald Reagan visited, he compared the South Bronx to a bombed-out London after the Battle of Britain. Thanks to a huge influx of government funds and a stronger economy, the South Bronx and the borough as a whole have taken steps away from poverty and violence. Still, for the most part, the South Bronx is not a traditional tourist destination and **is not a safe place to walk around, especially at night.**

YANKEE STADIUM

E. 161st St., at River Ave. Subway: 4, B, D to 161st St. Station right outside stadium. Map 28, A5, 26. ☎718-579-4531. Tours daily at noon. Admission $10, 14 and under and seniors $5. More expansive (and expensive) tours available. Call for details. No tours when there is a home day game or during the post season.

Babe Ruth's success as a hitter inspired the construction of the Yankees' own ballpark in 1923, and to this day "The House That Ruth Built" remains one of the Bronx's main attractions. Even though his team plays in this landmark of professional sports, George Steinbrenner has made a living threatening to move the Yankees to New Jersey. Apparently, Derek Jeter is a worthier investment than the South Bronx.

ART AND ANTIQUE MARKET

Subway: 6 to Third Ave.-138th St.

Antique roadshow buffs looking for a good deal might consider taking a look in the northeastern Bronx on Bruckner Blvd., between Alexander and Willis St.

BRONX PARK

Perhaps the highlight of the Bronx is this park featuring both the Bronx Zoo and New York Botanical Garden, both the best of their kind in the city.

BRONX ZOO

Entrances on Bronx Park S., Southern Blvd., E. Fordham Rd., and the Bronx River Pkwy. Subway: 2, 5 to West Farms Sq.-E. Tremont Ave. Follow Boston Rd. for 3 blocks until the Bronx Park S. gate. Bus: Bx9, Bx12, Bx19, Bx22, and Q44 pass various entrances to the zoo. Liberty Lines bus leaves from Madison Ave. in Midtown for the Bronxdale entrance to the zoo ($3 each way); ☎ 718-652-8400 for Liberty Lines info. Map 28, C4, 23. Zoo contact ☎ 718-367-1010 or 220-5100; 718-220-5188 for disabled access info. Open daily M-F 10am-5pm, Sa-Su 10am-5:30pm. Parts of the zoo closed Nov.-Apr. $11, seniors $8, ages 2-12 $8; W free (but donation suggested). Many attractions priced individually. Full pass (not for camel rides) $20, seniors and children $16.

The Bronx Zoo/Wildlife Conservation Park, also known as the New York Zoological Society, is perhaps the borough's biggest attraction. The largest urban zoo in the United States, it provides a home for over 4000 animals. While the odd building dots the zoo, this environmentally conscious park prefers to showcase its stars within the 265-acre expanse of natural habitats created for each species' dwelling pleasure. The timber rattlesnake and Samantha the python (the largest snake in the US) are in the **World of Reptiles,** but more benign beasts wander free in the Park's "protected sanctuary," occasionally allowing for startlingly close interaction between inhabitant and visitor. Indian elephants frolic unfettered in **Wild Asia,** which can be toured by monorail ($2 per ride), while white-cheeked gibbons tree-hop in **Jungle World.** More apes can be seen at the **Congo Gorilla Forest,** which also features okapi, but that requires a separate entrance. Other noteworthy habitats include the **Himalayan Highlands** and the **World of Darkness.** The new Tiger Mountain, featuring Siberian stripped cats, is now open. You can ride a camel for $5. Kids imitate animals at the hands-on **Children's Zoo,** where they can climb a spider's web or try on a turtle shell. If you tire of the kids, the crocodiles are fed Mondays and Thursdays at 2pm, sea lions daily at 11am and 3pm.

NEW YORK BOTANICAL GARDEN

Dr. Theodore Kazimiroff Blvd. Subway: 4 to Bedford Park Blvd.-Lehman College; B, D to Bedford Park Blvd. Walk 8 blocks east or take the Bx26 bus. Bus: Bx19 or Bx26. Train: Metro-North Harlem line goes from Grand Central Terminal to Botanical Garden station, which is right outside the Moshalu gate. Conservatory gate on Kazimoff Blvd. a bit north of Fordham Rd. ☎ 212-532-4900 for Metro-North line info. Map 25, C3, 12. ***Zoo contact:*** *☎ 718-817-8700. Open Apr.-Oct. Tu-Su 10am-6pm; July-Aug. Th and Sa grounds open until 8pm; Nov.-Mar. Tu-Su 10am-4pm. $3, students and seniors $2, children 2-12 $1; W all day and Sa 10am-noon free. Certain exhibits throughout the garden incur an additional charge; "passports" ($10; students and seniors $7.50, children $4) allow you to see all exhibits. Various tours (both paid and free) depart daily—inquire at the Visitor Center.*

North across E. Fordham Rd. from the zoo sprawls the beautiful, elaborate New York Botanical Garden. Snatches of forest and water attempt to recreate the area's original landscape. The 250-acre garden, an outstanding horticultural preserve, serves as both a research laboratory and a plant and tree museum.

Scope out the 40-acre **hemlock forest**—the last of the forests that once covered the city—in its natural state, the **Peggy Rockefeller Rose Garden, the T.H. Everett Rock Garden** and waterfall, and a hands-on children's adventure garden. Although it costs a few extra dollars to enter, the **Conservatory** deserves a visit; the gorgeous domed greenhouse contains a few different ecosystems of exquisite plant life. If you go exploring in this jungle by yourself, get a garden map. The crowded 30min. **tram ride** ($1) lets you glimpse most of the major sights. **The Mertz Library** features a rotating exhibit and an orchid terrarium in the lobby.

FORDHAM AND BELMONT

Fordham University is the Bronx's largest college, and its beautifully peaceful grounds offer refuge from the fast-paced surroundings. Belmont, well-positioned for a visit after a day at the Bronx Zoo or the New York Botanical Garden, is the Bronx's Little Italy.

FORDHAM UNIVERSITY

441 E. Fordham Rd., between Webster Ave. and Dr. Theodore Kazimiroff Blvd. Subway: B, D to Fordham Rd./Grand Concourse. Map 28, C3, 11. ☎ 718-817-1000.

Opened in 1841 by John Hughes as St. John's College, 80-acre Fordham has matured into one of the nation's foremost Jesuit schools. Robert S. Riley built the campus in classic collegiate Gothic style in 1936—so Gothic, in fact, that *The Exorcist* was filmed here. The Fordham Rams basketball and baseball teams play at Rose Hill Gymnasium and Coffey Field, respectively. Deck yourself out with Rams memorabilia from the bookstore in McGinley Center, on the north side of campus.

EAST FORDHAM ROAD SHOPPING AREA (FORDHAM CENTER)

E. Fordham Rd., from Webster Ave. to University Ave. Subway: 4 to Fordham Rd./Jerome Ave. or B, D to Fordham Rd./Grand Concourse. Map 28, B3, 10.

Perhaps the busiest shopping district in the Bronx, the strip is one long marketplace. Music blaring from storefront speakers attracts customers. Street vendors vie with department and specialty stores, while wizened women dish out *helado* alongside bargain beepers and gold figurines of the Madonna.

HALL OF FAME FOR GREAT AMERICANS

181st St. and Martin Luther King Jr. Blvd. (125th St.), on the campus of Bronx Community College. Map 28, B3, 9. ☎ 718-289-5161. Subway: 4 to Burnside Ave. Open daily 10am-5pm. Free.

This hall features over 100 bronze busts of America's immortals solemnly whiling away the years, among them Alexander Graham Bell, Abraham Lincoln, Booker T. Washington, and the Wright brothers.

BELMONT

Centering on Arthur Ave. and E. 187th St., near the Southern Blvd. entrance to the Bronx Zoo. Subway: B, D to Fordham Rd./Grand Concourse; then walk 11 blocks east (or take Bx12) to Arthur Ave. and head south. Map 28, C4.

This uptown "Little Italy," with its two-story rowhouses and narrow alleyways, cooks up some of the best Italian food west of Naples. **Arthur Avenue** is home to some wonderful homestyle southern Italian cooking. Boisterous crowds devour pasta at **Dominick's,** between 186th and 187th St. (p. 189). To get a concentrated sense of the area, stop into **Arthur Avenue Retail Market,** 2334 Arthur Ave., between 186th and Crescent St. (Map 28, C4, 22.) With its cafe, butcher, grocer, cheese shop, deli, tobacconist, and other stalls selling Italian necessities, this indoor market is indeed a Little Italy unto itself. The **Church of Our Lady of Mt. Carmel,** 627 187th St., at Belmont Ave., holds high mass in Italian daily at 10:15am, 12:45, and 7:30pm. (Map 28, C3; ☎ 718-295-3770) The church lights up the street and the neighborhood every July 15th with its festival of the Lady of Mt. Carmel. Signs of a recent Kosovar influx permeate the area—the Kosovar flag's red background and spidery bird grace the window fronts of many stores and eateries.

EDGAR ALLAN POE COTTAGE

E. Kingsbridge Rd. and Grand Concourse, 5 blocks west of Fordham University. Subway: 4 to Kingsbridge Rd./Jerome Ave. or B, D to Kingsbridge Rd./Grand Concourse. Map 28, B3, 8. ☎ 718-881-8900. Open Sa 10am-4pm, Su 1-5pm. $3, students and seniors $2.

The morbid writer lived spartanly in the cottage from 1846 to 1849 with his tubercular cousin/wife, Virginia (whom Poe married when he was 26 and she 13). Here Poe wrote *Annabel Lee, Eureka,* and *The Bells,* a tale of the neighboring Fordham bells. The museum displays a slew of Poe's manuscripts and macabrabilia.

KINGSBRIDGE AND BEDFORD PARK

Subway: 4 to Bedford Park Blvd.-Lehman College. Map 28, B2.

This neighborhood is located north of Fordham and contains two schools worth noting. Founded in 1931 as Hunter College, **Herbert H. Lehman College,** 250 Bedford Park Blvd. W., bounded by W. 198th St. and Jerome Ave., is a fiefdom in the CUNY empire (Map 28, B2; ☎ 718-960-8000). The UN Security Council met in the gymnasium building in 1946. In 1980, the Lehmans endowed the first cultural center in the Bronx, the **Lehman Center for the Performing Arts,** on the Bedford Park Blvd. side of campus. Just north of Lehman is the **Bronx High School of Science,** 75W. 205th St., an established center of academic excellence that has produced five Nobel Prize winners (the most of any high school in the world).

RIVERDALE AND VAN CORTLANDT PARK

In direct contrast to much of the poverty-stricken borough, Riverdale (Map 28, B1) features some extremely wealthy residences and a triumvirate of esteemed private schools—**Fieldston School** on Fieldston St., at Manhattan College Pkwy.; **Horace Mann,** 231 W. 246th St.; and **Riverdale,** 5250 Fieldston Rd. Sycamore Ave., between W. 252nd and W. 254th St., is the **Riverdale Historic District.** Physically and spiritually close to neighboring Westchester county, Riverdale's shady suburbs seem light-years away from Manhattan.

VAN CORTLANDT PARK

Sprawling east of Broadway and north of Van Cortlandt Park S., all the way to the Westchester border. Subway: 9 to Van Cortlandt Park-242nd St. Map 28, C1. ☎ 718-430-1890. The park's ***special events office*** *(☎ 718-430-1848) offers info about the many concerts and sports activities that take place during the warmer months. Park closes at 10pm.*

Van Cortlandt Park spreads across 1146 acres of ridges and valleys in the northwest Bronx. Apart from soccer, football, and cricket fields, the sprawling park also has two golf courses, tennis courts, baseball diamonds, a kiddie recreation area, a large swimming pool, and barbecue facilities. Hikers and mountain bikers have plenty of clambering options: the **Cass Gallagher Nature Trail** in the park's northwestern section leads to rock outcroppings from the last ice age amid what is arguably the most untamed wilderness in the city. The **Old Putnam Railroad Track,** once the city's first rail link to Boston, now leads past the quarry that supplied marble for Grand Central Terminal. Ballplayers have a choice between the baseball and softball diamonds of the **Indian Field recreation area** (laid atop the burial grounds of pro-rebel Stockbridge Indians who were ambushed and massacred by British troops during the Revolutionary War) or the **Parade Grounds.** New controversy has been raised by the city's plans to build a water treatment plant in the Park's southeast corner. Talk to anyone in the neighborhood and they will give you an earful on one side of the issue or the other.

VAN CORTLANDT HOUSE

Broadway, at W. 246th St. Subway: 9 to Van Cortlandt Park-242nd St. Map 28, B2, 4. ☎ 718-543-3344. Open Tu-F 10am-3pm, Sa-Su 11am-4pm. $2, seniors and students $1.50, under 12 free.

This national landmark, built in 1748 by the prominent political clan of the same name, is the oldest building in the Bronx. George Washington held his 1781 meeting with Rochambeau in this building, determining his strategy in the last days of the Revolutionary War. He also began his triumphal march into NYC from here in 1783. The stone house today features various rooms decorated in period styles, the nation's oldest dollhouse, and a colonial-era garden and sundial.

MANHATTAN COLLEGE

From the corner of Broadway and 242nd St., take 242nd St. uphill all the way. Subway: 1 to 242nd St. Map 28, B1, 3. ☎ 718-862-8000; www.manhattan.edu.

As you walk up 242nd St., you'll see the red-brick buildings and chapel of this 140-year-old private liberal arts institution. The campus sprawls over stairs, squares, and plateaus like a life-sized game of Snakes and Ladders. Hardy souls who ascend the campus's peaks can take in a cinemascopic view of the Bronx. The college takes its name from its original location, 131st St. and Broadway in Manhattan. The Manhattan College Jaspers are named after the first baseball coach, Brother Jasper of Mary, who may have invented the 7th-inning stretch.

WAVE HILL

Independence Ave., at W. 249th St. ☎ 718-549-3200; www.wavehill.org. Subway: 1, 9 to 231st St., then bus Bx7 or Bx10 to 252nd St. Walk across the Henry Hudson Pkwy. and turn left; walk to 249th St., turn right and walk to Wave Hill Gate. Map 28, B1, 1. Open Apr. 15-Oct. 14 Tu-Su 9am-5:30pm; June-July open W until dusk; Oct. 15-Apr. 14 Tu-Su 9am-4:30pm; mid-Apr. to mid-Oct. $4, students and seniors $2, Tu free, Sa free until noon; mid-Oct. to mid-Mar. free. Wheelchair- accessible.

This Riverdale pastoral estate commands a broad and amazing view of the Hudson River and the Palisades. Samuel Langhorne Clemens (a.k.a. Mark Twain), conductor Arturo Toscanini, and Teddy Roosevelt all resided in Wave Hill House. Horticultural enthusiasts will enjoy the greenhouses and spectacular formal gardens. The **Wild Garden's** hillside garden and gazebo date from at least 1915; it is inspired by the informally planted English wild garden as championed by the Irish writer William Robinson (1838-1935), one of the most influential garden designers of the 19th century. The **T. H. Everett Alpine House** features a collection of high-altitude and small, choice rock garden plants. Also on the grounds are Glyndor House and the Wave Hill House, both of which feature exhibitions of contemporary art.

WOODLAWN AND WOODLAWN CEMETERY

East of Van Cortlandt Park. Subway: 4 to Woodlawn. Map 28, C2. Open daily 9am-4:30pm.

Huge and bucolic Woodlawn Cemetery, with winding asphalt paths that curl around the ornate gravemarkers alongside a few rare weeping beech trees, contains the gravesites of numerous famous individuals. The list of prominent Americans buried at Woodlawn includes Oscar Hammerstein, composer; Fiorello LaGuardia, mayor of New York; Roland H. Macy, department store founder; Herman Melville, novelist; Joseph Pulitzer, publisher and founder of America's first professional school of journalism; Harry and Gertrude Whitney, builders of the Whitney Museum of American Art; and F.W. Woolworth, dime store millionaire. Music lovers pay tribute at the resting places of jazz legends Miles Davis, Duke Ellington, and Lionel Hampton. Woodlawn, to the north, is a neighborhood filled with Irish expatriates.

PELHAM BAY PARK

In the northeast corner of the Bronx. Subway: 6 to Pelham Bay Park. Map 28, E3. Rangers ☎ 718-430-1890. Open dawn to dusk. ***Stables:*** *Shore Rd. at City Island Dr.; take Bx29 from the Pelham Bay Park station. ☎ 718-885-0551. Open daily 9am-dusk. $25 per hr.* ***Bartow-Pell Mansion:*** *895 Shore Rd., opposite the golf courses. ☎ 718-885-1461. Open W and Sa-Su noon-4pm. $2.50, students and seniors $1.25, under 5 free.*

New York City's largest park, **Pelham Bay Park** boasts over 2700 acres of green saturated with playing fields, tennis courts, golf courses, wildlife sanctuaries, **Orchard Beach** (p. 233), and even training grounds for the city's mounted police force. The knowledgeable **park rangers** lead a variety of history- and nature-oriented walks. From the **Pelham Bay stables,** you can take a guided ride around the park on horseback. The Empire/Greek Revival **Bartow-Pell Mansion Museum** sits amid a prize-winning formal English garden landscaped in 1915. The house's wonders include a free-standing spiral staircase and a pond, complete with goldfish and spouting cherub.

CITY ISLAND

Subway: 6 to Pelham Bay Park; board bus Bx29 outside the station and get off at the 1st stop on City Island. Map 28, F4.

Go out on a fishing boat or eat seafood at one of the many restaurants lining City Island Ave., the main artery. The food chain stops dead in its tracks at the nearby **Pelham Cemetery** on the west end of Reville Rd. Emblazoned on the gate is: "Lives are commemorated...deaths are recorded...love is undisguised...this is a cemetery." Ponder this statement as you wait for the Bx29 bus, which leaves every 30min.

STATEN ISLAND

Staten Island has a lot to offer, but tourism here is often limited. Its many parks are vast and lush, and there are beaches, historical sites and lovely gardens. The **Staten Island Ferry** (leaves from South Ferry in Manhattan; Subway: N, R to Whitehall St. or 1, 9 to South Ferry) is itself a sight not to be missed. It offers the best and cheapest ($0) tour on NY's upper harbor, leaving every 30min. at peak hours (once an hour other times). Because of the hills and the distances (and some dangerous neighborhoods in between), it's a bad idea to *walk* from one site to the next. **Make sure to**

plan your excursion with the bus schedule in mind. You can pick one up from the VISIT booth on the Manhattan side of the ferry, or from the **Staten Island Chamber of Commerce,** 130 Bay St. (☎718-727-1900. Bear left from the ferry station onto Bay St. Open M-F 9am-5pm.) The Chamber also sells street maps for $2.

SNUG HARBOR CULTURAL CENTER

Cultural Center: 1000 Richmond Terr. Bus S40. ☎718-448-2500; www.snug-harbor.org. Free tours of the grounds offered Apr.-Nov. Sa-Su 2pm, starting at the Visitors Center. Map 29, B1, 4. ***Botanical Garden:*** *☎718-273-8200; www.sibg.org. Open daily dawn-dusk.* ***Chinese Scholar's Garden:*** *open Apr. to mid-Nov. Tu-Su 10am-5pm. $5; seniors, students, under 12 $4. Tours: W, Sa-Su on the hour noon-4pm.* ***Newhouse Center:*** *☎718-448-2500 ext. 508. Open W-Su noon-5pm. Call ahead for extended summer hours. Suggested donation $2.* ***Noble Collection:*** *☎718-447-6490. Open Sa-Su 1-5pm and for groups by appointment.* ***Children's Museum:*** *☎718-273-2060. Open Tu-Su noon-5pm. $4, under 1 free; W seniors free.*

Founded in 1801, Sailors' Snug Harbor originally served as a home for retired sailors (the iron fence that barricades it originally kept old mariners from quenching their thirst at nearby bars). Purchased by the city and opened in 1976 as a cultural center, the national landmark now includes 28 historic buildings scattered over 83 amazingly well-kept acres of wonderfully placid, unpopulated parkland. The **Connie Gretz Secret Garden, the New York Chinese Scholar's Garden,** and the **White Garden** (which offers tea every other Sunday) are a few of the horticultural displays making up the Center's **Staten Island Botanical Garden.** The Chinese Scholar's Garden is assuredly tranquil. In addition, the Center often hosts artistic displays as well as plays, recitals and concerts. Free summer concerts take place Sundays on the North Lawn; the **Newhouse Center for Contemporary Art** shows revolving exhibits of contemporary art; the **John A. Noble Maritime Collection** houses Noble's artwork focusing on NY's working waterfront; the **Children's Museum** features interactive exhibits.

HISTORIC RICHMOND TOWN

441 Clarke Ave. Bus S74 to Richmond Rd. and St. Patrick's Pl., 30min. Map 29, C4, 8. ☎718-351-1611; www.historicrichmondtown.org. Open June-Aug. M, W-F 10am-5pm, Su 1-5pm; Sept.-May Su and W-Sa 1-5pm. $5, seniors $4, ages 5-17 $3.50, under 5 free.

A huge, recreated village complex documenting three centuries of Staten Island culture and history, Historic Richmond Town's reconstructed 17th- to 19th-century dwellings feature artifacts from the Staten Island Historical Society's collection. Authentic "inhabitants" (costumed master craftspeople and their apprentices) give well-informed tours of the grounds. Especially noteworthy is **Voorlezer's House,** the oldest surviving elementary school in the US (built in 1695). The museum rotates the buildings it opens to the public, so call in advance to find out what you can see and to get info about the summertime "living history" events.

MORAVIAN CEMETERY

2205 Richmond Rd., at Todt Hill Rd., in Dongan Hills. Bus S74 to Todt Hill Rd. Map 29, C3, 6. Gates open daily 8am. Richmond Rd. gates close 4:30pm, Todt Hill gates 6:30pm.

Widely recognized for its beautifully manicured grounds, lakeside view, and natural knolls and valleys, the 113-acre non-sectarian cemetery offers a setting of beautiful serenity. Commodore Cornelius Vanderbilt (the ferry's creator) and his monied clan lie here in an ornate crypt designed in 1886 by Richard Morris Hunt. The grounds around the Vanderbilt mausoleum were landscaped by Frederick Law Olmsted, designer of Central Park.

RICHMOND COUNTY BANK BALLPARK AT ST. GEORGE

75 Richmond Terr., next door to the Ferry. ☎ 718-720-9265; www.siyanks.com. Call or check website for schedule and ticket information.

A newly acquired minor-league Yankees farm team was moved to Staten Island five years ago and has quickly established itself as a force in the Class A league. The three-year old ballpark offers a chance to see a home run hit into the Atlantic Ocean! Games played almost daily in summer. The grounds are often open during afternoon practices. Try to catch a game against the Baby Bombers' crosstown rivals, the Mets-affiliated Brooklyn Cyclones.

INSIDE

museums by neighborhood **128**
museum directory **128**
galleries **142**
soho **143** chelsea **144**
midtown and the upper east side **145**
brooklyn **146** queens **147** the bronx **147**

Museums & Galleries

For many visitors to New York, the city has no greater attraction than its wide array of museums and galleries. On any given day, one can enjoy the work of an up-and-coming artist in a Williamsburg gallery (p. 146), experience New York's history at the Lower East Side Tenement Museum (p. 137), or catch a rerun of *Diff'rent Strokes* at the Museum of Television and Radio (p. 139). New York's museums can be as diverse in their geography as they are in their cultural offerings: with the Metropolitan Museum of Art in Manhattan (p. 128); the Brooklyn Museum of Art (p. 131); and the Museum of Modern Art in Queens (p. 130), three of the city's five boroughs can boast world class art collections.

During the annual **Museum Mile Festival** (☎212-606-2296) in mid-June, Fifth Ave. museums keep their doors open until late at night, stage engaging exhibits, involve city kids in mural painting, and fill the streets with music. Many museums also sponsor film series and live concerts throughout the year (see **Entertainment,** p. 214). Be aware that many major museums, including the Met, the Cloisters, the Frick, and the Whitney, are not open on Monday. The MoMA is closed Tuesday and Wednesday.

MUSEUMS BY NEIGHBORHOOD

FINANCIAL DISTRICT
Museum of Jewish Heritage (139)
Nat'l Museum of the American Indian (140)
New York City Police Museum (141)

LOWER EAST SIDE
LES Tenement Museum (137)

SOHO
New Museum of Contemporary Art (140)
New York City Fire Museum (140)

GREENWICH VILLAGE
Forbes Magazine Galleries (134)
Nat'l Museum and Archive of Lesbian, Gay, Bisexual & Transgender History (140)
Parsons Exhibition Center (141)

EAST VILLAGE
Merchant's House Museum (137)

MURRAY HILL
Pierpont Morgan Library (141)

MIDTOWN
American Craft Museum (134)
International Center of Photography (136)
Japan Society (137)
Museum of Television and Radio (139)

HELL'S KITCHEN
Intrepid Sea-Air-Space Museum (136)

UPPER EAST SIDE
The Asia Society (134)
Cooper-Hewitt Nat'l Design Museum (135)
El Museo del Barrio (138)
Frick Collection (132)
Guggenheim Museum (131)
The Jewish Museum (137)
Metropolitan Museum of Art (128)
Mount Vernon Hotel Museum & Garden (138)
Museum of American Illustration (138)
Museum of the City of New York (139)
National Academy of Design Museum (140)
Whitney Museum of American Art (133)

UPPER WEST SIDE
American Museum of Natural History (130)
The Children's Museum of Manhattan (135)
New York Historical Society (141)

HARLEM
Studio Museum (142)

WASHINGTON HEIGHTS
Audubon Terrace Museum Group (135)
The Cloisters (132)

BROOKLYN
Brooklyn Children's Museum (135)
Brooklyn Museum of Art (131)
New York Transit Museum (141)
Waterfront Museum (142)

QUEENS
American Museum of the Moving Image (134)
Isamu Noguchi Garden Museum (136)
MoMA (130)
Museum for African Art (138)
P.S.1 Contemporary Art Center (142)

THE BRONX
The Bronx Museum of the Arts (135)

STATEN ISLAND
Alice Austen House Museum & Garden (133)
Jacques Marchais Museum of Tibetan Art (136)

MUSEUM DIRECTORY

Major museums are listed below in *Let's Go's* order of preference; **Other Collections** are listed in alphabetical order.

METROPOLITAN MUSEUM OF ART

1000 Fifth Ave., at 82nd St. Subway: 4, 5, 6 to 86th St./Lexington Ave. Map 15, A4, 69. Recorded info ☎212-535-7710, upcoming concerts and lectures ☎212-570-3949; TTY 212-570-3828; www.metmuseum.org. Open Su and Tu-Th 9:30am-5:15pm, F-Sa 9:30am-8:45pm. Foreign Visitors Desk: maps, brochures, and assistance in a number of languages; ☎212-570-3583. Gallery tours and talks daily. Free. Inquire at the main info desk for schedules, topics, and meeting places, or call ☎212-570-3930. Key to Met Audio Guides $6, children under 12 $4, discounted for groups. Suggested donation $12, students and seniors $7, members and under 12 (with adult) free. Disabled access ☎212-535-7710. Wheelchairs at the coat-check areas; enter through the 81st St. entrance.

Founded in 1870 by a group of distinguished art collectors, philanthropists, civic leaders, and artists, the Met's more than two million works of art spanning over 5000 years make it one of the largest and finest museums in the world. Don't rush the Metropolitan experience; you could camp out here for a month and still realize that you haven't seen everything that this phenomenal museum has to offer. You can't stop at the exhibits either—there are free guided tours, lectures, concerts, films, gallery talks and children's programs.

Those braving the Met without the guidance of tour and audio guides (info listed above) may want to focus on examining a limited number of collections in depth. The **European paintings** collection is perhaps the greatest of its kind with a whopping 2500 works. The centrally located entrance to these labyrinthine galleries of Old Masters and their artistic heirs is at the top of the main staircase on the second floor. Jacques-Louis David's larger-than-life portrait of the French chemist Lavoisier and his wife hangs on this first chamber's western wall. Farther ahead are familiar masterpieces by van Gogh, Cézanne, Vermeer, and Monet, not to mention such seminal works as van Eyck's *The Crucifixion* and *The Last Judgement;* El Greco's luminous *View of Toledo;* Botticelli's *The Last Communion of Saint Jerome;* and Brueghel's starkly realistic *The Harvesters.*

If oils don't set your interest aflame, you may want to try the scarabs to the right of the main entrance in the **Egyptian Art** section. The department's 36,000 pieces, most of which are on permanent display, date from the Paleolithic Era (300,000 BC) to the Roman Period (AD 400) and include compellingly beautiful vestiges of ancient Egyptian culture: Middle and New Kingdom jewelry, mummies in their wrappings, the Old Kingdom tomb of Pernab, and the fully intact **Temple of Dendur,** a monument reassembled with precision after its trip from the shore of the Nile to the Museum Mile.

Nearby, the arts of Africa, Oceania, and the Americas come alive. Beautifully carved wooden sculptures from sub-Saharan Africa and the Pacific Islands tell of ancient lineages, everyday customs, and seasonal celebrations. The artifacts of gold, silver, copper, and ivory date back from the second millennium BC.

Directly above the northern wing and the Egyptian galleries stands the largest and most comprehensive collection of **Asian Art** in the West: monumental Chinese Buddhist sculptures and ancient statuettes reside near an exquisite and preeminently serene recreation of a Ming scholar's garden. On the same level of the building, huge winged guardian icons flank a passageway in the **Ancient Near Eastern Art** gallery. They originally guarded Ashurnasirpal's palace at Nimrud in the 9th century BC. Unique bas-reliefs of the Assyrian kings, with their entourages of bird-men and eunuchs, adorn the walls.

Another must-see exhibit is the world-renowned **Costume Institute,** at the north end of the museum's ground floor. This collection of 75,000 costumes and accessories, spanning five continents and five centuries, has offered such interesting rotating exhibits as the 2003 "Goddess" show.

The list of stupendously well-appointed galleries continues from there. The **American Art** exhibition includes such classics as Sargent's *Madame X,* as well as works by Gilbert Stuart (the renowned painter of George Washington), Mary Cassatt, James McNeill Whistler, and others. Also worth a gander is one of the most famous canvases in all of American art: the 1851 painting *Washington Crossing the Delaware,* by Emanuel Gottlieb Leutze. The department of **Greek and Roman Art** combines the traditional museum complement of ancient marble torsos and heads with wall paintings from Roman villas, Greek painted urns, and superb glass- and silver-wares.

Many of the artifacts in the department of **Musical Instruments** are playable and can be heard in recordings, live concerts, and lectures. One historic American pipe organ is used in a recital on the first Wednesday of each month, from October to May. Another noteworthy seasonal display is the annual **Christmas tree** that goes up at the end of November on the first floor, covered with the Met's stunning collection of papier-mâché angels and accompanied by a Neapolitan nativity crêche.

MUSEUM OF MODERN ART (MOMA)

45-20 33rd St., at Queens Blvd., in Long Island City, Queens. Subway: 7 to 33rd St./Queens Blvd. Map 26, 20. ☎212-708-9400; TTY 247-1230; www.moma.org. Open Su-M, Th and Sa 10am-5pm, F 10am-7:45pm. Gallery talks Su-M, Th, Sa 2pm; F 2pm, 6pm. $12, students and seniors $8.50, under 16 free. Pay what you wish F 4pm-7:45pm. ***In 2005, the MoMa will move back from Queens to 11 W. 53rd St., between Fifth and Sixth Ave.***

In May 2002, the 53rd St. MoMA in Manhattan shut its doors and moved across the East River to a royal blue factory in an industrial section of Queens. Inside the cavernous space of a converted Swingline stapler factory, temporary exhibitions of the museum's vast permanent collection will continue until the Manhattan location reopens in early 2005.

The MoMA commands one of the world's most impressive collections of post-Impressionist, late 19th-century, and 20th-century art. Founded in 1929 by scholar Alfred Barr in response to the Met's refusal to display cutting-edge work, the museum's first exhibit—held in a Fifth Ave. office building—displayed then-unknowns Cézanne, Gauguin, Seurat, and van Gogh. But as the ground-breaking works of 1900 to 1950 moved from cult to masterpiece status, the MoMA also shifted from revolution to institution. In 2000, the museum reclaimed its innovative edge by commissioning Japanese architect Yoshio Taniguchi to expand and renovate the museum—a $650-million project that will more than double the museum's size.

Despite borough-hopping, the MoMA continues to display cutting-edge art alongside the museum's big-name permanent collection. Some of the collection's most renowned works are Picasso's *Les Demoiselles d'Avignon;* Dali's *Persistance of Memory;* Rodin's *John the Baptist;* van Gogh's *The Starry Night;* Duchamp's Dadaist *To Be Looked at (from the Other Side of the Glass) with One Eye, Close To, for Almost an Hour; White on White* by the Russian Constructivist Malevich; Henri Matisse's *Dance (First Version);* Mark Rothko's *Red, Brown, and Black;* and Andy Warhol's signature pieces, the gold *Marilyn Monroe* and the *Campbell Soup Cans.* With over 3500 pieces, MoMA owns much more 20th-century art than it will ever have space to display. In 2003, MOMA's Picasso-Matisse show was the toast of the town. Tickets get you into Gramercy Theater screenings and P.S. 1 (not including summer Warm Up). Call or look online for schedules for "Brown Bag Lunches," discussions, slide presentations and lectures.

AMERICAN MUSEUM OF NATURAL HISTORY

Central Park W., between 77th and 81st St. Subway: B, C to 81st St. Entrances at 77th St., Columbus Ave., Central Park W., and 81st St. Map 18, D4, 33. ☎212-769-5100; www.amnh.org. Open daily 10am-5:45pm. Rose Center: Open F 10am-8:45pm. Wheelchair-accessible. Highlight tours 6 per day from 10:15am-3:15pm, usually leaving 15min. past the hr. Free. Imax ☎212-769-5200. Museum suggested donation $10, students and seniors $7.50, children $6. ***Admission combos:*** *Combo-ticket (Museum and Imax) $15, students and seniors $11, ages 2-12 $9. Double Feature $21, students and seniors $15.50, children $12.50. Museum, Rose Center, Space Show $19, students and seniors $14, children $11.50.*

Think back to elementary school. Remember how most class trips were really boring, but there was always one excursion each year that you absolutely would not skip? For generations of New York's schoolchildren, the Natural History Museum has been the can't-miss opportunity to marvel at huge dinosaur skeletons, stargaze at the Hayden Planetarium, or buy mineral slabs and rubber snakes from the gift shop.

Even after fifth grade ends, you're never too old for the Natural History Museum, one of the world's largest museums devoted to science. The fourth-floor **dinosaur halls,** which display real fossils in 85 percent of the exhibits (most museums use fossil casts), draw throngs of adults and children alike. The bones of T. Rex, Triceratops, and the rest of the gang are overwhelmingly impressive. Don't forget to check out the informative explanations.

If the dinos grow tedious, chart the development of world cultures as displayed in life-sized dioramas on the second floor or dodge the 90 ft. blue whale suspended from the ceiling of the first floor. The **Alexander White Natural Science Center,** the museum's only room holding *live* animals, explains the ecology of New York City to children, while the **Discovery Room** offers artifacts they can touch. The newly renovated **Fossil Halls** on the fourth floor display the single largest and most diverse array of vertebrate fossils in the world: visitors follow a giant "family tree" of vertebrates that covers over 500 million years of vertebrate evolution. The museum also houses an **Imax** cinematic extravaganza on one of New York's largest movie screens—four stories high and 66 ft. wide.

The **Rose Center for Earth and Space** houses the 87 ft. sphere of the **Hayden Planetarium**. From the outside at night, the Planetarium simulates a floating globe within a glass and steel box. Call ahead or visit the website for a listing of current exhibits. 2003 highlights included exhibitions about chocolate, Albert Einstein, and coral reefs.

BROOKLYN MUSEUM OF ART

200 Eastern Pkwy., at Washington Ave. Subway: 1, 2 to Eastern Pkwy.-Brooklyn Museum. Map 23, D2, 12. ☎ 718-638-5000; www.brooklynart.org. Open W-F 10am-5pm, Sa-Su 11am-6pm; also open 1st Sa of the month 11am-11pm. Audio Tours $3. $6, students and seniors $3, under 12 free; free on 1st Sa of each month after 5pm.

In any other city in the United States, the Brooklyn Museum would have the largest and most impressive art collection in town. In fact, the only negative comment that can be made about the BMA is that it isn't the Met. Even so, it fully deserves to be considered as one of the city's finest cultural destinations.

The Brooklyn Museum is home to a magnificent collection of art from all over the world. The art of the Pacific Islands and the Art of the Americas exhibits take up the central two-story space on the first floor—the towering totem poles covered with human/animal hybrids could fit nowhere else. When it opened in 1923, the impressive African art collection was the first of its kind in an American museum.

The third floor holds outstanding ancient Egyptian galleries; only London's British Museum and Cairo's Egyptian Museum have larger Egyptian collections. Crafts, textiles, and period rooms on the fourth floor tell the story of American upper-class interiors from the 17th to the 19th centuries, including the Moorish Room, a lush bit of exotica from John D. Rockefeller's Manhattan townhouse. John Singer Sargent and the Hudson River School grace the fifth floor's American Collection. European art from the early Renaissance to post-Impressionism periods, including works by Renoir and Monet, also appear on the floor. Galleries downstairs host temporary exhibits and weekend talks.

In 1999, the Brooklyn Museum found itself at the center of a worldwide debate on censorship when Mayor Giuliani attempted to suppress a show of controversial modern art. After a number of courts ruled against the Mayor's efforts to cut off the BMA's funding, the show went on and was met with critical acclaim and lines snaking down Eastern Parkway.

In addition to offering a wide selection of educational programs, the Museum hosts a free night of art and entertainment on the first Saturday of each month.

GUGGENHEIM MUSEUM

1071 Fifth Ave., at 89th St. Subway: 4, 5, 6 to 86th St./Lexington Ave. Map 15, A3, 9. ☎ 212-423-3500; wheelchair access info ☎ 423-3539; www.guggenheim.org. Open Su-W and Sa 10am-5:45pm, Th 11-6pm F 9:30am-8:30pm. $15, students and seniors $10, under 12 free; F 6-8:30pm pay what you wish.

The Guggenheim's most famous exhibit is surely the building itself, an inverted white quasi-ziggurat, designed by Frank Lloyd Wright and hailed as a modern architectural masterpiece. The interdependent gallery spaces make up a spiral design that recalls a citrus fruit's membrane, or a large shopping mall's parking garage.

The founders—philanthropist Solomon R. Guggenheim and artist-advisor Hilla Rebay—insisted on a new kind of art to accompany this new kind of space. The Museum of Non-Objective Painting, as the Guggenheim was first known, was originally influenced by the radical new forms of art being developed by such artists as Vasily Kandinsky, Paul Klee, and Piet Mondrian. The Guggenheim's large collection of modern and postmodern paintings includes significant works in Cubism, Surrealism, American Minimalism, and Abstract Expressionism. Each spin of the museum's spiral holds one sequence or exhibit, while a portion of the **Tower Galleries** houses the **Thannhauser Collection.** Donated by Justin K. Thannhauser in 1976, the group of 19th- and 20th-century works includes several by Picasso and Matisse, and a beautiful collection of Impressionist-era paintings by van Gogh, Gauguin, Manet, and Cézanne. The rest of the permanent collection features geometric art, including that of Mondrian and his Dutch De Stijl school, German Josef Albers' Bauhaus experiments, and the works of Russian modernists. The collection also holds several Degas sculptures and works by Kandinsky, Klee, and Kirchner.

In 1992, under the leadership of director Thomas Krens, the Guggenheim significantly expanded its operations. The original building was restored and supplemented by a new tower, adding considerable overall exhibition space while allowing Wright's great rotunda and the monitor building to be seen in all their splendor.

FRICK COLLECTION

1 E. 70th St., at Fifth Ave. Subway: 6 to 68th St. Map 15, A5, 38. ☎212-288-0700; www.frick.org. Open Su 1-6pm, Tu- Th and Sa 10am-6pm, F 10am-9pm. Wheelchair-accessible. Group visits by appointment only. Audio guides free. Guidebooks $1. Slide show on the history of the collection and the grounds runs every hr. on the half-hour. $12, seniors $8, students $5. No children under 10 admitted; children under 16 must be accompanied by an adult.

Designed by Thomas Hastings in the style of an 18th-century mansion, the former residence of industrialist Henry Clay Frick now houses a magnificent ensemble of fine art, opened to the public in 1935. This extraordinary collection, two-thirds of which belonged to Frick himself, includes impressive Western masterpieces from the early Renaissance through the late 19th century. Paintings by the world's greatest Old Masters are displayed here, in addition to vases, 18th-century French sculptures, Renaissance bronzes, and porcelains.

The distinguished list of artists on view at the Frick includes Renoir, van Eyck, Goya, Whistler, El Greco, Holbein, Corot, and Titian. Don't miss the West Gallery's stately self-portrait of Rembrandt and the three Vermeer paintings (only 36-40 survive worldwide). Note the gold desk-watch in the Garden Court, which conforms to the odd 10-hour-day standard mandated by the French revolution. Frick's favorite organ music sometimes plays in the relaxing Garden Court (p. 217). The Frick Collection also operates an **art reference library,** at 10 E. 71st St., which is one of the leading institutions for research in the history of art.

THE CLOISTERS

Fort Tryon Park in Washington Heights. Subway: A to 190th St. Map 19 (inset), A2, 1. ☎212-923-3700. Open Mar.-Oct. Tu-Su 9:30am-5:15pm; Nov.-Feb. Tu-Su 9:30am-4:45pm. Tours Mar.-Oct. Su noon, Tu-F 3pm. Suggested donation $10, students and seniors $5. Includes same-day admission to the Met's main building in Central Park.

Crowning a hilltop at the northern tip of Manhattan, this tranquil branch of the Metropolitan Museum of Art incorporates pieces of 12th- and 13th-century French monasteries into its own medieval design. The Cuxa Cloister, taken from a 12th-century Benedictine monastery, is an especially beautiful portion of the museum. John D. Rockefeller donated the site (now Fort Tryon Park) and much of the Cloisters' rich collection of medieval art, including frescoes, panel paintings, and stained glass. Don't miss the sublimely detailed Unicorn Tapestries, which relate the hunt for a magic unicorn; the Treasury, where the museum's most fragile offerings are found;

and the Robert Campin altarpiece, one of the first known oil paintings. When the museum tires you out, make like a monk and sit in the two small gardens. The museum offers "Gallery Talks" and workshops for families in the summertime. Call for details.

WHITNEY MUSEUM OF AMERICAN ART

945 Madison Ave., at 75th St. Subway: 6 to 77th St. Map 15, A5, 32. ☎800-944-8639, or 212-570-3676; www.whitney.org. Open W-Th and Sa 11am-6pm, F 1pm-9pm, Su 11am-6pm. Wheelchair-accessible. $12, students and seniors $9.50, under 12 free; F 6-9pm pay what you wish. ***Another branch:*** *Located in the Altria building, 120 Park Ave., at 42nd St. (☎917-663-2453). Gallery open M-W, F 11am-6pm, Th 11am-7:30pm. Sculpture court open M-Sa 7:30am-9:30pm, Su 11am-7pm. Free.*

When the Metropolitan Museum declined a donation of over 500 works from Gertrude Vanderbilt Whitney in 1929, the wealthy patron and sculptor formed her own museum. In 1966, the collection settled into its present-day digs—a futuristic fortress-style building designed by Marcel Breuer.

This museum, unique in its historical mandate to champion the works of living American artists, has assembled the largest collection (12,000 objects) of 20th- and 21st-century American art in the world. Even the modern-art skeptic will be impressed by Jasper John's *Three Flags;* Joseph Stella's *Brooklyn Bridge;* Ad Reinhardt's *Abstract Painting, Number 33;* Edward Hopper's *Early Sunday Morning;* and Georgia O'Keeffe's flower paintings. The mezzanine-level galleries, accessible from the top floor, host Alexander Calder's *Circus* collection.

OTHER COLLECTIONS

ALICE AUSTEN HOUSE MUSEUM AND GARDEN

2 Hylan Blvd., on north end of Staten Island. Bus S51 to Hylan Blvd. Walk 1 block east toward the water. Map 29, D2, 5. ☎718-816-4506. Open Mar.-Dec. Th-Su noon-5pm; grounds open daily until dusk. Suggested donation $2.

This 18th-century cottage was the home of photographer Alice Austen, who took more than 8000 photographs of her upper-middle-class life. After the 1929 stock market crash, Austen languished in the poorhouse until the

Temple of Dendur

Museum of Natural History

Guggenheim Museum

the hidden deal

You May Pass Go!

Located in the *Forbes* magazine headquarters are the **Forbes Magazine Galleries,** 60 Fifth Ave., at 12th St. This gem comes courtesy of a multimillionaire financier who turned over his personal collection to the public. The late Malcolm Forbes' irrepressible penchant for the offbeat permeates this array of eclectic exhibits.

The standing collection includes an insane labyrinth of model boats, soldiers, and trophies. Of particular note is a room tracing the history of the game *Monopoly*—check out the "Oligopoly" version made just for Forbes, using properties he actually owned. Here, too, stands the world's largest collection of Fabergé objets d'art. The Forbes has 12 of those famous eggs; even the Kremlin has a paltry 10, while Queen Elizabeth lags behind at two. Other rooms feature a constant barrage of changing exhibitions. Sometimes, when they land on Boardwalk, they throw a little something to the kids hanging out on Baltic Ave. *(Subway: N, R to 8th St.-NYU; 4, 5, 6, L, N, Q, R, W to 14th St.-Union Sq. Map 10, E2, 11. ☎212-206-5548. Open Tu-W and F-Sa 10am-4pm. Free.)*

Staten Island Historical Society discovered her work and published it in *Life* months before her death. This quiet museum displays Austen's photos and has a garden with great views of the Verrazano-Narrows Bridge.

AMERICAN CRAFT MUSEUM

40 W. 53rd St., between Fifth and Sixth Ave. Subway: B, D, F, V to 47th-50th St.-Rockefeller Center; E, V to Fifth Ave./ 53rd St. Map 14, D3, 38. ☎212-956-3535; www.americancraftmuseum.org. Open M-W 10am-6pm, Th 10am-8pm, F-Su 10am-6pm. Wheelchair-accessible. $7.50, students and seniors $4, under 12 free; Th 6-8pm pay as you wish.

No wooden *tchotchkes* here. Three floors of phenomenal ceramic, glass, metal, wood, fiber, and origami displays by contemporary artists feature changing exhibits ranging from cinary urns to fiber pieces.

AMERICAN MUSEUM OF THE MOVING IMAGE

35th Ave., at 36th St., Astoria, Queens. Subway: G, R, V to Steinway St. Walk 1 block down Steinway St., turn right onto 35th Ave. Map 26, 17. ☎718-784-0077; www.movingimage.us. Open W-Th 11am-5pm, F 11am-7:30pm, Sa-Su 11am-6pm. $10, students and seniors $7.50, children 5-18 $5, under 4 free. Includes free screening tickets.

This museum, dedicated to the art of film and television production, contains displays of cameras, projectors, and movie-related memorabilia. One exhibit features over 20 outfits worn by Robert DeNiro; another, the jowl-enhancing mouthpiece that Marlon Brando wore in the *Godfather*. On the third floor, you can create your own digitally animated film sequence, dub your voice into scenes from *My Fair Lady*, or alter sound effects from movies like *Terminator 2*. Demonstrations of film- and TV-related processes add depth to the displays. The ground floor houses a rotating gallery often featuring interactive, cutting-edge moving image technology.

THE ASIA SOCIETY

725 Park Ave., at 70th St. Subway: 6 to 68th St. Map 15, B5, 41. ☎212-517-2742; www.asiasociety.org. Open Tu-Th and Sa-Su 11am-6pm, F 11am-9pm. Wheelchair-accessible. Tours Sa 12:30pm. $7, students and seniors $5, under 16 free, noon-2pm daily and F 6-9pm free.

The Asia Society exhibits Asian art from Iran and Japan to Yemen and Mongolia, in addition to works by Asian-American artists. Highly interactive exhibits make great use of multimedia.

AUDUBON TERRACE MUSEUM GROUP

613 W. 155th St. Enter from plaza on Broadway between W 155th St. and 156th. Subway: 1 to 157th St. Map 19, A3, 3. **Hispanic Society:** *☎212-926-2234. Open Tu-Sa 10am-4:30pm, museum only Su 1-4pm. Library closed in Aug. Free.* **Numismatic Society:** *☎212-234-3130. Open Tu-F 9am-4:30pm. Free.* **Academy of Arts and Letters:** *☎212-368-5900. Open only twice a year to the public: 2-3 weeks in mid-Mar. and again starting mid-May. Th-Su 1-4pm, but call ahead for more info.*

Once part of John James Audubon's estate and game preserve, the regal terrace now contains an unlikely trio of museums. The **Hispanic Society of America** includes mosaics, ceramics, and paintings by El Greco, Velázquez, and Goya. In addition to the vast collection of Spanish tiles and the building's own ornate design, students of Spanish and Portuguese arts and culture will enjoy the 100,000-volume research library. The less-trammeled **American Numismatic Society's** exhibition room features coinage and paper money from prehistoric times to the present. The **American Academy of Arts and Letters** honors American artists, writers, and composers. Only open to the public twice a year, the Academy exhibits the works of its honorees and new members.

THE BRONX MUSEUM OF THE ARTS

1040 Grand Concourse, at 165th St. Subway: 4, B, D to 161 St.-Yankee Stadium; 4 to 167th St. Map 28, B5, 27. ☎718-681-6000. Open W noon-9pm, Th-Su noon-6pm. Suggested donation $5, students and seniors $3. W free.

Located in the rotunda of the Bronx Courthouse, the museum's two small galleries exhibit works by contemporary artists as well as by local talent, focusing on Latino, African-American, and female artists. The museum encourages the community to create textual and visual responses to the permanent collection, mounting the (often nutty) viewer feedback alongside the original work.

BROOKLYN CHILDREN'S MUSEUM

145 Brooklyn Ave., at St. Mark's Pl. Subway: 1 to Kingston Ave.; C to Kingston-Throop Ave.; A to Nostrand Ave. Map 20, D3, 2. ☎718-735-4402; www.brooklynkids.org. Open July-Aug. Tu–F 1pm-6pm, Sa-Su 11am-6pm; Sept.-June W-F 2-5pm, Sa-Su 10am-5pm. Suggested donation $4; July-Aug. free after 5pm.

Founded in 1899, the Brooklyn Children's Museum is the oldest museum of its kind in America. The many exciting interactive exhibits tackle myriad subjects, from culture and history to the natural sciences. The *Together in the City* exhibit discusses the communal life of New Yorkers. Ten different galleries make for an exciting day for any child. Rotating exhibits like *Dinosaurs*, *Toolville*, and *Totally Tots* are also worth the trip.

THE CHILDREN'S MUSEUM OF MANHATTAN

212 W. 83rd St., off Amsterdam Ave. Subway: 1, 2 to 79th St., 86th St./Broadway. Map 18, C4, 21. ☎212-721-1234; www.cmom.org. Open W-Su 10am-5pm. Wheelchair-accessible. Adults and children $6, seniors $3, under 1 free.

Founded in 1973 by Harlem and Upper West Side artists and educators in response to the elimination of music and cultural programs in public schools, this museum is full of fun interactive exhibits for kids. Check out the *Body Odyssey* exhibit that allows you to explore the wonders of the human body or solve a mystery with real forensic techniques in "The Kloos Family Mystery," sponsored by CourtTV.

COOPER-HEWITT NATIONAL DESIGN MUSEUM

2 E. 91st St., at Fifth Ave. Subway: 4, 5, 6 to 86th St./Lexington Ave.; 6 to 96th St./Lexington Ave. Map 15, A3, 7. ☎212-849-8400; www.si.edu/ndm. Open Su noon-6pm, Tu-Th 10am-5pm, F 10am-9pm, Sa 10am-6pm. Wheelchair-accessible. $8, students and seniors $5, under 12 free; F 5-9pm free. **Library:** *☎212-849-8330. Library open daily by appointment until 5:30pm.*

Founded in 1897 by the Hewitt sisters, the National Design Museum was the first, and remains the only, museum in the US devoted exclusively to historical and contemporary design. Housed by the splendid Carnegie Mansion since 1967, the museum contains over 250,000 objects—one of the world's largest collections of design. Unfortunately, the vast majority of this permanent collection is never on display to the public; tourists instilled with a preternatural fascination for 19th-century pottery should make an appointment to explore these extensive archives privately. Public exhibitions are small but engaging and unusual.

INTERNATIONAL CENTER OF PHOTOGRAPHY

1133 Ave. of the Americas, at 43rd St. Subway: B, D, F, V, to 42nd St./Ave. of the Americas. Map 1, C4, 76. ☎212-857-0000; www.icp.org. Open Tu-Th 10am-5pm, F 10am-8pm, Sa-Su 10am-6pm. Wheelchairs available upon request. $10, students and seniors $7, under 12 free. Voluntary contribution F 5pm-8pm.

Housed in a Midtown skyscraper, ICP is the city's only photography museum. The center showcases historical and contemporary works, from fine art to photojournalism. The two floors rotate exhibits every three months. A small, chic restaurant sells slightly overpriced food on the bottom floor.

INTREPID SEA-AIR-SPACE MUSEUM

Pier 86, at 46th St. and 12th Ave. Subway: A, C, E to 42nd St.-Port Authority. Take the M42 west to 42nd. St. and Hudson River (Twelfth Ave.). Walk north to museum. ☎212-245-0072; www.intrepidmuseum.com Open Apr. 1-Sept. 28 M-F 10am-5pm, Sa-Su 10am-6pm; Oct. 1-Mar. 31 Tu-Su 10am-5pm. Last admission 1hr. before closing. $14; seniors, students ages 12-17, and veterans $10; ages 6-11 $7; ages 2-5 $2; active duty servicemen and under 2 free. Wheelchair patrons half-price.

A dream come true for kids of all ages who dream about wartime heroics, the museum features the veteran WWII and Vietnam War aircraft carrier *Intrepid*, the Vietnam War destroyer *Edson*, and the only publicly displayed guided-missile submarine, *Growler*. Pioneer's Hall displays models, antiques, and film shorts of flying devices from the turn of the century to the 1930s. Visitors can climb aboard the *Intrepid's* 900 ft. flight deck to view old and new warplanes—including a declassified CIA A-12 Blackbird, the world's fastest spy plane. The excitement doesn't stop there: check out the Iraqi tanks parked near the gift shop (captured in the first Gulf War) or the piece of the Berlin Wall outside.

ISAMU NOGUCHI GARDEN MUSEUM

***Interim location until 2005:** 36-01 43rd Ave., at 36th St., Long Island City, Queens. Subway: 7 to 33rd St./Queens Blvd. Map 26, 22. ☎718-204-7088; www.noguchi.org. Open Apr.-Oct. W-F 10am-5pm, Sa-Su 11am-6pm. Lengthy free tour 2pm. Courtesy shuttle leaves Sa-Su from the Asia Society, 70th St. and Park Ave. in Manhattan, every 30min. 11:30am-3:30pm; return trips every hr. noon-5pm. Suggested donation $5, students and seniors $2. **After 2005, permanent location change:** 32-37 Vernon Blvd., at 10th St. and 33rd Rd., in Long Island City, Queens. Subway: N, W to Broadway.*

The temporary location features rotating exhibits from the permanent collection and an indoor Japanese rock garden. Noguchi's breathtaking and wide-ranging work includes the sculptures that stand around the shimmering water of *The Well*, Italian playground slides, and *akari* lamps—mulberry paper and bamboo lanterns—that can be purchased at the museum. Not on exhibit at the museum, but perhaps indicative of the artist's vision, is Noguchi's *Sculpture to Be Seen From Mars*, a 2 mi. long face carved in the dirt next to Newark Liberty International Airport.

JACQUES MARCHAIS MUSEUM OF TIBETAN ART

338 Lighthouse Ave., at Nugent St., Staten Island. Bus S74 to Richmond Rd. and Lighthouse Ave.; turn right and walk up the fairly steep hill. Map 29, C4, 7. ☎718-987-3500; www.tibetanmuseum.com. Open daily 1-5pm. $5, seniors and students $3, under 12 $2.

This serene hilltop museum's bronzes, paintings, and sculpture from Tibet and its surrounding areas make up one of the largest private collections of Tibetan art in the West. The terraced sculpture gardens look down on the distant Lower Bay. Programs on Asian culture (fees vary) cover topics ranging from environmental consciousness to meditation.

JAPAN SOCIETY

333 E. 47th St., at First Ave. Subway: E, V, 6 to 51st St. Map 14, F3, 56. ☎ 212-832-1155; www.japansociety.org. Gallery tours Tu and Th 12:30pm. Open Tu-F 11am-6pm, Sa-Su 11am-5pm. $5, students and seniors $3.

Junzo Yoshimura's design—a plain, Western facade with an entirely Asian interior—embodies the attempt to bring together the people of Japan and the US. An interior pool garden on the first floor, complete with stones and bamboo trees, evokes the spirit of a traditional Japanese home. The second-floor gallery exhibits traditional and contemporary Japanese art. The Society also sponsors Japanese language courses, lectures, meetings with notable leaders, a film series, and performances.

THE JEWISH MUSEUM

1109 Fifth Ave., at 92nd St. Subway: 6 to 96th St. Map 15, A3, 6. ☎ 212-423-3200; wheelchair access info ☎ 423-3225; www.thejewishmuseum.org. Open Su-W 11am-5:45pm, Th 11am–8pm, F 11am-3pm. $10, students and seniors $7.50, under 12 free. Th 5-9pm pay what you wish. Free gallery talks usually M-Th at 12:15, 2:15, and 4:15pm. Inquire at admissions desk. Free audio guides on 4th fl.

The gallery's permanent exhibit about the Jewish experience throughout history, *Culture and Continuity: The Jewish Journey*, begins with ancient Biblical artifacts and ceremonial objects and moves on to contemporary masterpieces by Marc Chagall, Frank Stella, and George Segal. The installation culminates in hypermodernity with a deconstructivist mezuzah and an interactive Talmud exhibit. Popular rotating exhibits emphasize interpretation of art through the lens of social history.

LOWER EAST SIDE TENEMENT MUSEUM

90 Orchard St., at Broome St. Subway: F, J, M, Z to Delancey St.-Essex St. Map 11, D3, 32. ☎ 212-431-0233; www.tenement.org. Visitor Center and Gift Shop open daily 11am-5:30pm. Note that the tenement is accessible by guided tour only. Tours of the tenement leave from the Visitor Center. 1hr. long. Every 30min. Tu-W and F 1-4pm and Th 4:30, 5, and 6pm; Sa-Su every 20min. 11am-4:30pm. July and Aug. M tours 1, 2, 3, 4pm. Special Tours periodically through the week. Call or see website for details. Walking tours leave from the Visitors Center Th 6pm, Sa-Su 1, 2:30 pm. $8-9, students and seniors $6-7 (depending on which apartment is visited).

Three tours explore meticulously restored apartments that recreate the lives of the immigrant families who once inhabited the tenement. One tour focuses on a Depression-era family; another, on turn-of-the-century garment workers; the third involves a costumed guide taking you to the Confino apartment. The 1hr. neighborhood walking tours focus on historical buildings and immigrant experiences—past and present—in the Lower East Side. This museum is one of the finest investigations of New York history around.

MERCHANT'S HOUSE MUSEUM

29 E. 4th St., between Lafayette Ave. and Bowery. Subway: 6 to Bleecker St. ☎ 212-777-1089; www.merchantshouse.com. Open M and Th-Su 1-5pm. $6, students and seniors $4.

This three-floor museum is located in the preserved townhouse of Seabury Tredwell, a well-off 19th-century merchant. It features furniture, clothing, and other belongings of the Tredwell family.

MOUNT VERNON HOTEL MUSEUM AND GARDEN

421 E. 61st St., between York and First Ave. Subway: 4, 5, 6, N, R, W to 59th St.-Lexington Ave.; F to Lexington Ave./63rd St. Map 15, C6, 64. ☎212-838-6878. Open Sept.-July Tu-Su 11am-4pm. $5, students and seniors $4, under 12 free.

This reconstruction of the rooms of the Mount Vernon Hotel (1826-1833) illuminates early 19th-century hotel life by offering tours, lectures, and concerts. Summer Garden evenings, every Tuesday at 6pm in June and July ($12 adults, $5 children), offer games and music from the period for both adults and children, as well as an open bar ($10). Call the museum for further schedule information.

EL MUSEO DEL BARRIO

1230 Fifth Ave., at 104th St. Subway: 6 to 103rd St./Lexington Ave. Map 19, C7, 40; Map 15, A2, 1. ☎212-831-7272; www.elmuseo.org. Open W-Su 11am-5pm. Suggested contribution $5, students and seniors $3, under 12 free.

This bilingual museum and expansive Latino cultural institution, founded in 1969 by Puerto Rican artists and activists, features art and culture from throughout the Caribbean and Latin America. The permanent collection includes works by Santos de Palo, hand-crafted wooden saint figures from Latin America, and a vast exhibit, titled Voyagers of the Caribbean, on pre-Columbian and Taino art and ceramics dating back to AD 1200. Artistic treasures such as the colorful Chicano prints and Haitian Vodun flags complement contemporary exhibits celebrating Latin American culture's past and present. Recent exhibitions include Puerto Rican artist Rafael Turino's 'Painter of the People.'

MUSEUM FOR AFRICAN ART

36-01 43rd Ave., Long Island City, Queens. Subway: 7 to 33rd St./Queens Blvd. ☎718-784-7700; fax 784-7718; www.africanart.org. Open Tu-F 10:30am-5:30pm, Sa-Su noon-6pm. $5, students and seniors $2.50. Su free. ***In 2005, the museum will move permanently to Manhattan.***

This museum features two major exhibits a year, along with smaller exhibitions of stunning African and African-American art on such themes as storytelling, magic, religion, and mask-making. Objects on display span centuries and come from all over Africa. Many hands-on, family-oriented workshops on African culture are offered, providing instruction in traditional activities such as weaving and drumming. Call or visit the website for details.

MUSEUM OF AMERICAN ILLUSTRATION

128 E. 63rd St., between Lexington and Park Ave. Subway: 4, 5, 6, N, R, W to 59th St.-Lexington Ave.; F to Lexington Ave./63rd St. Map 15, B6, 56. ☎212-838-2560. Open Tu 10am-8pm, W-F 10am-5pm, Sa noon-4pm. Free.

Established in 1981 by the Society of Illustrators, this treasure of a museum owns over 1500 works by such legendary artists as Rockwell, Pyle, and Wyeth. A small, rotating exhibit in the main gallery focuses on the interplay between past, present, and future in the field of illustration. Your favorite artists' sketchbooks are also on sale at the front of the museum.

MUSEUM OF THE CHINESE IN THE AMERICAS

70 Mulberry St., between Bayard and Canal St. Subway: N, R, Q, W, J, M, Z, or 6 to Canal St. ☎212-619-4785; www.moca-nyc.org. Open Tu-Su noon-5pm. $3, students and seniors $1, children under 12 free.

First museum dedicated to the history of the Chinese and their descendants in the Western hemisphere, this museum houses a number of art, historical, and architectural exhibits like Ken Chu's installation '*Tong Zhi/Comrade: Out in Asia America*. The museum gift shop sells Chinese books, prints, and other trinkets.

MUSEUM OF THE CITY OF NEW YORK

1220 Fifth Ave., at 103rd St. Subway: 6 to 103rd St./ Lexington Ave. Map 19, C7, 41. ☎212-534-1672; www.mcny.org. Open W-Sa 10am-5pm, Su noon-5pm. Suggested contribution $7; seniors, students, and children $4, families $12.

This fascinating museum recounts the Big Apple's history. The vast collection includes an extensive photography exhibit documenting New York's evolution in the first half of the 20th century, a display on the 1898 consolidation of the boroughs, a toy gallery, and various temporary exhibits. Rotating exhibits like the 'Harlem Lost & Found' and 'Roaring into the Twenties: The New York Woman' complement the permanent displays nicely. Don't miss the reconstructed rooms from the Rockefeller mansion on the fifth floor.

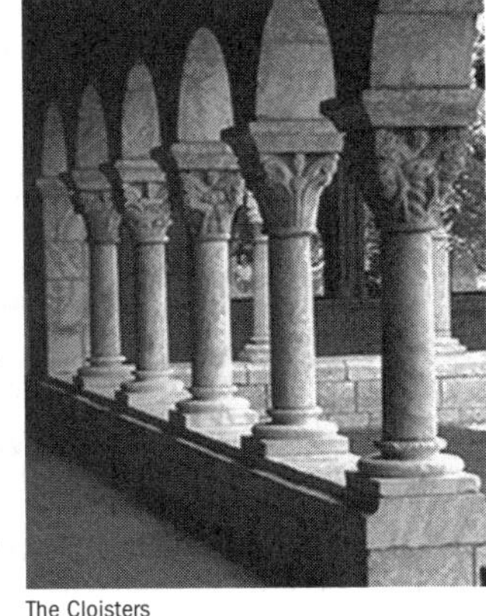
The Cloisters

MUSEUM OF JEWISH HERITAGE

18 First Pl., at Battery Park City. Subway: 4, 5 to Bowling Green; N, R to Whitehall St.; J, M, Z to Broad St.; 1, 2 to Wall St./William St. Map 7, B5, 16. ☎212-968-1800; www.mjhnyc.org. Open Su-W 10am-5:45pm, Th 10am-8pm, F and on eve of Jewish holidays 10am-3pm; Apr.-Oct. F 10am-5pm. Closed on Jewish holidays. $7, students and seniors $5, under 5 free.

This sleek, six-sided building recalling the Star of David pays painful yet uplifting tribute to the Jewish people. The collection of poignant personal artifacts complements hours of personal narratives to present a larger picture of Jewish life. The museum also owns some 2000 photos and 24 original documentary films. While the exhibits on the Holocaust are inherently upsetting, they are tempered by the hopeful final displays.

P.S. 1, Queens

MUSEUM OF TELEVISION AND RADIO

25 W. 52nd St., between Fifth and Sixth Ave. Subway: B, D, F, V to 47th-50th St.-Rockefeller Center/Sixth Ave. or E, V to Fifth Ave./53rd St. Map 14, D3, 39. ☎212-621-6600; daily activity schedule ☎212-621-6800; www.mtr.org. Open Tu-W and F-Su noon-6pm, Th noon-8pm. $10, students and seniors $8, under 13 $5. ISIC and AAA members free.

More archive than museum, this shrine to modern media contains over 100,000 TV and radio programs that are easily accessible through a computerized cataloguing system. The entrance fee includes up to 2hr. of screening room usage. In addition, the museum hosts film screenings focusing on topics of social, historical, popular, or artistic interest. Pick up a daily schedule at the front counter.

Max Protech Gallery

NATIONAL ACADEMY OF DESIGN MUSEUM

1083 Fifth Ave., between 89th and 90th St. Subway: 4, 5, 6, to 86th St./Lexington Ave. Map 15, A3, 8. ☎ 212-369-4880; www.nationalacademy.org. Open W-Th noon-5pm, F-Su 11am-6pm. Wheelchair-accessible. $8, seniors, students, and under 16 $4.50.

Founded in 1825 to "promote the fine arts through exhibition and instruction," the Academy both shows exhibits and trains young artists. Such notables as Winslow Homer, Frederic Edwin Church, John Singer Sargent, and Thomas Eakins represent the 19th century in the permanent collection.

NATIONAL MUSEUM AND ARCHIVE OF LESBIAN, GAY, BISEXUAL AND TRANSGENDER HISTORY

208 W. 13th St., 1st fl., between Seventh and Eighth Ave. Subway: 1, 2, 3 to 14th St./Seventh Ave.; A, C, E, L to 14th St./Eighth Ave. Map 10, B2, 6. ☎ 212-620-7310; www.gaycenter.org. Open Th 6-9pm and by appointment.

This museum, devoted to artwork that explores lesbian, gay, bisexual, and transgendered life, is housed in the Lesbian and Gay Community Services Center (p. 305). It includes a wide variety of exhibits that range from works by lesbian artists to photos of transgendered lives. The museum will play host to the New York City Erotic Art Fair from May 21-23, 2004.

NATIONAL MUSEUM OF THE AMERICAN INDIAN

1 Bowling Green. Subway: 4, 5 to Bowling Green. Map 7, C5, 17. ☎ 212-514-3888; www.si.edu/nmai. Open daily 10am-5pm, Th closes at 8pm. Free.

Housed in the stunning Custom House, this excellent museum exhibits the best of the Smithsonian's vast collection of Native American artifacts. Exhibitions are entirely conceived and designed by Native American artists and craftsmen.

NEW MUSEUM OF CONTEMPORARY ART

583 Broadway, between Prince and W. Houston St. Subway: N, R to Prince St.; C, E to Spring St./Ave. of the Americas (Sixth Ave.); 6 to Spring St./Lafayette St.; F, S, V to Broadway-Lafayette St. Map 9, D1, 11. ☎ 212-219-1222; www.newmuseum.org. Open Su, Tu-W and F-Sa noon-6pm, Th noon-8pm. $6, students and seniors $3, under 18 free. Th 6-8pm $3.

Since the New Museum was founded in 1977, its support of the newest and most controversial contemporary art has made it one of the world's premier modern art museums. Free lectures, symposia, panel discussions, and film screenings accompany most major exhibitions. Gallery talks are held in which an artist discusses his or her work. Three galleries feature innovative pieces in many media. Recent shows include a group exhibition entitled 'Black President: The Art and Legacy of Fela Anikulapo-Kuti' that explores the cultural impact of the famous Nigerian musician and activist who died in 1997.

NEW YORK CITY FIRE MUSEUM

278 Spring St., between Varick and Hudson St. Subway: 1, 9 to Houston St. Map 9, A3, 23. ☎ 212-691-1303; www.nycfiremuseum.org. Open Su 10am-4pm, Tu-Sa 10am-5pm. Suggested donation $5, students and seniors $2, under 12 $1.

Housed in a renovated 1904 firehouse, the museum satisfies the hero—or the pyromaniac—in kids and adults and alike. Impressive relics of fire-fighting past are on display, such as a hand-pulled truck from when George Washington was a volunteer NYC firefighter. The first permanent Sept. 11 exhibit, 'If They Could Speak,' is also on display. Guided, educational group and children tours available by reservation.

NEW YORK CITY POLICE MUSEUM

100 Old Slip, between Water and South St. Subway: 4, 5 to Bowling Green; 1, 2 to Wall St./William St.; N, R to Whitehall St. Map 7, E4, 21. ☎ 212-480-3100; www.nycpolicemuseum.org. Open Tu-Sa 10am-5pm. Wheelchair-accessible. Suggested admission $5, seniors $3, ages 6-19 $2, under 6 free. Call for group rates.

The police museum houses an extensive collection of memorabilia, most of which has never been on public display. An impressive array of badges, guns, and criminal profiles appeals to the public's desire for luridness. The *Vintage Weapons and Notorious Criminals* exhibit features the machine gun used by Al Capone's gang to assassinate Frankie Yale. Adults can arrange a turn on the Firearms and Tactics Simulator (FATS), used to train members of the police force (Available at 12:30, 1:30, and 2:30pm; groups should call to reserve). Two new exhibits feature the history of women in the police force, and the use of forensics and DNA. One wing is dedicated to the officers who lost their lives on Sept. 11.

NEW YORK HISTORICAL SOCIETY

2 W. 77th St., at Central Park W. Subway: 1, 2 to 79th; B, C to 72nd St./Central Park W., 81st St. Map 18, D4, 56. ☎ 212-873-3400; www.nyhistory.org. Museum open Labor Day-Memorial Day Tu-Su 11am-5pm; Memorial Day-Labor Day Tu-Su 11am-6pm. Wheelchair-accessible. Library open Labor Day-Memorial Day Tu-Su 10am-5pm; Memorial Day-Labor Day Tu-Su 10am-5pm. Gallery talks 1, 3pm. $6, students and seniors $4, children free.

Founded in 1804, this block-long Neoclassical building houses both New York's oldest continuously operated museum and a library. The Society's extensive, six-million-object collection, displayed in the **Henry Luce III Center** on the fourth floor, includes 132 Tiffany lamps (displayed furniture store style), George Washington's bed, Napoleon's chair, and 435 Audubon watercolors. The museum's minimalist approach may appeal to some visitors, while frustrating others: pieces are lined up behind glass and accompanied by little explanation.

NEW YORK TRANSIT MUSEUM

Corner of Schermerhorn St. and Boerum Pl. Subway: 1, 2, 3, 4, 5, M, N, R to Court St./ Borough Hall. Map 22, 20. ☎ 718-243-3060; www.mta.info/mta/museum. Open Tu-F 10am-4pm, Sa-Su noon-5pm. $3, children and senior citizens $1.50, seniors free W noon-4pm. ***Closed until fall 2003.***

Ever wonder what it was like to sit in a subway car from the 1930s? We have. Do you think about tokens a lot? We do. Does the Transit Museum fulfill our subterranean longings? It does. And it's even more awesome than we could have anticipated! Housed in the now-defunct Court St. subway station, this museum meticulously describes the birth and evolution of New York's mass transit system, from subways to buses to commuter rails. The walk-through exhibit includes old subway maps, turnstiles, and even the trains themselves. The museum is currently closed for renovations. Once it reopens, watch for a new art gallery, computer lab, and reference library. Embrace your inner subway nerd.

PARSONS EXHIBITION CENTER

2 W. 13th St., at Parsons School of Design on Fifth Ave. Subway: 4, 5, 6, L, N, Q, R, W to 14th St.-Union Sq. Map 10, E2, 10. ☎ 212-229-8987. Open M-F 9am-6pm. Free.

These ever-changing exhibitions of student and faculty work include photography, computer art, painting, and sculpture.

PIERPONT MORGAN LIBRARY

29 E. 36th St., at Madison Ave. Subway: 6 to 33rd St./Park Ave. S. Map 13, E2. ☎ 212-685-0610; www.morganlibrary.org. ***Closed for renovations until 2006.***

P.S.1 CONTEMPORARY ART CENTER

22-25 Jackson Ave., at 46th Ave., Long Island City. Subway: 7 to 45th Rd.-Courthouse Sq.; E, V to 23rd St.-Ely Ave.; G to 21st St./Jackson Ave. Map 26, 18. ☎718-784-2084; www.ps1.org. Open W-Su noon-6pm. Wheelchair-accessible. Suggested donation $5, students and seniors $2.

P.S.1, the first public school in then-independent Long Island City, has been converted into a cutting-edge art space—even the staircase landings are used as display areas. Rotating exhibits continue to keep up the museum's reputation for being at the vanguard of contemporary art. A partnership with MoMA has provided P.S.1 with access to the museum's resources while giving the larger institution street cred. The fourth floor offers a spectacular view of Manhattan and the surrounding area. In the summer, P.S.1 holds Saturday afternoon jammies in their art-stuffed courtyard (Live DJs, food and drink available. Weather-permitting).

STUDIO MUSEUM

144 W. 125th St., between Adam Clayton Powell Jr. Blvd. (Seventh Ave.) and Lenox (Sixth) Ave. Subway: 2, 3 to 125th St./Lenox (Sixth) Ave. Map 19, C5, 23. ☎212-864-4500. Open Su noon-6pm, W-F noon-6pm, Sa 10am-6pm. Gallery talks and tours Sa at 1pm. $7, students and seniors $3, members and under 12 free.

Born in 1967 at the height of the civil rights movement, the Studio Museum is dedicated to the collection and exhibition of works by contemporary black artists. It features two exhibitions per year of multimedia works, installations, paintings, sculptures, and photographs. The museum is currently undergoing a major growth spurt that will add gallery space, an auditorium, and a cafe.

WATERFRONT MUSEUM

290 Conover St., at Barge #79, Pier 45, in Red Hook, Brooklyn. Subway: A, C, F to Jay St.-Borough Hall; M, N, R to Court St.; then bus #B61 to Beard St.; walk 1 block in the opposite direction from bus; turn left onto Conover St. The museum is 2 blocks in the direction of the waterfront. Free shuttle bus from surrounding Brooklyn neighborhoods (see website for details). Map 24, 5. ☎718-624-4719; www.waterfrontmuseum.org. Garden pier open daily 24hr. Call for barge hours. Free. Circus Su on the barge, rain or shine; June 1pm and 4:30pm; advance tickets $10, Tickets the day of the performance $5, any remaining seats at showtime $1.

This is not your typical museum. First, it's located on the Lehigh Valley Railroad Barge #79, the only functional wooden barge floating in the New York Harbor. Second, the museum focuses not only on the exhibits but on the barge, the pier, and the stunning view. The museum's proprietor pulled the barge out of a muddy bank himself and took years to restore it to its present state. The museum hosts a great **Sunset Concert Series** (July-Aug. Sa 8-11pm; doors open 7:30pm. Suggested donation $5).

GALLERIES

New York's galleries are the vanguard of contemporary art. What's even better, gallery proprietors won't necessarily expect you to buy anything (read: be able to afford anything on display). And they don't even charge for entrance—yes, sometimes the best of culture can be **free.**

To get started, ask for a free copy of *The Gallery Guide* (www.galleryguideonline.com) at any major museum or gallery. Published every two to three months, it lists the addresses, phone numbers, and hours of virtually every showplace in the city. Extensive gallery info can also be found in the "Choices" listings of the free *Village Voice*, the Art section of *Time Out* and *New York* magazines, the complimentary *The New York Art World* (www.thenewyorkartworld.com) available in select galleries, and in *The New Yorker*'s "Goings On About Town."

Most galleries are open Tuesday to Saturday, from 10 or 11am to 5 or 6pm. Galleries are usually only open on weekend afternoons in the summer; many are closed from late July to early September, as gallery types head to the Hamptons in droves for their late summer vacation.

SOHO

Subway: C, E to Spring St./Ave. of the Americas (Sixth Ave.); 6 to Spring St./Lafayette St.; N, R to Prince St.; 1, 2 to W. Houston St.; F, S, V to Broadway-Lafayette St.

Since SoHo galleries open and close with amazing rapidity, many of them unfortunately have had to cut their losses and sell out. Still, the avant-garde does make a stand here. The most cutting-edge offerings have trouble making it to the ground-level, commercial galleries that line West Broadway and Broadway, so if you want to see SoHo's more experimental art, explore the second or third floors of gallery-packed buildings. The addresses 560-594 Broadway, between W. Houston and Prince St., are known as the **Broadway Gallery Buildings;** they have many small galleries huddled inside. (Map 9, D1.) The following list is only a sampling of this art-packed neighborhood.

Artists Space, 38 Greene St., 3rd fl., at Grand St. (☎212-226-3970). Subway: 1, 9 to Canal St./Varick St.; A, C, E to Canal St./Ave. of the Americas (Sixth Ave.). Map 9, C3, 33. Nonprofit gallery open since 1972. Space used for several, smaller exhibits by emerging artists, as well as large exhibits by artists such as contemporary architecturalist Zaha Hadid. Slide file of unaffiliated artists gives those without backing a chance to shine. Open Tu-Sa 11am-6pm. Slide file open by appointment F-Sa. Closed end of July through the beginning of September.

Deitch Projects, 76 Grand St., between Greene and Wooster St. (☎212-343-7300). Subway: 1, 9 to Canal St./Varick St.; A, C, E to Canal St./Ave. of the Americas (Sixth Ave.). Map 9, C3, 43. A red and black firey arch greets you as you enter this 3-room exhibition space that often has group shows of up-and-coming artists. Open Tu-Sa noon-6pm.

Dia Center for the Arts, 141 Wooster St., between W. Houston and Prince St. (☎212-473-8072). Subway: N, R to Prince St. Map 9, C1, 7. Extension of the Chelsea gallery has been showing Walter De Maria's *The New York Earth Room* since 1977. Closed mid-June to early Sept. Open W-Sa noon-6pm. Another branch is located at 548 and 545 W. 22nd St., between 10th and 11th Ave. Same opening hours, but closed late July-Sept. only; admission (only charged for W. 22nd St. branch) $6, students and seniors $4, under 10 free.

The Drawing Center, 35 Wooster St., between Grand and Broome St. (☎212-219-2166). Subway: 1, 9 to Canal St./Varick St.; A, C, E to Canal St./Ave. of the Americas (Sixth Ave.). Map 9, C3, 31. Specializing exclusively in original works on paper, this nonprofit space sets up reliably high-quality exhibits. Both historical and contemporary works—everything from Picasso to Kara Walker, are on rotation. Open Tu-F 10am-6pm, Sa 11am-6pm; closed Aug. Suggested donation $3. The Drawing Room across the street at 40 Wooster showcases illustrations of emerging artists like Roza El-Hassan's 'Drawings'.

Illustration House, 96 Spring St., 7th fl., between Mercer and Broadway. (☎212-966-9444). Subway: 6 to Spring St./Lafayette St.; C, E to Spring St./Ave. of the Americas (Sixth Ave.). Map 9, D2, 21. Devoted to exhibiting original American illustrative paintings and drawings. Works by Rockwell and N.C. Wyeth can be found here. Open Tu-Sa 10am-6pm.

The Painting Center, 52 Greene St., 2nd fl., at Broome St. (☎212-343-1060). Subway: 6 to Spring St./Lafayette St.; C, E to Spring St./Ave. of the Americas (Sixth Ave.). Map 9, C3, 29. Small gallery features colorful paintings of all shapes and sizes. Open Tu-Sa 11am-6pm.

Pop International Galleries, Inc., 473 W. Broadway, between Prince and W. Houston St. (☎212-533-4262; www.popinternational.com). Subway: 6 to Spring St./Lafayette St.; C, E to Spring St./Ave. of the Americas (Sixth Ave.).; N, R to Prince St. Map 9, C1, 5. Comparatively commercial space offers works by pop art icons such as Warhol, Lichtenstein, and Haring as well neo-pop sensations Britto, Burton Morris, and Marco. Also a large selection of vintage Beatles, Eric Clapton and Associated Press photos. Special exhibit for sports-lovers features paintings of boxing great Muhammed Ali. Open M-Sa 10am-7pm, Su 11am-6pm.

Staley-Wise, 560 Broadway, 3rd fl. room 305, at Prince St. (☎212-966-6223; www.staley-wise.com). Subway: N, R to Prince St. Map 9, D2, 19. Focus on fashion photography by the greats such as Louise Dahl-Wolfe, Helmut Newton, Man Ray, David LaChapelle, and Robert Doisneau. Open Sept.-June Tu-Sa 11am-5pm; July-Aug. M-F 11am-5pm.

The Work Space, 96 Spring St., 8th fl., between Broadway and Mercer St. (☎212-219-2790). Subway: 6 to Spring St./Lafayette St.; C, E to Spring St./Ave. of the Americas (Sixth Ave.). Map 9, D2, 22. Adequate art space for unknown, up-and-coming artists situated in a law firm's reception area. Open M-F 10am-5pm; winter also Sa 1-5pm.

CHELSEA

Subway: A, C, E, L to 14th St./Eighth Ave.; C, E to 23rd St./Eighth Ave. Map 13.

Cheaper rents have lured many of the original SoHo galleries to Chelsea's warehouses; the area west of Ninth Ave., between 17th and 26th St., is full of display spaces. Be sure to check out the 11-floor treasure trove of contemporary works at 529 W. 20th St., between 10th and 11th Ave. The area between Fifth and Sixth Ave. and 17th and 21st St., with its professional developing labs, is known as the **Photography District.** Outposts of cutting-edge art have recently emerged in **Chelsea's** reclaimed industrial spaces, centered around W. 14th St. between Ninth and Tenth Ave. and W. 22nd St. between 10th and 11th Ave.

303 Gallery, 525 W. 22nd St., between 10th and 11th Ave. (☎212-255-1121). Subway: C, E to 23rd St./Eighth Ave. Map 13, A5, 47. Open Tu-Sa 10am-6pm.

535 W. 22nd St., 535 W. 22nd St., between 10th and 11th Ave. Subway: C, E to 23rd St./Eighth Ave. Map 13, A5, 47. Home to an assortment of galleries, including the **CRG Gallery** (☎212-229-2766; www.crggallery.com) and the **Frederieke Taylor Gallery** (☎646-230-0992; www.frederieketaylorgallery.com).

D'Amelio Terras, 525 W. 22nd St., between 10th and 11th Ave. (☎212-352-9460; www.dameliotерras.com). Subway: C, E to 23rd St./Eighth Ave. Map 13, A5, 47. Open Labor Day-Memorial Day Tu-Sa 10am-6pm; Memorial Day-Labor Day M-F 10am-6pm.

DCA Gallery, 525 W. 22nd St., between 10th and 11th Ave. (☎212-255-5511; www.dcagallery.com). Subway: C, E to 23rd St./Eighth Ave. Map 13, A5, 47. Open Tu-F 10am-6pm, Sa noon-6pm; closed Aug.

Dia Center for the Arts, 548 W. 22nd St., between 10th and 11th Ave. (☎212-989-5566; www.diacenter.org). Subway: C, E to 23rd St./Eighth Ave. Map 13, A5, 51. A space with a definite knack for tapping into the pulse of contemporary art. Four fl. of long-term (3-9 mo.) exhibits cover a balanced range of media and styles. The roof holds an ongoing video installation piece, *Rooftop Urban Park Project*, as well as a cafe with a decent view of Chelsea. Poetry readings and lectures are held occasionally; call for schedule. Open W-Su noon-6pm; closed mid-June to mid-Sept. Bookstore open W-Su 11am-6pm. $6, students and seniors $3.

Gavin Brown's Enterprise, 436 W. 15th St., between Ninth and Tenth Ave., on the south side of the street behind an unmarked glass door (☎212-627-5258). Subway: A, C, E to 14th St./Eighth Ave.; 1, 2, 3 to 14th St./Seventh Ave. Map 13, B6, 101. This interactive space, hip to the point of incomprehensibility, doubles as gallery and social area. Open Tu-Sa 10am-6pm.

I-20, 529 W. 20th St., 11th fl. (☎212-645-1100; www.I-20.com). Subway: 1, 9 to 18th St./Seventh Ave. Map 13, A5, 54. This gallery, which exhibits high-quality contemporary art in a beautiful 11th-floor space, also commands a stirring view of the river and piers below. Open Tu-Sa 10am-6pm.

Matthew Marks Gallery, 522 W. 22nd St., between 10th and 11th Ave. (☎212-243-0200; www.matthewmarks.com). Subway: C, E to 23rd St./Eighth Ave. Map 13, A5, 53. One of the leading lights of the Chelsea gallery scene, with exhibits by major modern and contemporary artists (Willem de Kooning, Ellsworth Kelly, Nan Goldin) in the 2 large spaces. Open late June to mid-Sept. Tu-Sa 10am-6pm; mid-Sept. to late June M-F 11am-6pm. **Another branch** is at 523 W. 24th St., also between 10th and 11th Ave.

Max Protetch, 511 W. 22nd St., between 10th and 11th Ave. (☎212-633-6999; www.maxprotetch.com). Subway: C, E to 23rd St./Eighth Ave. Map 13, A5, 48. Started as an exhibition space for architectural drawings, Protetch now hosts impressive and intelligent contemporary shows of painting, sculpture, and all things in between. Open Tu-Sa 10am-6pm; closed Aug.

The Museum at the Fashion Institute of Technology, Seventh Ave., at 27th St. (☎212-217-5800). Subway: 1, 9 to 18th St./Seventh Ave. Map 13, C4, 29. A heavenly place for fashion buffs houses several changing exhibits pertaining to all things sartorial, from photography to mannequin displays. Open Tu-F noon-8pm, Sa 10am-5pm.

Sonnabend, 536 W. 22nd St., between 10th and 11th Ave. (☎212-627-0489). Subway: C, E to 23rd St./Eighth Ave. Map 13, A5, 52. Originally located in SoHo, this famous gallery has shown works by well-known American and European contemporary artists for 40 years. Open Tu-Sa 10am-6pm; closed Aug.

MIDTOWN AND THE UPPER EAST SIDE

Midtown's public art is also some of its most interesting. The recently restored NY Public Library Reading Room's **Cloud Scenes** ceiling mural (p. 78; Map 10, D4); Roy Lichtenstein's 68 ft. pop-art masterpiece **Mural with Blue Brush Stroke** in the Atrium of the Equitable Building, 787 Seventh Ave., between 51st and 52nd St. (Map 10, C3); and Thomas Hart Benton's 1932 mural **America Today** in the AXA Financial Center Building, 1290 Sixth Ave., at E. 51st St. (Map 10, D3) are all worth a peek.

The area's galleries themselves, of course, exude a more rarified glamour. **Madison Avenue,** between E. 63rd and E. 81st St., boasts numerous ritzy showplaces. Another group of galleries sits on **57th Street,** between Madison and Park Ave. (Map 10, E2). The stylish Art Deco **Fuller Building,** 41 E. 57th St., harbors 12 floors of galleries with frequent turnover. (Map 14, E2, 25. Most open M-Sa 10am-5:30pm, but call individual galleries to make sure; Oct.-May most closed M.)

Acquavella, 18 E. 79th St., between Madison and Fifth Ave. (☎212-734-6300). Subway: 6 to 77th St. This majestic brownstone houses Impressionist, post-Impressionist, and postwar contemporary paintings, drawings, and sculpture. Picasso, Degas, Cézanne, Giacometti, Monet, and Pollack are found here. Open M-F 10am-5pm.

Christie's, 20 Rockefeller Plaza, at 49th St. (☎212-636-2010). Subway: B, D, F, V to 47th-50th St.-Rockefeller Center. Map 14, D3, 46. This famous international auction house flaunts an impressive collection of valuable wares, ranging from a Giovanni painting to a dress worn by Marilyn Monroe. The 6 galleries and auctions are open to the public. 2-3 sales per wk. during the height of the season; summer months are much slower. Call ahead for a schedule. Open M-Sa 10am-5pm, Su 1-5pm.

Hirschl and Adler Galleries, 21 E. 70th St. between Madison and Fifth Ave. (☎212-535-8810). Subway: 6 to 68th St. 2 fl. of rotating exhibitions show a variety of 18th- and 19th-century European and American art as well as modernist and contemporary works. Open late Sept.-Memorial Day Tu-F 9:30am-5:15pm; Memorial Day-late Sept. M-F 9:30am-4:45pm. Closed Sa, Su, Rosh Hashanah, and Yom Kippur.

Leo Castelli, 59 E. 79th St., between Park and Madison Ave. (☎212-249-4470; www.castelligallery.com). Subway: 6 to 77th St. Showing a selection of contemporary artists such as Jasper Johns and Ed Ruscha. Open mid-Aug. to late June Tu-Sa 10am-6pm; late June to mid-Aug. Tu-F 11am-5pm. Occasionally closed between exhibitions; call ahead.

M. Knoedler & Co., Inc., 19 E. 70th St., between Madison and Fifth Ave. (☎212-794-0550; www.knoedlergallery.com). Subway: 6 to 68th St. Established in 1846, M. Knoedler & Co. is One of the oldest and most respected galleries in the city. Mounts exhibits such as *Frankenthaler: New Paintings*. Open Labor Day-Memorial Day M-Sa 9:30am-5:30pm; Memorial Day-Labor Day M-F 9:30am-5pm.

Pace Gallery, 32 E. 57th St., between Park and Madison Ave. (Pace Prints and Primitive ☎212-421-3237, Pace-MacGill ☎212-759-7999, and Pace Wildenstein ☎212-421-3292; www.paceprints.com). Subway: N, R to Fifth Ave./59th St.; 4, 5, 6 to 59th St./Lexington Ave. Map 14, E2, 27. 4 fl. spread out over this 10-story building are dedicated to the promotion of widely disparate forms of art, ranging from West African sculpture to American contemporary painting. The 10th fl. is home to the Pace Master Prints, works by well-known artists such as Picasso, Miro, Matisse, and Cézanne. Open Oct.-May Tu-Sa 9:30am-6pm; June-Sept. M-Th 9:30am-6pm.

Sotheby's, 1334 York Ave., at 72nd St. (☎212-606-7000, ticket office 606-7171; www.searchsothebys.com). Subway: 6 to 68th St. One of the city's oldest and most respected auction houses, offering everything from Degas to Disney. Auctions open to anyone, but a few of the more popular require a ticket (first come, first served). They also have several galleries for works soon to be auctioned off. Open Labor Day to late June M-Sa 9am-5pm, Su 1-5pm; mid-June to Labor Day closed Sa-Su.

BROOKLYN

The few Bohemian pilgrims that moved into **Williamsburg** in the 80s have seen the area transform into a full-scale artistic mecca. The neighborhood boasts over 30 galleries—with new ones constantly springing up—that provide a forum for cutting-edge artists who have yet to break into the commercialized world of downtown Manhattan. As a result, the art here is current and fresh. Many of the galleries cluster around Bedford Ave. and Grand St., but smaller gems are tucked deeper into Williamsburg.

Aquatic Creations, 99 N. 10th St., between Wythe and Berry Ave. (☎718-302-9080; www.aquaticcreationsinc.com). Subway: L to Bedford Ave. Map 21, 8. There is a shark at this place. It's in a big cubic tank. There are also other tanks: some with fish, some with water, many with both. Fish, sharks, and cutting-edge artwork are all for sale and on display at this warehouse-style gallery. Open daily noon-8pm.

Brooklyn Bridge Anchorage, Cadman Plaza W., on the corner of Hicks and Old Fulton St. (☎718-802-1215). Subway: A, C to High St. Map 22, 9. A gallery/performance space housed within the bridge's cavernous suspension cable storage chambers. Cutting-edge, multimedia installations make good use of the vaulted, 80 ft. ceilings. Creative Time runs the under-bridge space, which it uses for hip music performances. Open mid-May to mid-Oct. Th-Tu noon-8pm, W noon-7pm. Creative Time open Th-F 3-8pm, Sa-Su 1-6pm.

Lunar Base, 197 Grand St., between Bedford St. and Driggs Ave. (☎718-599-2905). Subway: L to Bedford Ave. Map 21, 34. Amid many other galleries, this one boasts bold abstract and contemporary works from international artists. Open Th-Su 1-7pm.

Pierogi, 177 N. 9th St., between Bedford and Driggs Ave. (☎718-599-2144; www.pierogi2000.com). Subway: L to Bedford Ave. Map 21, 18. Hosts 2 big-name solo shows a month, but the front files still display hundreds of affordable works by emerging artists. Those lucky enough to visit one of the openings can expect free pierogis. Open M and F-Su noon-6pm.

Plus Ultra, 235 S. 1st St., between Roebling and Havermeyer Ave. (☎718-387-3844). Subway: L to Bedford Ave. Map 21, 35. Small gallery aims to show slightly irreverent, accessible pieces in a conscious interplay with art history. Sounds convoluted, but the elegant simplicity speaks for itself. Open Sa-Su noon-6pm.

Rome ARTS, 103 Havermayer St., between 1st and Grand St. (☎718-388-2009). Subway: L to Bedford Ave. Map 21, 36. Tiny space constantly switching up its cutting edge exhibits by up-and-coming artists. Open Sa-Su noon-6pm.

Schroeder Romero, 173A N. 3rd St., between Bedford St. and Driggs Ave. (☎646-389-3213). Map 21, 32. Gem of a gallery hidden above a loading dock with no sign on the door. Its mission is to promote solo exhibitions. Open Sa-Su noon-6pm.

The Williamsburg Art and Historical Center, 135 Broadway 2nd fl., between Bedford and Driggs Ave. (☎718-486-7372). Subway: J, M, Z to Marcy Ave.; L to Bedford Ave. Map 21, 43. The epicenter of the Williamsburg arts scene, this historic building's beautiful 2nd-floor gallery exhibits the work of local and international artists. A monthly musical performance and biannual international show keep this center bustling with artists from all backgrounds. Theater and music events also featured; call for details. Open Sa-Su noon-6pm.

QUEENS

Long Island City is the center of the Queens arts scene. In addition to these spaces, don't miss P.S.1 (p. 142). The courtesy shuttle **Queens Artlink** runs on weekends from the Museum of Modern Art in Manhattan to major Queens sites. The route connects P.S.1, the Isamu Noguchi Museum (p. 136), Socrates Sculpture Park (p. 113), and the American Museum of the Moving Image (p. 134). (☎718-708-9750; www.queensartlink.com. Runs Sa-Su 11:30am-5:30pm.)

New York Center for Media Arts, 45-12 Davis St., off Jackson Ave., under the 7 line (☎718-472-9414; www.nycmediaarts.org). Subway: E, V to 23rd St.-Ely Ave.; G to 21st St.; 7 to 45th Rd.-Courthouse Sq. Map 25, A2. Spacious converted warehouse featuring rotating installations of multimedia artwork. Exhibits rotate every few months. Open Th-Su noon-6pm.

Holocenter (Center for the Holographic Arts), 45-10 Court Sq. (☎718-784-5065; www.holocenter.com). Subway: E, V to 23rd St.-Ely Ave.; G to 21st St.; 7 to 45th Rd.-Courthouse Sq. Map 25, A1. An exhibition space dedicated to artwork involving holograms. Open by appointment.

Jamaica Center for Arts, 161-04 Jamaica Ave., at 161st St. (☎718-658-7400; www.jcal.org). Subway: E, J, Z to Jamaica Center. Map 25, D3, 10. The small gallery offers workshops and art exhibits by local and international artists. Also organizes talks and classes. Open M-Tu and F-Sa 9am-6pm, W-Th 9am-8pm.

THE BRONX

Lehman Art Gallery, 250 Bedford Park Blvd., between West and Goulden Ave. On the campus of Herbert Lehman College (northwest side), in the Fine Arts Building (☎718-960-8731). Subway: 4 to Bedford Park Blvd.-Lehman College; B, D to Bedford Park Blvd.-Allerton Ave. Map 28, B2, 7. Housed in a building designed by Marcel Breuer, the gallery's past exhibitions have included examinations of femininity in contemporary Asian art, and paintings commemorating Puerto Rican victims of domestic violence. Every June, Lehman holds a children's show displaying art made by local youngsters in the museum's education program. Open Sept.-May Tu-Sa 10am-4pm; June and July M-F 10am-4pm; Aug. by appointment only.

INSIDE

listings by type of food **150**

listings by neighborhood **153**

financial district and civic center **153**

chinatown **154** little italy **156** nolita **157**

lower east side **158**

tribeca **160** soho **160**

greenwich village **161** east village **164**

chelsea and herald square **169**

union square, gramercy, and murray hill **171**

the theater district and hell's kitchen **173** midtown **174**

upper east side **175** upper west side **176**

morningside heights **178** harlem and washington heights **179**

brooklyn **181** queens **187**

the bronx **189** staten island **191**

Food & Drink

If this isn't the first chapter you're reading, you've made a mistake: flights and hotel rooms are important, but they mean nothing if you don't know where to have lunch. New York is a diner's paradise and New Yorkers treat their gustatory urges with gusto (i.e. they like to eat). Whether expense-accounting your way through a seven-course tasting menu in Midtown or scouring Queens for the best kebab vendor, you'll be able to find a perfect meal in New York. Don't be shy about leaving Manhattan; many of the city's best restaurants (and best deals) are in Brooklyn and Queens. If you're sure that ritz and glitz are totally out of your budget, think again. Every summer, many of New York's best restaurants participate in the **NY Restaurant Week,** during which the price of lunch corresponds to the current year. For example, the 2004 price will be $20.04—definitely a deal at places like Lutece, Gramercy Tavern, and Peter Luger (see p. 180). Reservations tend to go quickly. For dates and participating restaurants, call ☎212-484-1200 or visit www.nycvisit.com.

ORGANIZATION

We have prefaced the food listings with a chart of our favorite restaurants categorized **by cuisine.** These "*Let's Go* Picks" feature an extraordinary marriage of low prices with high quality. We base our appraisals on price, quality, and atmosphere. For more complete listings of good eats, turn to the **By Neighborhood** section.

Price ranges found in food listings are based on the average price of entrees:

❶	❷	❸	❹	❺
under $7	**$7-12**	**$13-18**	**$19-30**	**$31+**

LISTINGS BY TYPE OF FOOD

NEIGHBORHOODS: CHI Chinatown; **GV** Greenwich Village; **TBC** TriBeCa; **SoHo** SoHo; **EV** East Village; **UGM** Union Square, Gramercy, and Murray Hill; **UES** Upper East Side; **UWS** Upper West Side; **NOL** NoLIta; **QUE** Queens; **ST** Staten Island; **BX** Bronx; **THE** Theater District; **CHE** Chelsea and Herald Square; **MH** Morningside Heights; **LIT** Little Italy; **MID** Midtown; **LES** Lower East Side; **HAR** Harlem and Washington Heights; **FD** Financial District and Civic Center.

AFRICAN

Keur N'Deye (184) CB ❷
Madiba Restaurant & Shebeen (184) CB ❷
La Marmite (179) HAR ❷
Massawa (179) MH ❷

AMERICAN, STANDARD

@SQC (184) UWS ❹
12th St. Grill (186) CB ❸
Around the Clock (168) EV ❶
Barking Dog Luncheonette (175) UES ❷
Bendix Diner (164) EV ❷
betterburger (169) CHE ❷
Big Nick's Burger & Pizza Joint (176) UES ❷
Blue 9 Burger (165) EV ❶
Brooklyn Moon (184) BH ❶
Cargo Cafe (191) ST ❸
Chat 'n' Chew (171) UGM ❷
Corner Bistro (161) GV ❶
Crif Dogs (165) EV ❶
Dallas BBQ (176) UES ❸
Dizzy's (185) CB ❷
DuMont Restaurant WIL ❸
EJ's Luncheonette (175) UES ❷
elmo (170) CHE ❷
Empire Diner (170) CHE ❷
French Roast Cafe GV ❸
Good Enough to Eat (177) UWS ❷
Gray's Papaya (177) UWS ❶
Green Kitchen (168) UES ❶
Grilled Cheese (158) LES ❶
Island Burgers and Shakes (173) THE ❷
It's A Wrap (177) UWS ❷
Jackson Diner (187) QUE ❷
Jackson Hole (175) UES ❷
Jesse's Place HAR ❷
Josie's (177) UWS ❸
Junior's (184) CB ❷
Mama's Food Shop (166) GV ❷
Merchants NY (175) UES ❸
Nathan's (186) SB ❶
Papaya King (175) UES ❶
Paul's Boutique (158) LES ❶
Peanut Butter & Co. (163) GV ❶
Peter Luger (180) WIL ❺
Pink Tea Cup (163) GV ❷
Pommes Frites (167) EV ❶
Ranch 1 (171) UGM ❶

AMERICAN, STANDARD, CONT'D

Roll n' Roaster (186) SB ❶
Rush Hour (159) NOL ❶
Space Untitled (161) SoHo ❶
Tom's Restaurant (179) MH ❶
Viand (176) UES ❷
Waverly Restaurant (168) GV ❶
Yaffa's Tea Room (160) TBC ❸

AMERICAN, NEW

Bubby's (160) TBC ❷
Cafe Colonial Restaurant (157) NOL ❷
Cafe Gitane (157) NOL ❷
Chef & Co. (170) CHE ❷
City Grill (176) UWS ❸
Esperanto Cafe (162) GV ❶
Food Bar (171) CHE ❷
Henry's (177) UWS ❸
Jerry's (160) SoHo ❷
L Cafe (182) WIL ❷
Pink Pony (159) NOL ❷
Toast (179) MOH ❷

ASIAN, MISCELLANEOUS

Elvie's Turo-Turo (165) EV ❶
Faan (185) SB ❷
Kum Gang San (188) QUE ❷
Rice (157) NOL ❶
River (177) UWS ❷
Wild Lily Tea Room (170) CHE ❷
X.O. Cafe & Grill (156) CHE ❶

BAGELS/BIALYS

Bagel Buffet GV
Ess-a-Bagel (174) MID
H&H Bagels (164) UWS
Kossar's Bialys (159) LES
La Bagel Delight (164) BK

BAKERIES

Damascus Bakery (185) CB
De Lillo Pastry Shop (190) BX
Galaxy Pastry Shop (189) QUE
Hong Kong Egg Cake Co. (156) CHI
The Hungarian Pastry Shop (179) MH
Little Pie Co. (171) CHE
The Magnolia Bakery (163) GV
Moishe's Bake Shop (168) EV
Something Sweet (168) EV
Taipan Bakery (156) CHI

BAKERIES, CONT'D

Veniero's (169) EV

CAFES

Alt.Coffee (168) EV
Cafe La Fortuna (178) UWS
Cafe Lalo (178) UES
Cafe Mona Lisa (163) GV
Cafe Mozart (178) UES
Caffe Dante (163) GV
Caffe Palermo (157) LIT
Coffee Shop Bar (173) UGM
Galaxy Global Eatery (173) UGM
Gray Parrot Cafe (183) WIL
Greenpoint Coffee House (183) WIL
drip (178) UES
Food Bar (171) CHE
The Grey Dog (163) GV
Miro Cafe (161) BC
La Bella Ferrara (157) LIT
The Read Cafe and Bookshop (183) WIL
Rue des Crèpes (170) CHE
Tia Café (183) WIL
St. Alp's Teahouse (156) CHI
Sunburst Espresso Bar (173) UGM
Sweet-n-Tart Cafe (155) CHI
Yaffa's Tea Room (160) TBC

CARIBBEAN/JAMAICAN

Brisas del Caribe (160) SoHo ❶
Christie's Bakery (185) CB ❶
Day-O (162) GV ❸
Negril (170) CHE ❸

CENTRAL/EASTERN EUROPEAN

Little Poland (166) EV ❶
Primorski Restaurant (187) SB ❶
Restaurant Karpaty (181) WIL ❶
Veselka (168) EV ❶
Varenichnaya (187) BK ❶

CHINESE

Chao Zhau Restaurant (188) QUE ❶
DragonTown (188) QUE ❷
Excellent Dumpling House (154) CHI ❶
Fried Dumpling (154) CHI ❶
Flushing Noodle (187) QUE ❶
Hop Kee (155) CHI ❸
H.S.F. Restaurant (155) CHI ❷
Ivy's Cafe (177) UWS ❷
Joe's Shanghai (154) CHI ❷
Joe's Shanghai (187) QUE ❷
Kelley & Ping Grocery (161) & Noodle SoHo ❷
Red Hot Szechuan BK ❷
Shanghai Cuisine (155) CHI ❷
Szechuan Gourmet QUE ❷
Tiengarden (159) LES ❷
Vegetarian Dim Sum House (155) CHI ❶

DELICATESSENS

Katz's Delicatessen (158) LES ❷
Second Ave. Delicatessen (164) EV ❷
Stage Deli (168) MID ❷
Tino's Delicatessen (190) BX ❶

FRENCH

Brasserie Centrale (168) THE ❸
Chez Brigitte (162) GV ❷
CityCrepe UWS ❷
The Crooked Tree (165) EV ❶
Jules (166) EV ❸
Patois (185) CB ❷
Tartine (163) GV ❷

GAY HANGOUTS

Big Cup (171) CHE ❷
Caffe Raffaella (164) CHE ❷
Food Bar (171) CHE ❷
Lips (164) GV ❸

GREEK

Uncle George's (189) QUE ❷
Telly's Taverna (188) QUE ❷
Zorba's Souvlaki Plus (189) QUE ❶
Zygos Taverna (189) QUE ❷

INDO-PAKISTANI

Chip Shop and Curry Shop (186) CB ❷
Curry in a Hurry (172) UGM ❶
Minar (170) CHE ❶
Mughlai (177) WES ❸
Pakistan Tea House (160) TBC ❶
Salaam Bombay (160) TBC ❸
Tandoori Club (174) ID ❷

ITALIAN

Arthur Avenue Cafe (190) BX ❶
Becco (174) THE ❹
Bleu Evolution (179) HAR ❷
Caffe Pane e Cioccolato (161) GV ❷
Cucina di Pesce (165) EV ❷
Dominick's (189) BX ❷
Emilia's (190) BX ❸
Frank (164) EV ❷
Fresco by Scotto (174) MID ❷
Giovanni's (190) BX ❷
La Focacceria (166) EV ❶
La Mela (157) LIT ❷
Manganaro's (174) UGM ❷
Max (165) EV ❷
Pasquale's Rigoletto (190) BX ❸
Più Bello (188) QUE ❶
Rocky's Italian Restaurant (157) LIT ❸
Sidestreet Saloo (191) ST ❷
Thirty One (188) QUE ❷
Two Boots Restaurant (167) EV ❶
Vinny's of Carroll Gardens (185) BK ❷
Zigolini's (153) FD ❷

NEIGHBORHOODS: CHI Chinatown; **GV** Greenwich Village; **TBC** TriBeCa; **SoHo** SoHo; **EV** East Village; **UGM** Union Square, Gramercy, and Murray Hill; **UES** Upper East Side; **UWS** Upper West Side; **NOL** NoLIta; **QUE** Queens; **ST** Staten Island; **BX** Bronx; **THE** Theater District; **CHE** Chelsea and Herald Square; **MH** Morningside Heights; **LIT** Little Italy; **MID** Midtown; **LES** Lower East Side; **HAR** Harlem and Washington Heights; **FD** Financial District and Civic Center.

JAPANESE

Dojo Restaurant (165) EV ❶
Miyako (182) WIL ❷
Mottsu (158) NOL ❷
Sapporo (174) MID ❷

KOREAN

Kang Suh (169) CHE ❸
Kim Neh (188) QUE ❶
Manna (162) GV ❷

KOSHER

Moishe's Bake Shop (168) EV
Yonah Schimmel Knishery LES

LATIN AMERICAN

Alma (185) BK ❸
Beso (186) CB ❷
Blue Moon Mexican Cafe (169) CHE ❷
Brisas del Caribe (160) SoHo ❶
Burritoville (176) UWS ❸
Cafe Habana (158) NOL ❷
Caliente Cab Co. (162) GV ❶
Chango (172) CHE ❷
Coco Roco (186) CB ❸
EL Cafetal (188) QUE ❷
El Sombrero (158) LES ❷
El Teddy's (160) TBC ❺
Flor's Kitchen (166) EV ❶
Gabriela's (177) UWS ❸
Hispanola (179) HAR ❷
Kitchen/Market (169) CHE ❷
La Caridad 78 Restaurant (180) UWS ❶
La Caridad (177) UWS ❷
La Fonda Boricua (180) HAR ❷
La Taza de Oro (170) CHE ❷
Lupe's East L.A. Kitchen (161) SoHo ❷
Mama Mexico (177) UWS ❸
Mary Ann's (170) CHE ❷
National Cafe (165) EV ❶
Original Fresco Tortillas (173) UGM ❶
Rincon Salvadoreño (188) QUE ❷
Santa Fe Grill (185) CB ❷
Vera Cruz (183) WIL ❷

MALAYSIAN

Nyonya (155) CHI ❷
Sentosa (159) LES ❶

MEDITERRANEAN (NOT ITALIAN)

That Little Cafe (159) NOL ❷
Suba (159) LES ❹

MIDDLE EASTERN

Amir's Falafel (178) MH ❶
Caravan (184) CB ❷

MIDDLE EASTERN, CONT'D

Fountain Cafe (184) CB ❶
Mahmoun's (162) GV ❶
Moustache (162) GV ❶
Olive Tree Cafe (162) GV ❶
Rainbow Falafel (173) UGM ❶
Sahara East (167) EV ❶
Yaffe Cafe (168) EV ❶

PIZZA

Arturo's Pizza (162) GV ❸
Friendly's Gourmet Pizzeria (153) LM ❶
Grimaldi's (184) CB ❷
Joe's Pizza (158) LES ❶
John's Pizzeria (161) GV ❷
John's Pizzeria and Restaurant (188) QUE ❷
Koronet Pizza (178) MH ❶
Lombardi's Coal Oven Pizza (157) LIT ❷
Pino's La Forchetta (186) CB ❶
Pizza Mercato (163) GV ❶
Sal's Pizzeria (182) WIL ❷
Totonno Pizzeria Napolitano (187) SB ❶

PUBS AND TAVERNS

Hourglass Tavern (174) UGM ❸
Molly's (172) UGM ❷
Pete's Tavern (172) UGM ❸
St. Dymphna's (167) EV ❷

SEAFOOD

Chip Shop and Curry Shop (186) CB ❷
Reef Restaurant (190) BX ❷
A Salt and Battery (165) EV ❷

SHOPS AND MARKETS

Aji Ichiban (Munchies Paradise) (156) CHI
Chinatown Ice Cream Factory (156) CHI
Ciao Bella (158) NOL
Cosenza's Fish Market (190) BX
Dean and Deluca (161) SoHo
Di Palo's (157) LIT
Doughnut Plant (159) LES
Dynasty Supermarket Corp. (156) CHI
Economy Candy (159) LES
F & B (171) CHE
Fairway (180) HAR
Grace's Marketplace (176) UES
Great Wall Market (189) QUE
Kitchen/Market (169) CHE
The Lemon Ice King of Corona (189) QUE
Mangia (174) MID
Milano Market (179) MH
Minamoto Kitchen (174) MID
NYC ICY (168) CHE

SHOPS AND MARKETS, CONT'D

Le Pain Quotidien (176)	UES
The Pickle Guys (159)	LES
Sahadi Importing Co. (184)	CB
Ten Ren Tea & Ginseng Co. (156)	CHI
Teuscher Chocolatier (175)	MID
World of Nuts and Ice Cream (176)	UES
Yonah Schimmel Knishery (160)	LES
Yong Da Fung Food Herbal (189) Products Inc.	QUE
Zabar's (178)	UWS

SOUL

Copeland's (179)	HAR ❸
Sylvia's (180)	HAR ❷
Manna's Too! (179)	HAR ❶

THAI

Jai-Ya (187)	QUE ❷
Planet Thailand (181)	WIL ❷

THAI, CONT'D

Pad Thai Noodle Lounge (170)	CHE ❷
Thailand Restaurant (155)	CHI ❷

VEGAN/VEGETARIAN/HEALTHY

Bliss (181)	WIL ❶
Candle Cafe (175)	UES ❷
Eva's (162)	GV ❶
Kate's Corner (166)r	EV ❷
Soy Luck Club (163)	GV ❶
Tiengarden (159)	LES ❷
Vegetarian Dim Sum House (155)	CHI ❶
Whole Earth Bakery & Kitchen (168)	EV ❶
Zen Palate (171)	UGM ❷

VIETNAMESE

Bo-Ky (154)	CHI ❶
Dong Hae Ru (188)	QUE ❷
Doyers Vietnamese (154)	CHI ❶
Saigon Grill (176)	UES ❷

LISTINGS BY NEIGHBORHOOD

Neighborhoods are listed in geographical order (from south to north in Manhattan and from north to south in Brooklyn), and restaurants within each area are in alphabetical order (except for thumbpicks, which are listed first and in order of our preference). **Restaurants take major credit cards unless otherwise noted.**

FINANCIAL DISTRICT AND CIVIC CENTER

Lower Manhattan eateries tailor their schedules to the lunch breaks of Wall St. brokers. Fast-food joints abound on Broadway near Dey and John St.; food pushcarts offer tempting summertime deals on falafel, burritos, and gyros, but be wary of what you eat on the street.

Friendly's Gourmet Pizzeria, 49 & 59 Nassau St. (☎212-962-0220). Subway: N, R, W to Rector St.; 1, 2, to Wall St./William St.; 4, 5 to Wall St./Broadway; J, M, Z to Broad St. Map 7, C3, 10. This pizzeria has been serving the Wall Street area since 1965 and owner Joe and his staff take the 'Friendly' title seriously. Breakfast sandwiches starting at $1 (egg on a roll) and the lunch special of 2 huge New York Style slices with a 12 oz. soda ($3.50) make this spot a Financial District favorite. Free delivery. Open M-F 7am-7pm, Sa 9am-5pm. ❶

Rosario's Italian Bistro, 38 Pearl St., between Broad and Whitehall St. (☎212-514-5763). Subway: N, R to Whitehall St. Map 7, D5, 19. With 2 small eating areas and a large dining room, the whole family can sit down and enjoy Italy's finest. Panini sandwiches are a bit pricey ($8), but pasta is some of the cheapest around. Baked ziti and spaghetti ($4.50). Open daily 11am-3pm. ❷

Sophie's Restaurant, 205 Pearl St. (☎212-269-0909). Subway: N, R, W to Rector St.; 1, 2, to Wall St./William St.; 4, 5 to Wall St./Broadway; J, M, Z to Broad St. Map 7, D3, 11. An oasis in the Financial Districts' many rows of Chinese, Italian, and Indian restaurants. With the smells of rice and beans, spicy island chicken and pork, plantains, and empanadas wafting through the doorway, this hot lunch spot is hard to pass up. Come before the peak lunchtime hours because the line for takeout and seating is exceptionally long. Huge food portions ($7) are worth any wait. Open daily 10:30am-4:00pm. ❷

Zigolini's, 66 Pearl St., at Coenties Alley (☎212-425-7171). Subway: N, R to Whitehall St. Map 7, D5, 20. Tasty sandwiches ($5-8) and great pasta ($7), with deli counter in the back. Open M-F 7:30am-5pm. ❷

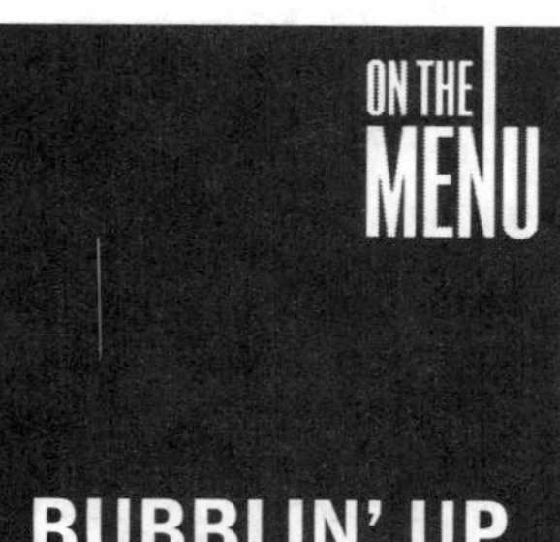

BUBBLIN' UP

In my travels up and down the city streets, I've found that my thirst has often been quenched by the newest beverage fad to hit New York: bubble tea. Bubble tea originated in Taiwan in the late 1980s and in the past five years it has become the overwhelming beverage of choice in Taiwan and Hong Kong. As a result of large Asian populations in the city, several bubble tea salons have recently opened.

Leading the Bubble Tea charge in New York City is the chain of Saint Alp's teahouses that have established outposts on Mott St. and on Third Ave. and E. 10th St. So what is Bubble Tea? The tea is a colorful frothy liquid (it is usually served cold), almost like a smoothie, and flavors range from Black Tea to Taro. That probably doesn't mean anything to you, so go ahead and try some wacky flavor.

But what about the bubbles? The bubbles in bubble tea are actually tapioca pearls. While you are probably having flashbacks to something your grandmother forced you to eat when you were seven, rest assured that tapioca pearls are not phlegmy globs of nastiness

(cont'd on pg. 155)

CHINATOWN

Subway: J, M, Z to Canal St./Centre St.; N, Q, R, W to Canal St./Broadway; 4, 6 to Canal St./Lafayette St.

Fresh food abounds in Chinatown. Open-air markets selling live turtles, eels, and crabs spill onto the sidewalks above **Canal Street.** Some of the best seafood and produce in the city can be found in the markets on **Mott Street.** The neighborhood's 300-plus restaurants serve fantastic east- and southeast-Asian cuisines at prices agreeable to the even the most frugal diner. English truly is a second language here, so be patient with waiters and salespeople. Many restaurants are **cash only** and don't serve alcohol.

Doyers Vietnamese Restaurant, 11-13 Doyers St., between Bowery and Pell St.; follow the steps downstairs. (☎212-693-0725). Map 8, D6, 39. Hidden on a street once known as New York's 'Bloody Angle,' Doyers (formerly known as Vietnam) has the best Vietnamese cuisine in the city, served ridiculously quickly by a friendly staff. The inexpensive noodle soups, cool summer rolls, and thin rice noodle dishes bring back many repeat customers. Try the squid. Serves beer. Open daily 11am-9:30pm. ❶

Fried Dumpling, 106 Mosco St., between Mulberry and Mott St. (☎212-693-1060). It wouldn't be an exaggeration to call this hole-in-the-wall the best bargain in New York City. For half the price of a ride on the subway, you can get either 5 dumplings or 4 pork buns. Only other items on the menu are soy milk ($1) and a very good hot-and-sour soup ($1). ❶

Joe's Shanghai, 9 Pell St., between Bowery and Mott St. (☎212-233-8888). Map 8, D6, 36. From fried turnip cakes ($3.25) to crispy whole yellowfish ($13), this branch of the Queens legend serves tasty Shanghai specialties. Delicious *xiao long bao* (crab meat and pork dumplings in a savory soup) $7. Be prepared for communal tables, long lines on weekends, and prices slightly above a typical Chinatown restaurant. For a really authentic experience, check out Joe's Queens location (13621 37th Ave., Flushing). Serves beer. Open daily 11am-11:15pm. Cash only. ❷

Bo-Ky, 80 Bayard St., between Mott and Mulberry St. (☎212-406-2292). Map 8, C5, 31. Tourists rarely grace this Vietnamese joint specializing in soups (most under $5). The curry chicken noodle ($4.50) will clear that nasty head cold instantly. *Pho,* the beef broth king of Vietnamese soups, will fill you up without emptying your wallet ($3-5). Open daily 8am-9:30pm. Cash only. ❶

Excellent Dumpling House, 111 Lafayette St., just south of Canal St. (☎212-219-0212). Map 8, A5, 19. Small, unassuming, crowded. Splendid food, fast service. Terrific veggie and meat dumplings fried, steamed, or boiled ($4.25 for 8). Huge bowls of noodle soup $3.75-5.50. Ask about the house favorites. Serves beer. Open daily 11am-9pm. Cash only. ❶

Hop Kee, 21 Mott St., at the corner of Mosco St. (☎212-964-8365). Map 8, C6, 40. Good Chinese food, bare-bones ambience. Spicy beef chow fun $5.25, roast pork with oyster sauce, $9.50. Open daily 11am-4am. Cash only. ❸

H.S.F. Restaurant, 46 Bowery, between Bayard and Canal St. (☎212-374-1319). Map 8, D5, 29. Wonderful dim sum ($3-5) served 11am-5pm. Buffet special lets you cook up vegetables, dumplings, and other ingredients in a pot of boiling broth at your table ($20 per person; after 5pm). Dazzling seafood selection in 22 fishtanks. Open daily 8:30am-11pm. ❷

Nyonya, 194 Grand St., between Mulberry and Mott St. (☎212-334-3669). Map 8, C3, 14. Popular, excellent Malaysian dishes in cool, wood-lined interior (seats 40-50). Delectably spicy *nasi lemak* ($4) puts chili anchovies and curry chicken in a bed of coconut rice. For an unusual dessert, ask for the "ABC"—a species of shaved-ice sundae with red bean, corn, palm seeds, and jelly rose syrup. Serves beer and wine. Open Su-Th 11am-11:30pm, F-Sa 11am-midnight. Cash only. ❷

Shanghai Cuisine, 89-91 Bayard St., at Mulberry St. (☎212-732-8988). Map 8, C5, 33. House specialty of braised soy duck with 8 treasures ($34) must be ordered one day in advance; it might be the richest dish you'll ever taste, so attack it only in large groups. With less intense dishes like spicy pepper salt prawns ($13) and mixed vegetables ($7). Serves beer and wine. Open daily noon-10:30pm. Cash only. ❷

Sweet-n-Tart Cafe, 76 Mott St., at Canal St. (☎212-334-8088). Map 8, C5, 26. In addition to inexpensive standard Chinese fare, this crowded cafe offers *tong shui,* sweet Chinese "tonics" (soups) believed to have medicinal value: dry bean curd with ginkgo for healthy skin ($2.35), lotus seeds in herbal tea with egg for liver and kidneys ($3). One of the early restaurants to jump on the bubble tea bandwagon. Open daily 9am-11:30pm. Cash only. ❶

Thailand Restaurant, 106 Bayard St., between Baxter and Mulberry St. (☎212-349-3132). Map 8, B5, 25. Chinatown's first Thai restaurant is simple and quiet, a welcome departure from the bustle of the streets outside. Chicken and shrimp pad thai $7, ground pork with ginger and roasted peanuts $7. Many vegetarian options. Homemade Thai desserts like sweet rice with egg custard and coconut milk ($1.50). Open daily 11:30am-11pm. ❷

Vegetarian Dim Sum House, 24 Pell St., at Doyers St. (☎212-226-6572). Map 8, D6, 35. No real animals on the menu in this small and appropriately

(cont'd from prev. pg.)

that will churn your stomach. At first, they may be a little disconcerting. After all, no one is prepared for a forceful rush of tapioca pellets to shoot into their mouth while they are drinking, but after a few sips it becomes fun and tasty (it's a party in your mouth).

While the exotic beverages alone are worth the trip, bubble tea salons are also relaxed places where friends can go to sit and talk. The wait staff never pressures its clientele to leave and this is a major plus considering how intent most cafes and restaurants are on quick customer turnover. Adding to the overall laid-back vibe are the musical offerings that most teahouses offer. While it may be embarrassing to actually own Justin Timberlake's album, you can count on being serenaded by the best in power pop (while writing this, I'm listening to Sean Paul's "Like Glue"). These are great for rainy days and dates.

Locations include: **Tea & Tea:** 10th St. and Second Ave. and Mott St. (right off of Bayard St.); **Pearl:** 4th St. and Sixth Ave.; **Sammy's Noodle Shop:** 11th St. and Sixth Ave.; **Jenny's Café:** St. Mark's between First and Avenue A.

-Eric Goldwyn, 2004

green eatery; soy and wheat by-products, taro root, and mushroom disguise themselves as beef, chicken, and fish. Fantastic dumplings (3 for $2) should please both vegetarians and carnivores alike. Most entrees $6-10. Ice-cold lotus-seed or lychee drink $2. Open daily 10:30am-10:30pm. Cash only. ❶

X.O. Cafe & Grill, 96 Walker St., between Canal and Centre St. (☎212-343-8339). Map 8, A5, 20. Tasty, authentic, and cheap Chinese cuisine. Happy Hour 3-6pm daily with 10% off of everything. Try the filling broiled chicken congee (rice porridge) bowl $3.50 and shrimp rice noodles $2.75. Great place for desserts and drinks. Cash only. Open M-Th and Su 11am-10pm, F-Sa 11-10:30pm. ❶

SHOPS

Chinatown Ice Cream Factory, 65 Bayard St., at Elizabeth St. (☎212-608-4170). Map 8, D5, 32. Unbeatable homemade ice cream in exotic flavors like lychee, taro, ginger, red bean, and green tea. 1 scoop $2.20, 2 $4, 3 $4.80. Open summer M-Th 11:30am-11:30pm, F-Su 11:30am-midnight; rest of the year daily noon-11pm.

Hong Kong Egg Cake Co., on the corner of Mott and Mosco St. Map 8, C6, 37. Located in a small red shack–just follow the line wrapped around the corner. Cecelia Tam will make you 12 bite-size, sweet egg cakes ($1) fresh from the skillet that she's been working for 20 years. Open in good weather.

Taipan Bakery, 194 Canal St., between Mott and Mulberry St. (☎212-732-2222). Map 8, C5, 24. One-stop bake shop with fantastic pastry selection for dirt-cheap prices, including 4 kinds of egg custard tarts (75¢). Shoulder your way to the back to try the plain sweet bun (60¢). Also serves non-Chinese favorites. The steady hordes of customers almost ensure warm, fresh pastry every time you come. Open daily 7:30am-8:30pm.

Aji Ichiban (Munchies Paradise), 37 Mott St., at Pell St. (☎212-233-7650). Map 8, C6, 34. Japanese chain selling dried and spiced fruit (preserved plums $3.50-5 for ½ lb.) and a mouth-watering selection of Japanese candies in bulk. Pricey, but where else can you buy a fistful of Super Lemons? Open daily 10am-8:30pm.

Dynasty Supermarket Corp., 69 Elizabeth St., at Hester St. (☎212-966-4943). Map 8, D4, 18. One of the most extensive markets in the area and an air-conditioned refuge from the tumult of the street. Live, fresh fish market inside, with nets used to capture tomorrow's lunch and dinner. Find ginseng, sea cucumber, chicken feet, exotic flavored gummy candies, and Hostess cupcakes all in 1 stop. Open daily 9:30am-8:30pm.

St. Alp's Teahouse, 51 Mott St., between Bayard and Pell St. (☎212-766-9889). Map 8, C5, 28. See feature (p. 154). Serves bubble tea, drink of trendy Taiwanese worldwide (iced drinks with marble-sized tapioca pearls sucked through a wide straw). Black tea with milk and pearls $2.85. Artificial-tasting fruit-flavored drinks. Thick buttered toast $1.50. Open daily 10am-midnight.

Ten Ren Tea and Ginseng Company, 75 Mott St., between Canal and Bayard St. (☎212-349-2286). Map 8, C5, 23. Comfortable and classy, with huge selection of rare teas (both cheap and pricey varieties). Ginseng $10-200 for ½ lb. To beat the summer heat, get the Green Tea Powder ($4-6.50) and add a packet's worth to a cold bottle of water or a chilled glass of pineapple, orange, or tomato juice. Even try it in your toothpaste or facial cleanser to take advantage of alleged health benefits like enhanced immune function and easier digestion. Open daily 10am-8pm. **Ten Ren's Tea Time** cafe, up the street at 79 Mott St., sells decent iced-tea tapioca drinks, including tapioca shaved ice ($4-4.50).

LITTLE ITALY

Subway: 6 to Spring St./Lafayette St.; J, M, Z to Canal St./Centre St.; N, Q, R, W to Canal St./Broadway; 4, 6 to Canal St./Lafayette St.; S to Grand St.; F to E. Broadway; F, V, S to Broadway-Lafayette St.

Snobby travelers, beware: Little Italy is an unabashed tourist trap. But even though there may be a countless number of better (and less appallingly over-priced) restaurants throughout the city, the three blocks of Mulberry St.

between Grand and Canal St. still have a certain unmistakable charm. At 7pm, the street comes to life; arrive a bit earlier for one of the better tables. Reservations are essential on the weekends. Three tips for choosing a restaurant or cafe: first, just because someone famous ate there doesn't mean it's good; second, just because it's really old doesn't mean it's good; and third, just because the waiters all have heavy Italian accents...well, you know. A full meal can run $60-70, particularly if you have wine with dinner. Save money with sizable appetizers (antipasti) or a snack at one of the many shops and groceries.

Lombardi's Coal Oven Pizza, 32 Spring St., between Mott and Mulberry St. (☎212-941-7994). Map 8, C2, 11. Claiming to be nation's oldest pizzeria (opened 1905), Lombardi's credits itself with creating the famous NY-style thin-crust, coal-oven pizza. Large pie feeds 2 ($13.50). Toppings ($3 for 1, $5 for 2, $6 for 3) are worth it. Reservations for groups of 6+. Open M-Th 11:30am-11pm, F-Sa 11:30am-midnight, Su 11:30am-10pm. Cash only. ❷

La Mela, 167 Mulberry St., between Broome and Grand St. (☎212-431-9493). Map 8, C3, 13. Raucous dining, chummy staff. Generous portions served family style. Inexpensive, house wine ($20 for 1.5L). Huge dessert concoction (ice cream, cake, coconut, glazed bananas) $8, feeds 2. Pasta $6-8, entrees $11-15. Open Su-Th noon-2am, F-Sa noon-3am. ❷

Rocky's Italian Restaurant, 45 Spring St., at Mulberry St. (☎212-274-9756). Map 8, C2, 10. True neighborhood joint buzzes with strains of the Old Country. Lunch menu (until 5pm) offers pizza hero ($4.50) and sandwiches ($4.50-9). Pasta $7-13, entrees $10-19. Great chicken with garlic sauce ($14). Cheap wine (carafe $16). Open Tu-Su 11am-11pm; kitchen closes at 10:30pm. ❸

CAFES

Caffe Palermo, 148 Mulberry St., between Hester and Grand St. (☎212-431-4205). Map 8, C4. Largest of the cafe offerings along Mulberry. Opens onto the street during summer, with espresso bar up front. Most pastries $3-5. Staff takes pride in tiramisu ($5), good *cannoli* ($2.75), and cappuccino ($3.25). Open Su-Th 10am-midnight, F-Sa 10am-2am.

La Bella Ferrara, 110 Mulberry St., between Canal and Hester St. (☎212-966-1488). Map 8, C5, 21. Name, cribbed from Grand St.'s larger, factory-like Caffe Ferrara, basically means "better Ferrara." Local choice for after-dinner dessert. Pastries $2-2.50, cakes $4.50, cappuccino $3. Open daily 10am-midnight. Cash only.

SHOPS

Di Palo's, 206 Grand St., at Mott St. (☎212-226-1033). Map 8, C3, 15. Deli specializing in mouth-watering cheese. Homemade soft, fleshy mozzarella ($4.89 per lb.) is their mainstay, but goat cheese and *ricotta fresca* are delicious, too. Breads, meats and pastas. Open M-Sa 9am-6:30pm, Su 9am-3:30pm.

NOLITA

Subway: 6 to Spring St./Lafayette St.; F, S, V to Broadway-Lafayette St.; N, R to Prince St.

NoLIta (North of Little Italy) is a budding pocket of culinary action. Good eats, you'll pay the price. If not, there are plenty of inexpensive choices for lunch or dinner.

Rice, 227 Mott St., between Prince and Spring St. (☎212-226-5775). Map 8, C2, 9. Fantastic food on rice. Basics—basmati, brown, sticky, Japanese, and Thai black—are all here. So are more exotic species like the Bhutanese red and green rice ($1-3.50). Sauces range from mango chutney to aleppo yogurt ($1). Ratatouille or chicken satay are among other enticing toppings ($4-9.50). Open daily noon-midnight. Cash only. ❶

Cafe Colonial Restaurant, 276 Elizabeth St., at Houston St. (☎212-274-0044). Map 8, C1, 4. Great entrees options like the veggie burger ($7.25) and soft-shell crab sandwich ($10). Open daily 8am-11pm. ❷

Cafe Gitane, 242 Mott St., at Prince St. (☎212-334-9552). Map 8, C1, 5. A focal point of NoLIta life, this cafe is a prime spot to see and be seen. Rack of glossy fashion mags invites the fashionable to linger. Salads ($5.25-9), grilled eggplant with goat cheese and pesto on rice pilaf ($8), tiramisu ($4.50). Open daily 9am-midnight. Cash only. ❷

Cafe Habana, 229 Elizabeth St., between Prince and Spring St. (☎212-625-2002). Map 8, C2, 6. Inexpensive but retro stylish. Local artsy types call this place home on warm summer evenings. *Tostadas de pollo* ($7.50) and Cuban sandwiches ($6.50). Vegetarian plate ($7), grilled steak ($10.50). Open daily noon-midnight. ❷

Mottsu, 285 Mott St., between Prince and Spring St. (☎212-343-8017). Map 8, C1, 2. One of the neighborhood's only sushi restaurants. Fresh sushi and sashimi at low prices. Tuna rolls $2.50. Lunch M-F noon-3pm; dinner M-Th 5-11pm, F-Sa 5-11:30pm, Su 5-10pm. ❷

SHOPS

Ciao Bella, 285 Mott St., between Prince and Spring St. (☎212-431-3591). Map 8, C1, 3. Some of the best ice cream in the city: dense, smooth and rich. Their location is little more than a storefront, but benches outside invite customers to linger. Small $4, large $4.50. Gourmet smoothies $6. Open M-Sa 11am-11:30pm, Su 11am-10pm.

LOWER EAST SIDE

Eating is something readily done in these parts. The Lower East Side is crammed with opportunity to fill up. Get up at it.

Paul's Boutique, 99 Rivington St. (☎646-805-0384) at Ludlow St. Subway: F, J, M, Z to Delancey St.-Essex St.; F, V to Lower East Side/Second Ave. The world-renowned rap troupe the Beastie Boys had a rehearsal space at this location, formerly the site of Paul's Boutique (the boutique). Then the NY-native emcees released their second album, *Paul's Boutique* (the CD). Paul's Boutique (the cafe) is delicious in its design (curved copper ceiling above a sunlit and mellow, if meticulous, seating area). Croissant sandwiches with fresh mozzarella ($4) and salads of great size ($6.50) satisfy. Beer and wine make for a good lazy afternoon as do the incident chess board and copies of the paper. Open M-Th 9am-10pm, F-Sa 9am-midnight, Su 9am-8pm. ❶

El Sombrero, 108 Stanton St., at Ludlow St. (☎212-254-4188). Subway: F, J, M, Z to Delancey St.-Essex St. Map 11, E1, 18. Divine budget Mexican food with kitschy aura. Vegetable enchiladas ($8) make a satisfying meal, but you'll marvel at the fajitas Mexicana ($12). Margaritas (small $3) and beer ($2-4). Hours vary, but opens daily around 10am and closes at approx. midnight during the week and 3am on the weekends. Cash only. ❷

Grilled Cheese, 168 Ludlow St., between Stanton and E. Houston St. (☎212-982-6600). Subway: F, J, M, Z to Delancey St.-Essex St. Map 11, E1, 17. The namesake sandwich of Grilled Cheese the restaurant is grilled cheese the sandwich. Delicious, ungreasy, grilled and cheesy variations on the original are superb and huge (with portabellos $5!). Well-shaken shakes ($3-4) and salads too ($4-6). They have checkers and Connect Four to play while your cheese is grilling. Open M-Sa noon-midnight, Su noon-10pm. ❶

Joe's Pizza, 51 Essex St., just south of Grand St. (☎212-777-3545). Subway: F, J, M, Z to Delancey St.-Essex St. Joe's serves pizza in the traditional manner: cheese, tomato sauce, crust, and slices cost $1.50 which is uncommonly low. They have Internet access which is uncommonly strange. What's more said access is particularly cheap ($3 per hr.) and you will be using a computer constructed by and sharing bandwidth with the kid Patrick who lives upstairs. Jamaican patties offer themselves for purchase ($1.50) alongside heros, pastas, and calzones. Open daily 10am-6:30pm. ❶

Katz's Delicatessen, 205 E. Houston St., between Orchard and Ludlow St. (☎212-254-2246). Subway: F, V to Lower East Side-Second Ave. Map 11, D1, 8. LES institution since 1888. Every president in the last 3 decades has proudly received a Katz salami. Sit at the table where Bill Clinton lunched. Orgasmic food (as Meg Ryan confirmed in *When Harry Met Sally*), but you pay extra for the atmosphere. Knishes and franks $2.40, sandwiches around $10. Open Su-Tu 8am-10pm, W-Th 8am-11pm, F-Sa 8am-3am. ❷

Pink Pony, 176 Ludlow St., between E. Houston and Stanton St. (☎212-253-1922). Subway: F, J, M, Z to Delancey St.-Essex St.; F, V to Lower East Side/Second Ave. C is for "ceilings" (high ones); A is for "appetizing, artful and alluring;" F is for "French-styled coffee house," and E is for "eat a sandwich for $7-9;" or "eat an entree for $9-13." Put it together and it spells CAFE, a place to read the paper, write a poem, watch a film screening from time to time in the back room or listen to live music (Tu evenings). Black and white photo exhibits are on the walls, which are made of wood. Lots of beer and wine. Open daily 10am-2pm. ❷

Rush Hour, 134 Ludlow St., between Rivington St. and Stanton St. (☎212-979-9211) Subway: F, J, M, Z to Delancey St.-Essex St. or F, V to Lower East Side/Second Ave. Small kitchen. Order breakfast in the morning; soups, quiche, sandwiches and salads perhaps a bit later. If you eat a burger here, it will be good and cost $4-5. Small graffiti-decorated, table-populated space out back. Open Su-Th 11am-2am, F-Sa 11am-4am. ❶

Sentosa, 3 Allen St., between Canal and Division St. (☎212-925-8018). Subway: F, V, S to Broadway-Lafayette St. Map 11, E4, 40. Really cheap Malaysian food with Singaporean (i.e. slightly more Chinese) twist in banal section of LES. Hainanese chicken rice $7, rice dishes $4. Open daily 9am-midnight. ❶

Suba, 109 Ludlow St., between Rivington and Delancey St. (☎212-982-5714). Subway: F, J, M, Z to Delancey St.-Essex St. Map 11, E2, 29. First floor: tapas lounge; 2 sub-basement ("suba") dining rooms: one has a moat, the other, a 20 ft. ceiling with skylight. Delectable Spanish style cuisine (apps $9, entrees $20). Su live flamenco performances ($30 min. of food and drink); M film screenings ($29 for the film and 3-course dinner). First monthly Tu is "Dinner in the Dark." Everything is pitch black; waiters wear night-vision goggles. No visual sensory input always makes Spanish food better. Open Su-Th 6pm-1am, F-Sa 6pm-4am. ❹

That Little Cafe (Dishful Caterers), 147 E. Houston St., between First and Second Ave. (☎212-475-5302). Subway: F, V to Lower East Side/Second Ave. "That Little Cafe" is a clever name because if you say "do you want to go to that little cafe" simply because you are too lazy to recall the cafe you mean, you will always end up here instead! It's a stratagem that makes everyone happy because the food is unusually well-made. Cafe is brand new—a rotating menu is planned for the first several months. Mediterranean elements, Asian influences, ginger beer! Sandwiches and salads $7-9. Entrees $10-13. Open daily 8am-2pm. ❷

Tiengarden, 170 Allen St., between Rivington and Stanton St. (☎212-388-1364). Subway: F, V to Lower East Side-Second Ave. Map 11, D2, 22. Vegan restaurant makes health food a spiritual experience by excluding the 5 impurities that could damage your *chi.* Spicy organic tofu ($7.50) with plenty of flavor. Open M-Sa noon-10pm. Cash only. ❷

SHOPS

Kossar's Bialys, 367 Grand St., between Essex and Norfolk St. (☎212-473-4810). Subway: F, J, M to Delancey St.-New York's best bialy emporium. You can get two onion bialys for a buck, or 13 for $6. Open all night on Sa, Kossar's offers LES' cheapest late-night nosh. Open Su-Th 6am-10pm, F 6am-4:30pm, Sa 11pm-6am.

Economy Candy, 108 Rivington St., between Ludlow and Essex St. (☎212-254-1531). Subway: F, J, M, Z to Delancey St.-Essex St. Map 11, E2, 26. Candy warehouse selling imported chocolates, jams, and countless confections at rock-bottom prices. Huge bag of dried cantaloupe $5; 10 lb. bag of assorted candy $12. Open Su-F 9am-6pm, Sa 10am-5pm.

The Pickle Guys, 49 Essex St., (☎888-474-2553) between Grand and Hester St. Subway: F, J, M, Z to Delancey St.-Essex St. Map 11, E3, 38. Glorious gherkins sold straight out of vats, from super-sour to sweet (individual $0.50-2; quart $6). Made under supervision of Rabbi Shmuel Fishelis. Open Su-Th 9am-6pm, F 9am-4pm.

Doughnut Plant, 379 Grand St., at Norfolk St. (☎212-505-3700). Subway: F, J, M, Z to Delancey St.-Essex St. A young man, down on his luck and irked at the notion of returning to his home in the Carolinas, made a batch of his old grandfather's doughnut recipe, took them to the city's poshest food market (Dean and Deluca), and soon found himself supplying doughnuts to most every classy joint in town. The young man, Marc Israel, is now an established doughnut godfather. His is the home of the doughnut: hand-made and organic ($2 a piece and as big as the as the head of a small child). Open 6:30am until there are no more doughnuts (anytime between 2:30pm and 6:30pm).

Yonah Schimmel Knishery, 137 E. Houston St., between Forsyth and Eldridge St. (☎212-477-2858). Subway: F, V to Lower East Side-Second Ave. Map 11, D1, 3. The knish has been an art form since 1910 at Rabbi Schimmel's LES institution. 12 varieties of these Eastern European potato-filled pastries are available for $2. Open Su-Th 9am-7pm, F-Sa 9am-midnight.

TRIBECA

Restaurants here cater to middle-aged adults with money to burn. For really cheap fare, head to the borders of TriBeCa–especially around **Chambers and Church Street.** (which have a handful of **halal** eateries).

Salaam Bombay, 317 Greenwich St., at Reade St. (☎212-226-9400). Subway: 1, 2, 3, 9 to Chambers St. Map 9. At *Let's Go,* we consider ourselves something of connoisseurs of Indian cuisine. Having sampled much of the city's expansive offerings of South Asian fare, trust us when we tell you that Salaam Bombay is the best Indian restaurant in the 5 boroughs. Ask the extremely personable manager for nightly recommendations and you won't leave disappointed. If you're not adventurous, try the lamb chops ($23) or chicken tikka ($12). Unbeatable weekend buffet $12.95. Full bar. Open M-F 11:30am-3pm and 5:30pm-10:45pm, Sa-Su noon-3pm and 5:30pm-10:45pm. ❸

Bubby's, 120 Hudson St., at N. Moore St. (☎212-219-0666). Subway: 1, 9 to Franklin St. Map 9, B6, 47. Rough brick walls and 2 walls of windows add to cafe's stylish unfinished simplicity. Great weekend brunch and pies draw locals. Entrees $9-15. Open M-F 8am-4:30pm and 6-11pm, Sa-Su 9am-4:30pm and 6-10pm. ❷

El Teddy's, 219 W. Broadway, between Franklin and White St. (☎212-941-7070). Subway: 1, 9 to Franklin St. Map 9, C6, 48. Look for Statue of Liberty headdress and windows of light-up whirligigs. Creative Mexican cuisine with strong dose of Cali health food. Soups and salads $7-9, quesadillas $11. Brims by night with carousing bar patrons. Open M-Th noon-3pm and 6-10:30pm, F noon-3pm and 6pm-midnight, Sa 5:30pm-midnight, Su 5:30-10pm. ❺

Pakistan Tea House, 176 Church St., between Duane and Reade St. (☎212-240-9800). Map 9, C7, 49. Ever-busy hole-in-the-wall eatery serves tandoori dishes and other traditional Pakistani favorites. Combo plates ($4-6) are an amazing deal. All meat is halal. Open daily 10am-4am. ❶

Yaffa's Tea Room, 19 Harrison St., at Greenwich St. (☎212-274-9403). Subway: 1, 9 to Franklin St. Map 9, A6, 46. Eclectic arrangement of used furniture. High tea from M-Sa 2-6pm ($20) includes cucumber, salmon, or watercress finger sandwiches, fresh-baked scones, dessert sampler, and pot of tea; reservations required. Sandwiches $8-11, salads $6-11.50, entrees $9-21. Open daily 8:30am-midnight. ❸

SOHO

Food is all about image in SoHo. It comes in a variety of exquisite and pricey forms. Often the best deal in SoHo is lunch, when the neighborhood shows its cozy, good-natured front. **West Houston** between MacDougal and Thompson St. reveals some delicious finds. Strolling along any of the side streets, such as **Sullivan Street,** is a good bet for people-watching and latte-sipping.

Brisas del Caribe, 489 Broadway, at Broome St. Subway: 6 to Spring St./Lafayette St.; C, E to Spring St./Ave. of the Americas (Sixth Ave.). Map 9, D3, 36. Very cheap Caribbean food in decidedly un-SoHo setting. Locals patronize this dive for french fries ($2), hot sandwiches ($3.25-6.50), and excellent roast pork ($3.50). Open daily 8am-4pm. ❶

Jerry's, 101 Prince St., between Mercer and Greene St. (☎212-966-9464). Subway: N, R to Prince St. Map 9, D2, 16. Popular spot with fun zebra decor. The calamari salad ($11) will add spice to your life. Great sandwich selection. Weekend brunch 10:30am-4:45pm. Open M-W 9am-11pm, Th-F 9am-11:30pm, Sa 10:30am-11:30pm, Su 10:30am-5pm. ❷

Kelley and Ping Asian Grocery and Noodle Shop, 127 Greene St., between W. Houston and Prince St. (☎212-228-1212). Subway: N, R to Prince St. Map 9, C1, 8. Filling noodle dishes for $8-11 in hollowed-out SoHo warehouse space decorated with Asian food products. Wraps $4. Soups $6.50-9.50. Also has a tea counter. Open daily 11:30am-11pm. ❷

Lupe's East L.A. Kitchen, 110 Sixth Ave., at Watts St. (☎212-966-1326). Subway: 1, 9 to Canal St./Varick St.; A, C, E to Canal St./Ave. of the Americas (Sixth Ave.); C, E to Spring St./ Ave. of the Americas (Sixth Ave.). Map 9, B3, 25. Small, casual cantina with extremely filling burritos and enchiladas ($8-10). Super Vegetarian Burrito ($8) and chicken mole ($9). 4 types of hot-pepper sauce. Brunch ($4-8) served Sa-Su 11:30am-4pm. Open Su-Tu 11:30am-11pm, W-Sa 11:30am-midnight. ❷

Ruben's Empanadas, 505 Broome St., between Thompson St. and W. Broadway. (☎212-334-3351). Subway: C, E to Spring St. Map 9, C3, 28. Since 1975 Ruben has cooked up tasty empanadas for the Soho community and has turned the snack shop into a local favorite. Every kind of meat, vegetable, or dessert empanada ($1.50-$4.00). Open M-F 8am-8pm, Sa-Su 9am-7pm. ❶

Space Untitled, 133 Greene St., between Prince and W. Houston St. (☎212-260-8962). Subway: N, R to Prince St. Map 9, C1, 6. Huge, warehouse-like cafe with plenty of chairs and tables. Salads and sandwiches $5-7.50. Sumptuous desserts $1.75-4.50. Coffee $1.50-4. Wine and beer $4.50. Open M-F 7am-9pm, Sa 8am-10pm, Su 8am-8pm. ❶

CAFE

Miro Cafe, 474 Broadway, between Broome and Grand St. (☎212-431-9391). Subway: N, R to Prince St. Map 9, D3, 39. Serves heaping sandwiches on delicious fresh-baked bread ($7-9), large salads ($8), beer ($5), wine, and baked goods to Broadway's hungry shoppers. Wide coffee bar selection ($1.25-4). Open daily 7am-9pm.

SHOPS

Dean and Deluca, 560 Broadway, at Prince St. (☎212-226-6800; www.deandandeluca.com). Subway: N, R to Prince St. Map 9, D2, 18. More gallery than grocery, with food too pretty to eat. Delectable cakes, tarts, and sushi. Open M-Sa 10am-8pm, Su 10-7pm.

GREENWICH VILLAGE

The West Village's artistic spirit spawns many creative eateries and makes stumbling around looking for food as much fun as dining. Around the intersection of Bleecker and Carmine St. are a cluster of Italian restaurants. On Hudson St. you'll find a number of gourmet shops that serve great sandwiches.

John's Pizzeria, 278 Bleecker St., between Seventh Ave. S. and Morton St. (☎212-243-1680). Subway: 1, 9 to Christopher St. Map 10, C4, 55. Widely regarded as Manhattan's best pizzeria; a great place to sit down and enjoy a pie. 2 sizes–small and large $10-20. No slices. Open M-Th 11:30am-11:30pm, F-Sa 11:30am-12:30am, Su noon-11:30pm. Cash only. ❷

Corner Bistro, 331 W. 4th St., on the corner of Jane St., at Eighth Ave. (☎212-242-9502). Subway: A, C, E, L to 14th St./Eighth Ave. Map 10, A2, 3. Huge, hungry lines crowd this joint for their unbelievable hamburgers. Most famous for their greasy, out-of-this-world $5.50 Bistro Burger (cheese, onions, bacon). Cold beer $2-3. Open M-Sa 11:30am-4am, Su noon-4am. Cash only. ❶

Caffe Pane e Cioccolato, 10 Waverly Pl., at Mercer St. (☎212-472-2944). Subway: N, R to 8th St. If Caffe Pane were an animal, it would be one that served flawless pasta ($7-9; entrees $8-10). If it were a color, it would be a shade that had outstanding service and a contagiously peaceful aura. If it were a fruit it would be a grape to make yummy wine and also a special kind of fruit that makes delicious cheese cake ($4). If it were a restaurant (which it really is!) it would serve brunch noon-4pm on weekends and be open M-Sa 11am-midnight, Su noon-10pm. ❷

Arturo's Pizza, 106 W. Houston St., at Thompson St. (☎212-677-3820). Subway: 1, 9 to Houston St. Map 10, E5, 87. Arturo's has provided great, cheap pizza and divey class for decades. Divine big, cheesy pies ($10-17), but no slices. Entrees $11-28. Live jazz M-Th 8pm-1am, F-Sa 9pm-2am, Su 7pm-midnight. Open M-Th 4pm-1am, F-Sa 4pm-2am, Su 3pm-midnight. ❸

Caliente Cab Co., 21 Waverly Pl., at Greene St. (☎212-529-1500) Subway: N, R to 8th St. Magnificently stuffed burritos ($7) and drinks that recall the glory days of Cancun ($2-4 beer, drinks $4-7) are what you will find here. Find a fiesta in your mouth! Lunch special: all you can eat for $6–en fuego! Open daily noon "until late" (1am to 4am). ❶

Chez Brigitte, 77 Greenwich Ave., between Seventh Ave. and Bank St. (☎212-929-6736). Subway: 1, 2, 3 to 14th St./Seventh Ave. Map 10, B3, 23. This famous, hole-in-the-wall French diner-cum-bistro has no pretensions with its $7-9 French entrees. Just as its menu boasts, it "serves 250 people, 11 people at a time" with diner-style counter service. Fabulous brunch special daily 11am-6pm daily of omelette and potatoes, salad and beverage ($7). Fresh, hearty sandwiches on French bread ($5-7). Open daily 11am-10pm. Cash only. ❷

Day-O, 103 Greenwich Ave., between Jane and W. 12th St. (☎212-924-3168). Map 10, B2, 5. Spicy Caribbean and Southern cuisine with both soul and funk. For a truly decadent (while economical) sampling of Day-O's finest, try their all-you-can-eat brunch of twenty-odd items including fried catfish, southern fried chicken, and salmon croquettes (only $11.95). Brunch Sa 11:30am-3pm, Su 11:30am-4pm. Firebird Jerk Chicken Wings $8. BBQ Ribs $17. Open Su-W noon-10:30pm, Th-Sa noon-1am. ❸

Esperanto Cafe, 114 MacDougal St., between Bleecker St. and W. 3rd St. (☎212-475-5400). Subway: A, C, E, F, V, S to W. 4th St. Here since Esperanto was the answer to Orwell's 1984. That year and that language have come and gone (more or less), but village hippies, young screen-writers and NY intellectuals still wax philosophic betwixt these hallowed wooden enjoying espresso ($2), sandwiches ($5) and desserts (like pumpkin-ginger cheese cake, $4.25). Open daily 24hr. ❶

Eva's, 11 W. 8th St., between MacDougal St. and Fifth Ave. (☎212-677-3496). Subway: A, C, E, F, V, S to W. 4th St. Map 10, D3, 34. Refreshing fast-service health food. Protein heavy plates, good for the gym rat. Lean steak sandwiches $5. Massive veggie plate with falafel, grape leaves, and eggplant salad $6. Vitamin store in back. Open M-Sa 11am-11pm, Su 11am-10pm. ❶

Gray's Papaya, Corner of W. 8th St. and 6th Ave. (☎212-260-3532). Subway: A, C, E, F, V, S to W. 4th St. Always open and always serving the best hotdogs in NYC. Recession special (maintained even in times of more favorable economic conditions) gives you 2 dogs and a drink (try the coconut champagne) for $2.45. Sauerkraut and onions, of course. Other fruit drinks too. Some breakfast stuff served in the morning. Open always as we said before. ❶

Mahmoun's, 119 MacDougal St., between W. 4th and 3rd St. (☎212-674-8685). Subway: A, C, E, F, V, S to W. 4th St. Best falafel ($2) and schwarma ($4) sandwiches you can find. The cool part: these sandwiches come in a pocket and Mahmoun's, with its small, typically village- styled stand-up service station in the back is like a little pocket for hungry people! Performative food preparation for dozens of years! Also baklava, grape leaves, and other Middle Eastern delectables. Go here when you are tired or not tired: open daily 11am-5am. ❶

Manna, 289 Mercer St., between E. Eighth and Mercer St. (☎212-473-6162). Subway: N, R to 8th St. Hole-in-the-wall Korean kitchen with good Kimchi and amazing Bi Bim Bap (assorted stuff over rice, $7). Eat and read Korean newspapers. Open M-F 11am-9:30pm, Sa noon-8pm. ❷

Moustache, 90 Bedford St., between Barrow and Grove St. (☎212-229-2220). Subway: 1, 9 to Christopher St. Map 10, B4, 51. Sumptuous Middle Eastern fare served on copper tabletops. Inhale the enticing, fresh smell of warm pita and try the succulent leg of lambwich ($7.50). Lentil soup ($3.50), salads ($4-9.50), tabouleh ($3.50), falafel sandwich ($5.50). Open daily noon-11pm. ❶

Olive Tree Cafe, 117 MacDougal St., between Bleecker St. and Minetta L. (☎212-254-3480). Subway: A, C, E, F, V, S to W. 4th St. Map 10, D5, 77. Superb Middle Eastern food with endless stimulation. You can watch old movies on the wide screen, rent chess and backgammon sets ($1 per person per hr.), doodle with chalk on the slate tables, or survey Village nightlife from the patio. Falafel sandwich $2.75; chicken kebab platter with salad, rice pilaf, and vegetable $8.75; delicious egg creams $2. Open daily 11am-4am. ❶

Peanut Butter & Co., 240 Sullivan St., at 3rd St. (☎212-677-3995). Subway: A, C, E, F, V, S to W. 4th St. Map 10, D4, 59. All sandwiches ($4-7) include fresh peanut butter ground daily. Open Su-Th 11am-9pm, F-Sa 11am-10pm. ❶

Pink Tea Cup, 42 Grove St. between Bleecker and Bedford St. (☎212-807-6755). Subway: A, C, E, L to 14th St./Eighth Ave.; 1, 2, 3 to 14th St./Seventh Ave. The delectable aroma of greasy, home-style fried chicken can be smelt miles away–about as long as the line extends on weekends. Be prepared for a hefty wait, later to be forgotten by savory chicken and apple fritters ($9.25)–the perfect brunch for even those not of Confederate blood. Amazing pancakes ($5.50), salmon croquettes ($8.50). Open M-Th 8am-midnight, F-Su 8am-1am. ❷

Pizza Mercato, 11 Waverly Pl., at Mercer St. (☎212-420-8327). Subway: N, R to 8th St. Just darn good pizza. Fresh ingredients and crazy range of toppings: zucchini? hot sausage? fresh garlic? capers rosemary chicken? A slice is $1.50 (you cannot find better in the city). This pizza is good if you feel like a *meal* of pizza. Also heros and Italian dishes (chicken parmigiana $5). Open daily 10:30am-11pm. ❶

Soy Luck Club, 115 Greenwich Ave. at Jane St. (☎212-229-9191). Subway: 1, 2, 3 to 14th St./Seventh Ave. Map 10, B2, 4. Heaven for the soy fanatic and the health conscious. Delicious, frothy drinks and warm, grilled sandwiches. Grab an iced vanilla mint soy latte or a honey ginger latte ($4) and a panini ($5-7) and grab a seat on the outdoor bench. Open M-F 10am-10pm, Sa-Su 10am-11pm. ❶

Tartine, 253 W. 11th St., at W. 4th St. (☎212-229-2611). Subway: 1, 2, 3 to 14th St./Seventh Ave.; 1, 9 to Christopher St. Map 10, B3, 21. Bring your own wine to complement a fine Continental lunch, brunch, or dinner in this secluded West Village bistro. Serene sidewalk seating. Huge crowds wait in line for a chance to delight in Tartine's delicately prepared, reasonably priced entrees (chicken sauteed in lemon and sage $13). *Prix-fixe* Su brunch $9.75. Open Tu-Sa 9am-10:30pm, Su 9am-10pm. Cash only. ❷

CAFES

Cafe Mona Lisa, 282 Bleecker St. at Seventh Ave. (☎212-929-1262). Subway: 1, 9 to Christopher St. Map 10, C4, 55. Oversized mirrors, old stuffed chairs, eccentric furniture pieces. Perfect spot for a novel and a delectable crepe on a rainy day. Well-brewed beverages ($1.25-4.50) and other cafe fare (sandwiches and crepes $7-11). Open daily 11am-2am.

Caffe Dante, 79-81 MacDougal St., between W. Houston and Bleecker St. (☎212-982-5275). Subway: A, C, E, F, V, S to W. 4th St. Map 10, D5, 81. A Village staple, with black-and-white photos of Italy and atmospheric lighting. *Frutta di bosco* (cream pastry with fruit) for $5.50, coffee-based drinks ($2-6), *gelati* ($6). Open Su-Th 10am-2am, F-Sa 10am-3am.

The Grey Dog, 33 Carmine St., between Bleecker and Bedford St. (☎212-462-0041). Subway: A, C, E, F, V, S to W. 4th St. Map 10, C5, 72. Hip can be cheap, as this cafe's happy young patrons know. Doggies everywhere, covering the walls and leaving (painted) tracks on the tables. Medium coffee just $1. Salads and sandwiches also reasonable ($5.50-8). Open M-F 6:30am-11:30pm, Sa-Su 7am-12:30am.

SHOPS

The Magnolia Bakery, 401 Bleecker St., at W. 11th St. (☎212-462-2572). Subway: 1, 9 to Christopher St. Map 10, A3, 20. Little West Village corner bakery with cupcakes so famous that they imposed a limit (one dozen per person, $1.50 each)! Can also do any kind of cake. Open M 10am-11:30pm, Tu-F 9am-11:30pm, Sa-Su 9am-12:30pm.

GAY/GAY-FRIENDLY RESTAURANTS AND HANGOUTS

Caffe Raffaella, 134 Seventh Ave S., north of Christopher St. (☎212-929-7247). Subway: 1, 9 to Christopher St. Map 10, B3, 25. This unpretentious old-world-style cafe serves Italian food to a largely gay, male clientele. Beautiful, plush, antique chairs in jeweled tones make observing eye-candy a delightful pastime. Huge, sumptuous desserts satisfy any sweet tooth. Sip steamed milk with *orzata* (sweet almond syrup, $3) while reclining in the embrace of an over-stuffed chair. Sandwiches $6.50-9. Pizza $8-10. Crepes $7-8. Cakes and pastries $4-5. Open daily 11am-2am. ❷

the hidden deal

City of Bagels

NYC's bagels are legendary. Crisp on the outside and chewy on the inside, a bagel is a New York breakfast tradition and a great snack. Here are three of the best places to buy a bagel in the city:

H&H Bagels, 2239 Broadway, at 80th St. (☎212-595-8003; www.handhbagel.com). Map 18, C4, 25. H&H has fed Upper West Siders for years with bagels (95¢) that are reputedly the best in Manhattan. Be forewarned: H&H doesn't have a toaster and only sells spreads in tubs. **Also at:** 639 W. 46th St., between 11th and 12th Ave. (☎212-595-8000). Both locations open 24hr. ❶

Ess-a-Bagel, 831 Third Ave., between 50th and 51st St. (☎212-980-1010). Real New-York-style deli. Bagels 70¢, $8.40 for a baker's dozen. Open M-F 6am-9pm, Sa-Su 8am-5pm. ❶

La Bagel Delight, 252 7th Ave., at 5th St., Brooklyn (☎718-768-6107). With four locations in Brooklyn, the Italian Stallions of La Bagel are an institution throughout the borough. Also at: 90 Court St., 122 7th Ave., and 3623 Ft. Hamilton Pkwy. All locations open M-F 6am-6pm, Sa-Su 6am-6pm. ❶

Lips, 2 Bank St., at Greenwich Ave. (☎212-675-7710). Subway: A, C, E, L to 14th St./Eighth Ave.; 1, 2, 3 to 14th St./Seventh Ave. Map 10, B3, 22. Italian-Continental cuisine with a sassy twist. Impromptu performances from a high-heeled staff in a room festooned with lips, and nightly cabaret entertainment shows. What more could a boy dressed as a girl want? Try the Rupaul for dinner ($14) or the Miss Understood to start ($7.50). Entrees $12-22. M and Tu $2 margaritas, Tu Karaoke. Open Su-Th 5:30pm-midnight, F-Sa 5:30pm-2am; Su brunch 11:30am-4pm. ❸

EAST VILLAGE

St. Mark's Place hosts a slew of inexpensive and popular village institutions. **Avenue A** throbs with bars and sidewalk cafes at night. Living up to East Village's famous reputation for ethnic cuisine are the row of Indian restaurants that line **East 6th Street.,** between First and Second Ave.; the Japanese eating spots on **East 9th Street** and **Stuyvesant Street,** between Second and Third Ave.; and the Eastern European restaurants along **Second Avenue.**

Second Ave. Delicatessen, 156 Second Ave., at 10th St. (☎212-677-0606). Subway: 6 to Astor Pl. Map 12, C2, 21. *The* definitive New York deli. See p. 67 for historical info on the deli. The Lebewohl family has proudly maintained this strictly kosher joint since 1954. No outside food allowed inside eatery. Meals served with array of pickles. Try the chopped liver ($6.50), *babka* ($3.25), *kasha varnishkes* ($4), or mushroom barley ($4), all reputed to be among the best in the city, or go for the classic pastrami or corned beef sandwiches ($8-11). Act like you know and order your Dr. Brown's black cherry soda with a lemon twist (tell them you learned the trick from Eddie). Open M-Sa 10am-8:30pm, Su 11am-7pm. ❷

Bendix Diner, 167 First Ave., between E. 10th and E. 11th St. (☎212-260-4220). Subway: 6 to Astor Pl.; L to First Ave. Bendix is a severely funked-up diner. Shapes of the booths, tables and counter are typical, but such features as the large art, colorful surfaces, and gigantic diorama of NY replete with brooklyn bridge (not to scale) make Bendix stand out. Menu is "Thai Chow and American Grub" (pad thai, curry soups, fried chicken, most every sandwich ever). Entrees, sandwiches $6-$13 and huge. Everything is good except the water. Just kidding. That's good too. Hooray for Bendix! Open M-F 9am-11pm, Sa-Su 9am-midnight. ❷

Frank, 88 Second Ave., between E. 5th and 6th St. (☎212-420-1232). Subway: 6 to Astor Pl. Map 12, C3, 70. Let's be Frank. We will be an Italian bistro that paradoxically needs a whole lot more space (because there is always a wait to eat), yet derives an indubitably essential charm from the closeness (and cuteness) of its quaint quarters. Our food will be as good as beer is to an alcoholic reneging on rehab. (Pasta, entrees, specials $10-15, cheaper at lunchtime) A wine list more artful than souffle. Wait! Let's not *be* Frank, *Let's Go* to Frank. I think I'll go there now! Open M-Th 10:30am-4pm and 5pm-1am; F-Sa 10:30am-4pm and 5pm-2am; Su 10:30am-4pm and 5pm-midnight. ❷

Cucina di Pesce, 87 E. 4th St., between Second and Third Ave. (☎212-260-6800). Subway: 6 to Astor Pl. Map 12, C1, 74. Classic little Italian place with oil paintings, rosily lit nooks, a beautiful garden, fireplace, skylight, and sidewalk seating. The serenity is disturbed only by the astoundingly good food which (silently) screams taste. Portions are large in size and on quality making Cucina di Pesce quite cheap for what you get. Spinach penne (with asparagus, sundried tomatoes, and fontina cheese) $8; salmon with sauteed mushrooms and pasta $11. Free mussels at the bar are a deal surpassed only by the early bird dinner special: full dinner with soup, entree, and glass of wine $10 (M-F 4-6:30pm, Sa-Su 4-6pm). Hours work nicely for those wishing to take in a great off-Broadway show at New York Theatre Workshop (p. 226), a couple of doors down. Or for those simply wishing to eat and still have 5 or so hours until midnight. Open daily 2:30pm-midnight. ❷

National Cafe, 210 First Ave., at E. 13th St. (☎212-473-9354). Subway: L to First Ave. Map 12, D1, 8. Great home cooking, Cuban style. The lunch special, also (if predictably) Cuban style, is perhaps the best in the city; from 10:30am-3pm, serves an entree of the day, rice and beans or salad, plantain, a cup of soup, and bread for $5. Everything on garlic-heavy menu well under $10. Open M-Sa 11am-10pm. ❶

A Salt and Battery, 80 2nd Ave., between E 4th and 5th St. (☎212-254-6610; www.asaltandbattery.com). Subway: F to Lower East Side/Second Ave. or 6 to Astor Pl. A real British-feeling fish 'n' chips shop that gives out huge portions of good food. Fried cod starts as low as $3.50. Many kinds of fish, sizes, and other stuff (shrimp, chicken pot pie, shepherd's pie, etc.). "In cod we trust ..." har har har. Open daily 11:30am-11pm. ❷

Blue 9 Burger, 92 Third Ave., between E. 12th and E. 13th St. (☎212-979-0053). At Blue 9 Burger, the writing is on the wall. It explains that they don't freeze their meat, do believe in simple, quality fast food preparation, have a predilection for the color blue, and charge $3.90 for a "Blue 9" (special double cheeseburger). Meals are $6. Mango chili sauce for the fries is holy to those who revere Taste, "God of Deliciousness." Burgers, fries, and shakes only. Free soda refills, my friend. Open Su-W 11am-1:30am, Th-Sa 11am-2am. ❶

Crif Dogs, 113 St. Marks Pl., between First Ave. and A. (☎212-614-2728). Subway: 6 to Astor Pl.; L to First Ave. Hot dogs are so good! They are even better at Crif Dogs (a small, impeccably clean cavern) because everyone who works there is a secret magician...of making hot dogs! Simple dog ($1.50), bacon, jalapeños, and cheese ($3.50). Cheap beer ($2 cans of Bud). Also a chest full of board games and old school Ms. Pac Man. Open Su-M noon-midnight, Tu-Th noon-2am, F-Sa noon-4am. ❶

The Crooked Tree, 110 St. Mark's Pl., between First Ave. and Ave. A. (☎212-533-3299). Subway: 6 to Astor Pl.; L to First Ave. Small family-owned creperie with recipes procured in the Alps of France. Cozy, photo-filled interior is nice, but the interior of the crepes (brie, tomato, and arugula ($7) or nutella and banana ($5) are some favorite interiors) are of equivalent visual merit and superior taste. Salads, sandwiches, and belgian waffles too! Open daily 10am-midnight. ❶

Dojo Restaurant, 26 St. Mark's Pl., between Second and Third Ave. (☎212-674-9821). Subway: 6 to Astor Pl. Map 12, C2. One of the area's most popular restaurants and hangouts. Incredible variety of (largely) vegetarian and Japanese foods with St. Mark's Pl. ambience. Soy burgers with brown rice and salad $3.50. *Dojo* salad with carrot dressing $5. *Yakisoba* $5-7. Open Su-Th 11am-1am, F-Sa 11am-2am. Cash only. ❶

Elvie's Turo-Turo, 214 First Ave., at E. 13th St. (☎212-473-7785). Subway: L to First Ave. Map 12, D1, 8. Filipino food served point-and-eat style. You see, *Turo Turo* means "point point." The name of the restaurant is also an encouragement. Dishes at which you may wish to point include *pancit* (a stir-fried rice noodle dish), an excellent chicken

Chinatown

Krispy Kreme

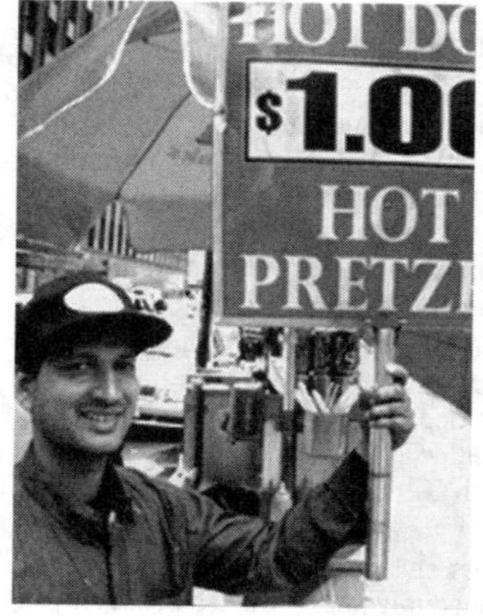

Street Vendor

adobo, and barbecued pork and chicken. 1 dish (plus rice) $4, 2 for $5.75. Open M-Sa 11am-10pm, Su 11am-9pm. ❶

Flor's Kitchen, 149 First Ave., at E. 9th St. (☎212-387-8949; www.florskitchen.com). Subway: 6 to Astor Pl.; L to First Ave. Map 12, D2, 41. Tiny, brightly colored Venezuelan restaurant serving up all sorts of *arepas* (filled corn cakes $3-4) and *empanadas* ($2.75). Good beet soup (bowl $4.50) and grilled kingfish ($8.50). Entrees $8-13. Open M-Th 11am-11pm, F-Sa 11am-midnight, Su 10am-10pm. ❶

Jules, 65 St. Mark's Pl., between First and Second Ave. (☎212-477-5560). Subway: 6 to Astor Pl.; L to First Ave. Hip French bistro with soft lighting and a bar brought over from the old country. White wine sangria is brilliant. Mushroom risotto is deadly good. Lunch entrees $9-12, dinner is a tad more. $3 beer and house wine. Live music begins nightly at 8 or 9pm: afro-latin jazz and Brazilian grooves mostly. Lots of regulars mean reservations are a good idea on weekend nights. Open daily 10:30am-2am. ❸

Kate's Corner, 56 Ave. B, at E. 4th St. (☎212-777-7059). Subway: F, V to Lower East Side-Second Ave. Map 12, E3, 86. Good vegan restaurant with hearty food. Colorful, couch-lined, chill. Veggie fare like tofu teriyaki ($10), Southern-fried unchicken cutlets ($10), and unturkey club ($7). A lot of vegan options too! Wanting beer and wine is a good reason to go to Kate's. Open daily 9am-1am (or 2am). ❷

La Focacceria, 128 First Ave., between St. Mark's Pl. and E. 7th St. (☎212-254-4946). Subway: 6 to Astor Pl. Map 12, D2, 77. Serving delectable Sicilian eats for 85 years. The *vesteddi* (fried ricotta and kashkaval cheese, $2.50) and Sicilian-style eggplant sandwiches ($5) are exceptional. Open M-Th 11am-10pm, F-Sa 1-11pm. ❶

Little Poland, 208 Second Ave., between 12th and 13th St. (☎212-777-9728). Subway: L to First Ave. or Third Ave. Map 12, C1, 6. Try a side order of *kielbasy* ($3.25) at the diner-style bar, or grab a booth. Unsurpassed dumpling-like pierogis with "special sauce" and generous portions of applesauce and sour cream ($6.20 for full order (8 'rogis), $4.20 for a half). The 8 kinds of steaming daily soups—served in a brimming bowl with freshly baked and buttered challah—present the best deal ($3 for bowl, $2 for cup). Open daily 7:30am-10pm. ❶

Mama's Food Shop, 200 E. 3rd St., between Ave. A and B (☎212-777-4425). Subway: F, V to Lower East Side-Second Ave. Map 12, E4, 103. Mama says "shut up and eat." After shutting up, you can eat fried chicken or salmon (each $7) with sides like honey-glazed sweet potatoes and broccoli or couscous ($1 each). Vegetarian dinner includes any 3 sides ($7). Bread pudding and cobbler come by the half-pint ($3). Dozens of old portraits, tables and comfy chairs belong in a living room and are found here. You don't really have to shut up if you do not care to. Open M-Sa 11am-11pm. Mama's twin **Step Mama's,** across the street at 199 E. 3rd St. (☎212-228-2663; Map 12, E4), sells sandwiches, soups, and sides. ❷

Max, 51 Ave. B, between E. 3rd and 4th St. (☎212-539-0111). Subway: F, V to Lower East Side-Second Ave. Map 12, E3, 107. Eating in the back garden is like having dinner in an old Italian-American neighborhood: clothes hang off faux washing lines. Food (pasta $9-11, entrees $11-15) tastes lovingly handmade. Open daily noon-midnight. Cash only. ❷

Pommes Frites, 123 Second Ave., between E. 7th St. and St. Mark's Pl. (☎212-674-1234). Subway: 6 to Astor Pl. Map 12, C2, 64. Hole-in-the-wall eatery selling lovely Belgian fries. With over 30 sauces to choose from it is an indecisive person's nightmare and yet this person's tongue will rejoice once the tough call is finally made. Tandoori mayo and mango chutney are extra tasty (this recommendation is aimed primarily at indecisive people). Regular fries $3.75, large $5. Open Su-Th 11:30am-1am, F-Sa 11:30am-2am. ❶

Sahara East, 184 First Ave., between E. 11th and E. 12th St. (☎212-353-9000). At first glance, Sahara East may seem just like the thousands of other skinny, yellow-painted, hummus-serving joints in the city. If you conclude thus, you will find yourself mistaken: an elaborate backyard unfolds before your very eyes; and the unmistakable perfume of the hookahs means 2 things: you can order a hookah for $10 (dozens of flavors) and you can smoke inside (a rare oasis for the tobacco-lover in the city's non-smoking desert). Food is very good (falafel platter $7). Lunch specials $5-7. Open daily 11am-4am. ❷

St. Dymphna's, 118 St. Mark's Pl., between First Ave. and Ave. A (☎212-254-6636). Subway: L to First Ave. Map 12, E2, 52. Cozy and old-fashioned pub with full bar and a lush garden out back. Named after the patron saint of the mentally ill. Sumptuous homemade burgers $8. Open for lunch M-F 10am-4pm; dinner daily 5pm-midnight; brunch Sa-Su 10am-5pm. Bar open daily until 4am. ❷

Two Boots Restaurant, 37 Ave. A, at E. 3rd St. (☎212-505-2276). Subway: F, V to Lower East Side-Second Ave. Map 12, E4, 102; 104. Boots refer to Italy and Louisiana. Swinging combo of Cajun and Italian draws locals with its hybrid pizzas named after excellent bit-part film and TV-characters. Po'boys $5-6. Nearby take-out pizzeria ($3 slices), **Two Boots To Go,** 42-44 Ave. A (☎212-254-1919) has an attached, amazingly well-stocked video store. **Den of Cin** (below the video store) is a screening room/performance space (☎212-254-0800). Two more Two Boots on Bleecker St. and 7th Ave. (see Greenwich Village). Open M-Sa 11am-1am, Su noon-midnight. ❶

Di Palo's

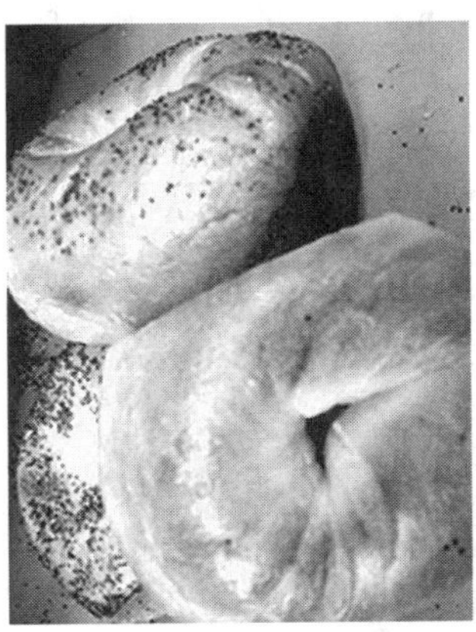

Bagels

Dining Out

24hr. Food

Famished from a night of clubbing? Too busy to eat during the day? No need to go hungry: the city that never sleeps can't stop eating. Chelsea's **Empire Diner** (p. 170), the East Village's **Veselka,** (p. 168) and **Yaffa Cafe** (p. 168), Flushing's **Kum Gang San** (p. 188), and Astoria's **Uncle George's** (p. 188) never close. The UWS boasts **Gray's Papaya** (p. 177), **H&H Bagels** (p. 164), **Tom's Restaurant** (p. 179), and **Big Nick's** (p. 176). Here is more round-the-clock dining:

EAST VILLAGE

Around the Clock, 8 Stuyvesant St., between Second and Third Ave. (☎212-598-0402). Subway: 6 to Astor Pl. Map 12, C2, 25. Spacious bar atmosphere and affordable grub. Pancakes with fresh fruit $5.50. ❶

GREENWICH

Cafe De L'Université, 1 University Pl., at Washington Sq. N (☎212-995-0111). Subway: N, R to 8th St.-NYU. Map 10, E4, 60. NYU haunt. ❶

Waverly Restaurant, 385 Sixth Ave., between W. 8th St and Waverly Pl. (☎212-675-3181). Subway: 1, 9 to Christopher St. Map 10, C3, 32. Diner-style. Grilled cheese $4, pancakes $4.50. ❶

French Roast Cafe, 456 Sixth Ave., at W. 11th St (☎212-533-2233). Subway: F, L, V to 14th St./Sixth Ave. Map 10, C3, 27. Fancy eats. Sauteed trout $14. ❸

Veselka, 144 Second Ave., at E. 9th St. (☎212-228-9682). Subway: 6 to Astor Pl. Map 12, C2, 25. Big, beautiful murals adorn this Ukrainian restaurant. Enormous menu includes 7 kinds of soups, as well as salads ($3.50-7.75), blintzes ($7.25), Ukrainian meatballs ($8.25), and other Eastern European fare. Combo special gets you soup, salad, stuffed cabbage, and 4 melt-in-your-mouth pierogis ($8.25). Open 24hr. ❶

Whole Earth Bakery and Kitchen, 130 St. Mark's Pl., between First Ave. and Ave. A (☎212-677-7597). Subway: 6 to Astor Pl. Map 12, E2, 52. Inspired by owner's 87-year-old mother—home cooking with vegan tweak. Shockingly tasty baked goods (all without egg, naturally). Ask for flavorful tofu/garlic spread on other items. Cookies (50¢-$2), fruit cobbler ($1.50), oil/sugar-free muffins ($1.50). Open M-F 8am-midnight, Sa-Su 10:30am-midnight. ❶

Yaffa Cafe, 97 St. Mark's Pl., between First Ave. and Ave. A (☎212-674-9302 or 677-9001). Subway: 6 to Astor Pl. Map 12, D2, 44. Cocktail garden party meets Middle Eastern leisure lounge. Sandwiches $4.50-7, salads around $6, veggie entrees $7, chicken entrees $9. Super weekend brunch $9. Beer $3.50. The beautiful outdoor garden is open all summer and quite beautiful. Open 24hr. ❶

CAFES

Alt.Coffee, 139 Ave. A, at E. 9th St. (☎212-529-2233). Subway: 6 to Astor Pl. Map 12, E2, 51. Haven for artists, anarchists, and alterna-types galore. All sorts of (non-alcoholic) drinks ($1.50-3.75), sandwiches, and vegan cookies ($2.25). Internet access $10 per hr. Local art on walls; lots of comfy couches and chairs. Yes, you can smoke here. Open M-Th 8:30am-1:30am, F 8:30am-3am, Sa 10am-3am, Su 10am-1:30am.

SHOPS

Moishe's Bake Shop, 115 Second Ave., between E. 6th and 7th St. (☎212-505-8555). Subway: 6 to Astor Pl. Map 12, C3, 67. For 30 years, this bake shop has served up strictly kosher breads and cookies. Challah $2.75. Open Su 7am-8pm, M-Th 7:30am-8:30pm, F 7am until 1hr. before sunset.

NYC ICY, 21 Ave. B, between E. 2nd and E. 3rd St. (☎212-979-9877). Subway: F to Lower East Side/Second Ave. Not quite sorbet, not quite ice cream: the New York City Icy Company has discovered the Icy and it's selling like wildfire! (Patent pending?) Tiny closet of an icy-store has friendly folks scooping the icies made on the premises just for you. Brilliant, uncommon flavor combos ($2 for 2 scoops, $3 for 4!) and slushy "icy tea" ($3). Open Sa-W 11am-midnight, F-Sa 11am-2am.

Something Sweet, 177 First Ave., at 11th St. (☎212-533-9986). Subway: L to First Ave. Map 12, C2, 35. Delectable, inventive sweets. Indulge in a tropical fruit tart ($2.50), a mousse tart ($2.50), or *crème brûlée* ($2.50). Cakes and other great stuff (more than $2.50). Open M-Sa 8am-10pm, Su 9:30am-5:30pm.

Veniero's, 342 E. 11th St., between First and Second Ave. (☎212-674-7070; www.venierospastry.com). Subway: L to First Ave. Map 12, D2, 34. Italian pastry shop established in 1894. Spacious cafe seating, superb at making cheese cake. A NYC classic and if you want a cake too pretty to eat (but to tasty too look at) you can find your culinary quandary here. *Cannolis* $2.25, cheesecakes $3.50-4. Open Su-Th 8am-midnight, F-Sa 8am-1pm.

CHELSEA AND HERALD SQUARE

The heart of Chelsea dining is **Eighth Avenue,** between 14th and 23rd St., a center of great cafes and stylish restaurants.

Kang Suh, 1250 Broadway, between Fifth and Sixth Ave. (☎212-564-6845). Subway: B, D, F, N, Q, R, V, W to Herald Sq. Map 13, D3, 15. The real deal: homestyle Korean cookin' with quick, efficient service. The delectable *hwe dup bap* (spicy sashimi salad with rice, $16.95) and the stellar juicy BBQ draw Koreans in hordes. Open 24hr. ❸

Kitchen/Market, 218 Eighth Ave., at 21st St. (☎212-243-4433; www.kitchenmarket.com). Subway: C, E to 23rd St./Eighth Ave. Map 13, B5, 61. Bear with the narrow confines–the Mexican dishes (takeout only) are well worth the squeeze. Books, Mexican paraphernalia, and a staggering array of international hot sauces also sold. Burrito stuffed with a filling of your choice, pinto beans, rice, and green salsa ($7.75). Open M-F 9am-10:30pm, Sa-Su 11am-10:30pm. ❷

Kum Gang San, 49 W. 32nd St., between Fifth and Sixth Ave. (☎212-967-0909). Subway: B, D, F, N, Q, R, V, W to Herald Sq. Map 13, D3, 13. This beautiful, immaculate haven of scrumptious Korean food features a sushi bar downstairs and a one-with-nature decor replete with stones, waterfalls, and greenery. Live classical piano music (sometimes featuring a bass) provides the perfect soothing accompaniment to delicious *galbi* (BBQ short ribs $22.95) or spicy tofu stew ($9.95). Open 24hr. ❹

Better Burger, 178 Eighth Ave. (☎212-989-6688). Claims to do the basics "better," and delivers on its word. Skimps on seating, but not on ingredients, offering organic ostrich burgers ($6.45) organically fed, antibiotic, and hormone-free, farm-raised salmon fillet ($15.95), and soy cheese ($1). Ask about their organic condiments, which include jalapeno-honey mustard and Cajun ketchup. ❷

Blue Moon Mexican Cafe, 150 Eighth Ave., between 17th and 18th St. (☎212-463-0560). Subway: A, C, E, L to 14th St./Eighth Ave. Map 13, B5, 70. Small

(cont'd from p. 168)

Bagel Buffet, 406 Sixth Ave., between 8th and 9th St. (☎212-477-0448). Subway: 1, 9 to Christopher St. Map 10, C3, 30. Not just bagels. Philly Cheesesteak $4.25. ❶

MIDTOWN

Stage Deli, 834 Seventh Ave., between W. 53rd and 54th St. (☎212-245-7850). Subway: E to Seventh Ave./53rd St. Map 14, C2, 14. With heaping sandwiches ($8-13) and giant slices of cheesecake ($10), this is the perfect spot to share a late-night meal with someone special. Closed daily 2-6pm. ❷

THEATER DISTRICT

Brasserie Centrale, 1700 Broadway, at W. 53rd St. (☎212-757-2233). Subway: E to Seventh Ave./53rd St. Map 14, C2, 13. Upscale French and American cuisine at all hours. Burger ($10) and escargot ($9) to recharge your batteries after a night of partying hard. ❸

UPPER EAST SIDE

Green Kitchen, 1477 1st Ave. at E. 77th St. (☎212-988-4163). Subway: 6 to 77th St. Map 15, C4, 27. A wide variety of standard diner fare served up in old-school fashion. They even have a rotating pie case. Burgers $4-8, sandwiches $6.25. ❶

cafe, popular both for the Mex-Cali fusion food and the margaritas. Generous portions, vegetarian-friendly dishes. Giant burritos $9; entrees $11-13. One alcoholic drink with weekend brunch (Sa-Su 11:30am-4pm); omelettes or french toast $8, pancakes $7. Open Su-Th noon-11pm, F-Sa 11:30am-midnight. ❷

Chef & Co., 8 W. 18th St. (☎646-336-1980). This world-famous catering company with a resume that includes the TONY awards, the Daytime EMMYs, etc., offers that day's catering items buffet-style to the public. Because the company caters 30-40 events daily, selection is fantastic. Open M-F 11am-4pm. ❷

elmo, 156 Seventh Ave. (☎212-337-8000). Perennially packed. Auspiciously American. Forget the popularity of the ethnic twist, elmo offers down 'n' dirty American food in a colorful yet minimalist setting. Even the joint's name is hidden, with only the label "Restaurant" across the top. Try the mac & cheese ($6.95), the fried chicken ($13.95) or the classic grilled cheese ($6.95). Open Su-Th 11am-11pm, F-Sa 11am-2am. ❷

Empire Diner, 210 10th Ave., at W. 22nd St. (☎212-243-2736). Map 13, A5, 50. Subway: C, E to 23rd St./Eighth Ave. Chelsea's slightly overpriced (but what isn't?) answer to the 1950s-style diner. Eat outside with the throngs of gallerygoers on the sidewalk patio seats in the afternoon, or grab a late-night grease-bomb at the diner counter inside. Sandwiches ($5-10.75), root beer floats ($4.75), decent selection of microbrews ($4.50). Open 24hr. ❷

La Taza de Oro, 96 Eighth Ave., between 14th and 15th St. (☎212-243-9946). Subway: A, C, E, L to 14th St./Eighth Ave. Map 13, B6, 110. Authentic Puerto Rican diner with extensive, daily changing menu. Daily special *mofongo* (green plantains mashed and fried with pork and gravy) $5.50. Roast chicken $6.50, octopus salad $10.75. Open M-Sa 6am-11:30pm. ❷

Mary Ann's, 116 Eighth Ave., at 16th St. (☎212-633-0877). Subway: A, C, E, L to 14th St./Eighth Ave. Map 13, C6, 103. Huge portions of inventive Mexican food in white-walled restaurant slung with lights. Entrees $8-12. $1 Corona with entree on Th. Happy Hours M-Th 4-7pm, jumbo margaritas $5. Open M-Tu noon-10:30pm, W-Th 11:30am-11pm, F-Sa 11:30am-11:30pm, Su noon-10pm. Cash only. ❷

Minar, 5 W. 31st St., between Fifth Ave. and Broadway (☎212-684-2199). Subway: B, D, F, N, Q, R, V, W to Herald Sq. Map 13, D3, 17. Long, narrow Indian restaurant packs in many neighborhood South Asians for lunch and dinner. Spicy vegetable curries ($4.25) and regular curries ($5.25-5.50) are served at counter with small salad and choice of bread or rice. Some South Indian fare as well, including 12-dosa selection ($3.50-6.50). Open M-F 10am-7:30pm, Sa 10am-5:30. ❶

Negril, 362 W. 23rd St., between Eighth and Ninth Ave. (☎212-807-6411). Subway: C, E to 23rd St./Eighth Ave. Map 13, B4, 28. Colorful decor, great Jamaican food, and a lively bar with 12 kinds of martinis. The jerk chicken ($8) is tender and spicy. Moderately priced ($8-13.50) lunch entrees. Add $1 for dinner entrees after 5pm. Open Su-Th noon-midnight, F-Sa noon-4am. ❸

Pad Thai Noodle Lounge, 114 Eighth Ave., between 15th and 16th St. (☎212-691-6226). Subway: A, C, E, L to 14th St./Eighth Ave. Map 13, B6, 104. Properly named, this cozy restaurant offers fuschia velvet chairs, budget prices and 4 types of pad thai ($9.95). Curry sauces are also splendid. ❷

Rue des Crepes, 104 Eighth Ave., between 15th and 16th St. (☎212-242-9900). Subway: A, C, E, L to 14th St./Eighth Ave. Map 13, B6, 105. A taste of Paris in the heart of Chelsea. Savory crepes made with buckwheat flour. Try the merguez sausage (spicy Moroccan sausage, white bean, and roasted garlic, $9.25) and the turkey, fontina, and spinach ($9.25). Dessert options include banana Nutella ($5.99) and brie and red grape ($6.99). Open M-Th 10am-11pm, F-Sa 11am-midnight, Su 11am-10pm. ❷

Wild Lily Tea Room, 511-A W. 22nd St., between 10th and 11th Ave. (☎212-691-2258; www.wildlilytearoom.com). Subway: C, E to 23rd St./Eighth Ave. Map 13, A4, 49. Sparse menu full of Asian (or Asian-inspired) ingredients like shiitake mushrooms and mesclun greens. Sip a jasmine or green mattcha iced tea ($5 for a tall glass) while you wax philosophical in the minimalist Tea Room, featuring a circular pond full of koi fish and floating flowers. Occasionally features live music. Entrees $11-13, green tea mochi ice cream $5.35. Open Tu-Su 11am-10pm. ❷

SHOPS

Little Pie Co., 407 W. 14th St., between Ninth and 10th Ave. (☎212-414-2324). Subway: A, C, E, L to 14th St./Eighth Ave. Map 13, B6, 107. Small and perfect. Grab a 5" old-fashioned apple pie ($5 of fresh apples and great crust) to go, or snack on it on the red diner-style bar counter. Open M-F 10am-8pm, Sa-Su noon-7pm.

F & B, 269 W. 23rd St., between Seventh and Eighth Ave. (☎212-486-4441). Subway: 1, 9 to 23rd St./Seventh Ave.; C, E to 23rd St./Eighth Ave. Map 13, C4, 30. Street food, European-style, with brushed-metal decor. Name stands for "frites and beignets." Hot dogs ($2.35-5.50, most $3.50) include very generous toppings. Amazing juicy *frites* ($2.25-3.25) with 12 choices of dip (60¢). Veggie dogs can be substituted for most hot dogs. Try the refreshing cool dog (vanilla ice cream in a sponge cake bun, $3.50). Open daily 11am-11pm.

GAY/GAY-FRIENDLY RESTAURANTS AND HANGOUTS

For restaurants with a largely gay crowd, one need not look farther than any of the well-adorned restaurants on Eighth Ave., between 14th and 23rd St.

Big Cup, 228 Eighth Ave., between 21st and 22nd St. (☎212-206-0059). Subway: C, E to 23rd St./Eighth Ave. Map 13, B5, 61. Bright, campy colors and comfy velvet chairs make this a great place to curl up with a cup of joe ($1.30) and wink at cute Chelsea boys. Sandwiches $6.50. Open M-Th 7am-1am, F-Sa 8am-2am, Su 8am-1am. ❷

Food Bar, 149 Eighth Ave., between W. 17th and W. 18th St. (☎212-243-2020). Subway: A, C, E, L to 14th St./Eighth Ave.; 1, 9 to 18th St./Seventh Ave. Map 13, B5, 69. A sharply dressed, almost all-male crowd adorns this popular, very chic gay hangout. Tasty, relatively cheap sandwiches, salads, and all-day breakfast $6-11; large-portioned dinner entrees $10-18. Minimalist decor. Min. $10 order at night. Open M-F 11am-4pm, daily 5pm-11:30pm. ❷

UNION SQUARE, GRAMERCY, AND MURRAY HILL

A small cluster of Pakistani and Indian restaurants and other ethnic cuisine restaurants battle for customers on Lexington and Third Ave., in the upper 20s and lower 30s (an area jocularly known as Curry Hill). Trendy, upscale restaurants (**Union Square Cafe** and **Bluewater Grill** are among New York's finest eating spots, although hardly the sort of place one would call 'budget') and yuppie watering holes cluster around Union Sq. and Park Ave. S. The open space at the square's north end hosts the **Union Square Greenmarket** (Map 13, E6), where dozens of small businesses and farms bring fresh-baked goods, produce, and country charm to the area. Products vary with the season, but you can almost always expect a slab of good focaccia for under $3, homemade jams, and a staggering variety of organic apples.

Ranch 1, 864 Broadway, between 17th and 18th St. (☎212-979-1111). Subway: N, R, W, Q, 4, 5, 6, L to Union Sq. Map 13. Scattered throughout Manhattan, Ranch 1 offers the most satisfying and least intestinally-unpleasant fast-food experience in the city. Grilled chicken is the order of the day, and a double chicken sandwich with cheese and hot sauce will fill you for less than $10. ❶

Chat 'n' Chew, 10 E. 16th St., between Fifth Ave. and Union Sq. W. (☎212-243-1616). Subway: 4, 5, 6, L, N, Q, R, W to 14th St.-Union Sq. Map 13, D6, 114. A giant ice cream sundae out front hails customers to try their "Real American homestyle," down-home food recalling a '50s sitcom. Heaping plates of macaroni and cheese ($8), classic grilled cheese with tomato ($6), cornmeal fried oysters ($6). "Not your Mother's Meatloaf" $11. Open M-Th 10am-midnight, F-Sa 10:30am-11:30pm, Su 10:30am-11pm. ❷

Zen Palate, 34 Union Sq. E. at E. 16th St. (☎212-614-9291). Subway: 4, 5, 6, L, N, Q, R, W to 14th St.-Union Sq. Map 13, E6, 117. Peaceful decor in deep natural colors offers calm, zen-like dining for the non-impoverished health nut. Sit cross-legged at a low table on the mezzanine level and savor the wheel of dharma ($14.50), a mandala of mushroom tempura propped up in a bed of creamy mashed yams, or the crepe de fleur ($17.50), a huge pinenut and soy-protein patty crowned by a crispy crepe bundle. Cheapie bar and noodle

Zabar's

Tavern on the Green

Gray's Papaya

counter on 1st fl., swankier mood-lit upper floors with slightly pricier, excellent Asian-inspired vegetarian/vegan cuisine. Open M-Th and Su 11am-10:45pm, F-Sa 11am-11:45pm. ❷

Chango, 239 Park Ave. S., between 19th and 20th St. (☎212-477-1500). Subway: 6, N, R, W to 23rd St. This fiery Mexican joint offers innovative fare in a chic, trendy environment. Try the killer crab quesadillas ($10) and jalapeno dusted onion rings ($4). Fabulous "Mariachi Brunch" with complimentary bread basket of bunuelos, guava butter, and unlimited Bloody Marias (Sa and Su until 3pm). Su nights feature $2 tacos! Open Su 12pm-10pm, M-W 12pm-11pm, Th-Sa 12pm-12am. ❷

Curry in a Hurry, 119 Lexington Ave., at 28th St. (☎212-683-0900). Subway: 6 to 28th St./Park Ave. S. Map 13, E3, 24. Lots of tasty food at good prices—one of our favorite Curry Hill locales. Apparently also a favorite of New York City cab drivers. Order at the counter and shoulder your way upstairs. Chicken or lamb curries $5; vegetarian dishes $2.75-4; platters (main dishes, basmati rice, *naan,* salad) $6.50-8.50. Open daily noon-midnight. ❶

Havana Central, 22 E. 17th St., between Broadway and Fifth Ave. (☎212-414-2298). Subway: 4, 5, 6, N, R, Q, W to Union Sq. Lively, bustling atmosphere serving up delectable, cheap Cuban fare. Make-your-own-paella bar and fabulous mojitos. After work crowd is rowdy and ready to down sangria. Most dishes under $12. Open daily noon-midnight. ❷

Kitchen 22, 36 E. 22nd St. between Broadway and Park Avenue S. (☎212-228-4399). Subway: 6, N, R, W to 23rd St. Top notch American bistro food in *prix fixe* packages. 3-course gourmet meals for $25 and martinis for $7.50! Delicious courses include Pan-seared salmon, roasted beet salad and sauteed mahi mahi. Open daily 5pm-11pm. ❹

Molly's, 287 Third Ave., between 22nd and 23rd St. (☎212-889-3361). Subway: 6 to 23rd St./Park Ave. S. Map 13, F4, 46. Wooden beams and dim lighting give Molly's the ambience of an Irish countryside pub; the sawdust covering the floor just adds to the feel of being in Killarney. Good burgers ($8-10), stellar corned beef & cabbage ($9.50), pint of (what else?) Guinness ($4.50). Open M-W 11:30am-midnight, Th-Su 11:30am-2am; kitchen closes at midnight.❷

Pete's Tavern, 129 E. 18th St., at Irving Pl. (☎212-473-7676). Subway: 4, 5, 6, L, N, Q, R, W to 14th St.-Union Sq. Map 13, E5, 95. "NY's oldest original bar," serving alcohol since 1864. Photos on the wall document its speakeasy Prohibition days. Legend has it that O. Henry wrote *The Gift of the Magi* in the 1st booth as you enter. On warm nights, you can take your beer outside to the sidewalk. Sandwiches $7-7.50; entrees $10.75-15.50. Kitchen open daily 11am-1am. ❸

Rainbow Falafel, 26 E. 17th St., at Union Sq. W. (☎212-691-8641). Subway: 4, 5, 6, L, N, Q, R, W to 14th St.-Union Sq. Map 13, E5, 115. No-nonsense falafel closet with Seinfeld Soup-Nazi atmosphere attracts salivating hordes every weekday lunch hr. Room holds only 4 customers and 3 employees at a time. Impeccable, fresh falafel sandwiches $3; extra toppings (fried cauliflower or eggplant) $1. Perfectly oiled grape leaves $3.25. Spinach pies $2. Open M-Sa 8am-7pm. ❶

Sushi Samba, 245 Park Ave. S., between 19th and 20th St. (☎212-475-9377). Subway: 6, N, R, W to 23rd St. You'll have to empty your pockets to eat here, but its cutting edge sushi redefines raw fish. Sushi rolls incorporate unique ingredients like eggplant, fresh mozzarella, lemon mayo, and mango. Orange decor attracts hipsters in the masses. Has even appeared in *Sex and the City*. Main courses $17-$29. Try their $20.03 lunch specials featuring various sushi combos. Open M-W 11:45am-1am, Th-Sa 11:45am-2am, Su 1pm-midnight. ❹

Tibetan Kitchen, 444 Third Ave., between 30th and 31st St. (☎212-679-6286). Subway: 6 to 28th St./Park Ave. S. Map 13, E3, 26. This tiny gem claims to be North America's first Tibetan restaurant (born in 1982). Local specialties meatier than Chinese, with a dollop of Indian. Delicious *momo* (beef dumplings, $9) and *bocha* (buttered, salted tea, $3.25). Plentiful veggie dishes $6.75-8. 10% off on your birthday! Open M-F noon-3pm and 5-11pm, Sa 5-11pm. ❷

CAFES AND SHOPS

Coffee Shop Bar, 29 Union Sq. W. (☎212-243-7969). Map 13, E6, 122. Classic American diner fare with a Brazilian twist (eggs Ipanema $9). Ugly building, beautiful people. Irresistible Cuban *media noche* sandwich $9. Beers $4.50-8. They card (21+) in the wee hours, as the shop transforms into a hoppin' bar scene with yuppies and artists mingling. Open M 7am-2am, Tu 7am-4am, W-F 7am-5:30am, Sa 8am-5:30am, Su 8am-2am.

Galaxy Global Eatery, 15 Irving Pl., at 15th St. (☎212-777-3631). Map 13, E5, 121. Often mobbed by late-night post-concertgoers from neighboring Irving Plaza, this funky corner bar offers adventurous, globe-trotting cuisines during its mellower lunch hour. Most paper products (i.e. menus) printed on hemp. Vegetarian-friendly menu has hempnut *edamame* with mango sauce ($8), Indonesian *Gado Gado* ($9), smoked eel burger ($11), *chichi morada,* a sweet Peruvian drink ($3.50). Open Su 8am-3am, M-Sa 8am-4am.

Sunburst Espresso Bar, 206 Third Ave., at 18th St. (☎212-674-1702). Map 13, E5, 98. Locals stroll in for impressive sandwich selection ($4.25-$6.50), H&H bagels ($1.25), low-fat muffins ($1.75), and espressos ($1.25). Breakfast served all day. Dieters can delight at the delicious fat-free pancakes with fresh fruit ($4.95). Dreamy shakes and smoothies $3.25-5. Open M-Th 7am-11pm, F-Sa 7am-midnight, Su 8am-11pm.

THE THEATER DISTRICT AND HELL'S KITCHEN

Subway: 1, 2, 3, 7, A, C, E, N, R, S to 42nd St.-Times Sq. or Port Authority.

Your best budget bets generally lie along Eighth Ave., between 34th and 59th St. Those willing to spend more should try a meal on posh **Restaurant Row** on 46th St., between Eighth and Ninth Ave. (Map 14, B4-C4). The block caters to a pre-theater crowd, so arriving after 8pm will make it easier to get a table.

Island Burgers and Shakes, 766 Ninth Ave., between 51st and 52nd St. (☎212-307-7934). This place is just super. Playful, refreshing decor and good music. The real point, however, is that the burgers are so good that Island sells more than 150 lb. of meat a day. $5-8 for 1 of the more than 50 hamburgers on the menu (also craft your own). Also chicken, salads, stuff to drink. No fries, but it's OK (there are other sorts of potato products). Open daily noon-10:30pm, F until 11pm. ❷

Original Fresco Tortillas, 125 W. 42nd St., between 6th Ave. and Broadway. (☎212-221-5849). Map 14, C4, 77. This Chinese-owned eatery makes excellent Mexican food. 99¢ tacos and quesadillas for $2 are a splendid deal. No artificial spices, MSG, or preservatives. Open M-F 11am-9pm, Sa-Su noon-9pm. ❶

Becco, 355 W. 46th St., between Eighth and Ninth Ave. (☎212-397-7597). Map 14, B4, 58. Gourmet cuisine that makes you forget your budget. 70 wines priced at $20 a bottle allow for moderate splurges. $17 prix-fixe lunch (dinner $22) gets you a gourmet antipasto platter or caesar salad, plus unlimited servings of the 3 pastas of the day. Dinner $16 food min. per person, lunch $14. Open daily noon-3pm and 5pm-midnight. ❹

Hourglass Tavern, 373 W. 46th St., between Eighth and Ninth Ave. (☎212-265-2060). Map 14, B4, 57. Dark, crowded, 2-floor triangular Restaurant Row joint for the fast-moving. Servers flip an hourglass at your table when you sit down, and the 59min. time limit is strictly enforced when crowds are waiting. Changing prix-fixe entrees ($12-17) regularly feature fresh fish and filet mignon. Open M-Tu 5-11:15pm, W and Sa 4:30-11:30pm, Th-F 5-11:30pm, Su 4:30-10:30pm. ❸

Manganaro's, 488-494 Ninth Ave., between 37th and 38th St. (☎212-947-7325). Map 14, B5, 87. This Italian deli/restaurant promises a lively and delicious lunch break with the authentic flavor of pre-gentrified Hell's Kitchen. True to its reputation as home of the 6 ft. sub, Mangaro's prides itself on gargantuan portions. Sandwiches $5-12. Open M-Sa 9am-9pm, Su 11am-6pm. ❷

MIDTOWN

Keep in mind that in Midtown, cash is king. Here, CEOs run their corporate empires by wining and dining their clients; socialite shoppers drop as much money on a late lunch as on a Fendi tote. Budget travelers, however, needn't despair—from noon to 2pm, harried junior executives seeking quick eats swamp delis and cafes. Don't forget the huge food court at **Grand Central Terminal Dining Concourse,** between 42nd and 45th St., Lexington and Vanderbilt Ave. (Map 14, E4). If you do want to splurge, many top restaurants offer relatively reasonable prix-fixe lunch menus that include an appetizer, entree, and dessert.

Ess-a-Bagel, 831 Third Ave., between 50th and 51st St. (☎212-980-1010). One of a handful of true NY bagel shops. Bagels are a mere fraction of a dollar (about 4/5, to be exact). Sandwiches are fat, stuffed with taste-capable cold-cuts ($3.25-6). Eat a bagel, man. Open M-F 6am-9pm, Sa-Su 8am-5pm. ❶

Fresco by Scotto, 40 E. 52nd St., between Park and Madison Ave. (☎212-754-2700). Subway: 6 to 51st St.; E, V to Fifth Ave./53rd St. Map 14, E3, 50. Italian-inspired fare. Grilled pizzas $5-10, sandwiches $7.25-11.25. Huge salads $7-10. Open M-F 6am-6pm. ❷

Sapporo, 152 W. 49th St., between Sixth and Seventh Ave. (☎212-869-8972). Subway: B, D, F, V to 47th-50th St.-Rockefeller Center. Map 14, C3, 35. Simple Japanese diner. Entrees listed on the wall in Japanese; menu in English. Favorite spot for Broadway cast members and corporate types. Portions are quite big, especially the noodle soups. Sapporo ramen special $7.35. Open M-Sa 11am-11:00pm, Su 11am-10:00pm. Cash only. ❷

Tandoori Club, 66 W. 39th St., between 5th and 6th Ave. (☎212-869-2789) Stands out among midtown eateries for its gargantuan portions. Tons of rice and 3 types of veggie dishes $5. Meat combos $6-7. The interior is not the most stunning, but you get so much food, which is all really quite tasty. Open daily 10:30am-9:30pm. ❷

SHOPS

Minamoto Kitchen, 608 Fifth Ave., at 49th St. (☎212-489-6217). Subway: B, D, F, V to 47th-50th St.-Rockefeller Center. Map 14, D3, 43. Traditional Japanese pastry in all its gelatinous artistry. Wide selection of artful and delicate pastries, jellies, and jellied fruit. Enticing *kuzusasamochi* (sweet white bean paste with green tea powder) $2.20. $1 for individual pieces, up to $13 for larger pieces. Open Su-Th 10am-7:30pm, F-Sa 10am-8pm.

Mangia, 16 E. 48th St., between Madison and Fifth Ave. (☎212-754-7600). Subway: 6 to 51st St. Map 14, D3, 48. Upscale prepared-food market. Pretty cakes, pies, candy tidbits, and tartlets. Fresh-pressed cantaloupe, red grape, and lime juice $2.85 for 10 oz., $3.85 for 12 oz. Salads $8, fancy breakfast sandwiches with prosciutto $2.85. Open M-F 7am-7pm; restaurant open M-F 11:30am-4pm.

Teuscher Chocolatier, 620 Fifth Ave., on the promenade at Rockefeller Center (☎212-246-4416). Subway: B, D, F, V to 47th-50th St.-Rockefeller Center. Map 14, D3, 44. Chocoholic's paradise, featuring the freshest chocolates flown in from Zurich weekly and the prices to prove it. You can still, however, savor 1 piece for under $2. Marvelous champagne truffles. Open M-W 10am-6pm, Th 10am-7:30pm, F-Sa 10am-6pm, Su 11:30am-5:30pm.

UPPER EAST SIDE

Meals on the Upper East Side descend in price as you move east away from Fifth Ave.'s glitzy, mildly exorbitant cafes toward Lexington, Third, and Second Ave. Second and Third Ave., especially from the mid-70s to the mid-80s, boast about six restaurants per block.

Barking Dog Luncheonette, 1678 Third Ave., at 94th St. (☎212-831-1800). Subway: 6 to 96th St. Map 15, B3, 5. A haven for Upper East Siders and their four-legged friends, the Barking Dog is known for its huge portions of tasty comfort food. Try the crispy buttermilk-battered half chicken ($11) or the arugula and radicchio salad ($9). Sandwiches ($6-$8) and daily blue plate specials (M-F 5-7pm) which include soup/salad and dessert. Open daily 8am-11pm. Cash only. ❷

Burger Heaven, 804 Lexington Ave., at corner of 62nd St. (☎212-838-3580). Subway: 4, 5, 6 to 59th St./Lexington Ave. Map 15, B6, 54. Established in 1943, this burger joint serves good food teamed with quick and friendly service. Check out the 50s theme as you and your friends chomp on burgers and other sandwiches. Open Su-Th 6:30am-9:30pm, F-Sa 6:30am-10pm. ❷

Candle Cafe, 1307 Third Ave., at 75th St. (☎212-472-0970). Subway: 6 to 77th St. Map 15, B5, 33. This vegan's delight has an excellent Classic Caesar with tempeh bacon ($8) and a summer vegetable lasagna ($13). Check out their specialty drinks like the Carrot Apple Snap ($4) or the Green Goddess ($6). Asian dumplings $8. Open M-Sa 11:30am-10:30pm, Su 11:30am-9:30pm. ❷

Dallas BBQ, 1265 Third Ave., at 73rd St. (☎212-772-9393). Subway: 6 to 68th St. Map 15, B5, 35. Big portions, tasty rib and shrimp dishes. After-work crowds flock to Dallas BBQ for the fluffy cornbread and famous oversized frosty drinks. Piña coladas $7, daiquiris $7 that are bigger than Texas. Early-bird special with dinner for 2 comes with all the fixin's ($8.95). Open Su-Th 11:30am-midnight, F-Sa 11:30am-1am. ❸

EJ's Luncheonette, 1271 Third Ave., at 73rd St. (☎212-472-0600). Subway: 6 to 68th, 77th St. Map 15, B5, 34. Scrumptious all-day breakfast with many local fans, so be prepared to wait for a seat at peak hours. Good buttermilk or multigrain pancakes $6. Open M-Sa 8am-11pm, Su 8am-10:30pm. **Also at** 447 Amsterdam Ave., between 81st and 82nd St. (☎212-873-3444); 432 Sixth Ave., between 9th and 10th St. (☎212-473-5555). ❷

Jackson Hole, 232 E. 64th St., between Second and Third Ave. (☎212-371-7187). Subway: 6 to 68th St. Map 15, B6, 52. Stop by at either of the East Side locations after 3pm, and prepare to be faced with teeming hordes of private school kids munching on the burgers and fries. Open since the 1970s, Jackson Hole has become a neighborhood institution, and for good reason. Platters, $6-12. Open M-Th 10:30am-1am, F-Sa 10:30am-1:30am, Su 10:30am-midnight. **Also at** 91st St. and Madison Ave. (☎212-427-2820); 85th St. and Columbus Ave. (☎212-362-5177); 70th St. and Astoria Blvd. (☎718-204-7070). ❷

Merchants NY, 1125 First Ave., at 62nd St. (☎212-832-1551). Subway: 4, 5, 6 to 59th St./Lexington. Map 15, C6, 58. This romantic hotspot has an excellent menu as well as an excellent venue with live jazz, comfy couches, and candlelit dining rooms. Indulge in New England Lobster Ravioli ($14), Southern Buttermilk Fried Chicken ($14), or Braised New Zealand Lamb Shank ($16.50). Call ahead to reserve a table by the fireplace. Also great for after-work drinks at the downstairs bar. Open daily for lunch 11:30am-5pm; dinner Su-W 5pm-2am, Th-Sa 5pm-3am, Su brunch 11:30-4pm. ❸

Papaya King, 179 E. 86th St., at Third Ave. (☎212-369-0648). Subway: 4, 5, 6 to 86th St./Lexington Ave. Map 15, B4, 17. Bright and neon-lit with tropical-decor, this no-seating dive has served New York's favorite quick-lunch hot dogs ($1.45) since 1945. House special is 2 hot dogs and a 16 oz. tropical drink for $4, trumpeted as "nature's own revitalizer." Open Su-W 8am-midnight, Th-Sa 8am-1am. ❶

Saigon Grill, 1700 Second Ave., at 88th St. (☎212-996-4600). Subway: 4, 5, 6 to 86th St./Lexington Ave. Map 15, C3, 15. Some of NYC's best Vietnamese food at prices not commonly seen on the Upper East Side. Sizable vegetarian options. Entrees $7-14. Open daily 11:30am-11:30pm. **Also at** 2381 Broadway, at W. 87th St. (☎212-875-9072). ❷

Viand, 673 Madison Ave., at 61st St. (☎212-751-6622). Subway: N, R to 59th St.-Fifth Ave. Map 15, A6, 56. Unassuming coffee shop with famous turkey sandwich ($7.35). Many local fans; some say that top brokers make deals here over the excellent apple turnovers ($2). Open daily 6am-7pm. ❷

SHOPS

Grace's Marketplace, 1237 Third Ave., at 71st St. (☎212-737-0600). Subway: 6 to 68th St. Map 15, B5, 36. Lively gourmet shop crowded with the too-busy-to-cook set, Grace's provides fresh goodies with expensive price tags. Open M-F and Sa 7am-8:30pm, Su 8am-7pm.

Le Pain Quotidien, 1131 Madison Ave., between 84th and 85th St. (☎212-327-4900). Subway: 4, 5, 6 to 86th St./Lexington Ave. Map 15, A4, 21. Boutique bakery making some of NYC's favorite bread. Pick up a *baguette à l'ancienne* ($2.50), or sit for a soup and sandwich at the famous communal wooden tables (reserved for waiter service only). Open M-F 7:30am-7pm, Sa-Su 8am-7pm.

World of Nuts & Ice Cream, 767 Lexington Ave., between 60th and 61st St. (☎212-759-9324). Subway: 4, 5, 6 to 59th St./Lexington, N, R, W to Fifth Ave. Map 1, B6, 63. 'Come Visit Us & Be Happy' reads the storefront in this candy/nuts/ice cream/balloon specialty store. Feel like a kid again as you stand in front of the hundreds of drawers filled with anything from honey roasted pistachios and pine nuts, to an assortment of jelly beans and chocolate covered cookie dough. The creamy ice cream ($1.99 for a substantial small cup) can only be described as heavenly. Open M-F 8am-11pm, Sa 9am-11pm, Su 10am-11pm.

UPPER WEST SIDE

The Upper West Side offers a variety of ethnic cuisine. If you're not in the mood for fancy dining, check out the countless pizza shops and diners. Browse Columbus Ave., Amsterdam Ave., and Broadway, between 72nd and 86th St., for inviting sidewalk cafes.

Big Nick's Burger Joint and Pizza Joint, 2175 Broadway, at 77th St. (☎212-362-9238). Subway: 1, 2 to 79th St. Map 18, C5, 35. Cramped but clean source of tried and true pizza, plate-sized burgers ($5-6.75, or go for the 1 lb. sumo burger, $7.50), and breakfast dishes from an expansive menu. Free delivery. Open 24hr. **Also at** 70 W. 71st St., at Columbus Ave. (☎212-799-4444). ❷

Burritoville, 166 W. 72nd St., between Amsterdam and Columbus Ave. (☎212-580-7700). Fabulous burritos for cheap prices. Healthy substitutions allow for whole wheat tortillas and tofu sour cream, but still make a bangin' burrito ($6-7). Cramped seating on plastic chairs means you'll want your burrito to go, but if you eat in, you get free chips! Open daily 11am-midnight. ❶

City Grill, 269 Columbus Ave., between 72nd and 73rd St. (☎212-873-9400). Huge windows entice passersby to try the nouveau American fare. Delightful salads complement hearty meat options: try the lollipop tuna ($14.95) or veal chop ($17.95). Open daily 10:35am-12:45am. ❸

CityCrepe, 274 Columbus Ave., between 72nd and 73rd St. (☎212-787-6088). Follow your nose to this bustling, sweet-smelling creperie. Pick from a huge variety including basil pesto grilled chicken with greens ($6.95), tropical fruit with ice cream ($5.50) or breakfast crepes with eggs ($3.50). Heed the advice of the young, peppy staff and wash it down with a cinnamon roasted apple and banana smoothie ($4). Open Su 9am-10pm, M-W 7:30am-10pm, Th 7:30am-11pm, F-Sa 7:30am-midnight. ❷

Gabriela's, 311 Amsterdam Ave., at 75th St. (☎212-875-8532). Subway: 1, 2, 3, 9 to 72nd St./Broadway. This reasonably priced Mexican joint provides stellar guacamole and a vibrant ambience. Try the house specialty of *pollo Yucateco* (roast chicken; half $8.95, full $16.50). M-Th 11:30am-11pm, Su 11:30am-10pm, F-Sa 11am-midnight. ❸

Good Enough to Eat, 483 Amsterdam Ave., between 83rd and 84th St. (☎212-496-0163). Subway: 1, 2 to 86th St./Broadway. Map 18, C4, 18. Breads and desserts made in quaint setting. Try M Fried Chicken Night or T Belgian Night for satisfying comfort food. Vermont cheddar and apple omelette with buttermilk biscuits $7.50; strawberry almond waffles $9; healthy salads $12-15. Vegetarian options abound. Open M-Th 8am-4pm and 5:30-10:30pm, F 8am-4pm and 5:30-11pm, Sa 9am-4pm and 5:30-11pm, Su 9am-4pm and 5:30-10:30pm. ❷

Gray's Papaya, 2090 Broadway, at 72nd St. (☎212-799-0243). Subway: 1, 2, 3, 9 to 72nd St./Broadway. Map 18, C5, 47. Cheap, lively takeout with amazing deals on hot dogs. Never-ending "recession special" sells 2 franks and 1 fruit drink (banana daiquiri, pineapple, piña colada, papaya) for a mere $2.45. Open 24hr. ❶

Henry's, 2745 Broadway, at 105th St. (☎212-866-0600). Subway: 1 to 103rd St./Lexington Ave. Map 18, B1, 7. Pleasant neighborhood restaurant with fresh and carefully-prepared dishes. Try the duck confit spring roll ($8), the crab cakes with fruit salad ($18) and the Grand Marnier cheesecake with grapefruit and orange ($6). Open M noon-11pm, Tu-Th noon-midnight, F noon-1am, Sa 11am-1am, Su 11am-11pm. Bar opens with restaurant and closes 4am. ❸

It's a Wrap, 2012 Broadway between 68th and 69th St. (☎212-362-7922). Subway: 1, 2, 3, 9 to 72nd St./Broadway. This bright, welcoming take-out shop offers sumptuous gourmet wraps and fresh smoothies for affordable prices. Call from your cell phone and the "guy in the purple shirt" will deliver to Central Park for a spontaneous picnic. Try the Kansas City Cheesesteak or the Under the Tuscan Sun (both $6.95). Open daily 8am-11pm. ❷

Ivy's Cafe, 154 W. 72nd St., between Broadway and Columbus Ave. (☎212-787-3333 or 787-0165). Subway: 1, 2, 3, 9 to 72nd St./Broadway; B, C to 72nd St./Central Park W. Map 18, C5, 53. This Chinese-Japanese restaurant has served People's Republic leaders Jiang Zemin and Li Peng. Ignore the unimpressive decor and savor the steamed buns and prawns in minced garlic. Chinese menu dishes stand out alongside the large Japanese menu (teriyaki dishes $9.50-15.50; tempura $9-13.75), and $5 lunch specials. Sushi $1.50-2.50 per piece. Open M-Th 11:30am-11:30pm, F-Sa 11:30am-midnight, Su noon-11:30pm. ❷

Josie's, 300 Amsterdam Ave., at 74th St. (☎212-769-1212). Ideal for the health nut obsessed with organic produce, free range chicken, and whole grains. Entire menu is dairy-free, and huge selection for vegetarians. Lacks options for the butter-lovers, so only for the serious nutrition nut. House specialty is the tuna wasabi Burger ($16). Open M-W noon-11pm, Th-F noon-midnight, Sa 11:30am-midnight, Su 11am-11pm. ❸

La Caridad 78 Restaurant, 2197-2199 Broadway, at 78th St. (☎212-874-2780). Subway: 1, 2 to 79th St. Map 18, C4, 29. Legendary lunch spot serving both Cuban and Chinese food. Try the flavorful *chicarrones* (black beans and yellow rice) for delicious cooking that makes up for rather mediocre decor. Prices around (and often well below) $10. Lunch special M-F 11:30am-4pm $5. Open M-Sa 11:30am-midnight, Su 11:30am-10:30pm. Cash only. ❶

Mama Mexico, 2672 Broadway, at 102nd St. (☎212-666-0900). Subway: 1 to 103rd St./Broadway. Map 18, C2, 10. Lively Mexican diner with colored lanterns, murals on the wall, a *loud* mariachi band, and a vivacious crowd. Amazing margaritas in 14 tropical flavors ($6). Entrees $12-23. Reservations strongly recommended. Open Su-Th noon-midnight, F-Sa noon-2am. ❸

Mughlai, 320 Columbus Ave., at 75th St. (☎212-724-6363). Subway: 1, 2, 3, 9 to 72nd St./Broadway. Try the spicy Vindaloo ($13.95) and classic tikka masala dishes ($13.95). Attentive, quick service with good prices and pleasant ambience—one of the best Indian restaurants north of "Curry Hill." Lunch only on weekends. Open M-Th 5pm-11:30pm, Sa-Su 12pm-midnight. ❸

River, 345 Amsterdam Ave., between 76th and 77th St. (☎212-579-1888). Subway: 1, 2, 3, 9 to 72nd St./Broadway. Modern decor, mouthwatering pad thai ($11) and basil chicken ($12) make a dunk in this Pan-Asian River worthwhile. Dim sum available during lunchtime. Open Su-Th noon-10:45pm, F-Sa noon-11:45pm. ❷

@SQC, 270 Columbus Ave., between 72nd and 73rd St. (☎212-579-0100). Plush pillows, white candles, and large windows set the scene for a romantic encounter. Pricey Americana food with French and Asian influences; worth it for the intimate ambience. Most famous for their nationally acclaimed hot chocolate ($4). Average entree cost ($20-26). Open for breakfast. Open Su-Th 8:30am-11pm, F-Sa 8:30am-midnight. ❹

CAFES

Cafe Lalo, 201 W. 83rd St., between Broadway and Amsterdam Ave. (☎212-496-6031). Subway: 1, 2 to 79th St., 86th St./Broadway. Map 18, C4, 20. Snag prime seating by the huge French windows (open in the summertime), sip iced cappuccinos, and choose from the immense selection of cakes, pies, and tarts ($5.50 per slice). Featured in *You've Got Mail*. Full bar available. Open M-Th 8am-2am, F 8am-4am, Sa 9am-4am, Su 9am-2am.

drip, 489 Amsterdam Ave., between 83rd and 84th St. (☎212-875-1032; www.drip.com). Subway: 1, 2 to 79th St., 86th St./Broadway. Map 18, C4, 19. Hip daytime coffee shop transforms into super-hip nighttime hoppin' bar/singles scene. Pastel interior, comfy couches, students on laptops (wireless Internet $2 per hr.) and young ladies reading complimentary magazines. drip's **dating service** ($20 to sign up, $3 to request a date) has 30,000 participants in its database. Coffee $1.25-2, cocktails $5-7. Live music Tu 8-11pm. Open M-Th 8:30am-1am, F 8:30am-2am, Sa 8:30am-3am, Su 9am-midnight.

Cafe La Fortuna, 69 71st St., at Columbus Ave. (☎212-724-5846). Subway: 1, 2, 3, 9 to 72nd St./Broadway; B, C to 72nd St./Central Park W. Map 18, D5. The Upper West Side's oldest cafe. Can only be described with the word 'Italian.' Dimly lit with Italian opera music complementing the Italian bakery inside and Italian ice stand in front. Quaint garden in the back. Espresso $2.50; pies $4.50; sandwiches $6; and salads $4.75-7.75. In the summer, they sell ices out front ($1.50-4) in 8 delightful flavors. Open Su-Th noon-midnight, F noon-1am, Sa noon-1:30am. Cash only.

Cafe Mozart, 154 70th St., between Amsterdam and Columbus Ave. (☎212-595-9797). Subway: 1, 2, 3, 9 to 72nd St./Broadway; B, C to 72nd St./Central Park W. Map 18, C5, 54. Cozy, low-key cafe adorned with Christmas lights and featuring **free Internet** access! Outdoor dining in the summer. Gourmet coffee $1-2; *cannoli* $3.50; tiramisu $5.50. Live music (usually classical or jazz piano) M-Sa 9pm-midnight, Su 1-4pm and 9pm-midnight. Open M-F 8am-1am, Sa-Su 10am-1am.

SHOPS

Zabar's, 2245 Broadway, between 80th and 81st St. (☎212-787-2000). Subway: 1, 2 to 79th St. Map 18, C4, 23. This Upper West Side institution sells everything you need for a 4-star meal at home. Cheese of every imaginable sort, smoked salmon, and beautiful bread lure droves of shoppers into this gourmet grocery store. On weekend mornings, masses of hungry New Yorkers stand in line for bagels and coffee. Kitchen gadgets and dishware sold upstairs. Open M-F 8am-7:30pm, Sa 8am-8pm, Su 9am-6pm.

MORNINGSIDE HEIGHTS

Morningside Heights caters mostly to Columbia students, faculty, and their families. Consequently, hours run late and the prices reasonable. Walk along Broadway and find everything from old-fashioned coffee shops and New Age diners to romantic Italian restaurants and fast Chinese food.

Amir's Falafel, 2911A Broadway, between 113th and 114th St. (☎212-749-7500). Subway: 1 to 110th St., 116th St./Broadway. Map 19, A6, 27. Small and simple, with low-priced Middle Eastern staples like schwarma, *baba ghanoush,* and *musakaa* (cold eggplant salad). Substantial selections for veggie lovers. Sandwiches ($3-5) and vegetarian platters ($5.50) made with care. Open daily 11am-11pm. Cash only. ❶

Koronet Pizza, 2848 Broadway, at 110th St. (☎212-222-1566). Subway: 1 to 110th St./Broadway. Map 19, C5, 19. Famously mammoth slices nearly feed 2 for $2.50. Open Su-W 10am-2am, Th-Sa 10am-4am. Cash only. ❶

Massawa, 1239 Amsterdam Ave., at 121st St. (☎212-663-0505). Subway: 1, 9 to 116th St., 125th St./Broadway. Map 19, B6, 28. Ethiopian and Eritrean hand held cuisine. Meat and veggie dishes ($6-13) served with spongy *injera* bread or rice. Great luncheon buffet ($7), not to mention lunch specials with your choice of entree, vegetable du jour, salad and injera ($6-7). Open daily 11:30am-midnight. ❷

Toast, 3157 Broadway, between Tiemann Pl. and La Salle St., near 125th St. (☎212-662-1144). Subway: 1, 9 to 125th St./Broadway. Map 19, A5, 15. This loft turned restaurant caters to the artsy regulars who enjoy its fresh sandwiches ($4-9) and monkey-themed artwork. Check weekend brunch specials (10am-4pm). Beer on tap $4. Happy Hour daily 5-7pm. Live music W nights. Open M-F 11am-midnight, Sa-Su 9am-midnight. ❷

Tom's Restaurant, 2880 Broadway, at 112th St. (☎212-864-6137). Subway: 1, 9 to 110th St./ Broadway. Map 19, A7, 35. Mostly famous for its facade (prominently featured in *Seinfeld*), but still has decent food. Excellent choice for breakfast served all day long with huge pancakes ($4.35) and tasty 3-egg omelettes ($5) as options. Open Su-Th 6am-1:30am, F-Sa 24hr. Cash only. ❶

SHOPS

The Hungarian Pastry Shop, 1030 Amsterdam Ave., at 111th St. (☎212-866-4230). Subway: 1 to 110th St./Broadway. Map 19, B7, 38. Get your *phyla* at this friendly neighborhood hotspot. Eclairs, cake slices, and other goodies for around $2. Pleasant outdoor seating. Open M-F 7:30am-11:30pm, Sa 8:30am-11:30pm, Su 8:30am-10pm. Cash only.

Milano Market, 2892 Broadway, between 112th and 113th St. (☎212-665-9500). Map 19, A7, 34. Wide selection of Italian imports, including a decent array of Perugia chocolate bars ($2). Gourmet sandwiches at the deli counter, made with fresh daily cheeses ($4-7). Open daily 6am-1am.

HARLEM AND WASHINGTON HEIGHTS

Harlem's cuisine ranges from East and West African to Caribbean, Creole. But the star of the plate is some of the best soul food north of the Mason-Dixon Line. In Spanish Harlem, you'll find Puerto Rican and other Latin food. Washington Heights has the city's most authentic (and inexpensive) Latin fare.

Copeland's, 547 W. 145th St., between Broadway and Amsterdam Ave. (☎212-234-2357). Subway: 1 to 145th St./Broadway; A, B, C, D to 145th St./St. Nicholas Ave. Map 19, A4. Elegant dining room with pricey entrees ($10-25), leaves the lower-ambience "cafeteria" next door (549 W. 145th; ☎212-234-2356) as a better option with the same excellent soul food and more options (entrees $4-11). Open Tu-Th 4:30-11pm, F-Sa 4:30pm-midnight, Su noon-9pm; cafeteria open daily 8am-11pm. ❸

La Marmite, 2264 Frederick Douglass Blvd. (Eighth Ave.), between 121st and 122nd St. (☎212-666-0653). Subway: B, C to 116th St.; A, B, C, D to 125th St./St. Nicholas Ave. Map 19, B6, 29. Serves authentic French and African cuisine in a cramped, colorful setting with a homey feel. Be prepared for the bite in some of the spices. Popular lunch dishes (available until 4pm) include *thiebou djeun* ($8), a famous Senagalese dish of fried rice served with fish and vegetables. Famous *dibi* ($9) and *poisson grille* ($9) on dinner menu. Entrees $8-12. Open daily 24hr. ❷

Manna's Too!, 486 Lenox (Sixth) Ave., between 134th and 135th St. (☎212-234-4488). Subway: 2, 3 to 135th St./Lenox (Sixth) Ave. Map 19, A7, 37. Harlem's best buffet and salad bar. Soul food and fresh veggies. Homemade desserts are heavenly: try the sinful, enormous piece of double chocolate cake ($2). Open M-Sa 8am-10pm, Su 10am-8pm. Cash only. ❶

Bleu Evolution, 808 W. 187th St., off Ft. Washington Ave. (☎212-928-6006; www.metrobase.com/bleu). Subway: A to 181/Ft. Washington. Quirky and stylish. Victorian chairs stand at antique-looking tables, below lanterns and chandeliers lighting tapestries and old oil portraits. The Franco-Italian-inspired eats ($8-15) are well-made and big. The fried calamari is divine. Compelling patio out behind which connects to the Monkey Room. Open daily 11am-11pm. ❷

Hispanola, 839 W. 181st St., at Cabrini Blvd. (☎212-740-5222; www.hispanolarestaurant.com). Subway: A to 181/Ft. Washington Ave. Simon Bolivar sought after a vision of Pan-American unity and Hispanola serves pan-American cuisine. Hispanola is a classy establish-

the BIG $plurge

Serious Meat

If you're more into the old-school version of cool, Peter Luger ⑤, 178 Broadway, between Bedford and Driggs Ave., should satisfy even the most discriminating palate. This world-famous, family-run Williamsburg steakhouse has been serving USDA Prime steaks since 1887. Peter Luger's stands out with its fanatical culinary approach. The meat preparation and selection in this establishment is serious business: it's done only by family members who visit the wholesale markets on a daily basis. The institution emanates authenticity: its worn wooden floor, simple china and muted lighting will transport you to the legendary steak feasts of the 19th century. Scorning newfangled tendencies towards calorie-counting and vegetarianism, the Luger specializes in porterhouse steaks cooked for two ($63), three ($96) or four people ($128). Moreover, the restaurant doesn't take any plastic except for its own, much-coveted Peter Luger credit card. This very anti-trendiness draws in huge numbers of people: dinner reservations must be made 6-8 weeks ahead. **THE BEST RESTAURANT IN NYC!** (Subway: J, M, Z to Marcy Ave. Map 21, 44. ☎718-387-7400. Cash only.)

ment with a swank decor, an austere bar and *style*. The $14 lunch special is worth it. Cigars sold; takes you back to a warm evening on the isthmus. Weekends add to the food fusion from across the Pacific and offer a Sushi Bar upstairs. Happy Hour half-price drinks M-F 4pm-8pm. Open daily. ❷

Jesse's Place, 812 W. 181st St., at Pinehurst Ave. (☎212-795-4168). Subway: A to 181/Ft. Washington. The food is a continental mix: kebabs, rice, beans, pizzas, pastas, salads. Food is excellent. The interior is jazz: deep and encompassing. Bar is stately. Live jazz a few nights a week and for the Sa-Su brunch. Entrees $8-14. Open daily 11:30am-3am or 4am. Kitchen closes at midnight. ❷

La Caridad, W. 184th St. and Broadway (☎212-781-0431) Subway: A to 181/Ft. Washington Ave. Of the many Dominican restaurants in the area, La Caridad is a cut above. If you want a quick bite have a simple $3.50 sandwich. Lots of stews and cutlets (with rice) for $8-10. For a night to remember have a bottle from the wide-ranging wine list and a $30 lobster! Salsa and merengue jukebox with all the classics. Open Su-Th 6am-midnight, F-Sa 6am-2am. ❷

La Fonda Boricua, 169 E. 106th St., between Lexington and Third Ave. (☎212-410-7292). Subway: 6 to 103rd St./Lexington Ave. Map 19, D7, 42. Friendly Puerto Rican restaurant. with community art on brick walls. Lots of seafood, like the popular shrimp salad ($10). Dinner entrees $7-10. Daily lunch specials $5-8. Open M-Sa 10:30am-8pm. ❷

Sylvia's, 328 Lenox (Sixth) Ave., at 126th St. (☎212-996-0660). Subway: 3 to 125th St./Lenox (Sixth) Ave. Map 19, C5, 21. A Harlem and greater New York favorite alike, Sylvia's has grown from a beloved local restaurant to hotspot drawing European tour groups in buses. For over 40 years, Sylvia has accented her "World-Famous Talked-About BBQ Ribs Special" with sweet spicy sauce, alongside collard greens and macaroni and cheese ($11). Lunch special: salmon croquette, pork chop, fried chicken leg, collard greens, and candied yams ($7). Free live jazz and R&B Sa 11am-4pm. Gospel Brunch Su 11am-4pm. Open M-Sa 8am-10:30pm, Su 12:30pm-8pm. ❷

SHOPS

Fairway, 2328 12th Ave., at W. 132nd St., on the Hudson River (☎212-234-3883). Subway: 1 to 125th St./Broadway. Map 19, A5, 13. Super supermarket with fabulous food selection at wholesale prices. Fresh bakery, gourmet cheeses; tons of fruit and deli options. Daily grocery delivery service until 8pm. Open daily 8am-11pm.

BROOKLYN

WILLIAMSBURG AND GREENPOINT

One generally associates artists with starvation, but food and drink abound in Billyburg, especially along Bedford Ave. Venturing thence along side streets or over to the other side of the BQE, however, is well worth the wandering. North of Williamsburg, Greenpoint features authentic Polish fare plus some Thai and Japanese eats.

Oznot's Dish, 79 Berry St., at N. 9th St. (☎718-599-6596). Subway: L to Bedford Ave. Map 21, 14. Exterior resembles a glorious lovechild between the works of Gaudi, Dali, Picasso and some old-school Italian mosaic-makermen. The interior continues the vibe famously. Whoever Oznot was, he has inspired a culinary sanctuary that offers food (neo-Mediterranean fusion) as good as can be found in all of New York City. Daily specials command the menu (entrees $10-15). For cheap, try the lunch *mezze* platter of pita, hummus, and olives ($6.50). If you have another few bills, indulge in the excellent wine list or try an original bar recipe. Open daily 11am-4:30pm and 6pm-midnight. ❷

Planet Thailand, 115 Berry St., between N. 7th and 8th St. (☎718-599-5758). Subway: L to Bedford Ave. Map 21, 16. Huge, sassy, high-ceilinged space that's too trendy for a sign. Expansive menu with reasonably priced Thai entrees ($8) and new, slightly pricier Japanese menu (sushi dinner $11). If you go on a weekend night, be prepared for a wait: Planet Thailand takes no reservations and people flock from across the city for the delicious and well-spiced fare. DJ nightly 9pm. Open Su-W 11:30am-1am, Th-Sa 11:30am-2am. Cash only. ❷

Restaurant Karpaty, 119 Nassau Ave., just past Leonard. (☎347-296-0191) Subway: G to Nassau St. Picnic tables and ornate decoration consisting of potted plants, deer busts, flowers, paintings and wood-carving. Polish homecooking. Your Mom-for-a-meal scoops out huge portions of traditional meatloaf, stuffed cabbage, tripe soup, or some 'rogis. Stuff yourself for $3.50. Good luck finding a way to spend more than $6. Get your own utensils, free Kompot (pink apple cider), grab some bread, sit with some strangers and enjoy the veritable Polish kitchen. Open daily 10:30am-9pm or until food runs out, whichever is last. ❶

Bliss, 191 Bedford Ave., between 6th and 7th St. (☎718-599-2547). Subway: L to Bedford Ave. Map 21, 27. Almost-vegan hotspot (eggs and cheese in

That Place from Seinfeld

Flushing

Pizza in the Bronx

PATTY TALK

Many exciting features come to mind when you think about Brooklyn, like the Brooklyn Museum of Art and the lovely Botanical Gardens. One characteristic that stands out are the neighborhoods, all equipped with their own unique culture and traditions.

The largest community of West Indians outside of the Caribbean Sea can be found in New York and many of them settled in Brooklyn. A large portion of the residents are from the island of Jamaica, famous for the beef patty. Since the invention of seasoned ground beef in a flaky, yellow crust/pocket, the beef patty has spurred the creation of such other delectable delights as the chicken veggie, and saltfish and ackee patty.

'Great,' you say, 'So how do I get my hands on one of these treasures? But, not just any patty—I want the best one.' Well, look no further than this feature story. Here is some sound advice that will ensure you get the best tasting, most authentic patty in Brooklyn:

If the store seems like it's too small—don't worry, it's perfect.

If the store's name has nothing to do with beef or patties, don't worry, it's perfect.

some non-vegan dishes). Meat-free chili *con pan*. Specialty Bliss Bowl comes with vegetables, rice, potatoes, tofu, and more ($8). BYOB. Open M-F 9am-11pm, Sa-Su 10am-11pm. Cash only. ❶

Diner, 85 Broadway (☎718-486-3077). Subway: J, M, or Z to Marcy Ave. Once it was a dining car; now it's a restaurant called Diner. Dimly lit with Billy Holiday playing in the background. More specials than regular menu items keeps the gourmet palette fresh. Excellent produce. Burgers $8, specials up to $17. Lots of champagnes and mixed drinks. Fries are super. Open daily 11am-2am. ❸

DuMont Restaurant, 432 Union Ave. (☎718-486-7717). Subway: L to Lorimer St. Walk in and you will be knocked over with a wave of swank. The food is outstanding. A mere handful of plates remain on the menu day to day (of which the burger and the mac and cheese (both $8) are signature pieces). Specials dictated by the fresh fishes and meats of the day ($13-18). And the chef's knowing whims. Feels like a French speakeasy (if France had ever endured prohibition). Excellent service, a solid wine list, and splendid garden dining. Open daily for lunch/brunch 11am-3pm, for dinner 6pm-11pm. ❸

L Cafe, 189 Bedford Ave., between N. 6th and 7th St. (☎718-388-6792). Subway: L to Bedford Ave. Map 21, 26. Colorful joint embodying Williamsburg cool. Check out the flyers up front. Back garden (one of the nicest in the hood) is tented and heated in the winter. Rolling Rock beer $3.25 (several other brands $4); veggie burger $6. Sandwiches, named after artsy revolutionary types like Joni Mitchell and Leonard Cohen ($4.50-8). Open M-F 9am-midnight, Sa-Su 10am-midnight. Cash only. ❷

Miyako, 143 Berry St., at N. 6th St. (☎718-486-0837). Subway: L to Bedford Ave. Map 21, 20. Affordable sushi in a classy restaurant. Lunch entrees run $5-8 while vegetarian handrolls are only $3-5. Many locals swear by Miyako's *maki*. The traditional decor is almost striking in this neck of the woods. Hooray for paper lanterns! Williamsburg Roll $7. Open M-F 11:30am-11:30pm, Sa 4:30-11:30pm. ❷

Sal's Pizzeria, 544 Lorimer St., at Devoe St. (☎718-388-6838). Subway: L to Lorimer St. Williamsburgers will tell you that the best pizza around is to be had at Sal's. Though toppings can get expensive (mushroom $2.50), the trek is to be made for the tastes are so very rewarding; Williamsburgers know the deal. Italian entrees $9-13. Open daily 11am-11pm. ❷

Sea, 114 N. 6th St., between Berry and Wythe (☎718-384-8825; www.spicenyc.net). Subway: L to Bedford Ave. Map 21, 9. True to its name, Sea is mesmerizing to all the senses. Packed with customers from its opening night, Sea has won recognition for its design, which includes a reflecting pool, a floating flower boat, and bathroom "pods." Thai cuisine at a decent price (Pad thai $8). Live DJ spins Th-Su. 2 bars. Open M-F 11:30am-1am, Sa-Su 11:30am-2am. ❷

Vera Cruz, 195 Bedford Ave., between 6th and 7th St. (☎ 718-599-7914; www.come.to/VeraCruz). Subway: L to Bedford Ave. Map 21, 28. Mexican food with a charming indoor dining room and lively outdoor garden (open year-round with outdoor heaters). A special seafood chef cooks up the freshest catch of the day. The margaritas ($3-4) are unreal; they go through 25 gal. on an average F night. Happy Hour M-F 4-7pm. Open M-Th 4-11:30pm, F-Sa 4pm-midnight, Su 11am-11pm. ❷

CAFES

Gray Parrot Cafe, 212 Bedford Ave., between N. 5th and N. 6th. (☎ 718-486-9372). Subway: L to Bedford Ave. Map 21, 25. A perfect place to stop for 5min. or 3hr. The simple, art-bedecked space also features a splendid backyard with a stone wall fountain, a good dose of green, and some covered seating. The inventive sandwiches ($6-8) might include avocado, green apples, or even a portabello cutlet. Su brunch for $10. Open M-F 9am-10:30pm, Sa-Su 10am-10:30pm.

Greenpoint Coffee House, 195 Franklin St., at Green St. (☎ 718-349-6635). Subway: G to Greenpoint Ave. This old-fashioned, jazzy coffee bar that features Olde Brooklyn Sodas and Birch Beer ($2) really should be seen. Comfy booths, easy chairs and a long tables are about. Copies of the *New York Times* strewn over the place. Owners' new born baby has a nursery just off the main room! Tasty croissants and muffins ($1.75-2.50). Open daily 7am-10pm.

The Read Cafe and Bookshop, 158 Bedford Ave., between 8th and 9th St. (☎ 718-599-3032; www.thereadcafe.com). Subway: L to Bedford Ave. Map 21, 17. Quiet, cozy cafe (does its own baking) with bookshelves and magazines (you can buy and sell literary tomes from Goethe to 3D "Magic Eye" Stereographs). Lovely garden seating out back. Amazing homemade scones $1.75. All pastries half-price after 7:30pm. Live experimental music on F. Weekend brunch 11am-4pm for $7.50 with live classical guitar. Open M-F 8am-11pm, Sa-Su 9am-11pm.

Tia:cafe, 128 Bedford Ave., at N. 10th St. (☎ 718-3880-8058). Subway: L to Bedford Ave. A certain Japanese plastic minimalism of bright synthetic colors and a penchant for rectangles houses a more traditional Japanese tea house. Wide range of hot and cold teas ($3-5), desserts and tea snacks (dumplings, spring rolls $3-6) are displayed on the plexiglass enclosed menus. A good product all told. Backyard too.

(cont'd from prev. pg.)

If the store only sells one kind of patty—chances are that it's the best one that they make. Never expect to find Brooklyn's best beef patty at a shop that 'specializes' in beef, veggie, chicken, jerk shrimp, jerk chicken, curry shrimp, shepherd's pie, and kiwi strawberry patties. If you buy a patty from a shop that only sells one kind of patty or that sells at most three or four, you've most likely stumbled upon a taster's choice in patties.

If the patty crust doesn't melt in your mouth and/or flakes of it don't float down to your pant front or shirt pocket, then you're not eating the best. If you can't get a hot and spicy patty, and the only option is mild, then you're in the wrong place. When other patrons make it a point to get a patty with every other purchase they make in the shop—you're as good as golden (crust, that is, teehee).

If you just paid for your patty with a credit card, then it was most definitely subpar. Choice shops hardly ever take credit cards. Cash only leaves more time for baking!

These simple tips will leave you on your way to tasting the strength of a community that has journeyed thousands of miles to flourish in a new country.

BROOKLYN HEIGHTS, DOWNTOWN, AND FORT GREENE

Old-school Brooklyn (pizzerias and diners) mixes with Middle Eastern newcomers on **Atlantic Avenue. Fulton Street** around the **Fort Greene** area has a variety of cafes and ethnic food joints.

Grimaldi's, 19 Old Fulton St., between Front and Water St. (☎718-858-4300). Subway: A, C to High St. Map 22, 7. Delicious thin-crust brick-oven pizza with wonderfully fresh mozzarella, sold only by the pie. Sinatra haunts both decor and jukebox (it was one of his favorite joints). Small pies $12, large $14; toppings $2 each. Open M-Th 11:30am-11pm, F-Sa noon-midnight, Su noon-11pm. Cash only. ❷

Brooklyn Moon, 745 Fulton St., at S. Elliott Pl., in Fort Greene (☎718-855-7149). Subway: G to Fulton St.; C to Lafayette Ave. Map 22, 26. Comfy couches, amiably mismatched furniture. Self-titled "Life saving, heart wrenching $5 menu" (salmon burger with spicy fries highly recommended). Open mic night F at 10:30pm, occasional performances and readings by authors like Jamaica Kincaid and Amiri Baraka. Open M-Th noon-11:30pm, F-Sa 11:30am-2am, Su 11:30am-11:30pm. ❶

Caravan, 193 Atlantic Ave., between Court and Clinton St. (☎718-488-7111). Subway: 2, 3, 4, 5, M, N, R to Court St./Borough Hall. Map 22, 18. Middle Eastern/Mediterranean/French cuisine. Prix-fixe lunch ($10) includes entree, hummus and *baba ghanoush,* soup or salad, dessert, and Moroccan coffee. Belly-dancing and live band Sa at 8pm. May need reservation on Sa nights. Open M-F 11am-10pm, Sa-Su noon-midnight. ❷

Fountain Cafe, 183 Atlantic Ave., between Clinton and Court St. (☎718-624-6764). Subway: 2, 3, 4, 5, M, N, R to Court St./Borough Hall. Map 21, 19. Inexpensive, filling Middle Eastern food. Schwarma or shish kebab sandwich $4.65, falafel sandwich $3.25. Open daily 11am-10:30pm. ❶

JRG Fashion Cafe, 177 Flatbush Ave., at Pacific St. (☎718-399-7079). Subway: 2, 3, 4, 5, M, N, R, Q to Atlantic Ave. A hidden gem on a relatively barren strip of Flatbush Ave., JRG was opened by a promoter of fashion shows. As you gaze at some of the dresses from past extravaganzas (or sit on the charming deck with a unique view), enjoy delicious West Indian cuisine for dinner and stay for the fully-stocked bar. ❷

Junior's, 386 Flatbush Ave. Extension, at DeKalb Ave. (☎718-852-5257). Subway: D, M, N, Q, R to DeKalb Ave. Map 21, 22. A 1970 *New York* magazine article touted this Brooklyn institution as the home of "the world's finest cheesecake," and thousands of slices ($4.50) are still served each week. Choose from fine selections like plain, blueberry, pineapple, chocolate mousse, or the favorite strawberry cheesecakes. Get it by the slice or ask for the whole pie. 10 oz. steakburgers $8.50. Open Su-Th 6am-12:30am, F-Sa 6am-2am. ❷

Keur N'Deye, 737 Fulton St., at S. Elliott Pl., in Fort Greene (☎718-875-4937). Subway: G to Fulton St.; C to Lafayette Ave. Map 21, 25. Senegalese restaurant. *Tiebou dieun* (bluefish with vegetables stewed in a tomato sauce) is a popular regional specialty ($9). Meat entrees $8-9; vegetarian entrees $7.50. Open Tu-Su noon-10pm. ❷

Madiba Restaurant & Shebeen, 195 DeKalb Ave., between Carlton and Adelphi St. (☎718-855-9190). Subway: C to Lafayette Ave. Map 22, 23. New York's only South African restaurant offering 'non-stop fun' for its patrons. Laid-back crowd and staff makes for comfy eating experience. Prawns Peri-peri ($18), vegetable ($12) or chicken ($14) biryani. Fully stocked bar for the late night crowd. Kahlua coffee ($8). All-Star Shebeen band F at 9pm, M Caribbean Night. Brunch F-Sa 9am-10:30am; lunch daily noon-4pm; dinner M-Th 5:30pm-midnight, F-Sa 5:30pm-1am, Su 5:30pm-11pm. ❸

SHOPS

Sahadi Importing Company, 187-189 Atlantic Ave., between Court and Clinton St. (☎718-624-4550). Subway: 2, 3, 4, 5, M, N, R to Court St./Borough Hall. Map 22. Popular Middle Eastern emporium stocks spices and seasonings, dried fruits, and spreads and dips like hummus and baba ghanoush. Open M-F 9am-7pm, Sa 8:30am-7pm.

Brooklyn Ice Cream Factory, Fulton Ferry Pier, Old Fulton St. at Water St. (☎718-246-3963). Traditional parlor has quickly become considered New York's best ice cream. Small cone $2.50. Open daily noon-11pm.

Jacques Torres Chocolate, 66 Water St., between Dock and Main St. (☎718-875-9772). Subway: A, C to High St.; F to York St. Map 22, 3. The kids will love this one and not only because of the decadent chocolate covered almonds, chocolate croissants ($1.50), or assorted chocolate bars. At this chocolatier, patrons get to view the chefs making the delights through a viewing window (think Willy Wonka). Also enjoy hot chocolate or mocha cappuccino ($2). Open M-Sa 9am-7pm.

Damascus Bakery, 195 Atlantic Ave., between Court and Clinton St. (☎718-625-7070). Subway: 2, 3, 4, 5, M, N, R to Court St./Borough Hall. Map 22, 17. Henry and Dennis Halaby run a friendly bakery with many goods, Middle Eastern and otherwise. Package of fresh pita bread 50¢, spinach and feta pies $1.35, pistachio Turkish delight $8 per lb. Every kind of baklava from walnut to pistachio and more $1-1.50. Open daily 7am-7pm.

CARROLL GARDENS AND RED HOOK

Smith Street has been called New York's new 'Restaurant Row.' Such renown, however, doesn't come cheap. You won't be let down by almost any restaurant on the block, but the following spots are some of our more affordable favorites.

Alma, 187 Columbia St., at DeGraw St. (☎718-643-5400). Subway: F, G to Carroll St. Haute Mexican cuisine served with a lengthy tequila list and a spectacular rooftop view of Manhattan. Open Su-Th 11:30am-2:30 pm and 5:30-10:30pm, F-Sa 11:30am-2:30pm and 5:30-11:30pm. ❸

Faan, 209 Smith St., at Baltic St. (☎718-694-2277). Subway: F, G to Bergen St. Portraits of Mao watch over pan-Asian cuisine at some of the best prices on Smith St. Good Thai standards (entrees $7-8) with surprisingly superb sushi (full dinners $12-18). Bar Below (as you might have guessed, it's downstairs) is a good option for post-dinner drinks and lounging. Open M-F 11am-1am, Sa-Su 1pm-2am. ❷

Patois, 225 Smith St., between DeGraw and Douglass St. (☎718-855-1535). Subway: F, G to Bergen St. Map 22. Quaint French bistro with rather pricey entrees ($12-17) and delicious traditional starters like garlic snails, puff pastry, and spinach and chives (around $8). Open Tu-Th 6-10:30pm, F-Sa 6-11:30pm, Su 11am-3pm and 5-10pm. ❷

Vinny's of Carroll Gardens, 295 Smith St., between Union and Sackett St. (☎718-875-5600). Subway: F, G to Carroll St. A holdover from an older Smith St., Vinny's serves Italian food just how we like it: nice and heavy. Unbeatable chicken parmigiana. Open M-Sa 10am-9:30pm. ❷

PARK SLOPE AND PROSPECT HEIGHTS

Upscale **Park Slope** brims with good eats, especially off **Fifth Avenue.**

Santa Fe Grill, 60 Seventh Ave., at Lincoln Pl. (☎718-636-0279). Subway: Q to Seventh Ave.; 2, 3 to Grand Army Plaza. Bottomless chips and salsa, strong margaritas with little plastic dolphins and mermaids floating in them, and a menu on which every single thing is so good that choosing what to order can seem impossible (although you can't miss with the bocados especiales, $12.95). One of Park Slope's most beloved neighborhood restaurants is also one of New York's best. Open M-Th 5-11pm, F 5pm-midnight, Sa 3pm-midnight, Su 3-11pm. ❷

Christie's Bakery, 334 Flatbush Ave., at Sterling Pl. (☎718-636-9746). Subway: Q to Seventh Ave.; 2, 3 to Grand Army Plaza. A Christie's beef patty in coco bread ($1.75) might be the most satisfying budget meal in New York City. See feature for more about Brooklyn's patty culture. M-Sa 9am-10pm, Su 9am-8pm. ❶

Dizzy's, 511 Ninth St., at Eighth Ave. (☎718-499-1966). Subway: F to Seventh Ave. Best brunch in the Slope and everyone in a 10-mile radius knows it. Brave the lines on weekend mornings for the opportunity to borrow one of the diner's many newspapers, sip your coffee, and feast on some of the best steak and eggs ($12.95) you'll ever have. Also serves excellent burgers ($6). Open M-F 7am-10pm, Sa-Su 9am-10pm. ❷

Beso, 210 Fifth Ave., at Union St. (☎ 718-783-4902). Subway: N, R to Union St. Dinner is good, but brunch is something special at this Latin restaurant. Try the daily specials ($10-$12) and be sure to wash it down with one of the excellent (and creatively-flavored) mimosas ($4 glass; $12 pitcher). Open Su and Th-Sa 10am-3:30pm and 5-10pm. ❷

Chip Shop and Curry Shop, 381 Fifth Avenue, at 6th St. (☎ 718-832-7701). Subway: F, M, N, R to Fourth Ave./9th St. Map 23, A2, 7. This restaurant cooks up the Queen of England's favorite dishes for its lucky Brooklyn residents. Dine on your favorite fish and chips with choices of cod ($9), haddock ($10), and salmon ($9). Also try the adjoining Curry Shop's korma chicken with naan ($11) or a fantastic mango lassi ($3). Open daily until 10pm. Cash only. ❷

CocoRoco, 392 Fifth Ave., between 6th and 7th St. (☎ 718-965-3376). Subway: F, M, N, R to Fourth Ave.-9th St. Map 23, A2, 6. Expertly prepared Peruvian fare. House specialty *ceviche*. Mixed seafood *ceviche* $11, papaya *ceviche* $13. Rotisserie chicken specials. Open Su-Th noon-10:30pm, F and Sa noon–11:30pm. ❸

Pino's La Forchetta, 181 Seventh Ave., between 1st and 2nd St. (☎ 718-965-4020). Subway: F to Seventh Ave. Cheap, greasy, and delicious. As typically New York as a local pizzeria can get, with friendly staff dishing out slices ($1.75) and the best chicken rolls ($3) in Brooklyn. Don't leave without getting an Italian ice ($1). Open M-Th 10am-1am, F-Sa 10am-2am. ❶

Red Hot Szechuan, 347 Seventh Ave., at 10th St. (☎ 718-369-0700). Subway: F to Seventh Ave. Chinese takeout *par excellence*. If you're just visiting and have nowhere to have your food delivered, eat in and enjoy Chinese fare (entrees $6-$12) that's as good as anything in Chinatown.Open M-Th 11:30am-10:30pm, F-Sa 11:30am-11pm, Su 1-10:30pm. ❷

Tom's Restaurant, 782 Washington Ave., at Sterling Pl. (☎ 718-636-9738). Subway: 2, 3 to Eastern Pkwy. The perfect place to have breakfast or lunch before a visit to the Brooklyn Museum of Art or the Brooklyn Botanic Gardens. Open since 1936 and family-owned, Tom's might very well be the friendliest diner in all of New York. Staff brings you oranges and cookies while you eagerly await for eggs and pancakes ($3-$7) and the most authentic Brooklyn egg cream money can buy. Open M-Sa 7am-4pm. ❶

12th Street Grill, 1123 Eighth Ave., between 11th and 12th St. (☎ 718-965-9526). Subway: F to Seventh Ave./9th St. Map 23, B3, 16. American restaurant dabbling here and there in international cuisine, specializing in steak and fish. Hanger steak $17, PEI mussels in a light curry broth $9, Roasted pork tenderloin with chorizo sausage $16. Seasonal menu changes about every 2½ months. Prix-fixe menu M-Tu provides appetizer, main course, and dessert ($20). Open M-Th 5:30pm-11pm; F 5:30pm-midnight; Sa 11am-3pm and 5pm-midnight; Su 11am-3pm and 5-11pm. ❸

CONEY ISLAND AND BRIGHTON BEACH

Ethnic enclave Brighton Beach is full of Russian and Ukrainian food, while Coney Island is known for its pizza and hot dogs. **Restaurants take credit cards unless otherwise noted.**

Roll n' Roaster, 2901 Emmons Ave., at Nostrand Ave. (☎ 718-769-6000). Subway: Q to Sheepshead Bay. Classic Brooklyn sandwich is the same color as the 70s-style booths (brown and gold) but far tastier. Regular patrons play 'Spin 'n' Win,' the in-house lottery. Worth the trip to Sheepshead Bay. Serves beer. Open Su-Th 11am-1am, F-Sa 11am-3am. ❶

Nathan's, 1310 Surf Ave. between Stillwell and 15th St., in Coney Island (☎ 718-946-2202). Subway: F, Q, W to Coney Island. Map 20, B6, 9. 74 years ago, Nathan Handwerker became famous for underselling his competitors on the boardwalk. Handwerker's hot dogs cost a nickel, theirs a dime. His crunchy dogs have since become famous worldover. A classic frank now sells for $2.25, cheeseburger meal with fries ($5), 3-piece chicken tender meal with fries ($5). Sauerkraut and fried onions available upon request. Open M-Th 6am-2am, F-Su 6am-4am. ❶

Totonno Pizzeria Napolitano, 1524 Neptune Ave., between 15th and 16th St. (☎718-372-8606). Subway: F, Q, W to Coney Island. Map 20, B6, 7. A Coney Island legend serving pizza by the pie. Vies for coveted title of finest pizza in NYC. Pies $13-14.50. No slices. Open W-Su noon-8:15pm. Cash only. ❶

Primorski Restaurant, 282 Brighton Beach Ave., between 2nd and 3rd St. (☎718-891-3111). Subway: Q to Brighton Beach. Map 20, C6, 13. Serves Ukrainian *borscht* ($3.50). Very affordable lunch special (M-F 11am-5pm, Sa-Su 11am-4pm; $4). Russian music and disco M-Th 8pm-midnight, F-Sa 9pm-2am, Su 8pm-1am. Open daily 11am-2am. ❶

Varenichnaya, 3086 Brighton 2nd. St., off Brighton Beach Ave. (☎718-332-9797). Subway: Q to Brighton Beach. Fluency in Russian is not completely necessary, but would probably help you figure out what you're ordering. We couldn't really read anything on the menu, but were happy with the dirt cheap *pelmeni* (Siberian meat dumplings $3) and *vareniki* (some other thing $2.50). Open daily 10am-9pm. ❶

QUEENS

Multicultural Queens offers visitors some of the best and most reasonably priced ethnic cuisine in town: keep an eye out for such borough delicacies as Greek fish, Indian *daal*, Italian ices, and Jamaican beef. Greek restaurants in **Astoria** proliferate around the elevated station at Broadway and 31st St., where you can catch the N and W trains north to Ditmars Blvd. for still more dining options. **Flushing's** excellent Chinese and Korean eateries often use rarely seen ingredients—like skatefish, squid, and tripe—which more Americanized Asian restaurants tend to avoid. Come to **Jackson Heights** for great Indian food or to buy spices in bulk. Thai, Chinese, and Vietnamese abound in **Elmhurst,** where Broadway and Elmhurst Ave. are the centers of the feast. West Indian, Central American, and Caribbean cuisine represent **Jamaica**—Linden Blvd. and Jamaica Ave. are the best bets for a tropical fix.

Elias Corner, 24-02 31st St., Astoria (☎718-932-1510). Subway: N, W to Astoria Blvd. Map 26, 10. Fantastic seafood restaurant with distinctly Greek character—no menus, outdoor dining, fresh everything. Try the *tsatziki,* calamari, or grilled octopus as appetizers ($3-6 depending on plate size). Whole grilled fish $9-20. Often crowded. No reservations. Open daily 4-11pm or midnight. Cash only. ❷

Flushing Noodle, 135-42 Roosevelt Ave., Flushing (☎718-353-1166). Subway: 7 to Flushing-Main St. Map 27, F1, 12. One of Flushing's finest Chinese noodle shops. Try the spare ribs ($6.50) and venture next door to the King's Queen Bakery for scrumptious Chinese pastries and bubble teas. Noodles $3.75-5. Lunch specials $5 between 11am-3:30pm. Open daily 9am-10pm. ❶

Jackson Diner, 37-47 74th St., in Jackson Heights, between 37th and 38th Ave. (☎718-672-1232). Subway: E, F, G, R, V to Jackson Heights/Roosevelt Ave.; 7 to 74th St.-Broadway. Map 26, 24. Delicious Indian food in colorful, almost-trendy setting. Great *saag gosht* (lamb with spinach, tomato, ginger, and cumin; $11) and samosas ($3.50). Lunch specials $6-7.50. Weekend lunch buffet $9 (11:30am-4pm). Open M-F 11:30am-10pm, Sa-Su 11:30am-10:30pm. Cash only. ❷

Jai-Ya, 81-11 Broadway, Elmhurst (☎718-651-1330). Subway: G, R, V to Elmhurst Ave. Map 26, 25. Great Thai food with 3 degrees of spiciness, from mild to fiery. Soothing interior, budget prices, decidedly upscale look. Most dishes $6-11. Vegetarian options available. Lunch specials ($6-9) until 3pm. Open M-F 11am-midnight, Sa-Su noon-midnight. ❷

Joe's Shanghai, 136-21 37th Ave., Flushing (☎718-539-3838). Subway: 7 to Flushing-Main St. Map 27, F1, 7. Original Queens outpost of favorite Shanghai eatery. Famous soup-filled *xiao long bao* dumplings. Open Su-Th 11am-11pm, F-Sa 11am-midnight. Cash only. ❷

Chao Zhau Restaurant, 40-52 Main St., Flushing. Subway: 7 to Main St. Hordes of salivating New Yorkers crowd this Chinese restaurant with delicious soups, dim sum, noodle dishes, and creamy milk teas. Quick, attentive service and amazing lunch specials. Noodle soups $4.50, dim sum $2.25-2.50. Open daily 11am-midnight. ❶

Dong Hae Ru, 36-26 Union St., Flushing (☎718-358-3869). Subway: 7 to Main St. Friendly Korean ladies folding hand-made dumplings can be seen from the street. Succumb to the temptation and buy a handful ($6-8). Also try the Korean-Chinese specialty of *jjajjangmyun*, noodles in black bean sauce ($4.95). Open daily 10:30am-10:30pm. ❷

Dragon Town, 41-12A Main St., Flushing (☎718-358-1883). Subway: 7 to Main St. Whole chickens hanging upside down in the windows beckon the diner to this authentic Chinese joint. Try the roast pig & oyster ($12.95). Lo mein dishes are perfectly spiced ($3.50). Lunch specials (11am-4pm, $4.50). Open daily 9:30am-11pm. ❷

El Cafetal, 30-19 Astoria Blvd., Astoria (☎718-956-9519). El Cafetal may offer little seating and atmosphere, but they deliver home-cooked *camarones* and *huevos rancheros* that truly satisfy. Wash it down with some fresh beet, carrot, or orange juice. ❷

John's Pizzeria & Restaurant, 23-39 Astoria Blvd., Astoria (☎718-721-6904). Youthful customers abound at this popular pizza place, advertising "Bud 'n' Pizza." Mingle with the locals, shoot the breeze with the amicable pizzamen, and throw back a cold beer and a slice of pepperoni. Open M-Th 11am-11pm, F-Sa 11am-midnight, Su 3pm-11pm. ❷

Kim Neh, 39-12 Union St., Flushing (☎718-888-3100). Subway: 7 to Main St. Bright yellow checkered decor welcomes you to this sunny haven of cheap Korean takeout. Try the *ddukbbokki* (korean rice cakes) or the *kimbob* (Korean sushi) for traditional snack foods. ❶

Kum Gang San, 138-28 Northern Blvd., Flushing (☎718-461-0909). Subway: 7 to Flushing-Main St.; walk north on Main St. and take a right on Northern Blvd. Map 27, G1, 11. Elegant, marble-floor setting. Individual grills at table for Korean BBQ. Lunch special includes chicken teriyaki with salad, noodles, California roll, and dumplings ($7-9). Open 24hr. ❷

Più Bello, 70-09 Austin St., Forest Hills (☎718-268-4400). Subway: E, F, G, R, V to Forest Hills/71st Ave. Map 25, C2, 5. Family-owned restaurant. Smooth *gelato* and delicious cakes made on the premises. Entrees $7-8. Individual pizzas from $4. 20+ *gelato* flavors ($2.75-3.75 cup, $7 pint). Open M-Th 9am-1am, F-Sa 9am-2am, Su 10am-1am. ❶

Rincon Salvadoreño, 92-15 149th St., at Jamaica Ave., Jamaica (☎718-526-3220). Subway: E, J, Z to Jamaica Center-Parsons/Archer Ave. Map 25, D3, 8. Heaping portions of El Salvadorean specialties like *pupusas* (tortillas with pork, cheese, or beans) $1.25-2. Meat entrees $8-12. Live music Sa-M and Th at 8pm. ❷

San Han jin mi, 36-24 Union St., Flushing (☎718-539-3274). Unbelievably cheap prices for mouth-watering Korean stews. Try their *sullungtang* (oxtail stew) or their *soondooboo* (spicy tofu stew) for only $3 each! ❶

Szechuan Gourmet, 135-15 37th Ave., Flushing (☎718-888-9388). Subway: 7 to Main St. Szechuan food for the gourmet: crispy fried duck is tender and juicy (½ duck $8.95), and jellyfish with hot-and-sour sauce is a succulent delicacy ($4.95). Check out lunch specials (11:30am-4pm, $4.95). Open Su-Th 11:30am-midnight, F-Sa 11:30am-1am. ❷

Telly's Taverna, 28-13 23rd Ave., Astoria (☎718-728-9194). Popular Greek fish and steak house uses only the freshest ingredients to prepare their delectable fare (you can see the daily catches at the restaurant's front). Warm, boisterous staff recommend the octopus ($8). Open M-Th 3:30pm-midnight, F-Sa 3:30pm-1am, Su 1-m-midnight. ❷

Thirty One, 22-48 31 St., Astoria (☎718-728-8288). Clean Italian restaurant offers delicious panini sandwiches on fresh foccacia or ciabatta ($5-7), pastas, pizzas, and salads. Opt for their black linguini with seafood ($12.50) for a classic dish fantastically prepared. ❷

Uncle George's, 33-19 Broadway, at 34th St., Astoria (☎718-626-0593). Subway: N, W to Broadway; G, R, V to Steinway St. Map 26, 12. Crowded, noisy, and friendly restaurant serves round-the-clock hearty Greek fare. Watch whole animals roast on a spit. All entrees under $12. Regulars eat roast leg of lamb with potatoes ($9.50) or octopus sauteed with vinegar ($8.50). Open daily 24hr. ❷

Zorba's Souvlaki Plus, 29-05 23rd Ave., Astoria (☎718-956-7266). Bright green tables and an open grill offer customers a pleasant Greek-American dining experience. The house charm lies in souvlaki (chicken, pork or lamb on a stick, $2-4), but hamburgers, omelettes, and sandwiches are also available. ❶

Zygos Taverna, 22-55 31st St., Astoria (☎718-728-7070). Try the thinly sliced leg of lamb ($10.75), the taramosalata (Red Caviar, $4.50) or the moussaka (Baked Eggplant with Potato and Beef, $9.75). Open daily 11am-midnight. ❷

SHOPS

Great Wall Market, 41-22 Main St., Flushing (☎718-358-8889). Sells plump, juicy fruits that must hail from the garden of Eden. Huge mangoes, cherries, papayas and other exotic fruits entice passersby, and the extensive selection of fresh seafood does not disappoint.

The Lemon Ice King of Corona, 52-02 108th St., at Corona Ave., Corona (☎718-699-5133). Subway: 7 to 111th St.; walk 1 block to 108th and south 10 blocks. Map 27, B4, 21. Well worth the trek (it's near Flushing Meadow-Corona Park anyway). One of Queens' most famous sites, on par with the Unisphere. Juicy frozen treats served outdoors. Vast flavor selection includes bubble gum, blueberry, cantaloupe, cherry, and, of course, lemon ($0.80-2). Open daily 10am-12:30am.

Galaxy Pastry Shop, 37-11 30th Ave., Astoria (☎718-545-3181). Subway: N, W to 30th Ave. Map 26, 13. Hangout for young locals, with great pastries. Baklava $1. Outdoor cafe seating during summer. Open daily 6:30am-3am.

Yong Da Fung Health Food Herbal Products Inc., 41-53A Main St., Flushing (☎718-539-6143). Herbal roots, teas, rubs of every sort provide the natural cure for any ailment. Seek the advice of the wise staff to guide you through the maze of pungent bins.

THE BRONX

Though each of the Bronx's many neighborhoods has main commercial strips, Arthur Ave. in Belmont offers a cluster of classy restaurants. Subway: C, D to Fordham Rd. and walk 5 blocks east; or 2 to Pelham Pkwy., then bus Bx12 2 stops west.

The Bronx's cuisine reflects its diverse make-up, but the local Italian fare is the culinary magnet of the borough. The Italian immigrants settling in the Bronx brought, with their recipes, a tradition of hearty communal dining. **Belmont** (see **Sights,** p. 120) brims with raw bars (try **Cosenza's Fish Market,** see p. 190), pastry shops, pizzerias, restaurants, and mom-and-pop emporiums—all without the touristy frills of Manhattan's Mulberry St. For a 50¢ treat, try a dixie cup of Italian ice from street vendors.

Dominick's, 2335 Arthur Ave., near E. 186th St., in Belmont (☎718-733-2807). Subway: B, D to Fordham Rd./Grand Concourse or 4 to Fordham Rd./Jerome Ave. Take the Bx12 bus to Hoffman St.; 2, 5 to Third Ave.-149th St., then take the Bx55 bus to 183rd St. and Third Ave. Arthur Ave. is 1 block east. Map 28, C4, 17. Small family-style Italian eatery with no menu and no set prices, although regulars are glad to advise. Waiters seat you at a long table and simply ask what you want. House specials include linguine with mussels and marinara $7, marinated artichoke $7, veal *francese* $12. Ever-changing specials, entrees generally $8-15. Arrive before 6pm or after 9pm, or expect a 20min. wait. Open M, Th, Sa noon-10pm; W and F noon-11pm; Su 1-9pm. Cash only. ❷

Reef Restaurant (a.k.a. Johnny's Reef), 2 City Island Ave. (☎718-885-2086). Subway: 6 to Pelham Bay Park, then Bx29 to City Island. Map 28, F4, 25. Cheap, fresh seafood (steamed or fried) beside squawking seagulls. Toss a fry up in the air and watch the most graceful mid-air savagery ever as one lucky gull gets the treat. Johnny's Fish and Chips $9. Beer only $2! Open daily 11am-midnight, sometimes 1hr. later on weekends. Cash only. ❷

Tino's Delicatessen, 609 E 178 St., between Hughes and Arthur Ave. (☎718-733-9879). Subway: B, D to Fordham Rd./Grand Concourse or 4 to Fordham Rd./Jerome Ave. Take the Bx12 bus to Hoffman St.; 2, 5 to Third Ave.-149th St., then take the Bx55 bus to 183rd St. and Third Ave. Walk 5 blocks north. This is an Italian Deli. Let each of those words be emphasized so that the reader understands that there is nothing more quintessentially deli-like than Tino's. Everything looks good: the sausages the size of your head, the cheese the size of a really big head. Get a huge sandwich for under $5 or a hot Italian specialty. No space to sit, so eat on a stoop and think about stickball. Food is spectacular. Open M-Sa 7:30am-6:30pm, Su 7:30am-3:30pm. ❶

Arthur Avenue Cafe, (☎718-295-5033) There is not a gigantic piazza next door to gaze at as you sip your cappuccino and smoke a cigarette, yet in all other aspects this cafe is all it should be: splendid desserts, sandwiches ($6-9) and a full bar. Live traditional Italian music on F-Sa. Sidewalk seating in nice weather. ❷

Emilia's, 2331 Arthur Ave., near E. 186th St., in Belmont (☎718-367-5915). Subway: B, D to Fordham Rd./Grand Concourse or 4 to Fordham Rd./Jerome Ave. Take the Bx12 bus to Hoffman St.; 2, 5 to Third Ave.-149th St., then take the Bx55 bus to 183rd St. and Third Ave. Arthur Ave. is 1 block east. Map 28, C4, 16. Delicious food, large portions. Great calamari and *scungilli* ($15). Appetizers $5-9; pasta $11-15; entrees $13-18. Lunch special $10. Open M-F and Su noon-10pm, Sa noon-11pm. ❸

Giovanni's, 2343 Arthur Ave., between E. 186th St. and Crescent Ave. (☎718-933-4141). Subway: B, D to Fordham Rd./Grand Concourse; 4 to Fordham Rd./Jerome Ave. Take the Bx12 bus to Hoffman St.; 2, 5 to Third Ave.-149th St., then take the Bx55 bus to 183rd St. and Third Ave. Arthur Ave. is 1 block east. Map 28, C3, 15. Arguably Belmont's best brick-oven pizza (individual size $6-9, regular size $11-14)—no small distinction. Open Su-Th 11am-midnight, F-Sa 11am-1am. ❷

Pasquale's Rigoletto, 2311 Arthur Ave., near E. 186th St., in Belmont (☎718-365-6644). Subway: B, D to Fordham Rd./Grand Concourse; 4 to Fordham Rd./Jerome Ave. Take the Bx12 bus to Hoffman St.; 2, 5 to Third Ave.-149th St., then take the Bx55 bus to 183rd St. and Third Ave. Arthur Ave. is 1 block east. Map 28, C4, 18. Luscious arias, classy decor. Ask to have your favorite played, or sing it yourself on Sa amateur night (reserve 1 wk. ahead). Star customer Joe Pesci's photos adorn front door. Pasta $14; meat dishes $17; poultry $17; seafood $17-26. Open Su-F noon-9:30, Sa noon-10:30. ❸

SHOPS

Cosenza's Fish Market, 2354 Arthur Ave., between Frank Simeone Sq. and Crescent Ave. (☎718-364-8510). Subway: B, D to Fordham Rd./Grand Concourse or 4 to Fordham Rd./Jerome Ave. Take the Bx12 bus to Hoffman St.; 2, 5 to Third Ave.-149th St., then take the Bx55 bus to 183rd St. and Third Ave. Arthur Ave. is 1 block east. Map 28, C4, 14. Sells fish from $1-23 per lb. as well as every other kind of imaginable seafood. The smell is like being smacked in the face with a gigantic (but exceedingly fresh) fish. And it's not a bad smell—it's fish. Open daily 7:30am-5:30pm. Cash only.

De Lillo Pastry Shop, 606 E. 187th St., between Hughes and Arthur Ave. (☎718-367-8198). Subway: B, D to Fordham Rd./Grand Concourse or 4 to Fordham Rd./Jerome Ave. Take the Bx12 bus to Hoffman St.; 2, 5 to Third Ave.-149th St., then take the Bx55 bus to 183rd St. and Third Ave. Walk 5 blocks north. Map 28, C3, 20. Crowded, with excellent baked goods ($1-2), cappuccino ($2.25), and espresso ($1.25). Open daily 8am-7pm; July-Aug. closed M. Cash only.

STATEN ISLAND

Cargo Cafe, 120 Bay St., near the Staten Island Chamber of Commerce, away from the Ferry Terminal (☎ 718-876-0539). Map 29, C1, 3. Large exterior mural and open windows with uneven iron fencing give this bar/restaurant a funky feel. Art on walls and bar games add to chill atmosphere. Lunch special (daily special and beer) $5.25, dinner entrees $15-22. Jazz Tu-Th nights. Open daily noon-4am. ❸

Sidestreet Saloon, 11 Schuyler St., just off busy Richmond Ter. (☎ 781-448-6868). Map 29, C1, 2. Unassuming restaurant/bar has such Italian staples as penne with vodka sauce ($10) and chicken parmigiana with linguini ($11). Open daily 11:30am-midnight, bar open until 1-4am, depending on the crowd. ❷

INSIDE

bars and lounges **193**

lower east side **194** east village **195**
soho and tribeca **198** greenwich village **199**
chelsea and union square **201**
upper east side **203** upper west side **204**
brooklyn **205** queens **207** the bronx **207**

dance clubs **208**

Nightlife

Whether you prefer Times Square's blinding lights or a Harlem jazz club, a smoky Brooklyn bar or a Lower East Side be-seen-ery, allow yourself to succumb to the city's dark side. A number of publications print daily, weekly, and monthly nightlife calendars; try Time Out: New York, the Village Voice, New York magazine, The New York Press, and The New York Times (particularly the Sunday edition). The monthly Free Time calendar ($1.25) lists free cultural events throughout Manhattan.

BARS AND LOUNGES

No one bar scene defines New York City in the way that pubs define Ireland or cruisy Hollywood bars define Los Angeles. NYC doesn't merely have every type of bar, but does every type well. Bars listed by neighborhood are ordered alphabetically, but personal preference will depend on your own social or alcoholic slant. Gay and lesbian nightlife options are listed on p. 197, p. 200, p. 202, and p. 204. Some establishments are geared exclusively toward **lesbians or gay men,** and may frown on letting in hopefuls of the opposite sex. If you and a friend of the opposite sex want to go to any of these clubs together, it might be wise to avoid behaving like a heterosexual couple, especially in front of the bouncer. **All bars listed below, unless otherwise noted, are open only to those aged 21 or over, so make sure you bring at least two pieces of valid ID. Cover required only where indicated.**

LOWER EAST SIDE

On the whole, LES has some of the best bars in Manhattan. These are a few that we like.

bOb Bar, 235 Eldridge St., between E. Houston and Stanton St. Subway: F, V to Lower East Side-Second Ave. Map 11, D1, 9. Small and laid-back, with a hip-hop-inclined crowd and graffiti-esque paintings covering the walls. Happy Hour F 7-10pm, $3 beers. While Tu alternates between Latin, reggae, and hip-hop (free), Th, F, Sa are strictly hip-hop Cover $5 after 10pm; women $3). Anti-thugwear dress code in effect (no sports apparel, sports shoes or hats). Open daily 7pm-4am.

Fun, 130 Madison St., at Pike St. (☎212-964-0303). Subway: F to E. Broadway. Map 11, F4, 42. In-the-know hipsters chill at this "never a cover, never a guest list" hangout. Its whimsical decor (complete with hydraulic lifts for the bartenders and wall video projections) merit the self-titled "integrated sound and video environment." Drinks start at $9. VJs and DJs rotate nightly. Tu Playstation nights. Open M-Sa 8pm-4am.

Idlewild, 145 E. Houston St., between Forsyth and Eldridge St. (☎212-477-5005). Subway: F, V to Lower East Side-Second Ave. Map 11, D1, 5. JFK Airport's former name has lifted eclectic theme bar to new heights. Venue shaped like an airplane, replete with a fuselage-shaped interior, reclining seats with tray tables, and boarding ramp. Beer $4-5. Martinis $9. Open Su and Tu-W 8pm-3am; Th-Sa 8pm-4am.

Kush, 183 Orchard St., between E. Houston St. and Stanton St. (☎212-677-7328). Subway: F, J, M, Z to Delancey St.-Essex St.; F, V to Lower East Side/Second Ave. In the words of The Brazilian reclining upon the plush sofa in the dim corner while puffing his hookah ($15, various flavors): "This is a genuine displacement of the heart of the Middle East to the core of the Big Apple." Tu live music and belly dancing. DJs a few nights a week. Weekend nights are more semite-nomad feel meets the brothers of Sig-Chi than straight up grove of the Silk Road. Open daily 7pm-2pm (sometimes until 4am) Opens at 6pm in winter.

Lotus Lounge, 35 Clinton St., at Stanton St. (☎212-253-1144). Subway: F, J, M, Z to Delancey St.-Essex St. The ceilings are high. The slats are of soft wood and the lanterns are lit at Lotus Lounge. Bookshelves stretch across the back for a chill afternoon of knowledge acquisition. The bar is centrally located for an evening of delightful confounding. Beer $4-5 ($2 specials frequently). Live DJs every night. A cafe from 8am-4pm. A bar from 4pm-4am.

Max Fish, 178 Ludlow St., at Houston St. (☎212-529-3959). Subway: F, V to Lower East Side-Second Ave. Map 11, E1, 13. Great low-key hangout in a land of "see and be seen" bars. Perhaps the best jukebox in town, playing everything from the Fugees to the Stooges. Keeps all great bar things: pinball, pool tables, and relatively inexpensive drinks. Beer $3-4.50. Open daily 5:30pm-4am.

Motor City Bar, 127 Ludlow St., between Rivington and Delancey St. (☎212-358-1595). Subway: F to Delancey St.-Essex St. Map 11, E2, 28. Locals and musicians kick back on the Dodge Dakota car seats and vinyl bar stools at this rock-and-roll bar. Pinball and video games for the less conversation-savvy. Beer $4. DJ spins rock and roll, punk, and new wave nightly. Happy Hour daily 4-7pm. Open daily 4pm-4am.

The Slipper Room, 167 Orchard St., at Stanton St. (☎212-253-7246; www.slipper-room.com). Subway: F, V to Lower East Side-Second Ave. Map 11, D1, 11. Inspired by the LES variety acts that thrived from 1870 to 1930, this converted sneaker store's mixed bag of vaudeville entertainment includes everything from go-go girls to sketch comedy to sword-swallowers. Beer $4-5. An artsy crowds swarms into this recent addition to the Orchard St. scene during the weekend, especially for the F and Sa burlesques. Check website for performance schedules (Sa "big show" at 11). Cover $5 on nights with performances. Open daily 8pm-4am.

EAST VILLAGE

East Village nightlife has something for everybody. Go there. Seriously, don't be a chach..

The Anyway Cafe, 34 E. 2nd St., just west of Second Ave. (☎212-533-3412). Subway: F, V to Lower East Side-Second Ave. Subway: F, V to Lower East Side-Second Ave.; 6 to Bleecker St. Map 12, C4, 93. Sample Russian-American culture at this dark, relaxed, leopard-spotted hangout. Numerous literary readings M-F, as well as jazz F-Sa nights. Music nightly from 9pm. Friendly and free of pretension. Great place to kick back with homemade sangria and gourmet Russian specialties ($8-12). Open M-Th 5pm-2am, F-Sa 5pm-4am, Su noon-1am.

Beauty Bar, 231 E. 14th St., between Second and Third Ave. (☎212-539-1389). Subway: L to Third Ave. Map 12, C1, 3. Unless you knew this was a bar, it would be easy enough to walk by "Thomas Hair Salon." Cosmetics on the top shelf, big salon chairs with hair blowers and Tu-Su get a manicure and a cocktail for a mere $10 (while the specialist is around). Fairly cheap cocktails (Amaretto sour $4). Beer $3-4.50. Live DJs W-Sa 6pm. Usually live music 10pm. Happy Hour M-F 5-9pm, all drinks $1 off. Open Su-Th 5pm-4am, F-Sa 7pm-4am.

Bbar (Bowery Bar), 40 E. 4th St., at the Bowery (☎212-475-2220). Subway: F, V to Lower East Side-Second Ave. Map 12, C4, 88. Bowery's longtime flagship of cooler-than-thou-ness. The clientele is good-looking, has money to spend and will break your heart like a teenage beauty queen. The downtown socialite's mainstay. Garden patio. Beer $5. Tu night is "Beige," Erich Conrad's wonderfully flamboyant gay party. Open M-F 11:30am-3am, Sa 11:30am-4am, Su 10:30am-midnight.

d.b.a., 41 First Ave., between E. 2nd and 3rd St. (☎212-475-5097). Subway: F, V to Lower East Side-Second Ave. Map 12, D4, 99. For the serious beer drinker. With 19 premium beers on tap (around $5), well over 100 bottled imports and microbrews, classy bourbons and whiskeys ($6), and 45 different tequilas, this extremely friendly space lives up to its motto—"drink good stuff." Mellow jazz and sassy crowd. Popular outdoor beer garden open until 10pm. Su morning brunch: free bagels and lox while it lasts! Open daily 1pm-4am.

Delft, 14 Ave. B, between E. 2nd and E. 3rd St. (☎212-260-7100). Subway: F, V to Lower East Side/2nd Ave. Hopping joint, excellent DJs nightly. Basement lounge area often devolves into dancing. Young, attractive crowd never quite as good looking as the bartenders. Beer $6, drinks $8-10. Open daily 7pm-4am.

Drinkin'

Milady's

Wanna Party?

Industry, 509 E. 6th St., between Ave. A and B (☎212-777-5920). Subway: 6 to Astor Pl. Map 12, E3, 83. Labyrinth of wood, glass, and trees. Casually elegant dining turns into hip, late-night scene after 11pm. Expensive food. Drink (beer $5, mixed drinks $5.50) and feel really good about yourself. Open Su-W 6pm-2am, Th-Sa 6pm-3am.

Izzy Bar, 166 First Ave., at E. 10th St. (☎212-228-0444). Subway: L to First Ave. Map 12, D2, 37. Wooden-decor-laden, votive-lit hangout. Bartender Lauren can talk anyone out of a bad mood. Also one of the East Village's best music spots, with DJs spinning house or hip-hop Tu and Th, plus live jazz Su. Corona $5. Cover M-F $5, F-Sa $10. Open daily 7pm-4am.

Joe's Pub, 425 Lafayette St., between Astor Pl. and E. 4th St. (☎212-539-8777). Subway: 6 to Astor Pl. Map 12, E3, 84. Not so much a typical pub. It's at a *Pub*lic Theater spot in NoHo: the *Jo*seph Papp *Pub*lic Theater. Hmm. Norwegian acid-folk, classical chamber music and dance-contests are more common than you could possibly imagine! Performances start around 7-9pm. Cover for performances $10-30. Occasional 2-drink min. Open daily 6pm-4am.

Karma, 51 First Ave., between E. 3rd St. and E. 4th St. (☎212-677-3160). Subway: F to Lower East Side/2nd Ave. It's hard not to recline on the velvety sofas. So recline, my friend. While you are at it, get a hookah for $10 and drink the tasty drinks (beer $5, drinks $7-9). Signs encourage the inhalation of tobacco products with much vehemence since smoking licenses are precious and rare in NYC. Basement is a Persian Prince's pillow-laden sanctuary. Live DJs spin on the weekends. Open Su-Th 3pm-2am, F-Sa 3pm-4am.

KGB, 85 E. 4th St., at Second Ave. (☎212-505-3360). Subway: F, V to Lower East Side-Second Ave. Map 12, C3, 73. Tiny 2nd fl. space. Formerly a meeting place for the Ukrainian Communist Party, today a hangout for literati and Slavophiles. Retains original furnishings, including the Lenin propaganda banner and candle-illuminated photos of factories. Frequent readings by major and minor authors. Call for details. Over 20 different kinds of Stoli ($3 per shot). Open daily 7pm-4am.

Korova Milk Bar, 200 Ave. A, between E. 12th and 13th St. (☎212-254-8838). Subway: L to First Ave. Map 12, E1, 11. Mock-up of little Alex's "moloko plus" bar in Stanley Kubrick's *A Clockwork Orange,* replete with sultry naked female mannequins, lusciously shaped couches, Kubrick's movie playing on various screens, and an anarchist atmosphere. Perhaps too self-consciously hip, but where else can you actually buy a *moloko* ($8)? Open daily 7pm-4am.

Lakeside Lounge, 162 Ave. B, between E. 10th St. and E. 11th St. (☎212-529-8463). Subway: L to First Ave.; 6 to Astor Pl. It's a dim yet lively bar. Always a good crowd. Mostly locals. Lots of stuff on the walls. Photo booth. Tables in the back. 2 for 1 happy hour 4pm-8pm. Open 4pm-4am daily.

La Linea, 15 First Ave., between E. 1st and 2nd St. (☎212-777-1571). Subway: F, V to Lower East Side-Second Ave. Map 12, D4, 101. Long, narrow bar with 3 rooms: friendly, lantern-laden bar room, comfortable lounge area in the middle, and grotto-like back room. (It's a lounge sandwich of sorts!) Very good ambient music (live DJ Tu-Sa after 10pm). Beer $6. Happy Hour (daily 3-9pm) $1 off. Open Su-M 5pm-2am, Tu-Sa 3pm-4am.

Lit, 93 Second Ave., at E. 6th St. (☎212-777-7987). Subway: 6 to Astor Pl.; F to Lower East Side/2nd Ave. Rocker joint. Rockers perform rock music 4 nights a week downstairs. Rockers can listen to DJ's upstairs every night. Most drinks are $4, which is good for rockers. Mostly populated by "artists of the industry" (rockers, generally). Also an art gallery by day. Gallery open Tu-Sa 2pm-7pm. Bar open daily 5pm-4am.

Lucky Cheng's, 24 First Ave., between E. 1st and 2nd St. (☎212-473-0516). Subway: F, V to Lower East Side-Second Ave. Map 12, D4, 100. One of NYC's better-known drag clubs. Upstairs restaurant and downstairs bar decorated in over-the-top Asian kitsch, serviced by gorgeous "girls." Karaoke begins at 9:30pm (Sa midnight). Up to 25 bachelorette parties, cut-throat banana eating contests and 3-4 drag shows nightly. Martinis $7.50; plum wine $5. Bar open Su-Th 5pm-2am, F-Sa 5pm-4am.

McSorley's Old Ale House, 15 E. 7th St., at Third Ave. (☎212-473-9148). Subway: 6 to Astor Pl. Map 12, C2, 31. Their motto is, "We were here before you were born." Unless you're 149 years old, they're right. Bar has played host to such luminaries as Abe Lincoln, the Roosevelts (Teddy and Franklin), and JFK; women weren't allowed in until 1970. Occasionally frat-boyish, but that might just be your thing. Only 2 beers: light and dark. Double-fisters take note: mugs come cheaper 2 at a time ($3.50, or $2 per beer). Open 11am-1am

Musical Box, 219 Ave. B., between E. 13th and E. 14th St. (☎212-254-1731). Hidden behind an unmarked facade, Musical Box lurks upon the Avenue, concealing its sleek bar and spacious lounge space: a veritable living room with sofas a pool table and rugs that tie it all together. A chill and friendly crowd always crowds in here just chilling. Make friends on the patio out back! Open daily 5pm-4am.

Niagara, 112 Ave. A, at corner of E. 7 St. Subway: 6 to Astor Pl.; L to First Ave. (☎212-420-9517). Is a famous NY state waterfall an appropriate name for a bar? Maybe "bustling, art-filled space with beautiful dark wood furniture, industrious bartenders, and a downstairs lounge called 'Lei Lounge' which features a second DJ and a pretty lady dancing (tastefully) on the weekends" would be more appropriate. But perhaps Lei Lounge is an unacceptable moniker, thereby illegitimizing the whole name altogether... Just accept "Niagara" and accept the $5 beers and weekly art shows (Th). Please also accept that it has a photo booth. Open daily 4pm-4pm.

Nuyorican Poets Cafe, 236 E. 3rd St., between Ave. B and C. Subway: F, V to Lower East Side-Second Ave. (☎212-505-8183; www.nuyorican.org). Map 12, F4, 108. NYC's leading joint for poetry slams (check out F night slam at 10pm) and spoken-word performances; several regulars have been featured on MTV. Mixed bag of doggerel and occasional gems. If you don't like the poets, don't worry—there's likely to be a heckler in the house. Cover $5-12. Open Tu-Su 7:30pm-midnight, F-Sa 7:30pm-2:30am.

Remote Lounge, 327 Bowery, between 2nd and 3rd St. (☎212-228-0228; www.remotelounge.com). Subway: F, V to Lower East Side-Second Ave.; N, R to 8th St.-NYU, Prince St.; 6 to Bleecker St. Map 12, B3, 61. This technology-themed cocktail lounge is also a "new media art space" and claims to be the only bar in the city reviewed by *Popular Science.* Over 60 video cameras cover every sq. ft. of the space from multiple angles; this live video is displayed on over 100 output devices, such as CRTs, LCDs, large format plasma screens, and video projectors. Animation, special effects, web-based art, and interactive multimedia also displayed. Snag your own Cocktail Console, zoom in on the other patrons, and message them if you like what you see. Beer $5; mixed drinks $6; martinis up to $11. Call ahead for theme nights and performers. Cover around $4. Open daily 6pm-4am.

Sake Bar Decibel, 240 E. 9th St., between Stuyvesant St. and Second Ave. (☎212-979-2733). Subway: 6 to Astor Pl. Map 12, C2, 26. Quasi-hidden bar (the entrance is down a flight of stairs). Japanese charm meets the aggressive funk of a village basement. Have a romantic evening drinking over 60 kinds of *sake* ($4-6 per glass). Decibel is great for eating and drinking or drinking alone. Min. order $8 per person during busy weekend hours. Open M-Sa 8pm-3am, Su 8pm-1am.

Tenth Street Lounge, 212 E. 10th St., between First and Second Ave. (☎212-473-5252). Subway: L to First Ave. Map 12, D2, 38. Chic hangout with matching clientele. High ceiling, spacious bar, and large couches make this a gorgeous place for an early-evening drink. Beers $4-5; cocktails $6-10. Open M-Sa 5pm-3am, Su 3pm-2am.

Tribe, 132 First Ave., at St. Mark's Pl. (☎212-979-8965). Subway: 6 to Astor Pl. Map 12, D2, 46. Behind the frosted glass windows lies a chic, friendly bar with colorful but subtle back lighting. Comfortable lounging areas. Before midnight: super chill. Then it rapidly evolves into a party. Beer $5; cocktails $5-10. DJ nightly at 10pm: lots of hip-hop and old school; Tu Salsa/Latin. Open daily 5pm-4am.

GAY AND GAY-FRIENDLY NIGHTLIFE

The Cock, 188 Ave. A, at E. 12th St. (☎212-946-1871). Subway: L to First Ave. Map 12, E1, 13. A dark boy bar with a full offering of gay-oriented diversions. Call for the nightly change of entertainment fare. Computerized lights and "X-rated go-go boys." Tends to get crowded after 12:30. M nights are "Three"–drinks $3. Open Su and Tu-Sa 10pm-4am, M 9pm-4am.

Boiler Room, 86 E. 4th St., between First and Second Ave. (☎212-254-7536). Subway: F, V to Lower East Side-Second Ave. Map 12, C4, 89. Popular locale catering to alluring alternative types, NYU college students, and eager refugees from the sometimes stifling Chelsea clone scene. Predominantly gay male bar, but the crowd gets a bit mixed especially on weekends. Terrific jukebox and pool table give the evening a democratic spin. Open daily 4pm-4am.

Wonder Bar, 505 E. 6th St., between Ave. A and B (☎212-777-9105). Subway: L to First Ave.; 6 to Astor Pl. or Bleecker St. Map 12, E3, 82. As you walk in, it says "Wonder Bar" on the floor. This is the name and the game is a cool principally gay bar, with spectral lighting and a hopping crowd. Open daily 8pm-4am.

SOHO AND TRIBECA

Bar 89, 89 Mercer St., between Spring and Broome St. (☎212-274-0989). Subway: N, R to Prince St. Map 9, D3, 35. Upscale bar/restaurant serving average American fare to a stylish crowd. Salads $7-11; sandwiches $7.50-$11. Draft beers ($5.50); imports ($6.50-16). Mixed Drinks ($10-16). Check out the unisex bathroom, which features glass doors that only become opaque when latched precisely. Open Su-Th noon-1:15am, F-Sa noon-2:15am.

Cafe Noir, 32 Grand St., at Thompson St. (☎212-431-7910). Subway: 1, 9 to Canal St./Varick St.; C, E to Canal St./Ave. of the Americas (Sixth Ave.). Map 9, B4, 40. The patrons, the bartenders, and the street-front windows all provide this small bar/lounge/restaurant with a classy but unaffected feel. Draft beers $5-6. Entrees $12-20. Open daily noon-4am (including the kitchen).

Circa Tabac, 32 Watts St., between Sixth Ave. and Thompson St. (☎212-941-1781). Subway: C, E to Spring St./Ave. of the Americas (Sixth Ave.). Map 9, B3, 26. Claims to be the world's first, and perhaps only, cigarette lounge. The war on smoking has spread even to downtown NYC, but Circa Tabac remains a haven for cigarette lovers. Decor recalls a Prohibition-era speakeasy: a jazz soundtrack accompanies protective curtains and Art Deco pieces. State-of-the-art air purifiers and odor killers keep the air clear. 180 kinds of cigarettes ($5-25) available. Open Su-W 5pm-2am, Th-Sa 5pm-4am.

Denizen, 73 Thompson St., between Broome and Spring St. (☎212-966-7299). Subway: C, E to Spring St./Ave. of the Americas (Sixth Ave.). Map 9, B3, 24. This elegant and sexy bar/restaurant features some of the best Cosmopolitans the city has to offer ($9). Restaurant open M-F 5pm-midnight, Sa-Su noon-2am; bar stays open until 4am.

Fanelli's Cafe, 94 Prince St., at Mercer St. (☎212-226-9412). Subway: N, R to Prince St. Map 9, D2, 17. Casual neighborhood alternative to the trendy scene. Full menu with great burgers ($7.50). Standard bar fare, cheap brew ($4 for domestic drafts, $4.75 for imports and microbrews). Slightly older crowd than neighboring bars. Open M-Th 10am-1:30am, F-Sa 10am-3am, Su 11am-1:30am.

Lucky Strike, 59 Grand St., at W. Broadway (☎212-941-0772). Subway: 1, 9 to Canal St./Varick St.; C, E to Canal St./Ave. of the Americas (Sixth Ave.). Map 9, C4, 44. French lovelies meet western cowboys in this Soho hangout. Don't let the beautiful people stop you. They're too secure to be pretentious, so all are welcome. Good food and divine drinks ($5 and up). Vanilla shanti ($8.50) is a carnival in a martini glass. Spiced tea, mojito ($8). Open daily noon-4am.

MercBar, 151 Mercer St., between Prince and W. Houston St. (☎212-966-2727). Subway: N, R to Prince St. Map 9, D1, 10. Trendy bar with a good-looking crowd. Cozy couches and dim lighting. Looking for Love? Maybe the drink will suffice ($11). All beers $6. Mixed drinks start at $6. Open M-Tu 5pm-1:30am, W 5pm-2am, Th 5pm-2:30am, F-Sa 5pm-3:30am, Su 6pm-1:30am.

Milady's, 160 Prince St., at Thompson St. (☎212-226-9069). Subway: C, E to Spring St./Ave. of the Americas (Sixth Ave.). Map 9, B2, 15. A rough in the overbearing SoHo diamond mine. Down-to-earth staff serves up delicious food with more than affordable drinks. Beer bottles ($3.50), draft (3.50-$4.50), and SoHo's only pool table. Everything (even martinis) under $7. Food M-Th 11am-midnight, F-Sa 11am-1am, Su 11am-11pm. Open daily 11am-4am.

Naked Lunch Bar and Lounge, 17 Thompson St., at Grand St. (☎212-343-0828). Subway: 1, 2, A, C, E to Canal St. Map 9, B4,42. Adorned with the roach-and-typewriter theme found in the William S. Burroughs book of the same name. Uninhibited after-work crowd has no qualms about dancing in the large space set aside right by the bar. Unbeatable martinis like the Tanqueray tea $8. All beers $6. Free barbecues monthly in summer. Occasional $7 cover F-Sa after 10pm. $2 off all drinks during Happy Hour Tu-F 5-9pm. Open Tu-Sa 5pm-4am.

X-R Bar, 128 W. Houston St., at Sullivan St. (☎212-674-4080). Subway: 1, 9 to Houston St. Map 9, B1, 3. Comfortable but lively bar caters to young crowd. Snack on ruffled potato chips instead of traditional bar peanuts. Beers $4-5. Drinks $6-8. M-Tu live music, often New Orleans bluegrass, jazz, or folk; Th-Sa DJ. Happy Hour daily 3-7pm, all drinks $1 off. Open M-Sa 3pm-4am, Su 4pm-4am.

Zinc Bar, 90 W. Houston St. at LaGuardia Pl. (W. Broadway). (☎212-477-8337). Subway: 1, 2, 3, 9 to Houston St. Map 9, C1, 4. Jazz hole on the border of Soho and Noho serving up classic, Brazilian, Cuban, and African music to satisfy every ear. No cover, but 2-drink min. on most nights. Sets at 9, 11pm, 12:30am, late night M and F-Sa at 2am, Su at 1am. Open daily 6pm-3:30am.

GREENWICH VILLAGE

Absolutely 4th, 228 W. 4th St., at Seventh Ave. S. (☎212-989-9444). Subway: 1, 9 to Christopher St. Map 10, B4, 40. A sexy splash in the ocean of West Village nightlife. The plush, high-backed, fan-shaped booths are constantly rearranged for the upscale crowd, giving the bar a new feel every night. On warm days, you can lounge by the floor-to-ceiling open windows and taunt passersby. Drinks $5-10. Karaoke W, DJ on weekends. Open daily 4pm-4am.

Automatic Slims, 733 Washington St., at Bank St. (☎212-645-8660). Subway: 1, 9 to Christopher St. Map 10, A4, 37. Stop by this 60s diner-esque bar for a dose of nostalgia or a glass of beer. Famous for its swingin' singles scene. 20-somethings sit on red and white bar stools and tables with classic vinyl under glass. Weekends pack a more diverse crowd. American cooking served 6pm-midnight. Entrees $10-16. Open Tu-Sa 5:30pm-4am.

Bar 6, 502 Sixth Ave., between 12th and 13th St. (☎212-691-1363). Subway: 1, 2, 3 to 14th St./Seventh Ave.; L to 14th St./Ave. of the Americas (Sixth Ave.). Map 10, C2, 7. French-Moroccan bistro by day, sizzling bar by night. Perennially mobbed on summer nights; the animated crowd spills onto the sidewalk. Beers on tap ($4-5 per pint), most from local Brooklyn Brewery. Live DJ spins funk, reggae, and upbeat old school stuff F-Su nights for an upscale crowd. Open Su-Th noon-2am, F-Sa noon-3am.

Hell, 59 Gansevoort St., between Greenwich and Washington St. (☎212-727-1666). Subway: A, C, E, L to 14th St./Eighth Ave. Map 10, A2, 2. This sultry lounge decorated with red velvet curtains took its theme just a little too far with photos of famous people graffitied with red horns and mustaches. And unexpectedly, hell is primarily occupied by trendy, urban hipsters. Hard to find, but worth the trip. Both gay and straight crowd. Open Su-Th and Sa 7pm-4am, F 5pm-4am.

Jekyll and Hyde, 91 Seventh Ave., at Barrow St. (☎212-989-7001 or 800-992-4933; www.jekyllpub.com). Subway: 1, 9 to Christopher St. Map 10, B4, 46. Billed as NY's only haunted restaurant/bar. Every 10min., roaring monsters pop out of the wall; creepy actors come over to your table and act spooky. Impressive collection of "haunted" memorabilia, including a real Egyptian mummy. Nightmare-named, but traditional pub fare. Open Su-Th noon-2am, F-Sa noon-4am.

Kava Lounge, 605 Hudson St., between Bethune and W. 12th St. (☎212-989-7504). Subway: A, C, E, L to 14th St./Eighth Ave. Map 10, A3, 18. A few blocks removed from the West Village's colorful center, Kava attracts a tame and relaxed crowd. Named after *kava*, the ceremonial Polynesian beverage. Prides itself on its Polynesian theme (replete with tribal murals on the walls) and boasts a vast selection of Aussie and New Zealander wines. Good place to keep the evening low-key. 2-for-1 Happy Hour M-F 5-7pm. Open Su-Th 5pm-1am, F-Sa 5pm-3am.

The Slaughtered Lamb Pub, 182 W. 4th St., at Jones St. (☎212-627-5262). Subway: A, C, E, F, V, S to W. 4th St. Map 10, C4, 54. Transylvanian kitsch. Named after an English pub that rubbed a slaughtered lamb's blood on top of doors to ward of the "werewolf" spirit. Home to a "werewolf lounge," "dungeon" (game room) downstairs and wax museum rejects in the back room. Patronized by locals, tourists, and an NYU crowd. More than 150 types of beer ($5-25 per bottle) and ale. $3 special on rotating beers from 5pm-7pm. Open Su-Th noon-2am, F-Sa noon-4am.

inside
SECRETS TO...

Hooked on Hookah

Ever since Bloomberg forced smokers out of New York's restaurants and bars, the sweet highs of strawberry apple-flavored tobacco now have the added thrill of an illicit inhalation. With the passage of the Smoke-Free Air Act came the demise of a popular subculture of hookah bars, whose devotees ranged from students to Broadway stars to investment bankers. Sadly, tabbouleh and hummus now must be enjoyed alone, without the sweet fruit-flavored tobacco that defined these Middle Eastern establishments. *Let's Go,* however, has located one particular hookah bar that offers the brilliant solution to appease both the law and hooked-on-hookah customers: a hookah bar that only serves its delicious aromatic tobacco outdoors. Walk up rose-petaled stairs to the second floor Turkish restaurant **Kapadokya,** and dine outside on the narghile patio. Try the rose or honey flavored tobacco ($13.95). Bring dollar bills for the shaking hips of beautiful belly dancers. And pat yourself on the back for discovering such a delectable loophole.

***Kapadokya**, 142 Montague St., between Clinton and Henry St., Brooklyn (☎718-875-2211). Open daily 11am-11pm. Hookah available 6pm-11pm. Belly dancers Th-F 8:30 pm, Sa 9pm.*

The Village Idiot, 355 W. 14th St., between Eighth and Ninth Ave. (☎212-989-7334). Subway: A, C, E, L to 14th St./Eighth Ave. Map 10, A2, 1. Forget New York, this bar takes you back to a roadhouse off the interstate, especially with its non-Manhattan prices. $5 pitchers and $3 shots account for the stumbling, drunken hordes. As if the customers' drunken antics or the bras hanging from the bar weren't enough, the (female) staff occasionally dances on the bar to the loud country music. Open daily noon-4am.

The Whitehorse Tavern, 567 Hudson St., at W. 11th St. (☎212-243-9260). Subway: 1, 9 to Christopher St. Map 10, A4, 38. Boisterous students playing drinking games and locals who reminisce of the tavern's 20¢ beers, pay homage to the poet Dylan Thomas, who drank himself to death here, pouring 18 straight whiskeys through an already tattered liver. Great jukebox. Outdoor patio. Beer $3.50-5. Open Su-Th 6pm-2am, F-Sa 6pm-4am.

GAY AND GAY-FRIENDLY NIGHTLIFE

Bar d'O, 29 Bedford St., at Downing St. (☎212-627-1580). Subway: 1, 9 to Christopher St. Map 10, C5, 74. Mixed, cozy, dimly-lit bar/lounge/drag cabaret. Even without the fine chanteuses, this is a damn fine place for a drink. Go early for the atmosphere, around midnight for the shows. Don't try to leave in the middle of a show, or risk a nasty tongue-lashing. Superb performances by drag divas Joey Arias (an impeccable Billie Holiday) and Raven O Sa-Su, Tu nights 11pm. Cover Tu and Su $5, Sa $7. M night is "Pleasure" for lesbians. Cover $5-7. Open Sa-Su 6pm-4am, M-F 6pm-3am.

Chi Chiz, 135 Christopher St., at Hudson St. (☎212-462-0027). Subway: 1, 9 to Christopher St. Map 10, A4, 39. No name outside, but a hot spot for attractive, well-groomed African-American and Latino men. Finger foods (chicken fingers, cheese sticks) also available. Pool table in back. Bar packs a younger, rowdier crowd on weekends, and a mellower neighborhood crowd during the week. 2-for-1 Happy Hour daily 4-8pm. Open daily 4pm-4am.

Crazy Nanny's, 21 Seventh Ave. S., near LeRoy St. (☎212-929-8356). Subway: 1, 9 to Houston St. Map 10, C5, 73. As the door promises, this bar is for "Gay women, biologically or otherwise." Glamour dykes come here to shoot some pool, play video games, eat free popcorn, or just hang out. Ethnically diverse crowd. F-Sa 2 bars, 2 fl. Special parties occasionally (Th). Usually 5% male, more men come for W and Su karaoke. Voyeurs not appreciated. M Pool Tournament (sign up at 7pm). Tu bingo and $3 Coronas. Th Exotic Dancers. Happy Hour daily opening to 7pm; well and domestic beers half-price, all other drinks $1 off. Cover only F-Sa after 9pm; F $10, Sa $8. 2-drink min. Open M-F 4pm-4am, Sa-Su 3pm-4am.

The Cubbyhole, 281 W. 12th St., at W. 4th St. (☎212-243-9041). Subway: A, C, E, L to 14th St./Eighth Ave. Map 10, A3, 17. The bar's hanging fish, seaweed and flowers are reminiscent of something in between a magic underwater garden and a kindergarten classroom. Neighborhood feel. Intimate and funky. Formerly predominantly lesbian, now mixed crowd (gay and straight, male and female). Best deal in town—all you can drink special $5, Sa night 8:30pm-10pm. Certain drinks half-price at Happy Hour M-F 4-7pm, Sa 2-7pm, Su 2-10pm. Open M-F 4pm-3am, Sa-Su 2pm-3am.

The Duplex, 61 Christopher St., at Seventh Ave. S. (☎212-255-5438). Subway: 1, 9 to Christopher St. Map 10, C4, 53. A sprawling, renowned piano bar with its name in lights, always abuzz with performances by the talented waitstaff. New York's oldest continuing cabaret with famous alumni who began their careers on its stage (Joan Rivers, Woody Allen). Filled with merry theatrical throngs who can recite every lyric from *On the Twentieth Century,* and will. Mixed crowd mingles on the colorful outdoor "beach" patio in summertime. Outside cafe. Cabaret performance room and game room with pool, poker and darts upstairs. Joan Rivers still performs several times a year. Beer $4. Mixed drinks $4-8. Cover $5-25, depending on event. 2-drink min. per set. Open daily 4pm-4am.

Henrietta Hudson, 438 Hudson St., between Morton and Barrow St. (☎212-243-9079). Subway: 1, 9 to Christopher St. Map 10, B5, 69. A young, clean-cut lesbian crowd presides at this neighborhood bar. Pool table and 2nd bar in back room. Also gay male and straight friendly. 2-for-1 Happy Hour M-F 4-7pm. Busiest Th-Sa. M karaoke, DJ. W 80s, Th Reggae. Cover $5 Su-F after 9pm, Sa after 7pm. Open M-F 4pm-4am, Sa 1pm-4am, Su 3pm-4am.

Rose's Turn, 55 Grove St., between Bleecker St. and Seventh Ave. S (☎212-366-5438). Subway: 1, 9 to Christopher St. Map 10, B4, 48. Dim, downstairs, piano bar with open mic and perhaps the most musically talented bar staff in New York. Mixed drinks $4-8. Beer $4.50. Basement bar is packed Th–Sa; Su provides a small-to-medium crowd for a pleasant balance of liveliness and intimacy. Come F-Su 9pm-4am to hear singer Terri White (who also tends bar)—her voice is one of the city's undiscovered wonders. Open mic W-F 6:30-9pm. Cabaret upstairs—cover $5-15 with 2-drink min., depending on show. Other events include comedy acts. 2-for-1 Happy Hour M-F 4-8pm, Sa-Su 4-6pm. Open daily 4pm-4am.

Stonewall Inn, 53 Christopher St., at Seventh Ave. S. (☎212-463-0950). Subway: 1, 9 to Christopher St. Map 10, B4, 38. Legendary bar of the 1969 Stonewall Riots (p. 59). Join the lively and diverse crowd and the famed bartender "Tree" in this recently renovated bar to toast the brave drag queens who fought back. Enter the male amateur strip contest appropriately named "Meatpacking" and win $200. 3 bars—main, back and upstairs at the dance floor. 2-for-1 Happy Hour M-F 3-9pm, Sa-Su $4 Cosmos. Hors d'oeuvres served halfway through. Cover only for special shows. Open daily 3pm-4am.

CHELSEA AND UNION SQUARE

Lola, 30 W. 22nd St., between Fifth and Sixth Ave. (☎212-675-6700). Subway: F, V to 23rd St./Ave. of the Americas (Sixth Ave.); N, R to 23rd St./Broadway. Map 13, D5, 79. This sleek restaurant's entrees are expensive (lunch $10.50-14, dinner $25-33), and the lounge (2-drink minimum) hosts an upscale after-work crowd. However, known to give free shots on select days. Beers $5. True to their claim that "Lola is soul," they have live music every day: M varies, Tu jazz music, W-Sa R&B, funk, and soul. Open M 6pm-1am, Tu-F noon-3pm and 6pm-1am, Sa-Su 6pm-1am.

Old Town Bar and Grill, 45 E. 18th St., between Park Ave. S and Broadway (☎212-529-6732). Subway: 4, 5, 6, L, N, Q, R, W to 14th St.-Union Sq. Map 13, E5, 97. A dark, 105-year-old hideaway with wood and brass furniture. Seen on the old "Late Night with David Letterman" opening montage. Popular with a late-20s/early-30s crowd: beware of perpetual after-work and weekend mobs. Beer on tap $4, Heineken $3.75. Open M-Sa 11:30am-1am, Su 3pm-midnight.

Open, 559 W. 22nd St., at 11th Ave. (☎212-243-1851). Subway: C, E to 23rd St./Eighth Ave. Map 13, A4, 27. Hordes of upscale hipsters crowd into this little bistro/cafe after their gallery tours to enjoy the floor-to-ceiling window view of the Hudson River. Boys and girls alike drool over the hot bartenders. So trendy it'll make you paw for your copy of *ArtForum* and pull up a low stool to the bar. Imported specialties are pricey but perfect for the Continental who wishes to be seen. Fresh melons with prosciutto $6 during the weekend special brunch (Sa-Su 11:30am-4:30pm). Open M-F 11am-4am, Sa-Su noon-4am.

Passerby, 436 W. 15th St., between Ninth and Tenth Ave. (☎212-266-7321). Subway: A, C, E. L to 14th St.-Eighth Ave. Map 13, B6, 106. Once adjacent to owner Gavin Brown's gallery (now moved farther downtown), Passerby's mirror and neon floor panels create a dizzying space-age-meets-70s-disco optical illusion on the outskirts of the meat-packing district. Most drinks $8. Open Su-M 6pm-1am, Tu-W 6pm-2am, Th-Sa 6pm-4am.

Peter McManus, 152 Seventh Ave., at 19th St. (☎212-929-6196). Subway: 1, 9 to 23rd St./Seventh Ave. Map 13, C5, 76. Made famous by a *New York Times* article on the timeless appeal of ordinary bars. Ordinary drinks, ordinary clientele (with some tourists thrown in), slightly-higher-than-ordinary prices. Friendly, intimate atmosphere at this oldest family-owned bar in NYC (now in its 4th generation). Carved mahogany bar and leaded glass windows. A smattering of video games and a jukebox. Dinner specials $6-8 until midnight. Draught beers $2-4.50. Open daily 10:30am-3am.

Q Lounge, 220 W. 19th St., between Seventh and Eighth Ave. (☎212-206-7665). Subway: 1, 9 to 23rd St./Seventh Ave. Map 13, C5, 77. This pool hall's red-felt tables, jewel toned curtains and abundant mirrors await both the hustlin' type and those who just enjoy a game of eight-ball. Low-lying lounge ottomans and a 10 ft. square TV screen greet the rest. You must be over 21 to play after 6pm. $13 per hr. before 6pm, $14 after. Open M-Th 1pm-2am, F-Sa 1pm-4am, Su 2pm-2am.

GAY AND GAY-FRIENDLY NIGHTLIFE

Barracuda, 275 W. 22nd St., between Seventh and Eighth Ave. (☎212-645-8613). Subway: C, E to 23rd St./Eighth Ave. Map 13, C5, 71. Dramatic red lighting directs patrons from the bar to the cozy hangout room in the back, complete with sofas, a pool table, game machines and a dazzling collection of kitsch furniture. Drinks $4-7. 2-for-1 Happy Hour M-F 4-9pm. Open daily 4pm-4am.

The Big Apple Ranch, at Dance Manhattan, 39 W. 19th St., 5th fl., between Fifth and Sixth Ave. (☎212-358-5752). Subway: F, V to 23rd St./Ave. of the Americas (Sixth Ave.); N, R to 23rd St./Broadway. Map 13, D5, 81. A friendly crowd of urban cowboys and girls welcomes all to a romping evening of gay and lesbian two-stepping. $10 cover includes lesson. Sa only 8pm-1am, lessons 8-9pm.

g, 223 W. 19th St., between Seventh and Eighth Ave. (☎212-929-1085). Subway: 1, 9 to 18th St./Seventh Ave. Map 13, C5, 74. Glitzy, popular bar shaped like an oval racetrack—perhaps an appropriate architectural metaphor, given the pumped-up Chelsea clientele that speeds around this circuit trying to win glances. Fortunately, the famous frozen Cosmos satisfy the thirst of those logging their miles. Open daily 4pm-4am.

La Nueva Escuelita, 301 W. 39th St., at Eighth Ave. (☎212-631-0588; Her/She ☎212-631-1093). Subway: A, C, E to 42nd St.-Port Authority. Map 14, B5, 88. Drag Latin dance club that throbs with merengue, salsa, soul, hip-hop, and arguably the best drag shows in New York. Largely, but not entirely, gay Latin crowd. F, starting at 10pm, is Her/She Bar, with go-go gals, performances, and special events. Cover Th $5; F $12; Sa $15; Su 7-10pm $8, after 10pm $10. Open Th-Sa 10pm-5am, Su 7pm-4am.

Rawhide, 212 Eighth Ave at W. 21st St. (☎212-242-9332). Subway: C, E to 23rd St./Eighth Ave. Map 13, B5, 64. One-room heaven for leather daddies and the boys that cruise them. Popular with early risers and afternoon prowlers for its opening hours. Happy hour(s) 10am-9pm (domestic beers $3 and well drinks $3.50). Open M-Sa 8am-4am, Su noon-4am.

The Roxy, 515 W. 18th St., at 10th Ave. (☎212-645-5156). Subway: A, C, E, L to 14th St./Eighth Ave. Map 13, A5, 58. Currently *the* place to be on Sa nights. Hundreds of gay men dance and drink in the Roxy's gigantic, luxurious space. Upstairs, lounge/bar provides a different DJ and more intimate setting. Downstairs you'll find high ceilings, a beautiful dance floor, and lounge space. Beer $5. Drinks $6+. Gay rollerskating night Th. Cover $25. Prime hours are 11pm-6am.

SBNY, 50 W. 17th St., between Fifth and Sixth Ave. (☎212-691-0073). Subway: 1, 9 to 18th St./ Seventh Ave.; F, V to 23rd St./Ave. of the Americas (Sixth Ave.). Map 13, D6, 112. One of the most popular gay mega-bars, the newly-renamed **S**plash **B**ar **N**ew **Y**ork (formerly known simply as Splash) has an enormous 2-floor complex. Industrial decor provides a sleek backdrop for a very crowded scene, with a dance floor that completes the evening. Drinks $4-7. Cover varies, peaking at $7. Open Su-Th 4pm-4am, F-Sa 4pm-5am.

View, 232 Eighth Ave., at W. 22nd St. (☎212-929-2243). Subway: C, E to 23rd St./Eighth Ave. Map 13, B5, 60. The latest hot spot where you can see and be seen. Call for wild theme nights. Happy Hour M-F 4pm-8pm. Open M-F 4pm-4am, Sa 3pm-4am, Su noon-4am.

UPPER EAST SIDE

Unless you want to hang out with the private school, fake-ID crowd, you'll avoid this neighborhood and its yuppified pubs and their clientele of investment-banking former JV lacrosse benchwarmers. That said, if you're willing to wade through a crowd of jailbait girls and men whose heads are permanently misshapen from years of wearing white hats, these are the best places to drink, be merry, and sing along to "Livin' on a Prayer."

American Spirits, 1744 Second Ave., near 91st St. (☎212-289-7510). Subway: 4, 5, 6 to 86th St./Lexington Ave. Map 15, C3, 13. Cozy sports bar. Beer $4-5, mixed drinks $7-8. The specialty, however, is the karaoke, hosted by the inimitable 'Sexual Chocolate' on Tu, Th, F, and Sa; live music every 3rd Sa of the month. Happy Hour 4-8pm with $2 drafts and $3 well drinks. Open daily 3pm-4am.

The Big Easy, 1768 Second Ave., at 92nd St. (☎212-348-0879). Subway: 6 to 96th St./Lexington. Map 15, C3, 12. A post-grad hangout for those who miss their college glory years. With 2 beirut (a.k.a. beer pong) tables in back, special $2 Bud drafts and well drinks nightly 11pm-midnight. This place can get sloppy, but is a good spot for cheap, strong drinks before a long NYC night. Open daily 5pm-4am.

Brother Jimmy's BBQ, 1485 2nd Ave., between 77th and 78th St. (☎212-545-7427). Subway: 6 to 77th St. Map 15, B5, 26. The sign advertises "BBQ and booze," and this greasy-chops South Carolina kitchen serves up plenty of both. On Su, have all the ribs that you can eat in 2hr. for $19.95. If you're a Southerner, grab your ID and come back on W for 25% off your dinner. Most nights, however, the bar is where the action is (lightweights, watch out). Lots of original drinks. Happy Hour M-F 5-7pm. Children under 12 eat free. Open Su-Th noon-midnight, F-Sa noon-1am. Bar open Su until 1 am, M-Sa 4am.

in the know

Be Your Own Rock Star

Go to the hippest lounge in the City, and you're guaranteed to see some sort of rock star. But better yet, go to one of the bars listed below and be your own rock star! A cheap, entertaining (and legal) way to release pent-up frustration, karaoke is a must in NYC nightlife.

For a swanky experience, head to **BINY** (Best In New York) in SoHo. With plush, private rooms, lychee martinis and Japanese fusion cuisine, BINY offers karaoke with style. (8 Thompson St. Between Canal St. and Sixth Ave. ☎212-334-5490. Open M-Th 10pm-4am, F-Sa 11pm-4am, Su 9pm-4am.)

For a more divey, drunk experience try **Winnie's** in Chinatown. (104 Bayard St. between Baxter and Mulberry St. ☎212-732-2384. Open daily noon-4am.)

For karaoke the gay way, head to **Pieces Bar,** where you can belt out Britney tune, shoot some pool and watch the disco ball go 'round and 'round. (8 Christopher St. Between Gay St. and Greenwich Ave. ☎212-353-9500. Open Su-M 2pm-2am, Tu-Sa 2pm-4am.)

Mo's Caribbean Bar and Mexican Grill, 1454 Second Ave., at 76th St. (☎212-650-0561). Subway: 6 to 77th St. Map 15, C5, 31. Very lively, very friendly bar with great drink specials every night. Beer: imported $4.50, domestic $4. Happy Hour 4-7pm with the entire bar at half price! W Ladies' Night (females get $1 drafts and frozen margaritas). Live reggae band Tu 8pm-midnight with $3 Coronas and margaritas. Open M-F 4pm-4am, Sa-Su noon-4am.

Ship of Fools, 1590 Second Ave., between 82nd and 83rd St. (☎212-570-2651). Subway: 4, 5, 6 to 86th St./Lexington Ave. Map 15, C4, 23. Boasting some of the area's best buffalo wings, this sports bar's 35 TV screens will let you catch everything from baseball to rugby. If you're not satisfied with being a spectator, head to the back rooms for some darts or a game of pool. $4 well drinks and most bottled beers. Happy Hour M-F 3-7pm. Ladies Night Th 3-9pm. Open M-Th 3pm-4am, F-Su noon-4am.

UPPER WEST SIDE

Citrus Bar and Grill, 320 Amsterdam Ave. at 75th St. (☎212-595-0500). Subway: 1, 2, 3, 9 to 72nd St. "Latin fare with Asian flair," but the bar's true gem lies in its fresh purees of exotic fruits (white peach, prickly pear, kiwi, coconut) that can be added to fresh squeezed juice margaritas (glass $7.25, liter $19.75). Open M 5:30pm-11pm, Tu-Th 5:30pm-midnight, F-Sa 5:30pm-1am, Su 11:30am-11pm.

The Evelyn Lounge, 380 Columbus Ave., at 78th St. (☎212-724-2363). Subway: B, C to 81st St. Map 18, C4, 31. A somewhat upscale bar for the after-work set, with fireplaces and settees creating a homey setting upstairs. Drinks (martinis $9) are a bit pricey but cover the cost of comfy couches colonized by cultured cliques. Enticing bar menu $7-14. Downstairs features a DJ W-Sa, spinning hip-hop F-Sa. Open F-Sa 6pm-4am, closes earlier Su-Th.

Potion Lounge, 370 Columbus Ave., between 77th and 78th St. (☎212-721-4386). Subway: 1 to 79th; B, C to 81st St. Map 18, C4, 32. A silvery-blue lounge complete with local art on the walls, bubbles rising through pipes in the windows, and velvety sofas. The lounge takes its name from the colorful layered drinks ("potions" $10) it serves. Try the Fig Newton, which comes with a Hershey's Kiss at the bottom. Draught beers $5-6, martinis $9. DJs on weekends. Open Tu-Sa 6pm-4am.

Shark Bar, 307 Amsterdam Ave. between 74th and 75th St. (☎212-874-8500). Subway: 1, 2, 3, 9 to 72nd St. The soul food here is served in gigantic proportions, and the sports crowd is rowdy and borderline fanatic. Appetizers ($5.95-$8.95). Open Su-Tu 5pm-11:30pm, W noon-midnight, Th noon-12:30am, F 12:30pm-1:30am, Sa 5pm-1:30am.

Yogi's, 2156 Broadway, at 76th St. (☎873-9852). Subway: 1, 9 to 79th St. Map 18, C4, 38. Midriff-baring bartenders pour seriously cheap beer and alcohol (mugs $1.25-2.25; pitchers $5; shots from $2.50), as a constant stream of country music twangs out of the stereo. The bar's namesake bear greets outside. Open daily 11:30am-4am.

GAY AND GAY-FRIENDLY NIGHTLIFE

Chase, 255 W. 55th St. between Broadway and Eighth Ave. (☎212-333-3400). Subway: 1, 9 to 50th St./Broadway; C, E to 50th St./Eighth Ave. Map 14, C2, 6. Trendy and chic, Chase brings a little bit of Chelsea to Hell's Kitchen, drawing in well-groomed men and the neighborhood theatrical community. Happy Hour daily 4-7pm. Open daily 3pm-3am.

The Works, 428 Columbus Ave., at 81st St. (☎212-799-7365). Subway: B, C to 81st St. Map 18, C4, 27. An Upper West Side hangout for the Banana Republic set. The Works packs them in Th and Su, when aspiring guppies seek genuine bargains in $1 frozen margaritas and cosmos (Th 8pm-2am) and the $5 martini W. Open daily 2pm-3am.

INWOOD

Arka Lounge, 4488 Broadway, at W. 192 St. (☎212-567-9425) Subway: 1, 9 to 191st St. Big fish swim in convex fish tanks behind the curvy bar making them look even bigger. Low tables and padded walls. Arka is a classy Latin joint with live DJs W-Sa and live music on Su. W night is live Latin Jazz (not in the summers). Clean up before you arrive: F-Su dress code: no sneakers and collared shirts and pants (for men). Men alone must pay the $10 cover on weekends. Happy Hour until 8: buy one get one free (generally $7-10). Open Su 5pm-2am, W-Th 7pm-2am, F-Sa 7pm-4am.

Umbrella Lounge, 440 W. 202nd St. (☎212-942-5916) Subway: 1 to 207th St. Umbrellas on the ceiling, big umbrella candelabra, umbrellas in the tropical drinks. This converted mechanic-shop, with its 45ft. ceilings, is a stellar mix of exposed cinderblocks, life-sized photographic prints by the owner, high art painted on the walls and club lighting. One of the city's hippest Latin hangouts (but with an increasingly mixed crowd), many of the Yankees have been known to stop by for all-night dancing. Definitely worth the trek uptown. Drinks $7-9. Live music of DJ every night. Su is the most hopping. Open Su-M, W-Sa 9pm-4am.

BROOKLYN

In a development that's no surprise to its many loyalists, Brooklyn has emerged as the vanguard of New York hipness, pseudo-hipness, and straight-up-trying-too-hard-for-hipness. To legions of young drinkers, partiers, and other sociable types, Brooklyn's nightlife is a better option than the overpriced martinis and aging *Sex and the City* watchers of Manhattan. If you're really hardcore, you'll get drunk in Staten Island. But if you can't hack it on Hylan Blvd., check out the borough that knows when to sleep and when to stay up all night doing it proper.

66 Water Street Bar, 66 Water St. on corner of Main St. (☎718-625-9352). Subway: A, C to High St. or F to York St. Map 22, 4. The best DUMBO after hours starts with 66 Water Street's Happy Hour daily 3-7pm where your favorite beer is only $3. Serves up great, inexpensive grill food with chicken quesadillas ($10) and penne pasta with chicken ($12) among the items on the menu. This bar also sports a red-light small concert hall in the back for F and Sa night bands. Call ahead for the musical schedule. Open daily noon-4am.

Artland, 609 Grand St. (☎718-599-9706). Subway: L to Lorimer St. Like a big livingroom, Artland always has something going on: Tango lessons (W), Live Jazz (Th), In-house psychic (Sa), various means of promoting local art. Books to read, board games and pinball to play and a bar full of rare liquors to drink. Beer $2-5 a pint. The fruit-cluster-shaped lamps, Persian rugs, and overstuffed chairs are not to be missed in this place made for gathering. Open daily 1pm-4am (365 days a year!).

Blu Lounge, 197 N. 8th St., at Driggs Ave. (☎718-782-8005) Subway: L to Bedford Ave. Map 21, 22. Dark and candlelit, low tables, plush seating and mellow ambient sounds. Both sensually and literally intoxicating, specializing in martinis and claiming Williamsburg's best Bloody Mary ($7). Regulars say they can always count on striking up deep conversation with a stranger. Back room and second bar gets bumping at night. DJ F-Sa, live music most W-Th. Home of "The Best Happy Hour in Brooklyn," everything half-off 3pm-7pm. Open daily 3pm-4am. Cash only.

Brooklyn Ale House, 103 Berry St., at N. 8th St. (☎718-302-9811). Subway: L to Bedford Ave. Map 21, 12. Less self-consciously hip than the Williamsburg scene. Still what at first feels like a generic pub reveals a mustard colored wall covered with large still-lifes. This lively neighborhood joint welcomes all with a great draft beer selection ($5) and a daily $3 beer. Most every sort of whiskey to boot. Happy Hour M-F 3pm-7pm, $1 off beer and well. Open daily 3pm-4am.

Butta' Cup Lounge, 271 Adelphi Street, on DeKalb Ave. (☎718-522-1669). Subway: C to Lafayette Ave. Map 22, 24. This hot nightspot also doubles as a tasty restaurant that is a must for Su brunch. The kitchen cooks up southern soul favorites with a Caribbean flair. Th live DJ beginning at 6pm, on F they play classics, house, and soul, and Sa nights bring rotating guest DJs to the restaurant's 2 fl. Su-Th kitchen open 10am until 12am, venue open until 1am. F and Sa kitchen open 10am until 2am, venue open until 3am.

Enid's, 560 Manhattan Ave., at Driggs Ave. (☎718-349-3859). Subway: G to Nassau Ave. Refreshingly spacious with a comfy, partially deconstructed feel. Enid's has a good mixed crowd from Greenpoint's little Poland and Williamsburg's style mania. An old-fashioned phone booth, a collection of board games and big comfy sofas make lazy afternoon and late

Is This A Bar Mitzvah?

bOb Bar, Lower East Side

Hailing a Cab

nights equally appealing here. Many local beers on tap ($3-5), half-price at Happy Hour (5pm-7pm). No food save for Sa-Su brunch (trout, buckwheat pancakes $6-8). Open M-F 5pm-4am, Sa-Su 10am-4am.

Galapagos, 70 N. 6th St., between Kent and Wythe St., in Williamsburg (☎718-782-5188). Subway: L to Bedford Ave. Map 21, 11. Once a mayonnaise factory, this space is now one of the hipper cultural spots in the city. Great bar in an interesting futuro-sleek decor, complete with an enormous reflecting pool, makes for an interesting hangout that draws patrons from all over the city. Puts up parties, vaudeville performances on M, as well as Ocularis, their weekly film series (Su 7 and 9:30pm, M 8:30pm; Cover $5). DJs every Tu-Sa. Events sometimes charge $5 cover. Happy Hour M-Sa 6pm-8pm. Open Su-Th 6pm-2am, F-Sa 6pm-4am.

The Gate, 321 Fifth Ave., corner of Third St. (☎718-768-4329). The Gate was the bar the begin it all. A few short years ago, Park Slope was a nightlife wasteland. The Gate's goods selection of beers (all around $3), welcoming atmosphere, and large patio (always filled) paved the way for the Fifth Ave. renaissance. Open M-Th 4pm-4am, F-Su noon-4am.

Halcyon, 227 Smith St., between Butler and Douglass St. (☎718-260-9299). Map 24, 2. Best to get there by taxi to avoid walking south of Atlantic Ave. after dark. The hippest Brooklyn hangout south of Flatbush Ave., Halcyon combines record store, cafe, and lounge (and even furniture store). Laid-back atmosphere allows you to soak in the sounds of the DJ while playing one of their old board games like Twixt, or smoking in the back garden. BYOB. Open Su and Tu-Th noon-1am F-Sa noon-2am.

Loki Lounge, 304 Fifth Avenue, corner of Second St. (☎718-965-9600). Don't be put off by Loki's dark exterior: inside is one of Brooklyn's best bars. Laid-back, comfortable, and staffed by good bartenders, Loki is a bar that does all the important things well. With occasional live music. Open daily 4pm-4am.

Montero's Bar & Grill, 73 Atlantic Ave., at Hicks St., in Downtown Brooklyn (☎718-624-9799). Subway: 2, 3, 4, 5, M, N, R to Court St./Borough Hall. Map 22, 15. Loaded with nautical paraphernalia, this friendly dive still looks like the longshoremen's bar it once was. Beer $3. Open M-Sa 10am-4am, Su noon-4pm.

The Pencil Factory, 142 Franklin St., at Greenpoint Ave. (☎718-609-5858) Subway: G to Greenpoint Ave. This bar inhabits the corner across from an old pencil factory. It has a bit of an old-fashioned feel with long wooden tables, brick walls and a tin ceiling. Old pictures make it feel, well, old. There is a little one table snuggle room, perfect for long nights of toasting. With 10 beers on tap ($4 pints) and a dozen single malts ($4-16), the mostly local, 20s and up crowd is always smiling for one reason or another. Open M-F 3pm-4am, Sa-Su 1pm-4am.

Pete's Candy Store, 709 Lorimer St., between Frost and Richardson St. (☎718-302-3770). Subway: L to Lorimer St. Map 21, 23. A labor of the owner's love, this hand-painted bar includes a small performance room in the back and a "make-out" hallway. The lively local crowd flocks to the soda-shop-turned-bar for the free live music every night. Tu Bingo and W Quiz-Off (both 7-9pm) are extremely popular, but it's the Bucket of Joy (Stoli, Red Bull, 7-Up and straws) that makes this place more than worth the walk ($6). M night poetry readings are among the best in the city. Open Su-Tu 5pm-2am, W-Sa 5pm-4am.

Rain Lounge, 216 Bedford Ave., at N. 5th St. (☎718-384-0100). The faux-glitz of bubbles behind the bar and colored lighting make this truly a place for lounging. The loud dance music gets the diverse crowd on their feet. $4 pints and live DJs. Backyard covered in case of Rain. Open daily 5pm-4am.

Teddy's, 96 Berry St., at N. 8th St. (☎718-384-9787). Subway: L to Bedford Ave. Map 21, 13. An eclectic mix of artists and wizened Brooklynites visits Teddy's for its great jukebox and friendly atmosphere. A wide variety of specialty martinis, extensive wine list, and low-priced Brooklyn beers ($3-4). Hugely popular brunch Sa and Su 11am-4pm ($3-7). Food is quite good, sandwiches especially ($6-8). Fridays feature the Fresh Fish Fry. F-Sa live DJs. Open M-F 11:30am-midnight, Sa-Su 11am-2am.

Waterfront Ale House, 155 Atlantic Ave., between Henry and Clinton St. (☎718-522-3794). Subway: 2, 3, 4, 5, M, N, R to Court St./Borough Hall. Map 22, 16. A friendly neighborhood joint, and a great spot to go for beer and burgers. The 15 beers on tap change seasonally; try to get a pint of Brooklyn Brown. Specials like mussels in a *weiss* beer broth broaden the definition of pub grub. Mugs $3.50, pints $4.50. Live jazz Sa 11pm-2am. Happy Hour (pints $3) M-F 4-7pm. Open daily noon-11pm; bar open until 3 or 4am.

Union Pool, 484 Union Ave., off Skillman Ave. (☎718-609-0484). One of the funkiest places in Brooklyn. The backyard has a fountain, butterfly chairs, picnic tables and restored Ford pickups from the 50s. The bar, an old pool supply depot, is owned, run and populated by close friends so whimsical events from circus performances, local film festivals and BBQs are frequent. Live DJ every night at 10pm. Live music a few times a week, usually 9pm. $2 pints of Yuengling. Photobooth too. Open daily 5pm-4am.

Yabby's, 265 Bedford Ave., between Grand and N. 1st St. (☎718-384-1664). Subway: L to Bedford Ave. Map 21, 33. A mellow crowd packs into this converted auto-repair shop to lounge on the mismatched vintage furniture and hangout on the large outdoor patio. The vast outdoor space makes this a summer hot spot. F, Su live music; Th, Sa DJ. Open Tu-Th 3pm-2am, F 3pm-4am, Sa noon-4am, and Su noon-2am.

QUEENS

Cosmos Bar Cafe, 28-06 Astoria Blvd, in Astoria (☎718-721-5500). Coors Light banners welcome you to this true neighborhood "dive." Bar stools and loud bartenders promise a long evening of beer, local gossip and more beer. Open daily 3pm-2am.

Los Amigos Bar and Restaurant, 22-73 31st St., in Astoria (☎718-726-8708). This lively Mexican grill offers a bustling environment, chips 'n' salsa ($2) and plenty of cheap *cerveza* ($3.50). Round up your amigos and mosey on over. Open daily 11am-2am.

Sheehan's, 171-57 46th St., in Flushing (☎718-961-6161). The best sports bar in Queens...toss 'em back with the other baseball fans, complain about the Mets and belt out N'Sync at karaoke every Su (11pm-3am).

THE BRONX

The Bronx isn't the place to come if you're looking for the elusive city-that-never-sleeps nightlife, but if you find yourself on City Island, you'll know where to go. **The Boat Livery, Inc.,** 663 City Island Ave., at Bridge St., is the place to come if you want cheap beer, bloodworms, and fishing tackle. Bud $1. (☎718-885-1843. Subway: 6 to Pelham Bay Park, then bus Bx29 to City Island Ave. and Kilroe St. Map 28, F4, 24. Boat rental open 5am-4:30pm; bait shop open 5am-8pm; bar open 5am-10pm.)

The Bronx is the next Brooklyn. We predict that in 10 years, this book will be all about boroughs that begin with 'B.' BADOW!

Jimmy's Bronx Cafe, 281 W. Fordham Rd., at Major Deegan. (☎718-329-2000). Subway: 1 to 207 St. Transfer to the Bx12. Downtown glitz is fine, but this is where the real heart of New York parties. Lots of good loud music and locals getting freaky. Drinks $4-7. Open daily 10am-4pm.

DANCE CLUBS

Carefree crowds, hype music, unlimited fun, massive pocketbook damage—these foundations of the New York club scene make it an unparalleled institution of boogie. Some of the best parties stay underground, advertised only by word of mouth, or by flyer. Many parties move from space to space each week. The rules to clubbing in New York are simple. Door people, the clubs' fashion police, forbid anything drab or conventional—that means: don't wear khaki shorts and a purse across your chest. Above all, just look confident—attitude is at least half the battle. Come after 11pm unless you crave solitude, but the real party starts around 1 or 2am. A few after-hours clubs keep at it until 5-6am, or even later. Consider pre-partying at a bar or at home before you go out: drinks at most clubs are $8-11. Finally, **call ahead or check the club website** as you plan your night, to see what events are slated: New York club schedules change every few months.

FLYERS

Too good for our recommendations? Keep your eyes peeled as you travel the city by day to find nighttime options. Although NYC doesn't have the flyer culture that other big cities do, there are plenty of places to pick up party, club, or concert ads. There are advertisements all over the place listing club events; if you head out to the downtown area at night, you'll be handed enough flyers to keep even the Hilton sisters occupied for a month. Check local publications like the *Village Voice* and *Time Out* for their club info; Internet sites like **www.promonyc.com** may also be helpful. If it's a special type of music you're into, ask around at record stores—smaller, specialized stores generally have in-the-know staff.

Centrofly, 45 W. 21st St., between Fifth and Sixth Ave. (☎212-627-7770; www.centrofly.com). Subway: 1, 9 to 23rd St./Seventh Ave.; 6 to 23rd St./Park Ave. S.; F, V to 23rd St./Ave. of the Americas (Sixth Ave.); N, R to 23rd St./Broadway. Map 13, D5, 80. Where the beautiful people and music aficionados come to dance to the latest house and techno, often by big-name DJs. Although the patrons rave about the martinis ($11), it's the psychedelic lights and retro-chic decor that put the "fly" in Centrofly. Impressive menu served until 5am includes chocolate fondue ($9) and eggs benedict ($8) to replenish your energy after a night of dancing. Large number of rooms, many with their own theme: the soundproof room lets you carry on a conversation, the champagne room offers overpriced champagne and bottle service, and the Crazy Room is decorated with black squares and white circles (with mirrors). All seating, except for champagne room, is waitress service. Mixed drinks $8-10. Cover $10-25. Open M-Sa 10pm-5am.

Eugene, 27 W. 24th St., between Fifth and Sixth Ave. (☎212-462-0999). Subway: 1, 9 to 23rd St./Seventh Ave.; 6 to 23rd St./Park Ave. S; F, V to 23rd St./Ave. of the Americas (Sixth Ave.); N, R 23rd St./Broadway. Map 13, D4, 37. This fancy bar/club/lounge doubles as an expensive restaurant by day, but around 11pm the DJ comes on and the party heats up. Vegas-casino atmosphere, with lots of gold and yellow light. Plenty of dimly lit seating for more intimate moments. Drinks from $9. Call for cover during week, $20 Th-Sa. Open M-Sa 5pm-4am.

Filter 14, 432 W. 14th St., at Washington St. (☎212-366-5680). Subway: A, C, E, L to 14th St./Eighth Ave.; 1, 2, 3 to 14th St./Seventh Ave. Leave the pretension behind: everyone here is all about the music. Intimate, no-frills club with primarily house music. Funky crowd, but dress code not strictly in effect. Cover $5-12. Open Tu-Sa 10pm-4am.

Go, 73 Eighth Ave., between W. 13th and 14th St. (☎212-496-1200). Subway: 1, 2, 3, to 14th St./Seventh Ave.; A, C, E, L to 14th St./Eighth Ave. Map 13 B6, 109. Smaller club with beautiful people. The entirely white decor makes a perfect canvas for the "light DJ" to change the club's color scheme depending on his mood (blue, orange, purple., etc.). Rumored to be the favorite NYC nightspot of pop princess Britney Spears. Cover $20. Open Su and Th-Sa 10pm-4am.

Nell's, 246 W. 14th St., between Seventh and Eighth Ave. (☎212-675-1567; www.nells.com). Subway: A, C, E, L to 14th St./Eighth Ave.; 1, 2, 3 to 14th St./Seventh Ave. Map 13, C6, 111. With various themes from Cuban salsa to comedy, this bar/club packs in a diverse and often older crowd. Upstairs is a mellow space for mingling; downstairs is for dancing. Leather couches and dark wood recall a 1930s bar. Metal detector policy in effect. No sneakers, jeans, or work boots. Hours and cover vary daily. Check website for details.

Suite 16, 127 Eighth Ave., at W. 16th St. (☎212-627-1680). Subway: A, C, E, L to 14th St./Eighth Ave.; 1, 2, 3 to 14th St./Seventh Ave. Map 13, B6, 100. With no VIP area and a single open space, the fabulous dance party often spills over (or, more accurately, onto the couches and seating area). Standard club decor, but stunningly beautiful people. If you get through the door without any hassle, take it as a compliment. Cover varies during the week; F-Sa $20. Open M-Sa 11pm-4am.

Webster Hall, 125 E. 11th St., between Third and Fourth Ave. (☎212-353-1600; www.websterhall.com). Subway: 4, 5, 6, L, N, Q, R, W to 14th St.-Union Sq. Map 12, B1, 2. This popular (if somewhat mainstream) club offers 4 floors dedicated to R&B/hip hop, 70s and 80s/Top 40, house/techno/trance, and Latin. Sports bar and coffee bar to boot. One of NYC's only 19+ clubs. Cover Th $20 for men, free for women; F-Sa $30. Website has guest passes that get you $10-15 off. Open Th-Sa 10pm-6am.

INSIDE

dance **211**

film **214**

music **216**

classical music **216** jazz **218**

opera **221** rock, pop, punk, funk **221**

theater **223**

broadway **224** off-broadway **225**

comedy clubs **226** general entertainment venues **227**

live television **230** outdoor theaters **231**

sports **231**

spectator sports **231** participatory sports **233**

Entertainment

Let's Go lists New York's most essential venues and hot spots, but check local sources to get the scoop on current offerings. After all, it's the shows that are good, not the venues. Look through publications for the most up-to-date info on entertainment in the city: try the *Village Voice*, *Time Out: New York*, *New York* magazine, and *The New York Times* (particularly the Sunday edition). The monthly *Free Time* calendar ($2) lists free cultural events throughout Manhattan. Call the NYC Parks Department's 24hr. **entertainment hotline** (☎212-360-3456) for the lowdown on special events in parks throughout the city.

DANCE

COMPANIES

Alvin Ailey Dance Company, 211 W. 61st St. (☎212-767-0590; fax 212-767-0625; www.alvinailey.org). Founded in 1958 by pioneer of American modern dance Alvin Ailey, AADC is now headed by renowned artistic director Judith Jamison. Repertory regularly includes Ailey masterpieces such as *Revelations, Escapades,* and *Memoria,* as well as works by other choreographers, such as Lynne Taylor-Corbett's *Prayers from the Edge* and Ronald Brown's *Grace.* AADC tours extensively in the US and abroad; they will be performing in New York at the City Center (see p. 213) Dec. 3, 2003-Jan.4, 2004. Tickets $25-80.

on the cheap

Cheap seats...

Should **Ticketmaster** (☎212-307-7171) fail to get you cheap tix, try the standby ticket distributor, **TKTS,** or any of the following options:

Rush Tickets: Some theaters distribute them on the morning of the performance; others make student rush tickets available 30min. before showtime. Get there *early* to beat the long lines.

Cancellation Line: Some theaters redistribute returned or unclaimed tickets a few hours before curtain. However, this might mean sacrificing your afternoon.

Sold-out Shows: Even if a show is sold out to the general public, theaters reserve prime house seats for VIPs. When no one important shows up, the theater sells them to the masses.

Standing-room Only: Sold on the day of the show, usually $15-20. Call first, as some theaters don't have standing room.

Hit Show Club: 630 Ninth Ave., between 44th and 45th St. (☎212-581-4211; www.hitshowclub.com). Map 14, B4, 61. Free service distributes coupons redeemable at the box office for over 1/3 off regular ticket prices. Call for coupons via mail or pick them up at the club office.

American Ballet Theatre, at the Metropolitan Opera House, Lincoln Center (☎212-477-3030, box office ☎362-6000; www.abt.org). See p. 95 for directions. This 64-year-old company (once headed by Mikhail Baryshnikov, now under the direction of Kevin McKenzie) puts on such opulent ballet classics as *Swan Lake, Romeo and Juliet,* and *Don Quixote.* It also performs more contemporary works by established modern choreographers like Twyla Tharp. Check with the box office for dates of "ABTalks," when dance writer Elizabeth Kaye hosts pre-performance talks focusing on the story behind that night's performance and cast. The ballet also performs at the City Center (p. 213). Tickets $17-75. Box office open June-Aug. M-F 10am-6pm; Sept.-May M-Sa 10am-8pm, Su noon-6pm.

De La Guarda, at the Daryl Roth Theater, 20 Union Sq. E., at 15th St. (☎212-239-6200; www.delaguardaonline.com). Subway: 4, 5, 6, L, N, Q, R, W to 14th St.-Union Sq.; L to Third Ave. Map 13, E6, 119. Think disco in the rain forest with an air show overhead: De la Guarda is an Argentinian performance art troupe whose shows are perpetually sold out. Tickets ($45-50) standing room only; a limited number are sold for $20 2hr. before each show. Box office open Su 1-7:15pm, Tu-Th 1-8:15pm, F 1-10:30pm, Sa 1-10pm.

Martha Graham Center of Contemporary Dance, 316 E. 63rd St. (☎212-838-5886; fax 212-838-0339; www.marthagrahamdance.org), is home to the **Martha Graham Dance Company** and eponymous school. Led by artistic directors Terese Capucilli and Christine Dakin, the company is dedicated to preserving legacy of Graham's revolutionary technique through performance of her work and other derivative pieces. Performances held at the City Center (see p. 213) Apr. 20-25, 2004.

New York City Ballet, at the New York State Theater, Lincoln Center (☎212-870-5570; www.nycballet.com). Founded by George Balanchine and now headed by former premier *danseur* Peter Martins, the company has put on critically acclaimed performances of works like *Serenade and Apollo.* It's most famous, however, for that New York Christmas tradition—George Balanchine's staging of *The Nutcracker* (Nov. 28-Jan. 4), replete with a 1-ton Christmas tree and spring's Balanchine production of A *Midsummer Night's Dream.* Call theater for week's listing of student rush tickets. Reserve early for this classic. Tickets ($16-88) can be purchased at the NY State Theater. Box office open M 10am-7:30pm, Tu-Sa 10am-8:30pm, Su 11:30am-7:30pm.

The Parsons Dance Company, 229 W. 42nd St. (☎212-869-9275; fax 212-944-7417; www.parsonsdance.org). Company performs newly commissioned works by modern dance choreographer David Parsons, known for such celebrated works as *Kind of*

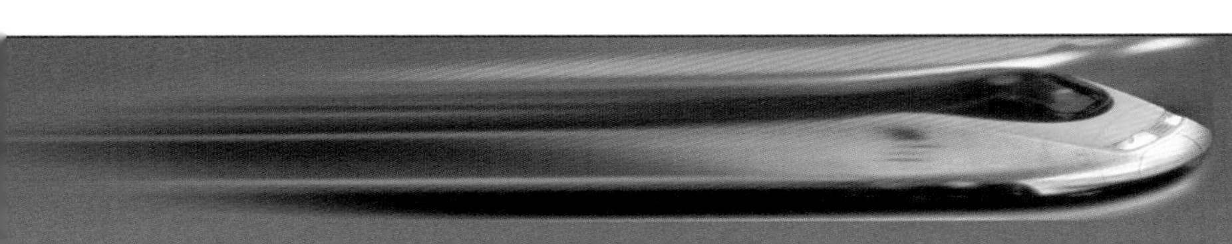

Blue, a tribute to 75th anniversary of birthday of Miles Davis, and *Closure.* Parsons also offers intensive summer programs and when company is in New York; see website for details on classes and performances.

VENUES

City Center, 130 W. 55th St., between Sixth and Seventh Ave. (☎212-581-1212 or outside NYC ☎877-581-1212). Subway: N, R, Q, W to 57th St./Seventh Ave.; B, D, E to Seventh Ave./53rd St.; 57th St./Ave. of the Americas (Sixth Ave.). Map 14, C2, 9. Manhattan's 1st performing arts center. Many companies perform here annually, including the Alvin Ailey American Dance Theater, Paul Taylor Dance Company, and American Ballet Theatre. Hosts events such as Rob Fisher and The Coffee Club Orchestra; long-time home of the Manhattan Theatre Club (p. 225), with its full season of plays and "Writers in Performance" series in City Center's Stage I and Stage II theaters. Box office open daily noon-8pm.

Dance Theater Workshop, 219 W. 19th St., between Seventh and Eighth Ave. (☎212-924-0077; www.dtw.org). Subway: 1, 9 to 18th St./Seventh Ave. Map 13, C5, 75. Supports emerging dancers, hosting innovative dance performances throughout the year. Students get one-third off regular ticket prices for most shows. Box office open M-F 10am-6pm.

Joyce Theater, 175 Eighth Ave., between 18th and 19th St. (☎242-0800; www.joyce.org). Subway: 1, 9 to 18th St./Seventh Ave. Map 13, B5, 67. *The* place to go for modern dance, the Joyce runs energetic, eclectic programming year-round. If you are in the city for a while, it may be worth it to buy a series of tickets to get a 40% discount. Such companies as the Parsons, Les Ballet Trockadero, and Pilobolus have all staged work at the Joyce. Tickets $25-40. Box office open daily from noon to 1hr. before 1st show (usually 7pm).

Mark Morris Dance Center, 3 Lafayette Ave., at Reade St., Downtown Brooklyn. (☎718-624-8400; www.mmdg.org). Subway: M, N, R, Q to Dekalb Ave. Map 22. Brooklyn-born Mark Morris leads one of America's leading dance troupes which finally has a permanent rehearsal space, right next to the **Brooklyn Academy of Music.** Check website for schedule. The center also offers dance classes for all ages.

Thalia Spanish Theater, 41-17 Greenpoint Ave., Sunnyside, Queens (☎718-729-3880; www.thaliatheatre.org). Subway: 7 to 40th St./Bowery St. Map 26, 23. Dedicated to the arts of Spanish-speaking cultures, the theater was showcasing exquisite dance performances long before the dance forms became popular. Thalia heats it up year-round with Tango, flamenco, and theater performances. Shows usually Th, Sa evenings and Sa 3pm. Dance performances F-Sa 8pm, Su 4pm. Tickets $25-30, students $22-25. Times and ticket prices change by show so call to double check.

...and more cheap seats

High 5 Tickets to the Arts: (☎212-445-8587; www.high5tix.org): Through this program, any junior high or high school student aged 13-18 can attend theater shows, concerts, and museum exhibitions for only $5. Proof of age required. Tickets, sold at all New York Ticketmaster locations, must be purchased at least 1 day before the performance.

Kids' Night on Broadway: (☎212-563-2929): Annual program, sponsored by TDF and the League of American Theatres, gives children aged 6-18 free admission (with purchase of 1 regularly priced ticket) on 4 specified nights. Tickets start selling in Oct.; performances Jan.-Feb.

CareTix: (☎212-840-0770, ext. 230): Sponsored by Broadway Cares/Equity Fights AIDS. Sells house seats for sold-out Broadway and off-Broadway shows, and for some non-theatrical events. Tickets are double the regular box office price, but it's for a good cause.

Audience Extras: (☎212-989-9550): Sells leftover tickets (many for prime house seats) to drama, dance, and musical performances. One-time membership fee $115, annual fee $85; after that, each ticket costs $3.50. Most tickets sold on a day-of-show basis.

FESTIVALS

Dances for Wave Hill, W. 249th St. and Independence Ave., Wave Hill, Bronx (☎718-549-3200). Subway: 1, 9 to 231st St. then Bx7 or Bx10 to 252 St. Map 28, B1, 2. Performances June and July every W, inspired by the Wave Hill landscape. Free with admission to **Wave Hill.** $4, students and seniors $2, under 6 and members free.

PARTICIPATORY EVENTS

Dancing on the Plaza, at Dana Discovery Center, Fifth Ave. and 110th St., Central Park (☎212-860-1370). See p. 86 for directions. Free dancing under the stars to sounds of salsa, classic disco, swing, and soul/R&B every Th in Aug. 6-8:30pm. First 45min. devoted to lessons for the toe-tied.

Midsummer Night Swing, outdoors in Lincoln Center Plaza, Columbus and 63rd St. (☎212-875-5766; www.lincolncenter.org). See p. 95 for directions. For the past 2 decades, some of the best names in jazz, big band, swing, Latin, and even line dancing have been coming to play at this exuberant month-long happening (late June-July). Come with or without a partner to dance the night away, see couples swishing around you, or merely to take in the ambience. If access to the plaza dance floor is sold out, you can strut your stuff (along with other hapless dancing feet) anywhere on the plaza. Tickets go on sale at the plaza at 5:45pm, but the line often begins at 5pm. Dancing 7:30-10pm; free lessons 6:30pm. Tickets $15(cash only); 6-night pass $78.

Warm Up, at P.S.1, 22-25 Jackson Ave., Long Island City, Queens (☎718-784-2084; www.ps1.org). See p. 142 for directions. Summer Saturdays seem slow? Popular showcase of DJs in P.S.1's outdoor courtyard should slake your thirst for dancing. For those who prefer others to do the dancing, performances in the museum begin at 6pm. Runs 3-9pm. Admission $5. Food and drinks offered for your enjoyment.

FILM

If you need any conclusive proof that Los Angeles indeed jocks New York's style, look no further than Tinseltown itself. Good movies often take place in New York City, while many movies set in California are bad. While we think this is no coincidence, you might be confused by such maddeningly intuitive logic. Fortunately, we have some statistics on our side: anywhere between 60 to 90 productions are on location in the city on a given day. The city encourages film production by granting free permits to those filmmakers who want to shoot on location; there is even a special police task force—the New York Police Movie and Television Unit—to assist with traffic re-routing and scenes involving guns or uniformed police officers.

Typical movie theaters showing big box office hits are easy to find in the city. Just look in any paper. The following listings are for theaters where you may find something special—institutes truly worthy of the world's theater capital.

American Museum of the Moving Image, 35th Ave., at 36th St., Astoria, Queens (☎718-784-0077; www.ammi.org). See p. 134 for directions. 3 full theaters showing everything from silent classics to retrospectives of great directors. $10, seniors and students $7.50, children under 12 $5. Free with admission to museum. Screenings Sa-Su; call for hours.

Angelika Film Center, 18 W. Houston St., at Mercer St. (☎212-995-2000; box office ☎995-2570). Subway: F, V, S to Broadway-Lafayette St.; N, R to Prince St.; 6 to Bleecker St.; C, E to Spring St./Ave. of the Americas (Sixth Ave.). Map 9, D1, 9; Map 10, F5, 89. "K" is for *Kultur:* 6 screens of alternative, independent, and foreign cinema. Handicapped seating available. Tickets $10, seniors and under 12 $6. Show up early on weekends; tickets frequently sell out far in advance.

Anthology Film Archives, 32 Second Ave., at E. 2nd St. (☎212-505-5181; www.anthologyfilmarchives.org). Subway: F, V to Lower East Side-Second Ave.; 6 to Bleecker St. Map 12, C4, 94. Housed in what used to be the Second Ave. Courthouse, this forum for independent films focuses on the contemporary, offbeat, and avant-garde, chosen from both US and foreign productions. The AFA hosts the annual **New York Underground Film Festival** (Mar.). Tickets $8, students and seniors $5. Tickets available day of show only, at the box office. Box office opens 30min. before 1st show of the day. Cash only.

BAMRose Cinemas, at the Brooklyn Academy of Music, 30 Lafayette Ave., Brooklyn. (☎718-636-4100; www.bam.org). Subway: 1, 2, 4, 5, Q to Atlantic Ave.; M, N, R, W to Pacific St. Map 22. New York's newest independent theater might also be its best. With a great selection of first-run and classic films, a tremendous array of special programs (including abundant opportunities to meet and hear filmmakers, actors, and the like), and a gorgeous space, BAMRose has lived up to the standard set by its well-established parent. $10, $7 students, $6 children and seniors.

Cinema Classics, 332 E. 11th St., between First and Second Ave. (☎212-677-5368; www.cinemaclassics.com). Subway: L to First Ave. Map 12, D2, 32. By day it may seem like your standard East Village cafe, but by night the screenings of arthouse films attract cineastes from all over. (Screenings around 8pm, 9pm and/or 10pm; $6). Beer $4, mixed drinks $5, coffee $2. Also an attached video store (open M-F 11:30am-7:30pm, Sa noon-6pm).

Cinema Village, 22 E. 12th St., between University Pl. and Fifth Ave. (☎212-924-3363). Subway: 4, 5, 6, N, R, W to 14th St.-Union Sq. Map 12, A1, 1. Features independent documentaries and hard-to-find foreign films. Wheelchair accessible. $9, students $7, children and seniors $5.50. Box office opens 30min. before first show, tickets available only day of show.

Film Forum, 209 W. Houston St., between Ave. of the Americas (Sixth Ave.) and Varick St. (☎212-727-8110). Subway: 1, 9 to Houston St.; E to Spring St./Ave. of the Americas (Sixth Ave.). Map 9, A1, 1. 3 screens with a strong selection in classics, foreign films, documentaries, and independent films. $9.75, under 12 $5, seniors $5 M-F before 5pm.

Millennium Film Workshop, 66 E. 4th St., between Bowery and Second Ave. (☎212-673-0090; www.millenniumfilm.org). Subway: F, V to Lower East Side-Second Ave. Map 12, C3, 71. More than just a theater, this media arts center presents an extensive program of experimental film and video, as well as offers classes and workshops on various aspects of filmmaking. Also has equipment available for use. Tickets $7. Call for showtimes.

Museum of Modern Art Film and Media, at the Gramercy Theatre, 127 E. 23rd St., between Lexington and Park Ave. (☎212-777-4900). Subway: F, J, M, Z to Essex St.-Delancey St. The renovating MoMA (p. 130) has launched its Film and Media exhibitions in its temporary new home at the historic Gramercy Theatre. Programs include an extensive inaugural international film preservation festival, a retrospective of the films of actress Delphine Seyrig, and a Richard Rodgers tribute, celebrating the centenary of the composer's birth. Admission $12, $8.50 for seniors and students (with ID). Friday screenings past 4 pm are "pay what you wish." Visitors will receive free admission to the theater with a MoMA QNS ticket stub dated from the previous 7 calendar days. A ticket stub from the Gramercy Theatre will also admit the bearer to MoMA QNS for up to 7 days from date of issue. Open M, Th, F 2pm; Sa-Su noon with additional screenings after 9pm.

New York Public Libraries: For a real deal, check out a library, any library. All show free films: documentaries, classics, and last year's blockbusters. Screening times may be a bit erratic, but you can't beat the price. (For complete info on New York libraries, see **Service Directory,** p. 326.)

Walter Reade Theater, 165 W. 65th St., at Lincoln Center (☎212-875-5600 or 496-3809; www.filmlinc.com). See p. 95 for directions. New York's performing arts octopus flexes yet another cultural tentacle with this theater next to the Juilliard School. Foreign and critically acclaimed independent films dominate. Home to June's acclaimed Human Rights Watch International Film Festival. Tickets $9.50, seniors $4.50 at weekday matinees, ages 5-12 $5. Children allowed only into "Movies for Kids" and "Reel to Real" screenings. Box office open daily 30min. before start of 1st film, closes 15min. after start of last show.

Ziegfeld, 141 W. 54th St., between Sixth and Seventh Ave. (☎212-765-7600). Subway: B, D, F to Rockefeller Center; N, R, Q to 57th St. Map 14, C2, 15. One of the largest screens left in America, showing first-run films. A must-visit for big-screen aficionados. Consult local newspapers for complete listings. Not handicapped accessible. $10, $6.50 for seniors (over 62) and under 11.

FESTIVALS

Bryant Park Film Festival, at Bryant Park, between 40th and 42nd St. and Sixth Ave. (☎212-512-5700). Subway: B, D, F, V to 42nd St./Ave. of the Americas (Sixth Ave.); 7 to Fifth Ave./42nd St. Map 14, D4. Running from mid-June to mid-Aug., this free outdoor series features classic revivals such as *On the Town, Bye Bye Birdie,* and *Young Frankenstein.* Movies begin M at sunset; rain date Tu nights.

New York Video Festival, at Walter Reade Theater in Lincoln Center (☎212-496-3809 or 875-5600; www.filmlinc.com). See p. 95 for directions. Runs in mid-July. $9.50, seniors $4.50 for weekday matinees, ages 5-12 $5. Prices may vary for special events. Call for ticket info.

Socrates Sculpture Park Film & Music Festival, at Socrates Sculpture Park, Long Island City, Queens (☎718-956-1819; www.socratessculpturepark.org). See p. 113 for directions. A series of free films from various cultures, preceded by musical performances and food from neighborhood restaurants. Performances start 7pm; movies start at sunset. Runs W evenings mid-July to late Aug. Call for schedule.

MUSIC

As one of New York's greatest filmmakers long ago realized, music is woven into the very fabric of the city. Woody Allen's *Manhattan* could not begin any other way than it does: the unity of the skyline and George Gershwin's *Rhapsody in Blue* is somehow completely obvious. Is it even surprising that Gershwin wrote the piece with its musical skeleton formed by the rhythm of his train rolling into New York?

From sweet vibrations to killer beats, New York is an unbeatable place to catch new music. Nearly every performer who comes to the States plays here, and thousands of local bands and DJs compete to make a statement and win an audience. Venues range from stadiums to concert halls to back-alley sound-systems. Every day of the year, clubs, bars, and smaller venues host everything from open-mic folk singers to "electronic" DJ recombinations. Annual festivals abound, such as summertime's **Next Wave Festival** that takes over the Brooklyn Academy of Music (see p. 228 for directions) with off-beat fusions of classical music, theater, and performance art.

CLASSICAL MUSIC

Musicians advertise themselves vigorously in New York City, so you should have no trouble finding the notes. Free recitals are common, especially in smaller spaces; just look in the *Voice, Time Out* and *The Free Time* calendar ($2) for listings of priceless events.

LINCOLN CENTER

Lincoln Center, between Columbus and Amsterdam Ave. and W. 62nd and 66th St. (see p. 95 for directions and background info), remains the great depot of New York's classical music. (☎212-875-5456; www.lincolncenter.org.) Regular tickets are pricey, but student and rush rates exist for select performances. You can buy all Lincoln Center tickets through **CenterCharge** (☎212-721-6500; open M-Sa 10am-8pm, Su noon-8pm) or online at **www.lincolncenter.org.** The **Alice Tully Hall** box office (☎212-875-5050; see p. 95 for directions) is open daily 11am to 6pm (opens Su at noon) and also until 30min. after the start of every performance. The **Avery Fisher Hall** box office (☎212-875-5030; see p. 95 for directions) is open daily from 10am to 6pm (opens Su at noon) and 30min. after the start of every performance.

Chamber Music Society, at Alice Tully Hall (☎212-875-5788; www.chambermusicsociety.org). Season Sept. 24-May 11. Tickets $27.50 and $37.50; some half-price student tickets can be purchased in advance. Student rush tickets ($10) also available at box office 1hr. before performance.

Great Performers Series, at Alice Tully and Avery Fisher Halls, and some other locations. A series that features quality classical music (with ticket prices to match), innovative programming, films, and occasional guests. 2004 Season includes 6 concerts of Louis Andriessen's work (May 1-15). Tickets generally $12-40, depending on event. Advance student tickets ($20) available through Avery Fisher Hall or Alice Tully Hall box offices; must be purchased at box office windows.

Mostly Mozart, at Alice Tully and Avery Fisher Halls. Summer festival (late July-late Aug.) features Mozart (plus some Schubert, Beethoven, and Haydn) performed by leading classical music performers. Tickets usually $25-50. 25% discount for Fleet customers. A few free events. Advance student tickets ($20) available through Avery Fisher Hall or Alice Tully Hall box offices or through Centercharge (☎212-721-6500).

National Chorale, at Avery Fisher Hall (☎212-333-5333). Choral music to make your soul soar. Season runs Dec. 5, 2003-Mar. 16, 2004. During the Christmas season, the Chorale puts on both the original Handel's *Messiah;* and a *Messiah* sing-in featuring audience participation. Tickets $27-88. Limited number of tickets may be available at Avery Fisher Hall box office to students with ID up until 3 days before performance (limit 2 tickets per ID).

New York Philharmonic, at Avery Fisher Hall (☎212-875-5656; www.newyorkphilharmonic.org). Perhaps the country's best orchestra. Previous Philharmonic directors include Leonard Bernstein, Arturo Toscanini, and Leopold Stokowski. Current director is Lorin Maazel. The '03/'04 season includes the series "Discovering the Revolutionary Genius of Charles Ives," "Beethoven Experience, all 9 Symphonies & 5 piano concertos" and fabulous holiday concerts. Season Sept. 18-June 21. Tickets $10-60. Limited number rush tickets ($10) may be available to students, senior citizens, and disabled persons on day of the performance, at the Avery Fisher Hall box office. ID is required, limit 2 tickets per ID; never available for F matinees or Sa evenings. Call ahead.

VENUES ELSEWHERE

Carnegie Hall, Seventh Ave., at 57th St. (CarnegieCharge: ☎212-247-7800). See p. 85 for directions. The New York Philharmonic's original home is still the favorite coming-out locale of musical debutantes. Top soloists and chamber groups are booked regularly. Some shows have $10 rush tickets for students and seniors—call for information. Box office open M-Sa 11am-6pm, Su noon-6pm.

Frick Collection, 1 E. 70th St., at Fifth Ave. (☎212-288-0700). See p. 132 for directions. The Frick Collection hosts free classical concerts twice a month from Sept. to May on Su and Tu at 5pm and 5:45pm respectively. Tickets limited to 2 per applicant (children under 10 not admitted), written requests must be received on the 3rd M before the concert and must be addressed to the Concert Department and enclosed in a stamped, self-addressed envelope. Or arrive 30min. early and try to take the seats of no-shows. Call the museum for a schedule. Museum open Su 1pm-6pm, Tu-Th and Sa 10am-6pm, F 10am-9pm. $12, seniors $8, students $5.

Metropolitan Museum of Art, 1000 Fifth Ave., at 82nd St. (☎212-570-3949 or 212-535-7710). See p. 128 for directions. The Met posts a schedule of performances covering the spectrum from traditional Japanese music and Russian *balalaika* to all-star classical music recitals Sept.-June. Call for info. Chamber music in bar and piano music in cafeteria F-Sa evenings; free with museum admission.

FESTIVALS

Concerts in the Park (☎212-875-5709; www.newyorkphilharmonic.org). See p. 86 for directions. In parks throughout the 5 boroughs and Long Island July-Aug. The Philharmonic plays magnificent outdoor concerts in parks during July. Concerts 8pm, followed by fireworks. Some (great) things in life *are* free.

Cooper-Hewitt Museum, 2 E. 91st St., at Fifth Ave. (☎212-849-8400). See p. 135 for directions. Free Cross-Currents concert series brings everything from classical to hip-hop to the museum's garden late June-July. Tu 6:30-8pm. July and August DJ dance parties F 6-9pm. Call ahead for schedule.

Apollo Theater

Carnegie Hall

Lenox Lounge

Bryant Park, (☎212-708-9491). See p. 78 for directions. "Summergarden," a contemporary classical music series, features Juilliard students performing behind the New York Public Library (p. 78). Sponsored by MoMA, this series used to be held in their sculpture garden. July-Aug. F-Sa at 6pm. Free.

MUSIC SCHOOLS

Visiting a music school promises low-cost, high-quality music—a panacea for a weary budget traveler's soul. Except for opera and ballet productions ($5-12), concerts at the following schools are free and frequent, especially during the school year (Sept.-May).

Bloomingdale School of Music, 323 W. 108th St., at Broadway (☎212-663-6021). Subway: 1 to Cathedral Pkwy. (110th St.)/Broadway. Map 18, B1, 2.

Juilliard School of Music, at Lincoln Center (☎769-7406; www.juilliard.edu). See p. 95 for directions. New York's most prominent music school. **Paul Recital Hall** hosts free student recitals Sept.-May almost daily. **Alice Tully Hall** (p. 95) holds larger student recitals, also free, Sept.-May most W at 1pm. Orchestral recitals and faculty performances, as well as chamber music, dance, and theater events take place regularly at Juilliard and never cost more than $10.

Manhattan School of Music, 122 Broadway, at Thames St. (☎212-749-2802). Subway: 1 to 116th St.

Mannes College of Music, 150 W. 85th St., between Columbus and Amsterdam Ave. (☎212-580-0210). Subway: 1, 2 to 86th St./Broadway. Map 18, C4, 17.

JAZZ

Since its beginnings, jazz has played a pivotal role in New York's music scene. Uptown at Minton's during the 50s, Charlie Parker, Dizzy Gillespie, and Thelonious Monk were overthrowing traditional swing and planting, arguably, the roots of such new musical movements as R&B and Rock n' Roll. Today, New York remains the jazz capital of the world. Its multitude of genres ranges from Big Band orchestras and traditional stylists to free, fusion, and avant-garde artists, thriving in venues throughout the city. Downtown's crowd is more young, funky, and commercialized; uptown in Harlem, you'll find a more intimate and smooth type of jazz. You can check out one of the many hazy dens that bred lingo like "cat" and "hip" (a "hippie" was originally someone on the fringes of jazz culture who talked the talk but was never really in the know), or more formal shows at Lincoln Center. Summer means open-air (often free) sets in parks and plazas. Check the papers to find listings of jazz venues around the city.

JAZZ CLUBS

You can expect high covers and drink minimums at the legendary jazz spots, but a few bars supply reliable up-and-comers free of charge. **Major credit cards accepted unless otherwise specified,** but call ahead to see which ones and bring cash just in case.

Apollo Theater, 253 W. 125th St., between Frederick Douglass and Adam Clayton Powell Blvd. (☎212-531-5301, box office ☎531-5305; www.apollotheater.com). Apollo Back Stage Tours (☎212-531-5337). Subway: A, B, C, D to 125th St./St. Nicholas Ave. Map 19, B5, 17. This Harlem landmark has heard Duke Ellington, Count Basie, Ella Fitzgerald, and Billie Holliday. A young Malcolm X shined shoes here. A big draw is Apollo's legendary and often televised Amateur Night ($13-30): the audience isn't shy about which acts they like (or don't). Some shows have age restrictions, but there are also many family shows. Order tickets through Ticketmaster (☎212-307-7171) or at the box office. Open M, Tu, Th, F 10am-6pm, W 10am-8:30pm. Call ahead for weekend hours.

Arthur's Tavern, 57 Grove St., between Bleecker and Seventh Ave. S (☎212-675-6879). Subway: 1, 9 to Christopher St. Map 10, B4, 45. A largely local crowd flocks to hear decent live jazz and blues played where Al Bundy jammed and Charlie Parker stomped. The dark and cavernous decor brightens with an animated crowd and swinging tunes. Features a full American-Italian menu. Drinks $7-8. No cover, but 2-drink minimum. Live jazz Tu-Sa 7-9pm, Dixieland jazz Su-M 8-11pm, blues/R&B Su-M 11pm-3am and Tu-Sa 9pm-3am. Open Su-M 8pm-3am, Tu-Th 6:30pm-3am, F-Sa 6:30pm-4am. Sets begin at 7pm. Cash only.

Birdland, 315 W. 44th St. between Eighth and Ninth Ave. (☎212-581-3080; www.birdland-jazz.com). Subway: 1, 2, 3, 7, 9, N, Q, R, S, W to 42nd St.-Times Sq. Map 14, B4, 64. Said by Charlie Parker to be the "jazz corner of the world," this dinner club serves up Cajun food and splendid jazz in a classy, neon-accented setting. The gumbo ($16) and the popcorn shrimp ($10) are as famous as the club itself. Music charge, including a complimentary drink $20-35. An additional $10 food/drink min. Reservations recommended for a table. Open daily 5pm-2am; 1st set nightly at 9pm, 2nd at 11pm.

Blue Note, 131 W. 3rd St., near Sixth Ave. (☎212-475-8592). Subway: A, C, E, F, V, S to W. 4th St. Map 10, D4, 58. The legendary jazz club is now more of a commercialized concert space, but the Blue Note still brings in many of today's all-stars (such as Take 6). Cover for big-name performers $20-70, M $10 for smaller acts. Students half-off cover Su-Th 10:30pm set only. For a great deal go during after-hours, when the cover for late-night jam sessions drops to $5 (F-Sa 1am-4am). $5 food/drink min. Set times 8pm and 10:30pm. Open Su-Th 7pm-midnight, F-Sa 7pm-4am.

Cotton Club, 656 W. 125th St., on the corner of Riverside Dr. (☎212-663-7980 or 800-640-7980; www.cottonclub-newyork.com). Subway: 1, 9 to 125th St./Broadway. Map 19, A5, 14. This jazz hall of greats like Lena Horne, Ethel Waters, and Calloway, is now often clogged with tourists. Swing Dance Big Band M evening. Buffet dinner and jazz show Th-Sa evenings. M and Th-Sa evenings 21+; brunch all ages; call for age restrictions at other events. Su brunch and Gospel Shows $25 (2 shows; noon and 2:30pm); jazz shows $32; dinner included. Call ahead (2 weeks is standard) for reservations and schedule.

Detour, 349 E. 13th St., between First and Second Ave. (☎212-533-6212; www.jazzat-detour.com). Subway: L to First Ave. Map 12, D1, 7. Municipally acclaimed nightly jazz and no cover—a perfect mix. Wheelchair-accessible. 2-drink min. Mixed drinks ($6), bottled beer ($4-5). Happy Hour daily 4-7pm, $3 beers. 21+. Open Su-Tu 4pm-2am, W-Sa 4pm-4am.

Fez, 380 Lafayette St., between 3rd and 4th St., under Time Cafe (☎212-533-2680). Subway: 6 to Bleecker St. Map 12, B4, 87. Lushly appointed, Moroccan-decorated performance club draws extremely photogenic crowd, especially on Th nights when Mingus Big Band holds court. $18, students pay $10 for 2nd set. Cover $5-30; 2-drink min. Reservations suggested. Sets 7:30pm and 10pm. Open Su-Th 6pm-2am, F-Sa 6pm-4am. Cash only at the door but credit cards accepted for food and drink.

Lenox Lounge, 288 Lenox (Sixth) Ave., between 124th and 125th St. (☎212-427-0253). Subway: 2, 3 to 125th St./Lenox (Sixth) Ave. Map 19, C5, 24. This lounge is quintessential Harlem: intimate, offbeat, and bursting with great jazz. Still sporting the original 1939 decor.

With smooth red booths and tiled floors, this lounge is one of Harlem's gems. Jazz, blues, and R&B Th-Su, jam session M night. 21+. Prices vary (up to $15 cover, 2-drink min. 3 shows 9, 10:45pm, 12:30am. Open daily 11am-4am.

101 Club, 101 Seventh Ave. S., at Grove St. (☎212-620-4000). Subway: 1, 9 to Christopher St. Map 10, B4, 44. Jumping spot is hard to pass by. Eclectic crowd listens to live jazz, funk, soul, and rock nightly. Beer $5.50. Mixed drinks $6-8. Happy Hour 6-9pm, all drinks half-price. 21+. No cover, but 1-drink min. Open Su-Th 6pm-3am, F-Sa 6pm-4am.

St. Nick's Pub, 773 St. Nicholas Ave., at 149th St. (☎212-283-9728). Subway: A, B, C, D to 145th St./St. Nicholas Ave. Map 19, B3, 4. Small and unpretentious with a dedicated crowd, this pub is one of Harlem's legends with live entertainment every night. Mixed drinks $6-7. The Sugar Hill Jazz Quartet hosts a great laid-back jam session M nights. Cover $3, or 2 people for $5 with 2-drink min. Bar opens at 12:30pm, shows M-Su 9:30pm until 2 or 3am.

Showman's Cafe, 375 W. 125th St., between St. Nicholas and Morningside Ave. (☎212-864-8941). Subway: A, B, C, D to 125th St./St. Nicholas Ave. Map 19, B5, 16. This cozy jazz club attracts a largely local crowd for nightly shows and friendly company. Showtimes M-Th 8:30, 10, 11:30pm; F-Sa 10:30pm, 12:30, 2:30am. 21+. 2-drink min. per person per show. Open M-Sa noon-4am.

Smoke, 2751 Broadway, between 105th and 106th St. (☎212-864-6662). Subway: 1, 9 to 103rd St.-Broadway. Map 18, B1, 6. Sultry cocktail lounge jumps with excellent jazz nightly. Although slightly congested, the intimate space swells with music and an animated atmosphere. M jam sessions, Tu Hammond organ and soul jazz, W Funk, Th electric acid jazz and fusion, Su Latin. Retro Happy Hour daily 5-8pm has $3 mixed drinks, $2 pint Woodpecker cider, $2 off other drinks. Happy Hammond Hour has live jazz Tu-Th 5-8pm. F-Sa smoke-free 9pm sets. 21+. F-Sa cover $16-20, depending on band. $10 drink min. per person per set. Sets usually at 9, 10pm, 12:30am. Open daily 5pm-4am.

Swing 46, 349 W. 46th St., between Eighth and Ninth Ave. (☎212-262-9554; www.swing46.com). Map 14, B4, 59. This jazz and supper club has jumped onto the big band wagon and delivers all kinds of smooth grooves like Swingtime M, Jump Tu, and Big Band Th. Su draws a devoted crowd with Buster Brown's Crazy Tap Jam. Dinner ($14-24) served daily 5pm-midnight. Happy Hour (half-price drinks) daily 5-7:30pm. 18+ to dance. Cover includes swing lessons at 9:15pm. Cover $15 for the bar, $10 main room, 2-drink or $12 min. (drinks $10-16). Sets begin at 10:30pm. Open daily 5pm-3am.

Village Vanguard, 178 Seventh Ave., between W. 11th and Greenwich St. (☎212-255-4037). Subway: 1, 2, 3 to 14th St./Seventh Ave. Map 10, B2, 24. Bright, red walls lead you downstairs to this windowless, wedge-shaped basement den 65-years-thick with memories of Lenny Bruce, Leadbelly, Miles Davis, and Sonny Rollins. Every M, the Vanguard Orchestra unleashes its torrential Big Band sound on sentimental journeymen at 9:30 and 11:30pm. All ages welcome. Cover Su-Th $15, F-Sa $20 plus $10 drink min. Sets Su-Th 9pm and 11pm. F-Sa 9, 11pm and sometimes 12:30am. Reservations recommended. Cash and traveler's checks only.

OTHER JAZZ VENUES

Jazz at Lincoln Center, Lincoln Center. (☎212-258-9800; www.jazzatlincolncenter.org). See p. 95 for directions. Year-round festival celebrating one of America's great music forms, led by Artistic Director Wynton Marsalis. Plans are afoot for a $128 million, 100,000 sq. ft. jazz-specific performance space above Central Park.

Saint Peter's Lutheran Church, 619 Lexington Ave., at 52nd St., at the Citicorp Center (☎212-935-2200). Subway: E, V, 6 to 51 St./Lexington Ave. Map 14, E2, 28. Su jazz vespers at 5pm, usually followed at 7pm by a jazz concert ($5-10 donation for the concert). Informal jazz concerts often held W evenings at 6pm. 1 night in Oct. is set aside for the annual All Night Soul session rocking from 5pm-5am. Call ahead for current schedule of St. Peter's offerings. Dale R. Lind, Pastor to the Jazz Community, oversees all tuneful good deeds.

SUMMER JAZZ AND FESTIVALS

The **JVC Jazz Festival** comes into the city from June to July. All-star performances of past series have included Elvin Jones, Ray Charles, Tito Puente, and Mel Torme. Tickets go on sale in early May, but many events take place outdoors in the parks and are free. Check the newspaper for listings. **Damrosch Park** at Lincoln Center, Columbus Ave., between 62nd and 66th St., hosts a large number of these concerts; so does **Bryant Park,** Sixth Ave., between 40th and 42nd St., which also hosts events throughout the summer. For directions to **Damrosch Park**, see p. 86; for directions to Bryant Park, see p. 78 (call ☎212-501-1390 or 496-9000 for info, or write to: JVC Jazz Festival New York, P.O. Box 1169, New York, NY 10023.) Annual festivals sponsored by major corporations bring in local talent and industry giants on the forefront of innovation. The concerts take place throughout the city (some free) but center around TriBeCa's **Knitting Factory** (p. 229).

Central Park Summerstage, at 72nd St. in Central Park (☎212-360-2777), divides its attention among many performing arts, including jazz. See p. 86 for directions. Call or pick up Central Park's calendar of events, available at the Dairy in Central Park (p. 87). The free concerts run from mid-June to early August.

The **World Financial Center Plaza** (☎212-945-0505 or 646-772-6835), occasionally hosts free concerts between June and September as part of the **Hudson River Festival.** See p. 52 for directions. The festival features such jazz performers as Little Jimmy Scott and the Kit McClure Big Band, an all-female jazz orchestra. The **South Street Seaport** (☎212-732-7678) sponsors a series of outdoor concerts from July to early September at Pier 17, Ambrose Stage, and the Atrium. See p. 54 for directions.

OPERA

Dicapo Opera Company, at the Dicapo Opera Theater, 184 E. 76th St., between Third and Lexington Ave. (☎212-288-9438; www.dicapo.com). Subway: 6 to 77th St. Map 15, B5, 29. This East Side opera company has been earning critical acclaim and standing ovations at every performance—it's easy to understand why tickets go very quickly (usually around $40, senior discounts available). Showtimes Th-Sa 8pm and Su 4pm.

The Metropolitan Opera Company, at the Lincoln Center's Metropolitan Opera House (☎212-362-6000; www.metopera.org). See p. 95 for directions. North America's premier opera outfit, performing on a stage as big as a football field. James Levine conducts the likes of Placido Domingo and Deborah Voigt in new productions and favorite repertory classics. Regular tickets can be as much as $195, so go for the upper balcony at around $65—the cheapest seats have an obstructed view. Tickets for M-Th performances ($60-165) are cheaper than weekend nights ($65-195). You can stand in the orchestra ($16) along with the opera buffs who've brought along the score, or all the way back in the Family Circle ($12). Season Sept.-May. M-Sa; box office open from Aug. 25. to the end of May, M-Sa 10am-8pm, Su noon-6pm. In summer, call for info on free park concerts.

The New York City Opera, at the New York State Theater, Lincoln Center (☎212-870-5630; 870-5570 or for tickets ☎496-0600). See p. 95 for directions. It may not be the juggernaut that the Met Opera is, but this smaller opera company has gained a reputation for inventive programming under the direction of Paul Kellogg. 2003-04 season includes classics such as *Madame Butterfly, Carmen,* and *The Magic Flute.* City now has a split season (Sept. 10-Nov. 24 and Mar. 11-Apr. 27), and keeps its ticket prices low year-round ($25-92). Limited number of rush tickets ($10) are available to students and seniors with valid ID; these can only be purchased at the New York State Theater Box Office on the day of performance. Box office open M 10am-7:30pm, Tu-Sa 10am-8:30pm, Su 11:30am-7:30pm.

ROCK, POP, PUNK, FUNK

Music festivals are hot tickets and provide the opportunity to see tons of bands at a (relatively) low price. The **CMJ Music Marathon** (☎917-606-1908; www.cmj.com) runs for four nights in the fall and includes over 400 bands and workshops on alternative music culture and college radio production. **The Digital Club Festival** (☎212-677-3530), a newly reconfigured indie-fest, visits New York in late July. The **Macintosh New York Music Festival** presents over 350 bands over a week-long period. For more electronic experimental sounds, check out

Creative Time's **Music in the Anchorage** (☎212-206-6674), a June concert series happening in the massive stone chambers in the base of the Brooklyn Bridge. See p. 104 for directions.

If arena rock is more your style, check out **Madison Square Garden** (☎212-465-6000), perhaps America's premier entertainment facility. See p. 76 for directions. MSG hosts over 600 events and nearly 6,000,000 spectators every year. New Jersey's **Meadowlands** (☎201-935-3900) and the **Nassau Coliseum** (☎516-888-9000) also stage high-priced performances. From June to early September the **Coca-Cola Concert Series** (☎516-221-1000) brings rock, jazz, and reggae concerts to Jones Beach. (Tickets $15-40. See **Long Island,** p. 279, for transportation info.)

Arlene Grocery and Butcher Bar, 95 Stanton St., between Ludlow and Orchard St. (☎212-358-1633; www.arlene-grocery.com). Subway: F, V to Lower East Side-Second Ave. Map 11, E1, 19. Hosts at least 3 bands back-to-back every night. Mostly local indie acts, but big names like Sheryl Crow have also played in this intimate space. Bob Dylan once stopped by, but only to use the bathroom. Stop by next door at the Butcher Bar–a leg of the "grocery" where drafts cost $5. M has Punk-rock Karaoke. 21+. Cover $7 Th-Su unless otherwise stated. Show starts 7pm.

The Bitter End, 147 Bleecker St., between Thompson and LaGuardia Pl. (☎212-673-7030; www.bitterend.com). Subway: A, C, E, F, V, S to W. 4th St.; F, V, S to Broadway-Lafayette St.; 6 to Bleecker St. Map 10, E5, 85. Small space hosting folk, country, and roots rock acts claims that artists like Billy Joel, Stevie Wonder, Woody Allen, and Rita Rudner performed here as unknowns. Look for their likenesses in the gaudy mural. Features prominently in Ethan Hawke's debut novel, *the Hottest State.* Usually 21+, sometimes 18+. Cover $5-12. Call for show times. Open Su-Th 7:30pm-2am, F-Sa 7:30pm-4am.

Bottom Line, 15. W. 4th St., at Mercer St. (info ☎212-228-7880; box office ☎228-6300; www.bottomlinecabaret.com). Subway: A, C, E, F, V, S to W. 4th St.; F, V, S to Broadway-Lafayette St.; 6 to Astor Pl.; N, R to 8th St.-NYU. Map 10, F4, 66. Large gothic venue with mixed bag of music entertainment–jazz, kitsch, country, theater, and rock-and-roll by over-the-hill singers. Crowd and mood vary: recent shows have run the gamut from Roger McGuinn to Broadway diva Betty Buckley. 21+ (double proof of age required), or come with parent/legal guardian. Some all-ages performances. Cover $15-25; shows nightly 7:30 and 10:30 pm.

Bowery Ballroom, 6 Delancey St., between Chrystie St. and Bowery (☎212-533-2111; or tickets ☎866-468-7619). Subway: J, M, Z to Bowery. Map 11, D3, 32. This medium-sized club retains some of the details from its original 1929 Beaux Arts construction. Attracts popular bands, and its stage has recently been graced by REM, the Black Crowes, and the Red Hot Chili Peppers. Cover and min. age restrictions vary with event. Tickets $10-20; you must buy them at least 1 day in advance. Box office at **Mercury Lounge** (see p. 223).

Cafe Wha?, 115 MacDougal St., between Bleecker and W. 3rd St. (☎212-254-3706). Subway: A, C, E, F, V, S to W. 4th St. Map 10, D5, 78. In the 1960s, this "beat/rock" club was famous for both its regular customers (Allen Ginsberg, Abbie Hoffman, and Bob Dylan) and its musical and comedy performers (Jimi Hendrix, Bruce Springsteen, Kool and the Gang, Bill Cosby, Richard Pryor). Mary Travers (of Peter, Paul and Mary fame) was a waitress here. Live music nightly. Beer $4.50, mixed drinks $5.50-$6.50. Tu Vintage Funk and Soul. W-Su Cafe Wha Band (rock, R&B, funk, reggae). 21+. Cover M and F-Sa $10, Tu $7, Th $5, W and Su free. Open Su-Th 8:30pm-2:30am, F-Sa 8:30pm-3am.

CBGB/OMFUG (CBGB's), 315 Bowery, at Bleecker St. (☎212-982-4052). Subway: F, V to Lower East Side-Second Ave.; 6 to Bleecker St. Map 12, C4, 92. Initials have stood for "country, bluegrass, blues, and other music for uplifting gourmandizers" since its 1973 opening, but the New York Dolls, Television, the Ramones, Patti Smith, and Talking Heads rendered this venue synonymous with punk. Music remains loud, raw, hungry. Shows nightly around 8pm. 16+. Cover $3-10. Next door, **CB's Gallery,** 313 Bowery (☎212-677-0455), has softer live music.

Continental, 25 Third Ave., at Stuyvesant St. (☎212-529-6924; www.continentalnyc.com). Subway: 6 to Astor Pl. Map 12, C2, 26. Dark club hosts loud set nightly. Come for noise, rock, and local punk. Iggy Pop, Debbie Harry, and Patti Smith have all played here recently. Check lamp posts and fliers for shows and times. Shot of anything $2 with a beer. Happy Hour daily, half-price drinks. Usually 21+. Cover, if required, up to $7.

Elbow Room, 144 Bleecker St., between Thompson St. and LaGuardia Pl. (☎212-979-8434). Subway: A, C, E, F, V, S to W. 4th St.; F, V, S to Broadway-Lafayette St.; 6 to Bleecker St. Map 10, E5, 85. Features 3-6 live bands nightly playing rock and live hip-hop to a house that seats 400. Call for nightly schedule. Usually 21+, sometimes 18+. Cover usually Tu-Th $7, F-Sa $10. Open Tu-Th 7:30pm-2:30am, F-Sa 7pm-4am.

Irving Plaza, 17 Irving Pl., at 15th St. (☎777-6800 or concert info ☎777-1224; www.irvingplaza.com). Subway: 4, 5, 6, L, N, Q, R, W to 14th St.-Union Sq; L to Third Ave. Map 13, E6, 120. A mid-sized club decorated in opulent chinoiserie style. Primarily musical acts (2003 included Interpol, the Flaming Lips, and El-P). Calendar also includes comedy, performance art, and other entertainment. Purchase tickets in advance for the bigger shows. "Savoy Sundays" feature live big bands and swing dancing ($13, seniors $5; doors open 7pm; bands play 8pm-midnight). Under 16 must come with parent or guardian. Cover varies, generally $15-25. Doors generally open at 8pm. Box office open M-F noon-6:30pm, Sa 1-4pm.

Mercury Lounge, 217 E. Houston St., between Essex and Ludlow St. (☎212-260-4700; www.mercuryloungenyc.com). Subway: F to Delancey St. Map 11, E1, 12. This converted gravestone parlor has attracted an amazing number and range of big-name acts, from folk to pop to noise, to its fairly small-time room. Past standouts include spoken-word artist Maggie Estep, Morphine, and Mary Lou Lord. Spectacular sound system attracts arbiters of hip to nightly shows. Cover varies. Box office open M-Sa noon-7pm. Cash only.

Roseland Ballroom, 239 W. 52nd St., between Broadway and Eighth Ave. (☎212-777-6800 or 777-6800). Subway: 1, 9 to 50th St.-Broadway; C, E to 50th St.-Eighth Ave. Map 14, C3, 32. Sizzling in the 40s as a swing dance hall, the ballroom is now a decently priced concert club featuring major-label alt-rock and hip-hop. Bob Dylan, Dave Matthews, Beck, Jamiroquai, and many others have recently played this newly renovated space. Tickets $15-30.

SOBs (Sounds of Brazil), 204 Varick St., at W. Houston St. (☎212-243-4940; www.sobs.com). Subway: 1, 9 to Houston St. Dinner club that has some of NYC's best live music. Weekly 'Basement Bhangra' has blown up in the past year, and SOBs continues to attract hip-hop's best talent. Recent acts have included Talib Kweli, Blackalicious, and Black Eyed Peas. Box office (located next door at 200 Varick St.) open M-F 11am-5pm, Sa noon-6pm. Cash only.

Southpaw, 125 Fifth Ave., between Sterling and St. John's Pl., Brooklyn. (☎718230-0236; www.spsounds.com). Subway: M, N, R, to Union St.; Q to Seventh Ave.; 2, 3 to Bergen St. New club in Park Slope hosts DJs, local musicians, and well-known talent. 2003 highlights included Sleater-Kinney, Elliott Smith, and Luna.

Tonic, 107 Norfolk St., between Delancey and Rivington St. (☎212-358-7501; www.tonic-nyc.com). Subway: F to Delancey St. Map 11, E2, 30. This converted wine brewery hosts a small-sized performance space for avant-garde musicians. In the downstairs lounge, enormous wine barrels have been carved open and filled with chairs and couches for seating. Su brunch with band. 18+. Cover performance space $6-12; downstairs lounge with DJ no cover; Su klezmer music brunch $10. Evening performance times vary. Lounge open daily 9pm-3am.

THEATER

Broadway war-horses like *The Phantom of the Opera* and *Les Misérables* have ushered armies of tourists, senior citizens, and suburbanites through the theater doors for interminable runs. The recent resurrection of Broadway has triggered an equally vibrant theater scene throughout the city—not only off-Broadway and off-off-Broadway, but also in dance and studio spaces, museums, cafes, parks, and even parking lots.

Broadway tickets usually start from $50, but many money-saving schemes exist (see **Cheap Seats,** p. 212). **TKTS** sells tickets for many Broadway and some larger off-Broadway shows at a 25-50% discount on the day of the performance. The lines begin to form an hour or so before the booths open, but they move fairly quickly. More tickets become available as showtime approaches, so you may find fewer possibilities if you go too early. (☎212-768-1818. Duffy Sq., at 47th St. and Broadway. Map 14, C4, 68. Tickets sold M-Sa 3-8pm for 8pm evening performances, Tu 2pm-8pm, W and Sa 10am-2pm for matinees, and Su 11am-7pm for matinees and evening performances.)

The **Theatre Development Fund** (☎212-221-0885; www.tdf.org.) offers discount vouchers for off- and off-off-Broadway productions, as well as for other events sponsored by small, independent production companies. Those eligible—students, teachers, performing-arts professionals, retirees, union and armed forces members, and clergy—must first join the TDF mailing list by sending in an application and $20. Once you are a member, which may take 6-8 weeks after you turn in the application, you can purchase four vouchers for $28. These are redeemable at the box office of any participating production.

You may reserve full-price tickets over the phone and pay by credit card using **Tele-Charge** (☎212-239-6200, outside NYC ☎800-432-7250; www.telecharge.com; 24hr.) for Broadway shows; **Ticket Central** (☎212-279-4200; www.ticketcentral.org) for off-Broadway shows; and **Ticketmaster** (☎212-307-4100, outside NYC ☎800-755-4000; www.ticketmaster.com; 24hr.) for all types of shows. All three services have a per-ticket service charge, so ask before purchasing. You can avoid these fees if you buy tickets directly from the box office.

BROADWAY

Subway: C, E to 50th St./Eighth Ave.; 1, 9 to 50th St./Broadway; N, R, W to 49th St./Seventh Ave.; A, C, E to 42nd St.-Port Authority; 1, 2, 3, 7, 9, N, Q, R, S, W to 42nd St.-Times Sq.

Most Broadway theaters are north of Times Square and are not actually on Broadway itself, but between Eighth Ave. and Broadway. Here's a list of some current blockbusters. For more information, go to www.nytheatre.com.

Aida, Palace Theatre, 1564 Broadway at 47th St., (www.disneyonbroadway.com). Map 14. Tickets $25-100.

Beauty and the Beast, Lunt-Fontanne Theatre, 205 W. 46th St., at Broadway (www.disneyonbroadway.com). Map 13, C4, 56. Megan McGinnis as Belle, Steve Blanchard as Beast. Tickets $30-85.

Cabaret, Studio 54, 254 W. 54th St., between Broadway and Eighth Ave. (www.cabaret54.com). Map 13, C2, 8. Tickets $45-90.

Chicago, Ambassador Theater, 215 W. 49th St. (www.chicagothemusical.com). Map 13, C4, 66. Excellent revival with stunning choreography by Anne Reinking. Winner of 6 1997 Tony Awards. $20 tickets available at box office 10am day of performance, subject to availability (2 per person, line forms early). Tickets $42.50-90.

42nd Street, Ford Center for the Performing Arts, 213 W. 42nd St. (www.42ndstreetbroadway.com). Winner of 2 Tony Awards. Tickets $30-100.

Hairspray, Neil Simon Theater, 250 W. 52nd St. (www.hairsprayonbroadway.com). Winner of 8 Tony Awards including Best Musical.

The Lion King, New Amsterdam Theater, 216 W. 42nd St., at Eighth Ave. (www.disneyonbroadway.com). Map 14, B4, 66. The intricate costumes and actors' graceful body movements make this elaborate show an aesthetic masterpiece. $20 rush tickets available 10am day of performance. Tickets $25-90.

Mamma Mia! Cadillac Winter Garden Theatre, 1534 Broadway at 50th St. (www.mamma-mia.com). Tickets $56-100.

Phantom of the Opera, Majestic Theater, 247 W. 44th St., between Broadway and Eighth Ave. (www.thephantomoftheopera.com). Map 14, C4, 73. Classic Broadway production. Tickets $20-85.

The Producers, St. James Theater, 246 W. 44th St., between Broadway and Eighth Ave. (www.producersonbroadway.com). Map 14, C4, 73. This Mel Brooks musical won a record 12 Tony Awards in 2001. Based on a 1967 movie, the extremely popular show stars Brad Oscar and Stephen Weber. Tickets $35-99.

Rent, Nederlander Theater, 208 W. 41st St., at Eighth Ave. (www.siteforrent.com). Map 14, B5, 89. Modern version of *La Bohème* set in NYC. $20 evening show tickets available after 5:30pm; line-up at the box office for 6pm lottery; 2 tickets per person, cash only. Tickets $35-80.

Urinetown, Henry Miller's Theater, 124 W. 43rd St. (www.urinetown.com), between Broadway and Sixth Ave. WInner of 3 Tony Awards and 3 Outer Critics Circle Awards. Tickets $35-95.

OFF-BROADWAY

Off-Broadway theaters, by definition, feature less mainstream presentations for crowds of 499 or fewer. Runs are generally short; nonetheless, shows occasionally jump to Broadway houses (as in the case of *Rent*). Many of the best off-Broadway houses huddle in the Sheridan Sq. area of the West Village, while others are located to the west of Times Square. Off-Broadway tickets cost $15-45. You may see shows for free by arranging to usher; this usually entails dressing neatly and showing up at the theater around 45min. ahead of curtain, helping to seat ticket-holders, and then staying after the performance to clean up. Speak with the house manager far in advance.

Listings and reviews appear the first Wednesday of every month in **Simon Says,** a *Village Voice* guide tailored to unconventional theater happenings around the city. Other publications with theater listings include *New York* magazine, the *New York Press*, the *New Yorker*, and *Time Out: New York*.

Actors Playhouse, 100 Seventh Ave. S., between Christopher and Bleecker St. (☎212-463-0060). Subway: 1, 9 to Christopher St. Map 10, B4, 49. For fans of the flesh and also, of comedy, "Naked Boys Singing" is in its 5th year of production. Tickets $35-65. Box office open 3-8pm on show days and Sa-Su noon-8pm.

Astor Place Theater, 436 Lafayette St., between E. 4th St. and Astor Pl. (☎212-800-258-3626). Subway: 6 to Astor Pl.; N, R to 8th St.-NYU. Map 12, C2, 31. Home to infectious *Blue Man Group*. Tickets $55-65. Box office open daily noon-8pm or until 15min. before last show. Shows Su 4, 7 and 10pm; Tu-Th 8pm; F 7 and 10pm; Sa 2, 5 and 8pm.

Charlie Pineapple Theater, 208 N. 8th St., at Driggs Ave., Brooklyn. (☎718-907-0577; www.charliepineapple.com). Subway: L to Bedford Ave. A small independent theater that houses a weekly improv troupe. Check the website for events and shows. A small cafe for intermissions serves beer and snacks. Call or check website for hours.

Cherry Lane Theater, 38 Commerce St., at Bedford St. (☎212-989-2020). Subway: 1, 9 to Christopher St., Houston St. Map 10, B5, 70. New York's oldest continuously-running off-broadway theater. This converted box-factory has hosted a slew of magnificent plays by famous playwrights such as Beckett, Albee, O'Neill, and others. Tickets $35-55. An alternative theater in the same building has more experimental productions. Tickets $12. Box office open Tu-F 3pm-8pm, Sa 3pm-10pm.

Joseph Papp Public Theater, 425 Lafayette St., between E. 4th St. and Astor Pl. (☎212-539-8750). Subway: 6 to Astor Pl.; N, R to 8th St.-NYU. Map 12, B3, 59. Built orginally as a library by J. J. Astor, it now houses 6 venues, which present a wide variety of productions and have hosted a decade-long marathon of Shakespeare's every last work, right down to *Timon of Athens*. **Shakespeare in the Park** (p. 231) tickets (which are free!) handed out at the box office. (Folks generally start lining up by 8 or 9am; 2 tix per person for that night's show only. Advance tickets available for purchase). Box office open Su-M 1pm-6pm, Tu-Sa 1pm-7:30pm.

Lamb's, 130 W. 44th St., between Sixth and Seventh Ave. (☎212-575-0300). Subway: 1, 2, 3, 7, 9, N, Q, R, S, W to 42nd St.-Times Sq.; B, D, F, V to 42nd St./Ave. of the Americas (Sixth Ave.). Map 14, C4, 75. A 349-seat theater and a 29-seater host family-oriented plays and musicals. Tickets $25-35.

Manhattan Theatre Club, at City Center, 131 W. 55th St., between Broadway and Seventh Ave. (☎212-399-3000 or 212-581-1212). Subway: N, R, Q, W to 57th St./Seventh Ave.; F to 57th St./Ave. of the Americas; B, D, E to Seventh Ave./53rd St. Map 14, C2, 7. A popular venue for new plays. Tickets $45-60.

New York Theatre Workshop, 79 E. 4th St., between Bowery and Second Ave. (☎212-460-5475; www.nytw.org). Subway: 6 to Astor Pl.; F, V to Lower East Side-Second Ave.; F, V, S to Broadway-Lafayette St. Map 12, C3, 72. Small (150-seat) theater. Line for cheap tickets ($10, 2 per person, cash only) 2hr. before curtain. Student tickets $15; seniors $28. Wheelchair accessible. Box office open Tu-Sa 1-6pm.

Orpheum, 126 Second Ave., between E. 7th St. and St. Mark's Pl. (☎212-477-2477; www.stomponline.com). Subway: 6 to Astor Pl. Map 12, C2, 31. Now playing *Stomp*: a percussive feast that uses household items for instruments. Shows: Tu-F 8pm; Sa 7 and 10:30pm; Su 3 and 7pm. Tickets $55-60. Box office open M 1-6pm, Tu-F 1-7pm, Sa 1-9pm, Su noon-6pm.

Primary Stages, 354 W. 45th St., between Eighth and Ninth Ave. (☎212-333-4052; www.primarystage.com). Subway: A, C, E to 42nd St.-Port Authority. Map 14, B4, 63. This theater, opening its 18th season, features new American plays. Box office open daily noon-6pm, when there is a show. Call for details.

Samuel Beckett Theater, 410 W. 42nd St., between Ninth and Tenth Ave. (☎212-574-2826). Subway: A, C, E to 42nd St.-Port Authority. Map 14, B4, 65. Mostly productions of contemporary drama, sometimes including post-performance discussions with members of the cast. Tickets $45, students and seniors $35. Box office open Su noon-3pm; Tu and Th-F noon-8pm; W noon-3:30 and 5-8pm; Sa noon-3pm and 5:30-8pm.

SoHo Repertory Theatre, 46 Walker St., between Broadway and Church St. (☎212-941-8632; reservations ☎946-5469). Subway: 1, 9 to Franklin St.; A, C, E to Canal St./Sixth Ave.; N, Q, R, W to Canal St./Broadway. Map 9, C5, 45. Tickets $8-25.

SoHo Think Tank Ohio Theater, 66 Wooster St., between Spring and Broome St. (☎212-966-4844). Subway: 1, 9 to Canal St./Varick St.; A, C, E to Canal St./Sixth Ave.; N, Q, R, W to Canal St./Broadway. Map 9, C3, 27. Provocative intellectual pieces combining theater, performance art, dancing, and sketch comedy. "Cafe Ohio" opens before shows at 6pm for "drinks and conversation." $15. Shows usually W-Sa at 7pm.

Theater for the New City, 155 First Ave., between E. Ninth and 10th St. (☎212-254-1109; www.theaterforthenewcity.com). Subway: 6 to Astor Pl. Map 12, D2, 39. New avant-garde productions. Dispatches a roving theater troupe throughout the city that performs in parks and streets (late July-Sept.; free; call for locations). Box office open 30min. before showtime. Houses a cool lefty, admirably irreverent bookstore. Tickets around $10. Shows Th-Su 8pm.

Union Square Theatre, 100 E. 17th St., at Union Sq. E. (☎212-505-0700). Subway: 4, 5, 6, L, N, Q, R, W to 14th St.-Union Sq. Map 13, E5, 96. A respectable off-Broadway theater, housed in what was once Tammany Hall. See p. 69 for more info about the building. Tickets $30-55. Box office open Su and Tu-Sa 1-6pm.

Vineyard Theater Company's Dimson Theatre, 108 E. 15th St., between Union Sq. E. and Irving Pl. (☎212-353-0303; www.vineyardtheatre.org). Subway: 4, 5, 6, L, N, Q, R, W to 14th St.-Union Sq. Map 13, E6, 123. A theater company that "thinks outside the box," Vineyard produces bold and idiosyncratic new plays and musicals, as well as operas for children and their families. Currently producing *Avenue Q* on Broadway. $15 per show with $50 season membership; under 30 $10 per show with $15 membership; $5 handling fee per order. Box office open M-F noon-6pm.

COMEDY CLUBS

Comic Strip Live, 1568 Second Ave., between 81st and 82nd St. (☎212-861-9386). Subway: 4, 5, 6 to 86th St./Lexington Ave. Map 15, C4, 24. Autographed headshots of all of the famous comics who have paid their dues at this club cover the better part of the lobby wall. Former regulars include just about everyone in the post-SNL pantheon, and today's hottest jokesters call this pub-style club home. $12 drink min. per person per show. 18+. Cover Su and Tu-Th $12, F-Sa $17. Try to make reservations on M starting at noon, especially for weekends. Shows Su-Th around 8:30pm, additional shows on weekends.

Dangerfield's, 1118 First Ave., between 61st and 62nd St. (☎212-593-1650). Subway: 4, 5, 6, N, R, W to Lexington Ave.-59th St. Map 15, C6, 59. Rodney's respectable comic-launching pad. HBO specials featuring Chris Rock and Jerry Seinfeld have been taped at the club.

Be prepared for a surprise—the lineup is only available the day of the show, and unannounced guest comedians appear occasionally. Ages 14 and under should be accompanied by adult. Cover Su-Th $12.50, F-Sa $15, Sa 10:30pm show $20. Shows Su-Th 8:45pm; F 8:30 and 10:30pm; Sa 8, 10:30pm, and 12:30am; doors open 1hr. before 1st show.

Gotham Comedy Club, 34 W. 22nd St., between Fifth and Sixth Ave. (☎212-367-9000; www.gothamcomedyclub.com). Subway: F, V to 23rd St./Ave. of the Americas (Sixth Ave.); N, R to 23rd St./Broadway. Map 13, D5, 78. One of New York's more upscale comedy clubs. 16+. Cover Su-Th $10, F-Sa $15. Usually a 2-drink min. Amateur night F 7pm, Sa 6:30pm. Shows Su-Th 8:30pm, F-Sa 8:30 and 10:30pm.

Stand Up New York, 236 W. 78th St., between Amsterdam Ave. and Broadway (☎212-595-0850). Subway: 1, 2 to 79th St. Map 18, C4, 30. Stand-up club with good lineup. Neighborhood man Jerry Seinfeld has performed here. 18+. 2-drink min. Cover $5-12. Shows Su-W 7 and 9pm; Th 7, 9, 11:30pm; F-Sa 8, 10pm.

Upright Citizens Brigade Theater, 161 W. 22nd St., between Sixth and Seventh Ave. (☎212-366-9176; www.ucbtheatre.com). Subway: 1, 9 to 23rd St./Seventh Ave. F, V to 23rd St./Ave. of the Americas (Sixth Ave.). Map 13, C4, 35. Funny, off-beat sketch and improv comedy, as seen on their Comedy Central show. The original gang shows up for Su performances. Tickets M-Th $5, F-Su $7, Su 9:30pm show free. 2-3 shows per night, usually 8 and 9:30pm.

GENERAL ENTERTAINMENT VENUES

92nd Street Y, 1395 Lexington Ave., at 92nd St. (☎212-996-1100; www.92y.com). Subway: 6 to 96th St./Lexington Ave. Map 15, B3, 11. Upper East Side cultural center. The Y's Kaufmann Concert Hall seats only 916 people and offers an intimate setting unmatched by New York's larger halls, with flawless acoustics and fantastic ambience. Notable series include Jazz in July, Chamber Music at the Y, Lyrics and Lyricists, and Young Concert Artists. Also hosts ongoing series of literary readings at the Poetry Center and some of the most engaging lectures in New York. $15-35 for tickets to all events. Visit the website for regularly updated schedules.

ABC No Rio, 156 Rivington St., between Clinton and Suffolk St. (☎212-254-3697; www.abcnorio.org). Subway: F, J, M, Z to Delancey St.-Essex St. Map 11, F2, 31. Nonprofit, community-run art space with a vibrant mural marking its entrance. Offers print-making studio, darkrooms, computer labs, and a library. Volunteer taught classes avail-

SOB's

Let's Go Mets!

Knitting Factory

able most weeknights. Center is open to the public and hosts many community events, from art exhibitions featuring local teenagers to hard-core and punk shows. No alcohol or beverages served. Cover $2-5. Call for changing schedule.

Beacon Theatre, 2124 Broadway, at 74th St. (☎212-496-7070). Subway: 1, 2, 3, 9 to 72nd St./Broadway. Map 18, C5, 41. Attached to the Beacon Hotel, this mid-sized venue hosts a wide variety of music acts, as well as other performances and plays. 2003 acts included Earth, Wind & Fire and Norah Jones. Call for schedule. Tickets usually $35. Box office open M-F 11am-7pm, Sa noon-6pm.

Brooklyn Academy of Music, 30 Lafayette Ave., between St. Felix St. and Ashland Pl. (☎718-636-4100; www.bam.org). Subway: 1, 2, 4, 5, Q to Atlantic Ave.; M, N, R, W to Pacific St. Map 22. Manhattan Express Bus ("BAM bus") departs from 120 Park Ave., at 42nd St., for each performance ($5, round-trip $10); call for more info. Oldest performing arts center in the country, with a colorful history of magnificent performances: Pavlova danced, Caruso sang, and Sarah Bernhardt played Camille here. Now focuses on new, non-traditional, multicultural programs—with the occasional early classical music performance. Jazz, blues, performance art, opera, and dance available. Late spring brings Dance Africa. BAM's annual Next Wave Festival, Oct.-Dec., features contemporary music, dance, theater, and performance art. Student rush $10, limit 2 tickets per ID; available at box office 2hr. before show. The Brooklyn Philharmonic Orchestra performs here Nov.-May. Some opera performances as well; call for schedule. Prices vary widely, usually $20-50.

Brooklyn Center for Performing Arts, 2900 Campus Rd. and Hillel Place, 1 block west of the junction of Flatbush and Nostrand Ave., on the campus of Brooklyn College (☎718-951-4500 or 718-951-4600; www.brooklyncenter.com). Subway: 2, 5 to Flatbush Ave.-Brooklyn College. Map 20, C4, 5. The likes of Ray Charles, Luciano Pavarotti, and Harry Belafonte have performed in this neighborhood favorite since its founding in 1954. Season Oct.-May. Limited discounted student rush tickets available to Brooklyn College and CUNY students at box office 1hr. before event—check website for details. Wheelchair accessible. Tickets usually $15-40. Box office open Tu-Sa 1pm-6pm and 1hr. before performance starts.

Cathedral of St. John the Divine (☎212-662-2133). See p. 96 for directions. Beautiful church offers impressive array of classical concerts, art exhibitions, lectures, plays, movies, and dance events. NY Philharmonic performs on occasion; soprano saxophonist Paul Winter gives annual Summer and Winter Solstice concerts. Prices vary. Box office open M-F 10am-2pm, Sa-Su 9am-5pm.

Colden Center for the Performing Arts, 65-30 Kissena Blvd., at Queens College in Flushing, Queens (☎718-793-8080). Subway: 7 to Flushing-Main St.; then buses Q17, Q25, or Q34 to the corner of Kissena Blvd. and the Long Island Expwy. Map 25, D2, 3. Beautiful 2143-seat theater hosts an excellent program of jazz, classical, and dance concerts Sept.-May. Summer box office open M-W 10am-4pm.

Collective Unconscious, 145 Ludlow St., between Rivington and Stanton St. (☎212-254-5277; www.weird.org). Subway: F, J, M, Z to Delancey St.-Essex St. Map 11, E2, 24. Popular off-off-Broadway performance space debuts performances from the downtown artistic community. Rev. Jen's Anti-Slam Comedy Act (W) brings in a big crowd; other nights run gamut from reading series to a "Famous Drunks in History" party. Tu film series; Su open mic. No alcohol served, but BYOB. Cover varies, usually $5-10. 1-1½hr. shows Th-Sa 8, 10pm, midnight.

Cultural Institutes. These cultural centers are valuable for their libraries, small but interesting exhibits, classes, and lectures. Some services are only open to members, but all the institutes have highly useful lists of cultural events throughout the city.

Alliance Française, Florence Gould Hall, 55 E. 59th St., between Park and Madison Ave. (☎212-355-6160 or 307-4100). Subway: 4, 5, 6 to 59th St./Lexington Ave., N, R to 5th Ave. Map 15, B6, 65. The cultural arm of the French Embassy offers Gallic lectures, classes, programs, and films. Admission $8, students $6. Tickets available day of screening at box office from 11am; first-come, first-served. Doors open 20min. before screening. Box office open Tu-F 11am-7pm, Sa-Su 11am-3pm.

Americas Society, 680 Park Ave., between 68th and 69th St. (☎212-249-8950). Subway: 6 to 68th St. Map 15, B6, 46. Concerts, visual arts exhibitions, and other educational programs offered. Gallery admission free. Exhibits rotate bimonthly. Educational programs $5, students and seniors $3. Concerts $15, students and seniors $10. Gallery open noon-6pm; call for event schedule.

Asia Society (p. 134) also has films from or about Asia. Call for schedule and ticket info.

China Institute, 125 E. 65th St., between Park and Lexington Ave. (☎212-744-8181; www.chinainstitute.org). Subway: 6 to 68th St. Map 15, B6, 51. Promotes the understanding of Chinese culture and history through classes, lectures, performances, and film series; its gallery showcases a broad spectrum of Chinese art and architecture from the Neolithic period to the present. Gallery open M, W, F-Sa 10am-5pm; Tu and Th 10am-8pm; Su 1-5pm. Closed major holidays and between exhibitions. $3, students and seniors $2. Tu and Th 6-8pm free. Call ahead or visit website for present schedules.

Goethe-Institut, 1014 Fifth Ave., between 82nd and 83rd St. (☎212-439-8700; www.goethe.de/newyork). Subway: 6 to 77th St.; 4, 5, 6 to 86th St./Lexington Ave. Map 15, A4, 22. Imports Germanic culture via films, concerts, classes, and lectures. Many events and exhibits are free. Closed for much of July-Aug. Office open M-Tu 9am-5pm, F 9am-4:15pm; gallery open M, W, F 10am-5pm; Tu and Th 10am-7pm; library open Tu and Th noon-7pm, W and F noon-5pm.

Italian Cultural Institute, 686 Park Ave., between 68th and 69th St. (☎212-879-4242; www.italcultny.org). Subway: 6 to 68th St. Map 15, B5, 44. Library open by appointment only. Reading room and institute open M-F 9am-1pm and 2-4pm.

Spanish Institute, 684 Park Ave., between 68th and 69th St. (☎212-628-0420; www.spanishinstitute.org). Subway: 6 to 68th St. Map 15, B5, 43. Housed in a 1927 landmark neo-Federal townhouse designed by McKim, Mead & White, the Institute was founded in 1954 to promote Spanish culture through lectures, symposia, events, language, and translation.

The Kitchen, 512 W. 19th St., between 10th and 11th Ave. (☎255-5793; www.thekitchen.org). Subway: C, E to 23rd St./Eighth Ave. Map 13, A5, 57. World-renowned arts showcase in an unassuming location. Features experimental and avant-garde film and video, as well as concerts, dance performances, and poetry readings. Ticket prices vary by event. Box office open M-F 10am-5pm.

Knitting Factory, 74 Leonard St., between Broadway and Church St. (☎212-219-3006). Subway: 1, 9 to Franklin St. Multi-level performance space features several shows nightly, ranging from avant-garde and indie rock to jazz and hip-hop. Also hosts a spectacular summertime jazz festival. Cover $5-25. Box office open for walk-up sales M-F 10am-2am, Sa noon-2am, Su 2pm-2am. Tickets available by phone M-F 10am-4pm, Sa noon-4am, Su 2pm-4am. Bar open 6pm-4am.

Merkin Concert Hall, 129 W. 67th St., between Broadway and Amsterdam Ave. (☎212-501-3330; www.ekcc.org). Subway: 1, 9 to 66th St. Map 18, C6, 60. An intimate theater, sometimes known as "the little hall with the big sound." This division of the Elaine Kaufman Cultural Center offers musically diverse programs. Season Sept.-June. Tickets usually $10-35. Call for student discounts. Box office open Jan.-Oct. Su-Th noon-7pm, F noon-4pm; Nov.-Jan. Su-Th noon-7pm, F 3pm-close.

The Point, 940 Garrison Ave., at the corner of Manida St., the Bronx. (☎718-542-4139; www.thepoint.org). Subway: 6 to Hunts Point Ave. Map 28, C5, 28. Bordering one of NY's poorest neighborhoods, The Point houses a growing artistic community and is home to dancer/choreographer Arthur Aviles. Monthly Latin jazz and hip-hop performances as well as studio facilities, a theater, summer programs for neighborhood youth, and art classes. Community-based efforts like the South Bronx Film and Video Festival enable Hunts Point to call itself "the artistic capital of the Bronx." Call for schedule of events. Open M-F 8:30am-7pm, Sa 10am-5pm. (See p. 314 for volunteer opportunities.)

Radio City Music Hall, 1260 Sixth Ave., at 50th St. (☎212-307-7171; see p. 78). Subway: 47th-50th St.-Rockefeller Center/Ave. of the Americas (Sixth Ave.). Map 15, D3, 36. Boasts a bill of great performers that reads like an invitation list to the Music Hall of Fame; Ella

Fitzgerald, Frank Sinatra, Ringo Starr, Linda Ronstadt, and Sting, among others, have performed at the legendary venue. Tickets generally start at $30. Box office open regularly M-Sa 10am-8pm, Su 11am-8pm. In summer, M-F 10am-8pm, Sa-Su noon-5pm.

St. Ann's Warehouse, 38 Water Street, near Dock St. (☎718-254-9601). Subway A, C to High St., F to York St. Map 22, 2. Not your typical DUMBO warehouse anymore, the Arts at St. Ann's have totally transformed this venue into a full-out theater with works such as *The Barber of Seville* and *Labalooza*, the new puppet theater festival. Call box office for ticket prices. Main office at 70 Washington St. (☎718-834-8794, ext. 10).

St. Mark's Church in-the-Bowery, 131 E. 10th St., between Second and Third Ave. (☎212-674-6377). Subway: 6 to Astor Pl. Map 12, C2, 19. Home to the **Ontological-Hysteric Theater** (☎212-533-4650), **Danspace Project** (☎212-674-8112), and **Poetry Project** (☎212-674-0910). While the Ontological Theater pioneered the wackiness of playwright Richard Foreman, Danspace has provided a venue for emerging dancers and experimental styles of movement since the 1920s (Isadora Duncan danced here). Poetry Project stages regular evening readings and closes June-Aug. Call for info on upcoming events, or check board outside; reserve for theater tickets and arrive 15min. early for the show. Tickets for Danspace usually $10-15, Poetry Project $4-7.

Symphony Space, 2537 Broadway, at W. 95th St. (☎212-864-5400; www.symphonyspace.org). Subway: 1, 2, 3, 9 to 96th St./Broadway. Map 18, B3, 12. Before and after performances, check out the *Barocco @ the Thalia Cafe*, chow on Mediterranean sandwiches and mingle with the evening's performers and artists. Most movies $9, seniors $8; other events usually $26-32. Box office open Tu-Su.

World Financial Center, in Battery Park City (☎212-945-0505 or 528-2733; www.worldfinancialcenter.com). See p. 52 for directions. A variety of festivals are held here year-round, but they are more common during the summer. Diversity is the only constant: there may be swing dancing one day and a Far East cultural exposition the next. Admission free.

FESTIVALS

Central Park Summerstage, at the Rumsey Playfield, at 72nd St., near Fifth Ave., in Central Park (☎212-360-2777; www.summerstage.org). See p. 87 for directions. Mid-June to mid-Sept., Summerstage hosts. free concerts, dance performances, and spoken word events. Past performers have included the Fugees, the Rocksteady Crew, the Gypsy Kings, and They Might Be Giants. Big names from all genres, but also an outstanding selection of up-and-coming performers.

Lincoln Center Festival, box office at Avery Fisher Hall, Lincoln Center (☎212-875-5928; www.lincolncenter.org). See p. 95 for directions. Cutting-edge dance, theater, opera, and music events throughout the Lincoln Center complex in July. 2003 performers included the Kirove Opera of St. Petersburg and the Chinese Opera. Tickets $20-75, depending on show. Ask for student discounts at the Avery Fisher Hall box office.

Lincoln Center Out-of-Doors (☎212-875-5108; www.lincolncenter.org). See p. 95 for directions. For 3 weeks in Aug., Lincoln Center sponsors a completely free performance arts festival. Performances run the gamut from dance to Chinese opera.

LIVE TELEVISION

For free tickets to live tapings of your favorite television shows, go to www.tvtickets.com—or contact the relevant network via telephone or website.

The Daily Show (Comedy Central), 513 W. 54th St., at 10th Ave. (☎212-586-2477). Subway: 1, 9, A, B, C, D to 59th St.-Columbus Circle. Map 14, A2, 3. Call for free tickets. The show tapes from M-Th. 18+, ID required. Doors open at 5:45pm.

Late Night with Conan O'Brien (NBC), at the G.E. Building in Rockefeller Center (☎212-664-3056). See p. 78 for directions. Ticket reservations are accepted in advance only by calling the NBC ticket office. Advance reservations limited to 4 tickets per group. For stand-by tickets, arrive no later than 9am on the morning of the taping, under the "NBC Studios" marquee at the 49th St. entrance of 30 Rockefeller Pl. Only 1 ticket per person. Stand-by tickets do not guarantee admission. 16+, ID required. No large bags.

Late Show with David Letterman (CBS), Ed Sullivan Theater, 1697 Broadway, at 53rd St. (☎212-975-1003). Subway: E to Seventh Ave./53rd St. Map 14, B2, 12. Cuddly-yet-acerbic host performs antics in front of a studio audience. If you are lucky enough to get tickets, bring a sweater–the studio is notoriously cold. To request 2 tickets, send a postcard with your name, address, and daytime and evening phone numbers to: Late Show Tickets, The Ed Sullivan Theater, 1697 Broadway, New York, NY 10019. Multiple requests will be discarded. Waiting time may be over 9 months. Tapings are M-Th. Stand-by tickets are available on the day of the show only by calling ☎212-247-6497 at 11am. Phones will be answered until allocation is gone. Only 2 tickets will be issued per caller and the recipient must have identification to match the name given when calling in. 18+. Ticketing may be subject to answering a trivia question about The Late Show.

Live with Regis and Kelly (ABC), W. 67th St. and Columbus Ave. (☎212-456-3537). Subway: 1, 2, to 66th St. Map 18, D6, 68. Send a postcard with name, address, phone number, approximate date of show you'd like to attend, and your request for up to 4 tickets to: Live Tickets, Ansonia Station, P.O. Box 777, New York, NY 10023-0777. Wait may be up to several months. For standby tickets arrive no later than 8am on the day of the show at W. 67th St. and Columbus Ave. (7 Lincoln Sq.). Standby tickets awarded on first-come, first-served basis.

Saturday Night Live (NBC), at the G.E. Building in Rockefeller Center (☎212-664-3056). See p. 78 for directions. *SNL* goes on hiatus June-Aug. Enter ticket lottery by sending an email to snltickets@nbc.com in August. If selected, you will get two tickets to a random week's show. Warning: they don't accept requests for a specific date and only award 2 tickets per household. For stand-by tickets, arrive no later than 7am on the morning of the taping, under the "NBC Studios" marquee at the 49th St. entrance of 30 Rockefeller Pl. You may choose a stand-by ticket for either the 8pm dress rehearsal or the 11:30pm live show. Only 1 ticket per person. Stand-by tickets do not guarantee admission. 16+.

OUTDOOR THEATERS

Queens Theatre in the Park, in the New York State Pavilion in Flushing Meadows-Corona Park (☎718-760-0064; www.queenstheatre.org). See p. 115 for directions. Film and performing arts center that hosts an annual Latino arts festival (late July to mid-Aug.), among other events. Call for dance and theater listings. Box office open Tu-Sa noon-6pm.

Shakespeare in the Park (☎212-539-8750). See p. 86 for directions. This renowned series is a New York summer tradition. 2 Shakespeare plays, one late June to mid-July and the second early Aug.-Sept., bring outstanding actors and directors to the outdoor Delacorte amphitheater in Central Park. Tickets available 1pm the day of performance at the Delacorte and 1-3pm at the Public Theatre at 425 Lafayette St.; try to get there by 10:30am. Stand-by line forms at 6pm. Limit 2 tickets per person. Doors open Su and Tu-Sa at 7:30pm; shows start at 8pm.

SPORTS

SPECTATOR SPORTS

BASEBALL

Created in 1962 to replace the much-mourned Giants and Dodgers (who had moved to California after the 1957 season), the **New York Mets** (short for "Metropolitans") set the still-unbroken major league record for losses in a season during their first year. Seven years later, however, the "Miracle Mets" captured the World Series. In 1986, carried by the arm of Dwight Gooden and the bat of Darryl Strawberry, the brash young Mets won their second World Championship.

The careers of both Gooden and Strawberry soon took tragic turns, and the Mets fortunes followed before rebounding over a decade later. In 2000, led by Mike Piazza, the greatest hitting catcher in baseball history, the Mets returned to the Fall Classic, where they were defeated in five games by their crosstown rivals, the New York Yankees. See p. 115 for information about the Mets' home, **Shea Stadium**. (☎718-507-6387. Tickets $13-30.)

Founded in 1903, the vaunted **New York Yankees** (team of Joe DiMaggio, Whitey Ford, Mickey Mantle, Babe Ruth, and Lou Gehrig) are baseball's most storied franchise. Possessing 26 World championships and 36 American League Championships, the Bronx Bombers have won more championships than any other team in American sports. Until the Arizona Diamondbacks ended their streak in 2001, the Yankees had won three straight World Series. The team plays ball at **Yankee Stadium** in the Bronx. See p. 118 for directions to stadium. (☎718-293-4300. Tickets $8-$65 usually available day of game; you can also find them on the web at www.tix.com.).

BASKETBALL

Although they've been unable to regain the heights of their 1969 Championship Season, the New York Knickerbockers (usually referred to as the **Knicks**) were a force in the NBA for much of the 1990s. After trading star center Patrick Ewing, the Knicks began a downward spiral and have not advanced to the playoffs for the past two seasons. The Knicks do their regular season dribbling at **Madison Square Garden** (☎212-465-5867; see p. 76) from early November to late April. Tickets start at $22 and are nearly impossible to come by unless you order well in advance. On the **collegiate level,** the Garden plays host to Big East Conference contender St. John's Red Storm during the winter and the NIT and Big East tournaments in March. Also playing at the Garden are the **New York Liberty** (☎212-564-9622) of the Women's National Basketball Association (WNBA). The season runs from June to August; tickets start at $8.

FOOTBALL

Both New York teams play across the Hudson at **Giants Stadium** (☎201-935-3900) in East Rutherford, New Jersey. The **Giants** surprised the entire football world when they captured the NFC title in 2000, only to lose the Super Bowl to the Baltimore Ravens. As with the Knicks, tickets are nigh impossible to get—season ticket holders have booked them all for the next 40 years, and the waiting list holds over 15,000 people. Befriend a fan, or view the action from a local sports bar. The **Jets,** with a respectable playoff run in 2001, are also worth watching. (Season runs early Sept.-early Jan. Tickets start at $25; cash only at the Meadowlands box office.)

HOCKEY

In a town known for its speed and turbulence, it's easy to understand why New Yorkers attend hockey games with such fervor. The **New York Rangers** hit the ice at Madison Square Garden. (MSG ☎212-465-6741; Rangers ☎308-6977; see p. 76 for directions. Season Oct.-Apr. Tickets, on sale Aug., start at $25; reserve well in advance.) The **New York Islanders** hang their skates at the Nassau Coliseum in Uniondale, Long Island. (☎516-794-9300. Season also Oct.-Apr. Tickets $27-70.)

HORSERACING

Fans seeking equine excitement can watch the stallions at **Belmont Park** (☎718-641-4700; see p. 120 for directions) May to July and September to mid-October, Wednesday to Sunday, and may even catch a grand slam event. The **Belmont Stakes,** run the first Saturday in June, is one leg in the Triple Crown. (The "Belmont Special" train leaves Penn Station twice per day. $8 round-trip, includes $1 off admission.) The **Aqueduct Racetrack,** near JFK Airport, has races from late October to early May, also Wednesday through Sunday. (☎718-641-4700. Subway: A to Aqueduct. Grandstand seating at both tracks $2.) Racing in New York is suspended in August, when the action goes upstate to Saratoga.

SOCCER

Buoyed by swelling youth interest and a strong US showing at the 2002 World Cup, soccer's recent rise in popularity has culminated in the birth of **Major League Soccer.** Since the league's 1996 inception, New Yorkers have been turning out to see the **New York/New Jersey Metrostars** play at **Giants Stadium,** 50 Rte. 120, East Rutherford, NJ. The Port Authority Bus Terminal in Manhattan, at Eighth Ave. and 41st St., offers bus service (20min.) to Giants Stadium. (Bus to Giant Stadium: 1st bus from New York leaves 2hr. in advance of the game; last one departs 30min. after event begins. Return service to New York begins immediately after game ends and continues to operate for up to 30min. after the event. Round-trip $7; one-way $4.25. For more information, contact New Jersey Transit at ☎800-772-2222. Tickets to see game: ☎888-4-METROTIX or 463-8768. Season late Mar. to early Sept. Tickets $18-36.)

TENNIS

Tennis enthusiasts who get their tickets three months in advance can attend the prestigious **US Open,** one of tennis's four Grand Slam events, held in late August and early September at the United States Tennis Association (USTA) Tennis Center in Flushing Meadows Park, Queens. (See p. 115 for directions. ☎718-760-6200. On sale by early June; call ☎866-673-6849. Tickets $33-69.)

PARTICIPATORY SPORTS

Whether trying to slim down at the health club or commuting to work via bicycle, endless amateur and recreational athletes twist and flex in New York. Although space in much of the city is at a premium, the **City of New York Parks and Recreation Department** (☎800-201-PARK/7275 for a recording of park events) manages to maintain numerous playgrounds and parks in all boroughs, for everything from baseball and basketball to croquet and shuffleboard. **Activities are listed in alphabetical order.**

BASKETBALL

Basketball is one of New York's favorite pastimes. Courts can be found in parks and playgrounds all over the city, and most are frequently occupied. Pickup basketball games can also be found in various parts of the city, each with its own rituals, rulers, and degree of intensity. **The Cage,** at W. 4th and Sixth Ave., is home to some of the city's best amateur players: rumor has it that scouts for college and pro teams occasionally drop by incognito to ferret out new talent. Other pickup spots worth checking out include Central Park, 96th and Lexington Ave., Tompkins Sq. Park, and 76th and Columbus Ave. Be aware that these games may get rough: before setting foot on the courts, make sure you know how to take care of yourself.

BEACHES

Manhattan Beach (¼ mi. long), on the Atlantic Ocean. Ocean Ave. to Mackenzie St. in Brooklyn (☎718-946-1373). Subway: D to Brighton Beach; then bus B1.

Orchard Beach and Promenade, in the Bronx's Pelham Bay Park (☎718-885-2275). Subway: 6 to Pelham Bay Park; then bus Bx5 (summer weekends only) or Bx12 (summer only) to Orchard Beach. Map 28, F3. A 1¼ mi. long sandy stretch facing Long Island Sound, Orchard Beach gets mobbed by snack stands and sun-seekers on hot summer days. Lifeguards keep watch Memorial Day-Labor Day daily 10am-6pm.

Rockaway Beach and Boardwalk (7½ mi. long), on the Atlantic Ocean (☎718-318-4000). See p. 117 for directions. Lifeguards Memorial Day-Labor Day daily 10am-6pm.

Staten Island: South Beach, Midland Beach, and **Franklin D. Roosevelt Boardwalk** (2½ mi.), on Lower New York Bay. Bus S51 from the ferry terminal. Map 29. Touted as one of NYC's "best beaches," South Beach offers spectacular views of the Narrows. Due to possible pollution, swimming after heavy rainfall is not recommended.

BICYCLING

From spring to fall, daily at dawn and dusk and throughout the weekend, packs of dedicated (and spandex-ed) cyclists navigate the trails and wide roads of **Central Park.** The circular drive is car-free Monday-Thursday 10am-3pm and 7-10pm, Friday 10am-3pm, and Friday 7pm until Monday 6am. On the West Side, between 72nd and 110th St., along the Hudson bank, **Riverside Park** draws more laid-back riders. Other excellent places to cycle on the weekends include the deserted **Wall Street** area and the unadorned roads of Brooklyn's **Prospect Park.** If you must leave your bike unattended, use a strong "U" lock. Thieves laugh at (and then cut through) chain locks. Don't leave quick-release items unattended; you will find them very quickly released. If you're in the area, don't miss **Bike New York** (☎212-932-2453; www.bikenewyork.org) on May 2, 2004. This bike ride through all five boroughs on traffic-free roads, alongside 28,000 other cyclists, is a 2-decade springtime tradition.

Metro Bicycle Stores, Lexington Ave., at 88th St. (☎212-427-4450; www.metrobicycles.com). Map 15, B3, 14. Seven convenient locations throughout the city. Entry-level mountain bikes and hybrids. $7 per hr., $35 per day, $45 overnight. Helmet rental $2.50 per bike. Daily rentals due back 30min. before store closes and overnight rentals next day at 10am. Credit card and valid ID required. Open Su-W and F-Sa 9:30am-6:30pm, Th 9:30am-7:30pm.

Pedal Pushers, 1306 Second Ave., between 68th and 69th St. (☎212-288-5592; www.pedalpusher.com). Subway: 6 to 68th St.-Lexington Ave. Map 15, C5, 47. Best rates in city. 3-speeds $4 per hr., $10 per day, $13 overnight; 10-speeds $5/$14; mountain bikes $6/$17/$25 overnight. Rent a helmet for an extra $1.40 per day. Now offering Central Park audio tours with CD or cassette player for $10. Overnight rentals require $150 deposit on major credit card; regular rentals only need major credit card, passport, or a NY state driver's license deposit. Open M and F-Su 10am-6pm, W 10am-7pm, Th 10am-8pm.

BOWLING

For some quality 10-pin, head to **Bowlmor Lanes,** 110 University Pl., between 12th and 13th St. (☎212-255-8188). You'll find bowling, music, and alcohol all in one place. Watch your game deteriorate as you knock a couple back with the NYU crowd. Subway: 4, 5, 6, L, N, R, Q, W to 14th St.-Union Sq. Map 10, E2, 13. Imported beer $6-7, domestic $5. 21+ after 6pm. Open M, F, Sa 11am-4am; Tu, W, Su 11am-1am; Th 11am-2am.

CLIMBING

You can climb to your heart's content in the center of Manhattan at the **ExtraVertical Climbing Center** in the Harmony Atrium, 61 W. 62nd St., between Columbus Ave. and Broadway. No experience necessary. (☎212-586-5382. Day pass $16, students $12, challenge climbs $9 for 2, equipment rental $6. Lessons $55-110. Monthly passes $75, students $50. Open summer M-F 1-10pm, Sa 10am-10pm, Su noon-8pm; winter M-F 5-10pm, Sa 10am-10pm, Su noon-8pm.) **North Meadow Recreation Center,** mid-park at 97th St. in **Central Park,** offers 4-week courses for $200 per person. (See p. 86 for directions. ☎212-348-4867 for reservations. Every Sa 10am.)

FISHING

See **Gone Fishin'** (to the right).

FITNESS

Membership at most of NYC's swank gyms is high-priced. Cheaper alternatives include public fitness centers and YMCA/YWCAs. **Public fitness centers,** or recreation centers, are run by the city government and feature most of the amenities, classes, and equipment of the brand-name gyms. Membership is an astounding $10-75 per *year* and there are over 30 branches throughout the city. In Manhattan, gyms include **Asser Levy,** E. 23rd St. (☎212-447-2020), between First Ave. and FDR Dr., and **Carmine** (☎212-242-5228), 1 Clarkson St., on Seventh Ave. The city's **YMCAs, YWCAs,** and **YM-YWHAs** are other options. Facilities at the following locations are high quality (call the Vanderbilt Y for other locations): **Vanderbilt YMCA,** 224 E. 47th St. (☎212-756-9600); **92nd St. YM-YWHA,** 1395 Lexington Ave. (☎212-415-5729), at 92nd St.; and **YWCA,** 610 Lexington Ave. (☎212-735-9753), at 53rd St.

GOLF

Although New York golf courses don't measure up to those at Pebble Beach, avid New York golfers jam all of the 13 well-manicured city courses during the weekends. Most are found in the Bronx or Queens, including **Pelham Bay Park** (☎718-885-1258; see p. 123), **Van Cortlandt Park** (☎718-543-4595; see p. 121), and **Forest Park** (☎718-296-0999; see p. 114). Greens fees are approximately $12-29 for NYC residents and $17-35 for non-NYC residents, depending on time of day and week. Reserve at least one week in advance for summer weekends. Long Island is home to some of the country's best public courses; **Bethpage** (☎516-249-7000) also features five top-notch ones. The Black course hosted the 2002 U.S. Open won by Tiger Woods. On the eastern tip of Long Island is **Montauk Downs** (☎631-668-5000), which is among the country's top 50 public courses.

HORSEBACK RIDING

Bet you didn't know you could do this in New York! **Central Park** horseback riding, for those well-versed in English equitation, operates out of **Claremont Stables,** 175 W. 89th St., between Columbus and Amsterdam Ave. (☎212-724-5100. Map 18, C3, 15. $50 per hr. Make reservations. Open daily 1hr. after sunrise to 1hr. before sunset.) **Lynne's Riding School,** 88-03 70th Rd. offers guided trail rides in Forest Park. (☎718-261-7679. Subway: J, Z to Woodhaven Blvd. $25 per hr. Open M-F 9am-4:30pm, Sa-Su 9am-6pm. Call and make an appointment.)

ICE-SKATING

The first gust of cold winter air brings out droves of aspiring Paul Wylies and Tara Lipinskis. While each of the rinks in the city has its own character, nearly all have lockers, skate rentals, and a snack bar.

Rockefeller Center, Fifth Ave. and 50th St. (☎212-332-7654). Subway: B, D, F, to Rockefeller Center. Map 14, D3. Famous and expensive sunken plaza that doubles as the chic American Festival Cafe during the warm months. Always crowded, with throngs of spectators around the outside edges. $20 gets you a pair of skates and entry to rink. Open Nov.1-Mar.1 weather permitting.

GONE FISHIN'

Let's suppose for a second that you're one of those people who likes the outdoors. You like sleeping under the stars, hiking through the woods, animals, killing animals, and fishing, which is like killing animals but somehow more acceptable. Its possible to do all of these things in New York, but really only advisable to fish. So let's go fishing!

Chances are, you left your fishing pole and bait at home. Fortunately, there are people who will not only provide these necessary implements, but also take you out on their boat for a morning or afternoon of fishing, asking only for money in return. This is the transfer of goods and services, the backbone of capitalism. Its also a lovely way to spend a summer afternoon!

A number of fishing boats leave from Emmons Ave. in Sheepshead Bay, Brooklyn each morning at around 8am and each afternoon at around 5pm. Prices vary widely, as do the lengths of trips. Your best bet would be to go down to the dock and comparison shop. You're sure to have a great time angling, and you'll enjoy the hilarious spectacle when you try to board your flight home with a dead fluke!

Fishing boats leave twice daily from Emmons Ave., between Ocean and Nostrand Ave. Subway: Q to Sheepshead Bay. Walk down Sheepshead Bay Rd. to Emmons Ave.

Sky Rink at Chelsea Piers, at W. 21st St. and the Hudson River (☎212-336-6100). See p. 74 for directions. Learn to skate or practice on one of the 2 full-sized indoor Olympic ice-skating rinks. Adults $12, ages 12 and under and seniors $8.50; free Sa 2-4pm mid-June to Aug. Skate rentals $5.50. General skating times mid-June to Aug. M 12:30-2:20pm and 4-7:30pm; Tu 12:30-2:20pm and 4-6:30pm; W and F 12:30-2:20pm and 4-6pm; Th 4-6:30pm; Sa noon-6:50pm; Su noon-5:50pm. Sept. to mid-June 11:30am-5:30pm.

Wollman Memorial Rink (☎212-396-1010). See p. 87 for directions. Located in a particularly scenic section of Central Park, near 64th St. $15 for 2hr., $25 all day; includes helmet and pads; $100 deposit required.

IN-LINE SKATING

There are many in-line skate rental locations throughout the city. For low prices and convenience, **Blades** (☎212-996-1644) has over eight stores in the Metropolitan area. (Flat rate $20; includes all protective gear. $200 deposit or credit is required. Open M-Sa 11am-8pm, Su 11am-6pm.) Blades also has various sister stores that feature the same prices and conditions—**Peck and Goodie Skates,** 917 Eighth Ave., between 54th and 55th St. (☎212-246-6123; Map 14, B2, 5), will also hold your shoes while you whiz past your favorite New York sights. They also offer private lessons for a fee of $40 per hr. (Open M-Sa 10am-8pm, Su 10am-6pm.) Good places to skate in the city include Battery Park, West St. between Christopher to Horatio St., Chelsea Piers, and East River Promenade between 60th and 81st St. Central Park has several roller zones including the Outer Loop, a slalom course near Tavern on the Green.

ROWBOATS

You can rent them at the Loeb Boathouse in **Central Park.** See p. 87 for directions. (☎212-517-2233. $10 per hr.; refundable $20 deposit. Open daily Apr.-Sept. 10am-5pm, weather permitting.)

RUNNING

When running in **Central Park** during no-traffic hours (see **Bicycling,** above), stay in the right-hand runners' lane to avoid being mowed down by reckless pedal-pushers. **Stay in populated areas and stay out of the park after dark.** Recommended courses include the 1½ mi. soft-surface track around the Reservoir (between 84th and 96th St.) and a picturesque 1.72 mi. route along West Dr., starting at Tavern on the Green, heading south to East Dr., and circling back west on 72nd St. Another beautiful place to run is **Riverside Park,** which stretches along the Hudson River bank from 72nd to 116th St.; **don't stray too far north.** For information on running clubs, clinics, and racing events around the city, call the **New York Roadrunner's Club,** 9 E. 89th St., between Madison and Fifth Ave. (☎212-860-1333). They host races in Central Park on summer weekends.

THE NEW YORK CITY MARATHON

On the first Sunday in November, two million spectators line rooftops, sidewalks, and promenades to cheer 22,000 runners in the **New York City Marathon** (16,000 racers actually finish). The November 3 race begins on the Verrazano Bridge and ends at Central Park's Tavern on the Green. Call the **NY Roadrunner's Club** (contact info above) for info on signing up.

SWIMMING

Two of the city's nicer pools include **John Jay Pool**, east of York Ave. at 77th St. (☎212-794-6566), and **Asser Levy Pool** at E. 23rd St. and Asser Levy Pl., next to the East River. (☎212-447-2020). Subway to John Jay Pool: 6 to 77th St. Pool is four blocks east from station. Subway to Asser Levy Pool: 6 to 23rd St./Lexington Ave.

Walk five blocks east from station. Both pools listed above are safe, clean and free but you must bring your own lock and a proper bathing suit, although Asser Levy's heated indoor pool is open only to members. All outdoor pools are open early July through Labor Day, 11am or noon to 7pm, depending on the weather. Call ☎800-201-7275 for other locations. Indoor pools can be somewhat safer than outdoor pools, but most require some sort of annual membership fee ($10 or more).

INSIDE

shopping by type **239**

shopping by neighborhood **241**

financial district and civic center **241**

chinatown and little italy **241** lower east side **242**

soho **243** greenwich village **244**

east village **246** chelsea and the flatiron district **248**

herald square **249** midtown **250**

upper east side **251** upper west side **251**

brooklyn **252**

Shopping

With everything you could ever imagine, from the world's (former) largest department store to the hottest new boutique to the hardest-to-find underground used-clothing store, spending money in NYC has never been easier—perhaps a bit *too* easy. This is your guide to the largest, the cutest, and the hippest. Find a department store; find a designer flagship store; find an out-of-print import CD; find the cheapest, tightest shirt for tonight; find $10 Prada bags and Rolex watches (or reasonable facsimiles thereof).

SHOPPING BY TYPE

ABBREVIATIONS. CB-Central Brooklyn; **CHE**-Chelsea, Flatiron District; **CHI**-Chinatown, Little Italy; **EV**-East Village; **GV**-Greenwich Village; **HAR**-Harlem; **HS**-Herald Square; **LES**-Lower East Side; **LM**-Lower Manhattan; **MID**-Midtown; **SoHo**-SoHo; **UES**-Upper East Side; **UWS**-Upper West Side; **WIL**-Williamsburg.

ACCESSORIES

Adorned (246)	EV
Bird (253)	BC
Girlprops.com (243)	SoHo
It's a Mod, Mod World (246)	EV
Language (242)	LM
Manhattan Portage (247)	EV
Tiffany & Co. (251)	MID
Ugly Luggage (253)	WIL

ARMY/NAVY SURPLUS

Uncle Sam's Army Navy (245)	GV
Weiss and Mahoney (249)	CHE

ART SUPPLIES AND STATIONERY

Untitled (243)	SoHo

ASIAN

The Oriental Culture Enterprise (242)	CHI
Pearl River (242)	CHI

BEAUTY AND HAIR PRODUCTS

Astor Place Hairstylist (246)	EV
Girdle Factory (253)	WIL
Kiehl's (246)	EV
Sephora (243)	SoHo

BOOKSTORES

Applause Theater & Cinema Bks (252)	UWS
Argosy Bookstore (251)	UES
Biography Bookstore (244)	GV
Bluestockings (242)	LES
Books of Wonder (248)	CHE
Clovis Press (253)	WIL
The Complete Traveller Bookstore (249)	HS
The Drama Book Shop (250)	MID
Gotham Book Mart (250)	MID
Hacker Strand Art Books (250)	MID
Murder Ink/Ivy's (252)	UWS
Oscar Wilde G & L Bookshop (244)	GV
Revolution Books (249)	CHE
St. Mark's Bookshop (247)	EV
See Hear (247)	EV
Shakespeare and Company (245)	GV
Strand Annex (241)	LM
Strand Bookstore (245)	GV

CLOTHING, CLUBBING

House of Trance (246)	EV
Metropolis (247)	EV

CLOTHING, DESIGNER

Allan and Suzi (251)	UWS
Bergdorff-Goodman (250)	MID
Bird (253)	BC
Find Outlet (242)	CHI

CLOTHING, GENERAL

Bloomingdale's (251)	UES
Century 21 (241)	LM
Diop Tailoring and Fashion (253)	CB
Domsey's (253)	WIL
Find Outlet (242)	CHI
H&M (249)	HS

CLOTHING, VINTAGE

17@17 Thrift Shop (248)	CHE
Andy's Chee-pee's (244)	GV
Beacon's Closet (252)	WIL
Cheap Jack's Vintage Clothing (244)	GV
Encore (251)	MID
FAB208 (248)	EV
Girdle Factory (253)	WIL
Love Saves the Day (247)	EV
Metropolis (247)	EV
Physical Graffiti (248)	EV
Tatiana Designer Resale Boutique (248)	EV
Tokyo 7 Consignment Store (248)	EV
Tokyo Joe (248)	EV

COLLECTIBLES/ANTIQUES

Las Venus Lounge (243)	LES
Lot 76 NYC (247)	EV
Love Saves the Day (247)	EV
Maxilla & Mandible (252)	UWS
Rita Ford Music Boxes (251)	MID
Sugar Hill Thrift Shop (252)	HAR

COMPUTERS AND ELECTRONICS

J&R Music /Computer World (241)	LM

DEPARTMENT STORES

Barneys New York (251)	MID
Bergdorff-Goodman (250)	MID
Bloomingdale's (251)	UES
Century 21 (241)	LM
Domsey's (253)	WIL
Lord and Taylor (250)	MID
Macy's (249)	HS
Saks Fifth Avenue (251)	MID

GAY

Bluestockings (242)	LES
Oscar Wilde G & L Bookshop (244)	GV

MALLS

Fulton Mall (253)	CB
Girdle Factory (253)	WIL
Pier 17 Pavilion (241)	LM

MUSIC

Beat Street (253)	BC
Disc-o-Rama (244)	GV
Downtown Music Gallery (246)	EV
Generation Records (244)	GV
Gryphon Record Shop (252)	WS
House of Trance (246)	EV
J&R Music/Computer World (241)	LM
Jammyland (246)	EV
Kim's Video and Audio (246)	EV
Midnight Records (248)	CHE
Other Music (247)	EV

MUSIC CONT'D.	
Reminiscence (249)	CHE
Rock and Soul (249)	HS
Second Coming Records (245)	GV
Throb (248)	EV
PERIODICALS AND NEWSPAPERS	
Clovis Press (253)	WIL
Universal News and Cafe Corp. (243)	SoHo
PETS	
JBJ Discount Pet Shop (243)	LES
The Barking Zoo (248)	CHE
POSTERS AND COMICS	
Forbidden Planet (244)	GV
See Hear (247)	EV
Village Comics (245)	GV
SEWING SUPPLIES	
K. Trimming Co. (243)	SoHo
Tender Buttons (251)	MID
SEX (AND SEXY) SHOPS	
Condomania (244)	GV
La Petite Coquette (244)	GV
The Leather Man (244)	GV
Religious Sex (247)	EV
SPECIALTY STORES	
Bentley Manhattan (250)	MID
Hammacher Schlemmer (250)	MID
KCDC (253)	WIL
Las Venus Lounge (243)	LES
The Pop Shop (242)	CHI
Rita Ford Music Boxes (251)	MID
Spokes & Strings (253)	CB
Village Chess Shop (245)	GV
TOYS AND GAMES	
F.A.O. Schwarz (250)	MID
Village Chess Shop (245)	GV
VIDEO STORES	
Kim's Video and Audio (246)	EV

SHOPPING BY NEIGHBORHOOD

Shops are listed in alphabetical order.

FINANCIAL DISTRICT AND CIVIC CENTER

On the whole, the southernmost portion of Manhattan is not known for its shopping, but it can claim having two of the best stores in the city.

Century 21, 22 Cortlandt St., between Broadway and Church St. (☎212-227-9092). Subway: 1, 2, 4, 5, A, C, J, M, Z to Fulton St./Broadway-Nassau St. Map 7, C3, 8. A shopper's dream—a department store with discounted designer wares. See feature on following page. Open M-W and F 7:45am-8pm, Th 7:45am-8:30pm, Sa 10am-8pm, Su 11am-7pm.

J&R Music World/Computer World, 23 Park Row, between Ann and Barclay St. (☎212-732-8600 or 238-9000). Subway: N, R to City Hall; 4, 5, 6 to Brooklyn Bridge-City Hall. Map 7, C2, 4. Block-long cluster of separate, competitively priced stores to meet most imaginable electronics needs. Open M-W and F-Sa 9am-7pm, Th 9am-7:30pm, Su 10:30am-6:30pm.

Pier 17 Pavilion, near the river on Fulton St. Subway: 1, 2, 4, 5, A, C J, M, Z to Fulton St./Broadway-Nassau St. Map 7, F3, 14. Expansive shopping mall and restaurant arcade.

Strand Annex, 95 Fulton St., between William and Gold St. (☎212-732-6070). Subway: N, R to City Hall; 4, 5, 6 to Brooklyn Bridge-City Hall. Map 7, D3, 9. Younger sibling of Fifth Ave. landmark, the Strand Annex has great remaindered-books section with hearty supply of $1 used books. Open M-F 9:30am-9pm, Sa-Su 11am-8pm.

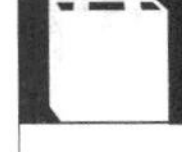

CHINATOWN AND LITTLE ITALY

So long as authenticity doesn't concern you, Chinatown is the perfect place to bargain hunt. You can find Asian imports, $5 burned CDs, and that Kate Spade bag you've been eyeing. And if the stores along Canal St. don't have the nice black vinyl bag with the Prada logo, ask them to stick one on—they're probably in the back.

North of Little Italy (NoLIta) is rife with fashionable boutiques. You might like them, but your wallet won't.

the hidden deal

Tired of the teeming masses that conspire to box you out from that cashmere, zebra-lined Dolce and Gabbana blazer? Unwilling to resort to fisticuffs to get your hands on that silk Versace dress? Just looking to spend an afternoon in Bay Ridge?

Although it still offers the best deal in Manhattan, Century 21 is far from hidden. Legions of locals and tourists alike overrun the Cortlandt Street landmark at all hours of the day. If you're overwhelmed by "New York's best-kept secret," you might consider checking out Century 21's best-kept secret, its branch in Brooklyn.

Stocked with many of the same designer wares as the Manhattan location but without the hordes of people clawing at them, the Brooklyn Century 21 can often be a better option than its sister store. It does get extremely crowded on weekends and holidays, but you can usually bargain hunt without distraction on a weekday afternoon.

472 86th St., Brooklyn. ☎718-748-3266. Subway: R to 86th St. Open M-W 10am-8pm, Th 10am-9pm, F 10am-8pm, Sa 10am-9:30pm, Su 11am-7pm. ***Additional locations in New Jersey and Long Island.***

Find Outlet, 229 Mott St., between Prince and Spring St. (☎212-226-5167). Subway: 6 to Spring St. Map 8, C2, 8. This outlet store sells wares from costly NoLIta boutiques at a substantial discount. Often 50-80% off the original. Open Th-Su noon-7pm. **Also at** 361 W. 17th St. (☎212-243-3177).

Language, 238 Mulberry St., between Prince and Spring St. (☎212-431-5566). Subway: 6 to Spring St. Map 8, C2, 7. Wonderful—though not affordable—women's clothing and froufrou accesories, all stylish and whimsically varied. Where else does one see a silver moped on display next to a gold-trimmed leather jacket and Amazon feather-masks? Open M-W 11am-7pm, Th 11am-7pm, Su noon-6pm.

The Oriental Culture Enterprise, 13-17 Elizabeth St., 2nd fl., between Bayard and Canal St. (☎212-226-8461). Subway: J, M, N, R, Z, 4, 5, 6 to Canal St. Map 8, D5, 27. Specializing in Chinese literature, but also sells tapes, newspapers, calligraphy equipment, musical instruments, and a selection of older pop music. Open daily 10am-7pm.

Pearl River, 277 Canal St., at Broadway (☎212-431-4770). Subway: N, R, J, M, Z, 4, 5, 6 to Canal St. Map 8, A4, 17. Chinese department store sells all the basic necessities, along with a few hard-to-find luxuries: silk slippers, paper lanterns, huge bamboo mats, and the miraculous Japanese buckwheat pillow. All cheap, all under 1 roof. Open daily 10am-7:30pm.

The Pop Shop, 292 Lafayette St., at Jersey St. (☎212-219-2784). Subway: B, D, F, Q to Broadway-Lafayette St. Map 8, B1, 1. 1980s pop artist Keith Haring's cartoonish, socially conscious work can be found on posters and postcards all over the city, but where else can you find pillows shaped like the figures in Haring's paintings ($85), Haring-decorated T-shirts (starting at $15), and everything else pop? Opened in 1985, the shop was painted by the late artist in his distinctive thick-brushed style, and all proceeds benefit the Keith Haring Foundation. Open M-Sa noon-7pm, Su noon-6pm.

LOWER EAST SIDE

Shopping on the Lower East Side is slowly becoming an expensive venture. Up-and-coming designers and select shops often display their handmade, cutting-edge wares in stores that look more like museums. Trendy boutiques abound on Stanton and Ludlow St. Orchard St., between Houston and Delancey St., offers a melange of thrift stores and high fashion.

Bluestockings, 172 Allen St., between Rivington and Stanton St. (☎212-777-6028; www.bluestockings.com). Subway: F, J, M, Z to Delancey St.-Essex St.

Map 11, D2, 23. An extremely gay-friendly, volunteer-run independent women's bookstore and cafe that "promotes empowerment of women through words, art and activism." The store doubles as a space for lectures, readings, workshops, and politically oriented meetings. Groups using the space include a "Dyke Knitting Circle" and a women's graduate dissertation support group. Website lists the nightly activities. Volunteer training 1st Sa of every month; call ahead to reserve a spot. Open Su, W-Sa 2:30-9pm.

JBJ Discount Pet Shop, 151 E. Houston St., at Eldridge St. (☎212-982-5310). Subway: J, M, Z to Bowery. Map 11, D1, 7. Sells bizarre pets at discount rates. Their petite pests have made it big: the Madagascar hissing roaches appeared in *Men In Black,* and many other species have debuted on David Letterman. The owners have a sense of humor, evidenced by the sign reading "Hug me" in the South American boa cage. Open M-Sa 10am-6:30pm.

Las Venus Lounge 20th Century Pop Culture, 163 Ludlow St., at Stanton St. (☎212-982-0608). Subway: F, J, M, Z to Delancey St.-Essex St. Map 11, E1, 16. A wild vintage store, this lounge sells everything from giant lily lamps to 1960s porn magazines. Scenesters stroll into this romantic hotspot on the weekend, kick back on the pleather couches, and transform what seems like an overcrowded vintage furniture store into a spontaneous party. Open Su-W noon-9pm, Th noon-11pm, F-Sa noon-midnight.

SOHO

SoHo is upscale, but you can still find some deals at the district's used clothing stores and streetside stands. Check out the daily "fair" that sets up shop in a lot on **Wooster and Spring Street.** The bargain hunt continues on Broadway with a wide selection of used clothing stores, like **Alice Underground.** (481 Broadway, between Broome and Grand St. Map 9, D3, 37.)

Girlprops.com, 153 Prince St., between W. Broadway and Thompson St. (☎212-505-7615). Subway: C, E to Spring St./Ave. of the Americas (Sixth Ave.); N, R to Prince St. Map 9, C2, 14. Heaven for accessory-lovers with every variety of hair clip, lariat, body glitter, rhinestone belt, feather boa, make-up, or tiara currently in style. Individually inexpensive—but beware, those sparkly bobby pins do add up. Most under $10. Open Su-Th 11am-10pm, F-Sa 11am-midnight.

K. Trimming Co., 519 Broadway between Spring and Broome St. (☎212-431-8929 or 226-3539). Subway: C, E to Spring St./Ave. of the Americas (Sixth Ave.); 6 to Spring St./Lafayette St.; N, R to Prince St. Map 9, D3, 34. Huge warehouse filled with every variety of sewing product you could ever want: doilies, swaths of colored fabrics, embroidered trimmings, pom-poms, etc. A fashion magnet for the aspiring SoHo designer in all of us. Open Su-Th 9am-7pm, F 9am-1:30pm, closed Sa.

Sephora, 555 Broadway, between Spring and Prince St. (☎212-625-1309). Subway: C, E to Spring St./Ave. of the Americas (Sixth Ave.); 6 to Spring St./Lafayette St.; N, R to Prince St. Map 9, D2. An overwhelming array of cosmetic products, including a vast selection of perfumes, powders, and exfoliators. Knowledgeable staff make finding that perfect skincare regime a breeze. They also carry men's fragrances and skincare products. Open M-Sa 10am-8pm, Su 11am-7pm.

Universal News and Cafe Corp., 484 Broadway, between Broome and Grand St. (☎212-965-9042). Subway: C, E to Spring St./Ave. of the Americas (Sixth Ave.); 6 to Spring St./Lafayette St. Map 9, D3, 38. Over 7000 foreign and domestic magazine titles, covering everything from fashion to fishing to politics. Doubles as a cafe with decent fare. Open daily 5am-midnight.

Untitled, 159 Prince St., between W. Broadway and Thompson St. (☎212-982-2088). Subway: C, E to Spring St./Ave. of the Americas (Sixth Ave.); N, R to Prince St. Map 9, C2, 13. Based in SoHo since 1970, this fine-arts store specializes in design and typography. An amazing library of postcards, each $0.85, is catalogued for your convenience. Open M-Th 10am-8pm, F-Sa 10am-9pm, Su 10am-8pm.

GREENWICH VILLAGE

Andy's Chee-pee's, 691 Broadway, between E. 4th St. and Great Jones St. (☎212-420-5980). Subway: N, R to 8th St.-NYU. Map 10, F4, 37. Not really cheap at all, but worth a peek, if only for that vintage clothing aroma. Open M-Sa 11am-9pm, Su noon-8pm.

Biography Bookstore, 400 Bleecker St., at W. 11th St. (☎212-807-8655). Subway: 1, 9 to Christopher St. Map 10, A3, 19. Biography-browsing at its best with friendly, knowledgeable staff. Search through the stacks and discover biographical gems on all sorts of fascinating (and boring) people, from Elvis to Princess Diana to probably even your grandma. Strong gay/lesbian section, as well as best-sellers, travel books, film, and drama. Open M-Th 11am-10pm, F-Sa 11am-11pm, Su 11am-7pm.

Cheap Jack's Vintage Clothing, 841 Broadway, between 13th and 14th St. (☎212-777-9564). Subway: 4, 5, 6, L, N, Q, R, W to 14th St.-Union Sq. Map 10, F2, 14. Yet another vintage store using the word "cheap" a bit too loosely. Jack's sells racks of worn jeans, leather jackets, and other vintage "gems." Open M-Sa 11am-8pm, Su noon-7pm.

Condomania, 351 Bleecker St., at W. 10th St. (☎212-691-9442). Subway: 1, 9 to Christopher St. Map 10, B3, 42. The Village's radical legacy made it the birthplace of the birth-control movement—and a sex-shop haven. "America's first condom store" stocks over 150 types of condoms in every imaginable color and texture, as well as various other accoutrements. Pick up some X-rated fortune cookies, a condom lollipop, a box of "Penis Pasta," or their best-selling pecker sipping straws with your order. Friendly staff answers all questions and gives safe-sex tips. Open Su-Th 11am-11pm, F-Sa 11am-midnight.

Disc-O-Rama, 186 W. 4th St., between MacDougal St. and 6th Ave. (☎212-206-8417). Subway: A, C, F to W. 4th St. Although they won't always have everything you want, Disc-o-Rama rarely charges more than $10 for a new CD. Such a ridiculous bargain, coupled with an impressive used CD collection, makes Disc-o-Rama our favorite music shop in NYC. Open M-Th 10:15am-10:45pm, F 10:15am-11:45pm, Sa 10:45am-12:45am, Su 11:45am-8:15pm.

Forbidden Planet, 840 Broadway, at 13th St. (☎212-473-1576). Subway: 4, 5, 6, L, N, Q, R, W to 14th St.-Union Sq. Map 10, F2, 15. A repository of all things sci-fi. Comics, posters, models, toys, Playstation games (to buy, sell, and trade), and art books. Pubescent boys congregate here to play role-playing games. Open M-Sa 10am-10pm, Su 11am-8pm.

Generation Records, 210 Thompson St., between Bleecker and 3rd St. (☎212-254-1100). Subway: A, C, E, F, V, S to W. 4th St. Map 10, E4, 83. Coolest goth hangout in town. All kinds of alternative and underground rock on CD and vinyl; the hard-core and industrial/experimental selection is especially impressive. Fairly low prices (CDs $11-13) and the best assortment of hard-to-find imports in the Village. Great deals on used merchandise downstairs (CDs usually $6 or less). Open M-Th 11am-10pm, F-Sa 11am-1am, Su noon-10pm.

La Petite Coquette, 51 University Pl., between 9th and 10th St. (☎212-473-2478). Subway: N, R to 8th St.-NYU. Map 10, F2, 35. This shop offers all things beaded, embroidered, laced, fringed, and tied. Celebrity photos on the walls testify that La Petite Coquette will elude your budget, but the prices won't drive away the true lingerie enthusiast. Come for their post-Valentine's Day sale when most items are 40% off. Open M-W 11am-7pm, Th 11am-8pm, F-Sa 11am-7pm, Su noon-6pm.

The Leather Man, 111 Christopher St., between Bleecker and Hudson St. (☎212-243-5339). Subway: 1, 9 to Christopher St. Map 10, B4, 47. A sex shop, not a superhero or knife store. The dim, freaky upstairs is dominated by leather apparel, handcuffs, and bondage equipment, but braving the spiral staircase downstairs drops you in a new world of kink. Open M-Sa noon-10pm, Su noon-8pm.

Oscar Wilde Gay and Lesbian Bookshop, 15 Christopher St., at Sixth Ave./Gay St. (☎212-255-8097). Subway: 1, 9 to Christopher St. Map 10, C3, 29. Originally in SoHo, this cozy shop claims to be the world's 1st gay and lesbian bookstore. In addition to a number of rare and 1st edition books, the store stocks a multitude of CDs, videos, travel guides and magazines. Will also special order any book. Open daily 11am-7pm.

Second Coming Records, 231 and 235 Sullivan St., between Bleecker and W. 3rd St. (☎212-228-1313). Subway: A, C, E, F, V, S to W. 4th St. Map 10, D4, 76. Heaven-sent vinyl, and lots of it. The CD stock accommodates a wide range of alternative and popular releases, both new and used. Also good for alternative imports and bootlegs. Open M-Th 11am-7pm, F-Sa 11am-9pm, Su noon-7pm.

Shakespeare and Company, 716 Broadway, at Washington Pl. (☎212-529-1330; www.shakespeareandco.com). Subway: N, R to 8th St.-NYU. Map 10, F3, 65. There's more than just words at this New York institution. Shakespeare & Co. carries high-quality literature, high-brow journals, and a great selection of vintage crime, art, and theater books that won't cost you a pound of flesh. Open Su-Th 10am-11pm, F-Sa 10am-midnight.

Astor Place Hair

Strand Bookstore, 828 Broadway, at E. 12th St. (☎212-473-1452). Subway: 4, 5, 6, L, N, Q, R, W to 14th St.-Union Sq. Map 10, F2, 16. The world's largest used bookstore. A must-see, with 8 mi. of shelf space that holds nearly 2 million books including rare titles and 1st editions. 50% off review copies and paperbacks. Vast collection of art books. Check the outdoor carts for extreme bargains. Ask for a catalog, or better yet, get lost in the shelves on your own. Open M-Sa 9:30am-9:20pm, Su 11am-9:20pm.

Strand Bookstore

Uncle Sam's Army Navy, 37 W. 8th St., between Fifth and Sixth Ave. (☎212-674-2222). Subway: N, R to 8th St.-NYU. Map 10, D3, 33. Eclectic supply of military garb from around the world (we're talkin' *East* German uniform pants). Selection of helmets $14-19 (sometimes on sale for $12). Also houses good selection of less official wear including work pants "that will never tear" ($15). Open M-W 10am-9pm, Th-Sa 10am-10pm, Su 11am-9pm.

Village Chess Shop, 230 Thompson St., between Bleecker and W. 3rd St. (☎212-475-9580). Subway: A, C, E, F, V, S to W. 4th St. Map 10, E4, 82. The Village's keenest intellects square off in rigorous strategic combat while sipping coffee ($1) and juice ($1.50). Play is $1 or $1.50 for clocked play per hr. per person. Don't swear, or you'll be penalized $1.25. Also has a wide variety of chess sets for sale, including several breathtaking antique chess sets. Open daily noon-midnight.

Village Comics, 214 Sullivan St., between Bleecker and W. 3rd St. (☎212-777-2770). Subway: A, C, E, F, V, S to W. 4th St. Map 10, D4, 80. The requisite comics jostle for space with collectible figurines, sci-fi trinkets, and horror-movie doodads. Porn movies and magazines in the back. Open M-Tu 10am-7:30pm, W-Sa 10am-8:30pm, Su 11am-7pm.

St. Mark's Place

EAST VILLAGE

As might be expected from an area populated by self-styled avatars of hipness, the East Village shopping scene is dominated by small, specialized stores. Those looking for brand names would be better off in SoHo, but those seeking vintage clothing shall find. St. Mark's Pl. shops sell a fantastic assortment of silver jewelry and odd trinkets. **Record Stores** line both sides of St. Mark's Pl., mostly between Third Ave. and Ave. A. Barely organized shelves/racks/drawers can keep you browsing for hours, but you'll find the best price for used and new CDs—as well as a decent variety of records. Make sure to check out **Sounds.** (20 St. Mark's Pl., between Second and Third Ave. Map 12, C2. ☎212-677-3444. Open daily noon-11pm.) **CD & Cassette Annex,** down the street, is also noteworthy. (16 St. Mark's Pl., between Second and Third Ave. Map 12, C2. ☎212-677-2727. Open daily noon-usually 11pm.) Boutiques along 9th St., off Ave. A, sell handmade, fashionable one-of-a-kinds.

Adorned, 47 Second Ave., between E. 2nd and 3rd St. (☎212-473-0007). Subway: F, V to Lower East Side-Second Ave. Map 12, C4, 91. Comfortable, safe, and friendly place to add bauble to your body and "make you beautiful, not mutilated." Some of the best artists in the city. Nose piercing $15; navel $20. Jewelry not included, but there's a wide variety for sale. Skilled, traditional *henna* work (hands and feet) from $20. Tattoos $75 and up. Open Su-Th 1pm-9pm, F-Sa 1pm-10pm.

Astor Place Hairstylist, 2 Astor Pl., at Broadway (☎212-475-9854). Subway: 6 to Astor Pl.; N, R to 8th St.-NYU. Map 12, B3, 57. World's largest haircutting establishment is famed for low-priced, production-line approach to style. It's also king of cool and the only place to go if you feel the NYC flavor. Run DMC, Adam Sandler, and Joan Rivers are some of the celeb clientele, whose photos adorn the front windows. 85 people work in the 3-story complex. Haircuts $11-25; Su $2 extra. Open daily M-Sa 8am-8pm.

Downtown Music Gallery, 211 E. 5th St., between Second and Third Ave. (☎212-473-0043). Subway: F, V to Lower East Side-Second Ave. Map 12, C3, 69. Dense, diverse selection of CDs and records should please most non-mainstream music enthusiasts. Knowledgeable, helpful staff. Genres include jazz, folk, classical, and electronic. Open Su-Th noon-9pm, F-Sa noon-11pm.

House of Trance, 122 St. Mark's Pl., between First Ave. and Ave. A (☎212-533-6700). Subway: 6 to Astor Pl. Map 12, D2, 48. Step into blacklight-lit ambience to chill with Goa-trancers, the modern-day version of psychedelic flower children. Trance records set the mood. Dayglo T-shirts $17-20, camisoles $17. Open daily 11am-midnight.

It's a Mod, Mod World, 85 First Ave., between E. 5th and 6th St. (☎212-460-8004). Subway: F, V to Lower East Side-Second Ave. Map 12, D3, 79. Beaded day-glo-painted temple to life's unnecessary but wonderful delights. Fabulous selection of gift items and jewelry. *Barbie* doll installations on display (available for sale), as well as clocks made of cereal and candy boxes ($20). Open M-Th noon-10pm, F-Sa noon-11pm, Su noon-8pm.

Jammyland, 60 E. 3rd St., between First and Second Ave. (☎212-614-0185; www.jammyland.com). Subway: F, V to Lower East Side-Second Ave. Map 12, D4, 96. Wide selection of reggae, dub, dance hall, ska, and other Jamaican innovations. Decent world music supply. Open Su noon-8pm, M-Th noon-10pm, F-Sa noon-midnight.

Kiehl's, 109 Third Ave., between E. 13th and 14th St. (☎212-677-3171). Subway: 4, 5, 6, L, N, Q, R, W to 14th St.-Union Sq.; L to Third Ave. Map 12, C1, 4. Specialty cosmetics store (over 150 yr. old!) with luxurious prices to match their products (toner $15, lip balm $5). Their policy of giving out free (and conveniently travel-sized) samples, however, is possibly one of New York's best deals–and might just convince you to buy something. Currently expanding and retaking their original home (for the first 107 yr.) next door. Pictures of lots of babies on the wall; despite the misleading t-shirts, all are not all little Kiehls. Open M-Sa 10am-7pm, Su 10am-6pm.

Kim's Video and Audio, 6 St. Mark's Pl., between Second and Third Ave. (☎212-598-9985). Subway: 6 to Astor Pl. Map 12, C2, 30. 3 floors of hip entertainment selections. Ground fl. has startlingly strong selection of independent and import CDs, with beats ranging from 1970s Jamaican dub to avant-jazz. 2nd fl. holds new and used vinyl, as well as a tremendous video showcase specializing in independent and foreign films. Open daily 9am-midnight (video until 10).

Lot 76 NYC, 76 E. Houston St., between Elizabeth St. and Bowery (☎212-505-8699). Subway: F, V to Lower East Side-Second Ave. Map 12, E4. Take home a piece of the subway, legally: this outdoor store sells NY subway signs. It also sells old Coke machines, antique chairs, and objects that simply defy description! Pieces often rented for film sets, photo shoots and other visually memorable endeavors. Open daily 10am-6pm, weather permitting.

Love Saves the Day, 119 Second Ave., at E. 7th St. (☎212-228-3802). Subway: 6 to Astor Pl. Map 12, C3, 35. Selling vintage clothing ($15 shirts) and random collectibles (we spotted ALF memorabilia and old issues of *Life* magazine) since 1966. Open daily 1-8:30pm.

Manhattan Portage, 333 E. 9th St., between First and Second Ave. (☎212-995-5490; www.manhattanportage.com). Subway: 6 to Astor Pl. You don't have to be a DJ or a bike messenger to carry these utility bags. Urban Outfitters sells them all over the country now—here's where they got their start. $35-70. Open Su-Th noon-7pm, F-Sa noon-8pm.

Metropolis, 43 Third Ave., between E. 9th and 10th St. (☎212-358-0795). Subway: 6 to Astor Pl. Map 12, C2, 23. Selection of new and vintage clubwear and shoes, heavy on the funk and slightly cyber-y. Complete with DJ booth; make sure to pick up flyers at the front of the store on the way out. Open daily noon-10pm. **Also at** 96 Ave. B, between E. 6th and 7th St. (☎212-477-3941).

Other Music, 15 E. 4th St., between Lafayette St. and Broadway (☎212-477-8150; www.othermusic.com). Subway: 6 to Bleecker St. Map 12, B3, 60. Specializing in the alternative and avant-garde. Obscure stuff abounds. Avoid steep import prices with sizeable used-CD section. Posters and flyers keep clientele updated on where to see their favorite performers; staff is an even better source of information. Overall point: best music store in the city. Open M-F noon-9pm, Sa noon-8pm, Su noon-7pm.

Religious Sex, 7 St. Mark's Pl., between Second and Third Ave. (☎212-477-9037). Subway: 6 to Astor Pl. Map 12, C2, 28. Supplies vinyl corsets, opulent boas, and sequined tutus to local fetishists. Amazing array of kinky outerwear that delights in the outlandish and dabbles in the gothic. 4-inch PVC stiletto heels $49. Open M-W noon-8pm, Th-Sa noon-9pm, Su 1-8pm.

See Hear, 59 E. 7th St., between First and Second Ave. (☎212-505-9781). Subway: 6 to Astor Pl. Map 12, D3, 76. Both literally and figuratively underground. Sells rock music books, 'zines, music mags, and comics. Good place to get old copies of *Mojo* magazine. Open daily noon-8pm.

St. Mark's Bookshop, 31 Third Ave., at E. 9th St. (☎212-260-7853; www.stmarksbookshop.com). Subway: 6 to Astor Pl. Map 12, C2, 22. Ultimate East

Chinatown Bargain-hunting

Generation Records

FAO Schwarz, Midtown

Village bookstore. Excellent selection of books, with an emphasis on current literary theory, fiction, and poetry. Good selection of mainstream and avant-garde magazines. Helpful staff. Open M-Sa 10am-midnight, Su 11am-midnight.

Throb, 211 E. 14th St., between Second and Third Ave. (☎212-533-2328). Subway: L, N, Q, R, W, 4, 5, 6 to 14th St.-Union Sq.; L to Third Ave. Map 13, F6, 125. House, drum 'n' bass, trip-hop, psychedelic trance, and more. Caters to folks who are serious about their beats. Wax for the DJs, CDs for the audiophiles, flyers for those looking to party, and a hip staff to assist the (gasp) unfamiliar. Open M-Sa noon-9pm, Su 1-9pm.

VINTAGE AND CONSIGNMENT STORES

FAB208, 75 E. 7th St., between First and Second Ave. (☎212-673-7581). Subway: 6 to Astor Pl. Map 12, D3, 78. Carries both vintage wear and new clothes under the FAB208NYC label. Prices range from $15 earrings to $165 for "one-of-a-kind recycled vintage silk pieces." Open Su 2-7pm, Tu-Sa noon-7:45pm.

Physical Graffiti, 96 St. Mark's Pl., between First Ave. and Ave. A (☎212-477-7334). Subway: 6 to Astor Pl.; L to First Ave. Map 12, D2, 48. 20s-60s vintage clothing. Wide price range. Men's shirts from $22, designer vintage dresses up to $150. Open M-Th 1-9pm, F 1pm-10:30pm, Sa-Su noon-11pm.

Tatiana Designer Resale Boutique, 111 St. Mark's Pl., between First Ave. and Ave. A (☎212-375-8728; www.tatianas.com). Subway: 6 to Astor Pl.; L to First Ave. Map 12, D2, 48. New and vintage jewelry, shoes, dresses, accessories, suits, handbags, and furs from elite designers such as Chanel, Versace, Emanuel Ungaro, Moschino, Hermes, Cartier, and Fendi. Most of the items come directly from fashion shows and showroom floors. Gucci vintage wallet $160, used Armani suit $225. Open daily 1pm-10pm.

Tokyo 7 Consignment Store, 64 E. 7th St., between First and Second Ave. (☎212-353-8443). Subway: 6 to Astor Pl. Map 12, D3, 78. Sells used designer clothes with such labels as Prada, Gucci, Betsy Johnson. $200-600. Open M-Sa noon-8:30pm, Su noon-8pm.

Tokyo Joe, 334 E. 11th St., between First and Second Ave. (☎212-473-0724). Subway: 6 to Astor Pl.; L to First Ave. Map 12, D2, 33. Consignment store with extremely well-priced brand-name clothing, as well as hard-to-find Japanese brands like Pluto Cat on the Earth. Open daily noon-9pm. **Also at** 240 E. 28th St., between Second and Third Ave.

CHELSEA AND THE FLATIRON DISTRICT

Ladies' Mile, in the Flatiron District between Broadway and Sixth Ave., was once a major shopping district: Macy's first store was here, at Sixth Ave. and 14th St. It still remains a shopping hub, and those seeking to avoid the hordes farther uptown will find the chain stores here somewhat less crowded.

17 @ 17 Thrift Shop, 17 W. 17th St., between 5th and 6th Ave. This thrift shop offers secondhand goods and clothing in an elegant setting. A silent auction on vintage Emilio Pucci clothing will cost you upwards of $400, but a paperback book–only 50¢. Open M-Tu and F 11am-6pm, W-Th 11am-7pm, Sa 11am-5pm.

The Barking Zoo, 172 Ninth Ave., between 20th and 21st St. (☎212-255-0658). Adorable pet store sells premium goods a bit off the beaten path. Find organic, holistic products such as doggy lamb jerky ($14.99) and all-natural pet shampoo. For accessories, try the jewelled dog leashes ($25) and army suits for dogs. M-F 11am-8pm, Sa 10am-6pm, Su 12pm-5pm.

Books of Wonder, 16 W. 18th St., between Fifth and Sixth Ave. (☎212-989-3270). Subway: F, V to 23rd St./Ave. of the Americas (Sixth Ave.). Map 13, D5, 84. A jewel of a children's bookstore, with an amazing antique book section and stuffed animals galore. Hosts a variety of programs related to children's books; storytime Su at noon. Open Sept.-June M-Sa 10am-7pm, Su noon-6pm; July-Aug. M-Sa 11am-7pm, Su noon-6pm.

Midnight Records, 263 W. 23rd St., between Seventh and Eighth Ave. (☎212-675-2768; www.midnightrecords.com). Subway: 1, 9 to 23rd St./Seventh Ave. Map 13, C4, 31. A mail-order and retail store specializing in hard-to-find rock records. Posters plaster the walls; every last nook of the store is crammed with its 10,000-plus collection of records. Lots of 60s and 70s titles. LPs, mostly $9-20, can be ordered online via the website. $1 records line the wall outside. Open Tu and Th-Sa noon-6pm.

Reminiscence, 50 W. 23rd St., between Fifth and Sixth Ave. (☎212-243-2292). Subway: N, R to 23rd St./Broadway. Map 13, D4, 38. Happily stuck in a 1970s groove, the Japan-based store features a wide selection of campy gifts, retro trinkets (inflatable flamingo cups $5; mini discoballs $3), 70s jewelry, and vintage gear (jeans $12-18, leather mini-skirts $12-18). Open M-Sa 11am-7:30pm, Su noon-7pm.

Revolution Books, 9 W. 19th St., between Fifth and Sixth Ave. (☎212-691-3345). Subway: F, V to 23rd St./Ave. of the Americas (Sixth Ave.); 4, 5, 6, L, N, Q, R, W to 14th St.-Union Sq. Map 13, D5, 82. America's largest explicitly revolutionary bookstore stocks literature on radical struggles worldwide. Large collection of works on Marx, Mao, and Malcolm X. Wares range from political science volumes to manifestos, posters to children's books. Meaty selection of anti-war and anti-Bush paraphernalia and literature. Not-for-profit and mostly staffed by clued-in volunteers. Open M-Sa 10am-7pm, Su noon-5pm.

Weiss and Mahoney, 142 Fifth Ave., at 19th St. (☎212-675-1915). Subway: F, V to 23rd St./Ave. of the Americas (Sixth Ave.). Map 13, D5, 83. A "peaceful" army/navy store selling surplus gear and camping equipment. The fashion militant can indulge in cargo pants ($20 for camo pants) and the mountain trampers can peruse a decent selection of outdoor gear. The brooding weapons lovers can sift through all sorts of knives. Buy Carhartts at decent prices ($27-40 depending on the style). Open M-F 9am-7pm, Sa 10am-6pm, Su 11am-5pm.

HERALD SQUARE

Dominated by Macy's, once the world's largest store, Herald Sq. is full of department stores.

The Complete Traveller Bookstore, 199 Madison Ave., at 35th St. (☎212-685-9007). Subway: 6 to 33rd St. Map 13, E2, 6. Arnold and Harriet Greenberg stock a wide selection of guidebooks, language manuals , travel clocks and also carry a well-kept selection of antique travel guides *(Baedekers, A&C Blacks)* and travelogues about distant lands. Wheelchair accessible. Open M-F 9am-6pm, Sa 10am-6pm, Su 11am-5pm. Open M-F 10am-7pm, Sa 10am-6pm, Su 12pm-5pm.

H&M, 1328 Broadway, at 34th St. (☎212-564-9922). Subway: B, D, F, N, Q, R, V, W to 34th St.-Herald Sq. Map 13, D2, 4. When this Swedish chain opened its first New York branch, lines formed round the block. Knock-offs of the latest styles and accessories, both at ridiculously low prices (we spotted an eyelash comb for $1.50). Maneuvering through the crowd is difficult and dizzying but made worthwhile by end-of-season clearance sales driving bargain prices down to pocket change (Tops $4.99). Open M-Sa 10am-9pm, Su 11am-8pm. **Also at** 640 Fifth Ave., at 51st St. (open M-F 10am-8pm, Sa 10am-9pm, Su 11am-7pm), and 558 Broadway, between Prince and Spring St. (open M-Sa 10am-9pm, Su 11am-5pm).

Macy's, 151 W. 34th St., between Broadway and Seventh Ave. (☎212-695-4400; www.macys.com). Subway: B, D, F, N, Q, R, V, W to 34th St.-Herald Sq. Map 13, C2, 3. This New York institution alternately provides thrills and frustration. Just don't get in the way of crazed shoppers on sale days (almost every W and Sa). Its labyrinthine interior lets you purchase a book, grab a snack or an all-out meal, get a facial or a haircut, have your jewelry appraised, exchange currency, purchase theater tickets, and get lost. Open M-Sa 10am-8:30pm, Su 11am-7pm. (See also **Sights,** p. 75.)

Rock and Soul, 462 Seventh Ave., between 35th and 36th St. (☎212-695-3953). Subway: 1, 2, 3, to 34th St.-Penn Station/Seventh Ave. Map 13, C2, 31. Past the bling bling (shiny jewelry) appropriately entitled "Gold and Soul" and the hottest, most up-to-date DJ equipment in the front, you'll find a pathway to full crates of vinyls. Great if you're looking for old-school classics or new releases in soul, R&B, reggae, or hip-hop. Open M-Sa 9:30am-7pm.

MIDTOWN

High-priced boutiques, the most fashionable that New York has to offer, line Fifth Ave. south of Central Park.

Bentley Manhattan, corner of 49th St. and Madison Ave. (☎212-680-5500). The man behind the desk knows about cars, which is good because these machines go for $250,000-450,000. They sit in the window taunting passersby with their unparalleled craftsmanship. If you have enough cash, you can customize every surface free: (types of leather, paint colors, feel of the steering-wheel). T-shirts and keychains with more human prices also sold! This place is ridiculous. Open M-F 11am-6pm, Sa 11am-3pm (not in summer).

Bergdorff-Goodman, 754 Fifth Ave. at 58th St. (☎212-872-3000). Subway: N, R, W to Fifth Ave./59th St. Map 14, D2, 18. In addition to housing all of high fashion's top designers, this legendary mansion of clothing (and pomp), splendid in its marble and chandelier surroundings, is every celebrity's one-stop shopping choice when they want to be left alone. Open M-W 10am-7pm, Th 10am-8pm, F-Sa 10am-7pm, Su noon-6pm.

The Drama Book Shop, 250 40th St., between Seventh and Eighth Ave. (☎212-944-0595; www.dramabookshop.com). Subway: 1, 2, 3, 7, 9, N, Q, R, S, W to 42nd St.-Times Square; A, C, E, to 42nd St.-Port Authority. Map 14, C5, 90. If it ever appeared on-stage, it's probably in print here. Find half the city's aspiring actors and the monologues they seek, all in one compact location. A necessary stop for any theater, film or performing arts buff. Open M-Sa 10am-8pm, Su noon-6pm.

F.A.O. Schwarz, 767 Fifth Ave., at 58th St. (☎212-644-9400). Subway: N, R, W to Fifth Ave./59th St. Map 14, D2, 19. Like Tom Hanks in *Big,* adults can reclaim their inner spoiled brat in this child's ultimate fantasy world: everything that whirs, flies, or begs to be assembled appears in this huge hands-on toy store. Christmastime sees amusement-park-like lines outside and frenzied shoppers inside. For the young ones, storytime is held daily at 1, 3, and 5pm. Open M-W 10am-7pm, Th-Sa 10am-7pm, Su 11am-6pm.

Gotham Book Mart, 41 W. 47th St., between Fifth and Sixth Ave. (☎212-719-4448). Subway: B, D, F, V to 50th St.-Rockefeller Center. Map 14, D3, 47. The sign outside reads "Wise men fish here." Legendary and venerable, Gotham's renowned selection of new and used volumes of 20th-century writing has long made it a favorite of New York bibliophiles, and the occasional celebrity. This little renegade store smuggled censored copies of works by Joyce, Lawrence, and Miller to America. Then-unknowns LeRoi Jones, Tennessee Williams, and Allen Ginsberg all worked here as clerks. Open M-F 9:30am-6:30pm, Sa 9:30am-6pm.

Hacker Strand Art Books, 45 W. 57th St., between Fifth and Sixth Ave. (☎212-688-7600). Subway: Q to 57th St. Map 14, D2, 16. 5 flights up from the rumble of the street, this store is hard to find (look for street numbers) but worth the effort for the great selection. The wide array of books should satisfy art historians, birdhouse builders, and fans of prehistoric stoneware alike. Open M-Sa 9:30am-6pm.

Hammacher Schlemmer, 147 E. 57th St., between Third and Lexington Ave. (☎212-421-9000; www.hammacher.com). Subway: 4, 5, 6, N, R, W to Lexington Ave.-59th St. Map 14, E2, 26. Known for its unique and innovative products, Hammacher Schlemmer was the first to carry such items as the steam iron, electric razor, microwave, and cordless telephone. The innovations of tomorrow: transparent kayak ($1460), floating table tennis set $70. Open M-Sa 10am-6pm.

Lord and Taylor, 424-434 Fifth Ave., between 38th and 39th St. (☎212-391-3344). Subway: B, D, F, V to 42nd St./Ave. of the Americas (Sixth Ave.); 7 to Fifth Ave./42nd St. Map 14, D5, 94; Map 13, D1, 1. During an unusually balmy December in 1905, Lord and Taylor revived the Christmas spirit for gloomy city-dwellers by filling its windows with mock blizzards; thus was born the tradition of the display window as stage. Today the courtly, albeit claustrophobia-inducing store features 10 fl. of fashion frenzy, caring service, and free early-morning coffee. Scores of New Yorkers come to be shod at the acclaimed shoe department. Beware the disorienting, funhouse-style mirrored columns on the 1st fl. Open M-F 10am-8:30pm, Sa 10am-7pm, Su 11am-7pm.

Saks Fifth Avenue, 611 Fifth Ave., between 49th and 50th St. (☎212-753-4000). N, R, W to Fifth Ave./59th St. Map 14, D3, 45. This subdued, chic institution has aged well and continues to combine inflated prices with smooth courtesy. At Saks you truly get what you pay for; in this case, it's expensive clothes (look for Armani, Gucci, Prada, Hugo Boss, D&G, and Ferragamo). Keep an eye out for end-of-season sales. During Christmastime, crowds line up to see the window displays. Open M-W and Sa 10am-7pm, Th 10am-8pm, Su noon-5pm.

Tiffany & Co., 727 Fifth Ave., at 57th St. (☎212-755-8000). N, R, W to Fifth Ave./59th St. Map 14, D2, 21. Although you (like Holly Golightly) may not be able to afford any of the precious gemstones, this 5-story, world-renowned jewel sanctuary is still a sight for sore eyes. Open M-F 10am-7pm, Sa 10am-6pm, Su noon-5pm.

UPPER EAST SIDE

For the most expensive in New York shopping, stroll down Madison Ave. from the 60s to the 80s.

Argosy Bookstore, 116 E. 59th St., between Lexington and Park Ave. (☎212-753-4455). Subway: 4, 5, 6, to 59th St.; N, R to Fifth Ave. Map 15, B6, 66. This 6-floor bookstore specializes in old, rare, and out-of-print books, along with autographed editions, Americana, original book covers and bookends, and antique maps and prints (starting at $3). Look for the racks of $1 books outside. Open M-F 10am-6pm; Sept.-May. also Sa 10am-5pm.

Barneys New York, 660 Madison Ave., at 61st St. (☎212-826-8900). Subway: 4, 5, 6, to 59th St.; N, R to Fifth Ave. Map 15, A6, 61. An exclusive department store whose claim to fame is its discovery and cultivation of relative unknowns into cutting-edge designers. Mind-boggling prices make for great people-watching. Open M-F 10am-8pm, Sa 10am-7pm, Su 11am-6pm.

Bloomingdale's, 1000 Third Ave., at 59th St. (☎212-705-2000). Map 15, B6, 67. Subway: 4, 5, 6, to 59th St.; N, R to Fifth Ave. Founded in 1872 by 2 brothers, Bloomie's is "not just a store, it's a destination." This 1st "department" store also invented the designer shopping bag in 1961 and turned Ralph Lauren, Donna Karan, and Fendi into household names. If you can survive the mob of perfume assailants, dazed tourists, and casual shoppers, you'll love getting lost in this colorful store. Open M-F 10am-8:30pm, Sa and Su 10am-7pm.

Encore, 1132 Madison Ave., at 84th St., 2nd fl. (☎212-879-2850). Map 15, A4, 20. Secondhand designer clothes for men and women. Open M-W and F 10:30am-6:30pm, Th 10:30am-7:30pm, Sa 10:30am-6pm, Su noon-6pm; July to mid-Aug. closed Su.

Rita Ford Music Boxes, 19 E. 65th St., between Madison and Fifth Ave. (☎212-535-6717). Subway: 6 to 68th St. Map 15, A6, 50. The first, and only, store in the US to service, repair, and sell both antique and contemporary music boxes, Rita Ford's has been winding up beautiful music since 1947 and has designed exclusive boxes for the White House, the State Department, and overseas royalty. Choose a song from the store's wide selections to put in your box. Open M-Sa 9am-5pm.

Tender Buttons, 143 E. 62nd St., between Third and Lexington Ave. (☎212-758-7004). Subway: 4, 5, 6, to 59th St.; N, R to Fifth Ave. Map 15, B6, 57. For over 40 years, Tender Buttons has provided the Upper East Side with millions of button solutions. If you carelessly lost the button on your favorite Renaissance doublet, you will find a replacement here, as well as a handy guide to tell you exactly how much your blunder cost. Also has cuff links and buckles. Open M-F 10:30am-6pm, Sa 10:30am-5:30pm.

UPPER WEST SIDE

Allan and Suzi, 416 Amsterdam Ave., at 80th St. (☎212-724-7445). Subway: 1, 2 to 79th St.; B, C to 81st St. Map 18, C4, 26. From new, 70%-off Gaultier wear to fabulous Jimmy Choo shoes, this store's discounted haute couture will have you dressing sharp for the nightclubs—without breaking the bank. For the most chic fashion tips, seek the advice of the owners, former hosts of "At Home with Allan and Suzi" on the home shopping network. Note the large selection of authentic platform shoes and feather boas. Men's clothing includes Gucci, D&G, and Hugo Boss suits. Madonna, Courtney Love, and Tommy

the hidden deal

Harlem Haunts

Welcome or not, mega-stores have burrowed into Harlem's fertile cultural soil. The main Harlem shopping drag, 125th St., already stomachs the first off-shoots of major corporations. But while Old Navy and the Disney Store might suck the non-conformist spirit out of 125th St., the following depots are more original than their grafted neighbors. Check out these other stores—less money, less mega, and much less mall.

Liberation Bookstore, 421 Lenox (Sixth) Ave., at 131st St. (☎212-281-4615). Subway: 2, 3 to 125th or 135th St./Lenox (Sixth) Ave. Map 19, C5, 20. This small store houses a great selection of African and African-American history, art, poetry, and fiction. A good place to get involved with community activism. Open Tu-F 3-7pm, Sa noon-4pm. Cash only.

Sugar Hill Thrift Shop, 409 W. 145th St., between St. Nicholas and Convent Ave. (☎212-281-2396). Subway: 1 to 145th St./Broadway; A, B, C, D to 145th St./St. Nicholas Ave. Map 19, B4, 8. Ripe with quality vintage clothing, used household merchandise and antiques, this shop is definitely the sweet side of Sugar Hill. Come see what all the buzz is about. Open M-F 10am-6pm, Sa noon-5pm.

Hilfiger have been spotted shopping here. A caveat: these threads may not be as mind-numbingly expensive as regular boutique garments, but they still aren't cheap. Open daily noon-7pm.

Applause Theater and Cinema Books, 211 W. 71st St., between Broadway and West End Ave. (☎212-496-7511). Subway: 1, 2, 3, 9 to 72nd St./Broadway. Map 18, C5, 51. Great selection of scripts, screenplays, and new and used books on everything about theater and cinema, from John Wayne to tap dancing. Over 4000 titles, some of them out of print. Look out for their intermittent $1 sales, 50%-off shelves, and the odd celebrity. Knowledgeable staff. Open M-Sa 10am-9pm, Su noon-6pm.

Gryphon Record Shop, 233 W. 72nd St., between Broadway and West End Ave. (☎212-874-1588). Subway: 1, 2, 3, 9 to 72nd St. Map 18, C5, 46. A relaxed place with wall-to-wall shelves of classical, Broadway, and jazz LPs, many rare or out of print. Hundreds of $1 records and books, with particularly great books on music and theater. Staff has the knowledge to match. Open M-F 9:30am-8pm, Sa 11am-8:30 pm, Su noon-6pm.

Maxilla & Mandible, 451 Columbus Ave., between 81st and 82nd St. (☎212-724-6173). Subway: 1, 9 to 79th St.; B, C to 81st St. Map 18, C4, 22. The world's "first and only osteological store" houses shells, fossils, eggs, preserved insects and bones for sale. For the little tykes, purchase souvenir-size "dinosaur dung" ($3) or real shark teeth ($5). Beyond the gallery lies the real business, where paleontologists and artists create traveling museum exhibits. Open Jan.-June Su-M, W-Sa 11am-7pm; July-Dec. M-Sa 11am-7pm.

Murder Ink/Ivy's, 2486 Broadway, between 92nd and 93rd St. (☎212-362-8905; www.murderink.com). Subway: 1 to 96th St. Map 18, C3, 14. Claiming to carry every mystery in print, Murder Ink is a whodunit-addict's dream. Next door is Ivy's, a conventional neighborhood bookstore. Ask to see their first edition of *Catcher in the Rye*, but please don't ask to touch (it's valued at 5 digits). Open M-Sa 10am-10pm, Su 11am-7pm.

BROOKLYN

Beacon's Closet, 88 N. 11th St., in Williamsburg (☎718-486-0816). Subway: L to Bedford Ave. A new, bigger location for one of Brooklyn's most famous vintage/thrift stores. Huge selection from funked-out hipster styles to design men's shirts. Go. It's worth it. Open M-F noon-9pm, Sa-Su 11am-8pm.

Beat Street, 494 Fulton St., at Duffield St., in Fort Greene. (☎718-624-7465). Subway: 1, 2, 4, 5 to Nevins St.; A, C, G to Hoyt St./Schermerhorn. Hip-hop par excellence with great vinyl to boot. Open M-W 10am-7pm, Th-Sa 10am-7:30pm, Su 10am-6pm.

Bird, 430 Seventh Ave., between 14th and 15th St., in Park Slope (☎718-768-4940). Subway: F to Seventh Ave. A fashionable women's clothing store that also sells accessories and bags. Open Tu-F noon-8pm, Sa-Su noon-6pm; call ahead otherwise.

Clovis Press, 229 Bedford Ave., between 4th and 5th St., in Williamsburg (☎718-302-3751). Subway: L to Bedford Ave. Map 21, 30. The labyrinthine store vends a great selection of new and used books, magazines (lots of hip lefty 'zines), art, and locally published editions into its cozy confines. Random doo-dahs and $1 books spill out onto the street in haphazard displays. Open daily noon-ish to 9pm-ish.

Diop Tailoring & Fashions, 3221 Church Ave., corner of New York Ave. (☎718-469-0904). Subway 2, 5 to Church Ave/Nostrand Ave. Map 20, D4, 4. This African fashion discount store specializes in custom designed men's and women's clothing in beautiful African fabrics. They also sell African drums, other small instruments, and footwear. Headwraps for only $5. Open daily 10am-8pm.

Domsey's Trading, 431 Kent Ave., between S. 8th and 9th St., in Williamsburg (☎718-384-6000). Subway: J, M, Z to Marcy Ave. Map 21, 41. Poorly paid Manhattanites and hipsters alike head to Domsey's, located far from the main drag of Williamsburg. Astounding bargains await the diligent shopper in this sprawling warehouse with a vast selection. Check out the tuxedos for $15 and corduroy Levis in all sorts of colors ($5). A more chaotic store, **Domsey's Warehouse Outlet,** has opened next door at 496 Wythe Ave., where clothing is sold by the lb. Both locations open M-F 8am-5:30pm, Sa 8am-6:30pm, Su 11am-5:30pm; annex of Domsey's Warehouse closes Su 3:30pm.

Fulton Mall, Fulton St. from Adams St. to Flatbush Ave. (☎718-858-5118). Info center located near Bond St. Subway M, N, R, 2, 3, 4, 5 to Borough Hall/Court St., Map 22, 21. This seven-block strip of over 200 stores is one of the country's largest outdoor shopping malls. In addition to department stores (Macy's) and chains (Foot Locker), also has many smaller businesses from the Brooklyn community.

Girdle Factory, 218 Bedford Ave., at N. 5th St., in Williamsburg. Subway: L to Bedford Ave. Map 21, 29. A cavernous collective of small spaces, inhabited by cafes (**Verb Cafe** is cozy, good smelling with cheap coffee, bread snacks and iBooks all around), a beauty salon **(Hello, Beautiful),** shops, a great bookstore (**Spoonbill Sugartown Bookstore,** which holds readings and book parties now and then) and chairs for relaxation. The **Internet Garage** charges 15¢ per min. The store after which the alternative complex was named, **The Girdle Factory,** sells hip vintage clothes. Open daily noon-9pm.

KCDC, 97 N. 10th St., Ste. 104, between Berry and Wythe Ave. Subway: L to Bedford Ave. Map 21, 9. At first glance, KCDC resembles a typical skate shop selling bags, T-shirts, shoes and videos. Then you notice the skater art gallery (exhibitions change monthly), which leads you to the–get this–*half pipe*. Try doing that paying Manhattan rent. Open daily noon-8pm.

Spokes & Strings, 170 Havemeyer St. at S. 2nd St. (☎718-599-2409). Subway: J, M or Z to Marcy Ave. This is a little bike shop that offers rentals ($25 for the day), fix-ups and tunings. They have their own line of handmade bikes called NYC, built for the city and of the finest acquired parts (often for half the projected commercial value). Also do custom construction. Take a look; rent a bike; pedal about. Call for hours.

Ugly Luggage, 214 Bedford Ave., at 5th St., in Williamsburg. (☎718-384-0724). Subway: L to Bedford Ave. Map 21, 24. Even with a bright orange storefront, this vintage store is surprisingly inconspicuous. Full of retro accessories, such as fake snakeskin phones and archaic typewriters and cool, low, box-shaped and cabineted pieces of furniture for which there is no proper name but the tragically undescriptive "table." Open M-F 1-8pm, Sa-Su 1pm-6pm.

INSIDE

hostels **257**
bed and breakfasts **257**
hotels **258**
accommodations by price **258**
accommodations by neighborhood **258**
long-term accommodations **274**

Accommodations

If you know someone who knows someone who lives in New York, get that person's phone number and ask to stay with them. The cost of living in New York can rip the seams out of your wallet. At true full-service establishments, one night will cost at least $125, with an additional hotel tax of 13.4%. Many reasonable choices are available for about $70 a night, but priorities vary from person to person: those traveling alone may want to spend more to stay in a safer neighborhood. The young and the outgoing may prefer a budget-style place crowded with students; honeymooning couples may not.

Hostels offer fewer amenities than hotels, yet manage to preserve a greater feeling of camaraderie. Cheap YMCAs and YWCAs offer another budget option, but young backpackers may miss the intimacy and social life a hostel can offer. All of these places advise you to reserve ahead. Budget hotels are concentrated around Times Square, Lower Midtown, and the Upper West Side.

Crime-free neighborhoods in the city exist only in dreams; never leave anything of value in your room if you are staying in budget accommodations. Many places have safes or lockers available, some for an extra fee. Don't sleep in your car, and never, ever sleep outdoors anywhere in New York. The city has a hard enough time protecting its homeless population—tourists simply would not stand a chance.

The Internet is a great tool for finding New York accommodations. Many of the accommodations listed in this chapter have websites, and some offer discounts for Internet reservations—ask when calling. A number of online sites list accommodations; see the **Complete Guide to NYC Hotels** (www.manhattanusersguide.com/hotels); **New York citysearch.com** (www.newyork.citysearch.com); and **New York Today** (www.nytoday.com). For long-term accommodations, see p. 274.

HOSTELS

Hostels are generally laid out dorm-style, often with large single-sex rooms and bunk beds, although some offer private rooms for families and couples. They sometimes have kitchens and utensils, bike or moped rentals, storage areas, and laundry facilities. Guests must often rent or bring their own sheets or "sleep-sacks" (two sheets sewn together); sleeping bags are usually not adequate. There can be drawbacks: some hostels close during certain daytime "lockout" hours, have a curfew, don't accept reservations, impose a maximum stay, or, less frequently, require that you do chores. In New York, a bed in a hostel will average around $25. Most guests are students or of student age, often from outside the US, but the clientele can be surprisingly mixed.

Joining the youth hostel association in your own country (see www.iyhf.org) automatically grants you membership privileges in **Hostelling International-American Youth Hostels (HI-AYH),** a federation of national hosteling associations. HI-AYH (www.hiayh.org) operates a network of nearly 125 hostels in the United States, including an excellent hostel in New York with much space and many amenities (see p. 12). **One-year memberships** are free for those under 18, $25 for those 18-54, and $15 for those over 55; lifetime memberships are $250. See websites for details. Most student travel agencies (p. 300) sell HI cards, as do all of the national hosteling organizations.

Although you might not be as enthusiastic as the Village People, don't overlook the **Young Men's Christian Association (YMCA)** or the **Young Women's Christian Association (YWCA),** which have seven branches in New York City: three in Manhattan, two in Queens, and two in Brooklyn. These establishments are slightly more expensive than hostels but usually much more uniform and cleaner, with 24hr. security and daily housekeeping service; singles generally range from $40-75 per night, and rooms generally include access to a pool, fitness facilities, and television. However, you may have to share a room and use a communal bath or shower. Some YMCAs in New York accept women and families as well as men. Try to reserve at least two weeks ahead and expect to pay a refundable key deposit of about $10. For information and reservations, contact the individual branch or **The Y's Way,** 224 E. 47th St., New York, NY 10017 (☎212-308-2899; fax 212-308-3161; ymcanyc.org).

A very friendly alternative to hostels is **Homestay New York,** 630 E. 19th St., Brooklyn (☎718-434-2071; www.homestayny.com). Travelers are placed in homes of New York City residents, mostly in outer boroughs but all within 15-30min. (by subway) of Manhattan. Rates of $100-130 vary according to the room and include some meals, a Metrocard, and a phone card. Call or email for reservations at least 10 days ahead.

BED AND BREAKFASTS

Bed and Breakfasts (private homes that rent out one or more spare rooms to travelers) are a great alternative to impersonal hotel and motel rooms. They're hardly your stereotypical B&Bs—no sleepy New England village squares or big front porches—but Manhattan does have a wide selection. Many don't have phones, TVs, or showers with their rooms. Reservations should be made a few weeks ahead, and usually require a deposit. Most apartments listed have two-night minimums. Some B&Bs are "hosted," while others are "unhosted," meaning that the people renting you the room will not be there. Most B&B agencies list accommodations in boroughs other than Manhattan; these can be an excellent budget alternative. Prices vary according to borough, neighborhood, and accommodation size (but generally run singles $70-100; doubles $80-135), so call for specifics with a neighborhood and price range in mind. **Urban Ventures** (☎212-879-4229;

fax 517-5356; www.gamutnyc.com) is a full-service real estate brokerage serving the New York City area. **All Around the Town** (☎212-675-5600 or toll-free from within the US 800-443-3800) specializes in short-term furnished apartments, and **Bed and Breakfast of New York** (☎212-645-8134) offers weekly and monthly rates.

HOTELS

A single in a cheap hotel goes for as little as $60-80. Don't expect a large room, however. Most hotel rooms should be reserved in advance. Ask the hotel owner if you can see a room before you pay for it. You should be told in advance whether the bathroom is communal or private. Most hotels require a key deposit when you register. Check-in usually takes place between 11am and 6pm; check-out before 11am. You may be able to store your gear for the day even after vacating your room and returning the key, but many proprietors will not take responsibility for the safety of your belongings. Some hotels require a non-refundable deposit for reservations. However, the hotel may allow you to use your deposit on a future stay at the hotel.

ACCOMMODATIONS BY PRICE

Hotel prices vary by season and by room. The price ranges listed below are by no means exact.

ACCOMMODATIONS BY NEIGHBORHOOD

Let's Go lists prices excluding tax, unless otherwise noted. The following accommodations are the best hostels, YMCA/YWCAs, hotels, and B&Bs in New York. Quality, value, and safety have been taken account in ranking. Unless otherwise noted, all establishments accept major credit cards.

LITTLE ITALY

Pioneer Hotel, 341 Broome St., between Elizabeth St. and the Bowery (☎212-226-1482; fax 266-3525). Subway: J, M, Z to Bowery; S to Grand St. Map 8, D3, 16. Also called the SoHotel. This 100-year-old building is a good no-frills place for those drawn to the SoHo and East Village nightlife. All rooms have ceiling fans, sinks, and TVs. Rooms with private bath have A/C. Key $10 deposit. Check-in 1pm. Check-out 11am. Reservations recommended at least 6 wk. ahead during peak season. Singles from $69; doubles $89, with bath $99. ❷

GREENWICH VILLAGE

Larchmont Hotel, 27 W. 11th St., between Fifth and Sixth Ave. (☎212-989-9333; fax 989-9496). Subway: 4, 5, 6, L, N, Q, R, W to 14th St.-Union Sq. Map 10, D2, 9. Spacious, clean rooms in a whitewashed brownstone on a quiet block. A/C, closets, desks, TVs, and wash basins in all rooms. Shared bath. Continental breakfast included. Check-in 3pm. Check-out noon. Reserve 5-6 wk. ahead. Singles $70-95; doubles $90-115; queen-size bed $109-125. ❷

Washington Square Hotel, 103 Waverly Pl., at MacDougal St. (☎212-777-9515 or 800-222-0418; fax 979-8373). Subway: A, C, E, F, V, S to W. 4th St. Map 10, D4, 56. A/C, cable TV, and key-card entry to rooms. Clean, comfortable rooms all have private bath. Friendly, multilingual staff. 24hr. exercise room. Continental breakfast included. Check-in 3pm. Check-out noon. Reserve 2 months or more ahead for weekends, 1 month for weekdays. Singles $126-145; doubles $148-160; queen-size bed or 2 twins $160-180; quads $181-190. Roll-away bed $20. 10% ISIC discount. ❺

$40 AND UNDER (❶)

Central Park Hostel (271)
Chelsea Center Hostel (264)
Chelsea International Hostel (264)
Chelsea Star Hotel (264)
De Hirsch Residence (269)
International Student Center (271)
International Student Hospice (263)
Jazz on the Park (271)
Manhattan Youth Castle (269)
New York International HI-AYH Hostel (271)
New York University (259)
Sugar Hill International House (273)
Uptown Hostel (273)

$41-80 (❷)

The Amsterdam Inn (269)
Carlton Arms (261)
Columbia University (271)
Crystal's Castle Bed and Breakfast (272)
Hotel 17 (261)
Hotel Caribe (273)
Hotel Pickwick Arms (266)
Larchmont Hotel (258)
Murray Inn Hotel (261)
New York Bed and Breakfast (272)
Pioneer Hotel (258)
Portland Square Hotel (267)
St. Mark's Hotel (259)
West End Studios (271)
West Side Inn (269)
West Side YMCA (269)
YMCA-Flushing (274)

$81-100 (❸)

Americana Inn (266)
Best Western President Hotel (267)
Big Apple Hostel (267)
Broadway Inn (267)
Chelsea Pines Inn (265)
Chelsea Savoy Hotel (263)
Colonial House Inn (265)
Flushing Grand Hotel (273)
Gershwin Hotel (261)
Herald Square Hotel (265)
Hotel Belleclaire (269)
Hotel Newton (269)
Hotel Wolcott (265)
Madison Hotel (263)
New York Inn (267)
Skyline Hotel (267)
YMCA-Vanderbilt (266)

$101-120 (❹)

Chelsea Inn (263)
Hotel Grand Union (261)
Hotel Stanford (265)

$121 AND UP (❺)

Akwaaba Mansion (273)
Bed & Breakfast on the Park (273)
Hotel Chelsea (259)
Hotel Olcott (269)
Hotel Stanford (265)
Hudson Hotel (267)
Sheraton LaGuardia East Hotel (274)
Super 8 Hotel (265)
ThirtyThirty (261)
Washington Square Hotel (258)
Union Square Inn (261)

DORMITORIES

New York University, 14a Washington Pl. (☎212-998-4621; www.nyu.edu/housing/summer). Subway: N, R to 8th St.-NYU. Map 10, E4. You do not have to be enrolled in NYU summer school to get housing, but summer school students get priority and lower rates. Housing only available for individuals. Options in the East, Greenwich, and West Villages as well as near South Street Seaport. Min. age 17, unless an approved summer school student. Reception M-Tu 9am-5pm, W-Th 9am-7pm, Su 9am-2pm. 11- to 12-week max. stay. 3-week (consecutive) min. stay. Call for prices—doubles and triples about $200 per wk. ❶

EAST VILLAGE

St. Mark's Hotel, 2 St. Mark's Pl., at Third Ave. (☎212-674-2192; fax 420-0854). Subway: 6 to Astor Pl. Map 12, C2, 29. Functional, clean rooms in perhaps NYC's most exciting location. All 64 rooms with cable TV and private baths. Check-in before 10pm. Call ahead for reservations. Room with full bed $80; queen-size bed $90; 2 full-size beds $110. Cash and travelers checks only. ❷

Chelsea Center Hostel (East Village branch), on 12th St., between First Ave. and Avenue A. Run by the Center Hostel (p. 264)—call them for details.

UNION SQUARE, GRAMERCY, AND MURRAY HILL

Gershwin Hotel, 7 E. 27th St., between Madison and Fifth Ave. (☎212-545-8000; fax 684-5546; www.gershwinhotel.com). Subway: N, R to 28th St./Broadway; 6 to 28th St./Park Ave. S. Map 13, D4, 36. An absolute gem of a first-rate boutique hotel. Stunning pop art decor, genuine Warhol pieces in the museum lobby. The steal of the century; funkified chicness for relatively budget prices. Offers spaces for poetry, comedy, concerts, and open mic nights, and has its own art gallery. Private rooms with bathrooms, cable TV, A/C, and phones. Internet $1 per 4min. Reception 24hr. Check-in 3pm. Check-out 11am. Dorm rooms available: 8- to 12-bed dorms $29-59 per bed, 1 female dorm. Economy room (single or double occupancy only) $99; standard room (single or double occupancy only) $129; superior rooms $159-179; family room $219-250; 1-bedroom suite $299; triples and quads add $10 per person. $15 extra for Th-Sa. ❸

Carlton Arms Hotel, 160 E. 25th St., between Third and Lexington Ave. (☎212-679-0680; www.carltonarms.com). Subway: 6 to 23rd St./Park Ave. S. Map 13, E4, 45. For the unconventional and truly hip; bold, dramatic artwork covers every nook and cranny from the bathroom to the closets. Each room is decorated by a different artist. 11C is the "good daughter/bad daughter" room—half the room is festooned in teenybopper posters, the other half in horror-movie pics. 54 spacious rooms. Check-in noon. Check-out 11:30am. Reserve for summer 2 months ahead; confirm 10 days ahead. Singles $60, with bath $75; doubles $80-95; triples $99-110; quads $105-117. Pay for 7+ nights up front and get a 10% discount. ❷

ThirtyThirty, 30 E. 30th St., between Park Ave. S. and Madison Ave. (☎212-689-1900 or 800-497-6028; fax 689-0023; www.stayinny.com). Subway: N, R to 28th St./Broadway; 6 to 28th St./Park Ave. S. Map 13, E3, 23. Sleek, modern hotel in a prime location at relatively budget prices. Pet friendly! All rooms have A/C, cable TV, hair dryers, irons, and phones with voicemail. Check-in 3pm. Check-out 11am. Singles $125; doubles $165; suites $245. ❺

Hotel Grand Union, 34 E. 32nd St., between Park Ave. S. and Madison Ave. (☎212-683-5890; fax 689-7397; www.hotelgrandunion.com). Subway: 6 to 33rd St. Map 13, E3, 22. This functional, mainstream centrally-located hotel offers fairly spacious rooms with A/C, cable TV, mini-fridge, bathrooms, phones with voicemail. 24hr. security. Wheelchair accessible. Check-in and check-out noon. Singles/doubles $99; twin/triple $115; quad $141. ❹

Murray Hill Inn, 143 E. 30th St., between Third and Lexington Ave. (☎212-683-6900 or 888-996-6376; fax 545-0103; www.murrayhillinn.com). Subway: N, R to 28th St./Broadway; 6 to 28th St./Park Ave. S. Map 13, E3, 25. Gym/pool access $10-25. No elevator, 5 floors. All rooms have A/C, cable TV, and phones. 21-night max. stay. Check-in 3pm. Check-out noon. Singles $75, private bath $115; doubles $95-$125. ❷

Hotel 17, 225 E. 17th St., between Second and Third Ave. (☎212-475-2845; fax 677-8178; http://hotel17.citysearch.com). Subway: L to Third Ave. Map 13, F5, 99. This historic 120-room hotel served as the setting for Woody Allen's *Manhattan Murder Mystery;* Madonna had her portrait done in these eccentric accommodations. High-ceilinged, standard, antique-ish rooms with A/C and cable TV. All rooms with shared baths, some with fireplaces. Check-in 2pm. Check-out noon. No children under 18 admitted. Singles $70-75; doubles $80-100. Weekly rates: Singles $425; doubles $600. No credit cards. ❷

Union Square Inn, 209 E. 14th St., between Second and Third Ave. (☎212-614-0500; fax 614-0512; www.unionsquareinn.com). Subway: 4, 5, 6, L, N, Q, R, W to 14th St.-Union Sq.; L to 3rd Ave. Map 12, F6, 124. 5-floor walk-up with 40 renovated rooms, all with A/C and cable TV. Cafe in the lobby. Gym/pool access $10-25. Reception 24hr. Check-in 2pm. Check-out noon. Singles/doubles $139-150, depending on room size. ❺

Madison Hotel, 21 E. 27th St., at Madison Ave. (☎212-532-7373 or 800-9MADISON; fax 686-0092; www.madison-hotel.com). Subway: N, R to 28th St./Broadway; 6 to 28th St./Park Ave. S. Map 13, E4, 40. Clean and straightforward. A/C, cable TV, and private baths. Breakfast included. $5 cable deposit; $40 phone deposit. Check-in noon. Check-out 11am. Singles $99; doubles $121; rooms for 2-4 with 2 double beds $145. ❸

HOSTELS

International Student Hospice, 154 E. 33rd St., between Lexington and Third Ave. (☎212-228-7470; fax 228-4689). Subway: 6 to 33rd St./Park Ave. S. Map 13, E3, 20. Tons of bric-a-brac in a dilapidated brownstone. Rooms for 1-4 people; tiny hall bathroom. Call ahead. Check-in and check-out 24hr. 1-week max. stay. $30 per night. ❶

Algonquin Hotel

CHELSEA

Hotel Chelsea, 222 W. 23rd St., between Seventh and Eighth Ave. (☎212-243-3700; fax 675-5531; www.hotelchelsea.com). Subway: 1, 9 to 23rd St./Seventh Ave. Map 13, C4, 33. Story-filled grand old dame of bohemian hotels. Plaques outside commemorate such famous literary guests as Thomas Wolfe and Dylan Thomas. Fabulous collection of artwork in lobby. All rooms with A/C, cable, and phones; most have private bathrooms. Many rooms with kitchens. Reservations recommended, but cancel 72hr. ahead to avoid penalty fees. Singles from $135; doubles from $165; triples from $185. Suites available. Call for long-term rates. ❺

Carlton Arms Hotel

Chelsea Inn, 46 W. 17th St., between Fifth and Sixth Ave. (☎212-645-8989 or 800-640-6469; fax 645-1903; www.chelseainn.com). Subway: F, L, V to 14th St./Sixth Ave./Avenue of the Americas; 1, 9 to 18th St. Map 13, D6, 113. Charmingly mismatched antiques in spacious rooms. All rooms with A/C, cable TV, coffee makers, fridges, phones, and safes. Reception M-Th 9am-9pm, F-Sa 9am-11pm, Su 9am-7pm. Check-in 3pm. Check-out noon. Reservations recommended. Guest rooms with shared bath $79-109; studios $109-159; 1-bedroom suites $159-199; 2-bedroom suites $179-259. ❹

Chelsea Savoy Hotel, 204 W. 23rd St., at Seventh Ave. (☎212-929-9353; fax 741-6309; www.chelseasavoynyc.com). Subway: 1, 9 to 23rd St./Seventh Ave.; C, E to 23rd St./Eighth Ave. Map 13, C4, 34. Clean, functional, welcoming rooms. All with A/C, cable TV, hairdryers, irons, and private

Home Away From Home

baths. Reception 24hr. Group rates available. Often weekly specials, but only available by phone. Check-in 3pm. Check-out 11am. Reservations recommended. Wheelchair-accessible. Singles $99-115; doubles $135-175; quads $145-195. ❸

Chelsea Star Hotel, 300 W. 30th St., at Eighth Ave. (☎212-244-7827 or 212-877-827-6969; fax 279-9018; www.starhotelny.com). Subway: A, C, E to 34th St.-Penn Station/Eighth Ave. Map 13, B3, 8. Stay in one of the 16 theme rooms where Madonna reportedly lived as a struggling artist or choose a normal "luxe" room. Clean and coveted. Residents get keys. All rooms with shared bathrooms (20 rooms, 4 per bath). Safe deposit box $5. Reception 24hr. Check-in 1pm. Check-out 11am. Reserve at least 1 month ahead. 14-night max. stay. Dorms $30; singles $59; doubles $79; 5-person suites $159. ❶

HOSTELS

Chelsea Center Hostel, 313 W. 29th St., between Eighth and Ninth Ave. (☎212-643-0214; fax 473-3945; www.chelseacenterhostel.com). Subway: A, C, E to 34th St.-Penn Station/Eighth Ave.; 1, 2, 3, 9 to 34th St.-Penn Station/Seventh Ave. Map 13, B3, 9. To enter, ring the buzzer at the door. Room for 20 guests in this quiet co-ed residential-home-turned-hostel. Women-only and family-only rooms available upon request. 15 stay in a spacious basement room with a summer camp feel; the rest in a slightly-cramped bedroom on the main fl. The hostel office doubles as a common space. Lovely garden adds to the charm. 2 showers. Light breakfast included. Linen provided. Check-in 8:30am-10:45pm. Check-out 11am. Flexible lockout 11am-5pm. Cash and traveler's checks only. Dorms $30. ❶

Chelsea International Hostel, 251 W. 20th St., between Seventh and Eighth Ave., in Chelsea (☎212-647-0010; fax 727-7289; www.chelseahostel.com). Subway: 1, 9 to 23rd St./Seventh Ave.; C, E to 23rd St./Eighth Ave. Map 13, C5, 72. Enclosed hotel with funky youth travelers (mostly Scandinavians and other Europeans, but Americans allowed, too). Congenial staff offers pizza W night. Backyard garden. Extremely safe neighborhood, with police station right across the street. Sparsely-furnished, smallish, utilitarian rooms. Kitchens, laundry room, TV rooms. Internet access (19¢ per min.). Key deposit $10. Check-in 8am-6pm, passport required. Check-out 1pm. Reservations recommended. 4- and 6-person dorms $25; private doubles with double or bunk bed $60. ❶

GAY AND GAY-FRIENDLY ACCOMMODATIONS

Colonial House Inn, 318 W. 22nd St., between Eighth and Ninth Ave. (☎212-243-9669 or 800-689-3779; fax 633-1612; www.colonialhouseinn.com). Subway: C, E to 23rd St. Map 13, B5, 59. A very comfortable B&B in a classy Chelsea brownstone owned by Mel Cheren, former owner of legendary club Paradise Garage. Cheren's autobiography available for sale in lobby. All rooms have A/C, cable TV, and phones; some have baths and fireplaces. Sun deck with a "clothing optional" area. 24hr. desk and concierge. Continental breakfast included, and served in the lounge/art gallery. Internet access in lobby (20¢ per min.). Check-in 2pm. Check-out noon. Reservations are encouraged and require 2 nights' deposit within 10 days of reservation. Double bed "economy" room $80-99; queen-size bedroom $99-125, with private bath and fridge $125-140. ❸

Chelsea Pines Inn, 317 W. 14th St., between Eighth and Ninth Ave. (☎212-929-1023; fax 620-5646; www.chelseapinesinn.com). Subway: A, C, E to 14th St.; L to Eighth Ave. Map 13, B6, 108. This fabulous gay-owned and operated inn is a friendly, amenity-laden haven of cozy rooms decorated with vintage film posters. Gorgeous garden and "greenhouse" out back. A/C, cable TV, phones with answering machines, refrigerators, and showers in all rooms. Continental breakfast included, with fresh homemade bread. Reservations are essential. 3-day min. stay on weekends. Rooms with private showers and shared toilet $99-169; with queen-size bed and private bath $129-$159; with queen-size bed, private bath, day bed, stereos and breakfast area $139-$169. $20 for extra person. Call for special summer rates (beginning at $79). ❹

HERALD SQUARE

Hotel Stanford, 43 W. 32nd St., between Fifth Ave. and Broadway (☎212-563-1500 or 800-365-1114; fax 629-0043; www.hotelstanford.com). Subway: B, D, F, N, Q, R, V, W to 34th St.-Herald Sq. Map 13, D3, 14. This Korean District hotel's lobby has sparkling ceiling lights and a polished marble floor. Impeccable rooms with A/C, bathrooms, cable TV, phones, and refrigerators. Continental breakfast included. On 1st fl., beautiful, immaculate Korean bakery *Pari Pari Ko*, and bustling 24hr. Korean eatery *Gam Mee Ok* famous for traditional beef stew. Check-in 3pm. Check-out noon. Reservations recommended. Singles $120-150; doubles, twins $150-180; suites $200-250. ❹

Herald Square Hotel, 19 W. 31st St., between Fifth Ave. and Broadway (☎212-279-4017 or 800-727-1888; fax 643-9208; www.heraldsquarehotel.com). Subway: B, D, F, N, Q, R, V, W to 34th St.-Herald Sq. Map 13, D3, 16. Original *Life* magazine's Beaux Arts home, decorated with ubiquitous *Life* covers. Clean, small rooms include A/C, cable TV, phones with voicemail, and safes. If you bring the little ones, request the "Little Angel Protection" program, with a child-proof package and child-friendly rooms. Check-in 2pm. Check-out noon. Reserve 2-3 wk. ahead. Singles $85 (shared bathroom singles $60); doubles $99-109; triples $120-130; quads $120-140. 10% discount for ISIC card holders. ❸

Hotel Wolcott, 4 W. 31st St., between Fifth Ave. and Broadway (☎212-268-2900; fax 563-0096; www.wolcott.com). Subway: B, D, F, N, Q, R, V, W to 34th St.-Herald Sq. Map 13, D3, 18. Unexpectedly ornate lobby. 50s rock-and-roll legend Buddy Holly recorded 2 hit albums in now-defunct studios. Free coffee and muffins for breakfast. Rooms have A/C, bathrooms, cable TV, and phones with voicemail. In-room Internet $10 per 12hr. Safe deposit boxes. Self-service laundry. Check-in 3pm. Check-out 12:30pm. Singles/doubles $99-140; triples $115-160; suites for 3 $129-190. ❸

MIDTOWN

Super 8 Hotel, 59 W. 46th St., between Fifth and Sixth Ave. (☎212-719-2300 or 800-800-8000 for reservations; www.super8.com). Subway: B, D, F, V to 47th-50th St.-Rockefeller Center. Map 14, 78, 51. 193 classy but subdued rooms in the heart of Midtown, a few yards from Rockefeller Center. Health facility downstairs. Complimentary breakfast and phone calls, in-room safe, color TV, private baths, and A/C. Check-in 3pm. Check-out noon. Regular room with double bed averages $179 depending on availability, but sale price can be as low as $89. ❺

Hotel Pickwick Arms, 230 E. 51st St., between Second and Third Ave. (☎212-355-0300 or 800-742-5945; www.pickwickarms.com). Subway: 6 to 51st St.; E, V to 53rd St.-Lexington Ave. Map 14, F3, 55. Business types congregate in this well-priced, mid-sized hotel. Chandelier-lit marble lobby contrasts with tiny rooms and tinier hall bathrooms. Roof garden. Airport service available. A/C, cable TV, phones, and voicemail in all rooms. Internet $1 per 4min. Check-in 2pm. Check-out 1pm. Singles $75-115; doubles with bath $129; studios with double bed and sofa for 2 people $205. Additional person in room $20. Credit card needed to guarantee room. ❷

YMCA-Vanderbilt, 224 E. 47th St., between Second and Third Ave. (☎212-756-9600; fax 752-0210). Subway: 6 to 51st St.; E, V to Lexington Ave./53rd St. Map 14, F3, 83. Convenient with reasonable security. Clean and brightly-lit lobby bustles with international visitors. Small rooms have A/C and cable TV; usually enough bathrooms to go around. Free use of well-equipped gym, safe-deposit boxes, and friendly staff. 5 shuttles per day to airports. Luggage storage until departure $1 per bag. Check-in 3pm. Check-out 11am. Reserve 2-3 wk. ahead and guarantee with a credit card. 25-night max. stay. Singles $67; twin bunks $78; doubles $100. ❸

Americana Inn, 69 W. 38th St., between Fifth and Sixth Ave. (☎212-840-6700). Subway: B, D, F, N, Q, R, V, W to 34th St.-Herald Sq.; B, D, F, V to 42nd St./Ave. of the Americas. Map 14, D5, 92. Great location makes up for the drab exterior. Each of the 50 clean, simple rooms has A/C, sink, and TV. 5 shared baths on each fl. Internet access $1 per 5min. No smoking. Check-in 1pm. Check-out noon. Singles $65; doubles $75; triples $85. ❸

TIMES SQUARE AND THEATER DISTRICT

Hudson Hotel, 356 W. 58th St., between Eighth and Ninth Ave. (☎212-554-6000). Subway: 1, 9, A, B, C, D to 59th St.-Columbus Circle. Map 14, B2, 4. Chic, swank full-service hotel featuring customized greenhouses, utopian garden courtyard, and 2 popular bars. Each decadent room has down comforters, oak walls, art exhibits, mood lighting as well as an ultra-modern bathroom. Check-in 3pm. Check-out noon. Standard room $155-$225, with suite as much as $500, but there's an occasional $125 special. ❺

Best Western President Hotel, 234 W. 48th St., between Broadway and Eighth Ave. (☎212-246-8800). Subway: 1, 9 to 50th St./Broadway; C, E to 50th St./Eighth Ave. Map 14, C3, 34. Chain hotel offering yet another full-service lodging option. 16 fl., 334 tastefully decorated rooms. Friendly staff, comfortable lounge, and 2 restaurants make this an attractive choice. Gym across the street available for additional $20 per day. Check-in 3pm. Check-out noon. Reserve as soon as possible. Rooms with double bed $99-179. ❸

Skyline Hotel, 725 10th Ave., at 49th St. (☎212-586-3400). Subway: C, E to 50th St./Eighth Ave. Map 14, A3, 29. Large, well-kept rooms with full amenities: pool with panoramic view of the city, restaurant, and discounted parking. Farther away from Times Square than other hotels, which allows more space for less money, and still a stone's throw from the Theater District. Check-in 3pm. Check-out noon. Make reservations as early as possible; walk-ins welcome if there is space. Rooms with double bed $99-169, subject to availability. ❸

Broadway Inn, 264 W. 46th St., between Eighth Ave. and Broadway (☎212-997-9200 or 800-826-6300; fax 212-768-2807). Subway: 1, 2, 3, 7, 9, N, Q, R, S, W to 42nd St.-Times Sq. Map 14, C4, 70. Helpful staff and cozy common room/lobby contribute to friendly, quaint atmosphere. A/C, data jacks, private baths, and TVs in all rooms. Continental breakfast included. Free parking a great deal for anyone driving to the city. Free upgrades if available, discounts on B'way shows and some local restaurants. Check-in 3pm. Check-out noon. Singles $110-145; doubles $140-160 (high-end includes jacuzzi), suites (for 2 adults and 2 children 6-12 or 3 adults) $185-205. ❸

New York Inn, 765 Eighth Ave., between 46th and 47th St. (☎212-247-5400). Subway: C, E to 50th St. Map 14, B4, 60. Not luxurious, but clean, well-kept rooms with private baths, A/C and TVs. Frequented by South American and European crowd. Continental breakfast included. Check-in and check-out noon. Reserve 2 wk. ahead. Singles $80; doubles $93; 2 double beds $130. ❸

Portland Square Hotel, 132 W. 47th St., between Sixth and Seventh Ave. (☎212-382-0600 or 800-388-8988). Subway: 1, 2, 3, 7, 9, N, Q, R, S, W to 42nd St.-Times Sq. Map 14, C3, 69. Pretty, self-proclaimed "theater hotel" lodging theater-goers since 1904. Institutional but clean rooms offer a variety of options for the budget-minded. A/C and TVs in all rooms. Luggage lockers $1. Check-in 3pm. Check-out noon. Small singles and doubles with shared bath $85; roomier doubles with private bath $99; triples (with 2 double beds) $120. ❷

HOSTELS

Big Apple Hostel, 119 W. 45th St., between Sixth and Seventh Ave. (☎212-302-2603; fax 302-2605; www.bigapplehostel.com). Subway: 1, 2, 3, 7, 9, N, Q, R, S, W to 42nd St.-Times Sq. Map 14, C4, 71. This centrally located hostel is the budget traveler's best option. Clean, carpeted rooms, kitchen with refrigerator, luggage room, big deck (closed 2-6am) with grill, common rooms, and laundry facilities. Americans accepted with out-of-state photo ID or other convincing proof that they're tourists. Reception 24hr. Safe deposit available at reception (25¢). Internet access $1 per 8min. Check-in and check-out 11am. No reservations accepted Aug.-Sept. except through website or by fax—send credit card number. 21-day max. stay. Bunk in dorm-style room with shared bath $33 (same-sex available for single travelers, mixed for groups of friends); singles/doubles $90. ❸

UPPER EAST SIDE

Manhattan Youth Castle, 1596 Lexington Ave., between 101st and 102nd St. (☎212-831-4440; fax 722-5746; www.youthcastle.com). Subway: 6 to 103rd St./Lexington Ave. Map 16, B2, 3. Small, affordable accommodation in area bordering Spanish Harlem. Large, mostly co-ed rooms with bunk beds, communal bathrooms, and shared lockers. **Free Internet** access to guests. Recreation room. Key deposit $15. Check-in M-Tu 10am-6pm, W-Su 10am-9pm. Check-out M-Sa noon. Reservations recommended. 4-week max. stay. Call 2 months ahead for summer, otherwise 2 weeks is sufficient. Passport ID required. $28; $60 for 4 days. ❶

De Hirsch Residence, 1395 Lexington Ave., at 92nd St. (☎212-415-5650 or 800-858-4692; fax 415-5578). Subway: 6 to 96th St. Map 15, B3, 10. Comparatively large, clean, and convenient hostel affiliated with the 92nd St. YMHA/YWHA. Guests must be going to school or working full-time. Over 300 dormitory-style rooms: choose from singles and small or large doubles. Huge bathrooms, kitchens, and laundry machines on at least every other fl. All with A/C. Single-sex floors, strictly enforced, but visitors of the opposite sex allowed as long as they sign in at the front desk. 24hr. access and security. Discounted access to the 92nd St. Y's many facilities ($89 per month) and reduced rates for concerts. Organized activities such as walking tours of New York. Wheelchair-accessible. Reserve several months ahead. 1-month min. stay. 1-year max. stay. Singles $1095 per month; shared rooms $265-895 per person per month. ❶

UPPER WEST SIDE

Hotel Olcott, 27 W. 72nd St., between Central Park W. and Columbus Ave. (☎212-877-4200; www.hotelolcott.com). Subway: B, C to 72nd St./Central Park W. Map 18, D5, 58. Just off Central Park, with a beautifully grand lobby. Rooms are large, and feature A/C, cable TV, and kitchenettes. Internet access $1 per 4min. Check-in 3pm. Check-out 11am. 1 night's deposit required (check or money order). 1- to 2-person studios $130 (weekly $840); 1- to 2-person suites $150 (weekly $980); $15 per extra person (weekly $70). Special winter rates include studio $99 and suite $129. Check the website for additional specials. ❺

Hotel Newton, 2528 Broadway, between 94th and 95th St. Map 18, C2, 13. (☎212-678-6500 or 888-468-3558; www.newyorkhotel.com). Subway: 1, 2, 3, 9 to 96th St./Broadway. Clean rooms with A/C, TVs, and private baths. Check-in 2pm. Check-out noon. Children 17 and under stay free. $85-160 per night for 2 people; $10 per additional person. ❸

Hotel Belleclaire, 250 W. 77th St., at Broadway (☎212-362-7700 or 877-468-3522; www.hotelbelleclaire.com). Subway: 1, 2 to 79th St. Map 18, C4, 34. In landmark building with marble staircases. Modern lobby and rooms look spanking new. Scandinavian furnishings and fluffy comforters on sleek white beds make for chic comfortable stays. State-of-the-art gym. Room service. All 170 rooms have A/C, cable TV, and fridges. Check-in 3pm. Check-out noon. Economy rooms (shared bath) $109; other rooms $169-229. ❸

The Amsterdam Inn, 340 Amsterdam Ave., at 76th St. (☎212-579-7500; www.amsterdaminn.com). Subway: 1, 2 to 79th St. Map 18, C1, 36. The 28 rooms are small and clean. 1-floor walk-up to lobby. All rooms have A/C and color TV. Check-in 2pm. Check-out noon. Singles $75; doubles $95, with private bath $125. Call for seasonal rates. ❷

West Side Inn, 237 W. 107th St., between Broadway and Amsterdam Ave. (☎212-866-0061 or 866-0062; www.westsideinn.com). Subway: 1 to Cathedral Pkwy. (110th St.)/Broadway. Map 18, C1, 4. Decent, clean private rooms with shared kitchenettes and bathrooms on each fl., in a nice brownstone building. Rooms with A/C, fridges, and TVs available. Internet access $1 per 4min. Check-in 3pm. Check-out 11am. Call 2-3 wk. ahead. Bunkbeds in dorm rooms begin at $20, private rooms begin at $90. ❷

West Side YMCA, 5 W. 63rd St., at Central Park W. (☎212-875-4273 or 875-4173; www.ymcanyc.org). Subway: 1, 9, A, B, C, D to 59th St.-Columbus Circle. Map 18, D6, 69. Behind the Y's impressive Moorish facade stand 450 basic, small rooms. No beautiful decor here, but there is free access to 65,000 sq. ft. gym (including 2 pools, aerobics classes,

steam room/sauna and a very well-equipped fitness center). All rooms have A/C and cable TV. Wheelchair-accessible. Check-in 2:30pm. Check-out noon. 25-night max. stay. 1-month min. stay. 1-year max. stay. Singles with shared bath $72-89, private bath $105-140. ❷

West End Studios, 850 West End Ave., between 101st and 102nd St. (☎212-749-7104; fax 865-5130). Subway: 1 to 103rd St./Broadway. Map 18, B2, 11. Great for those needing only a bed to sleep on. Internet access $1 per 5min. Shared bathrooms only. Check-in 3pm. Check-out 11am. Reserve at least 3 wk. ahead. Prices vary depending on availability. Call ahead for that night's pricing. ❷

HOSTELS

Jazz on the Park, 36 W. 106th St./Duke Ellington Blvd., at between Manhattan Ave. and Central Park W. (☎212-932-1600; www.jazzhostel.com). Subway: B, C to 103rd St./Central Park W. Map 18, D1, 5. Clean, brightly-colored hostel with funky, fun decor and 210 beds. A/C and lockers. Enough activities that you might not actually leave the hostel: live jazz in the downstairs lounge, all-you-can-eat BBQs on the terrace on Sa in summer ($5), and Su gospel brunches. Internet access $1 per 5min. Linen, towels, and breakfast included. 24hr. laundry on premise. Check-in and check-out 11am. Reservations essential June-Oct. 10- to 12-bed dorms $27; 6- to 8-bed dorms $30; 4-bed dorms $32; private rooms (full or bunk bed) $80, prices include tax. ❶

New York International HI-AYH Hostel, 891 Amsterdam Ave., at 103rd St. (☎212-932-2300; www.hinewyork.org). Subway: 1 to 103 St./Broadway; B, C to 103rd St./Central Park W. Map 18, C2, 8. Largest US youth hostel in block-long landmark building, with 90 dorm-style rooms and 624 beds. Soft carpets, spotless bathrooms, and A/C. Kitchens, dining rooms, communal TV lounges, and large outdoor garden. Internet access. Linen and towels included. 14 night max. stay. Check-in noon. Check-out 11am. Credit card reservations required. Nov.-Apr. 10- to 12-bed dorms $29; 6- to 8-bed dorms $32; 4-bed dorms $35. Family rooms with queen and 2 bunks available. May-Oct. dorms $2 more. Nonmembers $3 more. 10+ groups should ask about private rooms. ❶

Central Park Hostel, 19 W. 103rd St., between Manhattan Ave. and Central Park W (☎212-678-0491; www.centralparkhostel.com). Subway: B, C to 103rd St./Central Park W. Map 18, D2, 9. Clean rooms with A/C and a nice TV lounge downstairs in this 5-story walk up classic brownstone. Shared bathrooms. Lockers available. Linen and towels provided. Key deposit $2. 13-night max. stay. Dorms $25; private doubles $75. ❶

International Student Center, 38 W. 88th St. between Central Park W. and Columbus Ave. (☎212-787-7706). Subway: B, C to 86th St./Central Park W. Map 18, D3, 16. Open only to those aged 18-30 (American non-NYC residents allowed); must show passport or driver's license. Aging brownstone on tree-lined street noted for frequent celebrity sightings. Lots of stairs. No-frills, tolerable dorms with showers and linens. Single, mixed-sex rooms available. Large basement TV lounge with kitchen, fridge, and affable atmosphere. Key deposit $10. Reception daily 8am-11pm. Reserve in winter only. Call after 10:30am on the day you wish to stay to check for availability. June-Aug. 7-night max. stay; Sept.-May 14 day max. stay. 8- to 10-bed dorm $20. Cash or travelers checks only. ❶

DORMITORIES

Columbia University, 1230 Amsterdam Ave., at 120th St. (☎212-678-3235; fax 678-3222). Subway: 1 to 116th St. Map 19, A6. Whittier Hall sets aside 10 clean rooms year-round, all equipped with full beds. 24hr. security. Not the safest neighborhood, but well-populated until fairly late at night. Shared bathroom; some rooms may have kitchens. Reserve in Mar. for May-Aug.; in July for Sept.-Dec. 1-week max. stay. 4-person max. Singles $60; doubles $75. Credit card deposit required. ❷

HARLEM

As you hunt down lodging in Harlem, don't be alarmed that none of the listed accommodations have very large signs. Signs are often difficult to see from the street, so following the numbers might be easier. The lack of a bold marking does not necessarily imply ill repute.

BED AND BREAKFASTS

New York Bed and Breakfast, 134 W. 119th St., between Lenox and Adam Clayton Powell Ave. (☎212-666-0559; fax 663-5000). Subway: 2, 3 to 116th St. or 125th St./Lenox (Sixth) Ave. Map 19, C6, 30. Run by Gisèle, this B&B features a double and single bed in every airy room; coffee, juice, and danish for breakfast. All rooms with shared baths. Check-in 1-7pm. Check-out 11am. Reserve at least 1 month ahead in summer. 2-night min. stay. June-Aug. doubles $75; triples $95. Expect about $10 less in off-peak season. Next door, Gisèle also owns **another B&B** at 140 W. 119th St., with essentially the same rates and conditions—$15 less, but no breakfast. She can also help with temporary job placement. ❷

Crystal's Castle Bed & Breakfast, 119 W. 119th St., between Lenox (Sixth) Ave. and Adam Clayton Powell Blvd. (☎212-722-3637; fax 280-2061). Subway: 2, 3 to 116th St. or 125th St./Lenox (Sixth) Ave. Map 19, C6, 31. Green-and-white brownstone located in the center of the lively Mount Morris Historic district. 2 clean rooms. Continental breakfast included. Check-out 1pm. Call at least 2 months ahead in summer; 1 month ahead in off-season. 25% deposit required. 1-week cancellation notice required. Singles $76; doubles $97; both $409 per week (plus tax). About $20 less off-peak. ❷

Hotel Caribe, 515 West 145th St., between Broadway and Amerdam. (☎212-368-9915). Subway A, B, C, D, to 145th/St. Nicholas; 1,9 to 145th/Broadway. Map 19, A1. Good for the early to bed and early to rise. No one leaves, enters, or re-enters the hotel after 2:00am without permission from the front desk. Flanked by two more hotels, Casablanca and Hamilton

Heights, all having the same owner, management team, and basic amenities. Hotel Caribe has a clean, safe, and friendly facility. Only 2 people per room. Check-out noon. Rooms with bathroom $75, large front rooms $75, small rooms with sink $55. ❷

HOSTELS

Sugar Hill International House, 722 St. Nicholas Ave., at 146th St. (☎212-926-7030). Subway: A, B, C, D to 145th St./St. Nicholas Ave. Map 19, B3, 5. Passport ID required (Americans allowed). Across from subway, in lively Sugar Hill. Brownstone with large and spacious rooms (25-30 beds total, 6-8 beds per room) and a quiet family feel. You'll check out the sights downtown and then 'come home' at the end of your day. Garden out back; adorable but spoiled dog. Friendly staff is a living library of Harlem history and culture. No smoking. Rooms for 2-9 people. All-female room available. **Free Internet** access. Facilities include kitchens, stereo, and library. Key deposit $10. Call in the morning. Check-in 9am-9pm. Check-out 11am. Reserve 1 month ahead during off season, no reservations accepted July-Sept. 2-week max. stay. Dorms $20-$25; doubles $50-$60. ❶

Uptown Hostel, 239 Lenox (Sixth) Ave., at 122nd St. (☎212-666-0559; fax 663-5000). Subway: 2, 3 to 125th St./Lenox (Sixth) Ave. Map 19, E6, 32. Also run by Gisèle (see **New York Bed and Breakfast,** above), who knows the neighborhood well and helps long-term travelers find apartments and temporary jobs. Bunk beds in clean, comfy rooms. Spacious hall bathrooms. Wonderful new common room and kitchen add to the family atmosphere. Free linens. Passport required. Key deposit $10. Check-in 9am-8pm. Lock-out June-Aug. 11:30am-4pm. Call as far ahead as possible in summer, 2 days ahead the rest of the year. Singles $17-20; doubles $65. ❶

BROOKLYN

Akwaaba Mansion, 347 MacDonough St., in Bedford-Stuyvesant. (☎718-455-5958; fax 774-1744; www.akwaaba.com). Subway: A, C to Utica Ave. Map 20, D2, 1. Monique Greenwood, former editor of Essence Magazine, owns this B&B, built in 1860 in Victorian style. It won an award from the New York Landmarks Preservation Society; there are frequent fashion and advertising shoots here. Akwaaba, an African word meaning 'welcome,' contains 18 rooms each with their own theme; all are decorated in African cultural decor. Library, TV room, tree-shaded patio, wrap-around sun porch, and breakfast in an elegant dining room. Rooms comfortably accommodate 2. All include private bath and A/C. Check-in 4-7pm. Check-out 11am. F jazz and Su brunch with Southern/African cuisine ($10). Reserve at least 1 month ahead. Rooms $120-135; weekends $135-150. ❺

Bed & Breakfast on the Park, 113 Prospect Park W., between 6th and 7th St., in Prospect Park (☎718-499-6115; fax 499-1385; www.bbnyc.com). Subway: F to Seventh Ave./ Ninth St., then 2 blocks east and 2 blocks north. A magnificently restored brownstone jam-packed with Victoriana, this decadent, aromatic opiate of a hotel lacks only adequate horse stables and gas lighting. Classy furnishings (rococo armoires, oriental carpets, damask) are museum-quality, but you can touch and even fall asleep on them. Gourmet breakfast in not-so-common room. 8 doubles (2 with shared bath), $100-375. ❺

QUEENS

Flushing Grand Hotel, 36-38 Main St., near Northern Blvd., in Flushing (☎718-888-8668 or 718-888-8698; fax 888-8768; www.flushinggrand.com). Subway: 7 to Flushing-Main St.; walk north on Main St. Map 27, F1, 1. Clean, comfortable rooms with large windows, right on the main strip. Check-in 24hr. Check-out noon. Singles $90; doubles $100; triples $115. $30 room and phone deposit. ❸

YMCA-Flushing, 138-46 Northern Blvd., between Union and Bowne Sts., in Flushing (☎718-961-6880; fax 718-461-4691). Subway: 7 to Flushing-Main St.; from there walk 10min. north on Main St. and turn right onto Northern Blvd. Map 27, G1, 10. The area between the Y and Flushing's nearby shopping district is lively and well populated, but the neighborhood deteriorates north of Northern Blvd. Carpeted, small, clean rooms with cable TV and A/C; shared bathrooms only. Access to all Y facilities (including gym, squash courts, and swimming pools) included. Key deposit $10. Check-in 3pm. Check-out noon. Reserve at least a month ahead for summer, 1 week otherwise. 25-night max. stay. Singles $50; doubles $70; triples $80. ❷

Sheraton LaGuardia East Hotel, 135-20 39th Ave., off Main St., Flushing (☎718-460-6666 or 888-268-0717; fax 718-445-2655). Subway: 7 to Flushing-Main St. Map 27, F1, 6. Another link in a big hotel chain, but if you've got to be in Queens, there's not much in terms of accommodations options. Cable TV, A/C, phone. Continental breakfast included. Check-in 3pm. Check-out noon. Doubles $180-245. ❺

LONG-TERM ACCOMMODATIONS

So you're one of millions looking for an apartment in NYC. The market is extremely tight, rents are high, brokerage fees exorbitant, and most landlords will not rent without a guarantor on the lease and all potential tenants present when the decision to rent is made. Even so, a NYC apartment isn't an impossible dream. Like everything else here, housing is possible with a little perseverance, ingenuity, and luck.

When house-hunting on your own gets too exhausting, some sites will help you find a place—for a fee. **Manhattan Lodgings** (☎212-677-7616; www.manhattanlodgings.com) puts visitors in contact with New York apartment tenants who want to rent out their respective pads for a few days or weeks. **New York Habitat,** 307 Seventh Ave., Ste. 306 (☎212-255-8018; fax 627-1416; www.nyhabitat.com) finds sublets, roommates and apartment rentals. **www.relocationcentral.com** helps with everything from apartment hunting to renting a moving van, while **www.roomiematch.com** finds a roommate for you.

APARTMENTS

TIPS

Unless you are planning on permanently relocating to New York, **subletting** an apartment for a limited period of time is your best bet. When New Yorkers feel the need to escape, they will rent out their (usually furnished) apartments for a month or more. For longer stays, it is easier to become a **roommate** in someone's apartment than to find your own lease. When apartment hunting in NYC, **act fast.** If you find something suitable (but perhaps not your dream apartment), take it immediately; it *will* be gone when you call back, and you're *not* going to find your dream place. However, do not rush your search: always thoroughly investigate the apartment and surrounding neighborhood to make sure you would feel comfortable living there. You can usually get a better value in Brooklyn and Queens. Hoboken, West New York, and Weehawken, across the Hudson, also offer more for your money, a view of the Manhattan skyline, and a quick $1.50 (cheaper than the subway) commute to the center of everything.

RESOURCES

Word of mouth can be the best—and probably the cheapest—way to find a place in NYC. Realtors are a good resource when the housing hunt becomes frustrating, but brokerage fees are extremely high—look for them in a phone book. For those with no friends or funds in New York, newspapers and the Internet provide an invaluable resource. Both the *Village Voice* (www.villagevoice.com) and *The New York Times* (www.nytimes.com) have helpful classified sections with real estate options. There are also myriad websites devoted to finding roommates, subletters, and apartments throughout the city—many of them, like www.1800roommates.com, are free. **Craig's List** (www.newyork.craigslist.org) let people post sublet/lease listings for free. Summer sublet postings abound at grad-student and alumni websites, as aspiring lawyers and doctors migrate out of their New York apartments for summer internships elsewhere: university housing forums such as **Hunter College's** listings (www.hunter.cuny.edu/~reslife/page3.html), and professional organizations such as The **NALP Foundation** (www.nalp.org), often have amazing temporary-housing sections.

If you're moving to New York and want help finding a **gay, lesbian, bi- or transsexual roommate,** it might be worthwhile to pay a visit to **Rainbow Roommates,** 268 W. 22nd St., between Seventh and Eighth Ave. (☎212-627-8612; www.rainbowroommates.com. Drop-in hours Tu-Sa 11am-7pm.) Rainbow Roommates provides you with a subscription to personalized listings that match the roommate criteria you have requested. (Updates sent daily by email or fax. Subscription $150 for 3 months.) You may also want to try **DG Neary Realty,** 57 W. 16th St., on the corner of Sixth Ave., which hosts "G.R.I.N."—the Gay Roommate Information Network. (☎212-627-4242; fax 989-1207). Registration fee is $50 for one year daily room listings. **Gay Roommate Information Network** (☎212-627-4242; home.earthlink.net/~gayroommate) matches gay roommates.

OTHER OPTIONS

DORMS

Many universities in New York rent out their vacant dorms to summer visitors. The length of stay varies depending on the school, but often you can stay for the entire summer. **NYU** (p. 259) and **Columbia** (p. 271) provide summer housing for non-affiliates. For a more complete list of colleges and universities in New York, see **www.ci.nyc.ny.us** or **www.greatcollegetown.com/college.html.** The following schools also offer summer housing, and are not necessarily endorsed by *Let's Go*:

Fordham University, 315 Keating Hall, 441 East Fordham Rd., Bronx, New York 10458 (☎718-817-4665; fax 817-4670; www.fordham.edu/summer).

Long Island University, Brooklyn Campus, 1 University Plaza, Brooklyn, NY 11201 (☎718-488-1011; Resident Hall Director 780-1552). Rates average $50 per night, but vary depending on length of stay.

New School University, Office of the Vice President for Student Affairs, 66 W. 12th St., 8th fl., New York, NY 10011 (☎212-229-5350; downtown@newschool.edu).

HOME EXCHANGE AND RENTAL

For shorter stays, home exchange and rental can be cost-effective options, particularly for families with children. Home rentals are much more expensive than exchanges, although they are remarkably cheaper than an extended stay at a comparably serviced hotel. In New York, most home exchanges and rentals come with kitchen, cleaning service, telephones, and TV. Unfortunately, it can be difficult to arrange an exchange or rental for more than one month. Both rentals and exchanges are organized by the following services.

HomeExchange.com, P.O. Box 30085, Santa Barbara, CA 93130 (☎800-877-8723; www.homeexchange.com).

The Invented City: International Home Exchange, 41 Sutter St., Ste. 1090, San Francisco, CA 94104 (☎800-788-2489 in the US, 415-252-1141 elsewhere; www.invented-city.com). For $50, your offer is listed in a catalog and you have access to a database of thousands of homes for exchange.

HOSTELS

Although many of New York's hostels have maximum stay limits, some do allow long-term stays. If a hostel doesn't have a maximum stay limit, ask, and perhaps you shall receive. Where stipulated, limits usually hover between 25 and 30 days; for a two- or three-month stay, it's always possible to stay at two or three different hostels for the duration of your trip. For a list of hostels, see **Accommodations By Neighborhood,** p. 258. The **De Hirsch Residence,** on the Upper East Side, rents rooms by the month (p. 269). In addition, **YMCA-Flushing** allows long-term stays with advance notice (p. 274).

INSIDE

long island **279**
hudson valley **287**
the catskills **289**
new jersey **289**
connecticut **292**

Daytripping

DESTINATION	HIGHLIGHTS	TRAVEL TIME
Oyster Bay	The Gold Coast	45min.-1hr.
Jones Beach	Waves, sand, sunbathers	1hr.
Fire Island	Beaches, gay scene	1½-2hr.
The Hamptons and Montauk	Beaches, rich people	2-3hr.
Tarrytown and Sleepy Hollow	Estates	45min.-1hr.
West Point	Boot camp	1-1½hr.
Bear Mountain State Park	Hiking, bears	2½-3hr.
Atlantic City, NJ	Casinos	2½-3 hr.
Foxwoods and Mohegan Sun (CT)	Casinos	1½-2hr.

LONG ISLAND

TRANSPORTATION

Trains: Long Island Railroad, LIRR (travel info ☎718-217-5477 or main office 718-558-7400; TTY ☎718-558-3022; daily 24hr.). Trains leave from Penn Station in Manhattan (34th St. at Seventh Ave.; subway: 1, 2, 3, 9 to 34th St.-Penn Station/Seventh Ave.; A, C, E to 34th St.-Penn Station/Eighth Ave.) and meet in Jamaica, Queens (subway: E, J, Z to Jamaica Center-Parsons/Archer).

LIRR also connects in Queens via the 7 line to Vernon Blvd.-Jackson Ave. (Long Island City), Hunters Pt. Ave., and Flushing-Main St. stations, as well as to Brooklyn's Flatbush Ave. station (subway: 1, 2, 4, 5, Q to Atlantic Ave.; M, N, R, W to Pacific St.) Fares vary daily and by zone. Rush hour peak tickets (Manhattan-bound 5am-9am, outbound 4-8pm) about $1.50-4 more than off-peak fares. Tickets can be purchased aboard trains, but you will be surcharged $2 if the station ticket office is open.

BUSES

MTA Long Island Bus (☎516-228-4000; open M-Sa 7am-5pm). Daytime bus service in eastern Queens, Nassau, and western Suffolk. Runs along major streets, but routes are complex and irregular–confirm your destination with the driver. Some buses run every 15min., others every hr. Fare $2 (Metrocard or exact change only); transfers 25¢, free with Metrocard. Disabled travelers and senior citizens pay half fare. Serves Jones Beach daily late June-early Sept.; 20-25min., every 20-40min. from the LIRR station in Freeport.

Suffolk Transit (☎631-852-5200; open M-F 8am-4:30pm). Runs from Lindenhurst to the eastern end of Long Island. The 10a, 10b, and 10c lines make frequent stops along the South Fork. No service Su. Buses run in summer from the LIRR station in Babylon to Robert Moses State Park on Fire Island, hourly M-F and every ½hr. Sa-Su. Fare $1.50, students with ID $1, seniors and the disabled 50¢, transfers 25¢, under 5 free.

Hampton Jitney (☎631-283-4600 or 800-936-0440; www.hamptonjitney.com). The luxury bus serving the Hamptons. More expensive, but more comfortable and comprehensive than other buses. Departs from various Manhattan locales. $27, round-trip $47. Reservations advisable; call in advance, especially on weekends.

OYSTER BAY

***By car:** Take Long Island Expwy. to Exit 41N. Take Rte. 106N and follow signs to Oyster Bay. **By train:** LIRR to Oyster Bay branch to Oyster Bay. **Taxi:** ☎516-921-2141.*

Oyster Bay, a town on the affluent North Shore with beautiful estates lining the seashore, is Long Island at its most picturesque. Depending on your source, the town got its name either for the plentiful oysters located in the offshore waters or for its harbor's oyster-like shape.

SIGHTS

The town's most illustrious resident was President Theodore Roosevelt. His summertime estate, **Sagamore Hill,** is the most precious jewel in the crown of Oyster Bay. (Sagamore Hill Rd., off Cove Neck Rd. To get there from the Long Island Expwy., get off at Exit 41N and take Rte. 106N for 4 mi. to Rte. 25A. Turn right on Rte. 25A east and travel 2½ mi. to the 3rd traffic light, then turn left onto Cove Rd. After 1½ mi., you'll see a sign for Sagamore Hill. Make the next right. By public transportation: take LIRR to Oyster Bay. 60-75min. Approximately $8 taxi ride from station to Sagamore Hill.) In 1905, Roosevelt met in the Queen Anne-style house with envoys from Japan and Russia, arranging talks for the Treaty of Portsmouth that effectively ended of the Russo-Japanese War. Roosevelt won the Nobel Peace Prize for his part in the negotiations. The house is packed with such memorabilia as samurai swords presented by a Japanese emperor, an impressive collection of "preserved" wildlife, and a rhinoceros foot inkwell. Stuffed deer, buffalo and zebra heads, an old family pet, and an elephant's foot trash can also adorn his home. (☎516-922-4788; www.nps.gov/sahi. Visitors Center open daily 9am-5pm. 50 min. tours of the house hourly 10am-4pm. Come early—tours limited to 14 people. Access to house $5, under 16 free. Grounds free.)

If the presidential ethos proves overwhelming, remember that the **Planting Fields Arboretum** is another coastal gem. (To get to Planting Fields, once in Oyster Bay, turn left at the light onto Lexington Ave. and turn left again at the next light to Mill River Rd. Follow the signs to Planting Fields Arboretum.) Purchased by insurance magnate William Robinson Coe and his wife in 1913, the 409-acre estate features two

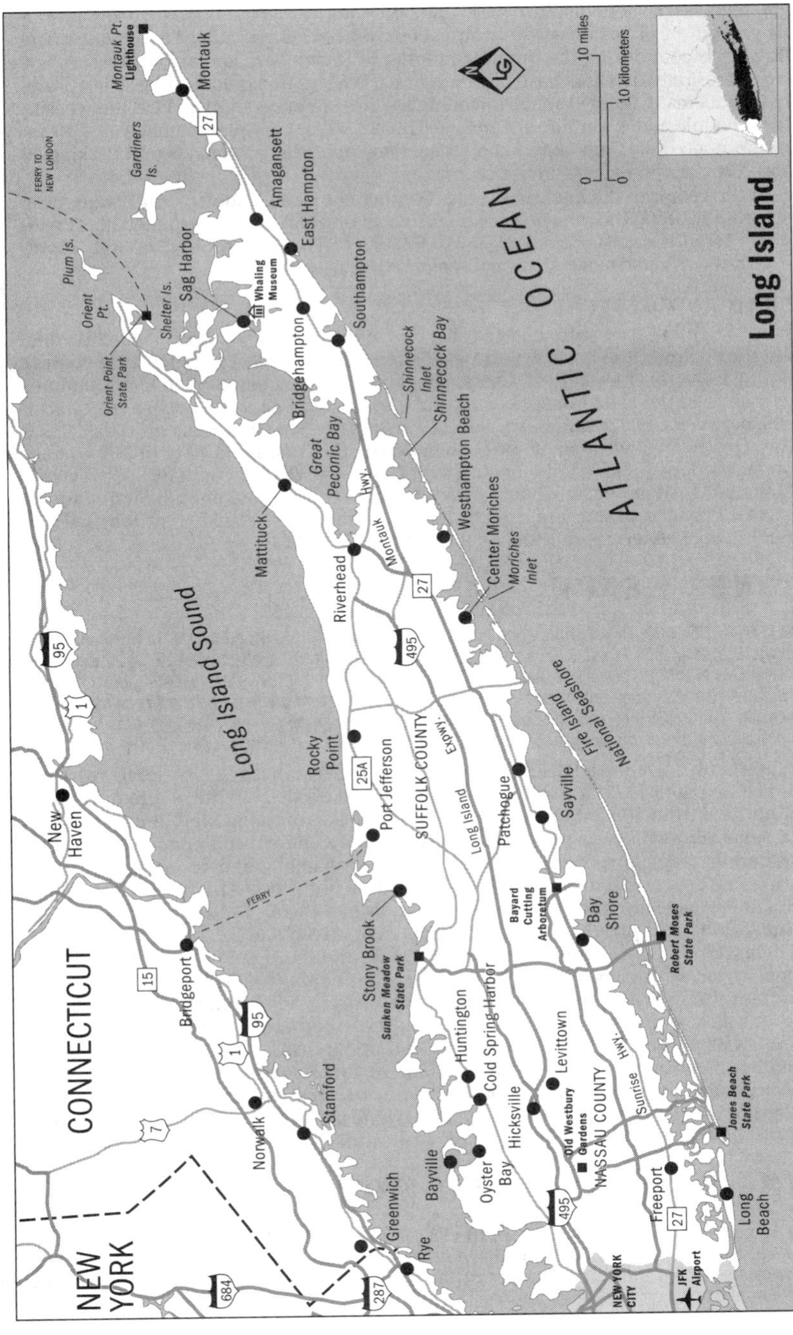

NEW YORK
CONNECTICUT
New Haven
Bridgeport
Norwalk
Stamford
Greenwich
Rye
Long Island Sound
FERRY
FERRY TO NEW LONDON
Plum Is.
Orient Pt.
Orient Point State Park
Shelter Is.
Gardiners Is.
Montauk Pt. Lighthouse
Montauk
Sag Harbor
Whaling Museum
Amagansett
East Hampton
Bridgehampton
Southampton
Mattituck
Great Peconic Bay
Riverhead
Montauk Hwy.
Rocky Point
Port Jefferson
Stony Brook
Sunken Meadow State Park
SUFFOLK COUNTY
Long Island Expwy.
Shinnecock Inlet
Shinnecock Bay
Westhampton Beach
Center Moriches
Moriches Inlet
Bayville
Oyster Bay
Huntington
Cold Spring Harbor
Hicksville
Levittown
Patchogue
Bayard Cutting Arboretum
Sayville
Bay Shore
Old Westbury Gardens
NASSAU COUNTY
Sunrise Hwy.
Fire Island National Seashore
ATLANTIC OCEAN
NEW YORK CITY
JFK Airport
Freeport
Long Beach
Jones Beach State Park
Robert Moses State Park
0 10 miles
0 10 kilometers
684
287
7
15
1
95
25A
495
27

Long Island

greenhouses, a rhododendron park, and other quirky highlights such as the "synoptic garden" of plants obsessively alphabetized according to their Latin names. The flowers bloom during the unlikely months of December, January, and February, when most city-dwellers have begun to forget what greenery looks like. The arboretum hosts many family events, including a summer concert series. Visit the website for schedule and event information. (☎516-922-8600; www.plantingfields.org. Arboretum open daily 9am-5pm. Main greenhouse open daily 10am-4:30pm. Parking $6 May- Sept. and weekends. Entrance free.)

At the center of the historic site sits **Coe Hall,** the Coes' Tudor revival estate. Constructed in 1921, the mansion has many rows of mind-boggling stained-glass windows from the 12th century. (☎516-922-9210. Tours Apr.-Sept. noon-3:30pm. Admission: $5, students with ID and seniors $3.50, ages 7-12 $1.)

FOOD AND OYSTERS

While its Gold Coast relics and sea-side charm draw a heavy tourist population during the summer, the bay town draws the masses with an oyster-shucking contest during its October Oysterfest. Oyster-shucking opportunities abound in the summer as well as at the local hot spot of 18 years, **Oyster Bay Fish and Clam Bar ❷,** 103 Rte. 106, between High St. and Berry Hill Rd. Oysters run $18 per dozen. (☎516-922-5522. Apr.-Oct. M-Th 3 pm-11pm, F-Sa 11am-midnight, Su 11am-11pm.) For pricier oysters on an outdoor patio, try the **South Street Oyster Bar ❸,** 100 South St., between W. Main and E. Main St. (☎516-922-1545. Open Tu-Th 5pm-midnight, F-Su noon-midnight.) For land-based fare, try the famous hamburgers ($4.25-6) at **Taby's ❶,** 28 Audrey St., between Spring and South St. (☎516-624-7781).

JONES BEACH

☎516-785-1600. ***By car:*** *Take Long Island Expwy. E or Grand Central Pkwy. E to Northern State Pkwy. E to Wantagh Pkwy. S to Jones Beach State Park. Alternatively, take Belt/Southern State Pkwy. E to Wantagh Pkwy. S to Jones Beach State Park. About 33 mi. Parking Lot 4 open until midnight, all other lots open until sundown. Parking M-F 8am-4pm and Sa-Su 6am-7pm $7, all other times free.* ***By train:*** *LIRR to Freeport, shuttle bus to Jones Beach. In the summer, the LIRR runs a summer package deal for the trip until Labor Day ($11 from Manhattan, call ahead for dates). Map 3.*

When New York State Parks Commissioner Robert Moses (p. 43) set to work on Jones Beach in 1921, it was a barren spit of land off the Atlantic shore of Nassau County. Within 10 years he had bought up the surrounding land, imported tons of sand, planted beach grass to preserve the new dunes, and completed dozens of buildings for purposes as diverse as diaper-changing and archery. His industrious efforts created 6½ mi. of popular public beaches. Although the water is not the bluest nor the sun the strongest, Jones Beach State Park's wealth of attractions and proximity to Manhattan still attracts an army of beachgoers. The parking fields accommodate 23,000 cars, and there are nearly 2500 acres of beachfront with eight different public beaches on the rough Atlantic Ocean and calmer Zachs Bay. Only 40min. from the city, barely a patch of sand shows under all the umbrellas and blankets in the summertime. Along the 1½ mile **boardwalk** you can find two Olympic-sized pools, softball fields, roller-skating, mini-golf, a fitness course, basketball, and nightly dancing. The **Tommy Hilfiger at Jones Beach Theater** inside the park often hosts big-name rockers such as Pearl Jam. (☎516-221-1000; www.tommyhilfigerjonesbeach.com. Box office open Tu-Sa 10am-6pm, Su noon-6pm, night of show until 9pm.)

THE HAMPTONS AND MONTAUK

By car: *Take the Long Island Expwy. (I-495) east to Exit 70-Manorville. Go south to Rte. 27 (a.k.a. Sunset Hwy. or Montauk Hwy.) and head east to Montauk (approx. 50 mi. on Rte. 27). Towns are located either directly off, or on, the highway.* ***By train:*** *LIRR from Penn Station serves all towns directly except Sag Harbor. Map 3.*

Located on the South Fork of Long Island, the Hamptons are a curious amalgam of the serene and the sexy. Summering Manhattanites, artists, writers, and displaced West Coast stars inhabit the Hamptons post-Memorial Day. The sex appeal and star power of this prized location for vacation houses translates into burgeoning development, crowded main streets, and conspicuous consumption.

A prized location for vacation houses, the Hamptons are best visited in the summer. Flowers are in bloom, the upper crust of society mills about on the sidewalks, and beachgoers bravely confront the ocean's waves. The Hamptons can be visited for a single day if you set out early in the morning. Most inns and guesthouses in the Hamptons run fairly steep, especially in the summer. If you must stay the night, Montauk's host of motels present the most realistic options. Nonetheless, it is imperative to call ahead. For a deal, try coming in the warm off-season weeks directly following Labor Day.

SOUTHAMPTON

From the Southampton LIRR station, head right out of the parking lot along Railroad Plaza to N. Main St.; turn left onto N. Main St. and walk to the stop sign; bear left and keep walking as N. Main becomes Main St., taking you to the center of town (about ½ mi. altogether). ***Taxis:*** *Atlantic Taxi ☎631-283-1900, Southampton 283-0242, Up Island Connection 287-7180. Map 3.*

Founded in 1640 as the first English colony in future New York State, beautiful Southampton features sprawling houses—many designed by Stanford White and other late 19th-century luminaries. On Dune Rd., by the ocean, enormous gates and rows of Normandy-esque hedges guard the beachfront mansions of some of the town's wealthiest residents. Most **beaches** require resident parking permits, but lots at the end of Beach Rd. D., off Meadow Lane, offer free parking. To get there from town, take Main St. south to Dune Rd. Make a left onto Dune Rd. and drive to First Neck Ln. Make a left, and find Meadow Lane to the right. Follow the road for 3-4 mi. Rd. D follows Rd. A, B, and C. For more information, pick up a detailed pamphlet at the **Chamber of Commerce,** 76 Main St. (☎631-283-0402. Open M-F 10am-4pm; Sa-Su 11am-4pm.)

Back in town, at the corner of Main St. and Meeting House Ln., the **Southampton Historical Museum** replicates an 1800s main street with a school-house, carpenter, cobbler, apothecary and blacksmith. (☎631-283-2494. Open May-Dec. Tu-Sa 11am-5pm, Su 1-5pm; Jan.-Apr. Tu-Sa 11am-5pm. $3, seniors $2, children 5-17 $1, under 6 free.)

The Venetian-style **Parrish Art Museum** is on the other side of Main St. This modern gallery houses a contemporary collection concentrating on American artists, particularly those who lived and worked near Southampton, like William Merritt Chase and Fairfield Porter. The Parrish is surrounded by a garden that showcases reproduced Roman busts. (☎631-283-2118. Open June to mid-Sept. M-Sa 11am-5pm, Su 1-and 5pm; late-Sept. to May M, Th-Sa 11am-5pm, Su 1-5pm. $5, seniors and students $3, under 18 free. Wheelchair-accessible.)

Just outside the picturesque town of Southampton, at the intersection of Hwy. 27 and Old Mill Rd., the tiny community of Water Mill hosts the original mill that was built "to supply the necessities of the towne" in 1644. The **Water Mill Museum** has been in its present location since 1726 and is open for tours. (☎631-726-4625. Open late May-June Sa-Su 11am-5pm; July-late Sept. M, Th-Sa 11am-5pm, Su 1-5pm. Admission: $3; children free.)

EAST HAMPTON AND AMAGANSETT

From the East Hampton train station: Walk along Newtown Ln. into town. From the Amagansett train station: Walk along Main St. into town. ***Taxis:*** *☎631-324-9696 or 324-0077. Map 3.*

The center of East Hampton is home to more art galleries, clothing stores, and colonial memorabilia outlets than one would care to imagine, but the town is great for strolling, window-shopping, and whiling away the hours. Many artists have found inspiration and refuge here, most prominently Jackson Pollock. To get to Main Beach, go down to Main St. and follow it back out of town. After passing the pond, instead of making a right onto the Montauk Hwy., continue straight through the light and drive about ¾ mi. to the ocean.

Nearby **Amagansett** is little more than a tiny Main St. If you want to glimpse some of the area's larger houses, head south of the highway to Further Ln. and examine the estates from the street. Back in town, the **Farmers' Market,** 367 Rte. 27 (Main St.), attracts locals and tourists alike to its fresh food sections, coffee shop, and pastries (☎631-267-3894. Open Memorial Day-Labor Day daily 7am-9pm; Labor Day-Memorial Day 6am-6pm.) Although Hamptons' beaches try to keep out ordinary folk by requiring parking permits, the **Atlantic Avenue Beach** is walkable from the center of town (approx. 1 mi.).

Amagansett hosts some great live music in the evenings. **The Stephen Talkhouse,** 161 Main St., hosts a wide range of performers from John Hiatt to De La Soul, as well as lesser-known acts. (☎516-267-3117; www.stephentalkhouse.com. Tickets: $5-100, depending on who's playing.)

SAG HARBOR

The LIRR does not stop at Sag Harbor, but the town is accessible via Bridgehampton. ***Taxis from the station:*** *Hampton Taxi ☎631-537-7400. Map 3.*

Sag Harbor sits on the north shore of the South Fork, one of the diamonds in the rough of Long Island. Founded in 1707, this port used to be more important than New York Harbor as its deep waters made for easy navigation. At its peak, the winsome village was the world's fourth-largest whaling port. James Fenimore Cooper began his first novel, *Precaution*, in a Sag Harbor hotel in 1824. During Prohibition, the harbor served as a major meeting place for smugglers and rum-runners from the Caribbean.

SIGHTS

In the past few years, an increasing number of tourists have returned to the quiet, tree-lined streets of salt-box cottages and Greek Revival mansions. Sag Harbor's former grandeur survives in the second-largest US collection of colonial buildings and in the cemeteries lined with the gravestones of Revolutionary soldiers and sailors. Check out the **Sag Harbor Whaling Museum** in the Masonic Temple, at the corner of Main and Garden St. A huge whale rib arches over the front door. Note the antique washing machine, made locally in 1864, and the excellent scrimshaw collection. (☎631-725-0770; www.sagharborwhalingmuseum.org. Open May-Sept. M-Sa 10am-5pm, Su 1-5pm; Oct.-Dec. Sa-Su noon-4pm. Tours by appointment year-round. $3, seniors $2, ages 6-13 $1, under 6 free.) The equally intriguing **Custom House,** the authentic 18th-century home across the street, features an extensive collection of period furniture and trivial keepsakes. (☎631-725-0250. Open June-Sept. Sa-Su 10am-5pm; July-Aug. daily 10am-5pm. Admission: $3, ages 7-14, seniors $1.50.) Less than a mile from the wharf is **Haven's Beach,** where it costs $10 to park.

For more information, go to the **Chamber of Commerce** that is housed in a large windmill in the center of the town. (☎631-725-0011; www.sagharborchamber.com. Open May-Oct. daily 10am-4pm.)

MONTAUK

LIRR to Montauk and head to the right out of the train station along the 2-lane road. This is Edgemere Rd., which leads straight to the village green, a 15-20min. walk. The Hampton Jitney makes more than a dozen trips daily. Map 3.

As the easternmost point of the South Fork, Montauk offers an unobstructed view of the Atlantic Ocean. Despite the slightly commercialized tourist/hotel areas and the 3hr. trip, the peaceful salt air is worth the effort.

SIGHTS

The 110 ft. **Montauk Point Lighthouse and Museum,** off the Montauk Hwy. (Rte. 27.), was built in 1796 by special order of President George Washington. The first public works project in the newly formed United States, the lighthouse guided many ships into the harbor, including the schooner *La Amistad.* If your lungs are willing, climb the 137 spiraling steps to the top for a view across the Long Island Sound to Connecticut and Rhode Island. (☎631-668-2544; www.montauklighthouse.com. Open June-Sept. M-F and Su 10:30am-6pm, Sa 10:30am-7:30pm; other times call for info. Admission: $6, seniors $5, under 12 $3.)

Those wanting to set out themselves for the open sea can try a half-day fluke-fishing cruise with **Viking** (☎631-668-5700; www.vikingfleet.com. $32, children $15, including equipment; times vary, see website) or **Lazybones** (☎631-668-5671; $30, children $20, including equipment; departs 7am and 1pm; reservations required). Both cruises depart from Montauk Dock. Back in town, off the main drag, an out-of-place high-rise apartment building looms. Real-estate developer Carl Fischer built this anomaly as part of his clearly misguided attempt to turn Montauk into a Miami Beach of the north.

For more information on things to do and see in Montauk, check out the **Chamber of Commerce,** 742 Montauk Hwy., in the center of town. (☎631-668-2428. Open daily 10am-5pm.)

FOOD

Gosman's Clam Bar, on West Lake Ln., through the Gosman's Dock sign by the ocean (☎631-668-5330). A good place to get a plate of mussels ($6) or a lobster (market price). Open daily noon-10pm. ❶

ACCOMMODATIONS

Hither Hills State Park is located 4 mi. west of Montauk along the highway and accessible from the village green in Montauk via taxi. It offers campsites located near lovely vistas, swimming, and picnicking spots. (☎631-668-2554. Park open daily 8am-dusk. Camping available early Apr. to mid-Nov. Reservations required—make them through MISTIX Corporation at ☎800-456-CAMP/2267. $24 per campsite per night.) While lodging anywhere on the South Fork requires some research and often reservations, clean rooms can be had at **Tipperary Inn** ❺, 432 West Lake Ln. (☎631-668-2010), accessible via the S-94 bus to Montauk Dock. The Inn provides A/C, TV, phone, and fridge. (Rooms for 2-6 people range M-Th $125-160, F-Su $395-450 in the summer.)

FIRE ISLAND

No cars ***are allowed on the island.*** **By train and ferry:** *LIRR to Sayville ($9.50). Take a taxi to the port. Ferries from Sayville (☎631-589-0810) go to Sailors' Haven (round-trip $9), Cherry Grove, and Fire Island Pines (round-trip $11, under 11 $5). LIRR to Bay Shore ($9.50). The Port is in walking distance down Maple Ave. Ferries from Bay Shore go to Kismet, Saltaire, Fair Harbor, Atlantic, Dunewood, Ocean Beach, Seaview, and Ocean Bay Park (round-trip $11.50, under 12 $5.50). LIRR to Patchogue ($10.75). Walk to ferry. Ferries from Patchogue (☎631-475-1665) go to Davis Park and Watch Hill (round-trip $11, under 11 $6). Bicycles are not allowed on the ferries. www.fireislandferries.com. To travel between towns, call one of many water taxi companies.* **Taxi:** *South Bay Water Taxi ☎631-665-8885. Prices vary.*

Tranquilly pristine towns dot Fire Island, southern Long Island's barrier against the temperamental Atlantic. Residents have done much to fend off the bright lights of the tourist industry, even as property values have soared. Some towns retain their original layout of closely packed bungalows without yards; citizens fought so fiercely to retain their quiet plots of land that not even the influential urban planner Robert Moses could build a road across the island. Since then, the state has protected most Fire Island areas by declaring them either state parks or federal "wilderness areas." The lack of infrastructure ensures both peace and inconvenience; visitors must often take water taxis to travel between towns. The separation has allowed Fire Island's 17 summer communities to forge distinct niches—middle-class residential clusters, openly gay communities (see below), and pockets of vacationing Hollywood stars.

The **Fire Island National Seashore** (☎631-289-4810 for the headquarters in Patchogue) is the official moniker for the stretches of coastline that hug the island. The beach is Fire Island's biggest draw and the daytime hot spot for summertime fishing, clamming, and guided nature walks. The **Fire Island Lighthouse Visitor Center** in Kismet houses the only monument on the isle. (☎631-321-7028. Small museum open daily 9:30am-5pm.) The facilities at **Sailor's Haven,** just west of the Cherry Grove community (☎631-597-6183), include a marina, a nature trail, and a famous beach. There are similar facilities at **Watch Hill** (☎631-289-9336; www.watchhillfi.com).

The **Sunken Forest,** named for its location behind the dunes, is another of the island's natural wonders. Located directly west of Sailor's Haven, its soil supports an unusual and attractive combination of gnarled holly, sassafras, and poison ivy. Some of the forest's specimens are over 200 years old. Atop the dunes, you can see the forest's trees laced together in a hulking, uninterrupted mesh.

OCEAN BEACH

The largest and most publicly accessible community on Fire Island, Ocean Beach provides a starting point for many tourists. Signs warn visitors to show some respect—no drinking in public, no walking around town without a shirt, and no "discourteous" public displays. Ocean Beach's main street is lined with gray-shingled buildings, restaurants, small groceries, and beachwear shops.

Take any side street (perpendicular to the main drag) all the way across the island to arrive at miles and miles of coastline. Once there, you can walk along the shore to see the beachfront homes that grow larger as you travel either way down the beach. The largest homes are located about 2 mi. west of Ocean Beach in posh **Saltaire** (a completely residential community), followed closely by the up-and-coming town of **Fair Harbor.** If you walk just over 2½ mi. east, you will reach two predominantly gay communities: the private bungalows and raised boardwalks of **Cherry Grove**, and the colossal homes of **Fire Island Pines** (see below for more).

ACCOMMODATIONS

Ferries run late into the night, but those so inclined can stay at **Clegg's Hotel ❷,** 478 Bayberry Walk. The hotel has clean rooms and a friendly, knowledgeable staff. Clegg's considers itself family-oriented and children stay for free. (☎631-583-5399. Room prices vary according to season, number of vacancies, view, and day of the week. Double $60 with shared bath, M-F; $350 with bay-room view during 2-night, peak-season Sa-Su stay.)

Nearby **Watch Hill** has a campground located across the Great South Bay from Patchogue. An annual lottery is held in April to determine who gets the 26 available units; check the website or call for more information. (☎631-289-9336; www.watchhillfi.com/camping.htm. Camping season mid-May to mid-Oct. Reservations required. Campground is for organized groups only. Max. 8 people per campsite, between 1-5 people must be 21+. $40 for min. 2-night stay, $20 for each additional night.)

CHERRY GROVE AND FIRE ISLAND PINES

Two prominent Fire Island resort hamlets, **Cherry Grove** and **Fire Island Pines** (called "the Pines"), host largely gay communities—and parties that rage late into the night. Crowded "streets," or wooden pathways, border spectacular Atlantic Ocean beaches. Weekdays provide an excellent opportunity to enjoy the island's beauty and charm in a low-key setting, with Thursdays and Sundays offering an ideal balance of sanity and scene; Friday and Saturday see mounting crowds and prices.

NIGHTLIFE

Gay nightlife on Fire Island has a very established rhythm that may be confusing to newcomers. Since neither Cherry Grove nor the Pines are very big, it's best just to ask around, either at your hotel or restaurant. In the wooded area between the Pines and the Grove is a loosely-bounded area that those in the know call the **Meat Rack.** Things go down amid the myriad walkways—**Gay Men's Health Crisis** (GMHC, p. 305) actually puts condoms in the trees to keep everyone safe. Another similar cruising location, sometimes called the **Dick Dock,** has recently sprung up on Harbor Walk, between Fire Island Blvd. and Ocean Walk.

CHERRY GROVE. More commercial than the Pines, the roadless Grove is lined with narrow, raised boardwalks leading to the small, uniformly shingled houses overflowing with men. Lesbian couples, however, make up the majority of the town's population. A night in Cherry Grove usually begins at the **Ice Palace,** attached to the Cherry Grove Beach Hotel, where you can disco until dawn. (☎631-597-6600. Open Sept.-June daily noon-10pm; July-Aug. daily noon-4am). Most go to the Pines for late-night partying; you can catch a water taxi from the docks at Cherry Grove.

FIRE ISLAND PINES. A 10min. walk up the beach from Cherry Grove, the Pines has traditionally looked down its nose at its uninhibited neighbor. Houses here are spacious and often stunningly modern, with an asymmetric aesthetic and huge windows. Boardwalks here are often poorly lit, so you may want to bring along a flashlight. Unfortunately, the Pines' active and upscale nighttime scene has a bit of a secret club feel to it—you need to be in the know or somehow be able to look like you know the program. **Tea Dance** (a.k.a. "Low Tea"), from 5-8pm, takes place inside and around the **Yacht Club bar/club** beside the **Pines** hotel (☎631-597-6500). Move on to disco **High Tea** at 8pm in the Pavilion (☎631-597-6131), the premier disco in Cherry Grove, but make sure you have somewhere to disappear to during "disco naptime" (after 10pm).

ACCOMMODATIONS

Both towns host establishments that advertise themselves as "guesthouses." Be aware that some of these may not be legally accredited (due to such things as fire code violations), and that some may not be lesbian-friendly. When planning lodging, be advised that many places require a two-night minimum on the weekends, so call ahead. **The Cherry Grove Beach Hotel** ❺ (☎631-597-6600; www.grovehotel.com) is a good bet, centrally located on the Main Walk of Cherry Grove and close to the beach. (Reservations are required. Open May-Oct. Economy room starts at $90 mid-week in July, but Sa-Su 2-night stay costs $400. M-F prices are lower: full price the 1st night and $30 each additional night.)

HUDSON VALLEY

TARRYTOWN AND SLEEPY HOLLOW

Take the New York State Thrwy. (I-87) to Exit 9 (Tarrytown), and take Rte. 9 into town. Trains: From Grand Central Station, 50min. local, 30min. express on Metro-North Hudson Line (☎212-532-4900). Trains run 6:30am-1:20am. $5.50 off peak, $7.50 rush hour. Map 3.

Less than 30 mi. north of the big city, the bucolic towns of Tarrytown and Sleepy Hollow epitomize the landscape and legends of 19th-century American Romanticism with their historical mansions, estates, farms, and churches.

SIGHTS

From the train station, cross the parking lot. Walk uphill on the other side of the police station to Main St. Taxis: Strongly recommended. Hoboken A-1 Taxi ☎201-659-9191, Hoboken Quick Service ☎201-792-7100, Hoboken Taxi ☎201-420-1480.

The Tarrytown area provided the inspiration for 19th-century author Washington Irving's tales—most famously, *The Legend of Sleepy Hollow*. An amateur landscape artist with an interest in architecture, Irving transformed a two-story Dutch cottage into his magnificent home. The estate, **Sunnyside,** is located at West Sunnyside Ln. off Rte. 9.; walk 2 mi. up Main St. to Rte. 9, and then south along Rte. 9. While the house offers a fascinating glimpse into Irving's life, the manicured grounds alone are worth the visit. Summer and special events include jazz festivals and candle-lit tours. (☎914-591-8763. $9, seniors $8, students 15-17 $5, 5 and under free. Grounds open Mar.-Dec. daily 10am-5pm; Sunnyside open M and W-Su 10am-5pm.)

A few miles north along Rte. 9 lies **Lyndhurst,** 635 S. Broadway, a Gothic Revival palace acquired by railroad tycoon Jay Gould in 1880. On the stately grounds surrounding the 19th-century mansion are rose and fern gardens, a carriage house, and the remains of what was once considered to be the nation's largest and finest private conservatory. The intricate rooms are interesting, but the gardens are the main draw. (☎914-631-4481; www.lindhurst.org. Open mid-Apr.-Oct. Tu-Su 10am-5pm; Nov.-Mar. Sa-Su 10am-4pm. Admission: $10, seniors $9, ages 12-17 $4, under 12 free; grounds alone $4.)

Approximately 10 mi. north of Tarrytown is Sleepy Hollow's **Union Church of Pocantico Hills,** 555 Bedford Rd. 3 mi. down Rte. 114 off Rte. 9. Nine vibrant stained-glass windows by Marc Chagall adorn the walls of this small church. Henri Matisse's last completed work, "Rose Window," hangs high above the altar. (☎914-631-2069. Open Apr.-Dec. M and W-F 11am-5pm, Su 2pm-5pm. Suggested donation $3.) Farther north along Rte. 9 lies **Phillipsburg Manor,** a 17th-century working farm and living history venue with rare breeds of cattle and sheep, costumed guides, and a working mill wheel. (☎914-631-3992. Open Apr.-Dec. M and W-Su 10am-5pm, but last admission is 4pm. $9, seniors $8, ages 5-17 $5, under 4 free.) Running out of Phillipsburg Manor are tours to the Rockefeller Estate, **Kykuit,** that explain the mansion's original art, sculpture, and furniture. Tours are pricey (ages 65 and under $20) and long (approx. 2¼hr.), but promise exquisite views.

WEST POINT

From New York City take I-87. Once over the Tappan Zee Bridge, take Exit 13N onto the Palisades Interstate Pkwy. heading north. Take the PIP north to its end (Bear Mountain traffic circle). Follow signs for Rte. 9W north (3rd exit off traffic circle). Exit 9W via West Point exit, Stony Lonesome exit, or Rte. 293 exit. Or try Short Line Bus (☎800-631-8405) from the New York Port Authority (roundtrip $26). Since the bus only runs a few times a day, call ahead and plan accordingly. Map 3.

History buffs, military zealots, and anyone fascinated by the prim, proper, and powerful should consider exploring West Point, America's oldest and most famous service academy. The academy is carved into the cliffs of the Hudson Highlands, the foothills of the Catskills. In addition to the immense campus' Revolutionary War sights, imposing Gothic buildings, and majestic vistas, West Point boasts an illustrious lists of graduates including Grant, Lee, MacArthur, and Eisenhower.

SIGHTS

The expansive and pristine **Visitors Center,** located just below **Thayer Gate,** is a good starting place for a tour. The center provides pamphlets and walking and driving tour maps. It also displays a brief instructional video, various army memorabilia, and a replica of a cadet's room complete with wax cadets. (☎845-938-2638. Open daily 9am-4:45 pm.) Just behind the Visitors Center lies the **West Point Museum.** The Gothic building houses one of the nation's largest and oldest collections of military memorabilia, with weapons and uniforms dating back to colonial times. (☎845-938-2203 or 938-3590. Open daily 10:30am-4:15 pm.)

The campus itself features two Revolutionary War sites—**Fort Clinton** and **Fort Putnam,** the latter originally under the command of George Washington. Also of interest is the assortment of war monuments, particularly **Trophy Point,** the storehouse for many intriguing US war relics, and the **Battle Monument,** rumored to be the largest polished granite shaft in the Western hemisphere. Other popular sites include the **Cadet Chapel,** which contains the world's largest organ, and **The Plain,** the famous West Point parade ground. It's approximately a 5 mi. walk through the sights. For security reasons, tours are no longer offered.

THE CATSKILLS

BEAR MOUNTAIN STATE PARK

Located at the intersection of the Palisades Pkwy. and Rte. 9W, 50 mi. north of the city. Short Line Buses (☎800-631-8405) run from Port Authority to the park and take about 1½ hr. (round-trip $22.) By train, Metro-North runs trains to Peekskill and Garrison. From there, you can take a $25 cab to the park. Map 3. Open year-round 8am-dusk.

Bear Mountain State Park's over 80 sq. mi. of wilderness and 140 mi. of marked trails include some of the taller Catskill Mountains, the expansive and sparkling Hessian Lake, a section of the Hudson River, and an enormous swimming pool. The other main attraction, the **Trailside Museums and Zoo,** is the oldest of its kind in the US. Visitors can safely view such injured and rehabilitated wildlife as a bobcat, two stir-crazy coyotes, and two black bears. The museums focus on the park's history, local geology, and nature study. (☎845-786-2701. Museum/zoo open daily 10am-4:30pm. $1, ages 6-12 50¢, under 6 free. $6 to park.) A statue of an "afoot and lighthearted" **Walt Whitman** stands along one of the zoo's shaded, meandering paths. Brimming with historical significance, the park also contains the earliest part of the Appalachian Trail and stars in a Bob Dylan song about a picnic gone horribly wrong (*Talking Bear Mountain Picnic Massacre Blues*). Paddleboats can be used on Hessian Lake. (Open Apr.-June Sa-Su 11am-5pm; June-Sept. M-F 11am-4pm, Sa-Su 11am-5pm. $4.50 per hr.) For further park information, call the Park Visitors Center. (☎845-786-5003. Open Apr.-Oct. 8am-6pm; Nov.-Mar. 8am-5pm.)

The **Bear Mountain Inn ❸,** evoking the Swiss-chalet style, stands in the center of the park. Although the standard rooms are not very large, they run relatively cheap; the inn also provides quieter, more remote lodges. (☎845-786-2731. Reservations strongly suggested. Standard double with queen-sized bed and bath $89, with 2 twin beds $99, lodge double with queen-sized bed $99.) Nestled in the Main Inn's enormous, yet strangely cozy second-floor lodge is a restaurant (❸) with an outdoor patio. The fare is pricey, however, and a picnic might be more budget-friendly. ($10-18 for dinner. Restaurant open for lunch daily 11:30am-4pm; for dinner Su-Th 5-9pm, F-Sa 5-10pm.)

NEW JERSEY

ATLANTIC CITY

Atlantic City lies halfway down New Jersey's eastern seashore, accessible via the Garden State Parkway and the Atlantic City Expressway, and easily reached by train from Philadelphia or New York. Amtrak, 1 Atlantic City Expressway (☎800-872-7245), is open daily 6am-9pm. To New York (5½hr., 11 per day, $54) and Philadelphia (2½hr., 30 per day, $48). Or New Jersey Transit (☎800-772-2222). Greyhound (☎340-2000). Buses travel between New York Port Authority and most major casinos (2½-3hr., round-trip from $26). Greyhound also has service from casinos to Philadelphia (18 per day, round-trip $14). New Jersey Transit (☎215-569-3752 or 800-582-5946) offers hourly service from the station on Atlantic Ave. between Michigan and Ohio St. to New York ($25, seniors $23). Gray Line Tours (☎800-669-0051; www.nycsightseeing.com; terminal open 24hr.) offers daytrips from New York (2½hr, $27).

For over 50 years, board-gaming strategists have been wheeling and dealing with Atlantic City geography, passing "Go" to collect their $200 and buying properties in an effort to control this coastal city as reincarnated on the *Monopoly* board. Meanwhile the opulence of Boardwalk and Park Place gradually faded into neglect and then into mega-dollar tackiness. Casinos rose from the rubble of the boardwalk in the 1970s, and nowadays Atlantic City's status is defined by waves of urban professionals looking for a fast buck and quick tan.

SIGHTS

All casinos on the Boardwalk fall within a dice toss of one another. The farthest south is the elegant **Hilton** (☎347-7111 or 800-257-8677; www.hiltonac.com), between Providence and Boston Ave., and the farthest north is the gaudy **Showboat** (☎343-4000 or 800-621-0200; www.harrahs.com), at Delaware Ave. and Boardwalk. Donald Trump's glittering **Trump Taj Mahal Hotel and Casino,** 1000 Boardwalk at Virginia Ave. (☎449-1000; www.trumptaj.com), is too ostentatious to be missed; neglected payments on this tasteless tallboy cast the financier into his billion dollar tailspin. In true *Monopoly* form, Trump owns three other hotel casinos in the city: the recently remodeled **Trump Plaza,** at Mississippi and the boardwalk (☎441-6000 or 800-677-7378; www.trumpplaza.com); **Trump World's Fair** (☎800-473-7829), on the Boardwalk; and **Trump Castle** (☎441-2000; www.trumpmarina.com), on Huron Blvd. at the Marina. In summer, energetic partiers go to "rock the dock" at Trump Castle's indoor/outdoor bar/restaurant, **The Deck** (☎877-477-4697). Many a die is cast at **Caesar's Boardwalk Resort and Casino,** 2100 Pacific Ave. (☎348-4411; www.caesarsatlatincity.com) at Arkansas Ave. The **Sands** (☎441-4000; www.acsands.com), at Indiana Ave., stands tall and flashy with its seashell motif. The newest casino in town is **The Borgata** (☎866-692-6742; www.theborgata.com), a golden scintillation near the Trump Marina Hotel Casino and Harrah's in the Marina District that has been in the works since 2000. All are open 24hr.

There's something for everyone in Atlantic City—thanks to the Boardwalk. Those under 21 **gamble for prizes** at one of the many arcades that line the Boardwalk, including **Central Pier Arcade & Speedway**, at the boardwalk and Tennessee (☎345-5219). It feels like real gambling, but the teddy bear in the window is easier to win than the convertible on display at Caesar's. The historic **Steel Pier** (☎898-7645 or 866-386-6659; www.steelpier.com), the boardwalk at Virginia Ave., juts into the coastal waters with a ferris wheel that spins riders over the Atlantic. It also offers the rest of the usual amusement park suspects: roller coaster, carousel, and games of "skill" aplenty. (Open daily noon-midnight; call the Taj Mahal for winter hours. Rides $2-5 each.) When and if you tire of spending money, check out the historic **Atlantic City Beach.** For more water fun, visitors invariably stumble upon at least one of the piers occupied by **Morey's Piers & Raging Waters Waterparks,** on the boardwalk at 25th Ave., Schellenger, and Spencer (☎522-3900 or 888-667-3971; www.moreyspiers.com). Just west of Atlantic City, **Ventnor City** offers more tranquil shores.

FOOD

Although not recommended by nutritionists, $0.75 hot dogs and $1.50 pizza slices are all over the Boardwalk. Some of the best deals in town await at the casinos, where all-you-can-eat lunch ($7) and dinner ($11) buffets abound. Tastier, less tacky food can be found a little farther from the seashore.

Inn of the Irish Pub, 164 St. James Pl. (☎345-9613; www.theirishpub.com), may not serve the healthiest food, but it tastes damn good. Start off with a 20th St. sampler (buffalo wings, fried mozzarella, potato skins, and chicken thumbs; $7). The daily lunch special (11:30am-2pm) includes a pre-selected sandwich and a cup of soup for $2. All-you-can-eat Su brunch $7. $6 dinner specials M-F 2-8pm and Sa-Su until 8pm. Domestic drafts $1. Open 24hr. Cash only. ❷

White House Sub Shop, 2301 Arctic Ave. (☎345-8599 or 345-1564 for pick-up; www.whitehousesubshop.com), at Mississippi Ave. Sinatra was rumored to have had these immense subs ($4-12) flown to him while he was on tour. Pictures of White House sub-lovers Joe Dimaggio, Wayne Newton, and Mr. T adorn the walls. Italian subs and cheesesteaks $6-12. Open Su-Th 10am-10pm, F-Sa 10am-11pm. Cash only. ❷

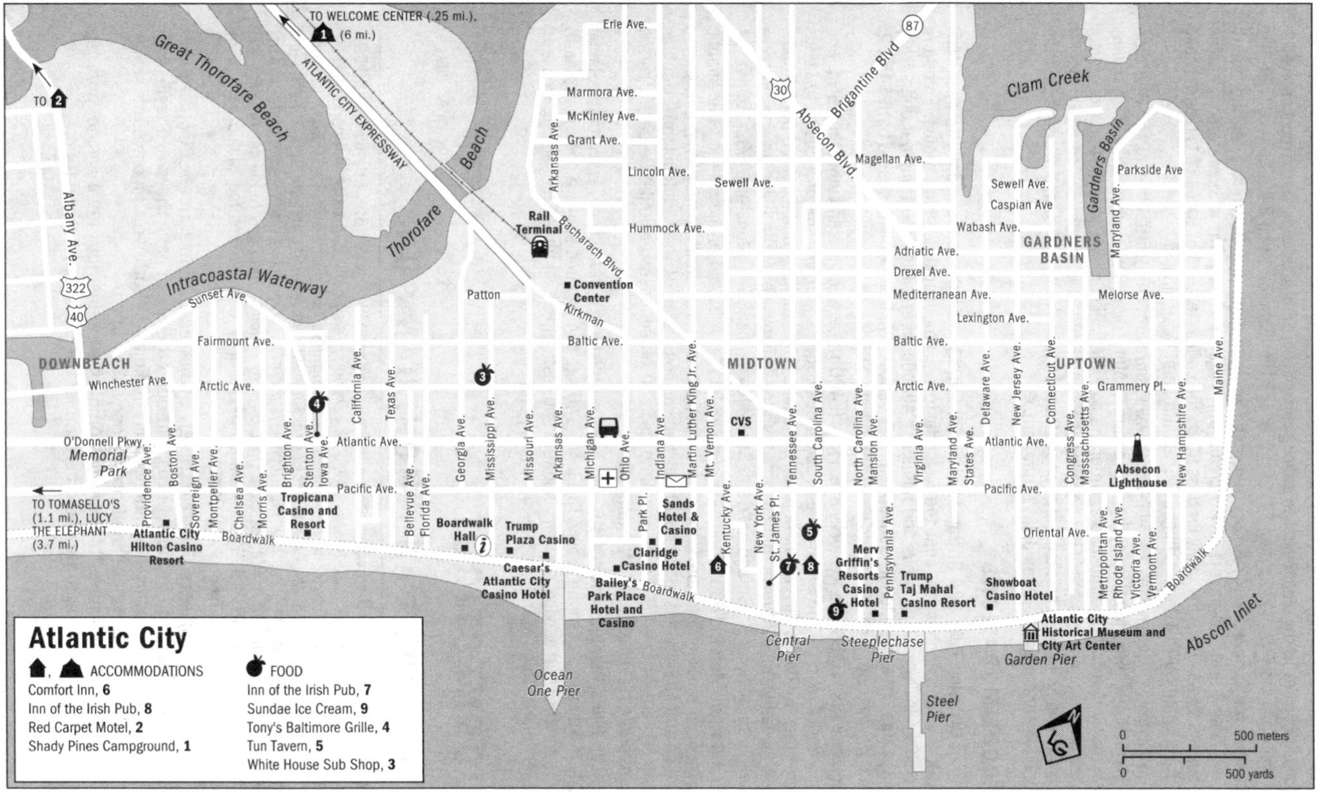
Atlantic City
ACCOMMODATIONS
Comfort Inn, 6
Inn of the Irish Pub, 8
Red Carpet Motel, 2
Shady Pines Campground, 1
FOOD
Inn of the Irish Pub, 7
Sundae Ice Cream, 9
Tony's Baltimore Grille, 4
Tun Tavern, 5
White House Sub Shop, 3
TO WELCOME CENTER (.25 mi.).
(6 mi.)
TO 2
TO TOMASELLO'S (1.1 mi.), LUCY THE ELEPHANT (3.7 mi.)
Great Thorofare Beach
Thorofare
Beach
Intracoastal Waterway
ATLANTIC CITY EXPRESSWAY
Clam Creek
Gardners Basin
GARDNERS BASIN
DOWNBEACH
MIDTOWN
UPTOWN
Absecon Inlet
Albany Ave.
Sunset Ave.
Fairmount Ave.
Winchester Ave.
Arctic Ave.
O'Donnell Pkwy.
Memorial Park
Atlantic Ave.
Pacific Ave.
Patton
Kirkman
Baltic Ave.
Bacharach Blvd.
Absecon Blvd.
Brigantine Blvd
Erie Ave.
Marmora Ave.
McKinley Ave.
Grant Ave.
Arkansas Ave.
Lincoln Ave.
Sewell Ave.
Hummock Ave.
Magellan Ave.
Adriatic Ave.
Drexel Ave.
Mediterranean Ave.
Lexington Ave.
Caspian Ave
Wabash Ave.
Parkside Ave
Maryland Ave.
Melorse Ave.
Grammery Pl.
Oriental Ave.
Providence Ave.
Boston Ave.
Sovereign Ave.
Montpelier Ave.
Chelsea Ave.
Morris Ave.
Brighton Ave.
Stenton Ave.
Iowa Ave.
California Ave.
Texas Ave.
Bellevue Ave.
Florida Ave.
Georgia Ave.
Mississippi Ave.
Missouri Ave.
Arkansas Ave.
Michigan Ave.
Ohio Ave.
Park Pl.
Indiana Ave.
Martin Luther King Jr. Ave.
Mt. Vernon Ave.
Kentucky Ave.
New York Ave.
St. James Pl.
Tennessee Ave.
South Carolina Ave.
North Carolina Ave.
Mansion Ave.
Pennsylvania Ave.
Virginia Ave.
Maryland Ave.
States Ave.
Delaware Ave.
New Jersey Ave.
Connecticut Ave.
Congress Ave.
Massachusetts Ave.
Metropolitan Ave.
Rhode Island Ave.
Victoria Ave.
Vermont Ave.
New Hampshire Ave.
Maine Ave.
Boardwalk
Rail Terminal
Convention Center
CVS
Absecon Lighthouse
Atlantic City Hilton Casino Resort
Tropicana Casino and Resort
Boardwalk Hall
Trump Plaza Casino
Caesar's Atlantic City Casino Hotel
Bailey's Park Place Hotel and Casino
Claridge Casino Hotel
Sands Hotel & Casino
Merv Griffin's Resorts Casino Hotel
Trump Taj Mahal Casino Resort
Showboat Casino Hotel
Atlantic City Historical Museum and City Art Center
Ocean One Pier
Central Pier
Steeplechase Pier
Steel Pier
Garden Pier
0 500 meters
0 500 yards

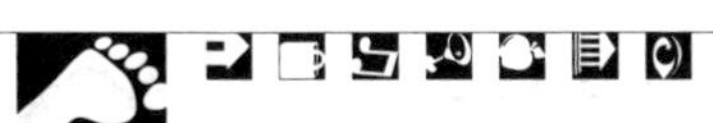

Tony's Baltimore Grille, 2800 Atlantic Ave. (☎345-5766), between Pacific and Baltic, at Iowa Ave. Tourists can't resist the old-time Italian atmosphere with personal jukeboxes, not to mention the $3-8 pasta and pizza. Seafood platter $12. Open daily 11am-3am. Bar open 24hr. Cash only. ❷

Sundae Ice Cream (☎347-8424), between South Carolina and Ocean Ave. on the boardwalk, makes over 20 flavors of ice cream and yogurt ($2.50). The chocolate chip cookie dough is terrific. If it's too chilly for dessert, try the coffee, tea, or hot cocoa ($1). Funnel cake $3.50. Open Su-Th 10am-midnight, F-Sa 10am-3am. Cash only. ❶

Tun Tavern, 2 Ocean Way (☎347-7800; www.tuntavern.com), attached to the Sheraton Hotel, across from the Atlantic City Convention Center. Locals and tourists alike enjoy nightly live music in a casual atmosphere. Order the $25 filet mignon with freshly steamed vegetables, or opt for the less costly but equally satisfying $6 big bowl of corn and crab chowder. W $5 pitchers and $0.25 chicken wings after 10pm. Th karaoke 9pm. F dance fl. opens 5:30pm for R&B performances. Open daily 11am-2am. ❹

ACCOMMODATIONS

Inn of the Irish Pub, 164 St. James Pl. (☎344-9063; www.theirishpub.com), between New York Ave. and Tennessee, near the Ramada Tower, has spacious, clean rooms. Enjoy the porch's relaxing rocking chairs and refreshing Atlantic breeze. The downstairs bar offers lively entertainment and a friendly atmosphere. Key deposit $7. Doubles with shared bath $45-52, with private bath $75-90; quads with shared bath $85-99. ❸

Comfort Inn, 154 South Kentucky Ave. (☎348-4000), between Martin Luther King Blvd. and New York Ave., near the Sands (see p. 290). Basic rooms with king-size or 2 queen-size beds and—true to Atlantic City swank—a jacuzzi. Breakfast, free parking, and a heated pool. Rooms with ocean views $20 extra, but come with fridge, microwave, and a bigger jacuzzi. Reserve well in advance for Sa-Su and holidays. Sept.-May rooms$59-69; June-Aug. $89-159. ❹

Red Carpet Motel, 1630 Albany Ave. (☎348-3171). A bit out of the way, off the Atlantic Expwy. on the way into town, the Red Carpet provides standard, comfortable, uninspiring rooms and free shuttles to the boardwalk and casinos. Cable TV, restaurant in lobby. Doubles $39-59; quads $55-79. Prices can jump to $130 on summer weekends. *Be careful in the surrounding neighborhood after dark.* ❸

Shady Pines Campground, 443 S. 6th Ave. (☎652-1516), in Absecon, 6 mi. from Atlantic City. Take Exit 12 from the Expwy. This leafy, 140-site campground sports a pool, playground, laundry, firewood service, and new showers and restrooms. Call ahead for summer weekend reservations. Open Mar.-Nov. Sites with water and electricity $33. ❷

CONNECTICUT

FOXWOODS AND MOHEGAN SUN

Foxwoods: Greyhound provides service to Foxwoods from New York. (625 8th Ave. ☎800-231-2222 or 212-971-6300. 9-12 buses daily. $23.) Driving is also convenient with free parking at the resort. From I-95 take Exit 92 to Rte. 2 West, and from I-84 take Exit 55 to Rte. 2 East. Once on Rte. 2 follow the signs to the casino. ***Mohegan Sun:*** *With free parking and shuttles from the lots in each of the Mohegan Sun's four lots, driving is the most convenient way to access the casino. From I-395 take Exit 79A to Rte. 2A East. Once on Rte. 2A follow the signs to the casino. (For specific information ☎888-226-7711). A variety of bus lines also services the casino from many points in the northeast. (☎888-770-0140).*

Foxwoods and **Mohegan Sun,** two tribally owned casinos in southeast Connecticut, bring a little bit of sin to the suburbs. Although they each have their own style, they share a tendency towards decadence that make them both worth a traveler's while, especially if said traveler can afford to lose a few dollars.

The 4.7 million square ft. **Foxwoods** complex contains not only a casino, but also three hotels, a spa, nightlife and entertainment areas, shopping and food.

While winning or losing money on the floor is uncertain, paying handsomely for lodging in the casino complex is a sure thing. The **Two Trees Inn ❺,** a short shuttle ride from the casino, is the least expensive of the three hotels in the complex. (☎800-442-1000. Rooms $99-210.) A better option for those who aren't cleaning up are the campgrounds that speckle the roadside along Rte. 2.

The central attraction is, of course, the seemingly endless gaming opportunities. The 6500 **slot machines** that clang and whirl ceaselessly are spread among the five casinos within the complex, as are the 17 **table games** including **Blackjack, Craps, Baccarat, Poker,** and **Roulette. Keno** and **Bingo** are also popular diversions. In addition, **Ultimate Race Book** allows one to place bets on horses, hounds, and *jai alai* at a dozen windows while watching the events on theater-quality displays. Additionally, Foxwoods provides 25 food and beverage venues offering everything from food on-the-go to gourmet dining. Hours and prices are highly variable, but information is easily at hand from one of the many information booths in the casino.

Nightlife and entertainment are never in short supply. The 1450-seat **Fox Theatre** hosts a variety of live performances, including past appearances by Frank Sinatra, Bill Cosby, and the Dixie Chicks. (☎800-200-2882. Prices and performance times vary with the show.) The **B.B. King Nightclub** is a popular destination for lovers of jazz, blues, and comedy, with live music and comedy shows. (☎800-200-2882. No cover. Open M-Th 8pm-1am, F-Sa 8pm-2am, Su noon-1am.) The **Pequot Museum,** 110 Pequot Terr., with its interactive exhibits and numerous life size displays including a mock-village is an interesting and instructive alternative way to spend an afternoon. (☎800-411-9671. Open daily 9am-5pm. $15, seniors $13, ages 6-15 $10.)

Mohegan Sun offers two of the world's largest casinos in distinctive environments as well as a wide variety of services, entertainment, lodging, and shopping. The entire complex is contained in one enormous interconnected sleek structure that is at odds with the interior design, which reflects the culture and heritage of the Mohegan Tribe.

INSIDE

embassies and consulates **295**
documents and formalities **295**
money **297**
health **298**
insurance **299**
packing **299**
getting to new york **300**
specific concerns **303**
public holidays in 2004 **307**

Planning Your Trip

EMBASSIES AND CONSULATES

Contact the nearest embassy or consulate to obtain information regarding visas and permits to the United States. Offices are only open limited hours, so call well before you depart. The US State Department provides contact information for US diplomatic missions on the Internet at http://foia.state.gov/MMS/KOH/keyofficers.asp. Foreign embassies in the US are located in Washington, D.C., but there are many consulates in New York. For a more extensive list of embassies and consulates in the US, consult the web site www.embassy.org. Consular services in New York are listed on p. 32.

DOCUMENTS AND FORMALITIES

PASSPORTS

REQUIREMENTS. All foreign visitors except Canadians need valid passports to enter the United States and to re-enter their own country. The US does not allow entrance if the holder's passport expires in under six months; returning home with an expired passport is often illegal, and may result in a fine. Canadians need to demonstrate proof of citizenship, such as a citizenship card or birth certificate.

NEW PASSPORTS. Citizens of Australia, Canada, Ireland, New Zealand, and the United Kingdom can apply for a passport at any post office, passport office, or court of law. Citizens of South Africa can apply for a passport at any Home Affairs office. Any applications must be filed well in advance of the departure date, although most passport offices offer rush services for a very steep fee.

PASSPORT MAINTENANCE. Be sure to photocopy the page of your passport with your photo, as well as your visas, traveler's check serial numbers, and any other important documents. Carry one set of copies in a safe place, apart from the originals, and leave another set at home. Consulates also recommend that you carry an expired passport or an official copy of your birth certificate in a part of your baggage separate from other documents. If you lose your passport, immediately notify the local police and the consulate of your home government. To expedite its replacement, it helps to have a photocopy. In some cases, a replacement may take weeks to process, and it may be valid only for a limited time. Any **visas** stamped in your old passport will be irretrievably lost. In an emergency, ask for **temporary traveling papers** that will permit you to re-enter your home country.

VISAS, INVITATIONS, AND WORK PERMITS

VISAS. Citizens of South Africa and most other countries need a visa—a stamp, sticker, or insert in your passport specifying the purpose of your travel and the permitted duration of your stay—in addition to a valid passport for entrance to the US. See http://travel.state.gov/visa_services.html and www.unitedstatesvisas.gov for more information. To obtain a visa, contact a US embassy or consulate; recent security measures have made the visa application process more rigorous, and therefore lengthy. Apply well in advance of your travel date.

Canadian citizens do not need to obtain a visa for admission to the US. Citizens of Australia, New Zealand, and most European countries can waive US visas through the **Visa Waiver Program.** Visitors qualify if they are traveling only for business or pleasure (*not* work or study), are staying for fewer than **90 days,** have proof of intent to leave (e.g. a return plane ticket), possess an I-94W form, are traveling on particular air or sea carriers, and possess a machine readable passport from a nation of which they are a citizen. See http://travel.state.gov/vwp.html for more information.

If you lose your I-94 form, you can replace it by filling out form I-102, although it's very unlikely that the form will be replaced within the time of your stay. The form is available at the nearest **Bureau of Citizenship and Immigration Services (BSIC)** office (www.bcis.gov), through the forms request line (☎800-870-3676), or online (http://www.bcis.gov/graphics/formsfee/forms/i-102.htm). **Visa extensions** are sometimes granted with a completed I-539 form; call the forms request line or get it online at http://www.immigration.gov/graphics/formsfee/forms/i-539.htm.

All travelers, except Canadians, planning a stay of more than 90 days also need to obtain a visa. Admission as a visitor does not include the right to work, which is authorized only by a **work permit.** Entering the US to study requires a special visa. For more information, see **Alternatives to Tourism,** p. 309.

IDENTIFICATION

When you travel, always carry two or more forms of identification with you, including at least one photo ID; a passport or a driver's license combined with birth certificate is usually adequate. Never carry all your ID together. Split them up in case of theft or loss, and keep photocopies of them in your bags and at home.

TEACHER, STUDENT AND YOUTH IDENTIFICATION. The **International Student Identity Card (ISIC),** the most widely accepted form of student ID, provides discounts on sights, accommodations, food, and transport; access to a 24hr. emergency helpline (in North America ☎877-370-4742; elsewhere call US collect ☎+1-715-345-0505); and insurance benefits for US cardholders (see **Insurance,** p. 299). The ISIC is preferable to an institution-specific card (such as a university ID) because it is more likely to be recognized and honored abroad. Applicants must be degree-seeking students of a secondary or post-secondary school and must be at least 12 years of age. Because of the proliferation of fake ISICs, some services (particularly airlines) require additional proof of student identity, such as a school ID or a letter signed by your registrar and stamped with your school seal.

The **International Teacher Identity Card (ITIC)** offers teachers the same insurance coverage and similar but limited discounts. For non-student travelers who are 25 years old or younger, the **International Youth Travel Card** (**IYTC;** formerly the **GO 25** Card) offers many of the same benefits as the ISIC.

Each of the cards costs $22 or equivalent. ISIC and ITIC cards are valid for 16 months; IYTC cards are valid for one year. Many student travel agencies (see p. 301) issue the cards, including STA Travel in Australia and New Zealand; Travel CUTS in Canada; USIT in the Republic of Ireland and Northern Ireland; SASTS in South Africa; Campus Travel and STA Travel in the UK; and Council Travel and STA Travel in the US. For more information, contact the **International Student Travel Confederation (ISTC),** Herengracht 479, 1017 BS Amsterdam, The Netherlands (☎20 421 28 00; fax 421 28 10; www.istc.org).

CUSTOMS

Upon entering the US, you must declare certain items from abroad and pay a duty on the value of those articles that exceeds the US customs allowance. Note that goods and gifts purchased at duty-free shops abroad are not exempt from duty or sales tax at your point of return and thus must be declared as well; "duty-free" merely means that you need not pay a tax in the country of purchase. Upon returning, you must similarly declare all articles acquired abroad and pay a duty on the value of articles in excess of your home country's allowance.

MONEY

CURRENCY & EXCHANGE

The currency chart below is based on August 2004 exchange rates between local currency and Australian dollars (AUS$), Canadian dollars (CDN$), New Zealand dollars (NZ$), South African Rand (ZAR), British pounds (UK£), US dollars (US$), and European Union euros (EUR€). Check the currency converter on financial websites such as www.bloomberg.com and www.xe.com, or a large newspaper for the latest exchange rates.

US DOLLAR ($)		
	AUS$1 = US$0.64	US$1 = AUS$1.55
	CDN$1 = US$0.71	US$1 = CDN$1.40
	NZ$1 = US$0.58	US$1 = NZ$1.72
	ZAR1 = US$0.13	US$1 = ZAR7.43
	UK£1 = US$1.60	US$1 = UK£0.62
	€1 = US$0.88	US$1 = €1.13

TRAVELER'S CHECKS

Traveler's checks are one of the safest and least troublesome means of carrying funds. American Express and Visa are the most widely recognized brands. Many banks and agencies sell them for a small commission. Check issuers provide refunds if the checks are lost or stolen, and many provide additional services, such as toll-free refund hotlines abroad, emergency message services, and stolen credit card assistance. They are readily accepted in New York. Ask about toll-free refund hotlines and the location of refund centers when purchasing checks, and always carry emergency cash.

American Express: Checks available with commission at select banks, at all AmEx offices, and online (www.americanexpress.com; US residents only). American Express cardholders can also purchase checks by phone (☎888-269-6669). AAA offers commission-free checks to its members. Checks available in US, Australian, British, Canadian, Japanese, and euro currencies. *Cheques for Two* can be signed by either of 2 people traveling together. For purchase locations or more information contact AmEx's service centers: in the US and Canada ☎800-221-7282; elsewhere US collect ☎+1 801-964-6665; UK ☎0800 587 6023; Australia ☎800 68 80 22; New Zealand ☎0508 555 358.

Visa: Checks available (generally with commission) at banks worldwide. For the location of the nearest office, call Visa's service centers: in the US ☎800-227-6811; in the UK ☎0800 51 58 84; elsewhere UK collect ☎020 7937 8091. Checks available in US, British, Canadian, Japanese, and Euro currencies.

Travelex/Thomas Cook: In the US and Canada call ☎800-287-7362; UK ☎0800 62 21 01; elsewhere UK collect ☎1733 31 89 50.

CREDIT, DEBIT, AND ATM CARDS

Credit cards often offer superior exchange rates—up to 5% better than the retail rate used by banks and other currency exchange establishments. Credit cards may also offer services such as insurance or emergency help, and are sometimes required to reserve hotel rooms or rental cars. **MasterCard** and **Visa** are the most welcomed; **American Express** cards work at some ATMs and at AmEx offices and major airports.

ATM cards are widespread in the US. Depending on the system that your home bank uses, you can most likely access your personal bank account from abroad. ATMs get the same wholesale exchange rate as credit cards, but there is often a limit on the amount of money you can withdraw per day (around US$500). There is typically also a surcharge of US$1-5 per withdrawal.

A **debit card** can be used wherever its associated credit card company (usually Mastercard or Visa) is accepted, yet the money is withdrawn directly from the holder's checking account. Debit cards often also function as ATM cards and can be used to withdraw cash from associated banks and ATMs throughout the US. Ask your local bank about obtaining one.

The two major international money networks are **Cirrus** (to locate ATMs US ☎800-424-7787; www.mastercard.com) and **Visa/PLUS** (to locate ATMs US ☎800-843-7587; www.visa.com). Most ATMs charge a transaction fee that is paid to the bank that owns the ATM.

HEALTH

For lists of doctors, hospitals, pharmacies, and emergency numbers, see **Service Directory**, p. 325.

MEDICAL ASSISTANCE ON THE ROAD

Medical care in the US is among the best in the world, and New York City is home to many of the country's best hospitals. In case of medical emergency, dial ☎**911** from any phone and an operator will send out paramedics, a fire brigade, or the police as needed. Emergency care is also readily available in the US and Canada at any emergency room on a walk-in basis. If you do not have insurance, you will have to pay for medical care (see **Insurance,** p. 299). Appointments are required for non-emergency medical services.

If you are concerned about obtaining medical assistance while traveling, you may wish to employ special support services. The *MedPass* from **GlobalCare, Inc.,** 6875 Shiloh Rd. East, Alpharetta, GA 30005, USA (☎800-860-1111; fax 678-341-1800; www.globalems.com), provides 24hr. international medical assistance, support, and medical evacuation resources. The **International Association for Medical Assistance to Travelers** (**IAMAT;** US ☎716-754-4883, Canada ☎519-836-0102; www.cybermall.co.nz/NZ/IAMAT) has free membership, lists English-speaking doctors worldwide, and offers detailed info on immunization requirements and sanitation. If your regular **insurance** policy does not cover travel abroad, you may wish to purchase additional coverage (see p. 299).

Those with medical conditions (such as diabetes, allergies to antibiotics, epilepsy, heart conditions) may want to obtain a **Medic Alert** membership (first year US$35, annually thereafter US$20), which includes a stainless steel ID tag, among other benefits, like a 24hr. collect-call number. Contact the Medic Alert Foundation, 2323 Colorado Ave., Turlock, CA 95382, USA (☎888-633-4298; outside US ☎209-668-3333; www.medicalert.org).

INSURANCE

Travel insurance generally covers four basic areas: medical/health problems, property loss, trip cancellation/interruption, and emergency evacuation. Your regular insurance policies may extend to travel-related accidents, but you may consider purchasing travel insurance if the cost of potential trip cancellation/interruption or emergency medical evacuation is greater than you can absorb. Prices for travel insurance purchased separately generally run about $40 per week for full coverage.

Medical insurance (especially university policies) often covers costs incurred abroad; check with your provider. **US Medicare** does not cover foreign travel, with the exception of travel to Canada and Mexico. **Canadians** are protected by their home province's health insurance plan for up to 90 days after leaving the country; check with the provincial Ministry of Health or Health Plan Headquarters for details. **Homeowners' insurance** (or your family's coverage) often covers theft during travel and loss of travel documents (passport, plane ticket, railpass, etc.) up to US$500.

ISIC and **ITIC** (see p. 296) provide basic insurance benefits, including $100 per day of in-hospital sickness for up to 60 days, $3,000 of accident-related medical reimbursement, and $25,000 for emergency medical transport. Cardholders have access to a toll-free 24hr. helpline (run by the insurance provider **TravelGuard**) for medical, legal, and financial emergencies (US and Canada ☎877-370-4742). **American Express** (US ☎800-528-4800) grants some cardholders automatic car rental insurance (collision and theft, but not liability) and ground travel accident coverage of $100,000 on flight purchases made with the card.

INSURANCE PROVIDERS. STA (see p. 301) offers a range of plans that can supplement your basic coverage. Other private insurance providers in the US and Canada include: **Access America** (☎866-807-3982; www.accessamerica.com); **Berkely Group** (☎800-797-4514; www.berkely.com); **GlobalCare Insurance Services Inc.** (☎800-821-2488; www.globalcare-cocco.com); and **Travel Assistance International** (☎800-821-2828; www.travelassistance.com). Providers in the **UK** include **Columbus Direct** (☎020 7375 0011; www.columbusdirect.co.uk). In **Australia,** try **AFTA** (☎02 9264 3299; www.afta.com.au).

PACKING

Pack lightly: put out only what you absolutely need, then take half the clothes and twice the money. As you pack, here are some important things to keep in mind.

CONVERTERS & ADAPTERS

In the US and Canada, electricity is **110V,** and 220V electrical appliances don't like 110V current. Visit a hardware store for an adapter (which changes the shape of the plug) and a converter (which changes the voltage). Don't make the mistake of using only an adapter unless appliance instructions explicitly state otherwise. See http://kropla.com/electric.htm for more info.

FILM & CAMERAS

Less serious photographers may want to bring a **disposable camera** or two rather than an expensive permanent one. Always pack film in your carry-on luggage, since higher-intensity X-rays are used on checked luggage; these can, despite disclaimers, fog film. All types of film for all types of cameras are available in Boston, but 35mm is the most common.

IMPORTANT DOCUMENTS

Don't forget your passport, traveler's checks, ATM and/or credit cards, and adequate ID (see p. 295). Also check that you have any of the following that might apply: an ISIC card, driver's license, and travel insurance forms.

GETTING TO NEW YORK

BY PLANE

Three major airports serve the New York metropolitan region. The largest, **John F. Kennedy Airport,** or JFK (☎718-244-4444), is 15 mi. from midtown Manhattan in southern Queens and handles mostly international flights. **LaGuardia Airport,** or LGA (☎718-533-3400), 9 mi. from midtown in northern Queens, is the second largest, offering domestic flights as well as hourly shuttles to and from Boston and Washington, D.C. **Newark Liberty International Airport,** or EWR (☎973-961-6000), 16 mi. from midtown in Newark, NJ, offers both domestic and international flights at budget fares often not available at the other airports (although getting to and from Newark can be expensive).

AIRFARES

Airfares to the US and Canada peak between during the summer; holidays are also expensive. It is cheapest to travel midweek (M-Th morning), as round-trip flights run US$40-50 cheaper than weekend flights.

Not fixing a return date ("open return") or arriving in and departing from different cities ("open-jaw") can be pricier than round-trip flights. Patching one-way flights together is the most expensive way to travel. Flights between major cities or regional hubs will tend to be cheaper.

When it comes to airfare, a little effort can save you a bundle. If your plans are flexible enough to deal with the restrictions, courier fares are the cheapest. Tickets bought from consolidators and standby seating are also good deals, but last-minute specials, airfare wars, and charter flights often beat these fares. The key is to hunt around, to be flexible, and to ask persistently about discounts. Students, seniors, and those under 26 should never pay full price for a ticket.

BUDGET & STUDENT TRAVEL AGENCIES

While knowledgeable agents specializing in flights to New York can make your life easy and help you save, they may not spend the time to find you the lowest possible fare—they get paid on commission. Travelers holding **ISIC and IYTC cards** (see p. 296) qualify for big discounts from student travel agencies. Most flights from budget agencies are on major airlines, but in peak season some may sell seats on less reliable chartered aircraft.

USIT, 19-21 Aston Quay, Dublin 2 (☎01 602 1600; www.usitworld.com). Ireland's leading student/budget travel agency has 22 offices throughout Northern Ireland and the Republic of Ireland. Offers programs to work in North America.

CTS Travel, 30 Rathbone Pl., London W1T 1GQ, UK (☎020 7290 0630; www.ctstravel.co.uk). A British student travel agent with offices in 39 countries including the US, Empire State Building, 350 Fifth Ave., Ste. 7813, New York, NY 10118 (☎877-287-6665; www.ctstravelusa.com).

STA Travel, 7890 S. Hardy Dr., Ste. 110, Tempe AZ 85284, USA (24hr. reservations and info ☎800-781-4040; www.sta-travel.com). A student and youth travel organization with over 150 offices worldwide (check their website for a listing of all their offices), including US offices in Boston, Chicago, L.A., New York, San Francisco, Seattle, and Washington, D.C. Ticket booking, travel insurance, railpasses, and more. In the UK, walk-in office 11 Goodge St., **London** W1T 2PF (☎0207 436 7779). In New Zealand, Shop 2B, 182 Queen St., **Auckland** (☎09 309 0458). In Australia, 366 Lygon St., **Carlton** Vic 3053 (☎03 9349 4344).

FLIGHT PLANNING ON THE INTERNET.

Many airline sites offer special last-minute deals on the Web. Other sites do the legwork and compile the deals for you—try www.bestfares.com, www.flights.com, www.lowestfare.com, www.onetravel.com, and www.travelzoo.com.

StudentUniverse (www.studentuniverse.com), **STA** (www.sta-travel.com) and **Orbitz.com** provide quotes on student tickets, while **Expedia** (www.expedia.com) and **Travelocity** (www.travelocity.com) offer full travel services. **Priceline** (www.priceline.com) allows you to specify a price and obligates you to buy any ticket that meets or beats it, but be prepared for antisocial hours and odd routes. **Skyauction** (www.skyauction.com) allows you to bid on both last-minute and advance-purchase tickets.

An indispensable resource on the Internet is the *Air Traveler's Handbook* (www.cs.cmu.edu/afs/cs/user/mkant/Public/Travel/airfare.html), a comprehensive listing of links to everything you need to know before you board a plane.

STANDBY FLIGHTS

Traveling standby requires considerable flexibility in arrival and departure dates and cities. Companies dealing in standby flights sell vouchers rather than tickets, along with the promise to get to your destination (or near your destination) within a certain window of time (typically 1-5 days). You call in before your specific window of time to hear your flight options and the probability that you will be able to board each flight. You can then decide which flights you want to try to make, show up at the appropriate airport at the appropriate time, present your voucher, and board if space is available. Vouchers can usually be bought for both one-way and round-trip travel. You may receive a monetary refund only if every available flight within your date range is full; if you opt not to take an available (but perhaps less convenient) flight, you can only get credit toward future travel. Carefully read agreements with any company offering standby flights as tricky fine print can leave you in a lurch. To check on a company's service record in the US, call the Better Business Bureau (☎212-533-6200). It is difficult to receive refunds, and clients' vouchers will not be honored when an airline fails to receive payment in time.

BY BUS

Getting in and out of New York can be less expensive and more scenic by bus or train than by plane. The hub of the Northeast bus network, New York's **Port Authority Terminal,** 41st St. and Eighth Ave., is a huge modern facility with labyrinthine bus terminals (☎212-564-8484. Subway: A, C, E to 42nd St.-Port Authority). Port Authority has good information and security services, but the surrounding neighborhood is somewhat deserted at night, and it pays to call a cab.

Greyhound (☎800-231-2222; www.greyhound.com) operates the largest number of lines, departing from **Boston** (4-6hr.; $42, $79 round-trip), **Montreal** (8-9hr.; $70, $109 round-trip), **Philadelphia** (2-3hr.; $21, $40 round-trip), and **Washington, D.C.** (4½-6hr.; $42, $79 round-trip). The fares listed require no advance purchase, but you can save money by purchasing tickets 14 days in advance. Ask about the three-day advance purchase two-for-one deal. A number of **discounts** are available on Greyhound's standard-fare tickets: students ride for 15% off with the Student Advantage Card (☎800-333-2920, www.studentadvantage.com to purchase the $20 card), senior citizens ride for 10% off, children under 11 ride for half-fare, and children under two ride for free in the lap of an adult (one per adult). A traveler with a physical disability may bring along a companion for free after clearing them by calling ☎800-752-4841.

The new phenomenon in discount travel is the emergence of the so-called 'Chinatown buses,' which transport people from one city's Chinatown to another's. New York is a hub for a number of these services, including the **Fung Wah Bus Company, Dragon Express,** and **Sunshine**. Check **www.ivymedia.com** for a fuller listing.

BY TRAIN

You can save money by purchasing your tickets in advance, so plan ahead. **Amtrak** (☎800-USA-RAIL/872-7245; www.amtrak.com) is the major provider of intercity passenger train service in the US. The web page lists up-to-date schedules, fares, and arrival and departure info. Many qualify for discounts: senior citizens (10-15% off); students (15% off) with a Student Advantage Card (see **By Bus,** p. 301, for how to purchase); travelers with disabilities (15% off); children 2-15 accompanied by a parent (50% off, up to 2 children); children under age two (free with each adult ticket purchased); current members of the US armed forces, active-duty veterans, and their dependents (15% off with $19.95 membership). "Rail SALE" offers online discounts of up to 70%; visit the Amtrak website for details and reservations.

Amtrak's trains connect NYC to most other parts of the country through **Penn Station,** 33rd St. and Eighth Ave. (Subway: 1, 2, 3, 9 to 34th St.-Penn Station/Seventh Ave.; A, C, E to 34th St.-Penn Station/Eighth Ave.) Routes run from Boston (4-5hr., $64), Washington, D.C. (3-4hr., $72), and Philadelphia (1½hr., $48). The **Long Island Railroad** (see p. 279) and **New Jersey Transit** both run out of Penn Station.

BY CAR

There are several major paths leading to Manhattan from outside of the city. From New Jersey there are three choices, each costing $6. The **Holland Tunnel** connects to lower Manhattan, the **Lincoln Tunnel** exits to Midtown in the West 40s and the **George Washington Bridge** crosses the Hudson River into northern Manhattan, offering access to either Harlem River Dr. or the West Side Hwy. From New England, take **I-95** and connect to the **Bruckner Expwy. (I-287);** if you are driving outbound, follow the I-95 signs because the Bruckner is not marked as I-287 until after its intersection with the **Cross Bronx Expwy.** Take the Bruckner to either the **Triborough Bridge** ($3.50 toll) or the **Cross Bronx Expwy.,** which crosses upper Manhattan to the upper west side of Manhattan, near the George Washington Bridge at Broadway and 175th St. The **speed limit** in New York State, as in most other states, is 55 mi. per hr. on highways (30 mi. per hr. on streets). As in most other states, wearing a seat belt is required by law. For information on renting a car, see the **Service Directory,** (p. 323).

SPECIFIC CONCERNS

OLDER TRAVELERS

Senior citizens are eligible for a wide range of discounts on transportation, museums, movies, theaters, concerts, restaurants, and accommodations. If you don't see a senior citizen price listed, ask, and you may be delightfully surprised. The books *No Problem! Worldwise Tips for Mature Adventurers*, by Janice Kenyon (Orca Book Publishers; $16) and *Unbelievably Good Deals and Great Adventures That You Absolutely Can't Get Unless You're Over 50*, by Joan Rattner Heilman (NTC/Contemporary Publishing; $15) are both excellent resources. For more information, contact one of the following organizations:

Elderhostel, 11 Ave. de Lafayette, Boston, MA 02111 (☎877-426-8056; www.elderhostel.org). Organizes 1- to 4-week educational adventures for those 55+.

The Mature Traveler, P.O. Box 1543, Wildomar, CA 92595 (☎909-461-9598; www.thematuretraveler.com; subscription $30). Monthly newsletter with deals, discounts, tips, and travel packages for the senior traveler.

TRAVELERS WITH DISABILITIES

Arrange transportation well in advance to ensure a smooth trip. Hertz, Avis, and National **car rental agencies** have hand-controlled vehicles at some locations. In the US, both **Amtrak** and major airlines will accommodate disabled passengers if notified at least 72 hours in advance. Hearing-impaired travelers may contact

Amtrak using teletype printers (☎800-523-6590). **Greyhound** buses will provide free travel for a companion under certain circumstances; if you are without a fellow traveler, call Greyhound (☎800-752-4841) at least 48 hours before you leave and they will make arrangements for you.

New York is much more accommodating for disabled travelers than it used to be. About 75 New York **subway stations** and all the buses have excellent wheelchair access. Call **NYC Travel Information** (☎718-596-8585) for details. **Access-A-Ride** door-to-door service is available for some (call ☎877-337-2017). Those with disabilities should inform airlines and hotels of their disabilities when making reservations, as some time may be needed to prepare special accommodations. Call ahead to restaurants, museums, and other facilities to find out if they are handicapped-accessible; the **Elevators and Escalator Accessibility Hotline** (☎800-734-6772) is available 24hr. Guide dog owners must license their dogs, and it's free with proper documentation; call **Veterinary Public Health Services** for details (☎212-676-2120; www.nyc.gov/html/doh/html/vet/vet.html).

For the hearing impaired community, the **Hands On! Organization** (☎212-822-8550, TTY 822-8549; www.handson.org) arranges sign language interpreting for many cultural events in NYC; **Hospital Audiences** (☎212-575-7676, 888-424-4685; TTY 212-575-7673; www.hospitalaudiences.org) provides an audio-description service for blind theatergoers. The **Mayor's Office for People with Disabilities** (☎212-788-2830; www.nyc.gov/html/mopd/home.html) will send the book *Access New York* free of charge to people who inquire via telephone. The 100-page large-type book provides resources and specific accessibility reviews for cultural institutions, theaters, nightlife and sports venues, and tours. **Society for the Advancement of Travel for the Handicapped (SATH),** 347 Fifth Ave., #610, New York, NY 10016, USA (☎212-447-7284; www.sath.org), is an advocacy group that publishes free online travel information and the travel magazine *OPEN WORLD* (US$18, free for members). Annual membership is $45, students and seniors $30.

WOMEN TRAVELERS

Women exploring NYC on their own inevitably face additional safety concerns. In general, NYC by day is safe, but from evening to morning some neighborhoods are definitely dangerous. Always trust your instincts: if you'd feel better somewhere else, move on. Always carry extra money for a phone call, bus, or taxi. Stick to centrally located accommodations and avoid late-night treks or subway rides.

Look as if you know where you're going (even when you don't) and consider approaching women or couples for directions if you're lost or feel uncomfortable. Your best answer to verbal harassment is no answer at all. Don't hesitate to seek out a police officer or a passerby if you are being harassed. The look on your face is the key to avoiding unwanted attention; have a New Yorker's attitude. These warnings should not discourage women from traveling alone—NYC women manage just fine.

Important emergency/crisis resources for women include the **NYC Domestic Violence Hotline** (☎800-621-4673); the **Crime Victims Treatment Center** at the **St. Luke's-Roosevelt Hospital Center** (☎212-523-4728); the **Victim Services Rape, Sexual Assault and Incest Hotline** (☎212-227-3000); and the **NYPD Sex Crimes Report Hotline** (☎212-267-7273). For general information and for information on rape crisis centers, counseling services, and advocacy issues, contact the **National Organization for Women of NYC (NOW-NYC** at 105 W. 28th St., #304, **New York,** NY 10001 (☎212-627-9895; fax 627-9891; www.nownyc.org).

Other major women's advocacy groups include the **Women's City Club of New York,** 33 W. 60th St., 5th fl. (☎212-353-8070; fax 228-4665; www.wccny.org) and the **Women's Advisors of NYC,** 100 Gold St., 2nd fl. (☎212-788-2738; www.nyc.gov/html/csw/html/wahome.html).

GAY AND LESBIAN TRAVELERS

New York has a plethora of publications dedicated to the gay and lesbian community, although the city's queer media seems to cater predominantly to gay men. *HomoXtra* (*HX* and *HX for Her*) and *Next* both have listings of nightlife and activities, and are available free at gay hangouts around the city. *Go NYC*, which published its first edition Spring 2002, promises to be a "cultural roadmap for the city girl." The free *LGNY* (no, that's not *Let's Go NY*, but *Lesbian-Gay NY*) and the *New York Blade News* are community broadsheets and are distributed throughout the boroughs; *Gay City News* (www.gaycitynews.com), which began in May 2002, also reports on New York events of interest to the gay community. Free copies of *MetroSource* (www.metrosource.com), a gay-oriented magazine with a wider scope including movie reviews, travel, and national news, can be found around Chelsea. The nationally distributed *Advocate* magazine has a New York section; also check out the *Village Voice* (www.villagevoice.com), which provides events, services, and occasional feature articles of interest to gays and lesbians. In addition, some **websites** will give you info that the printed rags don't reveal. Check out www.gmad.org, a resource for gay men of African descent, and www.pridelinks.com.

Bluestockings (p. 242) has an bulletin-board area for postings about anything from roommates wanted to rideshares to the Butchies concert in Syracuse; you can find events of specific interest to gay women posted as well.

The helpful **Gayellow Pages,** P.O. Box 533, Village Station, New York, NY 10014, has a special New York edition ($16) that list accommodations, organizations, and services in the city (☎212-674-0120; fax 420-1126; www.gayellowpages.com).

HEALTH AND SUPPORT SERVICES

Callen-Lorde Community Health Center, 356 W. 18th St., between Eighth and Ninth Ave. (☎212-271-7200; www.callen-lorde.org). Subway: A, C, E to 14th St.; L to Eighth Ave. Comprehensive general health services for the queer community, plus counseling and a health resource department. Callen-Lorde offers a sliding-scale fee structure for individuals without insurance coverage, and no one is turned away. Open M 12:30-8pm, W 2:30-8pm, Tu and Th-F 9am-4:30pm.

Gay Men's Health Crisis (GMHC), 119 W. 24th St., between Sixth and Seventh Ave. (☎212-367-1000; Geffen Center ☎367-1100, hotline ☎800-243-7692 or 807-6655; www.gmhc.org). Subway: 1, F to 23rd St. Healthcare, support groups, physician referrals, and counseling for men and women with HIV and AIDS. Walk-in counseling M-F 10am-6pm. GMHC's **Geffen Center** provides confidential (not anonymous) HIV testing. Open M-F 10am-9pm, Sa noon-3pm.

Gay and Lesbian National Hotline (☎212-989-0999; glnh@glnh.org; www.glnh.org). Information, peer counseling, and referrals for the gay or lesbian traveler. Open M-F 4pm-midnight, Sa noon-5pm. 24hr. recording.

Lesbian and Gay Community Services Center, 208 W. 13th St., between Seventh and Eighth Ave. (☎212-620-7310; www.gaycenter.org). Subway: A, C, E, to 14th St. The second-largest lesbian, gay, bisexual and transgender community center in the world, this enormous resource provides information and referral services as well as space for 300 groups, 27 programs and over 5000 visitors each week. Open daily 9am-11pm.

RELIGIOUS SERVICES

Church of St. Paul and St. Andrew, 263 86th St., at West End Ave. (☎212-362-3179). Subway: 1, 9 to 86th St. United Methodist Church dating from 1897. Check out the octagonal tower and the angles in the spandrels. Gay-friendly services Su 11am.

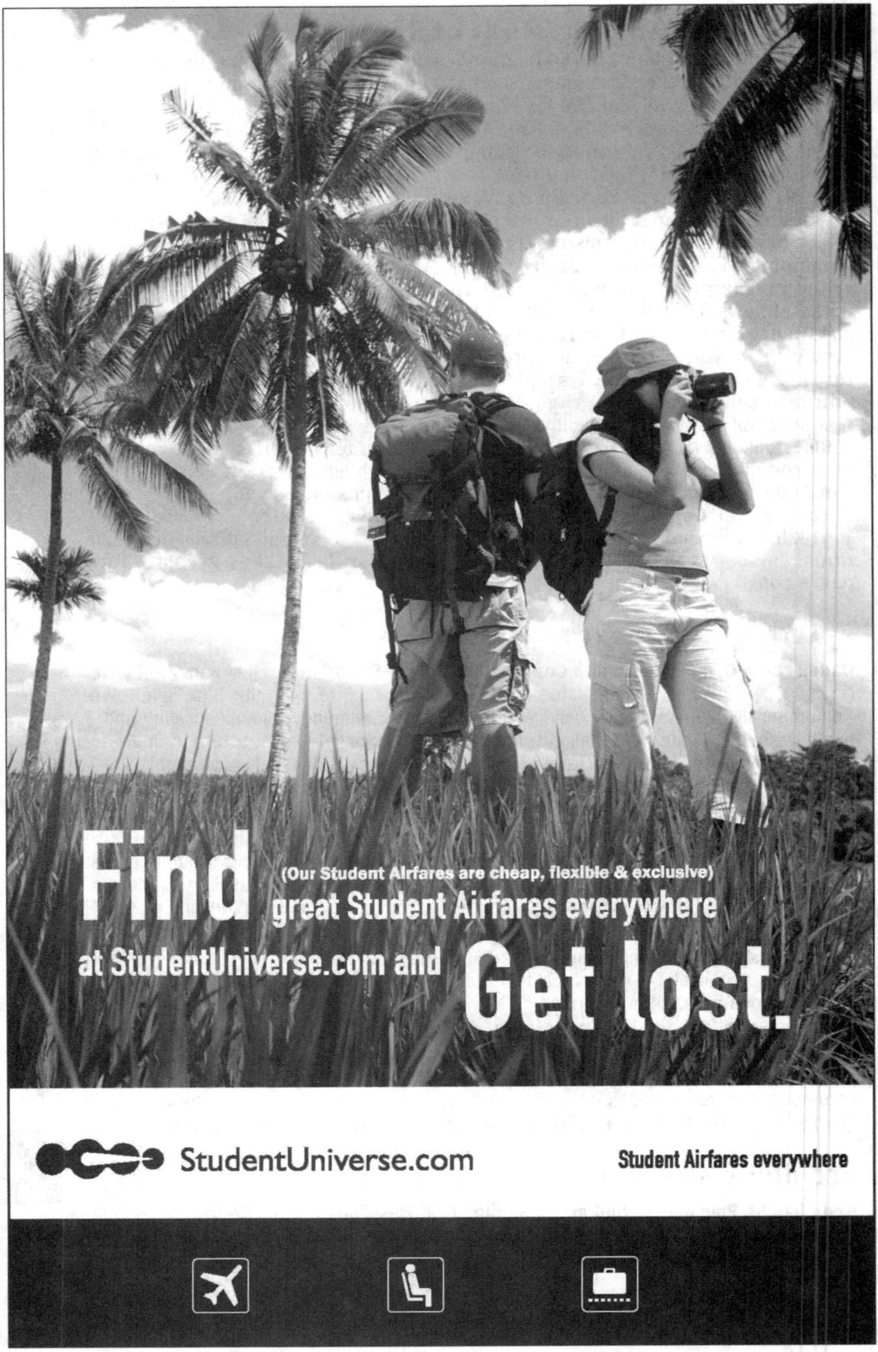
Find
(Our Student Airfares are cheap, flexible & exclusive)
great Student Airfares everywhere
at StudentUniverse.com and
Get lost.
StudentUniverse.com
Student Airfares everywhere

Congregation Beth Simchat Torah, 57 Bethune St. (☎212-929-9498; www.cbst.org). Subway: A, C, E to 14th St. Synagogue catering to the NY lesbian and gay community. Main services F at 8pm at the **Church of the Holy Apostle,** at 296 Ninth Ave. and 28th St. Additional services F at 8:30pm at Bethune St. location.

Metropolitan Community Church of New York, 446 W. 36th St., between 9th and 10th St. (☎212-629-7440). Subway: A, C, E to 34th St. This Christian church has been serving the queer community for 26 years. Services Su 10am, 12:30pm (in Spanish), 7pm; W 7pm.

DIETARY CONCERNS

Vegetarians won't have any problem eating cheap and well in New York. Excellent vegetarian restaurants abound, and almost every non-vegetarian place offers non-meat options (see **Food,** p. 149). The **North American Vegetarian Society** publishes information about vegetarian travel, including *The Vegetarian Journal's Guide to Natural Food Restaurants in the US and Canada* (P.O. Box 72, Dolgeville, NY 13329. ☎518-568-7970; www.navs-online.org). For more information, visit your local bookstore, health food store, or library. You may want to consult *The Vegan Guide to New York City* by Rynn Berry and Chris A. Suzuki (Pythagorean Books; US$10), *The Vegetarian Traveler* by Jed and Susan Civic (Larson Publications; US$16), and *Good and Cheap Vegetarian Dining in New York* by Arthur Brown and Barbara Holmes (US$10).

New York boasts an extensive selection of **halal** food; consult www.zabihah.com/ny.shtml to find your nearest halal restaurant, deli or grocery. Travelers who keep **kosher** should call a New York synagogue for information (your own synagogue or college Hillel office should have lists of NYC Jewish institutions). Chabad houses (centers for Lubavitch Hassidim and outreach) should also be able to either provide kosher food or direct you to it. Columbia's Beit Ayala Chabad Student Center is located at 510 W. 110th St., #5C (☎212-864-5010, ext.44), and the Upper East Side's Chabad *shuckles* is at 311 E. 83rd St., Ste. B (☎212-717-4613). They also provide general information and support, classes, and matchmaking for religious visitors.

PUBLIC HOLIDAYS IN 2004

DATE	HOLIDAY/FESTIVAL	INFORMATION
November 27, 2003	Thanksgiving Day	Businesses and government offices closed.
December 25	Christmas Day	Businesses and government offices closed.
January 1, 2004	New Year's Day	Businesses and government offices closed.
January 19	Martin Luther King, Jr.'s Birthday	City and state offices closed.
February 16	President's Day	Government offices closed.
April 11	Easter Sunday	Businesses closed.
May 31	Memorial Day	Businesses and government offices closed.
July 4	Independence Day	Businesses and government offices closed.
September 6	Labor Day	Businesses and government offices closed.
October 11	Columbus Day	Government offices closed.
November 11	Veterans Day	Government offices closed.

INSIDE

volunteering **312**
hunger **312**
homelessness **313**
youth and community programs **313**
other concerns **314**
studying **315**
universities **315**
film, theater, and music schools **316**
working **317**
long-term work **318**
short-term work **320**

Alternatives to Tourism

When Let's Go started out in 1961, about 1.7 million people in the world were traveling internationally each year; in 2002, nearly 700 million trips were made, projected to be up to a billion by 2010. New York City alone receives around 35 million tourists each year, making it one of the most heavily visited places on earth. The dramatic rise in tourism has created an interdependence between the economy, environment, and culture of many destinations and the tourists they host.

Those looking to **volunteer** in the efforts to resolve these issues have many options. Whether you're working in a homeless shelter or teaching in a educational program for disadvantaged kids, you can participate in projects on an infrequent basis or as the main component of your trip. Later in this section, we recommend organizations that can help you find the opportunities that best suit your interests, whether you're looking to pitch in for a day or a year.

In recent years, the cracks in New York's facade have been painted over with the wide brushstrokes of public safety; suddenly, those who had shunned New York for years were pouring into the city in droves. Even though New York is indeed far safer than it was less than a decade ago, the city is not without its share of troubles: a nice layer of paint might hide problems, but it won't make them go away. If it's important to you to make a contribution greater than your tourist dollars, you should by no means discount New York City as a very viable location to have an impact.

Given the tremendous economic boom of the last decade and New York's strange new place as 'America's City,' it's often forgotten that the riches of the 1990s not only had no effect on many New Yorkers, but might have actually made the lives of a number of them appreciably worse. In fact, homelessness in New York reached an all-time high in 2003 and the crisis shows little sign of abating. In the previous mayoral administration, services for needy New Yorkers were drastically and ruthlessly cut; today, it would be generous and misleading to say that most New Yorkers have access to even a minimal array of services. Although lacking the immediate gratification and visible progress of many volunteer opportunities in the developing world, an act of urban service is still terribly significant: for example, preventing homelessness by working in a tenant's advocacy group can be as satisfying as building a house with your own hands.

Other than volunteering, there are any number of other ways that you can integrate yourself with the communities you visit. One of the most popular options is **studying** at a local college. In addition to a number of liberal arts and technical colleges and universities, New York also has some of the country's most prestigious film and music schools. Many travelers also structure their trips by the **work** that they can do along the way—either odd jobs as they go, or full-time stints in cities where they plan to stay for some time. New York's short-term work options range from largely secretarial (and often mind-numbing) temp work to opportunities to be seen on the big screen as a movie extra. Those seeking longer commitments can often find jobs as babysitters and nannies or waiters and waitresses. Still, many others travel to NYC to take advantage of the city's place as a corporate center and the wide array of internship possibilities. For personal development, there are few places that rival New York's options.

For more information about sustainable tourism, www.worldsurface.com features photos and personal stories of volunteer experiences. More general information is available at www.sustainabletravel.org. For those who seek more active involvement, Earthwatch International, Operation Crossroads Africa, Cross Cultural Solutions, and Habitat for Humanity offer fulfilling volunteer opportunities all over the world.

Before handing your money over to any volunteer or study abroad program, make sure you know exactly what you're getting into. It's a good idea to get the name of **previous participants** and ask them about their experience, as some programs sound much better on paper than in reality. The **questions** below are a good place to start:

-Will you be the only person in the program? If not, what are the other participants like? How old are they? How much will you be expected to interact with them?

-Is room and board included? If so, what is the arrangement? Will you be expected to share a room? A bathroom? What are the meals like? Do they fit any dietary restrictions?

-Is transportation included? Are there any additional expenses?

-How much free time will you have? Will you be able to travel around the island?

-What kind of safety network is set up? Will you still be covered by your home insurance? Does the program have an emergency plan?

A NEW PHILOSOPHY OF TRAVEL

We at *Let's Go* have watched the growth of the 'ignorant tourist' stereotype with dismay, knowing that the majority of travelers care passionately about the state of the communities and environments they explore—but also knowing that even conscientious tourists can inadvertently damage natural wonders, rich cultures, and impoverished communities. We believe the philosophy of **sustainable travel** is among the most important travel tips we could impart to our readers, to help guide fellow backpackers and on-the-road philanthropists. By staying aware of the needs and troubles of local communities, today's travelers can be a powerful force in preserving and restoring this fragile world.

Working against the negative consequences of irresponsible tourism is much simpler than it might seem; it is often self-awareness, rather than self-sacrifice, that makes the biggest difference. Simply by trying to spend responsibly and conserve local resources, all travelers can positively impact the places they visit. Let's Go has partnered with **BEST** (**Business Enterprises for Sustainable Travel,** an affiliate of the Conference Board; see www.sustainabletravel.org), which recognizes businesses that operate based on the principles of sustainable travel. Below, they provide advice on how ordinary visitors can practice this philosophy in their daily travels, no matter where they are.

TIPS FOR CIVIC TRAVEL: HOW TO MAKE A DIFFERENCE

Travel by train when feasible. Rail travel requires only half the energy per passenger mile that planes do. On average, each of the 40,000 daily domestic air flights releases more than 1700 pounds of greenhouse gas emissions.

Use public mass transportation whenever possible; outside of cities, take advantage of group taxis or vans. Bicycles are an attractive way of seeing a community first-hand. And enjoy walking–purchase good maps of your destination and ask about on-foot touring opportunities.

When renting a car, ask whether fuel-efficient vehicles are available. Honda and Toyota produce cars that use hybrid engines powered by electricity and gasoline, thus reducing emissions of carbon dioxide. Ford Motor Company plans to introduce a hybrid fuel model by the end of 2004.

Reduce, reuse, recycle–use electronic tickets, recycle papers and bottles wherever possible, and avoid using containers made of styrofoam. Refillable water bottles and rechargable batteries both efficiently conserve expendable resources.

Be thoughtful in your purchases. Take care not to buy souvenir objects made from trees in old-growth or endangered forests, such as teak, or items made from endangered species, like ivory or tortoise jewelry. Ask whether products are made from renewable resources.

Buy from local enterprises, such as casual street vendors. In developing countries and low-income neighborhoods, many people depend on the "informal economy" to make a living.

Be on-the-road-philanthropists. If you are inspired by the natural environment of a destination or enriched by its culture, join in preserving their integrity by making a charitable contribution to a local organization.

Spread the word. Upon your return home, tell friends and colleagues about places to visit that will benefit greatly from their tourist dollars, and reward sustainable enterprises by recommending their services. Travelers can not only introduce friends to particular vendors but also to local causes and charities that they might choose to support when they travel.

VOLUNTEERING

Though New York City is considered wealthy in worldwide terms, there is no shortage of aid organizations to benefit the very real issues the region faces. New York has substantial homeless, hungry, disadvantaged populations that are often overshadowed by the city's bright lights. With such pressing needs being left unfulfilled, visitors to New York have the special opportunity to help improve lives in addition to being tourists. Volunteering can be one of the most fulfilling experiences in life, especially if you combine it with the thrill of traveling in a new place.

Most people who volunteer in NYC do so on a short-term basis, at organizations that make use of drop-in or once-a-week volunteers. These can be found in virtually every city, and are referenced both in this section and in our town and city write-ups themselves. The best way to find opportunities that match up with your interests and schedule may be to check with New York volunteer agencies and do internet searches. The **Volunteer Referral Center** places individuals in volunteer positions in organizations throughout the city, based on detailed personal interviews. **New York Cares** also specializes in public service placements. The **Mayor's Voluntary Action Center** (www.nyc.gov/html/mvac/home.html) has an extensive list of community service organizations. **Idealist** contains a searchable database of over 27,000 nonprofit and community organizations in 153 countries, including over 1000 in New York.

More intensive volunteer services may charge you a fee to participate. These costs can be surprisingly hefty (although they frequently cover airfare and most, if not all, living expenses). Most people choose to go through a parent organization that takes care of logistical details and frequently provides a group environment and support system. There are two main types of organizations—religious and non-sectarian—although there are rarely restrictions on participation for either.

HUNGER

Despite the tall buildings, trendy shops, and chic nightspots, many New Yorkers go hungry each day. Recent economic recessions and cutbacks are only making the problem worse. 45% more people were served in food pantries and soup kitchens in 2002 than in 2000. Following Sept. 11, 87% of these organizations reported an increased demand for food in the number of children requesting food. With so many people in need, volunteers are always in high demand to help put food in hungry mouths that may otherwise remain empty.

City Harvest, 575 Eighth Ave., 4th fl., at W. 38th St. (☎917-351-8700; http://cityharvest.org). This nonprofit organization, founded in 1981, is the largest and oldest food rescue program in the world. City Harvest is committed to feeding hungry people in NYC using a variety of innovative, practical, and cost-effective methods. Their primary approach is to rescue food that otherwise would be wasted and deliver it to those who serve the hungry. Volunteer opportunities vary widely in nature and level of commitment–you can help pick up food donations from the city's vendors and markets, drive the truck that collects the food, or provide administrative support to the organization.

Food Bank for New York City, 355 Food Center Dr., Bronx, NY 10474 (☎718-991-4300; www.foodbanknyc.org). Supplies food for 200,000 meals served each day to those in need. Volunteer opportunities are always available sorting food, working at special events, or assisting at one of the Food Bank's 1000 community food programs.

Yorkville Common Pantry, 8 E. 109th St., New York, NY 10029 (☎212-410-2264, ext. 110; www.ycp.org). Serves 1200 hot meals each week to those in need, in addition to offering a girls youth program, showers, laundry service, psychiatric help, and afterschool programs. Volunteers help prepare and serve meals, and assist with the pantry's other services.

HOMELESSNESS

Homelessness is one of New York's most widespread problems. In May 2003, over 38,000 people slept in shelters each night, 79% of whom were children and families. With New York's recent economic difficulties following Sept. 11, the number of those living on the streets or in shelters will likely be on the rise. Volunteers are always needed to enlist in the fight against this growing problem.

Common Ground Community, 505 Eighth Ave., 15th fl., New York, NY 10018 (☎212-389-9334; www.commonground.org). Volunteer opportunities are available to help Common Ground with its supportive housing programs that provide permanent homes to the formerly homeless, disabled, elderly, or poor.

Covenant House New York, 460 W. 41st St., New York, NY 10036 (☎212-613-0300; www.covenanthouseny.org). Provides food, shelter, health services, counseling, job training, respect, emotional support, 24hr. crisis assistance, and much more to homeless, abused, or at-risk youth, with locations in each of the 5 boroughs. There are a wide variety of opportunities for volunteers.

Habitat for Humanity New York City, 334 Furman St., at Joralemon St., in Downtown Brooklyn (☎718-246-5656). Through volunteer labor and tax-deductible donations of money and materials, Habitat builds and rehabilitates simple homes with the help of the future homeowners. Habitat homes, sold to partner families at no profit and financed with affordable, no-interest loans, have been built in Queens, the Bronx, Brooklyn, and Manhattan.

Neighborhood Coalition for Shelter, 157 E. 86th St., New York, NY 10028 (☎212-861-0704; www.ncsinc.org). The Neighborhood Coalition for Shelter offers a variety of services to New York's needy, including supportive housing, 24hr. service, shelter, counseling, and job and education specialists. Volunteers are always welcome for short, long, or one-time commitments.

Partnership for the Homeless, 305 Seventh Ave., New York, NY 10001 (☎212-645-3444; www.partnershipforthehomeless.org). Partnership for the Homeless is dedicated to breaking the cycle of homelessness by addressing the complex needs of homeless people through a variety of programs geared toward families, the elderly, veterans, those affected by HIV/AIDS, and several other at-risk groups. Volunteers staff shelters throughout the city and assist with the Partnership's many programs.

YOUTH AND COMMUNITY PROGRAMS

Despite the attractions and importance of each of New York City's boroughs, there is a wide disparity in resources and opportunities from neighborhood to neighborhood. Many of the poorer communities lack good educational and recreational programs, support services, and career or enrichment opportunities. It is remarkable how much an impact one person can make on improving the lives of those living in disadvantaged communities simply by volunteering their time.

Big Brothers, Big Sisters, 223 E. 30th St., New York, NY 10016 (☎212-686-2042; www.bigsnyc.org). By spending only 4hr. every other week hanging out with a local child, volunteers become mentors and friends to at-risk kids in an effort to support children growing up in single parent households.

City Year, 20 W. 22nd St., New York, NY 10010 (☎212-675-8881; www.cityyear.org). City Year volunteers participate in a broad range of public service programs primarily in the South Bronx, East Harlem, Lower East Side, and Harlem. Service work focuses primarily on youth development and enrichment, and mentoring. Participants must be US citizens.

East Harlem Tutor Program (EHTP), 2050 Second Ave., New York, NY 10029 (☎212-831-0650; www.ehtp.prg). This nonprofit program offers local Harlem children lessons in math, reading, writing, and computers. The need for volunteers is so great that there is even a waiting list for kids seeking tutors.

Forest Hills Community House, 108-25 62nd Dr., Forest Hills, NY 11375 (☎718-592-5757; www.fhch.org). The Forest Hills Community House supports the community through youth and elderly programs, and local support and education services. Volunteers are encouraged to participate in its wide range of programs that include tutoring, employment support, homelessness prevention, early childhood development, and youth outreach.

The Point Community Development Center, 940 Garrison Ave., Bronx, NY 10474 (☎718-542-4139; www.thepoint.org). The Point is a nonprofit organization operating in Hunts Point in the Bronx that is committed to promoting youth development, as well as cultural and economic revitalization. It offers South Bronx residents, afterschool programs, music instruction, visual arts workshops, entrepreneurial opportunities, community leadership projects, and much more. Volunteers are always welcome.

Union Settlement Association, 237 E. 104th St., New York, NY 10029 (☎212-828-6000; www.unionsettlement.org). With 16 locations in Harlem, Union Settlement's afterschool, childcare, summer job placement, nutrition, and economic development programs have a positive impact on nearly 12,000 people a year. Volunteers play a big role in making these achievements possible.

OTHER CONCERNS

City of New York Parks and Recreation, the Arsenal, Central Park, 830 Fifth Ave., New York, NY 10021 (☎212-NEW-YORK; www.nycgovparks.org). Those 18 and older can volunteer for the Urban Park Ranger Volunteer Program, operating in each of the 5 boroughs. Participants research local history, greet visitors, secure donations, write grants, and more.

God's Love We Deliver, 166 Ave. of the Americas (Sixth Ave.), at Spring St. (☎212-294-8100). This organization prepares and delivers fresh, nutritious meals to those living with AIDS who cannot shop and cook for themselves. Also offers internships for students.

Guggenheim Museum, 1071 Fifth Ave., New York, NY 10128 (☎212-423-3500; www.guggenheim.org). Volunteer opportunities are available in the curatorial, public affairs, visitor information, education, finance, and special events departments. Volunteers may also assist with the museum's outreach program, "Learning Through Art."

New York Civil Rights Coalition, 3 W. 35th St., New York, NY 10001 (☎212-563-5636; www.nycivilrights.org). College, law and graduate students are eligible to participate in the Coalition's efforts to defend civil rights and promote race relations through its Unlearning Stereotypes program. Volunteers work in groups of 2 to teach a semester-long course in local public schools that provides students the skills to combat prejudice.

Sanctuary for Families, P.O. Box 1406, Wall St. Station, New York, NY 10268 (☎212-349-6009; www.sanctuaryforfamilies.org). Sanctuary for Families provides shelter, support, respect, and clinical and legal services to victims of domestic violence and their children. Volunteers participate in many of the organization's programs including childcare, tutoring, special events coordination, and pro bono services (for professionals).

OTHER RESOURCES

New York Cares, 116 E. 16th St., 6th fl., at Lexington Ave. (☎212-228-5000; www.nycares.org). This organization creates more than 2000 opportunities each month for volunteers to serve on flexibly-scheduled, team-based service projects that the program coordinates in partnership with schools, social service agencies, and environmental groups.

Volunteer Referral Center, 161 Madison Ave., New York, NY 10016 (☎212-889-4805; www.volunteer-referral.com). Prospective volunteers are interviewed to determine their strengths and interests, and then are placed with a nonprofit organization that suits them anywhere in New York's 5 boroughs.

WEB RESOURCES

The following websites can also help find volunteer work in New York and abroad: www.amnesty-volunteer.org; www.communityservice.org; www.idealist.org; www.servenet.org; and www.volunteermatch.com.

STUDYING

New York City has more institutions of higher education than any other city in the world. Some 500,000 students worldwide flock to its 95 major universities, small colleges, and professional and specialty schools. Many schools such as **NYU** and **Columbia** have summer programs for visiting students, while **The Cooper Union for the Advancement of Science and Art** and **The Juilliard School** offer respected adult-education programs (see p. 315). For a complete list of academic institutions in the city, visit the official New York City website at www.nyc.gov or www.greatcollegetown.com/college.html. Some of these schools may also be helpful in finding long-term accommodations; call for details.

VISA INFORMATION. Two types of study visas are available: the **F-1,** for academic studies (including language school), and the **M-1,** for non-academic and vocational studies. In order to secure a study visa, you must already be accepted into a full course of study at an educational institution approved by the Immigration and Naturalization Services (INS). F-1 applicants must also prove they have enough readily-available funds to meet all expenses for the first year of study, and that adequate funds will be available for each subsequent year of study; M-1 applicants must have evidence that sufficient funds are immediately available to pay all tuition and living costs for the entire period of intended stay. See http://unitedstatesvisas.gov for more information. Applications should be processed through the American embassy or consulate in your country of residence (see **Visas, Invitations, and Work Permits,** p. 296).

UNIVERSITIES

Columbia University Continuing Education, Information Center, 303 Lewisohn, 116th St. and Broadway (☎212-854-9699; www.ce.columbia.edu). 35 acre campus boasts one of the largest library collections in the nation and state-of-the-art gym and recreational facilities (p. 97). Columbia offers several continuing-education options for those not enrolled in degree programs—students can enroll in individual classes or participate in a variety of other programs (Second-Majors, Summer Session, Creative Writing Studies, or Auditing). Info center open M-F 9am-6pm.

The Cooper Union for the Advancement of Science and Art, Cooper Sq. New York, NY 10003-7120 (☎212-353-4000; www.cooper.edu). The Adult Education department at Cooper Union (p. 66) offers non-credit classes in art, design, photography, language, and New York urban studies; the school also offers an extensive range of free and inexpensive public lectures, debates, cultural events, symposia, concerts, tours, and other community-oriented activities. Fall, spring, and summer sessions. See website for details, or call ☎212-353-4195 for a catalogue.

New School University, 66 W. 12th St., New York, NY 10011 (☎212-229-5600; www.newschool.edu). The Adult Education department at NSU (p. 61) offers more than 1500 credit and non-credit courses each semester. Credit and non-credit courses for adults are offered in: Business and Career Education, Writing, Social Sciences, Humanities, Culinary Arts, Foreign Languages, English Language Studies, Music, Recreation and Physical Fitness, Computers, Communication and Film, Theater and Dance, Photography, and Visual Arts. Most summer adult education courses begin in early June.

New York University (NYU), Office of Undergraduate Admissions, 22 Washington Sq. N., New York, NY 10003 (☎212-998-4500; www.nyu.edu). In addition to degree-program students, students from other colleges and universities and adults who want to earn college credits can register for summer classes at this Greenwich Village institution (p. 60). High school diploma or equivalent required. Over 1000 courses available. Courses are usually 6 wk. long (running late May to mid-June). Housing in residence halls available for additional fee. Call Office of Summer Sessions at ☎212-998-2292 for more info (M-F 9am-5pm, excluding university holidays).

Parsons School of Design, 66 Fifth Ave., New York, NY 10011 (☎212-229-8910 or 800-252-0852; fax 229-8975; www.parsons.edu). Offers a number of non-degree program options. Individual classes and summer intensives for credit and non-credit. Courses cover such topics as Digital Design, Fashion Studies, Fine Arts, Floral Design, Graphic Design, Interior & Architecture. Students can enroll in Continuing Education classes or take 6-week studio classes ("short courses"). 1-month summer intensive programs geared for high school and college students also available (June and July sessions).

School of Visual Arts, 209 E. 23rd St., New York, NY, 10010 (☎212-592-2000; www.schoolofvisualarts.edu). Offers continuing education courses, programs, and workshops. Subjects range from studio arts classes in advertising, computer art, film, interior design and photography, to liberal arts classes in art history, humanities, English as a Second Language, and cinema studies. The School of Visual Arts also offers Arts Abroad, Arts for Kids, and pre-college art programs. Student housing may be available for an additional fee.

EXCHANGE PROGRAMS

International Association for the Exchange of Students for Technical Experience (IAESTE), 10400 Little Patuxent Pkwy. Suite 250, Columbia, MD 21044-3519 (☎410-997-2200; www.aipt.org). 8- to 12-week programs in New York and across the U.S. for international college students with 2 years of experience in technical study. US$25 application fee.

FILM, THEATER, AND MUSIC SCHOOLS

Some people in the industry say that New York City is an even better place for aspiring actors than Hollywood. NYC boasts more small theaters and low-budget independent features, which will give unknown actors more opportunities. Backstage.com features casting notices for features, stage, indie-film, and TV productions. Keep in mind, though, that the entertainment industry is fickle: you had best look for a day job as well.

Prestigious performing-arts schools such as the **Columbia University School of the Arts** (☎212-854-2815; www.columbia.edu/cu/arts/film); **The American Musical and Dramatic Academy** (☎212-787-5300 or 800-367-7908; fax 799-4623; www.amda.edu); and **New York University, Department of Film Studies** (☎212-998-1600; fax 995-4061; www.nyu.edu/gsas/dept/cinema) generally take full-time students only. Still, such major schools often cast for short films and can provide valuable network opportunities. The schools listed below offer shorter-term programs.

FILM SCHOOLS

New York Film Academy, 100 E. 17th St., New York, NY 10003 (☎212-674-4300; www.nyfa.com). Offers classes in filmmaking, digital editing, film acting, screenwriting, and 3D animation. Courses last 4 wk. to 1 yr. Evening and summer classes offered. Branches in London and Los Angeles as well.

The School for Film and Television, 39 W. 19th St., 12th fl., New York, NY 10011 (☎212-645-0030 or 888-645-0030; fax 212-645-0039; www.filmandtelevision.com). Accredited film acting school. The full-time program lasts 2 years, but the Summer Acting Intensives program allows high-school and college students to earn college credits while learning cutting-edge on-camera performance techniques. 9-month part-time certificate programs also offered.

School of Visual Arts, 209 E. 23rd St., New York, NY 10010-3994 (☎212-592-2000; fax 592-2166; www.schoolofvisualarts.edu). Focuses on artistic, communication and entertainment fields. The Continuing Education department's flexible class schedule offers full-semester classes during the evening and the day, as well as intensive workshops and special programs. Summer programs also available.

MUSIC AND ACTING SCHOOLS

American Academy of Dramatic Arts (AADA) in New York, 120 Madison Ave., New York, NY 10016 (☎800-463-8990 or 212-686-9244). The Academy has provided stage, film, and television training for over a century. Evening, summer, and Saturday classes offered.

Circle in the Square Theatre School, Broadway and 50th St., New York City, NY 10019 (☎212-307-0388; www.circlesquare.org). Besides its regular and evening curriculum, offers 7-week (July-Aug.) program with intensive, professionally oriented curriculum of acting classes. Musical track available too.

The Juilliard School Evening Division, 60 Lincoln Center Plaza, New York, NY 10023-6588 (☎212-799-5040; fax 769-6420; juilliardatnight@juilliard.edu). World-famous performing-arts institution also offers evening classes to the public (p. 95). Classes are taught by renowned experts in the music and performing-arts worlds, including faculty members from the College Division. Class levels range from beginning to advanced. Most classes start after 5:30pm and finish by 8pm. Fall and spring semesters offered.

TVI Actors Studio, 165 W. 46th St., Ste. 509, New York, NY 10036 (☎212-302-1900 or 800-884-2772, ext. 2; fax 212-302-1926; www.tvistudios.com). Offers summer programs and year-round classes. Courses run for 2-10 wk.

WORKING

As with volunteering, work opportunities tend to fall into two categories. Some travelers want long-term jobs that allow them to get to know another part of the world as a member of the community, while other travelers seek out short-term jobs to finance the next leg of their travels. In New York City, those looking for long-term jobs should check out childcare, waiter/waitressing, bartending, and internship opportunities. For shorter job commitments, the best bet is probably temp work or potentially acting as a movie extra. Check the **classifieds** of New York's newspapers, particularly in the *Village Voice*, *New York Press*, and the Sunday edition of the *New York Times*. Also check **bulletin boards** in local coffee shops, markets, libraries, and community centers for help wanted posters (for a list of community centers, see **Community Resources,** p. 324). In addition, all of New York's colleges and universities have **career and employment offices;** even if you can't get into the office itself (some may require a school ID to enter), most have bulletin boards outside (for a list of colleges and universities in New York, see **Studying in New York,** p. 315). Sometimes a restaurant or store will post a sign in the window—keep your eyes peeled. As a last resort, it can be fruitful to **go door-to-door with your resume** and a cover letter, particularly if you're targeting a type of establishment that is concentrated in a given area (this works well in an area like SoHo, for example, for someone interested in finding work at a gallery). When finding a job in New York, the **Internet** is your best friend.

WORK PERMITS

A work permit is required for all foreigners planning to work in the US. In typical bureaucratic style, there are dozens of employment visas, most of which are nearly impossible to get. There are three general categories of work visas/permits: employment-based visas, generally issued to skilled or highly educated workers that already have a job offer in the US; temporary worker visas, which have fixed time limits and very specific classifications (for instance, "artists or entertainers who perform under a program that is culturally unique" or those with "practical training in the education of handicapped children"); and cultural exchange visas, which allow for employment by participants in either fellowships or reciprocal work programs with the aim of promoting cultural exchange. For more on the requirements for each type of visa, visit http://travel.state.gov/visa_services.html#niv. While the chances of getting a work visa may seem next to impossible, there is hope: the Council on International Educational Exchange (CIEE) facilitates a work/study/intern exchange program between the citizens of the US and those of Australia, China, France, Germany, Italy, Japan, Spain, Taiwan, and the UK. For a fee, CIEE will guide university students and recent graduates through the red tape of the visa application process; once in the US, they can also help you find employment. For more information, contact your local Council Travel office or visit the CIEE website (www.ciee.org).

LONG-TERM WORK

If you're planning on spending a substantial amount of time (more than 3 months) working in New York City search for a job well in advance. **Internships,** usually for college students, are a good way to learn valuable skills while experiencing New York life, although they are often unpaid or poorly paid (many say the experience, however, is well worth it).

CHILDCARE

Childcare can be a lucrative field, as babysitters and nannies are always in demand. Make sure you know what you're getting into, though, as some parents think you should also do housework. Websites such as **http://newyork.craigslist.org** and **http://babysitter.webshq.com** let both parents and potential babysitters advertise for free.

If you go through an agency, make sure you research the company thoroughly, as many of them make a killing on fees while providing little service or support to you (some also have a limit on what you can be paid by the family, and some don't do the background checks on the families that they claim to do). Major childcare agencies, not endorsed by *Let's Go*, include:

Adele Poston Domestic Agency, 16 E. 79th St., New York, NY 10021 (☎212-879-7474; fax 988-7191; www.adelepostonagency.com). In addition to childcare, provides butler, chauffeur, laundress, bartender, waiter/waitress, and housekeeper services. Call for details. Fees are 8 wk. salary for permanent placement, and—when placement is short-term—30% of salary (up to 8 wk.) for the length of employment.

The Baby Sitters' Guild, 60 E. 42nd St., Ste. 912, New York, NY 10165 (☎212-682-0227; fax 687-4660; www.babysittersguild.citysearch.com). References required. Open daily 9am-9pm.

Elite Nannies, Inc. (☎718-544-9800, 212-246-0600 or 866-354-8344 for those calling from out of state; www.elitenanny.com). Specializes in caregivers, babysitters, housekeepers, sick child care, and companions. Rigorously screened staff may be live-in or live-out, full-time or part-time. Call for fees. Open M-F 9am-6pm.

FOOD SERVICE

The highest-paid food service employees are generally **waiters** and **waitresses.** Waitstaff in New York City make $80-200 per shift, on average about $150 per shift or about $600-$700 per week. Professionals usually make more, depending on the restaurant. **Bartenders** can make up to $300 per shift.

Food service employees make less than minimum wage, but their salary is supplemented with **tips,** which can average upwards of $15 per hour. Since tipping is 15-20% of the bill, the more expensive the restaurant, the more tips for the waitstaff (although higher-class restaurants want experienced staff). If you are working as a **cashier** or **host,** you won't make much in tips and your salary will be close to minimum wage. **Bartenders** make great tips, but they work late and usually need certification and previous experience. The **American Bartending School** provides a one- to two-week 40hr. bartending course, as well as job placement. (252 W. 29th St., at Eighth Ave., 5th fl. ☎800-532-9222.)

For food-service job listings, check out the search engines listed under **Internet Resources** (p. 320). You may also want to check **www.bartender.com** and read the classified ads in the papers listed on p. 37.

INTERNSHIPS

New York City headquarters just about every industry and nonprofit sector imaginable, with the exception of government (and even then, there's the high-profile Mayor's Office and City Hall). In particular, NYC is the primary American home for publishing, advertising, theater, television, finance, fashion, and museum curating; it also houses offices for most international and nationwide nonprofit organizations. In other words, if you want it, it's here. While it's difficult to get paying, short-term positions at these offices, most are eager for interns; however, even interning and volunteering in the Big Apple is fiercely competitive. Be sure to contact your organization of choice early (around 3-6 months before you plan to arrive), and be prepared for an extensive application process.

Many websites provide nationwide databases of internship opportunities: **Internjobs.com** (www.internjobs.com); **Internsearch.com** (www.internsearch.com); **Internweb.com** (www.internweb.com); **Rising Star Internships** (www.rsinternships.com); **Studentintern.com** (www.studentintern.com); and **Wetfeet.com** (www.wetfeet.internshipprograms.com) all let you search their postings *and* post your resume for free. Don't overlook websites more dedicated to your field of interest, however. **Journalismjobs.com** (www.journalismjobs.com), for instance, focuses entirely on media jobs, while **Studentjobs.gov** (www.studentjobs.gov)—a joint project between the US Office of Personnel Management (OPM) and the US Department of Education's Student Financial Assistance office—lists jobs and internships with the federal government. The **Council on International Educational Exchange (CIEE)** may also be useful in finding an internship (p. 319). The list below includes some (but definitely not all) internships that are unique to New York City.

NEW YORK-SPECIFIC INTERNSHIPS

City of New York Parks and Recreation, the Arsenal, Central Park, 830 5th Ave., New York, NY 10021 (☎212-NEW-YORK; www.nycgovparks.org). The Parks Department works to keep the city's parks and playgrounds clean and safe, while also organizing cultural, social, and athletic activities such as nature walks, historic tours, and concerts. A wide range of internship opportunities are available in many different departments.

Government Scholars Program, NYC Department of Citywide Administrative Services, 1 Center St., Rm. 2425, New York, NY 10007 (☎212-NEW-YORK; www.nyc.gov/html/dcas/html/govscho6lars.html). College sophomores and juniors are eligible to participate in the Government Scholars Program, which combines an internship in City government with seminars on the workings of city government. Interns receive a $3,500 stipend for the 10-week summer program.

Guggenheim Museum, 1071 Fifth Ave., New York, NY 10128, (☎212-423-3500; www.guggenheim.org). Offers a variety of academic year and summer internships to undergraduates and graduates studying art history, conservation, education, film, media studies, museum studies, and similar fields. Stipends are awarded in some cases, depending on the program and applicant. International students are encouraged to apply.

New York City Government Summer Internship Program, NYC Department of Citywide Administrative Services, 1 Center St., Rm. 2425, New York, NY 10007 (☎212-NEW-YORK; www.nyc.gov/html/dcas/html/summerinternguide.html). Summer internships are available to college and graduate students in a long list of government departments, including the Cultural Affairs, Finance, Homeless Services, Human Rights, Small Business Services, Youth and Development, and Fire departments. The availability of stipends, and length of the internship (up to 13 wk.) varies with the specific placement.

INTERNET RESOURCES

Careerbuilder.com (www.careerbuilder.com). Over 400,000 jobs in database.

Craigslist (http://newyork.craigslist.org). Post your resume and search available jobs. Also provides community and apartment listings.

Foreignborn.com (www.foreignborn.com/career_ctr.htm). Foreignborn.com's career center lets you submit your resume for viewing by US-based companies looking specifically for foreign-born employees. Also has visa information.

HotJobs (www.hotjobs.com). Allows potential employees to post resumes and search a huge job database.

Monster.com (www.monster.com). Search database, post resume on highly acclaimed site.

SHORT-TERM WORK

Traveling for long periods of time can get expensive; therefore, many travelers try their hand at odd jobs for a few weeks at a time to make some extra cash to carry them through another month or two of touring around. For some extra cash, take on a temp position, or, if you're feeling lucky, register to act as a movie extra. Many places, especially due to the high turnover in the tourism industry, are always eager for help, even if only temporary.

MOVIE EXTRA OPPORTUNITIES

If you're interested in seeing your face on the silver screen, you should consider registering with a casting agent: New York is one of the most-filmed locations in the world, and casting directors will hire background extras regardless of experience. Many film producers select extras from a casting agency's album of headshots; registration fees at casting agencies are usually around $15-30. You don't have to belong to a union to land a gig, but union members do earn more than non-union extras—up to $200 for 8hr. of work if they make it into the movie, television show or commercial. The **Screen Actors Guild** office is located at 1515 Broadway, 44th fl., New York, NY 10036 (☎212-944-1030; fax 944-6774; www.sag.org). Still, non-union members can pick up about $50 a day. Sites such as **www.caryn.com** and **www.filmfaces.com** post casting calls for free. Below is a list of agencies that cast background actors in New York; see **www.nycasting.com** or **www.assistantdirectors.com** for more.

Actors Reps of New York, 1501 Broadway, Ste. 308, New York, NY 10036 (☎212-391-4668; fax 391-8499; www.actorsreps.com). Casts extras for all areas. Auditions M-F 11:30am-1pm and 4pm-5:30pm, Sa 11am-1pm.

Impossible Casting, 111 W. 17th St., New York, NY 10011 (☎212-352-9098).

Jimmy Hank Promotions, 209 W. 104th St., Ste. 2H, New York, NY 10025 (☎212-864-2132).

Kee Casting, 424 Park Ave. S., #128, New York, NY 10016 (☎212-725-3775). Casting Director: Karen E. Etcoff. Casts films and commercials.

Liz Lewis Casting Partners, 3 W. 18th St., 6th fl., New York, NY 10011 (☎212-645-1500).

Stark Naked Productions (Elsie Stark Casting), 39th 19th St., 12th fl., New York, NY 10011 (☎212-366-1903). Casts commercials and films.

Stickman-Ripps, Inc., 65 N. Moore St., Ste. 3A, New York, NY 10013 (☎212-966-3211).

Winsome Sinclair & Associates, 314 W. 53rd St., Ste. 106, New York, NY 10019 (☎212-397-1537). Casts films.

TEMPORARY WORK

One of the easiest (and most mindless) ways to earn money is as a temp worker. Offices often hire employees for short periods (anywhere from a few days to several months) through New York's many temp agencies (read: massive clearinghouses of unemployed but oh-so-skilled workers). Most jobs are secretarial in nature: data entry, filing, answering phones, etc. Agencies may be able to place you in full-time work after only a few weeks; if they do, health insurance is often included. Other companies may offer direct deposit (very handy), referral bonuses, and/or vacation pay. It is rare to find an agency which offers all these benefits, and if it does, the pay is usually rather low. You should shop around to find an agency that provides the benefits and pay package you desire.

Those with computer skills make the most money in the temping industry. You should know at least one major word-processing program and one major spreadsheet program to get some of the better temp jobs. Don't fret if you have neither: many tempers with only basic skills (filing, answering phones, etc.) are able to get started with temp agencies before learning computer and other skills on the job.

The **Red Guide to Temp Agencies** (www.panix.com/~grvsmth/redguide) provides great reviews of the city's temp agencies. The **New York Association of Temporary Staffing Services** (☎212-696-2070; www.staffingtoday.net/ny-metro/index.html) is a chapter of a nationwide organization that represents the interests of the staffing industry. The following temp agencies are not endorsed by *Let's Go:*

 **Atrium Staffing,** 420 Lexington Ave., Ste. 1410, New York, NY 10170 (☎212-292-0550; www.atriumstaff.com). Assignments in support and finance.

PS Inc., 1285 Ave. of the Americas, 35th fl., New York, NY 10019 (☎212-554-4263; www.ps-staffing.com). Offers Permanent Placement, Temporary Staffing, and Employee Leasing client programs.

Snelling Downtown, 150 Broadway, Ste. 902, New York, NY 10038-4381 (temping jobs ☎212-331-9200; permanent jobs ☎227-6705; www.snelling.com). Business, IT, and office temps.

The Supporting Cast, 10 E. 40th St., #1300, New York, NY 10016 (☎212-532-8888; www.supportingcast.com). Also offers permanent jobs.

Tiger Information Systems, 130 William St., New York, NY 10038 (☎212-412-0600; www.tiger-info.com). Offers temporary and permanent desktop, IT, project management and creative staffing..

FOR FURTHER READING ON ALTERNATIVES TO TOURISM

International Directory of Voluntary Work, by Whetter and Pybus. Peterson's Guides and Vacation Work, 2000 (US$16).

Work Abroad: The Complete Guide to Finding a Job Overseas, by Hubbs, Griffith, and Nolting. Transitions Abroad Publishing, 2000 ($16).

Invest Yourself: The Catalogue of Volunteer Opportunities, published by the Commission on Voluntary Service and Action (☎718-638-8487).

9026
4H28
19
DRIVERS WANTED
212-957-4646
NEW YORK
2K53
1N83

Service Directory

AIRLINES

Major airlines have numerous Manhattan offices; call for the closest location.

American, ☎800-433-7300.

Continental, ☎800-525-0280.

Delta, ☎800-221-1212.

Northwest, ☎800-225-2525.

United, ☎800-241-6522.

US Airways, ☎800-428-4322.

AIRPORTS

John F. Kennedy Airport (JFK), ☎718-244-4444. In Jamaica, Queens. See p. 28 for directions.

LaGuardia Airport (LGA), ☎718-533-3400. In East Elmhurst, Queens. See p. 28 for directions.

Newark Liberty Int'l Airport (EWR), ☎973-961-6000. In NJ. See p. 28 for directions.

AIRPORT TRANSPORT

See p. 27 for air transport information.

New York Airport Service, ☎212-875-8200. Serves JFK and LaGuardia.

Olympia Airport Express, ☎212-964-6233. Serves Newark.

SuperShuttle, ☎212-258-3826, 800-258-3826. Serves JFK, LaGuardia, and Newark.

AUTO ASSOCIATIONS

American Automobile Association (AAA) Travel Related Services (☎800-222-4357; www.aaa.com). Provides travel services, maps and guides to members, as well as emergency road service to all.

AUTO RENTAL

AAMCAR Rent-a-Car, 315 W. 96th St., between West End Ave. and Riverside Dr. (☎212-222-8500). Open M-F 7:30am-7:30pm, Sa 9am-5pm, Su 9am-7pm. **Also at** 506 W. 181st St., at Amsterdam Ave. (☎212-927-7000).

Avis, ☎800-230-4898. 18+. Under 25 $110 extra fee per day.

Dollar, ☎800-800-4000. 21+.

Enterprise, ☎800-736-8222. 18+. Under 21 extra fee.

Hertz, ☎800-654-3131, 800-831-2847. 18+. Under 25 $51 extra fee per day.

National, ☎800-227-7368.

Zipcar.com, www.zipcar.com.

BICYCLE RENTAL

See **Entertainment,** p. 234.

BUSES

See also **Metro Transit,** p. 326.

Green Bus Lines, ☎718-995-4700. Serves Jamaica and central Queens.

Greyhound, ☎800-229-9424.

Jamaica Buses, Inc., ☎718-526-0800. Serves Jamaica and Rockaway.

Liberty Lines Express, ☎718-652-8400. Serves the Bronx.

MTA/Long Island Bus, ☎516-228-4000.

New York Bus Service, ☎718-994-5500. Serves the Bronx.

Port Authority Terminal, ☎212-435-7000.

Queens Surface Corp., ☎718-445-3100.

TriBoro Coach Corp., ☎718-335-1000. Serves Forest Hills, Ridgewood, Jackson Hts., and Midtown.

CABS

See **Taxis,** p. 327.

CAR RENTAL

See **Auto Rental,** p. 323.

COMMUNITY CENTERS

Alliance for Downtown New York, ☎212-566-6700. The Alliance's **NYPD Downtown Center** has a 24hr. security phone number (☎212-306-5656).

United Community Centers, 613 New Lots Ave., between Hendrix St. and Schenck Ave., Brooklyn (☎718-649-7979). Similar to UNH.

United Neighborhood Houses of New York (UNH), 70 W. 36th St., 5th fl. (☎212-967-0322; fax 967-0792; www.unhny.org). Partnerships with community centers throughout the 5 boroughs.

CONSULATES

Australia, 150 E. 42nd St., 34th fl., at Broadway. (☎212-351-6500). No visa services.

British Commonwealth, 800 Second Ave., at Broadway (☎212-599-8478).

Canada, Main Concourse Level, 1251 Ave. of the Americas (Sixth Ave.), between 49th and 50th St. (☎212-596-1700).

Germany, 871 UN Plaza, 49th St., at First Ave. (☎212-610-9700).

France, 934 Fifth Ave., between 74th and 75th St. (☎212-606-3600/3680). Visa services, 10 E. 74th St., between Fifth and Madison Ave. (☎212-606-3681/3644).

Ireland, 345 Park Ave. (☎212-319-2555).

Israel, 800 Second Ave., at Broadway (☎212-499-5000).

New Zealand, 222 E. 43rd St., Suite 2510 780 Third Ave., Ste. 1904, at E. 48th St. (☎212-832-4038).

South Africa, 333 E. 38th St., 9th fl., between First and Second Ave. (☎212-213-4880).

UK, 845 Third Ave., between 51st and 52nd St. (☎212-745-0200).

CRISIS AND HELP LINES

See also **Emergency,** p. 325; **Hospitals,** p. 325; **Medical Clinics,** p. 326; and **Women's Health,** p. 327.

AIDS Information, ☎212-807-6655. Open M-F 10am-9pm, Sa noon-3pm.

Alcohol and Substance Abuse Info Line, ☎800-274-2042. 24hr. info and referrals.

CDC AIDS Hotline, ☎800-342-AIDS (2437) or 800-825-5448. Open daily 9am-9pm or 24hr. recording.

Crime Victims' Hotline, ☎212-577-7777. 24hr. counseling and referrals.

Gay and Lesbian Switchboard, ☎212-989-0999; glnh.@glnh.org. Open M-F 4-8pm, Sa noon-5pm. 24hr. recording.

Help Line, ☎212-532-2400. Crisis counseling and referrals. Open 24hr.

National Abortion Federation, ☎800-772-9100. Open M-F 8am-10pm, Sa-Su 9am-5pm.

Poison Control Center, ☎212-764-7667. Open 24hr.

Roosevelt Hospital Rape Crisis Center, ☎212-523-4728 or 877-665-7273. Open M-F 8am-7pm, Sa-Su 9am-5pm.

Samaritans, ☎212-673-3000 or 800-SUICIDE (784-2433) . Suicide prevention. Open 24hr.

Sex Crimes Report Line, ☎212-267-7273. NYPD-related. 24hr. information and referrals.

Terrorism Hotline, ☎800-543-3638. Open 24hr.

CURRENCY EXCHANGE

American Express branches:

- **Macy's Herald Square,** 151 W. 34th St., at Seventh Ave., on Macy's balcony level (☎212-695-8075). Open M-F 9am-5pm.
- **822 Lexington Ave.,** at 63rd St. (☎212-758-6510). Open M-F 9am-6pm, Sa 10am-4pm.
- **374 Park Ave.,** at 53rd St. (☎212-421-8240). Open M-F 9am-5:30pm.
- **1185 Sixth Ave.,** at 47th St. (☎212-398-8585). Open M-F 9am-6pm.
- **111 Broadway,** near Pine St. (☎212-693-1100). Open M-F 8:30am-5:30pm.
- **200 Fifth Ave.,** at 23rd St. (☎212-691-9797). Open M-F 8:30am-5:30pm and Sa 10am-4pm.
- **New York Marriot Marquis,** 1535 Broadway, 8th fl. lobby, between 45th and 46th St. (☎212-575-6580). Open M-F 9am-5pm.

Bank Leumi, 579 Fifth Ave., at 47th St. (☎917-542-2343). Open M-F 9am-3:30pm.

Cheque Point USA, 1568 Broadway, at 47th St. (☎212-750-2400). Other branches throughout the city; call for locations. Open daily 8am-7pm.

Travelex & Thomas Cook, 29 Broadway, at Morris St. (☎800-287-7362). Open M-F 9am-5pm.

DENTISTS

Emergency Dental Associates, ☎800-439-9299. Open 24hr.

NYU College of Dentistry, ☎212-998-9800. Open M-Th 9am-7pm, F 9am-3pm.

DISABLED RESOURCES

Access-A-Ride, ☎718-330-3322 or 337-2017. For public transport.

Directions Unlimited, ☎914-241-1700 or 800-533-5343.

Elevators and Escalator Accessibility, ☎800-734-6772. Open 24hr.

Moss Rehab Hospital Travel Information Service, ☎800-225-5667.

Society for Accessible Traveler Hospitality (SATH), 347 Fifth Ave., Ste. 610, New York, NY 10016 (☎212-447-7284).

Transit Authority Access, ☎718-596-8585.

DRY CLEANERS

Midnight Express Cleaners, ☎212-921-0111. Picks up laundry. Open M-F 8am-8pm, Sa 9am-noon; closed Sa July-Aug.

EMERGENCY

In an emergency, dial ☎**911.** See also **Crisis and Help Lines,** p. 325; **Hospitals,** p. 325; **Medical Clinics,** p. 326; and **Women's Health,** p. 327.

Ambulance: ☎212-988-8800.

Fire: ☎212-999-2222 or 718-416-7000.

Police (non-emergency): ☎646-610-5000 or 311.

ENTERTAINMENT INFO

See also **Ticket Services,** p. 327.

MovieFone, ☎212-777-3456.

NYC/ON STAGE Hotline, ☎212-768-1818.

Parks & Recreation Special Events Hotline, ☎212-360-3456 or 888-NY-PARKS (697-2757). Open 24hr.

HOSPITALS

See also **Crisis and Help Lines,** p. 324; **Emergency,** p. 325; **Medical Clinics,** p. 326; and **Women's Health,** p. 327.

Bellevue Hospital Center, 462 First Ave., at 27th St. (☎212-562-4141; adult ER ☎562-3015, pediatric ER ☎562-3025).

Beth Israel Medical Center, First Ave., at E. 16th St. (☎212-420-2000; adult ER ☎420-2840, pediatric ER ☎420-2860).

Bronx-Lebanon Hospital Center, 1650 Grand Concourse, at Cross-Bronx Expwy., the Bronx (☎718-590-1800). 2 ERs: 1650 Grand Concourse (☎718-518-5120), 1276 Fulton Ave., between E. 168th and 169th St. (☎718-960-8700).

Brooklyn Hospital Center, 121 DeKalb Ave., near Ashland Pl., in Brooklyn (☎718-250-8000; ER ☎250-8075).

Interfaith Medical Center, 1545 Atlantic Ave. in Brooklyn (☎718-613-4000). 555 Prospect Pl., near Franklin St., Brooklyn (☎718-935-7000). 2 ERs: St. Marks

(☎718-935-7110) and Atlantic Ave. (☎718-613-4444).

Jacobi Medical Center, 1400 Pelham Pkwy. S., at Seymour Ave., the Bronx (☎718-918-5000; adult ER ☎918-5800, pediatric ER ☎918-5875, psychiatric ER ☎918-4850).

Jamaica Hospital Medical Center, 8900 Van Wyck Expwy., at 89th Ave., in Jamaica, Queens (☎718-206-6000; ER ☎206-6066).

Mount Sinai Medical Center, Fifth Ave., at 100th St. (☎212-241-6500; ER ☎241-7171).

New York Columbia-Presbyterian Medical Center, 622 W. 168th St., between Fort Washington Ave. and Broadway (☎212-305-2500; ER ☎305-6204).

New York University Downtown Hospital, 170 William St., between Spruce and Beekman St. (☎212-312-5000).

New York University Medical Center, 560 First Ave., between 32nd and 33rd St. (☎212-263-7300; ER 263-5550).

INTERNET ACCESS

See also **By Email and Internet,** p. 34.

alt.coffee, 139 Ave. A, between 8th and 9th St. (☎212-529-2233). $10 per hr. Open M-F 7:30-1:30am, Sa-Su 10-2am.

Kinko's. Over 30 locations; call ☎800-254-6567 for the one you want. About 20¢ per min., but varies according to branch. Open 24hr.

LIBRARIES

Bronx Reference Center, 2556 Bainbridge Ave., at Dr. Sandy F. Ray Blvd. (☎718-579-4257). Open M and W 10am-8pm, Tu and Th 10am-6pm, F noon-6pm, Sa 10am-5pm.

Brooklyn Public Library, Grand Army Plaza, Brooklyn (☎718-230-2100). Open M-Th 9am-8pm, F-Sa 9am-6pm.

Donnell Library Center, 20 W. 53rd St., between Fifth and Sixth Ave. (☎212-621-0618). Open M, W, F 10am-6pm, Tu and Th 10am-8pm, Sa 10am-5pm.

Mid-Manhattan Library, 455 Fifth Ave., at 40th St. (☎212-340-0833). Open M, and W-Th 9am-9pm, Tu 11am-7pm, F-Sa 10am-6pm.

New York Humanities and Social Sciences Library, 11 W. 40th St., entrance on Fifth Ave. at 42nd St. (☎212-930-0830 or 869-8089). Open M and Th-Sa 10am-6pm, Tu-W 11am-7:30pm.

New York Public Library for the Performing Arts, 40 Lincoln Center Plaza (☎212-870-1630). Open M and Th noon-8pm, Tu-W and F-Sa noon-6pm.

Queens Borough Public Library, 89-11 Merrick Blvd., at 89th St., in Jamaica, Queens (☎718-990-0700). Open M-F 10am-9pm, Sa 10am-5:30pm; mid-Sept. to mid-May Su noon-5pm.

Schomburg Center for Research in Black Culture, 515 Malcolm X Blvd. (Sixth Ave.), on the corner of 135th St. (☎212-491-2200). Library open M and W noon-7pm, Tu and Th-F noon-6pm, Sa 10am-6pm; archives open M-Tu and F-Sa noon-5pm.

St. George Library Center, 5 Central Ave., at Hyatt St., on Staten Island (☎718-442-8560). Open M and Th noon-8pm, Tu-W 10am-6pm, F noon-6pm, and Sa 10am-5pm.

MEDICAL CLINICS

See also **Crisis and Help Lines,** p. 324; **Dentists,** p. 325; **Emergency,** p. 325; **Hospitals,** p. 325; **Pharmacies,** p. 326.

Callen-Lorde Community Health Center, 356 W. 18th St., between Eighth and Ninth Ave. (☎212-271-7200; www.callen-lorde.org). Serves the queer community. Open M 12:30-8pm, Tu and Th-F 9am-4:30pm, W 8:30am-1pm and 3-8pm.

D*O*C*S, 55 E. 34th St., at Park and Madison Ave. (☎212-252-6000). **Also at:** 1555 Third Ave., at 88th St. (☎212-828-2300); 202 W. 23rd St., at Seventh Ave. (☎212-352-2600). Open M-Th 8am-8pm, F 8am-7pm, Sa 9am-3pm, Su 9am-2pm.

Doctors Walk-in Clinic, 55 E. 34th St., between Park and Madison Ave. (☎212-252-6001, ext. 2). Open M-Th 8am-8pm, F 8am-7pm, Sa 9am-3pm, Su 9am-2pm. Last walk-in 1hr. before closing.

Gay Men's Health Crisis-Geffen Clinic, 119 W. 24th St., between Sixth and Seventh Ave. (☎212-807-6655). Open M-F 11am-8pm.

PHARMACIES

See also **Medical Clinics,** p. 326.

CVS, ☎800-746-7287.

Duane Reade, 224 57th St., at Broadway (☎212-541-9708). Open 24hr. **Also at:** 2465 Broadway, at 91st St. (☎212-799-3172); 1279 Third Ave., at 74th St. (☎212-

744-2668); 378 Sixth Ave., at Waverly Pl. (☎212-674-5357).

Rite-Aid, ☎800-748-3243.

POSTAL SERVICES

US Postal Service Customer Service Assistance Center, ☎212-967-8585 (M-F 8:30am-6pm), ☎800-725-2161 (24hr.).

General Post Office, 421 Eighth Ave., at W. 32nd St. (☎212-330-3002; www.usps.com), occupying the block. Use website to locate other post offices. Open daily 24hr.

REGISTRY OF MOTOR VEHICLES

All RMV branches below can be reached at ☎212-645-5550 or 718-966-6155.

11 Greenwich St., Battery Park Pl. and Morris St. (☎212-645-5550 or 718-966-6155). Open M-F 8:30am-4am. Many other locations in city; most use the same phone numbers, so call for the one nearest you.

SUBWAY

See also **Airport Transport,** p. 323; **Buses,** p. 324; and **Trains,** p. 327.

Bus Info, ☎718-330-3322.

General Info, ☎718-330-1234 in English, ☎718-330-4847 for other languages.

MetroCard Info, ☎800-638-7622 or 212-638-7622.

Reduced Fare Info, ☎718-243-4999, TDD ☎718-596-8273.

TAXIS

All City Taxis, ☎718-402-2323.

Taxi Commission, 40 Rector St. (☎212-676-1000; 24hr. 212-692-8294). Open M-F 9am-4:30pm.

Tel Aviv, ☎212-777-7777.

Tri-State, ☎212-777-7171.

TICKET SERVICES

See also **Entertainment Info,** p. 325.

Tele-Charge, ☎212-239-6200 (24hr.), (800-545-2559; www.telecharge.com).

Ticket Central, ☎212-279-4200. Open daily 1-8pm.

Ticketmaster, ☎212-307-4100; www.ticketmaster.com.

TKTS, ☎212-221-0031.

TOURIST INFO AND AID

34th Street Partnership, 250 W. 34th St., Penn Station, on south side of Amtrak Rotunda (☎212-967-3433). Open daily 9:30am-6:30pm.

Manhattan Mall Info Booth, at Sixth Ave. and 33rd St., 1st fl., Herald Sq. (☎212-465-0500). Open M, Th, F 10am-8pm; Tu, W, Sa 10am-7pm, Su 11am-6pm.

New York Convention and Visitors Bureau, 810 Seventh Ave., at 53rd St. (☎212-484-1222). Open M-F 8:30am-6pm, Sa-Su 9am-5pm.

New York State Department of Economic Development, 633 Third Ave., between 40th and 41st St. (☎212-803-2200 or 800-225-5697). Open M-F 9am-5:30pm.

Travelers' Aid of NY & NJ, at JFK Airport, in Terminal 6 (☎718-656-4870). Open daily 9am-8pm.

TRAINS

See also **Metro Transit,** p. 326.

Amtrak, ☎800-872-7245.

Long Island Railroad (LIRR), ☎718-217-5477 or 516-822-5477.

Metro-North Commuter Lines, ☎800-638-7646.

NJ Transit, ☎973-762-5100 or 800-772-2222 in NJ.

PATH, ☎800-234-7284.

WOMEN'S HEALTH

See also **Crisis and Help Lines,** p. 324; **Hospitals,** p. 325; and **Medical Clinics,** p. 326.

Eastern Women's Center, 38 E. 30th St., between Park and Madison Ave. (☎212-686-6066 or 800-346-5111). Exams by appointment only; walk-in pregnancy testing. Facility open Tu-Sa 7:30am-4:30pm; free pregnancy testing Tu-Sa 11am-4pm; switchboard open M-Sa 8am-5pm, Su 9am-4pm.

Planned Parenthood, Margaret Sanger Center, 26 Bleecker St., at Mott St. (☎212-965-7000). **Also at:** 44 Court St., Brooklyn and 349 E. 149th St., at Cortland Ave., the Bronx.

Women's Health Line, New York City Department of Health (☎212-230-1111). Open M-F 9am-9pm, Sa 8am-6pm.

Index

@SQC 178
101 Club 220
12th Street Grill 186
1811 Commissioner's Plan 42
24hr. food 168
303 Gallery 144
535 W. 22nd St. 144
57th St. 85
66 Water Street Bar 205
69th Regiment Armory 71
6th Street and Ave. B Garden 67
75½ Bedford Street 63
92nd Street Y 25
  entertainment venue 227

A

A Salt and Battery 165
AAA (American Automobile Association) 323
AAMCAR Rent-a-Car 323
ABC No Rio 227
abortion
  National Abortion Federation 324
  Planned Parenthood 327
Absolutely 4th 199
Abyssinian Baptist Church 99
accommodations 255
  by neighborhood 258
  by price 258
  home exchange and rental 276
  Internet resources 255
  long-term 274
Acquavella 145
Actors Playhouse 225
Adam Clayton Powell Jr. Blvd. (Seventh Ave.) 99
adapters 299
Adele 318
Adorned 246
Africa Rising sculpture 54
African Burial Ground 54
African food 150
AIDS
  help lines 324
  hotline 324
  information 324
airlines 323
airplane travel
  fares 300
  Internet resources 301
  standby 301
airport transport 27, 323
airports 323
AirTrain 28
Aji Ichiban (Munchies Paradise) 156
Alamo 66
alcohol 37
  abuse 324
  alcohol and substance abuse hotline 324
Algonquin Hotel 42, 78
Alice Austen House Museum and Garden 133
Alice Tully Hall 95, 216
  Chamber Music Society 216
  Great Performers Series 217
  Mostly Mozart 217
Alice Underground 243
All Around the Town 258
All City Taxis 327
Allan and Suzi 251
Alliance for Downtown New York 324
Alliance Française 228
Alma 185
Alphabet City 14
Alt.Coffee 168
alternatives to tourism 307, 309
Alvin Ailey Dance Company 211
Amagansett 283
Ambrose 55
America Today 145
American Academy of Arts and Letters 135
American Academy of Dramatic Arts 72
American Airlines 323
American Automobile Association (AAA) 323
American Ballet Theatre 212
American Bible Society, gallery 94
American Craft Museum 134
American Express 297
  NY branches 325
  wiring money 35
American Family Immigration History Center 49
American food
  new 150
  standard 150
American Museum of Natural History 130
American Museum of the Moving Image 113, 134, 214
  Queens Artlink 147
American Negro Theater 99
American Numismatic Society 135
American Spirits 203
Americana Inn 266
Americas Society 229
Amir's Falafel 178
Amsterdam Inn 269
Amtrak 303, 327
Ancient Arabic Order of the Nobles of the Mystic

Shrine 86
Andy's Chee-pee's 244
Angelika Film Center 214
Ansonia Hotel 96
Anthology Film Archives 214
Anyway Cafe 195
apartments 275
Apollo Theater 219
Applause Theater and Cinema Books 252
Apthorp Apartments 96
Aquatic Creations 146
architects
Bacon, Henry 69
Gilbert, Cass 43, 50, 53, 72
Hardenbergh, Henry 86, 95
Hunt, Richard Howland 92
Le Corbusier 101
Libeskind, Daniel 45
McKim, Charles 72
Mies Van der Rohe, Ludwig 44
Post, George 51
Roebling, John Augustus 104
Van Alen, William 84
van der Rohe, Ludwig Mies 82
White, Stanford 72, 92
Argosy Bookstore 251
Arka Lounge 204
Arlene Grocery and Butcher Bar 222
Armstrong, Louis 113
Around the Clock 168
Art and Antique Market, Bronx 119
art, modern
Guggenheim Museum 131
MoMA 130
Whitney Museum of American Art 133
Arthur Ashe Stadium 115
Arthur Avenue Cafe 190
Arthur's Tavern 219
artists
Barney, Matthew 84
Basquiat, Jean-Michel 59
Chagall, Marc 84
Chagall,Marc 137
Duchamp, Marcel 71
Haring, Keith 59
Lynds, Clyde 54
Matisse, Henri 71, 130, 132
O'Keeffe, Georgia 133
O'Keeffe,Georgia 104
Picasso, Pablo 61, 71, 130, 146
Picasso,Pablo 132
Rockwell, Norman 84
Rosenthal, Bernard 66
Sert, Jose Maria 79
Stella, Frank 137
Stella, Joseph 104
Vuchetich, Evgeniy. 84
Artists Space 143
Artland 205
Artlink. See Queens Artlink.
arts and entertainment
ticket services 327
Ticketmaster 327
arts clubs 92
arts. See entertainment.
Arturo's Pizza 162
Asia Society 134
films 229
Asian food 150
Asian fusion food 150
Asser Levy Pool 236
Astor Place 66
Astor Place Hairstylist 246
Astor Place Theater 225
Astoria 21
food 187
sights 112
Atlantic Avenue Beach 284
Atlantic City, NJ 289
Atlas 80
ATM cards 298
Auden, W. H. 105
Audience Extras 213
Audubon Terrace Museum Group 135
Automatic Slims 199
Avery Fisher Hall 95, 216
Great Performers Series 217
Mostly Mozart 217
National Chorale 217
New York Philharmonic 217
Avis 323
Avon Spa 81

B

B&Bs 257
Akwaaba Mansion 273
Bed & Breakfast on the Park 273
Bed and Breakfast of New York 258
Colonial House Inn 265
Crystal's Castle Bed & Breakfast 272
New York Bed and Breakfast 272
Bagel Buffet 169
bagels 164
bakeries 150
Bank Leumi 325
Bar 6 199
Bar 89 198
Bar d'O 200
Barking Dog Luncheonette 175
Barnes, Djuna 42
Barney, Matthew 84
Barneys New York 251
Barracuda 202
Barrio, El 20
bars 193
bars, famous
75½ Bedford Street 63
Chumley's 63
Stonewall Inn 63
Bartow-Pell Mansion Museum 123
baseball
Brooklyn Cyclones 112
historic sights 70
Keyspan Park 112
stadiums 231
tickets 232
Yankee Stadium 118
basketball 232
playing 233
Battery Park 50
Battery Park City
apartments 52
entertainment 230
Battle Monument 288
Bay Ridge 11
Bbar (Bowery Bar) 195
beaches 233
Haven's Beach 284
Jones Beach 282
Southampton 283
Beacon Theater 228
Beacon's Closet 252
Bear Mountain Inn 289
Bear Mountain State Park 289

Beat movement 59
Beat Street 253
Beauty and the Beast 224
Beauty Bar 195
Beaver Murals 66
Becco 174
Bed & Breakfast on the Park 273
bed and breakfasts. See B&Bs.
Bedford Park 121
Bedford-Stuyvesant 108
beer, local 103
Bellevue Hospital Center 325
Belmont 6, 120
  food 189
  food markets 190
  sights 120
Belt Pkwy. 6
Benchley, Robert 42
Bendix Diner 164
Bensonhurst 6, 11
Bentley Manhattan 250
Bergdorff-Goodman 250
Bernstein, Leonard
  City Center Theater 86
  Dakota Apartments 95
  grave 110
  Hell's Kitchen and *West Side Story* 95
Beso 186
Best Western President Hotel 267
Beth Israel Medical Center 325
Bethpage, golf 235
betterburger 169
bicycles
  routes 234
  stores and rental 234
Big Apple Circus 95
Big Apple Hostel 267
Big Apple Ranch 202
Big Cup 171
Big Easy 203
Big Nick's Burger Joint and Pizza Joint 176
Big Onion Walking Tours 24
Bike New York 234
Biography Bookstore 244
Bird 252
Birdland 219
birth control
  Planned Parenthood 327
Bisexual, Gay, and Lesbian
  travel information 325
Bitter End 222
Blades in-line skate store 236
Bleu Evolution 179
Bliss 181
Bloomberg, Michael 45, 54, 93
Bloomingdale School of Music 218
Bloomingdale's 251
Blu Lounge 205
Blue 9 Burger 165
Blue Moon Mexican Cafe 169
Blue Note 219
Bluestockings 242
boating tours 25
bOb Bar 194
Boiler Room 197
Bo-Ky 154
Books of Wonder 248
Borough Hall 107
Borough Park 6, 11
Botanic Garden 6
Bottom Line 222
Bowery Ballroom 222
Bowery Bar (Bbar) 195
bowling 234
Bowling Green 50
Bowlmor Lanes 234
Bowne & Co. 55
Bowne House 116
Bradford, William 42
Brasserie Centrale 169
Brighton Beach 11
  food 186
  sights 111
Brighton Beach Memoirs 111
Brisas del Caribe 160
Broadway Inn 267
Broadway shows 224
Bronx 6
  beaches 233
  entertainment 214, 229
  food 189
  food markets 190
  galleries 147
  museums 128
  nightlife 207
  sights 118–123
Bronx Museum of the Arts 135
Bronx Park 6
  sights 119
Bronx Reference Center 326
Bronx River Pkwy. 6
Bronx Zoo 6, 119
Bronx-Lebanon Hospital Center 325
Brooklyn 20, 42
  beaches 233
  Civic Center 105
  entertainment 213, 223, 228, 230
  food 181–186
  galleries 146
  museums 128
  nightlife 205–207
  shopping 252
  sights 102–112
Brooklyn Academy of Music 228
  BAMRose Cinemas 215
Brooklyn Ale House 205
Brooklyn Attitude 25
Brooklyn Botanic Garden 107
Brooklyn Brewery 103
Brooklyn Bridge 54, 104
Brooklyn Bridge Anchorage 146
Brooklyn Center for Performing Arts 228
Brooklyn Children's Museum 135
Brooklyn Civic Center 105
Brooklyn Cyclones 112
Brooklyn Eagle 104
Brooklyn Heights 10
  food 184
  food markets 184
Brooklyn Historical Society 106
Brooklyn Hospital Center

325
Brooklyn Ice Cream Factory 185
Brooklyn Moon 184
Brooklyn Museum of Art 131
Brooklyn Public Library 108, 326
Brooklyn-Queens Expwy. (BQE) 6
Brother Jimmy's BBQ 203, 204
Bryant Park 35, 78
 film festival 216
 Summergarden concert 218
Bubby's 160
Burger Heaven 175
Burger King 35
Burr, Aaron
 Erasmus Hall Academy 110
Burritoville 176
Bus 25
bus tours 25
buses 324
 See also Metro Transit
buses, NYC 30
Butta' Cup Lounge 205

C

Cabaret 224
Cadet Chapel 289
Cafe Colonial Restaurant 157
Cafe De L'Université 168
Cafe Gitane 158
Cafe Habana 158
Cafe La Fortuna 178
Cafe Lalo 178
Cafe Mona Lisa 163
Cafe Mozart 178
Cafe Noir 198
Cafe Wha? 222
cafes 151
 East Village 168
 Gramercy 173
 Greenwich Village 163
 Little Italy 157
 Murray Hill 173
 SoHo 161
 Union Square 173
 Upper West Side 178
 Williamsburg 183
Caffe Dante 163
Caffe Palermo 157
Caffe Pane e Cioccolato 161
Caffe Raffaella 163
Cage, basketball 233
Caliente Cab Co. 162
Callen-Lorde Community Health Center 305, 326
cameras 299
camping 285
Campos Plaza 67
Candle Cafe 175
car rental 31, 323
car services. See AAA.
Caravan 184
CareTix 213
Cargo Cafe 191
Caribbean food 151
Carlton Arms Hotel 261
Carnegie Hall 85
 classical music 217
 Rose Museum 85
Carroll Gardens 10
 sights 109
cars, NYC 31
Cartier 81
casinos 290, 292
Castle Clinton 50
Cathedral of St. John the Divine 96, 228
Catskills 289
CB's Gallery 222
CBGB/OMFUG (CBGB's) 222
CD & Cassette Annex 246
cell phones 34
Center for the Holographic Arts. See Holocenter.
CenterCharge 216
Central European food 151
Central Park
 Alice in Wonderland 90
 Andersen, Hans Christian 90
 Belvedere Castle 90
 Burnett Fountain 91
 Carousel 87
 Charles A. Dana Discovery Center 91
 Chess and Checkers House 87
 Children's District 87
 Claremont Stables 235
 climbing 234
 Conservatory Garden 91
 Conservatory Water
 Dairy 87
 Dancing on the Plaza 214
 Delacorte Theater 90
 entertainment 217, 221, 225, 230, 231, 236
 Great Lawn 90
 Harlem Meer Performance Festival 91
 horseback riding 235
 ice-skating 236
 Imagine mosaic
 jogging 236
 Lake 87
 Loeb Boathouse 236
 Mall 87
 Naumberg Bandshell 87
 Points North 90
 Ramble 90
 Reservoir 90
 rowboats 236
 Rumsey Playfield 87
 Shakespeare Garden 90
 Shakespeare in the Park 231
 Sheep Meadow 87
 sights 86–91
 Strawberry Fields 87
 Summerstage 221, 230
 Swedish Cottage Marionette Theater 90
 Tavern on the Green 87
 Tisch Children's Zoo 87
 Turtle Pond 90
 Wildlife Center 87
 Wollman Memorial Rink 87, 236
 Zoo 87
Central Park Hostel 271
Centrofly 208
Century 21 22, 241, 242
Chagall, Marc 137
Chamber Music Society 216
changing money 297
Chango 172
Channel Gardens 79
Chao Zhau Restaurant 188
Charles A. Dana Discovery Center 91
 Dancing on the Plaza 214
Charlie Pineapple Theater 225
Chase 204

Chat 'n' Chew 171
Chatham Square 56
Cheap Jack's Vintage Clothing 244
cheap tickets 212
Chef & Co. 170
Chelsea
entertainment 213, 227, 229, 236
food 169–171
food markets 171
galleries 144
gay bars 202
gay restaurants 171
hostels 264
hotels 263
nightlife 201–203
shopping 248
sights 72–74
Chelsea Center Hostel 264
Chelsea Inn 263
Chelsea International Hostel 264
Chelsea Market 73
Chelsea Piers 74
ice-skating 236
Chelsea Pines Inn 265
Chelsea Savoy Hotel 263
Chelsea Star Hotel 264
Chelsea Wine Vault 74
Chelseas Center Hostel (East Village branch) 261
Cheque Point USA 325
Cherry Grove 286
Beach Hotel 287
Cherry Lane Theater 42, 63, 225
Chez Brigitte 162
Chi Chiz 200
Chicago 224
Children's Historic House Museum, Prospect Park 107
Children's Museum of Manhattan 135
China Institute 229
Chinatown 12
food 154–156
food markets 156
ice cream 156
shopping 241
sights 56–57
Chinatown bus 301
Chinatown Ice Cream Factory 156
Chinese food 151
Chinese Ivory Carving, UN Building 84
Chip Shop and Curry Shop 186
Christie's 145
Christie's Bakery 185
Christmas tree lighting
Rockefeller Center 79
Christy, Liz 66
Chrysler Building 43, 84
Church of Our Lady of Mt. Carmel 121
Church of St. Jean Baptiste 92
Church of St. Luke's in the Fields 63
Church of St. Paul and St. Andrew 305
Church of the Holy Apostle 307
Church of the Holy Trinity 93
Church of the Transfiguration 72
churches
Abyssinian Baptist church 99
Cathedral of St. John the Divine 96, 228
Church of Our Lady of Mt. Carmel 121
Church of St. Jean Baptiste 92
Church of St.Luke's in the Fields 63
Church of the Holy Trinity 93
Church of the Transfiguration 72
First Presbyterian Church 117
Grace Church, in Queens 117
Plymouth Church of Pilgrims 105
Riverside Church 97
Russian Orthodox Cathedral of the Transfiguration 103
Saint Peter's Lutheran Church 220
St. Ann's and the Holy Trinity Episcopal Church 106
St. Anthony and Alphonsius Church 103
St. Bartholomew's Church 82
St. George Ukrainian Catholic Church 68
St. George's Episcopal Church 69
St. Mark's Church in-the-Bowery 66, 230
St. Nicholas Russian Orthodox Cathedral 93
St. Patrick's Cathedral 80
St. Paul's Chapel 52
St. Peter's Episcopal Church 73
Tabernacle of Prayer 117
Trinity Church 51
Cinema Classics 215
Cinema Village 215
Circa Tabac 198
Circle 25
Circle Line Tours 25
Cirrus 298
Citicorp Building 113
Citigroup Center 83
Citrus Bar and Grill 204
City Center 213
City Center Theater 85
City College 99
City Grill 176
City Hall 53
City Hall Park 53
City Island 6, 123
City of New York Parks and Recreation Department
hotline 233
CityCrepe 176
Civic Center 12
food 153
shopping 241
sights 52
Civil War 42
Claremont Stables 235
classical music
festivals 217
other venues 227
venues other than Lincoln Center 217
Clegg's Hotel 286
Clemens, Samuel Langhorne. See Twain, Mark.
climbing 234
Cloisters 132
Cloud Scenes ceiling, New York Public Library 145
Clovis Press 253

clubs, dance 208
clubs, social 70
Grolier Club 92
Knickerbocker Club 91
Lotos Club 92
Metropolitan Club 91
Union Club 91
University Club 81
CMJ Music Marathon 221
Cobble Hill 10
sights 109
Coca-Cola Concert Series 222
Cock, The 197
CocoRoco 186
Coe Hall 282
Coffee Shop Bar 173
Colden Center for the Performing Arts 228
Collective Unconscious 228
Colonial House Inn 265
Colonnade Row 67
Columbia University 42, 97, 271, 316
Columbus Circle 94
comedy clubs 226
Comic Strip Live 226
community resources
centers 324
women's centers 324
Complete Traveller Bookstore 249
Computer World 241
Concerts in the Park 217
Condomania 244
Coney Island 11, 111
Circus Sideshow 111
food 186
sights 111
Congregation Anshe Chesed 58
Congregation Beth Simchat Torah 307
Connecticut 292
consulates 32, 295
consulates, in NY 324
Continental 222
Continental Airlines 323
converters 299
converting currency 297
Cooper Square
Peter Cooper's statue 66
Cooper Union Foundation Building 66
Cooper-Hewitt National Design Museum 135, 217
Copeland's 179
Corner Bistro 161
Corona
sights 113
corporate art, Midtown 145
Cosenza's Fish Market 190
Cosmos Bar Cafe 207
Cotton Club 43, 219
Craigslist 320
Crane, Hart 104
Crazy Nanny's 200
Crif Dogs 165
crime
victim services 324
Crime Victim's Hotline 324
crisis lines 324
Cross-Bronx Expwy. (I-95) 6
Crown Building 81
Crystal's Castle Bed & Breakfast 272
Cuban food 152
Cubbyhole 201
Cube, Astor Place 66
Cucina di Pesce 165
cultural institutes 228
cummings, e.e. 42
currency exchange 297, 325
American Express 325
See also banks
Thomas Cook 325
Curry in a Hurry 172
Cushman Row 74
Custom House, Sag Harbor 284
customs 297
CyberCafe 35
Cyclone 23, 111

D

D*O*C*S 326
d.b.a. 195
D'Amelio Terras 144
Daily News 37, 84
building 84
Daily Show 230
Dakota Apartments 95
Dallas BBQ 175
Damascus Bakery 185
Damrosch Park 95
Dana Discovery Center. See Charles A. Dana Discovery Center
dance 211
dance companies 211
dance venues 213
festivals 214
participatory events 214
Dance Theater Workshop 213
Dances for Wave Hill 214
Dancing on the Plaza 214
Dangerfield's 226
Danspace Project 67, 230
Davis, Miles
grave 123
Day-O 162
daytripping 279
DCA Gallery 144
De Colores Community Yard and Garden 66
De Hirsch Residence 269
De La Guarda 212
De Lillo Pastry Shop 190
Dean and Deluca 161
Deitch Projects 143
Delacorte amphitheater 231
Delft 195
delicatessens 151
Delta Airlines 323
Den of Cin 167
Denizen 198
dentists 325
Department of Consumer Affairs 324
Department of Motor Vehicles 327
Detour 219
Dia Center for the Arts 143, 144
Dicapo Opera Company 221

Dick Dock 287
dietary concerns 307
Diff'rent Strokes 127
Digital Club Festival 221
Dimson Theatre. See Vineyard Theater Company's Dimson Theatre.
Diner 182
Dinkins, David 44
Diop Tailoring & Fashions 253
disabled travelers 303
 resources 325
 transportation 304
Disc-o-Rama 244
disposable cameras 299
Dizzy's 185
dog run, Tompkins Square Park 68
Dojo Restaurant 165
Dollar Rent-a-Car 323
Dominick's 189
Domsey's 253
Dong Hae Ru 188
dorms, long-term 275
Doughnut Plant 159
Down Under Manhattan Bridge Overpass. See DUMBO.
Downtown Brooklyn 10
 food 184
 food markets 184
Downtown Music Gallery 246
Doyers Vietnamese Restaurant 154
DragonTown 188
Drama Book Shop 250
Drawing Center 143
Dreiser, Theodore 42
drip cafe 178
driving 31
 speed limit 303
drugs 37
 abuse 324
dry cleaners 325
Duane Reade 326
Duchamp, Marcel 71
DUMBO 10, 105
 sights 104
DuMont Restaurant 182
Duplex 201
Dynasty Supermarket Corp. 156

E

Eagle Warehouse and Storage Co. 104
East Fordham Road shopping area (Fordham Center) 120
East Hampton 283
East Side Anarchists 68
East Village 14
 cafes 168
 entertainment 214, 215, 219, 222, 225, 226
 food 164–169
 food markets 168
 food, 24hr. 168
 gay bars 197
 hotels 259
 museums 128
 nightlife 195–197
 sights 65–68
Eastern European food 151
Eastern Women's Center 327
Easy Internet Cafe 35
Ebbets Field 110
Economy Candy 159
Ed 44
Edgar Allan Poe Cottage 121
EJ's Luncheonette 175
El Barrio 98
El Cafetal 188
El Museo del Barrio 138
El Sol Brillante 67
El Sombrero 158
El Teddy's 160
Elbow Room 223
Elderhostel 303
Eldridge St. Synagogue 58
Elias Corner 187
Ellington, Duke
 grave 123
Ellis Island 49
Elmhurst 21
 food 187
 sights 113
elmo 170
Elvie's Turo-Turo 165
embassies 32, 295
emergency 325
 crisis lines 324
 dentists 325
 help lines 324
 hospitals 325
 medical clinics 326
 pharmacies 326
 Planned Parenthood 327
emergency medical services 298
Emilia's 190
Empire Diner 170
Empire State Building 43, 74
Encore 251
Enid's 205
Enterprise Car Rental 323
entertainment 211
 Bronx 214, 229
 Brooklyn 213, 223, 228, 230
 Central Park 217, 221, 225, 230, 231, 236
 Chelsea 213, 227, 229, 236
 East Village 214, 215, 219, 222, 225, 226
 Gramercy 215
 Greenwich Village 222, 223
 Harlem 219, 220
 Lower East Side 222, 223, 227, 228
 Midtown 213, 215, 216, 217, 218, 219, 220, 223, 229, 230, 231, 235
 Queens 213, 214, 216, 228, 231
 resources 211
 SoHo 226
 Times Square 212
 Union Square 212, 223, 226
 Upper East Side 212, 217, 221, 226, 227
 Upper West Side 211, 214, 215, 216, 217, 220, 221, 227, 228, 229, 230, 231
 Village 214
 West Village 215, 219, 220, 225
 Williamsburg 225
entertainment info 325
Equitable Building 145
Erasmus Hall Academy

110
Esperanto Cafe, 162
Ess-a-Bagel 164, 174
etiquette 38
Eugene 208
Europe-USA Cellular Phone Rentals 34
Eva's 162
Evelyn Lounge 204
Everett, T. H., Alpine House 122
EWR. See Newark Liberty International Airport.
Excellent Dumpling House 154
exchange rates 297
ExtraVertical Climbing Center 234

F

F & B 171
F.A.O. Schwarz 250
Faan 185
FAB208 248
Fair Harbor 286
Falun Xiulian Dafa practice 56
Fanelli's Cafe 198
Fashion Institute of Technology 76
Federal Hall National Memorial 51
Federal Office Building 54
Federal Reserve Bank of New York 52
female travelers 304
Ferber, Edna 42
Fez 219
Fieldston School 121
Fifth Avenue 77
Filipino food 150
film 214, 299
  festivals 216
Film Forum 215
Filter 14 208
Financial District 11
  food 153
  museums 128
  shopping 241
  sights 49
financial security 36
Find Outlet 242
Fire Island 285
  Ocean Beach 286
Fire Island Lighthouse Visitor Center 286
Fire Island National Seashore 286
Fire Island Pines 286
Fire Island Pines. See Pines.
Firefighter's Prayer 77
First Presbyterian Church 117
First Shearith Israel Graveyard 56
Fitzgerald, Ella
  home 116
Fitzgerald, F. Scott 86
Flatbush
  orientation 11
  sights 109
Flatiron Building 43, 71
Flatiron District
  shopping 248
Flor's Kitchen 166
Flower District 77
fluke-fishing 285
Flushing 21
  food 187
  sights 116
Flushing Council of Culture and the Arts 116
Flushing Grand Hotel 273
Flushing Meadows-Corona Park 21, 114
  Queens Theatre in the Park 231
  tennis 233
Flushing Noodle 187
Flushing Town Hall 116
food
  24hr. establishments 168
  bagels 164
  Bronx 189
  Brooklyn 181–186
  Chelsea 169–171
  Chinatown 154–156
  Civic Center 153
  classified by cuisine 150
  East Village 164–169
  Financial District 153
  Gramercy 171
  Greenwich Village 161–164
  halal 307
  Harlem 179–180
  Herald Square 169–171
  kosher 307
  Little Italy 156
  Lower East Side 158–160
  Midtown 173–175
  Morningside Heights 178
  Murray Hill 171
  NoLITa 157
  Park Slope 185
  Queens 187–189
  SoHo 160
  Staten Island 191
  TriBeCa 160
  Union Square 171
  Upper East Side 175–176
  Upper West Side 176–178
  vegetarians 307
  Washington Heights 179–180
  Williamsburg 181–183
Food Bar 171
food markets
  Belmont 190
  Bronx 190
  Brooklyn Heights 184
  Chelsea 171
  Chinatown 156
  Downtown Brooklyn 184
  East Village 168
  Fort Greene 184
  Harlem 180
  Herald Square 171
  Little Italy 157
  Lower East Side 159
  Midtown 174
  Morningside Heights 179
  SoHo 161
  Upper East Side 176
  Upper West Side 178
football 232
Forbes Magazine Galleries 134
Forbidden Planet 244
Ford, Gerald 43
Fordham 6
  sights 120
Fordham University 120
Forest Hills 21
Forest Park 21, 114
  Dixie Dew Stables 235
  golf 235
  horseback riding 235
Fort Clinton 288
Fort Greene 10
  food 184

food markets 184
Fort Putnam 288
Fort Sumter 42
Fort Tryon Park 102
Fountain Cafe 184
Foxwoods 292
Frank 164
Franklin D. Roosevelt Boardwalk 233
Frederick Douglass Blvd. (Eighth Ave.) 99
French food 151
French Roast Cafe 168
Fresco by Scotto, on the go 174
Frick Collection 132
classical music 217
Fried Dumpling 154
friendliness etiquette 39
Friendly's Gourmet Pizzeria 153
Friends Meeting House 69
Fuller Building 71
Fulton Ferry 10, 104
Fulton Fish Market 55
Fulton Landing
sights 104
Fulton Mall 253
Fun 194
funk 221

G

g 202
Gabriela's 177
Galapagos 206
Galaxy Global Eatery 173
Galaxy Pastry Shop 189
galleries 142
Bronx 147
Brooklyn 146
Chelsea 144
Midtown 145
Queens 147
SoHo 143
Upper East Side 145
gardens
6th Street and Ave. B Garden 67
Brooklyn Botanic Garden 107
Campos Plaza 67
De Colores Community Yard and Garden 66
El Sol Brillante 67
Gilbert's Sculpture Garden 67
Liz Christy Bowery-Houston Garden 66
Miracle Garden 67
Planting Fields Arboretum 280
Garment District 14, 76
Gavin Brown's Enterprise 144
Gay and Lesbian Switchboard 305
gay bars
Chelsea 202
East Village 197
Greenwich Village 200
Upper West Side 204
Gay Men's Health Crisis 287
Gay Men's Health Crisis (GMHC) 305
gay resources
health and support services 305
gay restaurants 151
Chelsea 171
Greenwich Village 163
gay services
help line 324
gay travelers 303, 325
Gayellow Pages 305
Geffen Center 305
General Delivery 33
General Electric Building 79
General Grant National Memorial 97
General Post Office 76
General Theological Seminary 73
Generation Records 244
George Washington Bridge 101, 303
Gershwin Hotel 261
Giants Stadium
football 232
soccer 233
Gilbert, Cass 43, 50, 53, 72
Gilbert's Sculpture Garden 67
Gillespie, Dizzy
home 116
Giovanni's 190
Girdle Factory 253
Girlprops.com 243
Giuliani, Rudolph 44, 131
Glyndor House 122
GMHC. See Gay Men's Health Crisis.
Go 209
GO25 card. See International Youth Travel Card (IYTC)
Godfather, The 134
See Seton, Eliah.
Goethe-Institut 229
Gold, Joyce. Tours 24
golf 235
Good Enough to Eat 177
Gosman's Clam Bar 285
Gotham Book Mart 250
Gotham Comedy Club 227
Gotham, origin 42
Grace Church, in Queens 117
Grace's Marketplace 176
Gracie Mansion 93
Graffiti Wall of Fame 98
Gramercy 14
cafes 173
entertainment 215
food 171
hotels 261
Gramercy Park 70
Gramercy Theatre
Museum of Modern Art Film and Media 215
Grand Army Plaza 86
Grand Central Terminal 81
Dining Concourse 82, 174
Grant's Tomb 97
gratuity. See tipping.
graveyards
First Shearith Israel Graveyard 56
Moravian Cemetery 124
New York Marble Cemeteries 67
Pelham Cemetery 123
Gray 25
Gray Line Sight-Seeing 25
Gray Parrot Cafe 183

Gray's Papaya 162, 177
Great Performers Series 217
Great Wall Market 189
Greeley, Horace. Statue 53
Green Guerrillas 66
Green Kitchen 169
Greenpoint 10
Greenpoint Coffee House 183
Greenwich Village
- cafes 163
- entertainment 222, 223
- food 161–164
- food, 24hr. 168
- gay bars 200
- gay restaurants 163
- hotels 258
- museums 128
- nightlife 199–201
- shopping 244
- sights 59–63

Greenwood Cemetery 10
Grey Dog 163
Greyhound 301, 304, 324
Grilled Cheese 158
Grimadi's 184
Grimaldi's 22
Grolier Club 92
Ground Zero. See World Trade Center Site.
Gryphon Record Shop 252
Guggenheim Bandshell 95
Guggenheim Museum 131

H

H&H Bagels 164
H&M 249
H.S.F. Restaurant 155
Hacker Strand Art Books 250
Halcyon 206
Hall of Fame for Great Americans 120
Hamilton Grange 100
Hamilton Heights 100
Hamilton, Alexander 100
- Erasmus Hall Academy 110
- grave 51
- Hamilton Grange 100
- Knickerbocker Club 92

Hammacher Schlemmer 250
Hampton Jitney 280
Hamptons 282
- Amagansett 283
- East Hampton 283
- Hither Hills State Park 285
- Sag Harbor 284
- Southampton 283

Hardenbergh, Henry 86, 95
Harlem
- entertainment 219, 220
- food 179–180
- food markets 180
- orientation 20
- shopping 252
- sights 98–100

Harlem Meer Performance Festival 91
Harlem Renaissance 42, 43
- Striver's Row 100
- Sugar Hill 100

Harlem Spiritual tours 25
Hassidim 11
Haughwout Building 59
Havana Central 172
Haven's Beach 284
Hawthorne, Nathaniel 97
Hayden Planetarium 131
health 298
- See also medical services.

Heart of Brooklyn Trolley 25
Hell 199
Hell's Kitchen
- museums 128

Hello, Beautiful 253
help lines 324
Henderson Place Historic District 93
Henrietta Hudson 201
Henry's 177
Herald Square 14
- food 169–171
- food markets 171
- hotels 265
- sights 74–77

Herald Square Hotel 265
Hertz Car Rental 324
High 5 Tickets to the Arts 213
High Tea, Fire Island 287
Hirschl and Adler Galleries 145
Hispanic Society of America 135
Hispanola 179
Historic Richmond Town 124
history, New York 41
Hit Show Club 212
Hither Hills State Park 285
hockey 232
Holland Tunnel 303
Holocenter (Center for the Holographic Arts) 147
Homestay New York 257
Hong Kong Egg Cake Co. 156
Hop Kee 155
Horace Mann School 121
horseback riding 235
horseracing 232
hospitals 325
Hostelling International-American Youth Hostels (HI-AYH) 257
hostels 257
- Big Apple Hostel 267
- Central Park Hostel 271
- Chelsea Center Hostel 264
- Chelsea International Hostel 264
- Chelseas Center Hostel (East Village branch) 261
- International Student Center 271
- International Student Hospice 263
- Jazz on the Park 271
- long-term 277
- New York International HI-AYH Hostel 271
- Sugar Hill International House 273
- Uptown Hostel 273

Hotel 17 261
Hotel Belleclaire 269
Hotel Chelsea 73, 263
Hotel Grand Union 261
Hotel Newton 269
Hotel Olcott 269
Hotel Pickwick Arms 266
Hotel Stanford 265
Hotel Wolcott 265

hotels 258
Chelsea 263
East Village 259
Gramercy 261
Greenwich Village 258
Herald Square 265
Little Italy 258
Midtown 265
Murray Hill 261
Theater District 267
Times Square 267
Union Square 261
Upper East Side 269
Houghton Gallery 66
Hourglass Tavern 174
House of Trance 246
Hudson Hotel 267
Hudson River Festival 221
Hudson Valley
Sleepy Hollow 287
Tarrytown 287
Hughes, Langston 42, 98
Hunt, Richard Howland 92
Hunt, Richard Morris 124

I

I Love New York 43
I-20 144
ice cream
Chinatown 156
Lemon Ice King of Corona 189
NoLIta 158
Ice Palace 287
ice skating 235
identification 296
Idlewild 194
Illustration House 143
Indian Field recreation area 122
Industry 196
Inka Travel and Internet Cafe 35
insurance 299
Interfaith Medical Center 325
International Auto Show 77
International Building 80
International Center of Photography 136
International Exhibition of Modern Art, 1913 71
International Student Center 271
International Student Hospice 263
International Student Identity Card (ISIC) 296
International Teacher Identity Card (ITIC) 297
International Youth Travel Card (IYTC) 297
Internet access 35, 326
internships 319
Intrepid Sea-Air-Space Museum 136
Irving Plaza 223
Irving, Washington 42, 288
Isamu Nogochi Museum
Queens Artlink 147
Isamu Noguchi Garden Museum 136
Island Burgers and Shakes 173
It's a Mod, Mod World 246
It's a Wrap 177
Italian Cultural Institute 229
Italian food 151
ITIC card 297
itineraries 22
Ivy's Cafe 177
IYTC Card. See International Youth Travel Card (IYTC)
Izzy Bar 196

J

J & R Music World/ Computer World 241
Jackie Robinson Park 98
Jackson Diner 187
Jackson Heights 21
food 187
Jackson Hole 175
Jacob K. Javits Convention Center 77
Jacob Riis Park 118
Jacobi Medical Center 326
Jacques Marchais Museum of Tibetan Art 136
Jacques Torres Chocolate 185
Jai-Ya 187
Jamaica
food 187
Jamaica Bay Wildlife Refuge 117
Jamaica Center for Arts 147
Jamaica Hospital Medical Center 326
Jamaican food 151
James A. Farley Building 76
Jammyland 246
Japan Society 137
Japanese food 152
Japanese Peace Bell, UN Building 84
Jay, John
Erasmus Hall Academy 110
jazz 218
clubs 219
other venues 220
summer festivals 220
Jazz at Lincoln Center 220
Jazz on the Park 271
JBJ Discount Pet Shop 243
Jefferson Market Library 64
Jekyll and Hyde 199
Jerry's 160
Jesse's Place 180
Jets, football team 232
Jewish Museum 137
Jews
kosher 307
JFK Airport 28, 323
Jimmy's Bronx Cafe 208
Joe's Pizza 158
Joe's Pub 196
Joe's Shanghai
Chinatown 154
Queens 187
jogging. See running.
John F. Kennedy Airport. See JFK Airport
John Jay College of Criminal Justice 77

John Jay Pool 236
John's Pizzeria 161
John's Pizzeria & Restaurant (Queens) 188
Jones Beach 282
Tommy Hilfiger at Jones Beach Theater 282
Joseph Papp Public Theater 225
Josie Robertson Plaza 95
Josie's 177
Joyce Gold's Tours 24
Joyce Theater 213
JRG Fashion Cafe 184
Juilliard School 95, 218, 317
concerts and recitals 218
Jules 166
Jungle Fever 100
Junior's 184
JVC Jazz Festival 220

K

K. Trimming Co. 243
Kang Suh 169
Karma 196
Kate's Corner 166
Katz's Delicatessen 158
Kaufman-Astoria Studios 113
Kava Lounge 199
KCDC 253
Kelley and Ping Asian Grocery and Noodle Sho 161
Keur N'Deye 184
Keyspan Park 112
KGB 196
Kids, Washington Park movie setting 60
Kids' Night on Broadway 213
Kiehl's 246
Kim Neh 188
Kim's Video and Audio 246
Kimlau Square 56
King Manor Museum 117
King Park 117
Kingsbridge 121
Kingsland Homestead 116
Kinko's 326
Kitchen 22 172
Kitchen, The 229
Kitchen/Market 169
Knickerbocker Club 91
Knicks 232
Knitting Factory 229
jazz 221
Koch, Ed 44
Korean food 150
Koronet Pizza 178
Korova Milk Bar 196
kosher travelers 307
kosher food 152
Kossar's Bialys 159
Kum Gang San 169
Kum Gang San (Queens) 188
Kush 194
Kykuit 288

L

L Cafe 182
La Amistad 285
La Bagel Delight 164
La Bella Ferrara 157
La Caridad 180
La Caridad 78 Restaurant 177
La Focacceria 166
La Fonda Boricua 180
La Linea 196
La Marmite 179
La Mela 157
La Nueva Escuelita 202
La Petite Coquette 244
La Taza de Oro 170
Ladies' Mile 248
LaGuardia Airport 28, 300, 323
LaGuardia, Fiorello 43
grave 123
Lakeside Lounge 196
Lamb's 225
Langston Hughes Auditorium 99
Language 242
Larchmont Hotel 258
Las Venus Lounge 20th Century Pop Culture 243
Late Night with Conan O'Brien 230
Late Show with David Letterman 231
Latin American food 152
laundry
dry cleaners 325
Lazarus, Emma 47
Lazybones fluke-fishing cruise 285
Le Pain Quotidien 176
Leather Man 244
Lebewohl, Abe 67
Leffert's Homestead 107
Legend of Sleepy Hollow 288
Lehman Art Gallery 147
Lemon Ice King of Corona 113, 189
length 25
Lennon, John
site of shooting 95
Lennon, John. *Imagine* mosaic 87
Lenox Ave. (Sixth Ave. or Malcolm X Blvd.) 99
Lenox Lounge 219
Leo Castelli 145
lesbian resources
health & support services 305
lesbian services
help line 324
lesbian travelers 303, 325
Liberation Bookstore 252
Liberty Street Bridge 52
Libeskind, Daniel 45
libraries 326
Brooklyn Public Library 108
New York Public Libraries 215
Lich Gate 72
Lighthouse Park 102
Lin Ze Xu, statue 57
Lincoln Center 43, 95, 216
Alice Tully Hall 216
American Ballet Theatre 212

Avery Fisher Hall 95, 216
CenterCharge 216
Chamber Music Society 216
Damrosch Park 95
Great Performers Series 217
Guggenheim Bandshell 95
jazz 220
Josie Robertson Plaza 95
Juilliard School 95, 218
Lincoln Center Festival 230
Lincoln Center Out-of-Doors 230
Metropolitan Opera House 95
Midsummer Night Swing 214
Mitzi E. Newhouse Theater 95
Mostly Mozart 217
National Chorale 217
New York City Ballet 212
New York City Opera 221
New York Philharmonic 217
New York State Theater 95
New York Video Festival 216
Paul Recital Hall 218
Vivian Beaumont Theater 95
Walter E. Reade Theater 95, 215
Lincoln Tunnel 303
Lion King 224
Lips 164
Lit 196
literary figures
Barnes, Djuna 42, 64
Benchley, Robert 42, 78
Cooper, James Fenimore 284
Crane, Hart 104
cummings, e.e. 64
cummings,e.e. 42
Dos Passos, John 63
Dreiser, Theodore 42, 64
Faulkner, William 63
Ferber, Edna 42
Fitzgerald, F. Scott 86
Hawthorne, Nathaniel 97
Hemingway, Ernest 63
Hughes, Langston 42, 98
Irving, Washington 42
James, Henry 59
Melville, Herman 42
Millay, Edna St. Vincent 42
Miller, Arthur 73, 105
Moore, Clement Clarke 73
Nabokov, Vladimir 73
Parker, Diane 61
Parker, Dorothy 42, 78
Parker, Mel 61
Ross, Harold 42, 78
Salinger, J.D. 63
Simon, Neil 111
St. Vincent Millay, Edna 63
Steinbeck, John 63
Thomas, Dylan 73, 200
Twain, Mark 70, 73, 86, 92
Wharton, Edith 97
Whitman, Walt 42
Wollcott, Alexander 42
Woollcott, Alexander 78
Little Church Around the Corner. See Church of the Transfiguration.
Little Italy
cafes 157
food 156
food markets 157
hotels 258
orientation 12
shopping 241
sights 56–57
Little Pie Co. 171
Little Poland 166
Little Red Lighthouse 101
live television, tickets 230
Live with Regis and Kelly 231
Liz Christy Bowery-Houston Garden 66
local life in new york 37
Loeb Boathouse 236
Loki Lounge 206
Lola 201
Lombardi's Coal Oven Pizza 157
Long Island 279
Amagansett 283
Bethpage, golf 235
buses 280
East Hampton 283
Fire Island 285
Hamptons 282
Hither Hills State Park 285
Jones Beach 282
Montauk 282
Oyster Bay 280
Sag Harbor 284
Southampton 283
transportation 279
Long Island City 21
galleries 147
sights 112
Long Island Railroad (LIRR) 303, 327
Lord and Taylor 250
Los Amigos Bar and Restaurant 207
Lot 76 NYC 247
Lotos Club 92
Love Saves the Day 247
Lower 25
Lower East Side 13
entertainment 222, 223, 227, 228
food 158–160
food markets 159
museums 128
nightlife 194
shopping 242
sights 58
Lower East Side Tenement Museum 137
walking tours 25
Lower East Side Visitors Center 58
Lower Manhattan
sights 47–56
Lower Midtown
sights 68
Lucky Cheng's 196
Lucky Strike 198
Lunar Base 146
Lupe's East L.A. Kitchen 161
Lyndhurst 288
Lynne's Riding School 235

M

M. Knoedler & Co., Inc. 145
Macintosh New York Music Festival 221
Macy's 75, 249
4th of July fireworks 76
Tap-A-Mania 76
Thanksgiving Day Parade 75
Madiba Restaurant & Shebeen 184
Madison Avenue 91
Madison Hotel 263
Madison Square Garden 76
music 222
Madison Square Park 70
magazines, NYC 37
Magnolia Bakery 163
Mahayana Buddhist Temple 57
Mahmoun's 162

mail 32
Major Deegan Expwy. (I-87) 6
Major League Soccer 233
Mama Mexico 177
Mama's Food Shop 166
Manganaro's 174
Mangia 174
Manhattan
  neighborhoods 6
  sights 47–102
Manhattan Beach 233
Manhattan Bridge 57
Manhattan College 122
Manhattan Portage 247
Manhattan School of Music 218
Manhattan Theatre Club 225
Manhattan Youth Castle 269
Manna 162
Manna's Too!! 179
Mannes College of Music 218
Marathon, New York City 236
marathon. See New York City Marathon.
Marcus Garvey Park 98
Mark Morris Dance Center 213
markets, food. See food markets.
Martha Graham Center of Contempory Dance 212
Mary Ann's 170
Massawa 179
MasterCard 298
Matisse, Henri 71, 130, 132
Matthew Marks Gallery 144
Mature Traveler, The 303
Max 167
Max Fish 194
Max Protetch 145
Maxilla & Mandible 252
mayors
  Dinkins, David 44
  Giuliani, Rudolph 44, 131
  Koch, Ed 44
McKim, Charles 72
McSorley's Old Ale House 196
Meadowlands, NJ 222
Meat Rack 287
Meat-packing District 65
Medic Alert 299
medical services 298
  clinics 326
  crisis lines 324
  dentists 325
  emergency 325
  help lines 324
  hospitals 325
  pharmacies 326
  Planned Parenthood 327
Melville, Herman 42
MercBar 198
Merchant's House Museum 137
Merchants NY 175
Mercury Lounge 223
Merkin Concert Hall 229
Met Life Building 82
Metro Bicycle Stores 234
Metro Transit
  buses 324
  trains 327
  wheelchair access 304
MetroCard 29
Metro-North Commuter Lines 327
Metropolis 247
Metropolitan Club 91
Metropolitan Communtiy Church of New York 307
Metropolitan Life Insurance Tower 71
Metropolitan Museum of Art 128, 217
Metropolitan Opera Company 221
Mexican food 152
Midland Beach 233
Mid-Manhattan Library 326
Midnight Records 248
Midsummer Night Swing 214
Midtown
  corporate art 145
  entertainment 213, 215, 216, 217, 218, 219, 220, 223, 229, 230, 231, 235
  food 173–175
  food markets 174
  food, 24hr. 169
  galleries 145
  hotels 265
  museums 128
  sights 77–86
  Upper East Side 145
Mies Van der Rohe, Ludwig 44
Milady's 198
Milano Market 179
Millay, Edna St. Vincent 42
Millennium Film Workshop 215
Miller, Arthur 73, 105
Minamoto Kitchen 174
Minar 170
Miracle Garden 67
Mitzi E. Newhouse Theater 95
Miyako 182
Mo's Caribbean Bar and Mexican Grille 204
modern art. See art, modern.
Mohegan Sun 292
Moishe's Bake Shop 168
Molly's 172
MoMA 112, 130
  Queens Artlink 147
money
  currency exchange 325
Montauk 282, 284
  accommodations 285
Montauk Chamber of Commerce 285
Montauk Downs, golf 235
Montauk Point Lighthouse and Museum 285
Montero's Bar & Grill 206
Moore, Clement Clarke 73
Moravian Cemetery 124
Morgan, J.P.
  Pierpont Morgan Library 141
Morningside Heights 20
  food 178
  food markets 179
  sights 96
Morningside Park 97
Morris-Jumel Mansion 101

Moses, Robert 43
- Jones Beach 282
- Lincoln Center 95

Mostly Mozart 217
Motor City Bar 194
Mottsu 158
Mount Sinai Medical Center 326
Mount Vernon Hotel Museum and Garden 138
Moustache 162
movie settings
- *Rosemary's Baby* 96
- *Scent of a Woman* 113
- *West Side Story* 77

MovieFone 325
MTA Long Island Bus 280
Mughlai 177
Munchies Paradise. See Aji Ichiban.
Municipal 25
Municipal Art Society 25
Mural with Blue Brush Stroke 145
Murder Ink/Ivy's 252
Murray Hill
- cafes 173
- food 171
- hotels 261
- sights 72

Murray Hill Inn 261
Murray. 14
Museum at Fashion Institute of Technology 145
Museum for African Art 138
Museum Mile 91
- festival 127

Museum of American Illustration 138
Museum of Chinese in the Americas 138
Museum of Jewish Heritage 139
Museum of Modern Art Film and Media 215
Museum of Modern Art. See MoMA.
Museum of Television and Radio 139
Museum of the City of New York 139
museums
- SoHo 128

music 216
- classical music 216
- other venues 227

music boxes 251
Music in the Anchorage 222
music schools
- concerts 218

Musical Box 197
musicians
- Lennon, John. See Lennon, John.
- Louis Armstrong 116
- Mitchell, Joni 73
- Sugarhill Gang 100

N

Nabokov, Vladimir 73
Naked Lunch Bar and Lounge 198
Nassau Coliseum 222
Nathan's 186
National Abortion Federation 324
National Academy of Design Museum 140
National Arts Club 70
National Cafe 165
National Car Rental 324
National Chorale 217
National Museum and Archive of Lesbian, Gay, Bisexual and Transgender History 140
National Museum of the American Indian 50, 140
National Organization for Women 304
National Tennis Center 115
NBC Tour 78
Negril 170
Nell's 209
New 42
New Jersey
- Atlantic City 289

New Museum of Contemporary Art 140
New Ring Shout sculpture 54
New School 61
New York Airport Service 323
New York Airport Service express bus 28
New York Aquarium 112
New York Bed and Breakfast 272
New York Botanical Garden 119
New York Center for Media Arts 147
New York City Ballet 212
New York City Draft Riots 42
New York City Fire Museum 140
New York City Marathon 236
New York City Opera 221
New York City Police Museum 141
New York Columbia-Presbyterian Medical Center 326
New York Convention and Visitors Bureau 327
New York Harbor 11
New York in Its Infancy sculpture 54
New York in Revolutionary Times sculpture 54
New York Inn 267
New York International HI-AYH Hostel 271
New York Kayak Company 50
New York Liberty 232
New York Life Insurance Building 72
New York Marble Cemeteries 67
New York Mets 23, 112, 115, 231
New York Philharmonic 217
- Concerts in the Park 217

New York Post 37, 77

New York Public Libraries 215
New York Public Library 78, 326
  Cloud Scenes 145
New York Roadrunner's Club 236
New York Skyride 75
New York State Department of Economic Development 327
New York State Department of Motor Vehicles 31
New York State Pavilion 115
  Queens Theatre in the Park 231
New York State Theater 95
New York Stock Exchange 50
New York Theatre Workshop 225, 226
New York Times 37, 85, 211
New York Transit Museum 141
New York Underground Film Festival 215
New York Unearthed 50
New York University 316
  dorms 259
New York University (NYU) 316
New York University Downtown Hospital 326
New York Video Festival 216
New York Yankees 125
New York/New Jersey Metrostars 233
New Yorker 38, 42
Newark International Airport 323
Newark Liberty International Airport 28, 300
Newspaper Row 54
newspapers, NYC 37
Next Wave Festival 216
Niagara 197
nightlife 193
  Bronx 207
  Brooklyn 205–207
  Chelsea 201–203
  East Village 195–197
  Greenwich Village 199–201
  Lower East Side 194
  Queens 207
  SoHo 198
  Union Square 201–203
  Upper East Side 203
  Upper West Side 204
nightlife. See bars and clubs, dance.
NJ Transit 303, 327
NoLIta
  food 157
  ice cream 158
  shopping 241
North by Northwest 86
North Meadow Recreation Center
  climbing 234
Northwest Airlines 323
Nuyorican Poets Cafe 197
NY Computer Cafe 35
NYC ICY 168
NYC/ON STAGE Hotline 325
Nyonya 155
NYU dorms. See New York University

O

O'Keeffe, Georgia 104, 133
Ocean Beach 286
off-Broadway 225
old boys clubs 91
Old Putnam Railroad Track 122
Old Town Bar and Grill 201
Olive Tree Cafe 162
Olmsted, Frederick Law 86, 102
Olympia Airport Express 28, 323
One Times Square 85
Ontological Theater 67, 230
Open 201
opera 221
Orchard Beach and Promenade 233
Oriental Culture Enterprise 242
Original Fresco Tortillas 173
Orpheum 226
Oscar Wilde Gay and Lesbian Bookshop 244
Other Music 247
Oyster Bay 280
  Coe Hall 282
  food 282
  oysters 282
  Planting Fields Arboretum 280
Oyster Bay Fish and Clam Bar 282
Oznot's Dish 181

P.S.1 Contemporary Art Center 142
Pace Gallery 146
packing 299
Pad Thai Noodle Lounge 170
Painting Center 143
Pakistan Tea House 160
Panorama of the City of New York 115
Papaya King 175
Parade Grounds, Van Cortlandt Park 122
Park Avenue
  sights 81
Park Slope 10, 23
  food 185
Parker, Dorothy 42
parks
  Battery Park 50
  Bryant Park 78
  Carl Schurz Park 93
  Central Park 86–91
  Flushing Meadows-Corona Park 114
  Forest Park 114
  Fort Tryon Park 102
  Gramercy Park 70
  Jacob Riis Park 118
  Keyspan Park 112
  Lighthouse Park 102
  Madison Square Park 70

Morningside Park 97
Pelham Bay Park 6, 123
Prospect Park 23, 107
Riverbank State Park 100
Riverside Park 96
Sakura Park 97
Tompkins Square Park 68
Van Cortlandt Park 6, 121
Washington Square Park 60
Parrish Art Museum 283
Parsons Dance Company 212
Parsons Exhibition Center 141
Parsons School of Design 316
Pasquale's Rigoletto 190
Passerby 202
passports 295
Patchin Place 42, 64
PATH trains 303, 327
Patois 185
Paul Recital Hall 218
Paul's Boutique 158
pay phone 34
Peanut Butter & Co. 163
Pearl River 242
Peck and Goodie Skates 236
Pedal Pushers 234
Peking 55
Pelham Bay Park 6, 123
golf 235
Pelham Bay stables 123
Pelham Cemetery 123
Penn Station 76, 279, 303
Pete's Candy Store 206, 207
Pete's Tavern 172
Peter Luger 180
Peter McManus 202
Phantom of the Opera 224
pharmacies 326
Pharmacy 327
Phillipsburg Manor 288
phone calls
abroad from New York 33
local 34
Photography District 144
Physical Graffiti 248
Picasso, Pablo 61, 71, 130, 132, 146
Pickle Guys 159
Pier 17 Pavilion 241
Pierogi 146
Pierpont Morgan Library 141
Pink Pony 159
Pink Tea Cup 163
Pino's La Forchetta 186
Pioneer Hotel 258
Più Bello 188
Pizza Mercato 163
Plain, West Point 289
Planet Thailand 181
Planned Parenthood 327
Planning Your Trip 295
Planting Fields Arboretum 280
jazz festival 282
synoptic garden 282
Players Club 70
Plaza Hotel 86
PLUS 298
Plus Ultra 146
Plymouth Church of Pilgrims 105
Poe's house 121
Poetry Project 67, 230
Point, The 229
Poison Control Center 324
Police Headquarters 57
Polish food 151
Pommes Frites 167
pop 221
Pop International Galleries, Inc. 143
Pop Shop 242
Port Authority 27, 301, 324
Port Authority of NJ and NY 27
Portland Square Hotel 267
Post Office 327
post office, 24hr. 33
postal rate 33
Poste Restante. See General Delivery.
Potion Lounge 204
Precaution 284
prescription drugs 37
Pride Weekend 72
Primary Stages 226
Primorski Restaurant 187
Producers, The 224
Prometheus statue at Rockefeller Center 79
Prospect Park 23, 107
bicycling 234
Carousel 107
Children's Historic House Museum 107
Wildlife Center/Zoo 107
public pools 236
Puerto Rican Constitution Day 98
Pulitzer Fountain 86
punk 221

Q

Q Lounge 202
Queens 20
entertainment 213, 214, 216, 228, 231
food 187–189
galleries 147
museums 128
nightlife 207
Rockaway Beach 233
sights 112–118
Queens Artlink 147
Queens Botanical Garden 116
Queens Bus Map 21
Queens Historical Society 116
Queens Jazz Trail 116
Queens Museum of Art 115
Queens Public Library 326
Queens Theatre in the Park 231
Queens Wildlife Center/Zoo 115

R

Radical Walking Tours 24
radio 38
Radio City Music Hall 80
Rockettes 80
tickets 229

Rain Lounge 207
Rainbow Falafel 173
Ranch 1 171
rape
  crisis center 324
Rawhide 202
Read Cafe and Bookshop 183
Red Hook 10
  sights 109
Red Hot Szechuan 186
Reed, John 42
Reef Restaurant 190
Religious Sex 247
Reminiscence 249
Remote Lounge 195, 197
Renewal sculpture 54
Rent 225
rental car 323
RentCell.com 34
Restaurant Karpaty 181
Restaurant Row 173
restaurants. See food.
Revolution Books 249
Revolutionary War sites
  Fort Clinton, Fort Putnam 288
Rice 157
Richmond County Bank Ballpark 125
Rincon Salvadoreño 188
Rita Ford Music Boxes 251
Rite-Aid 327
River 177
Riverbank State Park 100
Riverdale 6
  sights 121
Riverdale School 121
Riverside Church 97
Riverside Park 96
  bicycling 234
  running 236
Roadrunner's Club, New York 236
rock 221
Rock and Soul 249
Rockaway Beach 117
Rockaway Beach and Boardwalk 233
Rockaways
  sights 117
Rockaways, The 21
rock-climbing. See climbing.
Rockefeller 97
Rockefeller Center 78
  Channel Gardens 79
  Christmas tree lighting 79
  General Electric Building 79
  ice-skating 79, 235
  International Building 80
  NBC Tour 78
  Prometheus statue 79
  Radio City Music Hall 80
  Tour 79
  Tower Plaza 79
Rockefeller Center, underground concourse 80
Rockefeller, John D. Jr.
  Fort Tryon Park 102
  Lincoln Center 95
  Riverside Church 97
  Rockefeller Center 78
Rockefeller, Peggy. Rose Garden 120
Rocky's Italian Restaurant 157
Roebling, John Augustus 104
Roll 'n' Roaster 186
rollerblading. See in-line skating.
Rome ARTS 146
Roosevelt Boardwalk. See Franklin D. Roosevelt Boardwalk.
Roosevelt Island 102
Roosevelt, Theodore
  and International Exhibition of Modern Art, 1913 71
  as police commissioner 42
  birthplace 70
  estate on Sagamore Hill 280
  in National Arts Club 70
  Nobel Peace Prize 280
  police department and crime 42
  Russo-Japanese War 280
  Wave Hill 122
Rosario's Italian Bistro 153
Rose Museum 85
Rose's Turn 201
Roseland Ballroom 223
Rosenthal, Bernard.
  Sculpture 66
Ross, Harold 42
rowboats 236
Roxy 202
Ruben's Empanadas 161
Rue des Crepes 170
Rumsey Playfield
  Summerstage 230
running
  New York City Marathon 236
  New York Roadrunner's Club 236
  routes 236
Rush Hour 159
rush tickets 212
Russian food 151
Russian Orthodox Cathedral of the Transfiguration 103

safety 36
  financial 36
  personal 36
  terrorism 36
Sag Harbor 284
Sag Harbor Chamber of Commerce 284
Sag Harbor Whaling Museum 284
Sagamore Hill 280
Sahadi Importing Company 184
Sahara East 167
Saigon Grill 176
Sailor's Haven 286
Saint Peter's, jazz vespers 220
Sake Bar Decibel 197
Saks Fifth Avenue 251
Sakura Park 97
Sal's Pizzeria 182
Salaam Bombay 160
Saltaire 286
Salvatore Ferragamo 81
Samuel Beckett Theater 226
San Han jin mi 188
Santa Fe Grille 185

Sara Delano Roosevelt Park 56
birds and birdcages 56
Saturday Night Live 44, 79, 231
SBNY 203
Schermerhorn Row 56
Schomburg Center for Research in Black Culture 99, 326
Schroeder Romero 146
Sea 182
seafood 282, 285
Seagram Building 44, 82
Second Avenue Deli 67, 164
Second Coming Records 245
See Hear 247
senior travelers 303
Sentosa 159
Sephora 243
Sert, Jose Maria 79
Service Directory 323
Sex Crimes Report Line 325
Shakespeare and Company 245
Shakespeare in the Park 90, 231
tickets 225
Shanghai Cuisine 155
Shark Bar 204
Shea Stadium 115
Shea Stadum 43
Sheehan's 207
Sheraton LaGuardia East Hotel 274
Ship of Fools 204
shopping
Brooklyn 252
Chelsea 248
Chinatown 241
Civic Center 241
Financial District 241
Flatiron District 248
Greenwich Village 244
Harlem 252
Little Italy 241
Lower East Side 242
NoLIta 241
SoHo 243
Upper East Side 251
Upper West Side 251
Showman's Cafe 220
Shubert Alley 85
Sidestreet Saloon 191
sights
Bronx 118–123
Brooklyn 102–112
Central Park 86–91
Chelsea 72–74
Chinatown 56–57
East Village 65–68
Greenwich Village 59–63
Harlem 98–100
Herald Square 74–77
Little Italy 56–57
Lower East Side 58
Lower Manhattan 47–56
Lower Midtown 68
Manhattan 47–102
Midtown 77–86
Murray Hill 72
Queens 112–118
SoHo 59
Staten Island 123–125
TriBeCa 58
Union Square and Gramercy 68–72
Upper East Side 91–94
Upper West Side 94–96
Washington Heights 100
West Village 63–65
Simon Says 225
Simon, Neil 111
skating. See ice-skating.
Skyline Hotel 267
skyscrapers
Chrysler Building 84
Citicorp Building 113
Citigroup Center 83
Crown Building 81
Daily News Building 84
Empire State Building 74
Flatiron Building 71
Fuller Building 71
Met Life Building 82
Metropolitan Life Insurance Tower 71
Trump Tower 81
Slaughtered Lamb Pub 199
Sleeping Hollow 287
Slipper Room 194
Smoke 220
smoking etiquette 38
Snug Harbor Cultural Center 124
SOBs (Sounds of Brazil) 223
soccer
tickets 233
Socrates Sculpture Park 112, 113
film and music festival 216
Queens Artlink 147
Socrates Sculpture Park Film & Music Festival 216
SoHo
cafes 161
entertainment 226
food 160
food markets 161
galleries 143
museums 128
nightlife 198
shopping 243
sights 59
Soho 13
SoHo Repertory Theatre 226
SoHo Think Tank Ohio Theater 226
Soldiers and Sailors Arch, Prospect Park 107
Something Sweet 168
Sonnabend 145
Sony Plaza 81
Sophie's Restaurant 153
Sotheby's 146
Sounds 246
South Beach 233
South Bronx 6
sights 118
South Street Oyster Bar 282
South Street Seaport
Ambrose 55
Bowne & Co. 55
Fulton Fish Market 55
museum 54
orientation 12
Peking 55
Schermerhorn Row 56
Visitors Center 55
South Street Seaport Museum
jazz festival 221
Southampton 283
Southampton Chamber of Commerce 283
Southampton Historical

Museum 283
Southpaw 223
Soy Luck Club 163
Space Untitled 161
Spanish Harlem 20, 98
Spanish Institute 229
special concerns
dietary concerns 307
Special Diets 307
specific concerns
bisexual, gay, and lesbian travelers 303, 325
disabled travelers 303
senior travelers 303
speed limit 303
Spokes & Strings 253
sports 231
participatory 233
spectator sports 231
sports entertainment. See entertainment.
St. Alp's Teahouse 156
St. Ann's and the Holy Trinity Episcopal Church 106
St. Ann's Warehouse 230
St. Anthony and Alphonsius Church 103
St. Bartholomew's Church 82
St. Dymphna's 167
St. George Library Center 326
St. George Ukrainian Catholic Church 68
St. George's Episcopal Church 69
St. John's Red Storm 232
St. Mark's Bookshop 65, 247
St. Mark's Church in-the-Bowery 66
entertainment 230
St. Mark's Hotel 259
St. Mark's Place 65
St. Nicholas Russian Orthodox Cathedral 93
St. Nick's Pub 220
St. Patrick's Cathedral 80
St. Peter's Episcopal Church 73
STA Travel 300
Stage Deli 169
Staley-Wise 144
Stand Up New York 227
standby flights 301
Staten Island 21
beaches 233
ferry 23, 48
food 191
museums 128
sights 123–125
Staten Island Chamber of Commerce 124
statue
Butterfield, Daniel 97
X, Malcolm 101
Statue of Liberty 47
statues
Alma Mater 97
Andersen, Hans Christian 90
Atlas 80
Bowling Green 50
Central Park 87
Columbus, Christopher 94
Cooper, Peter 66
Firefighter's Prayer 77
Greeley, Horace 54
Let Us Beat Swords into Plowshares 84
Lin Ze Xu 57
Mercury 81
Patience and Fortitude 78
Pomona 86
Robinson, Jackie 98
Seward, William 70
Sherman, William Tecumseh 86
Soldiers and Sailors Arch 107
Statue of Liberty 47
Stuyvesant, Peter 69
Surrogate's Court 54
The Garment Worker 76
statutes
Socrates Sculpture Park 113
Steinway Piano Factory 113
Stella, Frank 137
Stella, Joseph 104
Step Mama's 167
Stephen Talkhouse 284
Stonewall Inn, bar 201
Stonewall Riots 63
Strand Annex 241
Strand Bookstore 245
Striver's Row 100
Studio Museum 142
studying 315
Stuyvesant Square 69
Stuyvesant, Peter 41, 69
grave 66
Suba 159
subway 29
fares 29
history 43
MetroCards 30
safety 30
subway etiquette 38
Suffolk Transit 280
Sugar Hill 100
Sugar Hill International House 273
Sugar Hill Thrift Shop 252
suggested itineraries 22
Suite 16 209
Summergarden concert at Bryant Park 218
Summerstage 230
jazz 221
Sunburst Espresso Bar 173
Sung Tak Buddhist Association 58
Sunken Forest 286
Sunnyside 288
Sunset Park 6
Super 8 Hotel 265
supermarkets. See food markets.
SuperShuttle 28, 323
Surrogate's Court 54
sushi 152
Sushi Samba 173
Sweet-n-Tart Cafe 155
Swift, Hildegarde Hoyt 101
swimming 236
Swing 46 220
Sylvia's 180
Symphony Space 230
synagogues
Congregation Anshe Chesed 58
Eldridge St. Synagogue 58
Shearith Israel Synagogue 56
Temple Emanu-el 92
synoptic garden 282
Szechuan Gourmet 188

T

T. H. Everett Alpine House 122
Tabernacle of Prayer 117
Taby's 282
Taipan Bakery 156
Tales from the Road 108
Tammany Hall 54, 69
Tandoori Club 174
Tarrytown 287
Tartine 163
Tatiana Designer Resale Boutique 248
taxes, NYC 38
Taxi Commission 31, 327
taxis 30
Tea Dance 287
Teddy's 207
Tel Aviv Taxi 327
Tele-Charge 224, 327
telephone. See phone calls.
Telly's Taverna 188
Temple Emanu-el 92
temporary work 320
Ten Ren Tea and Ginseng Company 156
tennis 233
Tenth Street Lounge 197
Teresa Hotel 99
Terrorism Hotline 325
Teuscher Chocolatier 175
Thailand Restaurant 155
Thalia Spanish Theater 213
That Little Cafe (Dishful Caterers) 159
Thayer Gate, West Point 288
The Boat Livery, Inc. 207
The Cloisters 102
The Crooked Tree 165
The Gate 206
The Great Gatsby 86
The Hungarian Pastry Shop 179
The Pencil Factory 206
The Slipper Room 194
The Way We Were 86
The Works 204
theater 221, 223
  Broadway shows 224
  info lines 325
  live television 230
  off-Broadway 225
  other venues 227
  outdoor theaters 231
Theater District 85
  food, 24hr. 169
  hostels 267
  hotels 267
  sights 84
Theater for the New City 226
Theatre Development Fund (TDF) 224
Theodore Roosevelt Birthplace 70
Thirty One 188
ThirtyThirty 261
Thomas Cook 298
  branches in NY 325
  wiring money 35
Thomas, Dylan 73, 200
Throb 248
Tia
  cafe 183
Tibetan Kitchen 173
Ticket Central 224, 327
Ticketmaster 212, 224, 327
tickets 327
  basketball 232
  cancellation line 212
  cheap 212
  football 232
  hockey 232
  rush 212
  soccer 233
  sold-out shows 212
  standing-room only 212
  theater 221, 223, 224
  Ticketmaster 212
  TKTS 212
Tiengarden 159
Tiffany & Co. 251
time differences. See time zones.
Time Out New York 38, 211
time zones 33
Times Square
  entertainment 212
  hostels 267
  hotels 267
  sights 84
Tino's Delicatessen 190
Tipperary Inn 285
tipping, NYC 38
TKTS 212, 223, 327
Toast 179
Tokyo 7 Consignment Store 248
Tokyo Joe 248
Tom's Restaurant 179, 186
Tommy Hilfiger at Jones Beach Theater 282
Tompkins Square Park 68
Tonic 223
Toscanini, Arturo
  Wave Hill 122
Totonno Pizzeria Napolitano 187
tourist info 327
tours 24
Tower Plaza 79
Train travel 303
trains 327
  Amtrak 327
  See also Metro Transit.
tranportation
  trains 327
Transit Authority 327
transportation
  airlines 323
  airport transport 323
  airports 323
  buses 324
  for disabled travelers 304
  to and from airpot 27
transportation, within New York 29
travel agencies 300
traveler's checks 297
TravellCell.com 34
Tribe 197
TriBeCa
  food 160
  orientation 13
  sights 58
TriBeCa Grill 59
Trinity Church 51
Trophy Point 288
Trump International Hotel and Towers 94
Trump Tower 81
Twain, Mark 73, 86, 92

Wave Hill House 122
Tweed Courthouse 54
Tweed, William "Boss" 42, 54, 69
Twin Towers. See World Trade Center Site. 77
Two Boots Restaurant 167
Two Boots To Go 167

U

Ugly Luggage 253
Umbrella Lounge 205
Uncle George's 189
Uncle Sam's Army Navy 245
unicorns 132
Union Church of Pocantico Hills 288
Union Club 91
Union Pool 207
Union Square 14
entertainment 212, 223, 226
food 171
Greenmarket 69
hotels 261
nightlife 201–203
Union Square and Gramercy
sights 68–72
Union Square Greenmarket 171
Union Square Inn 261
Union Square Savings Bank 69
Union Square Theatre 69, 226
Unisphere 115
United Airlines 323
United Community Centers 324
United Nations Building 83
United Nations Secretariat building 44
United Neighborhood Houses of New York 324
United States Tennis Association (USTA) 233
Universal News and Cafe Corp. 243
University Club 81
Untitled 243
Upper East Side 15
entertainment 212, 217, 221, 226, 227
food 175–176
food markets 176
food, 24hr. 169
hotels 269
museums 128
nightlife 203
shopping 251
sights 91–94
Upper West Side
cafes 178
entertainment 211, 214, 215, 216, 217, 220, 221, 227, 228, 229, 230, 231
food 176–178
food markets 178
gay bars 204
museums 128
nightlife 204
orientation 15
shopping 251
sights 94–96
Upright Citizens Brigade Theater 227
Uptown Hostel 273
Urban Ventures 257
US Airways 323
US Custom House 50
US Open 233
US State Department 35
USTA National Tennis Center 115

V

Van Alen, William 84
Van Cortlandt Park 6, 121
golf 235
house 122
sights 121
van der Rohe, Ludwig Mies 82
Varenichnaya 187
Vaux, Calvert 86
Vegetarian Dim Sum House 155
vegetarians 307
Veniero's 169
venues
general entertainment 227
Vera Cruz 183
Verrazano-Narrows Bridge 11
Veselka 168
Viand 176
View 203
Viking fluke-fishing cruise 285
Village
entertainment 214
Village Chess Shop 245
Village Comics 245
Village Halloween Parade 60
Village Idiot 200
Village Vanguard 220
Village Voice 38, 211
Vineyard Theater Company's Dimson Theatre 226
Vinny's of Carroll Gardens 185
Visa 298
visas 296, 315
Vivian Beaumont Theater 95
volunteering 312
Voorlezer's House 124

W

Waldorf-Astoria Hotel 82
Walk-in Clinic 326
walking tours 24
Walt 104
Walter Reade Theater 95, 215
Warm Up 214
Washington Heights
food 179–180
museums 128
orientation 20
sights 100
Washington Square Hotel 258
Washington, George
battle in Bryant Park 78
in St. Paul's C hapel 53
Morris-Jumel Mansion 101
statue at Federal Hall 51
Washington Crossing the Delaware 129

- Washington Memorial Arch 60
- Watch Hill 286
- Water Mill Museum 283
- Waterfront Ale House 207
- Waterfront Museum 142
- Wave Hill 122
- Wave Hill House 122
- Waverly Restaurant 168
- Webster Hall 209
- Weeksville 109
- Weiss and Mahoney 249
- West End Studios 271
- West Point 288
- West Point Museum 288
- West Side Inn 269
- West Side YMCA 269
- West Village
  - entertainment 215, 219, 220, 225
  - sights 63–65
- Western Union 35
- Wharton, Edith 97
- when to go 22
- White, Stanford 72, 92
  - site of death 72
- Whitehorse Tavern 200
- Whitman, Walt 104
  - Bear Mountain State Park 289
  - *Brooklyn Eagle* 42
- Whitney Museum of American Art 133
- Whitney, Harry and Gertrude
  - grave 123
- Whole Earth Bakery and Kitchen 168
- Wild Lily Tea Room 170
- Williamsburg 10
  - cafes 183
  - entertainment 225
  - food 181–183
  - galleries 146
- Williamsburg Art and Historical Center 146
- Willow Street 106
- Wollcott, Alexander 42
- Wollman Memorial Rink 87, 236
- women travelers 304
- Women's Health Line 327
- women's resources
  - centers 324
  - health centers 327
  - Planned Parenthood 327
  - safety 304
- Wonder Bar 198
- Woodlawn 123
- Woodlawn Cemetery 123
- Woolworth Building 43
- Woolworth, F. W.
  - grave 123
- Work Space 144
- working 317
  - long term 318
  - short-term 320
  - temporary 320
- World Financial Center 52
  - entertainment 230
  - jazz festival 221
- World Financial Center Festival. See Hudson River Festival.
- World of Nuts & Ice Cream 176
- World Trade Center Site 52
- World's Fairs
  - Bryant Park, 1853 78
  - Queens Botanical Garden, 1939 116
  - Unisphere, 1964 115

- X, Malcolm
  - site of assasination 101
- X.O. Cafe 156
- X-R Bar 199

- Y's Way 257
- Yabby's 207
- Yacht Club bar/club 287
- Yaffa Cafe 168
- Yaffa's Tea Room 160
- Yankee Stadium 118
- Yeshiva University 102
- Yiddish Rialto 67
- YMCA 234
  - 92nd Street 25
  - Flushing 274
  - Vanderbilt 266
  - Westside 269
- YM-YWHA 234
- Yogi's 204
- Yonah Schimmel Knishery 160
- Yong Da Fung Health Food Herbal Products 189
- Young Men's Christian Association (YMCA). See YMCA
- Young Women's Christian Association (YWCA). See YWCA
- YWCA 234

Z

- Zabar's 178
- Zen Palate 171
- Ziegfeld 215
- Zigolini's 153
- Zinc Bar 199
- Zipcar 32, 324
- Zorba's Souvlaki Plus 189
- Zygos Taverna 189

Map Appendix

Astoria & Long Island City **394**
Brooklyn **386 - 387**
Brooklyn Heights & Downtown Brooklyn **389**
Carroll Gardens & Red Hook **391**
Central Park North **380**
Central Park South **381**
Chinatown & Little Italy **362 - 363**
Downtown Bus Routes **399**
East Village **370 - 371**
Flushing & Corona **395**
Greater New York **356 - 357**
Greenwich Village **366 - 368**
Harlem & Morningside Heights **384- 385**
Lower East Side **369**
Lower Manhattan **360 - 361**
Lower Midtown **372 - 374**
Manhattan **358**
Manhattan Neighborhoods **359**
Midtown **375 - 377**
New York Metropolitan Area **354 - 355**
Park Slope & Prospect Park **390**
Queens **392 - 393**
Soho & TriBeCa **364 - 365**
Staten Island **398**
The Bronx **396 - 397**
Upper East Side **378 - 379**
Upper West Side **382 - 383**
Uptown Bus Routes **400**
Washington Heights **384**
Williamsburg & Greenpoint **388**

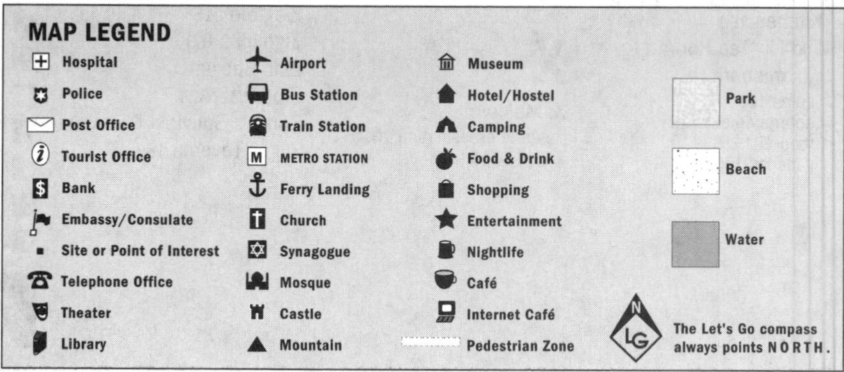

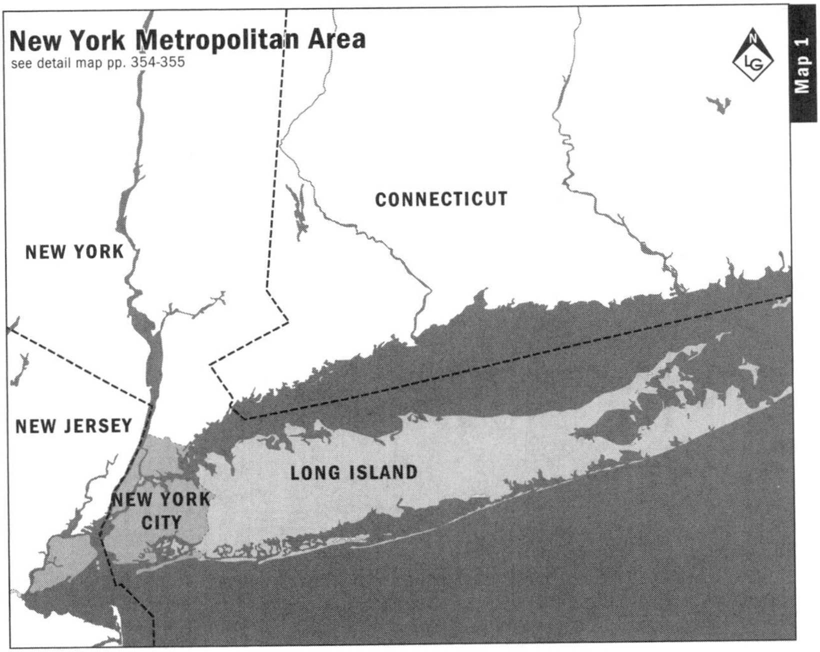
New York Metropolitan Area
see detail map pp. 354-355
Map 1
N
LG
CONNECTICUT
NEW YORK
NEW JERSEY
LONG ISLAND
NEW YORK CITY

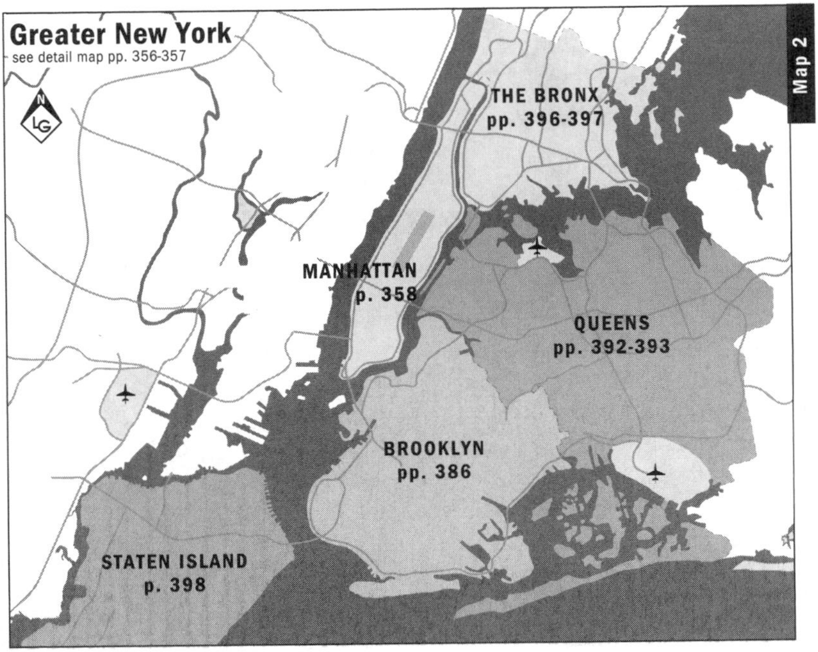
Greater New York
see detail map pp. 356-357
Map 2
N
LG
THE BRONX
pp. 396-397
MANHATTAN
p. 358
QUEENS
pp. 392-393
BROOKLYN
pp. 386
STATEN ISLAND
p. 398

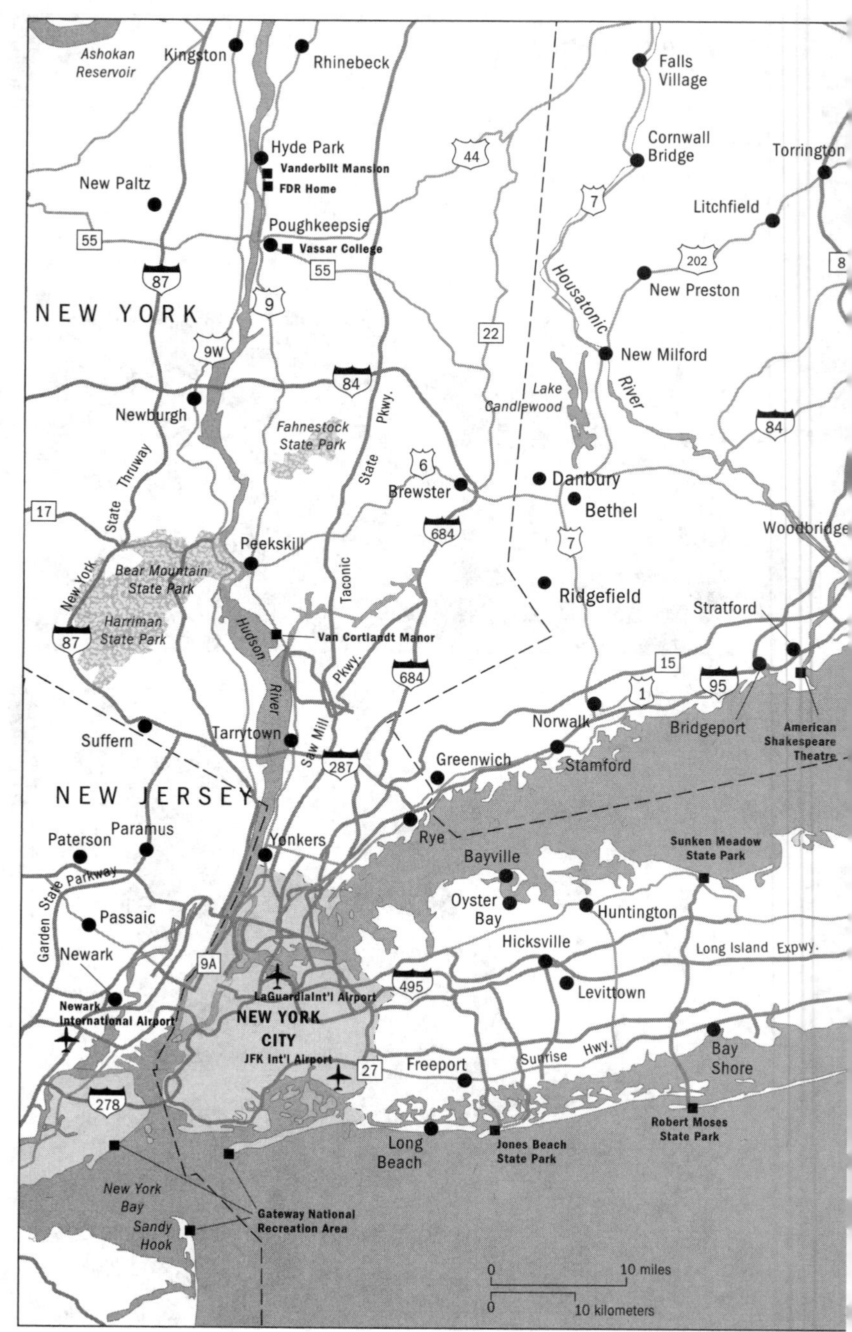
Ashokan Reservoir
Kingston
Rhinebeck
Falls Village
Cornwall Bridge
Torrington
Hyde Park
Vanderbilt Mansion
FDR Home
New Paltz
Litchfield
Poughkeepsie
Vassar College
New Preston
NEW YORK
Housatonic River
New Milford
Lake Candlewood
Newburgh
Fahnestock State Park
State Pkwy.
Taconic Pkwy.
Brewster
Danbury
Bethel
Woodbridge
New York State Thruway
Peekskill
Bear Mountain State Park
Harriman State Park
Ridgefield
Stratford
Hudson River
Van Cortlandt Manor
Saw Mill
Norwalk
Bridgeport
American Shakespeare Theatre
Suffern
Tarrytown
Stamford
Greenwich
NEW JERSEY
Paterson
Paramus
Yonkers
Rye
Bayville
Sunken Meadow State Park
Garden State Parkway
Passaic
Oyster Bay
Huntington
Newark
Hicksville
Long Island Expwy.
Levittown
LaGuardiaInt'l Airport
Newark International Airport
NEW YORK CITY
JFK Int'l Airport
Sunrise Hwy.
Bay Shore
Freeport
Long Beach
Jones Beach State Park
Robert Moses State Park
New York Bay
Sandy Hook
Gateway National Recreation Area
0
10 miles
0
10 kilometers
87
55
9
9W
84
22
44
7
202
8
6
17
684
15
1
95
287
9A
495
27
278

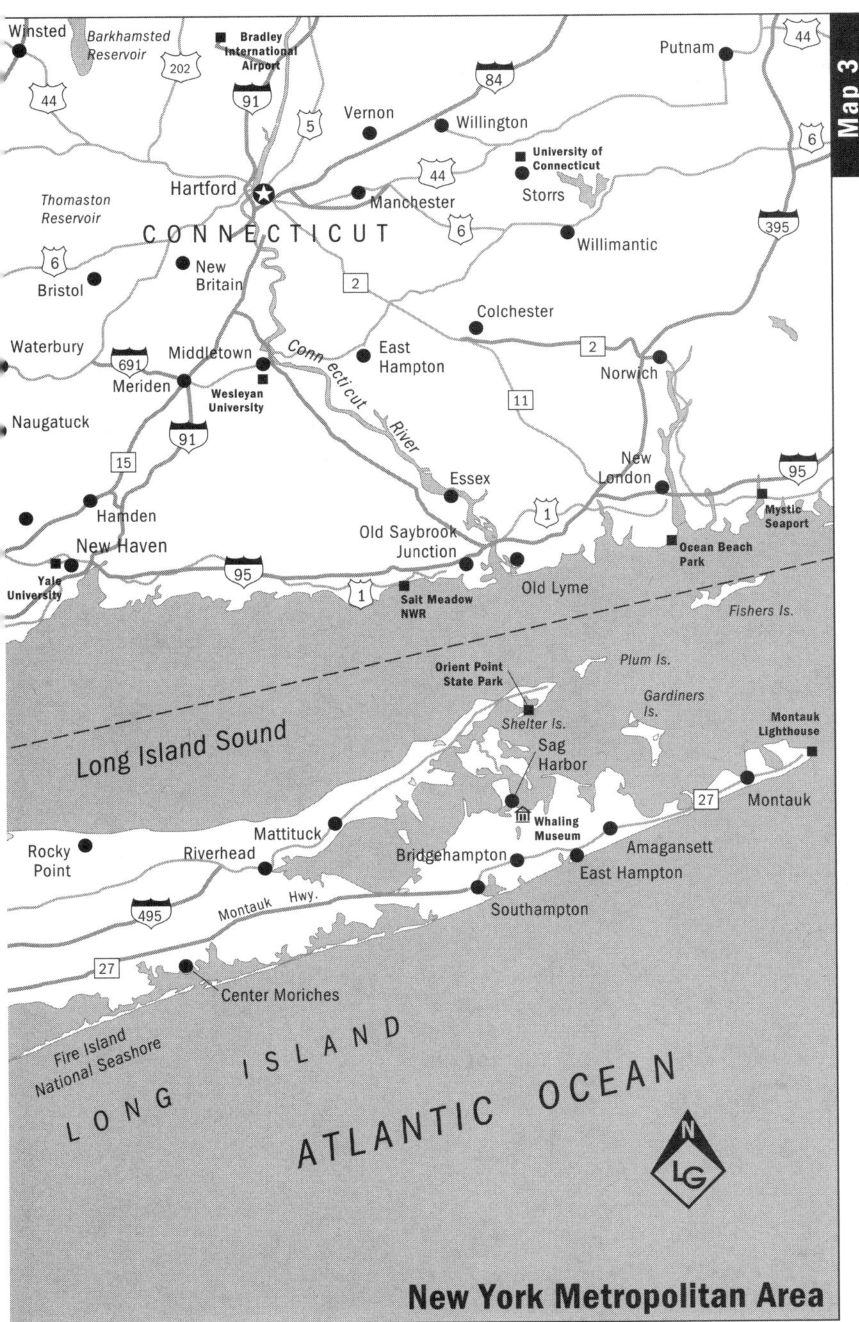
Map 3
Winsted
Barkhamsted Reservoir
Bradley International Airport
Putnam
Vernon
Willington
University of Connecticut
Storrs
Hartford
Manchester
Thomaston Reservoir
CONNECTICUT
Willimantic
New Britain
Bristol
Colchester
Waterbury
Middletown
East Hampton
Norwich
Meriden
Wesleyan University
Connecticut River
Naugatuck
Essex
New London
Hamden
Mystic Seaport
New Haven
Old Saybrook Junction
Ocean Beach Park
Yale University
Salt Meadow NWR
Old Lyme
Fishers Is.
Plum Is.
Orient Point State Park
Gardiners Is.
Shelter Is.
Montauk Lighthouse
Long Island Sound
Sag Harbor
Montauk
Whaling Museum
Mattituck
Amagansett
Rocky Point
Riverhead
Bridgehampton
East Hampton
Southampton
Montauk Hwy.
Center Moriches
Fire Island National Seashore
LONG ISLAND
ATLANTIC OCEAN
New York Metropolitan Area

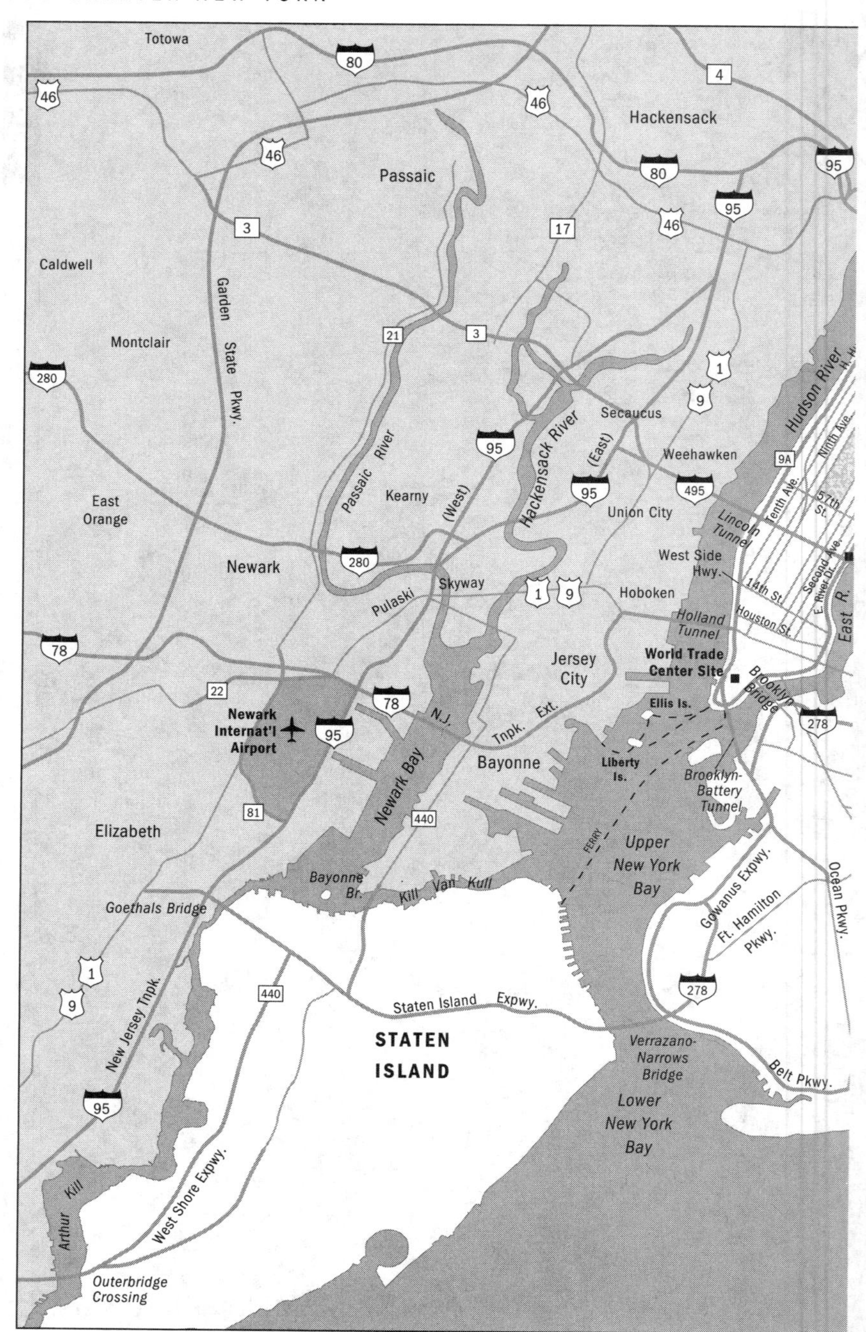
Totowa
Hackensack
Passaic
Caldwell
Montclair
Garden State Pkwy.
Secaucus
Weehawken
Hudson River
Ninth Ave.
Tenth Ave.
57th St.
Passaic River
Kearny
(West)
Hackensack River
(East)
Union City
East Orange
Lincoln Tunnel
West Side Hwy.
Second Ave.
E. River Dr.
Newark
Pulaski
Skyway
Hoboken
14th St.
Holland Tunnel
Houston St.
East R.
Jersey City
World Trade Center Site
Brooklyn Bridge
Newark Internat'l Airport
N.J.
Tnpk. Ext.
Ellis Is.
Bayonne
Liberty Is.
Newark Bay
Brooklyn-Battery Tunnel
Elizabeth
FERRY
Upper New York Bay
Bayonne Br.
Kill Van Kull
Goethals Bridge
Gowanus Expwy.
Ft. Hamilton Pkwy.
Ocean Pkwy.
New Jersey Tnpk.
Staten Island Expwy.
STATEN ISLAND
Verrazano-Narrows Bridge
Belt Pkwy.
Lower New York Bay
West Shore Expwy.
Arthur Kill
Outerbridge Crossing

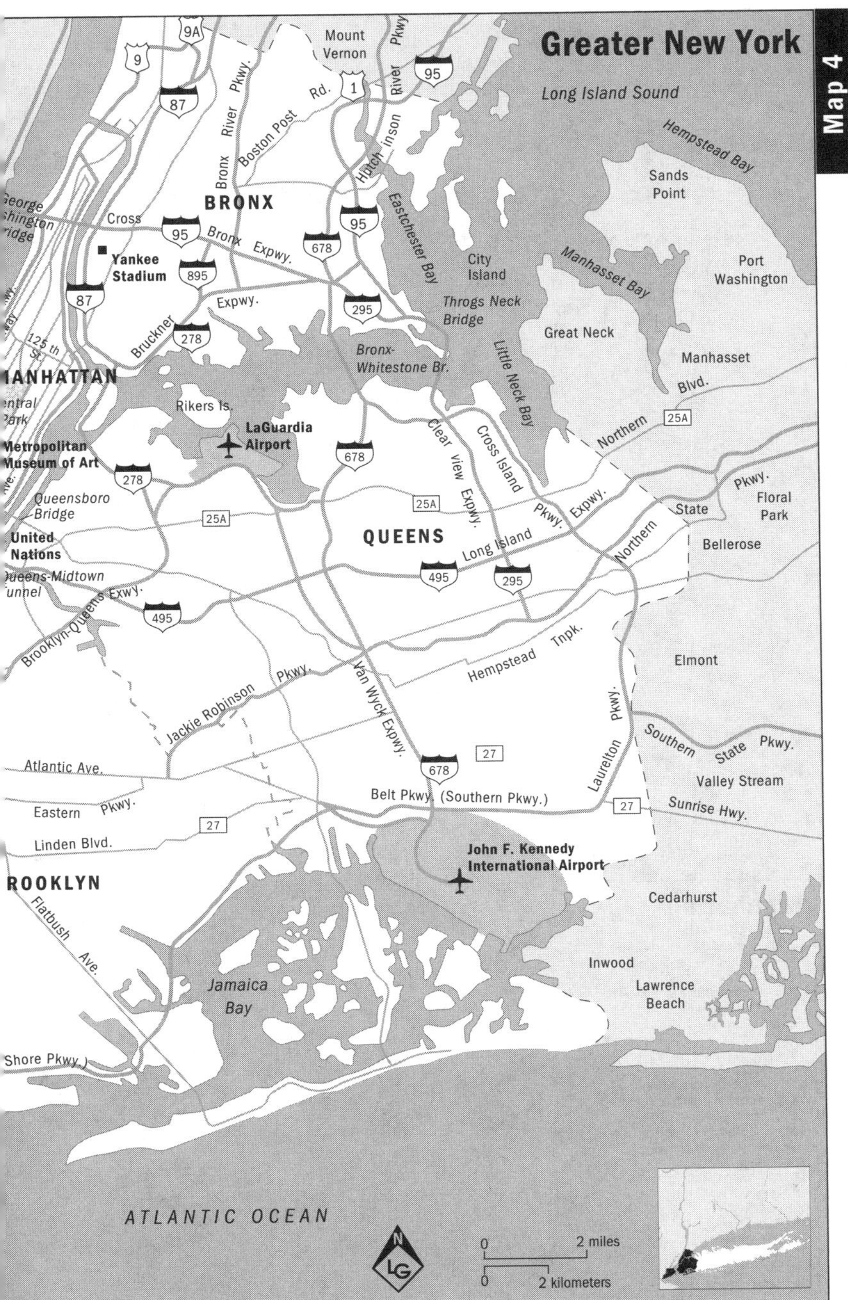
Greater New York
Map 4
Long Island Sound
Hempstead Bay
Sands Point
Port Washington
Manhasset Bay
Great Neck
Manhasset
Mount Vernon
BRONX
Yankee Stadium
City Island
Throgs Neck Bridge
Bronx-Whitestone Br.
Eastchester Bay
Little Neck Bay
MANHATTAN
Rikers Is.
LaGuardia Airport
Metropolitan Museum of Art
Queensboro Bridge
United Nations
QUEENS
Floral Park
Bellerose
Elmont
Valley Stream
Belt Pkwy. (Southern Pkwy.)
John F. Kennedy International Airport
BROOKLYN
Cedarhurst
Inwood
Lawrence Beach
Jamaica Bay
ATLANTIC OCEAN
0 2 miles
0 2 kilometers

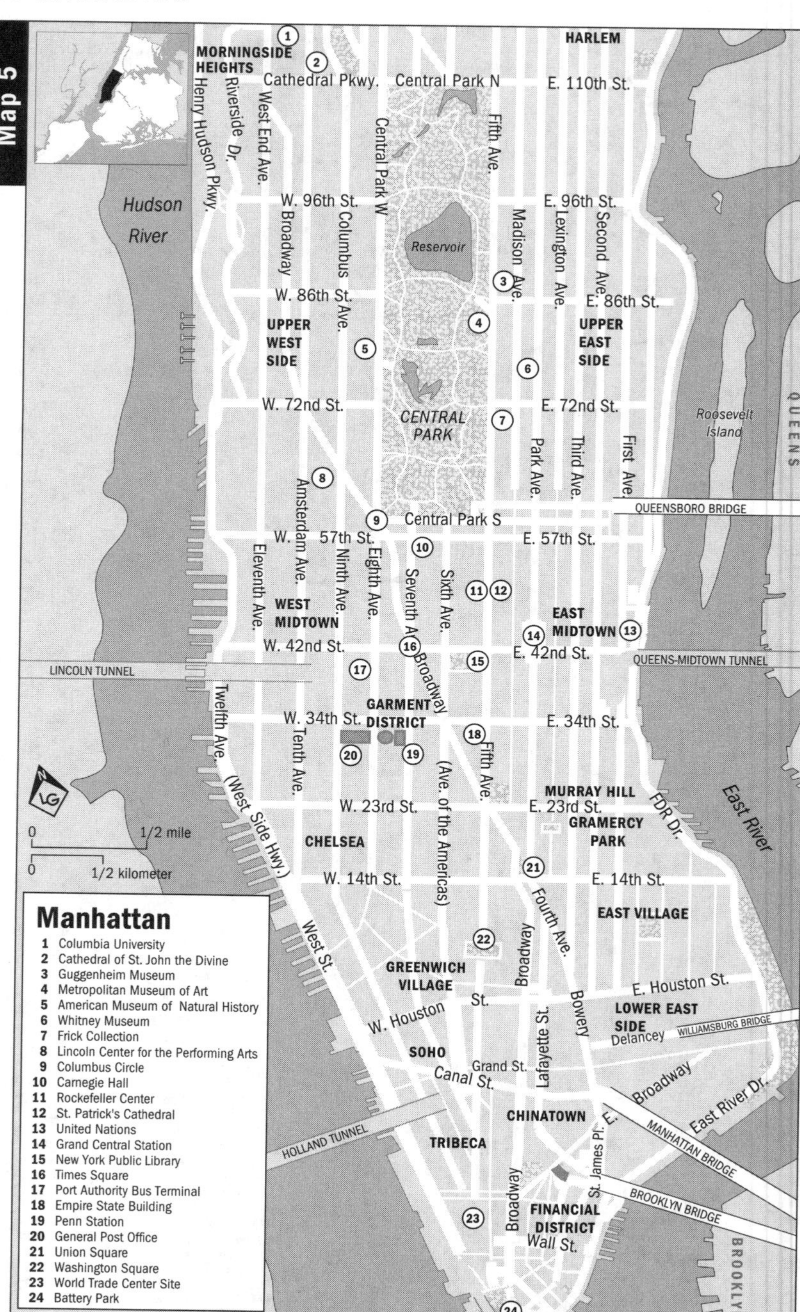
Map 5
Manhattan
1 Columbia University
2 Cathedral of St. John the Divine
3 Guggenheim Museum
4 Metropolitan Museum of Art
5 American Museum of Natural History
6 Whitney Museum
7 Frick Collection
8 Lincoln Center for the Performing Arts
9 Columbus Circle
10 Carnegie Hall
11 Rockefeller Center
12 St. Patrick's Cathedral
13 United Nations
14 Grand Central Station
15 New York Public Library
16 Times Square
17 Port Authority Bus Terminal
18 Empire State Building
19 Penn Station
20 General Post Office
21 Union Square
22 Washington Square
23 World Trade Center Site
24 Battery Park
HARLEM
MORNINGSIDE HEIGHTS
Cathedral Pkwy.
Central Park N
E. 110th St.
Henry Hudson Pkwy.
Riverside Dr.
West End Ave.
Central Park W
Fifth Ave.
Hudson River
W. 96th St.
E. 96th St.
Broadway
Columbus Ave.
Reservoir
Madison Ave.
Lexington Ave.
Second Ave.
W. 86th St.
E. 86th St.
UPPER WEST SIDE
UPPER EAST SIDE
W. 72nd St.
E. 72nd St.
CENTRAL PARK
Park Ave.
Third Ave.
First Ave.
Roosevelt Island
QUEENS
QUEENSBORO BRIDGE
Central Park S
W. 57th St.
E. 57th St.
Amsterdam Ave.
Ninth Ave.
Eighth Ave.
Eleventh Ave.
Seventh Ave.
Sixth Ave.
WEST MIDTOWN
EAST MIDTOWN
W. 42nd St.
E. 42nd St.
QUEENS-MIDTOWN TUNNEL
LINCOLN TUNNEL
Twelfth Ave.
GARMENT DISTRICT
W. 34th St.
E. 34th St.
Tenth Ave.
(Ave. of the Americas)
MURRAY HILL
(West Side Hwy.)
W. 23rd St.
E. 23rd St.
GRAMERCY PARK
FDR Dr.
East River
0
1/2 mile
1/2 kilometer
CHELSEA
W. 14th St.
E. 14th St.
EAST VILLAGE
West St.
Fourth Ave.
GREENWICH VILLAGE
E. Houston St.
W. Houston
St.
LOWER EAST SIDE
Delancey
WILLIAMSBURG BRIDGE
Lafayette St.
Bowery
SOHO
Grand St.
Canal St.
Broadway
East River Dr.
CHINATOWN
E.
St. James Pl.
MANHATTAN BRIDGE
HOLLAND TUNNEL
TRIBECA
BROOKLYN BRIDGE
FINANCIAL DISTRICT
Wall St.
BROOKLYN

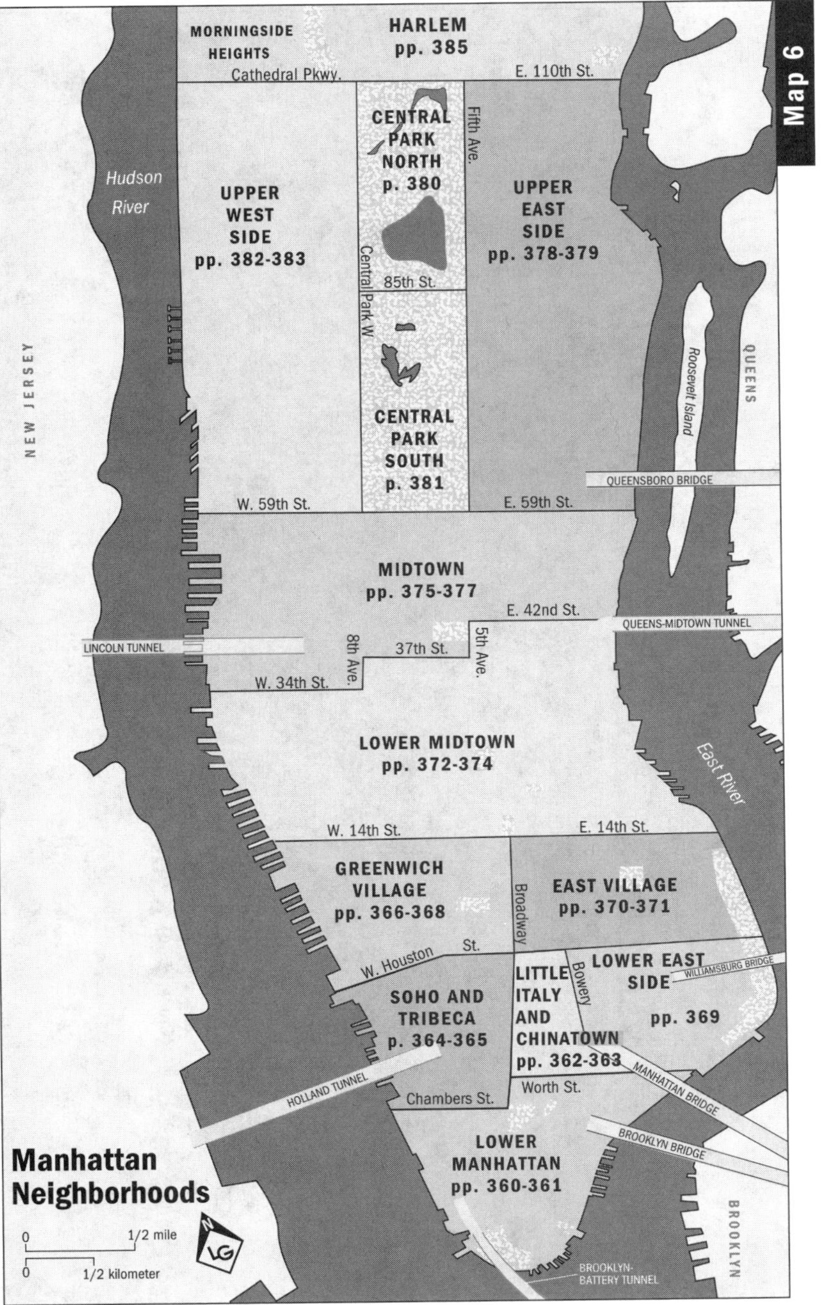
Map 6
MORNINGSIDE HEIGHTS
HARLEM pp. 385
Cathedral Pkwy.
E. 110th St.
CENTRAL PARK NORTH p. 380
Fifth Ave.
Hudson River
UPPER WEST SIDE pp. 382-383
UPPER EAST SIDE pp. 378-379
Central Park W
85th St.
NEW JERSEY
Roosevelt Island
QUEENS
CENTRAL PARK SOUTH p. 381
QUEENSBORO BRIDGE
W. 59th St.
E. 59th St.
MIDTOWN pp. 375-377
E. 42nd St.
QUEENS-MIDTOWN TUNNEL
LINCOLN TUNNEL
8th Ave.
37th St.
5th Ave.
W. 34th St.
LOWER MIDTOWN pp. 372-374
East River
W. 14th St.
E. 14th St.
GREENWICH VILLAGE pp. 366-368
Broadway
EAST VILLAGE pp. 370-371
W. Houston St.
LITTLE ITALY AND CHINATOWN pp. 362-363
Bowery
LOWER EAST SIDE pp. 369
WILLIAMSBURG BRIDGE
SOHO AND TRIBECA p. 364-365
HOLLAND TUNNEL
Chambers St.
Worth St.
MANHATTAN BRIDGE
BROOKLYN BRIDGE
LOWER MANHATTAN pp. 360-361
Manhattan Neighborhoods
0 1/2 mile
0 1/2 kilometer
BROOKLYN-BATTERY TUNNEL
BROOKLYN

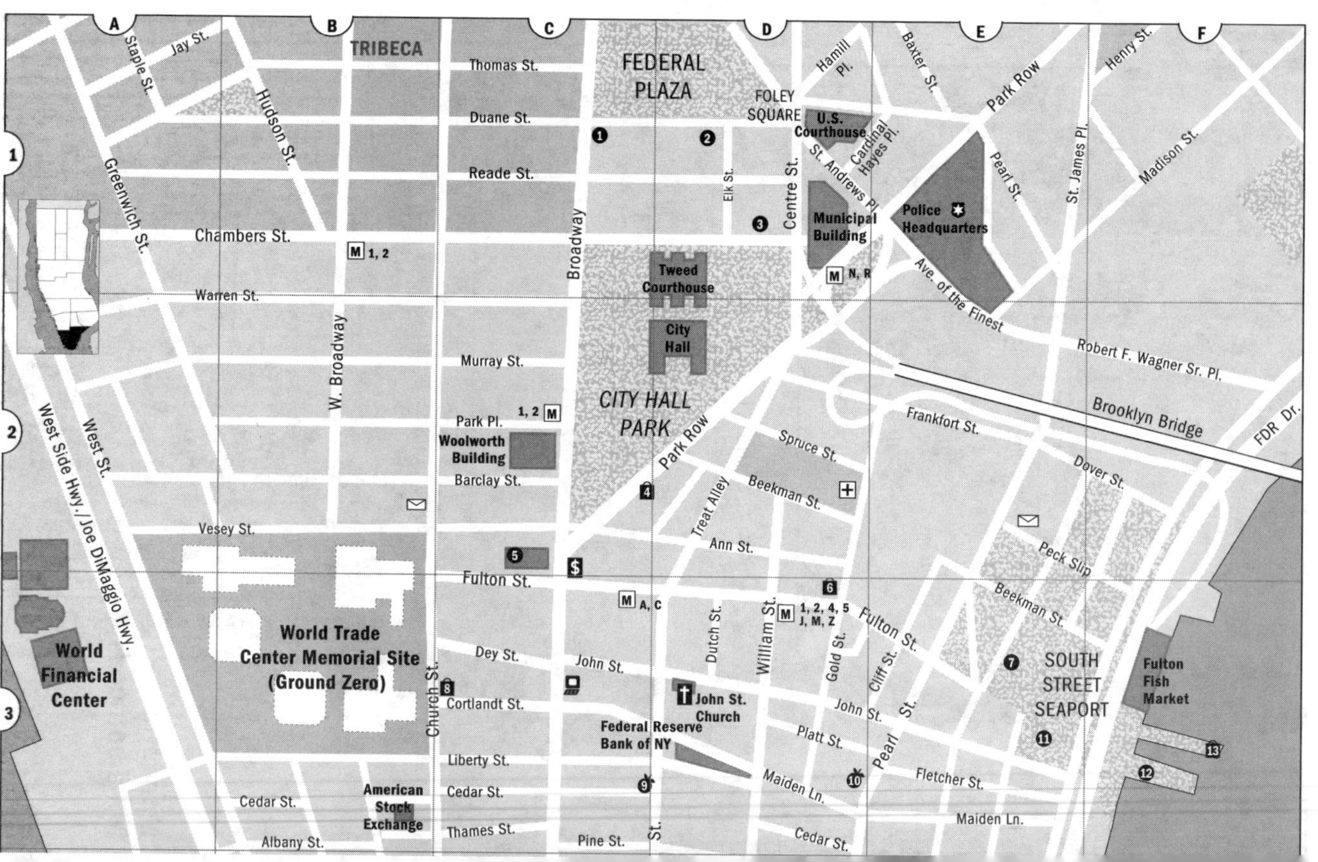
TRIBECA
FEDERAL PLAZA
FOLEY SQUARE
CITY HALL PARK
SOUTH STREET SEAPORT
U.S. Courthouse
Municipal Building
Police Headquarters
Tweed Courthouse
City Hall
Woolworth Building
John St. Church
Federal Reserve Bank of NY
American Stock Exchange
World Trade Center Memorial Site (Ground Zero)
World Financial Center
Fulton Fish Market
Brooklyn Bridge
FDR Dr.
Robert F. Wagner Sr. Pl.
Madison St.
Henry St.
St. James Pl.
Park Row
Pearl St.
Baxter St.
Ave. of the Finest
Cardinal Hayes Pl.
St. Andrews Pl.
Hamill Pl.
Centre St.
Elk St.
Frankfort St.
Dover St.
Peck Slip
Beekman St.
Spruce St.
Ann St.
Treat Alley
Fulton St.
Cliff St.
Gold St.
William St.
Dutch St.
John St.
Platt St.
Maiden Ln.
Fletcher St.
Cedar St.
Pine St.
Broadway
Thomas St.
Duane St.
Reade St.
Murray St.
Park Pl.
Barclay St.
Dey St.
Cortlandt St.
Liberty St.
Thames St.
Church St.
W. Broadway
Hudson St.
Chambers St.
Warren St.
Vesey St.
Albany St.
Jay St.
Staple St.
Greenwich St.
West St.
West Side Hwy./Joe DiMaggio Hwy.
N, R
1, 2, 4, 5
J, M, Z
A, C
1, 2
A
B
C
D
E
F
1
2
3

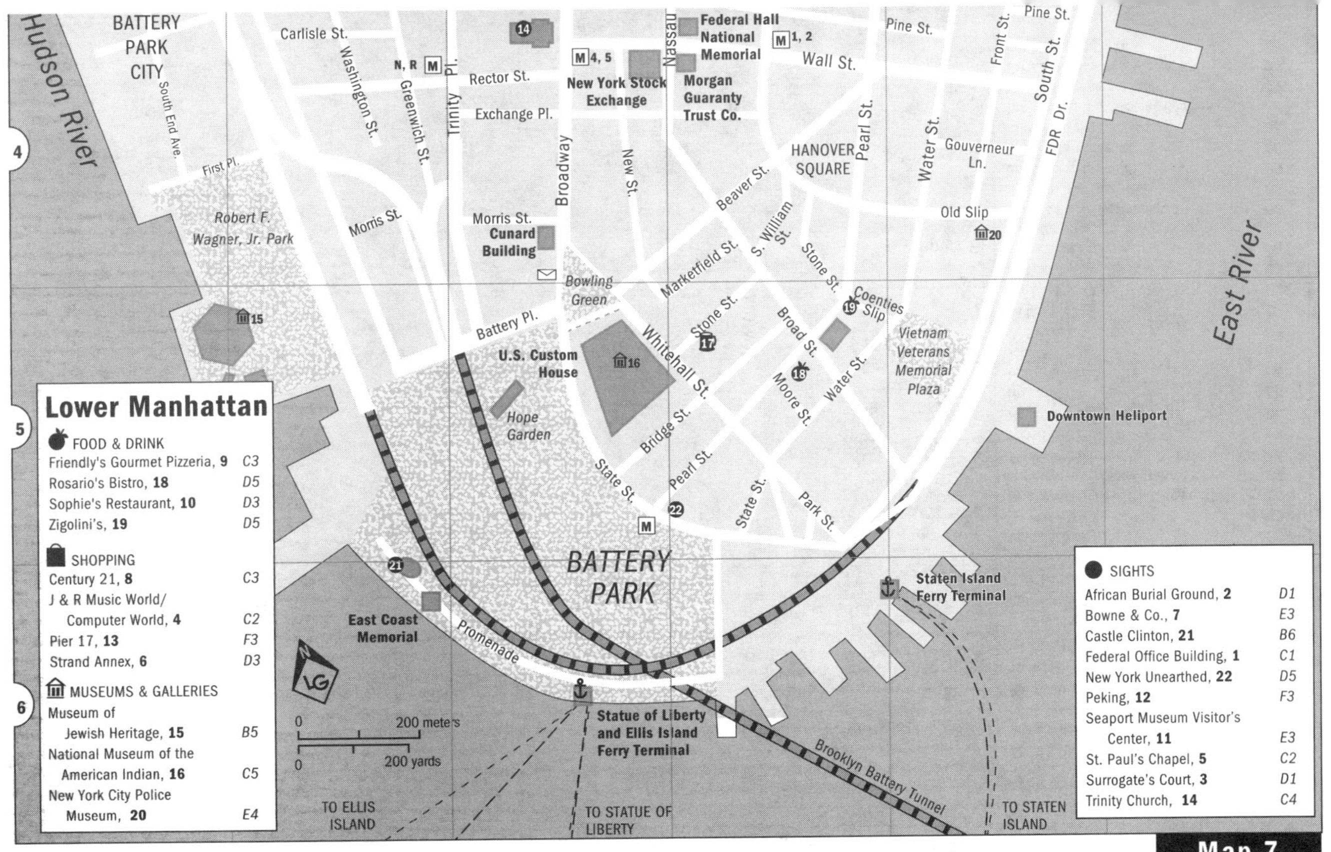
Map 7
Lower Manhattan
FOOD & DRINK
Friendly's Gourmet Pizzeria, 9 C3
Rosario's Bistro, 18 D5
Sophie's Restaurant, 10 D3
Zigolini's, 19 D5
SHOPPING
Century 21, 8 C3
J & R Music World/ Computer World, 4 C2
Pier 17, 13 F3
Strand Annex, 6 D3
MUSEUMS & GALLERIES
Museum of Jewish Heritage, 15 B5
National Museum of the American Indian, 16 C5
New York City Police Museum, 20 E4
SIGHTS
African Burial Ground, 2 D1
Bowne & Co., 7 E3
Castle Clinton, 21 B6
Federal Office Building, 1 C1
New York Unearthed, 22 D5
Peking, 12 F3
Seaport Museum Visitor's Center, 11 E3
St. Paul's Chapel, 5 C2
Surrogate's Court, 3 D1
Trinity Church, 14 C4
Hudson River
East River
BATTERY PARK CITY
BATTERY PARK
HANOVER SQUARE
Robert F. Wagner, Jr. Park
South End Ave.
First Pl.
Carlisle St.
Washington St.
Greenwich St.
Morris St.
Trinity Pl.
Rector St.
Exchange Pl.
Broadway
New St.
Nassau
Wall St.
Pine St.
Beaver St.
Marketfield St.
S. William St.
Stone St.
Broad St.
Whitehall St.
Bridge St.
Pearl St.
State St.
Moore St.
Water St.
Park St.
Coenties Slip
Old Slip
Gouverneur Ln.
Front St.
South St.
FDR Dr.
Federal Hall National Memorial
Morgan Guaranty Trust Co.
New York Stock Exchange
Cunard Building
Battery Pl.
Bowling Green
U.S. Custom House
Hope Garden
Promenade
East Coast Memorial
Vietnam Veterans Memorial Plaza
Downtown Heliport
Staten Island Ferry Terminal
Statue of Liberty and Ellis Island Ferry Terminal
Brooklyn Battery Tunnel
TO STATEN ISLAND
TO STATUE OF LIBERTY
TO ELLIS ISLAND
200 meters
200 yards
N, R
4, 5
1, 2
4
5
6

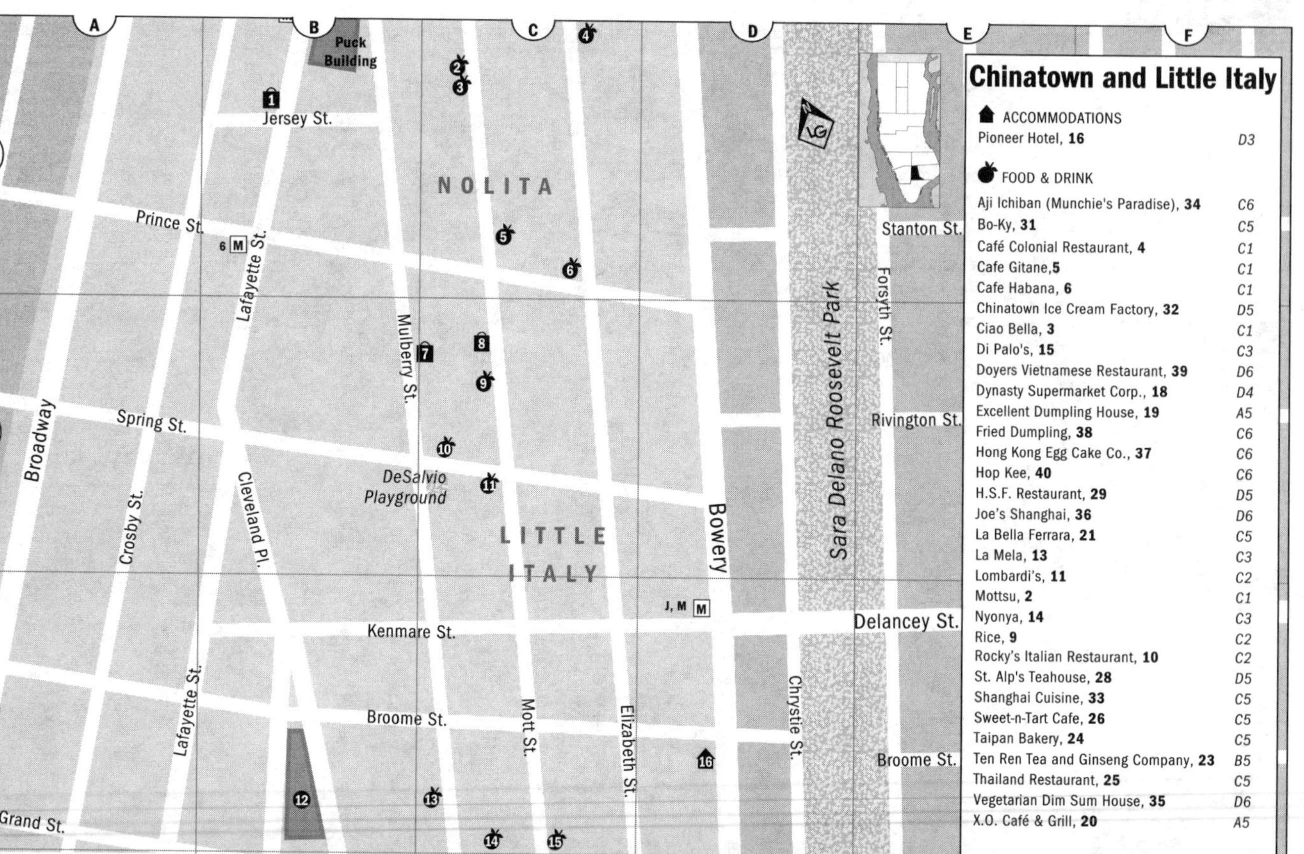
Chinatown and Little Italy
ACCOMMODATIONS
Pioneer Hotel, 16 D3
FOOD & DRINK
Aji Ichiban (Munchie's Paradise), 34 C6
Bo-Ky, 31 C5
Café Colonial Restaurant, 4 C1
Cafe Gitane,5 C1
Cafe Habana, 6 C1
Chinatown Ice Cream Factory, 32 D5
Ciao Bella, 3 C1
Di Palo's, 15 C3
Doyers Vietnamese Restaurant, 39 D6
Dynasty Supermarket Corp., 18 D4
Excellent Dumpling House, 19 A5
Fried Dumpling, 38 C6
Hong Kong Egg Cake Co., 37 C6
Hop Kee, 40 C6
H.S.F. Restaurant, 29 D5
Joe's Shanghai, 36 D6
La Bella Ferrara, 21 C5
La Mela, 13 C3
Lombardi's, 11 C2
Mottsu, 2 C1
Nyonya, 14 C3
Rice, 9 C2
Rocky's Italian Restaurant, 10 C2
St. Alp's Teahouse, 28 D5
Shanghai Cuisine, 33 C5
Sweet-n-Tart Cafe, 26 C5
Taipan Bakery, 24 C5
Ten Ren Tea and Ginseng Company, 23 B5
Thailand Restaurant, 25 C5
Vegetarian Dim Sum House, 35 D6
X.O. Café & Grill, 20 A5
A
B
C
D
E
F
1
2
3
Puck Building
Jersey St.
NOLITA
LITTLE ITALY
Prince St.
Lafayette St.
6 M
Mulberry St.
Spring St.
Broadway
Crosby St.
Cleveland Pl.
DeSalvio Playground
Bowery
J, M M
Kenmare St.
Broome St.
Mott St.
Elizabeth St.
Chrystie St.
Grand St.
Sara Delano Roosevelt Park
Forsyth St.
Stanton St.
Rivington St.
Delancey St.

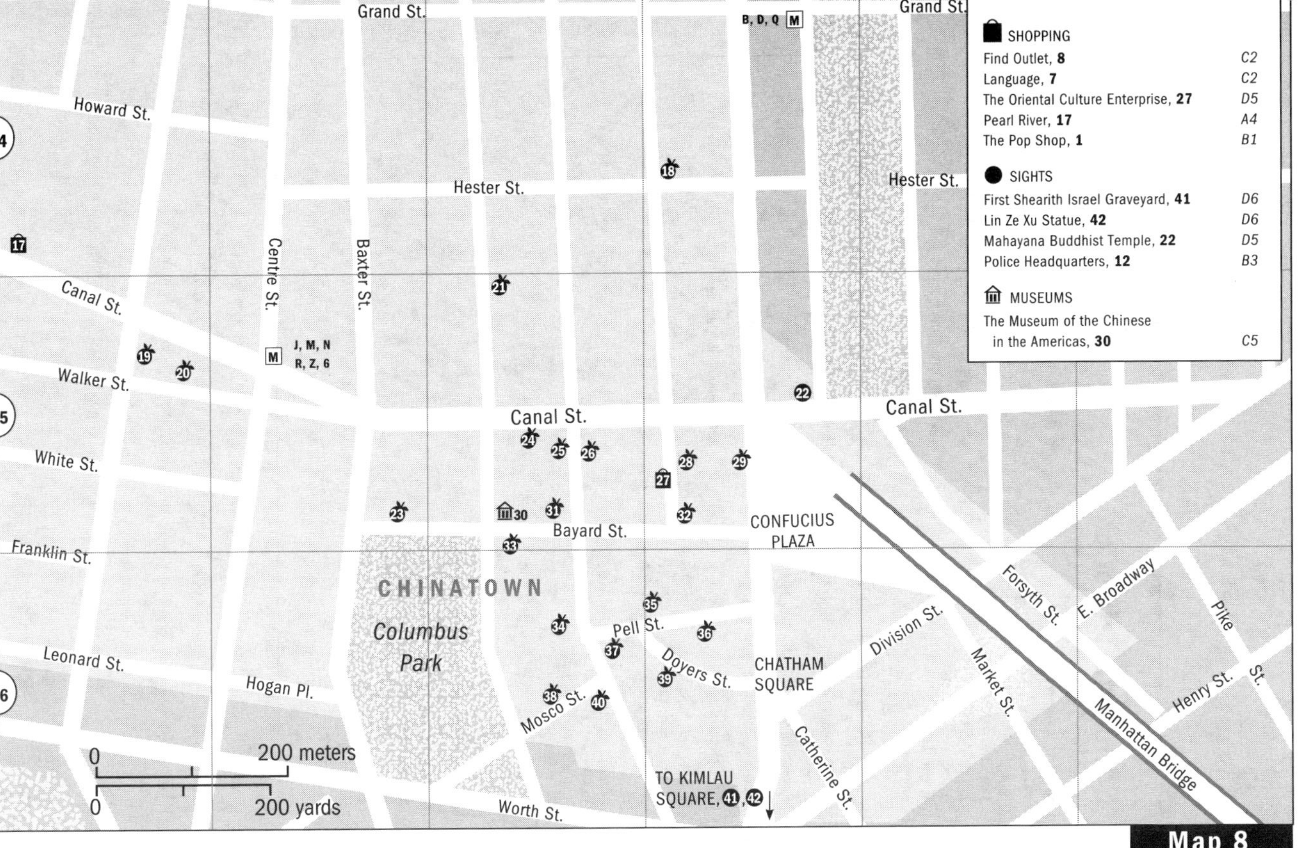
SHOPPING
Find Outlet, 8 C2
Language, 7 C2
The Oriental Culture Enterprise, 27 D5
Pearl River, 17 A4
The Pop Shop, 1 B1
SIGHTS
First Shearith Israel Graveyard, 41 D6
Lin Ze Xu Statue, 42 D6
Mahayana Buddhist Temple, 22 D5
Police Headquarters, 12 B3
MUSEUMS
The Museum of the Chinese in the Americas, 30 C5
Grand St.
B, D, Q
Howard St.
Hester St.
Centre St.
Baxter St.
Canal St.
J, M, N R, Z, 6
Walker St.
White St.
Bayard St.
CONFUCIUS PLAZA
Franklin St.
CHINATOWN
Columbus Park
Pell St.
Doyers St.
CHATHAM SQUARE
Division St.
Forsyth St.
E. Broadway
Pike St.
Henry St.
Market St.
Manhattan Bridge
Leonard St.
Hogan Pl.
Mosco St.
Catherine St.
TO KIMLAU SQUARE, 41, 42
Worth St.
0 200 meters
0 200 yards
4
5
6
Map 8

SoHo and TriBeCa

FOOD & DRINK

Brisas del Caribe, **34**	*D3*
Bubby's, **44**	*B6*
Dean and Deluca, **16**	*D2*
El Teddy's, **45**	*C6*
Ideya Restaurant, **28**	*C3*
Jerry's, **14**	*D2*
Kelley and Ping Asian Grocery and Noodle Shop, **7**	*C1*
Lupe's East L.A. Kitchen, **23**	*B3*
Miro Cafe, **37**	*D3*
Pakistan Tea House, **46**	*C7*
Penang, **18**	*D2*
Ruben's Empanadas, **26**	*C3*
Space Untitled, **5**	*C1*
Yaffa's Tea Room, **43**	*A6*

SHOPPING

Alice Underground, **35**	*D3*
Girlprops.com, **12**	*C2*
K Trimming, **32**	*D3*
Universal News and Cafe Corp., **36**	*D3*
Untitled, **11**	*C2*

NIGHTLIFE

Bar 89, **33**	*D3*
Cafe Noir, **38**	*B4*
Circa Tabac, **24**	*B3*
Denizen, **22**	*B3*
Fanelli's Cafe, **15**	*D2*
Lucky Strike, **41**	*C4*
MercBar, **9**	*D1*
Milady's, **13**	*C2*
Naked Lunch Bar and Lounge, **39**	*B4*
X-R Bar, **2**	*B1*
Zinc Bar, **3**	*C1*

ARTS & ENTERTAINMENT

Angelika Film Center, **8**	*D1*
Film Forum, **1**	*A1*
SoHo Repertory Theater, **42**	*C5*
SoHo Ohio Think Tank Theater, **25**	*C3*

MUSEUMS & GALLERIES

Arcadia Gallery, **30**	*C3*
Artists Space, **31**	*C3*
Deitch Projects, **40**	*C4*
Dia Center for the Arts, **6**	*C1*
Drawing Center, **29**	*C3*
Illustration House, **19**	*D2*
New Museum of Contemporary Art, **10**	*D1*
New York City Fire Museum, **21**	*A3*
The Painting Center, **27**	*C3*
POP International Galleries, Inc., **4**	*C1*
Staley-Wise, **17**	*D2*
The Work Space, **20**	*D2*

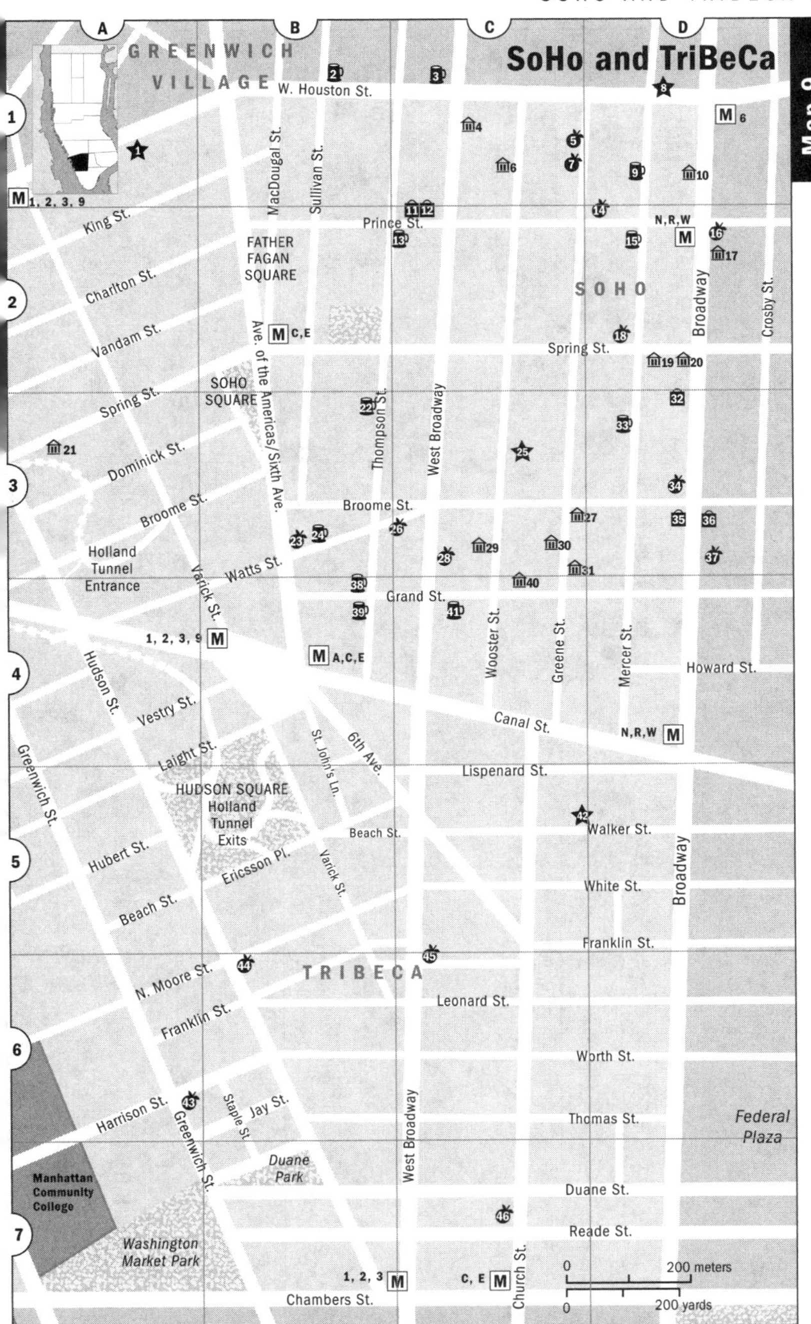
SoHo and TriBeCa
Map 9
GREENWICH VILLAGE
SOHO
TRIBECA
W. Houston St.
Prince St.
Spring St.
Broome St.
Grand St.
Canal St.
Howard St.
Lispenard St.
Walker St.
White St.
Franklin St.
Leonard St.
Worth St.
Thomas St.
Duane St.
Reade St.
Chambers St.
King St.
Charlton St.
Vandam St.
Dominick St.
Watts St.
Vestry St.
Laight St.
Hubert St.
Beach St.
Ericsson Pl.
N. Moore St.
Harrison St.
Jay St.
Staple St.
MacDougal St.
Sullivan St.
Thompson St.
West Broadway
Wooster St.
Greene St.
Mercer St.
Broadway
Crosby St.
Church St.
Varick St.
Hudson St.
Greenwich St.
St. John's Ln.
6th Ave.
Ave. of the Americas/Sixth Ave.
FATHER FAGAN SQUARE
SOHO SQUARE
HUDSON SQUARE
Holland Tunnel Entrance
Holland Tunnel Exits
Duane Park
Washington Market Park
Manhattan Community College
Federal Plaza
0
200 meters
200 yards

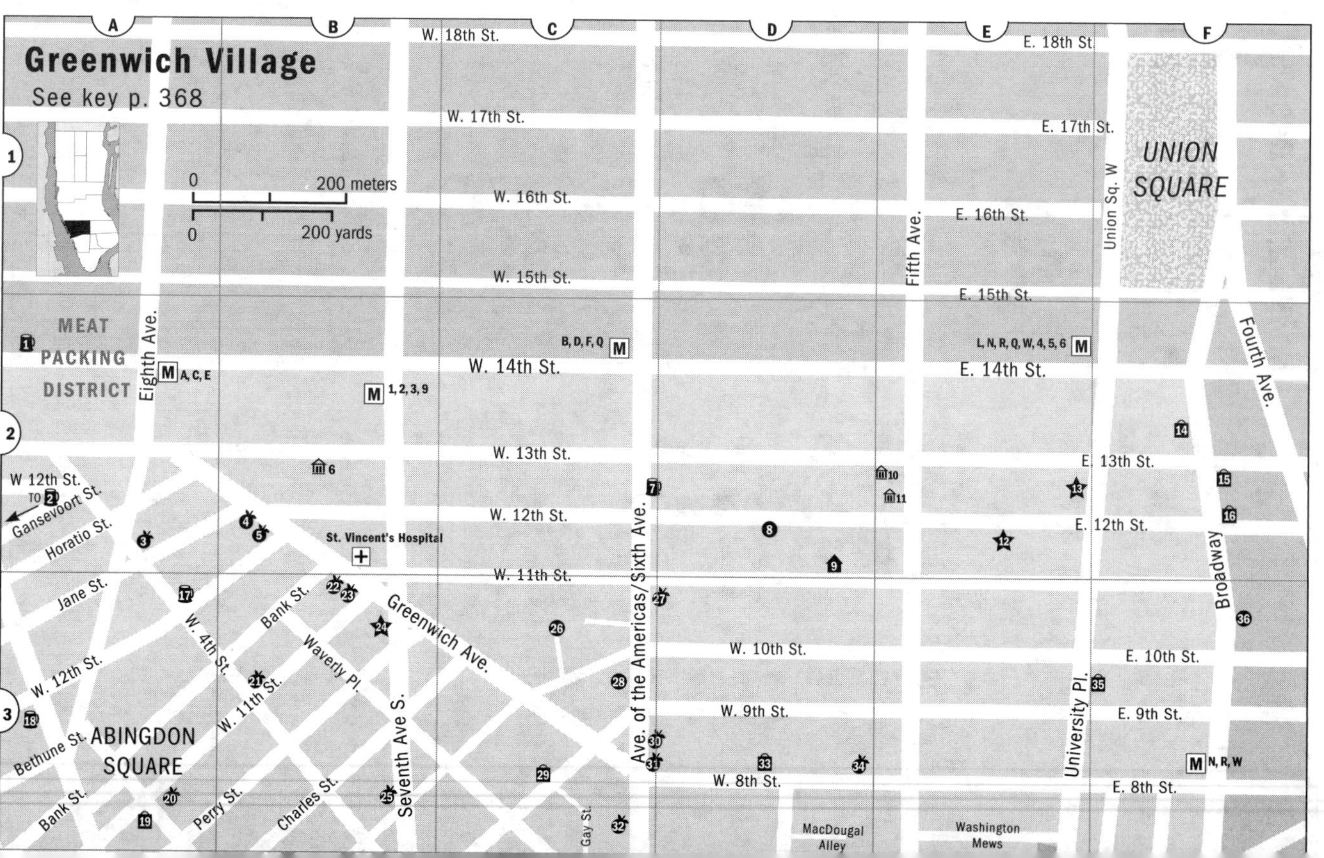

Greenwich Village
See key p. 368
0
200 meters
0
200 yards
MEAT
PACKING
DISTRICT
UNION
SQUARE
ABINGDON
SQUARE
W. 18th St.
E. 18th St.
W. 17th St.
E. 17th St.
W. 16th St.
E. 16th St.
W. 15th St.
E. 15th St.
W. 14th St.
E. 14th St.
W. 13th St.
E. 13th St.
W. 12th St.
E. 12th St.
W. 11th St.
W. 10th St.
E. 10th St.
W. 9th St.
E. 9th St.
W. 8th St.
E. 8th St.
Fourth Ave.
Broadway
Union Sq. W
University Pl.
Fifth Ave.
Ave. of the Americas/Sixth Ave.
Seventh Ave S.
Eighth Ave.
Greenwich Ave.
Waverly Pl.
Bank St.
W. 4th St.
W. 11th St.
Charles St.
Perry St.
Jane St.
Horatio St.
Gansevoort St.
W 12th St.
TO 2
Bethune St.
Gay St.
MacDougal Alley
Washington Mews
St. Vincent's Hospital
L, N, R, Q, W, 4, 5, 6
B, D, F, Q
1, 2, 3, 9
A, C, E
N, R, W
A
B
C
D
E
F
1
2
3

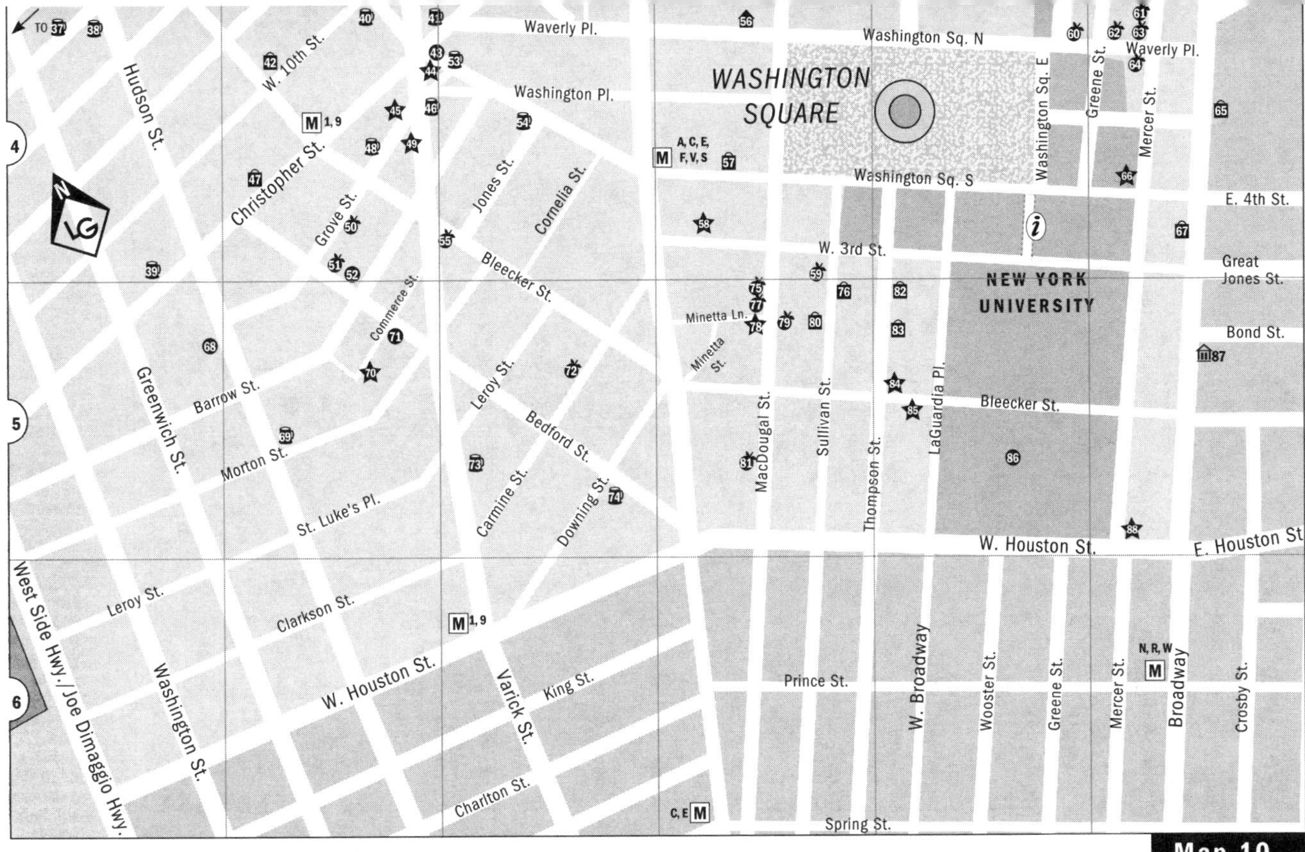

Map 10
WASHINGTON SQUARE
NEW YORK UNIVERSITY
Washington Sq. N
Washington Sq. S
Washington Sq. E
Waverly Pl.
Washington Pl.
Greene St.
Mercer St.
E. 4th St.
Great Jones St.
Bond St.
W. 3rd St.
Minetta Ln.
Minetta St.
MacDougal St.
Sullivan St.
Thompson St.
LaGuardia Pl.
Bleecker St.
W. Houston St.
E. Houston St
Hudson St.
W. 10th St.
Christopher St.
Grove St.
Jones St.
Cornelia St.
Commerce St.
Barrow St.
Greenwich St.
Morton St.
St. Luke's Pl.
Leroy St.
Bedford St.
Carmine St.
Downing St.
Clarkson St.
Varick St.
King St.
Charlton St.
Washington St.
West Side Hwy./Joe Dimaggio Hwy.
Prince St.
Spring St.
W. Broadway
Wooster St.
Broadway
Crosby St.
N, R, W
A, C, E, F, V, S
1, 9
C, E
TO 37
4
5
6

Greenwich Village

See map p. 366-367

ACCOMMODATIONS

Larchmont Hotel, **9** *D2*
Washington Square Hotel, **56** *D4*

FOOD & DRINK

Arturo's Pizza, **86** *E5*
Bagel Buffet, **30** *C3*
Caffe Dante, **81** *D5*
Caffe Pane e Cioccolato, **64** *F4*
Caffe Raffaella, **25** *B3*
Cafe Mona Lisa, **55** *C4*
Cafe de L'Université, **60** *E4*
Caliente Cab Co., **62** *F4*
Chez Brigitte, **23** *B3*
Corner Bistro, **3** *A2*
Day-O, **5** *B2*
Esperanto Cafe, **79** *D5*
Eva's, **34** *D3*
French Roast Cafe, **27** *C3*
Gray's Papaya, **31** *C3*
The Grey Dog Cafe, **72** *C5*
The Magnolia Bakery, **20** *A3*
John's Pizzeria, **55** *C4*
Lips, **22** *B3*
Mahmoun's, **75** *D5*
Manna, **61** *F4*
Moustache, **51** *B4*
Olive Tree Cafe, **77** *D5*
Peanut Butter & Co., **59** *D4*
The Pink Tea Cup, **50** *B4*
Pizza Mercato, **63** *F4*
Soy Luck Club, **4** *B2*
Tartine, **21** *B3*
Waverly Restaurant, **32** C3

SHOPPING

Andy's Chee-pee's, **67** *F4*
Biography Bookstore, **19** *A3*
Cheap Jack's Vintage Clothing, **14** *F2*
Condomania, **42** *B4*
Disc-o-Rama, **57** *D4*
Forbidden Planet, **15** *F2*
Generation Records, **83** *E5*
La Petite Coquette, **35** *F3*
The Leather Man, **47** *B4*
Oscar Wilde Bookstore, **29** *C3*
Second Coming Records, **76** *D5*
Shakespeare and Company, **65** *F4*
Strand Bookstore, **16** *F2*
Uncle Sam's Army Navy, **33** *D3*
Village Chess Shop, **82** *E5*
Village Comics, **80** *D4*

NIGHTLIFE

Absolutely 4th, **40** *B4*
Automatic Slims, **37** *A4*
Bar d'O, **74** *C5*
Bar 6, **7** *C2*
Chi Chiz, **39** *A4*
Crazy Nanny's, **73** *C5*
The Cubbyhole, **17** *A3*
The Duplex, **53** *C4*
Jekyll & Hyde, **46** *B4*
Hell, **2** *A2*
Henrietta Hudson, **69** *B5*
Kava Lounge, **18** *A3*
Rose's Turn, **48** *B4*
The Slaughtered Lamb Pub, **54** *C4*
Stonewall Inn, **41** *B4*
The Village Idiot, **1** *A2*
The Whitehorse Tavern, **38** *A4*

ARTS & ENTERTAINMENT

101 Club, **44** *B4*
Actors Playhouse, **49** *B4*
Angelika Film Center, **88** *F5*
Arthur's Tavern, **45** *B4*
The Bitter End, **84** *E5*
Blue Note, **58** *D4*
Bottom Line, **66** *F4*
Bowlmor Lanes, **13** *E2*
Cafe Wha?, **78** *D5*
Cherry Lane, **70** *B5*
Cinema Village, **12** *E2*
Elbow Room, **85** *E5*
Village Vanguard, **24** *B3*

SIGHTS

75½ Bedford Street, **71** *B5*
Chumley's, **52** *B4*
Church of St. Luke's in the Fields, **68** *A5*
Grace Church, **36** *F3*
Jefferson Market Library, **28** *C3*
Patchin Place, **26** *C3*
Picasso, **86** *E5*
Sheridan Square, **43** *B4*
New School, **8** *D2*

MUSEUMS & GALLERIES

Forbes Magazine Galleries, **11** *E2*
Parsons Exhibition Center, **10** *E2*
Leica Gallery, **87** *F5*
National Museum and Archive of Lesbian, Gay, Bisexual and Transgender History, **6** *B2*

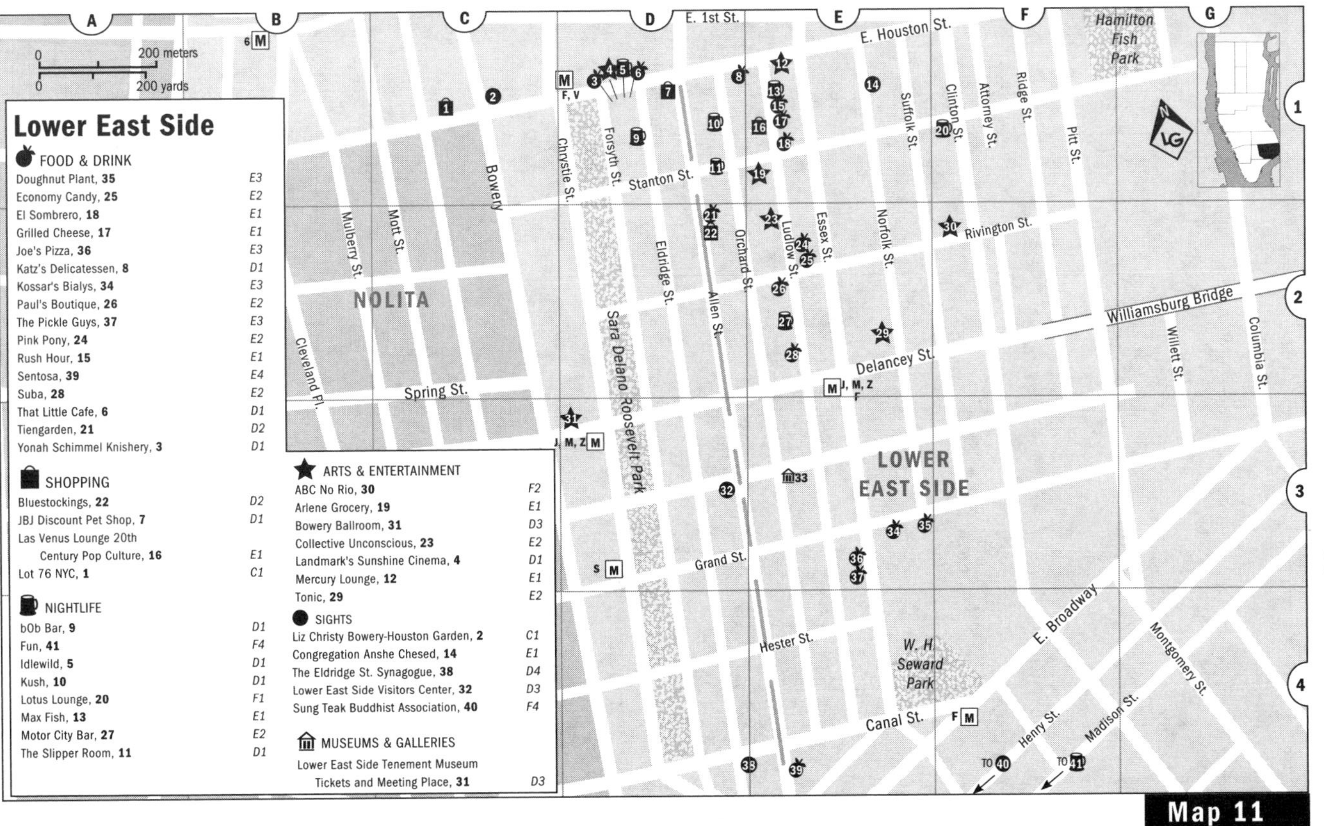
Map 11
Lower East Side
0 200 meters
0 200 yards
FOOD & DRINK
Doughnut Plant, 35 E3
Economy Candy, 25 E2
El Sombrero, 18 E1
Grilled Cheese, 17 E1
Joe's Pizza, 36 E3
Katz's Delicatessen, 8 D1
Kossar's Bialys, 34 E3
Paul's Boutique, 26 E2
The Pickle Guys, 37 E3
Pink Pony, 24 E2
Rush Hour, 15 E1
Sentosa, 39 E4
Suba, 28 E2
That Little Cafe, 6 D1
Tiengarden, 21 D2
Yonah Schimmel Knishery, 3 D1
SHOPPING
Bluestockings, 22 D2
JBJ Discount Pet Shop, 7 D1
Las Venus Lounge 20th Century Pop Culture, 16 E1
Lot 76 NYC, 1 C1
NIGHTLIFE
bOb Bar, 9 D1
Fun, 41 F4
Idlewild, 5 D1
Kush, 10 D1
Lotus Lounge, 20 F1
Max Fish, 13 E1
Motor City Bar, 27 E2
The Slipper Room, 11 D1
ARTS & ENTERTAINMENT
ABC No Rio, 30 F2
Arlene Grocery, 19 E1
Bowery Ballroom, 31 D3
Collective Unconscious, 23 E2
Landmark's Sunshine Cinema, 4 D1
Mercury Lounge, 12 E1
Tonic, 29 E2
SIGHTS
Liz Christy Bowery-Houston Garden, 2 C1
Congregation Anshe Chesed, 14 E1
The Eldridge St. Synagogue, 38 D4
Lower East Side Visitors Center, 32 D3
Sung Teak Buddhist Association, 40 F4
MUSEUMS & GALLERIES
Lower East Side Tenement Museum Tickets and Meeting Place, 31 D3
Hamilton Fish Park
E. 1st St.
E. Houston St.
Stanton St.
Rivington St.
Delancey St.
Spring St.
Grand St.
Hester St.
Canal St.
Williamsburg Bridge
Mulberry St.
Mott St.
Bowery
Chrystie St.
Forsyth St.
Eldridge St.
Allen St.
Orchard St.
Ludlow St.
Essex St.
Norfolk St.
Suffolk St.
Clinton St.
Attorney St.
Ridge St.
Pitt St.
Willett St.
Columbia St.
Cleveland Pl.
Sara Delano Roosevelt Park
NOLITA
LOWER EAST SIDE
W. H. Seward Park
E. Broadway
Montgomery St.
Henry St.
Madison St.
TO 40
TO 41

Map 12
East Village
UNION SQUARE
E. 14th St.
E. 13th St.
E. 12th St.
E. 11th St.
E. 10th St.
E. 9th St.
E. 8th St.
St. Mark's Pl.
E. 7th St.
E. 6th St.
E. 5th St.
E. 4th St.
E. 3rd St.
E. 2nd St.
E. 1st St.
E. Houston St.
Szold Pl.
Ave. D
Ave. C
Ave. B
Ave. A
First Ave.
Second Ave.
Third Ave.
Fourth Ave.
Columbia St.
Hamilton Fish
Tompkins Square Park
ALPHABET CITY
EAST VILLAGE
NOHO
COOPER SQUARE
Cooper Union
Stuyvesant St.
Astor Pl.
Lafayette St.
Great Jones St.
Bond St.
Bleecker St.
Jones Al.
Shinbone Al.
Wanamaker Pl.
8th St.
Waverly Pl.
University Pl.
W. 4th St.
W. 3rd St.
NEW YORK UINVERSITY
200 meters
200 yards

East Village

ACCOMMODATIONS

Chelsea Center Hostel, **9**	*D1*
St. Mark's Hotel, **29**	*C2*

FOOD & DRINK

A Salt and Battery, **72**	*C3*
Alt. Coffee, **49**	*E2*
Around the Clock, **25**	*C2*
Bendix Diner, **36**	*D2*
Blue 9 Burger, **5**	*C1*
Cucina di Pesce, **71**	*C3*
Crif Dogs, **44**	*D2*
The Crooked Tree, **46**	*D2*
Elvie's Turo-Turo, **8**	*D1*
Flor's Kitchen, **40**	*D2*
Frank, **67**	*C3*
Jules, **42**	*D2*
Kate's Corner, **82**	*E3*
La Focacceria, **73**	*D3*
Little Poland, **6**	*C1*
Mama's Food Shop, **98**	*E4*
Max, **102**	*F4*
Moishe's Bake Shop, **64**	*C3*
National Cafe, **8**	*D1*
NYC ICY, **103**	*F4*
Pomme Frites, **60**	*C3*
Sahara East, **10**	*D1*
Second Ave. Delicatessen, **21**	*C2*
Something Sweet, **35**	*D2*
St. Dymphna's, **50**	*E2*
Two Boots Restaurant, **97**, **99**	*E4*
Veniero's, **34**	*D2*
Veselka, **24**	*C2*
Whole Earth Bakery and Kitchen, **50**	*E2*
Yaffa Cafe, **43**	*D2*

SHOPPING

Adorned, **86**	*C4*
Astor Place Hair Stylist, **55**	*B3*
Downtown Music Gallery, **66**	*C3*
FAB208, **75**	*D3*
House of Trance, **47**	*D2*
It's a Mod, Mod World, **76**	*D3*
Jammyland, **92**	*D4*
Kiehl's, **4**	*C1*
Kim's Video and Audio, **30**	*C2*
Love Saves the Day, **61**	*C3*
Manhattan Portage, **41**	*D2*
Metropolis, **23**	*C2*
Other Music, **57**	*B3*
Physical Graffiti, **47**	*D2*
Religious Sex, **28**	*C2*
See Hear, **74**	*D3*
St. Mark's Bookshop, **22**	*C2*
Tatiana Designer Retail Boutique, **47**	*D2*
Tokyo 7 Consignment Store, **75**	*D3*
Tokyo Joe, **33**	*D2*

NIGHTLIFE

The Anyway Cafe, **88**	*C4E2*
Bbar (Bowery Bar), **84**	*C4*
Beauty Bar, **3**	*C1*
Boiler Room, **85**	*C4*
The Cock, **13**	*E1*
d.b.a., **93**	*D4*
Delft, **101**	*E4*
Industry, **79**	*E3*
Izzy Bar, **37**	*D2*
Joe's Bar, **80**	*E3*
Karma, **91**	*D4*
KGB, **70**	*C3*
Korova Milk Bar, **11**	*E1*
Lakeside Lounge, **48**	*E2*
La Linea, **96**	*D4*
Lit, **65**	*C3*
Lucky Cheng's, **95**	*D4*
McSorley's Old Ale House, **62**	*C2*
The Musical Box, **14**	*F1*
Niagara, **77**	*E3*
Nuyorican Poets Cafe, **104**	*F4*
Remote Lounge, **58**	*B3*
Sake Bar Decibel, **26**	*C2*
Tenth St. Lounge, **38**	*D2*
Tribe, **45**	*D2*
Webster Hall, **2**	*B1*
Wonder Bar, **78**	*E3*

ARTS & ENTERTAINMENT

Anthology Film Archives, **90**	*C4*
Astor Place Theater, **31**	*C2*
CBGB, **89**	*C4*
Cinema Classics, **32**	*D2*
Cinema Village, **1**	*A1*
Continental, **27**	*C2*
Detour, **7**	*D1*
Fez, **83**	*B4*
The Joseph Papp Public Theater, **56**	*B3*
Millennium Film Workshop, **68**	*C3*
NY Theatre Workshop, **69**	*C3*
Orpheum, **31**	*C2*
Theater for the New City, **39**	*D2*

SIGHTS

6th St. and Ave. B Garden, **81**	*E3*
Abe Lebewohl Park, **20**	*C2*
Campos Community Garden, **16**	*F1*
Casita Garden, **15**	*F1*
Colonnade Row, **17**	*B2*
Community Garden, **52**	*F2*
The Cooper Union Foundation Building, **59**	*C3*
The Cube, **18**	*B2*
De Colores Community Garden, **53**	*F2*
El Sol Brilliant Garden, **12**	*E1*
Gilbert's Garden, **54**	*F2*
Miracle Garden, **100**	*E4*
New York Marble Cemeteries, **87**, **94**	*C/D4*
St. George Ukrainian Catholic Church, **63**	*C3*
St. Mark's Church in-the-Bowery, **19**	*C2*
Tenth Street Garden, **51**	*F2*

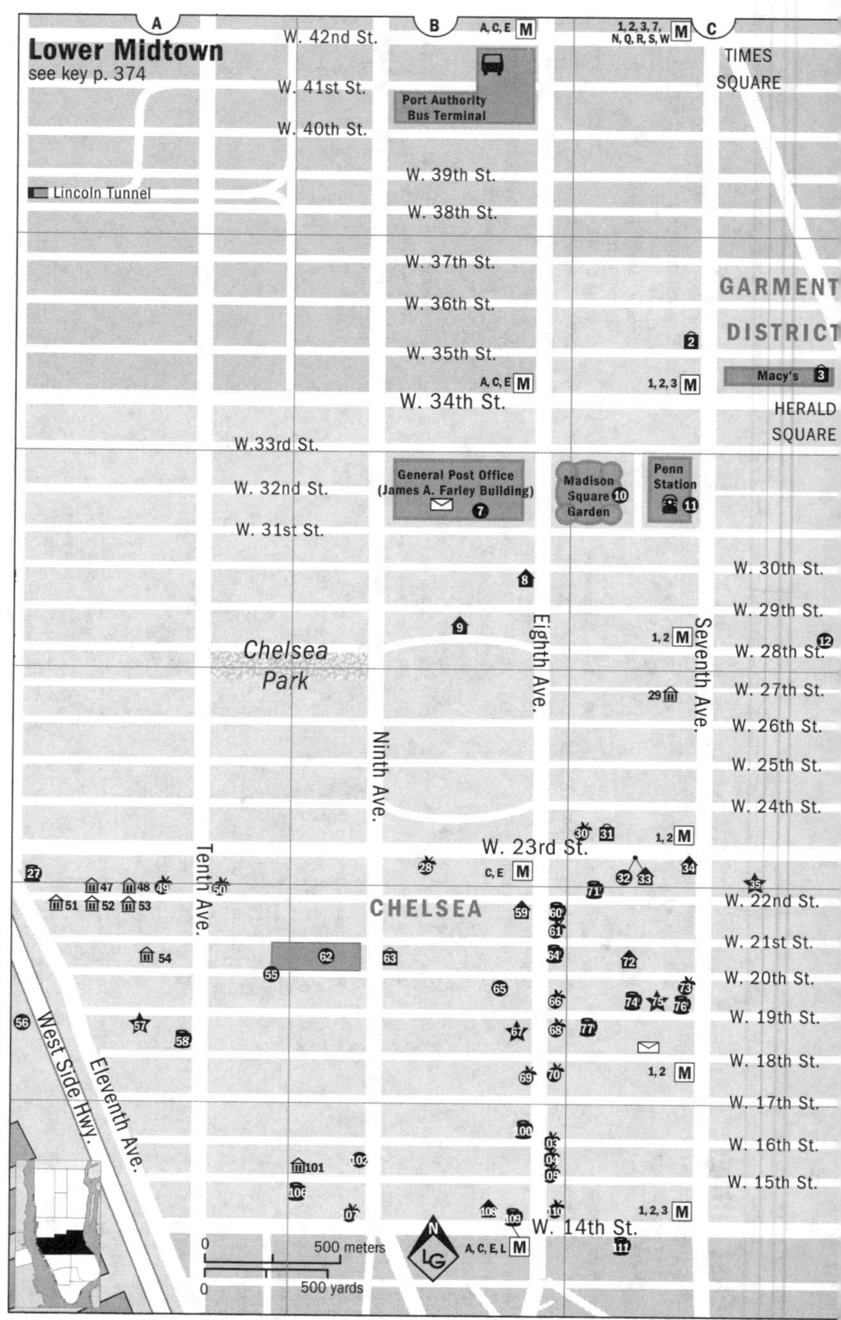

Lower Midtown
see key p. 374
A
B
C
W. 42nd St.
W. 41st St.
W. 40th St.
W. 39th St.
W. 38th St.
W. 37th St.
W. 36th St.
W. 35th St.
W. 34th St.
W.33rd St.
W. 32nd St.
W. 31st St.
W. 30th St.
W. 29th St.
W. 28th St.
W. 27th St.
W. 26th St.
W. 25th St.
W. 24th St.
W. 23rd St.
W. 22nd St.
W. 21st St.
W. 20th St.
W. 19th St.
W. 18th St.
W. 17th St.
W. 16th St.
W. 15th St.
W. 14th St.
A, C, E
1, 2, 3, 7, N, Q, R, S, W
TIMES SQUARE
Port Authority Bus Terminal
Lincoln Tunnel
GARMENT DISTRICT
Macy's
HERALD SQUARE
1, 2, 3
General Post Office (James A. Farley Building)
Madison Square Garden
Penn Station
Eighth Ave.
Seventh Ave.
Ninth Ave.
Tenth Ave.
Eleventh Ave.
West Side Hwy.
Chelsea Park
CHELSEA
1, 2
C, E
1, 2, 3
A, C, E, L
500 meters
500 yards

Map 13
Bryant Park
New York Public Library
American Standard Building
MURRAY HILL
E. 42nd St.
E. 41st St.
E. 40th St.
E. 39th St.
E. 38th St.
E. 37th St.
E. 36th St.
E. 35th St.
E. 34th St.
E. 33rd St.
E. 32nd St.
E. 31st St.
E. 30th St.
E. 29th St.
E. 28th St.
E. 27th St.
E. 26th St.
E. 25th St.
E. 24th St.
E. 23rd St.
E. 22nd St.
E. 21st St.
E. 20th St.
E. 19th St.
E. 18th St.
E. 17th St.
E. 16th St.
E. 15th St.
E. 14th St.
E. 13th St.
W. 13th St.
(VEHICULAR TUNNEL BELOW STREET)
Empire State Building
Madison Ave.
Park Ave.
Park Ave. S
Lexington Ave.
Third Ave.
Second Ave.
First Ave.
Fifth Ave.
Broadway
Avenue of the Americas / Sixth Ave.
Madison Square Park
GRAMERCY PARK
FLATIRON DISTRICT
Gramercy Park
Union Square
Union Sq. E.
Union Sq. W.
Irving Pl.
University Pl.
Stuyvesant Square
4, 5, 6, 7, S
B, D, N, Q, R, V, W
N, R
F, V
F, L, V
4, 5, 6, L, N, Q, R, W

Lower Midtown

see map pp. 372-373

ACCOMMODATIONS

Carlton Arms Hotel, **45** *F4*
Chelsea Center Hostel, **9** *B3*
Chelsea Inn, **113** *D6*
Chelsea International Hostel, **72** *C5*
Chelsea Pines Inn, **108** *B6*
Chelsea Savoy Hotel, **34** *C4*
Chelsea Star Hotel, **8** *B3*
Colonial House Inn, **59** *B5*
Gershwin Hotel, **36** *D4*
Herald Square Hotel, **16** *D3*
Hotel 17, **99** *F5*
Hotel Chelsea, **33** *C4*
Hotel Grand Union, **22** *E3*
Hotel Stanford, **14** *D3*
Hotel Wolcott, **18** *D3*
International Student Hospice, **20** *E3*
Madison Hotel, **40** *E4*
Murray Hill Inn, **25** *F3*
ThirtyThirty, **23** *E3*
Union Square Inn, **124** *F6*

FOOD & DRINK

Better Burger, **66** *B5*
Big Cup, **61** *B5*
Blue Moon Mexican Cafe, **70** *B5*
Chango, **91** *E5*
Chat 'n' Chew, **114** *D6*
Chef & Co., **85** *D5*
Coffee Shop Bar, **122** *E6*
Curry in a Hurry, **24** *E3*
elmo, **73** *C5*
Empire Diner, **50** *A5*
F & B, **30** *C4*
Food Bar, **69** *B5*
Galaxy Global Eatery, **121** *E6*
Havana Central, **86** *D5*
Kang Suh, **15** *D3*
Kitchen 22, **88** *E5*
Kitchen/Market, **61** *B5*
Kum Gang San, **13** *D3*
La Taza de Oro, **110** *B6*
Little Pie Co., **107** *B6*
Mary Ann's, **103** *B6*
Minar, **17** *D3*
Molly's, **46** *F4*
Negril, **28** *B4*
Pad Thai Noodle Lounge, **104** *B6*
Pete's Tavern, **95** *E5*
Rainbow Falafel, **115** *E6*
Ranch 1, **97** *E5*
Rue de Crepes, **105** *B6*
Sunburst Espresso Bar, **98** *F5*
Sushi Samba, **90** *E5*
Tibetan Kitchen, **26** *F3*
Wild Lily Tea Room, **49** *A5*
Zen Palate, **117** *E6*

SHOPPING

17@17 Thrift Shop, **87** *D5*
The Barking Zoo, **63** *B5*
Books of Wonder, **84** *D5*
The Complete Traveller Bookstore, **6** *E2*
H & M, **4** *D2*
Lord and Taylor, **1** *D1*
Macy's, **3** *C2*
Midnight Records, **31** *C4*
Reminiscence, **38** *D4*
Revolution Books, **82** *D5*
Rock and Soul, **2** *C2*
Throb, **125** *F6*
Weiss and Mahoney, **83** *D5*

NIGHTLIFE

Barracuda, **71** *C5*
Big Apple Ranch, **81** *D5*
Centrofly, **80** *D5*
Eugene, **37** *D4*
g, **74** *C5*
Go, **109** *B6*
Lola, **79** *D5*
Nell's, **111** *C6*
Old Town Bar and Grill, **94** *E5*
Open, **27** *A4*
Passerby, **106** *B6*
Peter McManus, **76** *C5*
Q Lounge, **77** *C5*
Rawhide, **64** *B5*
The Roxy, **58** *A5*
SBNY, **112** *D6*
Suite 16, **100** *B6*
The View, **60** *B5*

ARTS & ENTERTAINMENT

Dance Theater Workshop, **75** *C5*
Darryl Roth Theater, **119** *E6*
Gotham Comedy Club, **78** *D5*
Irving Plaza, **120** *E6*
Joyce Theater, **67** *B5*
The Kitchen, **57** *A5*
Museum of Modern Art Film and Media, **44** *E4*
Union Square Theatre, **116** *E6*
Upright Citizens Brigade Theater, **35** *C4*
Vineyard Theater Company's Dimson Theater, **123** *E6*

SIGHTS

69th Regiment Armory, **42** *E4*
American Academy of Dramatic Arts, **21** *E3*
Chelsea Market, **102** *B6*
Chelsea Piers, **56** *A5*
Church of the Transfiguration, **19** *D3*
Cushman Row, **55** *A5*
Empire State Building, **5** *D2*
Flatiron Building, **39** *D4*
Flower District, **12** *C3*
General Post Office (Farley Building), **7** *B3*
General Theological Seminary, **62** *B5*
Hotel Chelsea, **32** *C4*
Madison Square Garden, **10** *C3*
Metropolitan Life Insurance Tower, **43** *E4*
National Arts Club, **92** *E5*
New York Life Insurance Building, **41** *E4*
Penn Station, **11** *C3*
Player's Club, **93** *E5*
St. Peter's Episcopal Church, **65** *B5*
The Theodore Roosevelt Birthplace, **89** *E5*
Union Square Theatre, **96** *E5*
Union Square Savings Bank, **118** *E6*

MUSEUMS & GALLERIES

303 Gallery, **47** *A5*
535 W. 22nd St., **47** *A5*
D'Amelio Terras, **47** *A5*
DCA Gallery, **47** *A5*
Dia Center for the Arts, **51** *A5*
Gavin Brown's Enterprise, **101** *B6*
I-20, **54** *A5*
Matthew Marks, **53** *A5*
Max Protetch, **48** *A5*
The Museum at Fashion Institute of Technology, **29** *C4*
Sonnabend, **52** *A5*

Midtown

see map pp. 376-377

ACCOMMODATIONS

Americana Inn, **92** *D5*
Best Western President Hotel, **34** *C3*
Big Apple Hostel, **71** *C4*
Broadway Inn, **70** *C4*
Hotel Pickwick Arms, **55** *F3*
Hudson Hotel, **4** *B2*
New York Inn, **60** *B4*
Portland Square Hotel, **69** *C3*
Skyline Hotel, **29** *A3*
Super 8 Hotel, **78** *D4*
YMCA-Vanderbilt, **83** *F3*

FOOD & DRINK

Becco, **58** *B4*
Brasserie Centrale, **13** *C2*
Ess-a-Bagel, **54** *E3*
Fresco by Scotto, **50** *E3*
Hourglass Tavern, **57** *B4*
Island Burgers & Shakes, **30** *B3*
Manganaro's, **87** *B5*
Mangia, **48** *D3*
Minamoto Kitchoan, **43** *D3*
Original Fresco Tortillas, **77** *C4*
Sapporo, **35** *C3*
Stage Deli, **14** *C2*
Tandoori Club, **93** *D5*
Teuscher Chocolatier, **44** *D3*

SHOPPING

Bentley Manhattan, **62** *E3*
Bergdorff-Goodman, **18** *D2*
The Drama Book Shop, **90** *C5*
F.A.O. Schwarz, **19** *D2*
Gotham Book Mart, **47** *D3*
Hacker Art Books, **16** *D2*
Hammacher Schlemmer, **26** *E2*
Lord and Taylor, **94** *D5*
Saks Fifth Avenue, **45** *D3*
Tiffany & Co., **21** *D2*

NIGHTLIFE

Chase, **6** *C2*
La Nueva Escuelita, **88** *B5*

ARTS & ENTERTAINMENT

Birdland, **64** *B4*
Carnegie Hall, **8** *C2*
City Center, **9** *C2*
The Daily Show, **3** *A2*
Hit Show Club, **61** *B4*
Imperial Theater, **62** *B4*
Lunt-Fontanne Theatre, **67** *C4*
Lamb's, **75** *C4*
Late Show with David Letterman, **12** *B2*
Majestic Theater, **73** *C4*
Manhattan Theater Club, **7** *C2*
NBC Studios, **41** *D3*
Nederlander Theater, **89** *B5*
Neil Simon Theater, **31** *C3*
New Amsterdam Theater, **66** *B4*
Peck and Goodie Skates, **5** *B2*
Primary Stages, **63** *B4*
Roseland Ballroom, **32** *C3*
Samuel Beckett Theater, **65** *B4*
Shubert Theater, **73** *C4*
St. James Theater, **73** *C4*
Studio 54, **11** *C2*
Swing 46, **59** *B4*
TKTS, **68** *C4*
Ziegfeld, **15** *C2*

SIGHTS

A Fireman's Prayer, **72** *C4*
AXA Financial Center, **37** *D3*
The Algonquin Hotel, **79** *D4*
Chrysler Building, **81** *E4*
Citigroup Center/Saint Peter's, **28** *E2*
City Center Theater, **10** *C2*
Crown Building, **20** *D2*
Daily News Building, **85** *F4*
Equitable Life Building, **33** *C3*
GE Building, **42** *D3*
Grand Central Station, **80** *E4*
Jacob K. Javits Convention Center, **86** *A5*
John Jay College of Criminal Justice, **2** *A2*
MetLife Building, **80** *E4*
New York Public Library, **91** *D5*
The New York Times, **74** *C4*
Plaza Hotel, **17** *D2*
Radio City Music Hall, **36** *D3*
Seagram Building, **51** *E3*
Sony Plaza, **23** *D2*
St. Bartholomew's Church, **52** *E3*
St. Patrick's Cathedral, **40** *D3*
Trump International Hotel, **1** *B1*
Trump Tower, **22** *D2*
United Nations, **84** *F4*
University Club, **24** *D2*
Waldorf Astoria Hotel, **53** *E3*

MUSEUMS & GALLERIES

American Craft Museum, **38** *D3*
Christie's, **46** *D3*
Fuller Building, **25** *E2*
International Center of Photography, **76** *C4*
Japan Society, **56** *F3*
Museum of Television and Radio, **39** *D3*
Pace Gallery, **27** *E2*

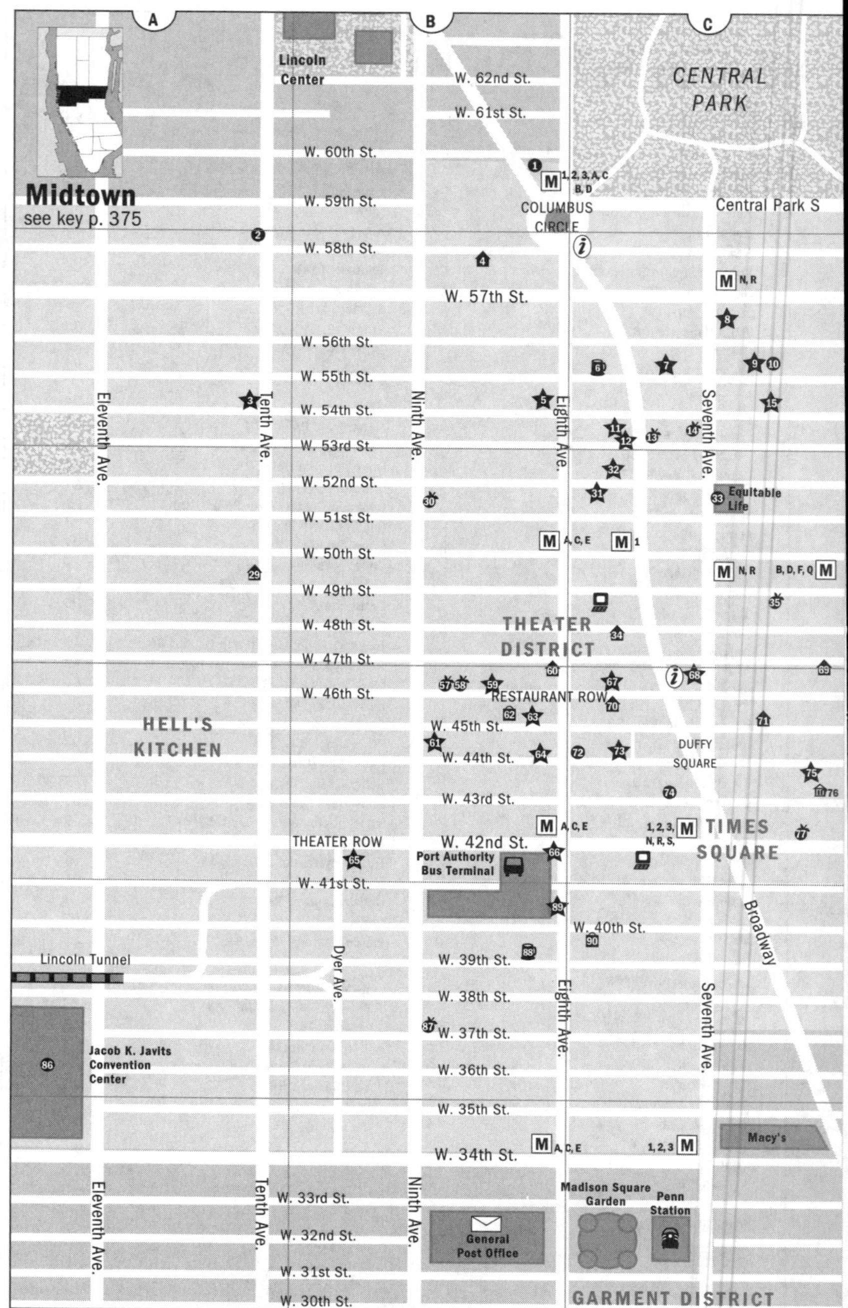
Midtown
see key p. 375
A
B
C
Lincoln Center
CENTRAL PARK
W. 62nd St.
W. 61st St.
W. 60th St.
W. 59th St.
COLUMBUS CIRCLE
Central Park S
W. 58th St.
W. 57th St.
W. 56th St.
W. 55th St.
W. 54th St.
W. 53rd St.
W. 52nd St.
W. 51st St.
W. 50th St.
W. 49th St.
W. 48th St.
W. 47th St.
W. 46th St.
W. 45th St.
W. 44th St.
W. 43rd St.
W. 42nd St.
W. 41st St.
W. 40th St.
W. 39th St.
W. 38th St.
W. 37th St.
W. 36th St.
W. 35th St.
W. 34th St.
W. 33rd St.
W. 32nd St.
W. 31st St.
W. 30th St.
Eleventh Ave.
Tenth Ave.
Ninth Ave.
Eighth Ave.
Seventh Ave.
Broadway
Dyer Ave.
Equitable Life
THEATER DISTRICT
RESTAURANT ROW
HELL'S KITCHEN
DUFFY SQUARE
TIMES SQUARE
THEATER ROW
Port Authority Bus Terminal
Lincoln Tunnel
Jacob K. Javits Convention Center
Macy's
Madison Square Garden
Penn Station
General Post Office
GARMENT DISTRICT
1, 2, 3, A, C, B, D
N, R
A, C, E
1
B, D, F, Q
1, 2, 3, N, R, S,
1, 2, 3

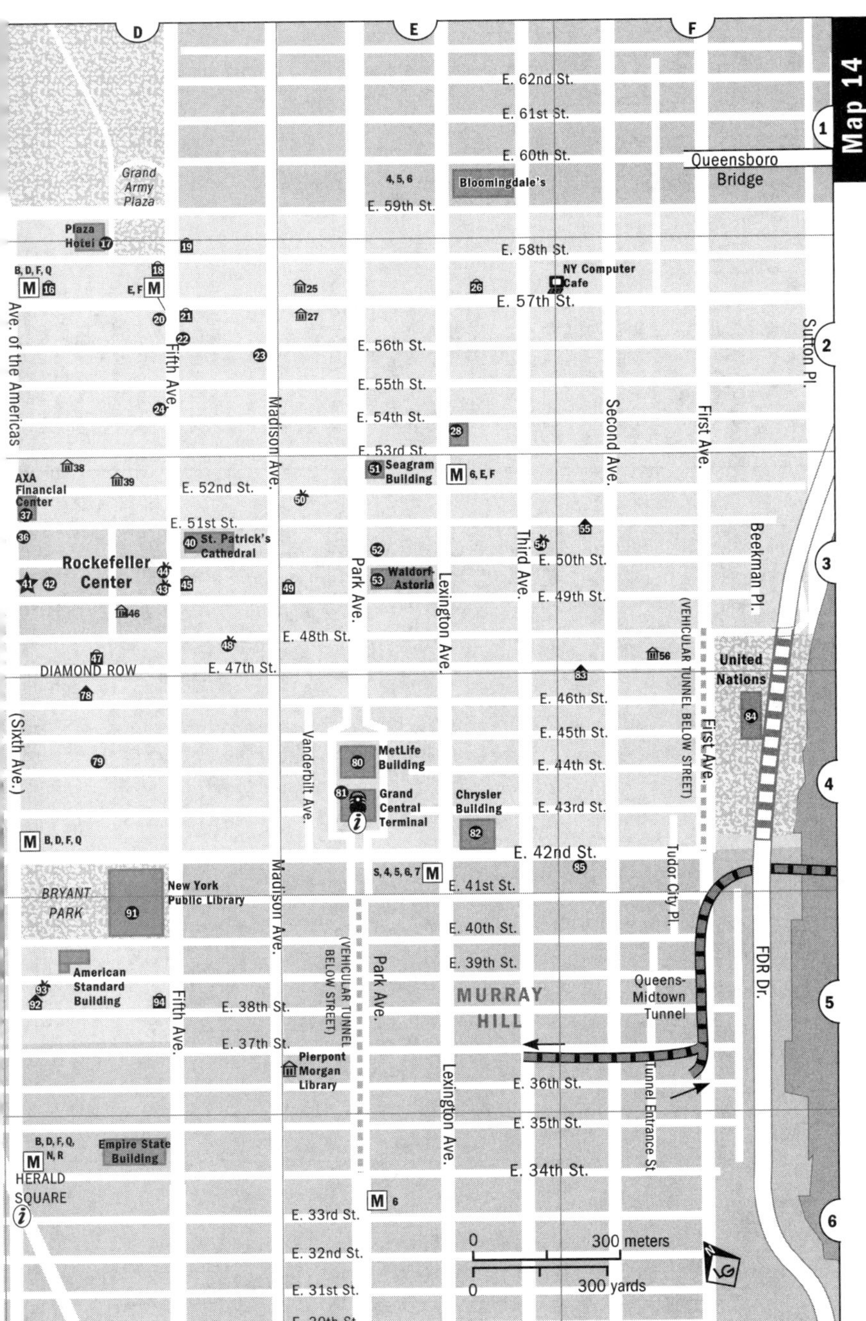
Map 14
D
E
F
1
2
3
4
5
6
E. 62nd St.
E. 61st St.
E. 60th St.
Queensboro Bridge
Grand Army Plaza
4, 5, 6
Bloomingdale's
E. 59th St.
Plaza Hotel
E. 58th St.
B, D, F, Q
E, F
NY Computer Cafe
E. 57th St.
Ave. of the Americas
Fifth Ave.
Sutton Pl.
E. 56th St.
E. 55th St.
E. 54th St.
Madison Ave.
Second Ave.
First Ave.
E. 53rd St.
Seagram Building
6, E, F
AXA Financial Center
E. 52nd St.
E. 51st St.
St. Patrick's Cathedral
Rockefeller Center
Beekman Pl.
Third Ave.
E. 50th St.
Park Ave.
Waldorf-Astoria
Lexington Ave.
E. 49th St.
E. 48th St.
(VEHICULAR TUNNEL BELOW STREET)
United Nations
DIAMOND ROW
E. 47th St.
E. 46th St.
E. 45th St.
(Sixth Ave.)
Vanderbilt Ave.
MetLife Building
E. 44th St.
Grand Central Terminal
Chrysler Building
E. 43rd St.
B, D, F, Q
E. 42nd St.
S, 4, 5, 6, 7
E. 41st St.
Tudor City Pl.
BRYANT PARK
New York Public Library
E. 40th St.
E. 39th St.
American Standard Building
MURRAY HILL
Queens-Midtown Tunnel
FDR Dr.
E. 38th St.
E. 37th St.
Pierpont Morgan Library
E. 36th St.
Tunnel Entrance St
E. 35th St.
B, D, F, Q, N, R
Empire State Building
E. 34th St.
HERALD SQUARE
6
E. 33rd St.
0
300 meters
E. 32nd St.
0
300 yards
E. 31st St.
E. 30th St.

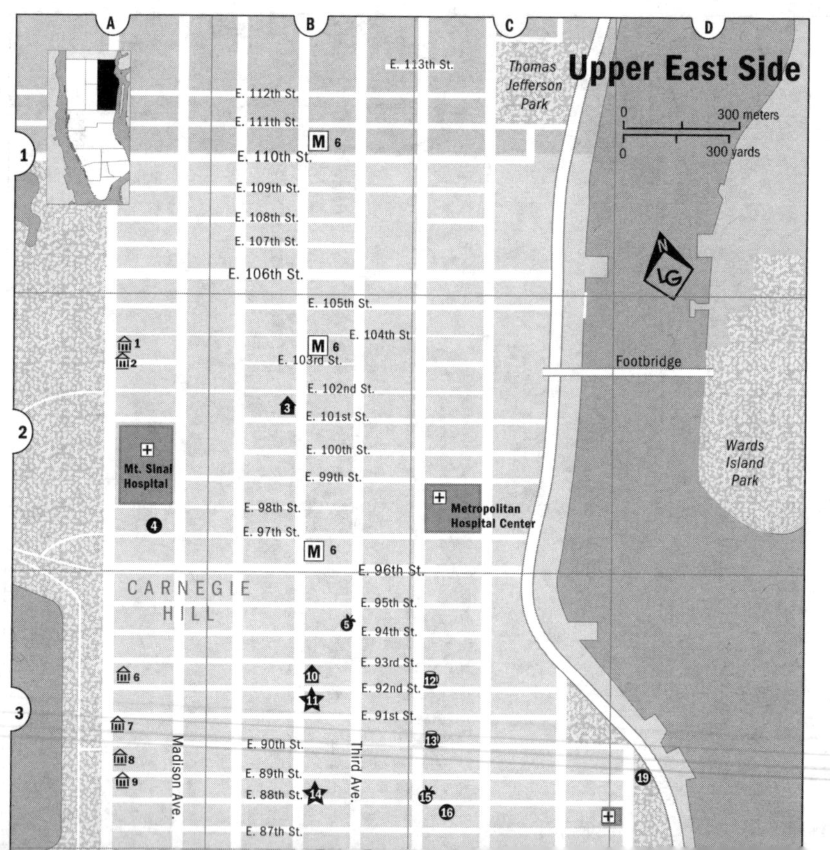

ACCOMMODATIONS	
De Hirsch Residence, **10**	B3
Manhattan Youth Castle, **3**	B2
FOOD & DRINK	
Barking Dog Luncheonette, **5**	B3
Burger Heaven, **54**	B6
Candle Cafe, **33**	B5
Dallas BBQ, **35**	B5
EJ's Luncheonette, **34**	B5
Grace's Marketplace, **36**	B5
Green Kitchen, **27**	C4
Jackson Hole, **52**	B6
Le Pain Quotidien, **21**	A4
Merchants NY, **58**	C6
Papaya King, **17**	B4
Saigon Grill, **15**	C3
Viand, **56**	A6
World of Nuts & Ice Cream, **63**	B6
SHOPPING	
Argosy Bookstore, **66**	B6
Barneys New York, **61**	A6
Bloomingdales, **67**	B6
Encore, **20**	A4
Rita Ford Music Boxes, **50**	A6
Tender Buttons, **57**	B6
NIGHTLIFE	
American Spirits, **13**	C3
The Big Easy, **12**	C3
Brother Jimmy's BBQ, **26**	B4
Mo's Caribbean Bar and Grille, **31**	C5
Ship of Fools, **23**	C4
ARTS & ENTERTAINMENT	
92nd Street Y, **11**	B3
Comic Strip Live, **24**	C4
Dangerfield's, **59**	C6
Dicapo Opera Theater, **29**	B5
John Jay Pool, **28**	C4

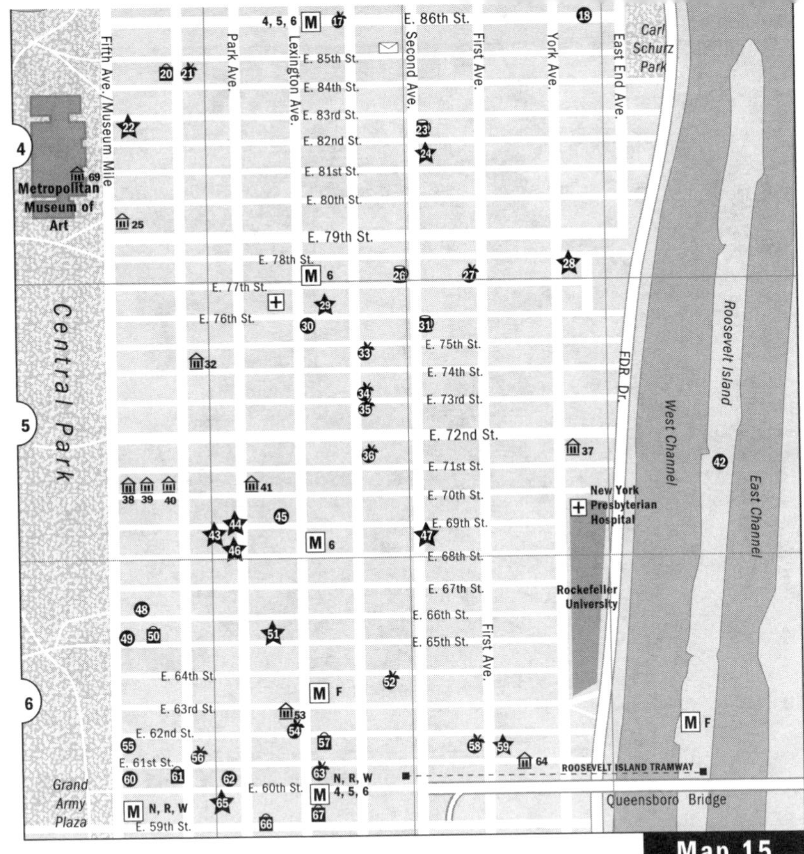

Metro Bicycle Stores, **14**	*B3*
Pedal Pushers, **47**	*C5*
Cultural Institutes:	
Alliance Française, **65**	*B6*
Americas Society, **46**	*B5*
China Institute, **51**	*B6*
Goethe-Institute, **22**	*A4*
Italian Cultural Institute, **44**	*B5*
Spanish Institute, **43**	*B5*

SIGHTS

Gracie Mansion, **19**	*D3*
Grolier Club, **62**	*B6*
Henderson Place Historic District, **18**	*C4*
The Church of Holy Trinity, **16**	*C3*
Knickerbocker Club, **55**	*A6*
Lotos Club, **45**	*B5*
Metropolitan Club, **60**	*A6*
Roosevelt Island, **42**	*D5*
Church of St. Jean Baptiste, **30**	*B5*
St. Nicholas Russian Orthodox Cathedral, **4**	*A2*
Temple Emanu-El, **49**	*A6*
Union Club, **48**	*A6*

MUSEUMS & GALLERIES

Acquavella Gallery, **25**	*A4*
The Asia Society, **41**	*B5*
The Cooper-Hewitt National Design Museum, **7**	*A3*
El Museo del Barrio, **1**	*A2*
Frick Collection, **38**	*A5*
Guggenheim Museum, **9**	*A3*
Hirschl & Adler Galleries, **39**	*A5*
The Jewish Museum, **6**	*A3*
Metropolitan Museum of Art, **69**	*A4*
M. Knoedler & Co., Inc, **40**	*A5*
Mt. Vernon Hotel Museum and Garden, **64**	*C6*
Museum of American Illustration, **53**	*B6*
Museum of the City of New York, **2**	*A2*
National Academy of Design Museum, **8**	*A3*
Sotheby's, **37**	*C5*
Whitney Museum of American Art, **32**	*A5*

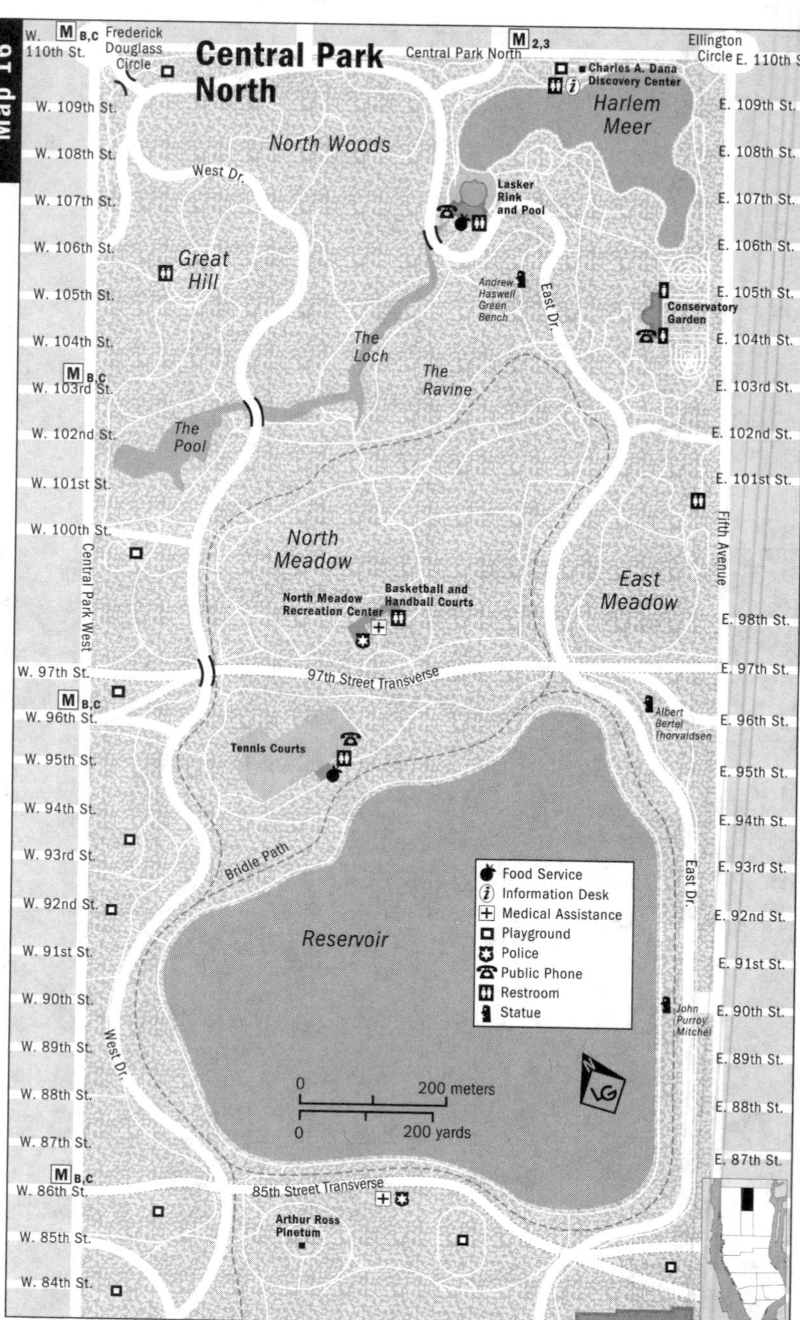

Map 16
Central Park North
W. 110th St.
Frederick Douglass Circle
B,C
Central Park North
2,3
Ellington Circle
E. 110th St.
Charles A. Dana Discovery Center
Harlem Meer
North Woods
West Dr.
Lasker Rink and Pool
Great Hill
Andrew Haswell Green Bench
East Dr.
Conservatory Garden
The Loch
The Ravine
The Pool
North Meadow
East Meadow
Fifth Avenue
Central Park West
North Meadow Recreation Center
Basketball and Handball Courts
97th Street Transverse
Albert Bertel Thorvaldsen
Tennis Courts
Bridle Path
Reservoir
John Purroy Mitchel
85th Street Transverse
Arthur Ross Pinetum
W. 109th St.
W. 108th St.
W. 107th St.
W. 106th St.
W. 105th St.
W. 104th St.
W. 103rd St.
W. 102nd St.
W. 101st St.
W. 100th St.
W. 97th St.
W. 96th St.
W. 95th St.
W. 94th St.
W. 93rd St.
W. 92nd St.
W. 91st St.
W. 90th St.
W. 89th St.
W. 88th St.
W. 87th St.
W. 86th St.
W. 85th St.
W. 84th St.
E. 109th St.
E. 108th St.
E. 107th St.
E. 106th St.
E. 105th St.
E. 104th St.
E. 103rd St.
E. 102nd St.
E. 101st St.
E. 98th St.
E. 97th St.
E. 96th St.
E. 95th St.
E. 94th St.
E. 93rd St.
E. 92nd St.
E. 91st St.
E. 90th St.
E. 89th St.
E. 88th St.
E. 87th St.
Food Service
Information Desk
Medical Assistance
Playground
Police
Public Phone
Restroom
Statue
0
200 meters
0
200 yards

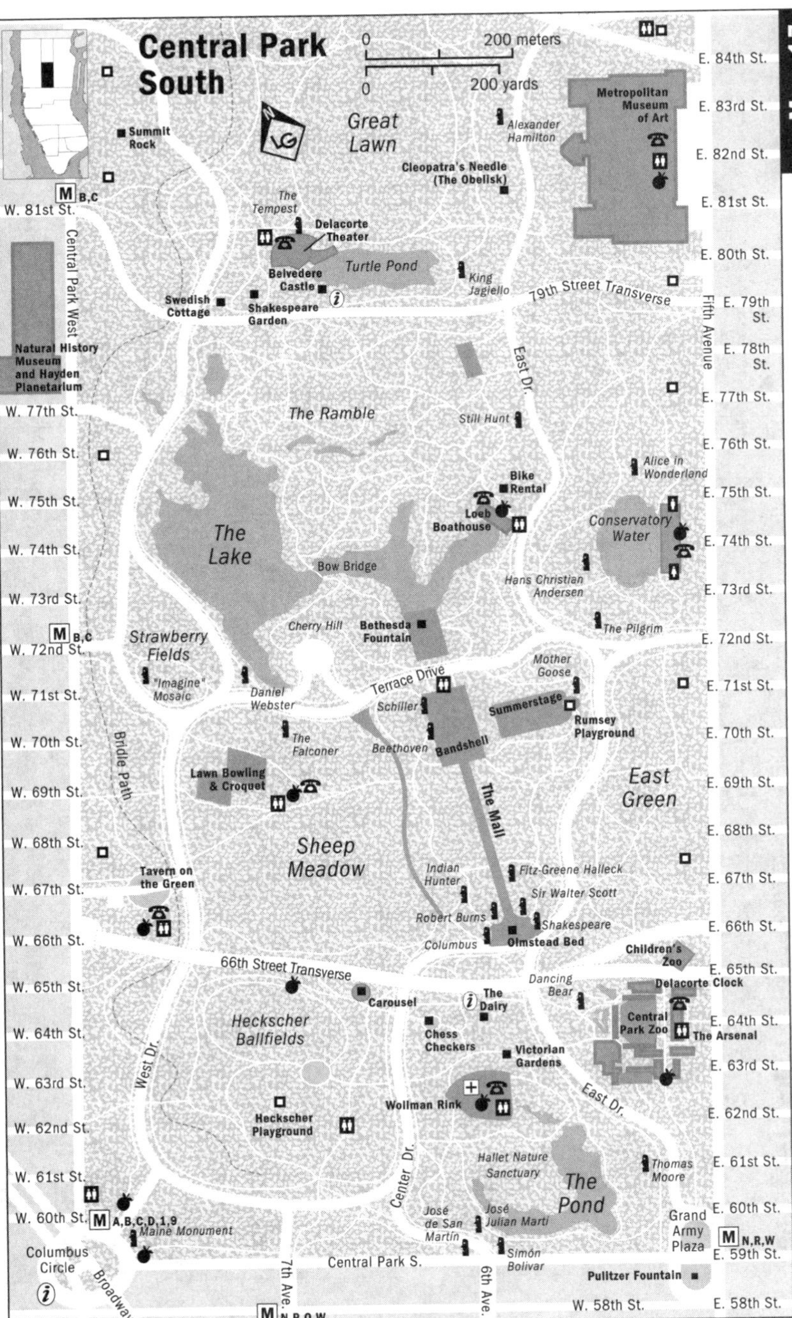
Central Park South
Map 17
0 200 meters
0 200 yards
Great Lawn
Summit Rock
Alexander Hamilton
Metropolitan Museum of Art
Cleopatra's Needle (The Obelisk)
The Tempest
Delacorte Theater
Turtle Pond
Belvedere Castle
King Jagiello
Swedish Cottage
Shakespeare Garden
79th Street Transverse
Central Park West
Natural History Museum and Hayden Planetarium
East Dr.
Fifth Avenue
The Ramble
Still Hunt
Alice in Wonderland
Bike Rental
Loeb Boathouse
Conservatory Water
The Lake
Bow Bridge
Hans Christian Andersen
Cherry Hill
Bethesda Fountain
The Pilgrim
Strawberry Fields
"Imagine" Mosaic
Daniel Webster
Terrace Drive
Mother Goose
Schiller
Summerstage
Rumsey Playground
The Falconer
Beethoven
Bandshell
Bridle Path
Lawn Bowling & Croquet
East Green
The Mall
Sheep Meadow
Tavern on the Green
Indian Hunter
Fitz-Greene Halleck
Sir Walter Scott
Robert Burns
Shakespeare
Columbus
Olmstead Bed
Children's Zoo
66th Street Transverse
Dancing Bear
Delacorte Clock
Carousel
The Dairy
Heckscher Ballfields
Chess Checkers
Central Park Zoo
The Arsenal
Victorian Gardens
West Dr.
East Dr.
Wollman Rink
Heckscher Playground
Hallet Nature Sanctuary
The Pond
Thomas Moore
Center Dr.
José de San Martín
José Julian Martí
Grand Army Plaza
Maine Monument
Simón Bolívar
Columbus Circle
Central Park S.
Pulitzer Fountain
Broadway
7th Ave.
6th Ave.
W. 58th St.
M B,C
M A,B,C,D,1,9
M N,R,W
M N,R,Q,W
W. 81st St.
W. 77th St.
W. 76th St.
W. 75th St.
W. 74th St.
W. 73rd St.
W. 72nd St.
W. 71st St.
W. 70th St.
W. 69th St.
W. 68th St.
W. 67th St.
W. 66th St.
W. 65th St.
W. 64th St.
W. 63rd St.
W. 62nd St.
W. 61st St.
W. 60th St.
E. 84th St.
E. 83rd St.
E. 82nd St.
E. 81st St.
E. 80th St.
E. 79th St.
E. 78th St.
E. 77th St.
E. 76th St.
E. 75th St.
E. 74th St.
E. 73rd St.
E. 72nd St.
E. 71st St.
E. 70th St.
E. 69th St.
E. 68th St.
E. 67th St.
E. 66th St.
E. 65th St.
E. 64th St.
E. 63rd St.
E. 62nd St.
E. 61st St.
E. 60th St.
E. 59th St.
E. 58th St.

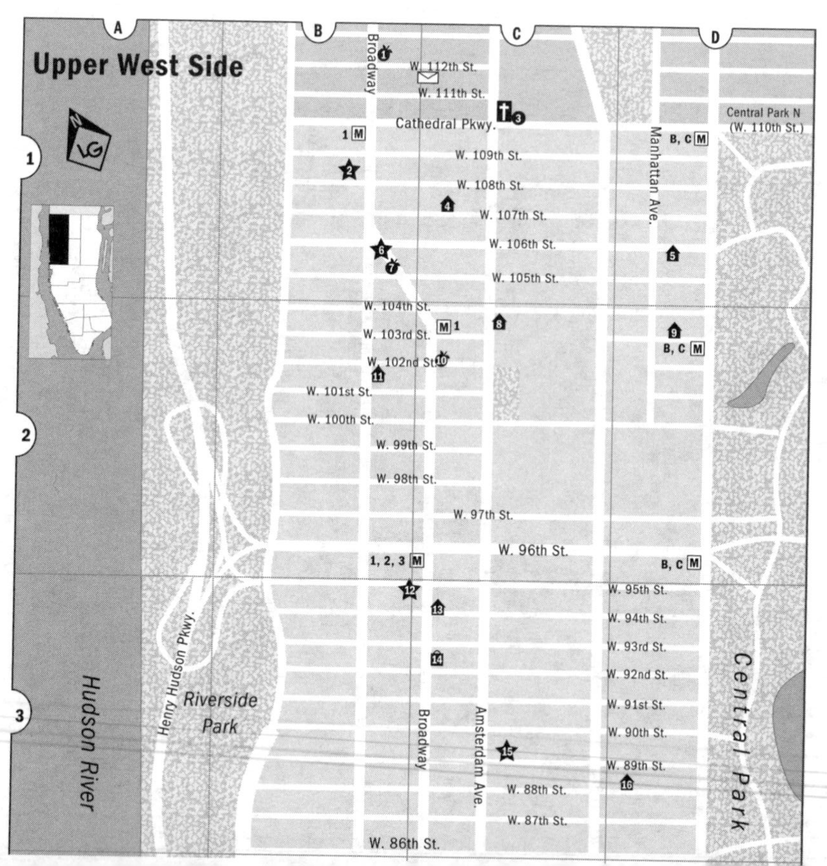

Upper West Side

ACCOMMODATIONS

The Amsterdam Inn, **36**	C5
Central Park Hostel, **9**	D2
Hotel Belleclaire, **34**	C5
Hotel Newton, **13**	C3
Hotel Olcott, **57**	D5
International Student Center, **16**	D3
Jazz on the Park, **5**	D1
New York International HI-AYH Hostel, **8**	C2
West End Studios, **11**	B2
West Side Inn, **4**	C1
West Side YMCA, **68**	D6

FOOD & DRINK

@SQC, **48**	C5
Big Nick's Burger and Pizza Joint, **35**	C5
Cafe Lalo, **20**	C4
Cafe Mozart, **53**	C5
City Crepe, **49**	C5
City Grill, **50**	C5
Dallas BBQ, **56**	C5
drip cafe, **19**	C4
Gabriela's, **43**	C5
Good Enough to Eat, **18**	C4
Gray's Papaya, **47**	C5
H&H Bagels, **25**	C4
Henry's, **7**	B1
It's A Wrap, **54**	C5
Ivy's Cafe, **52**	C5
Josie's, **42**	C5
La Caridad 78 Restaurant, **29**	C4
Mama Mexico, **10**	C2
Mughlai, **40**	C5
River, **37**	C5
Tom's Restaurant, **1**	B1
Zabar's, **23**	C4

SHOPPING

Allan and Suzi, **26**	C4
Applause Theater and Cinema Books, **51**	C5
Gryphon Record Shop, **46**	C5

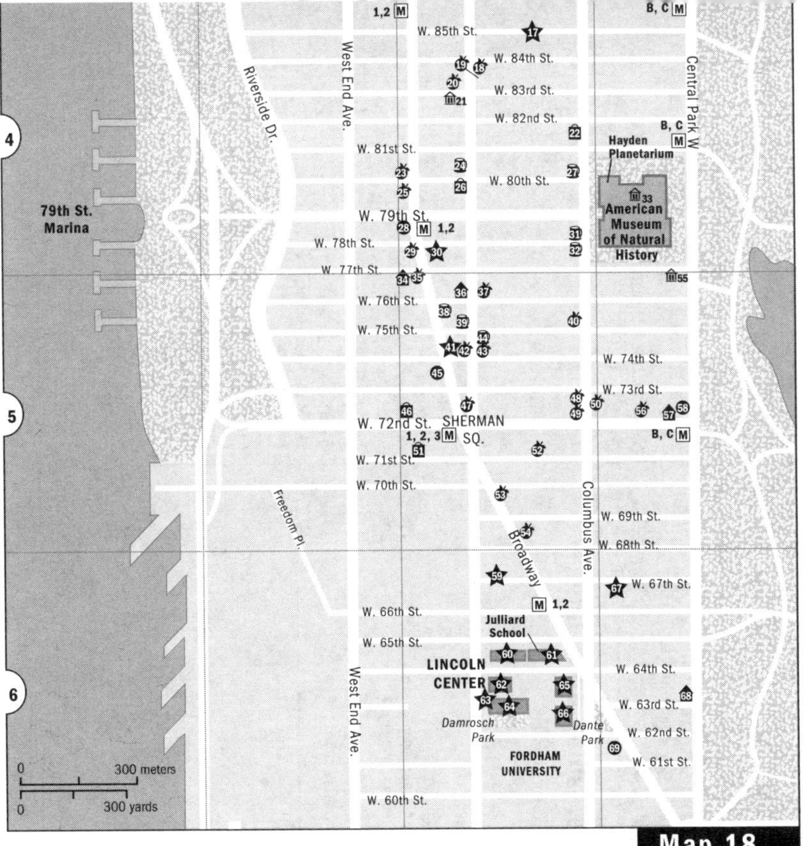

Maxilla & Mandible, **22** C4
Murder Ink/Ivy's, **14** C3

NIGHTLIFE

Brother Jimmy's, **24** C4
Citrus Bar, **39** C4
The Evelyn Lounge, **31** C4
Potion Lounge, **32** C4
Shark Bar, **44** C5
The Works, **27** C4
Yogi's, **38** C5

ARTS & ENTERTAINMENT

Beacon Theatre, **41** C5
Bloomingdale School of Music, **2** B1
Claremont Stables, **15** C3
Live with Regis and Kelly (WABC), **67** D6
Mannes College of Music, **17** C4
Merkin Concert Hall, **59** C6
Smoke, **6** B1
Stand up New York, **30** C4
Symphony Space, **12** B3
at Lincoln Center:
Alice Tully Hall, **61** C6
Avery Fisher Hall, **65** C6
Metropolitan Opera House, **64** C6
New York Public Library for the Performing Arts, **63** C6
New York State Theater, **66** C6
Vivian Beaumont Theater and Mitzi E. Newhouse Theater, **62** C6
Walter E. Reade Theater, **60** C6

SIGHTS

Ansonia Hotel, **45** C5
Apthorp Apartments, **28** C4
American Bible Society, **69** D6
Cathedral of St. John the Divine, **3** C1
Dakota Apartments, **58** D5

MUSEUMS & GALLERIES

American Museum of Natural History, **33** D4
The Children's Museum of Manhattan, **21** C4
New York Historical Society, **55** D4

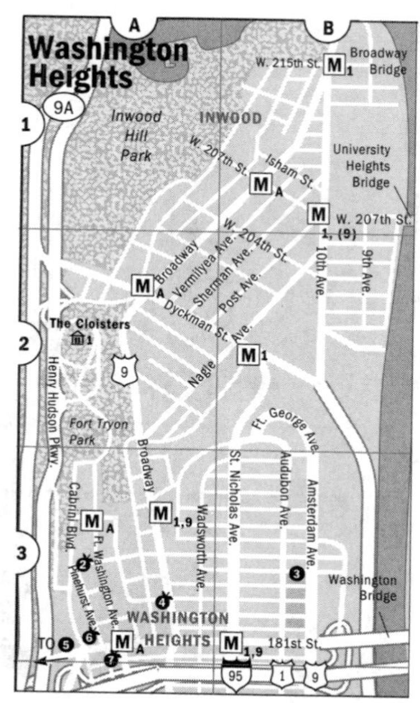

Washington Heights

FOOD & DRINK

Bleu Elevation, **2** — *A3*
Copeland's, **7** — *C4*
Hispanola, **6** — *A3*
La Caridad, **4** — *A3*

SIGHTS

Little Red Lighthouse, **5** — *A3*
Yeshiva University, **3** — *B3*

MUSEUMS & GALLERIES

Cloisters, **1** — *A2*

Harlem and Morningside Heights

ACCOMMODATIONS

Crystal's Castle Bed & Breakfast, **30** — *C6*
Hotel Caribe, **6** — *A4*
New York Bed and Breakfast, **29** — *C6*
Sugar Hill International House, **5** — *B3*
Uptown Hostel, **31** — *C6*

FOOD & DRINK

Amir's Falafel, **26** — *A6*
Fairway, **13** — *A5*
The Hungarian Pastry Shop, **35** — *B7*
Jesse's Place, **7** — *B4*
Koronet Pizza, **18** — *C5*
La Fonda Boricua, **39** — *D7*
La Marmite, **28** — *B6*
Manna's Too!!, **34** — *A7*
Massawa, **27** — *B6*
Milano Market, **32** — *A7*
Sylvia's, **20** — *C5*
Toast, **15** — *A5*
Tom's Restaurant, **33** — *A7*

SHOPPING

Liberation Bookstore, **19** — *C5*
Sugar Hill Thrift Shop, **8** — *B4*

ARTS & ENTERTAINMENT

Apollo Theatre, **17** — *B5*
Cotton Club, **14** — *A5*
Lenox Lounge, **23** — *C5*
Showman's Cafe, **16** — *B5*
St. Nick's Pub, **4** — *B3*

SIGHTS

The Abyssinian Baptist Church, **11** — *C4*
Audubon Ballroom, **1** — *A2*
Cathedral of St. John the Divine, **36** — *B7*
City College, **10** — *B4*
General Grant National Memorial, **24** — *A6*
Hamilton Grange, **9** — *B4*
Morris-Jumel Mansion, **2** — *B2*
Riverside Church, **25** — *A6*
The Schomburg Center for Research in Black Culture, **12** — *C4*
Teresa Hotel, **21** — *C5*

MUSEUMS & GALLERIES

Audubon Terrace Museum Group, **3** — *A3*
El Museo Del Barrio, **37** — *C7*
Museum of the City of New York, **38** — *C7*
Studio Museum, **22** — *C5*

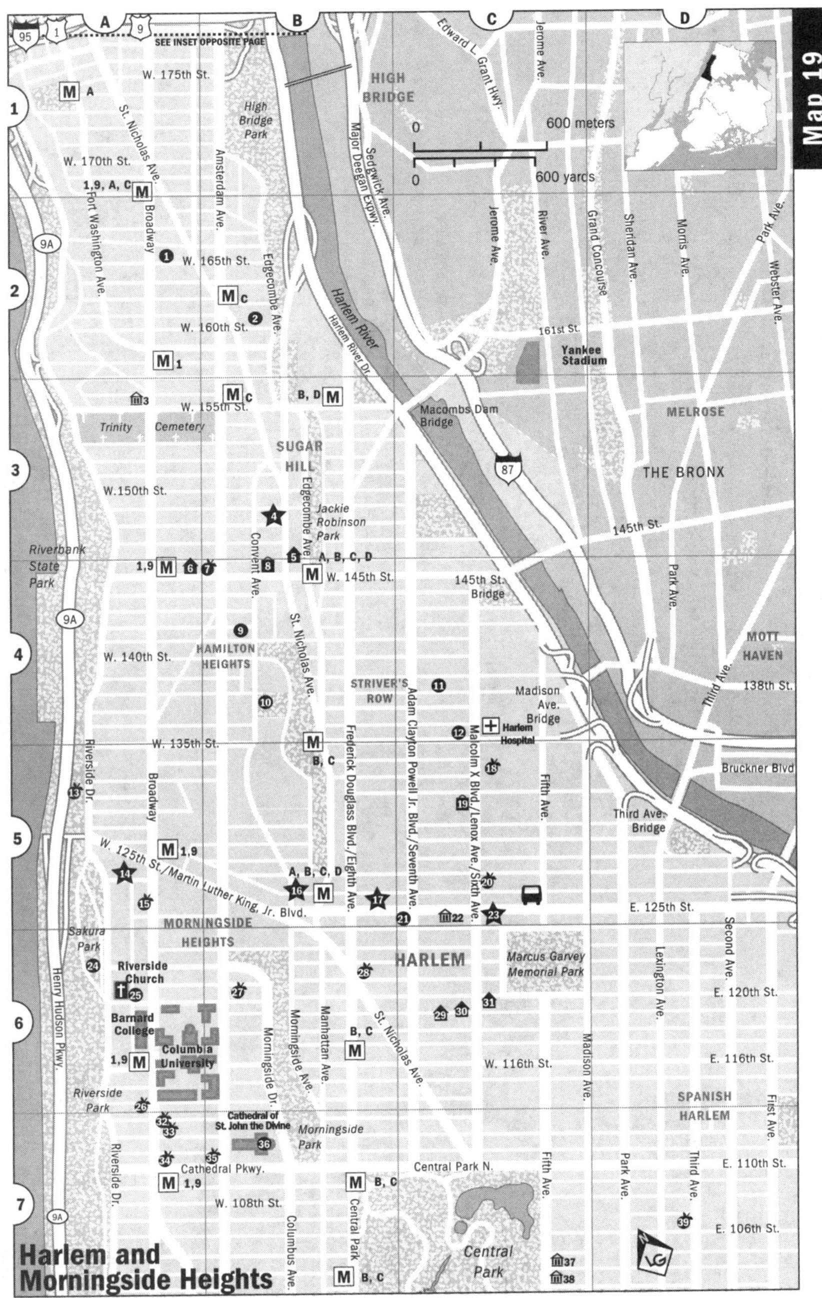
Map 19
SEE INSET OPPOSITE PAGE
W. 175th St.
High Bridge Park
HIGH BRIDGE
Edward L. Grant Hwy.
Jerome Ave.
600 meters
600 yards
W. 170th St.
St. Nicholas Ave.
Amsterdam Ave.
Sedgwick Ave.
Major Deegan Expwy.
Fort Washington Ave.
Broadway
W. 165th St.
Edgecombe Ave.
River Ave.
Grand Concourse
Sheridan Ave.
Morris Ave.
Park Ave.
Webster Ave.
Harlem River
Harlem River Dr.
W. 160th St.
161st St.
Yankee Stadium
W. 155th St.
Trinity Cemetery
Macombs Dam Bridge
MELROSE
SUGAR HILL
THE BRONX
W.150th St.
Jackie Robinson Park
145th St.
Riverbank State Park
Convent Ave.
W. 145th St.
145th St. Bridge
St. Nicholas Ave.
HAMILTON HEIGHTS
W. 140th St.
MOTT HAVEN
STRIVER'S ROW
Adam Clayton Powell Jr. Blvd./Seventh Ave.
Madison Ave. Bridge
Third Ave.
138th St.
Frederick Douglass Blvd./Eighth Ave.
Malcolm X Blvd./Lenox Ave./Sixth Ave.
Harlem Hospital
W. 135th St.
Riverside Dr.
Fifth Ave.
Bruckner Blvd
Third Ave. Bridge
W. 125th St./Martin Luther King, Jr. Blvd.
E. 125th St.
MORNINGSIDE HEIGHTS
Sakura Park
HARLEM
Marcus Garvey Memorial Park
Lexington Ave.
Second Ave.
Riverside Church
E. 120th St.
Henry Hudson Pkwy.
Barnard College
Columbia University
Morningside Dr.
Morningside Ave.
Manhattan Ave.
St. Nicholas Ave.
W. 116th St.
E. 116th St.
Madison Ave.
SPANISH HARLEM
Riverside Park
Cathedral of St. John the Divine
Morningside Park
First Ave.
Cathedral Pkwy.
Central Park N.
E. 110th St.
W. 108th St.
Columbus Ave.
Central Park
E. 106th St.
Harlem and Morningside Heights

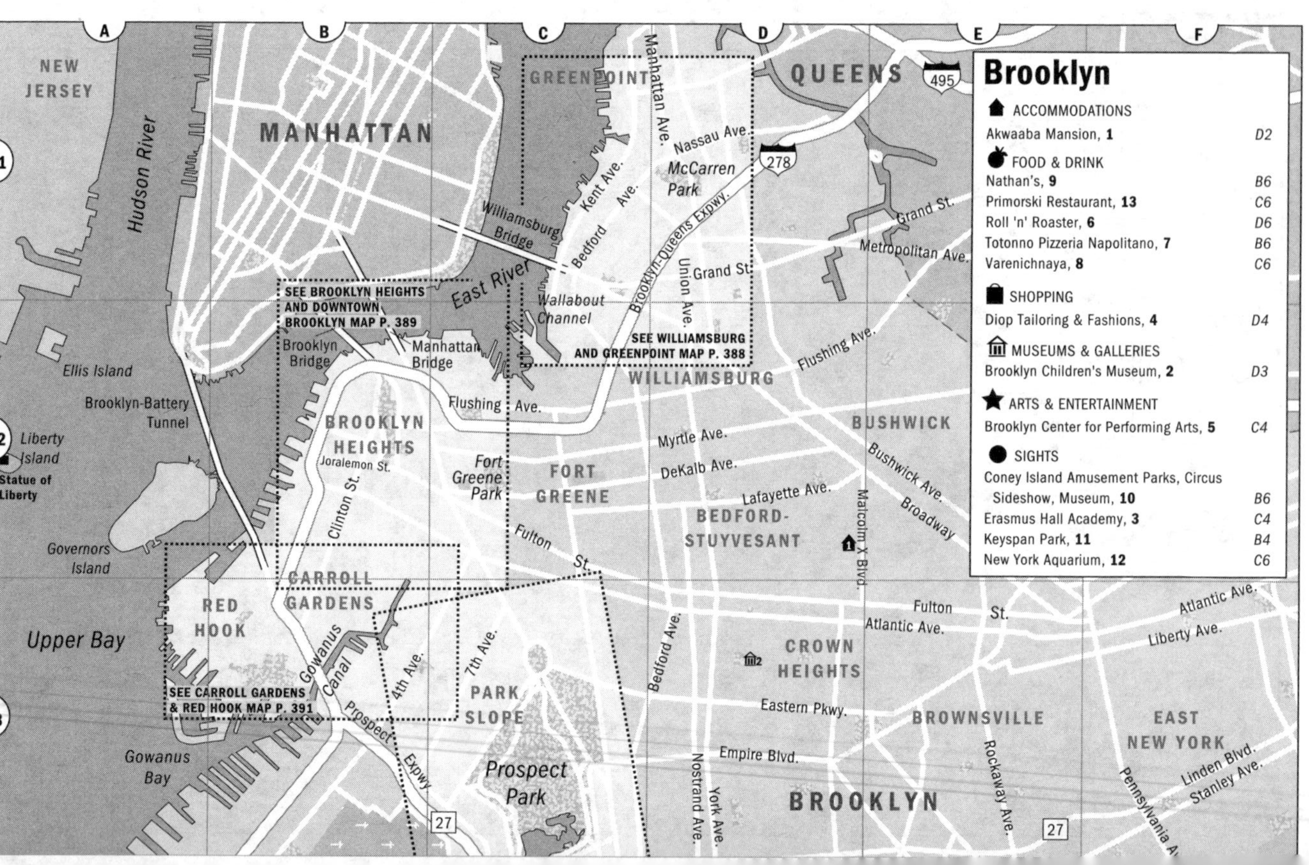
Brooklyn
ACCOMMODATIONS
Akwaaba Mansion, 1 D2
FOOD & DRINK
Nathan's, 9 B6
Primorski Restaurant, 13 C6
Roll 'n' Roaster, 6 D6
Totonno Pizzeria Napolitano, 7 B6
Varenichnaya, 8 C6
SHOPPING
Diop Tailoring & Fashions, 4 D4
MUSEUMS & GALLERIES
Brooklyn Children's Museum, 2 D3
ARTS & ENTERTAINMENT
Brooklyn Center for Performing Arts, 5 C4
SIGHTS
Coney Island Amusement Parks, Circus Sideshow, Museum, 10 B6
Erasmus Hall Academy, 3 C4
Keyspan Park, 11 B4
New York Aquarium, 12 C6
A
B
C
D
E
F
1
2
3
NEW JERSEY
Hudson River
MANHATTAN
QUEENS
GREENPOINT
WILLIAMSBURG
BUSHWICK
FORT GREENE
BEDFORD-STUYVESANT
CROWN HEIGHTS
BROWNSVILLE
EAST NEW YORK
BROOKLYN
BROOKLYN HEIGHTS
CARROLL GARDENS
RED HOOK
PARK SLOPE
Prospect Park
Fort Greene Park
McCarren Park
East River
Upper Bay
Gowanus Bay
Ellis Island
Liberty Island
Statue of Liberty
Governors Island
Brooklyn-Battery Tunnel
Brooklyn Bridge
Manhattan Bridge
Williamsburg Bridge
Wallabout Channel
Gowanus Canal
SEE WILLIAMSBURG AND GREENPOINT MAP P. 388
SEE BROOKLYN HEIGHTS AND DOWNTOWN BROOKLYN MAP P. 389
SEE CARROLL GARDENS & RED HOOK MAP P. 391
Brooklyn-Queens Expwy.
Prospect Expwy.
Manhattan Ave.
Nassau Ave.
Kent Ave.
Bedford Ave.
Union Ave.
Grand St.
Metropolitan Ave.
Flushing Ave.
Myrtle Ave.
DeKalb Ave.
Lafayette Ave.
Bushwick Ave.
Broadway
Malcolm X Blvd.
Fulton St.
Atlantic Ave.
Eastern Pkwy.
Empire Blvd.
York Ave.
Nostrand Ave.
Rockaway Ave.
Liberty Ave.
Linden Blvd.
Stanley Ave.
Joralemon St.
Clinton St.
4th Ave.
7th Ave.
278
495
27

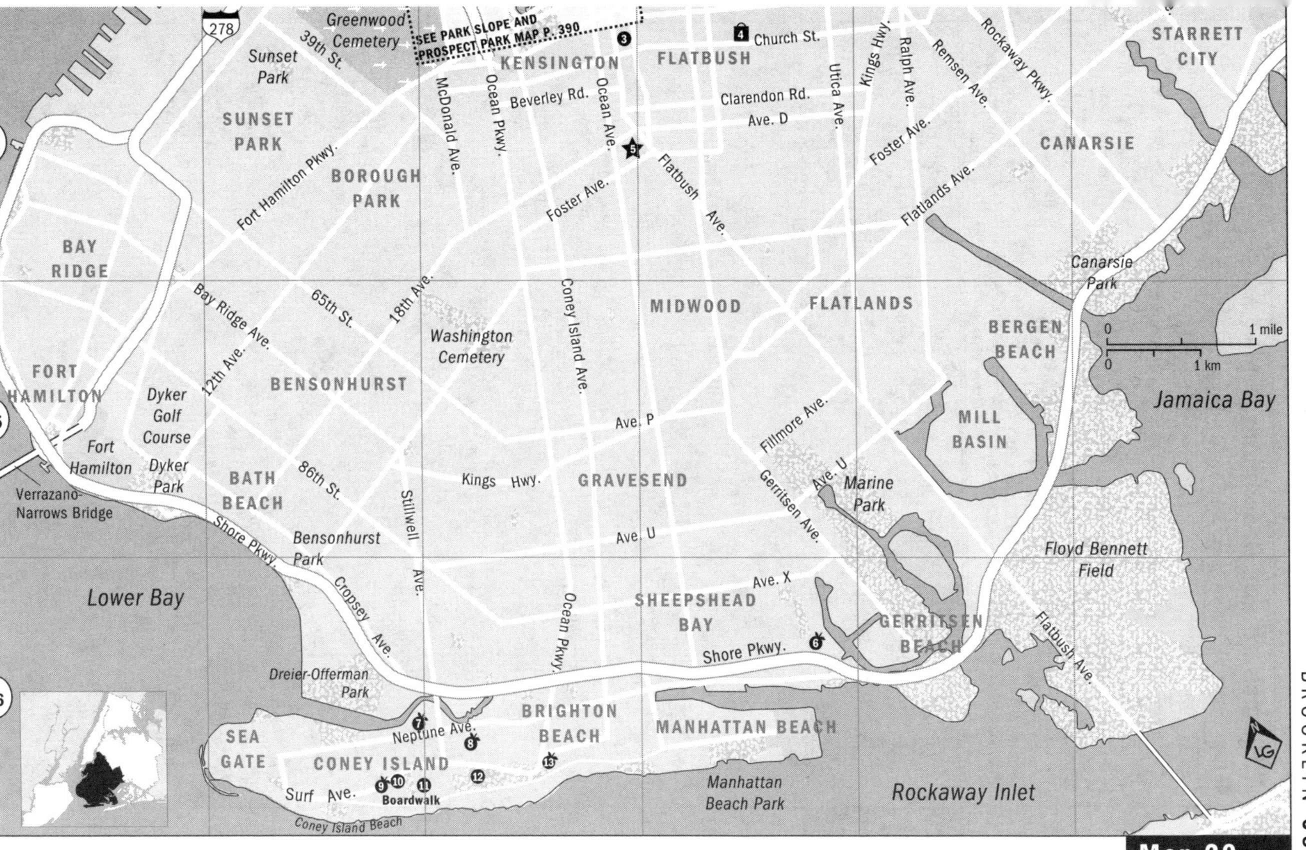

Map 20
SEE PARK SLOPE AND PROSPECT PARK MAP P. 390
278
Greenwood Cemetery
39th St.
Sunset Park
SUNSET PARK
KENSINGTON
FLATBUSH
Church St.
STARRETT CITY
McDonald Ave.
Ocean Pkwy.
Beverley Rd.
Ocean Ave.
Clarendon Rd.
Ave. D
Utica Ave.
Kings Hwy.
Ralph Ave.
Remsen Ave.
Rockaway Pkwy.
Foster Ave.
CANARSIE
Fort Hamilton Pkwy.
BOROUGH PARK
Foster Ave.
Flatbush Ave.
Flatlands Ave.
BAY RIDGE
Canarsie Park
Bay Ridge Ave.
65th St.
18th Ave.
Coney Island Ave.
MIDWOOD
FLATLANDS
BERGEN BEACH
1 mile
1 km
Washington Cemetery
FORT HAMILTON
12th Ave.
BENSONHURST
Dyker Golf Course
Jamaica Bay
Ave. P
Fillmore Ave.
MILL BASIN
Fort Hamilton
Dyker Park
BATH BEACH
86th St.
Stillwell Ave.
Kings Hwy.
GRAVESEND
Ave. U
Marine Park
Verrazano-Narrows Bridge
Gerritsen Ave.
Shore Pkwy.
Bensonhurst Park
Ave. U
Floyd Bennett Field
Lower Bay
Cropsey Ave.
Ocean Pkwy.
Ave. X
SHEEPSHEAD BAY
GERRITSEN BEACH
Flatbush Ave.
Shore Pkwy.
Dreier-Offerman Park
BRIGHTON BEACH
MANHATTAN BEACH
SEA GATE
Neptune Ave.
CONEY ISLAND
Surf Ave.
Boardwalk
Manhattan Beach Park
Rockaway Inlet
Coney Island Beach

Williamsburg and Greenpoint

FOOD & DRINK
Bliss, **26**
Diner, **41**
DuMont Restaurant, **36**
Gray Parrot Cafe Inc., **24**
Greenpoint Coffee House, **1**
L Cafe, **25**
Miyako, **19**
Oznot's Dish, **13**
Peter Luger, **43**
Planet Thailand, **15**
The Read Cafe and Bookshop, **16**
Restaurant Karpaty, **4**
Sal's Pizzeria, **37**
Sea, **18**
Tia Café, **14**
Vera Cruz, **27**

SHOPPING
Beacon's Closet, **9**
KCDC, **8**
Clovis Press, **29**
Domsey's, **40**
Girdle Factory, **28**
Spokes & Strings, **38**
Ugly Luggage, **23**

NIGHTLIFE
Artland, **39**
Blu Lounge, **21**
Brooklyn Ale House, **11**
Enid's, **5**
Galapagos, **10**
Pete's Candy Store, **22**
The Pencil Factory, **2**
Teddy's, **12**
Union Pool, **30**
Yabby's, **32**

ARTS & ENTERTAINMENT
Charlie Pineapple Theater, **20**

SIGHTS
Sts. Anthony and Alphonsus Church, **3**
Waterfront Walk, **6**

MUSEUMS & GALLERIES
Aquatic Creations, **7**
Lunar Base, **33**
Pierogi 2000, **17**
Plus Ultra, **34**
Rome, **35**
Schroeder Romero, **31**
The Williamsburg Art and Historical Center, **42**

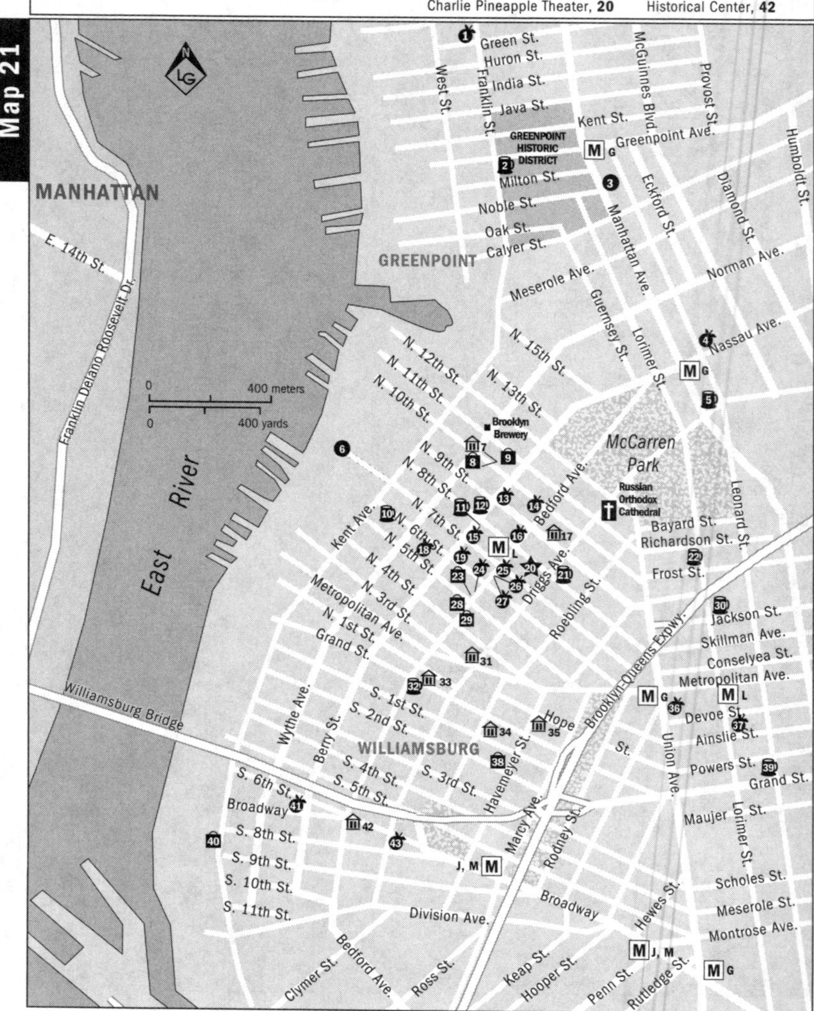

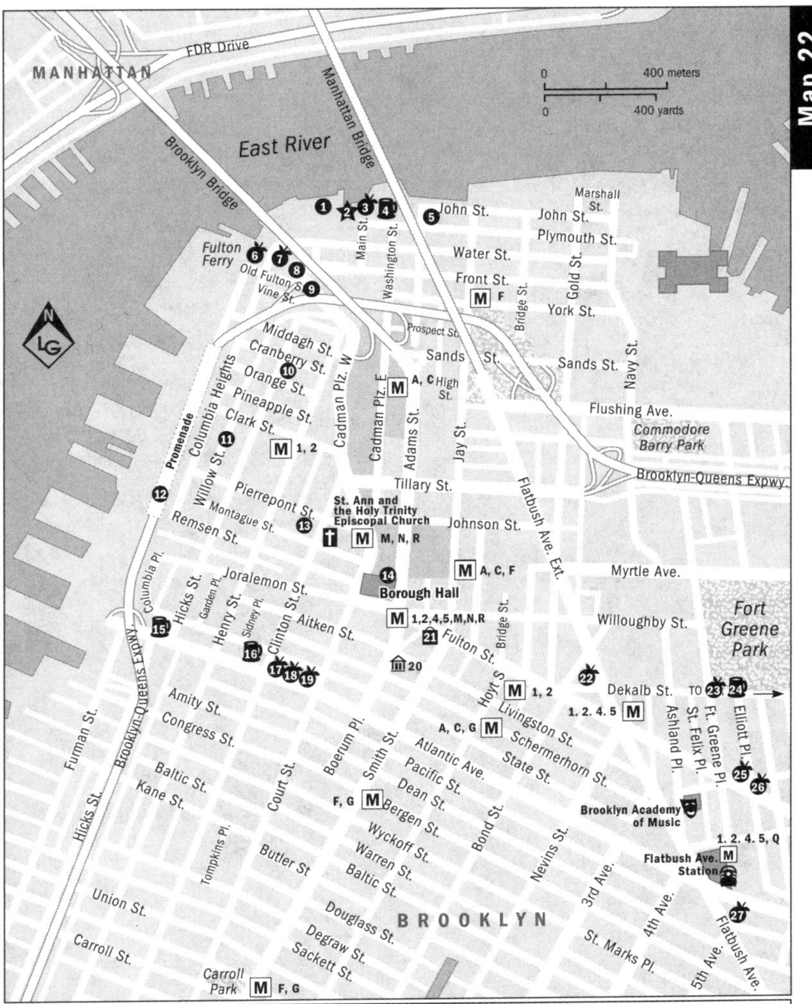

Brooklyn Heights and Downtown Brooklyn

FOOD & DRINK
Brooklyn Ice Cream Factory, **6**
Brooklyn Moon, **26**
Caravan, **18**
Damascus Bakery, **17**
Fountain Cafe, **19**
Grimaldi's, **7**
Jacques Torres Chocolate, **3**
JRG Fashion Cafe, **27**
Junior's, **22**
Keur N'Deye, **25**
Madiba Restaurant, **23**

SHOPPING
Fulton Outdoor Mall, **21**

NIGHTLIFE
66 Water Street, **4**
Butta Cup Lounge, **24**
Montero's Bar & Grill, **15**
Waterfront Ale House, **16**

ARTS & ENTERTAINMENT
St. Ann's Warehouse, **2**

SIGHTS
135 Plymouth St., **5**
Borough Hall, **14**
Brooklyn Bridge Anchorage, **9**
Brooklyn Historical Society, **13**
The Eagle Warehouse and Storage Co., **8**
Empire & Fulton Ferry Park, **1**
Plymouth Church of Pilgrims, **10**
Willow Street, **11**
Waterfront Promenade, **12**

MUSEUMS
New York Transit Museum, **20**

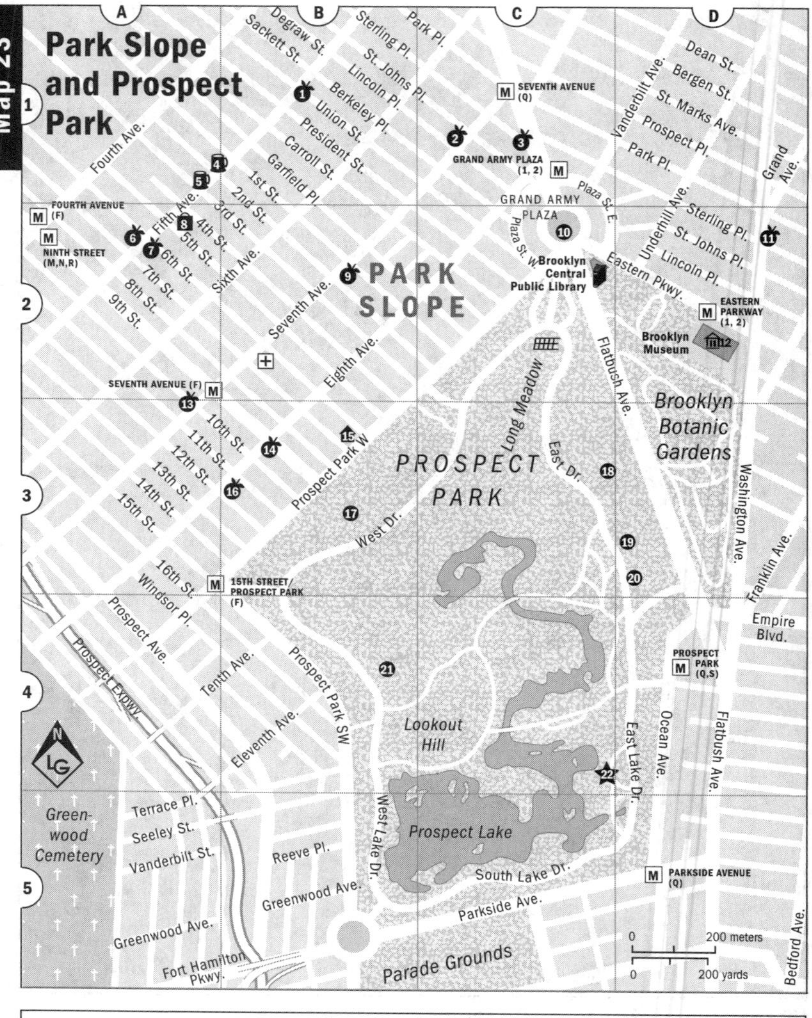

Park Slope and Prospect Park

ACCOMMODATIONS

Bed & Breakfast on the Park, **15**	*B3*

FOOD & DRINK

12th Street Grill, **16**	*B3*
Beso, **1**	*B1*
Chip & Curry Shop, **7**	*A2*
Christie's Bakery, **3**	*C1*
CocoRoco, **6**	*A2*
Dizzy's, **14**	*B3*
Pino La Forchetta, **9**	*B2*
Red Hot Szechuan, **13**	*A3*
Santa Fe Grille, **2**	*C1*
Tom's Restaurant, **11**	*D2*

SHOPPING

Inka Travel & Internet Café, **8**	*A2*

NIGHTLIFE

The Gate, **5**	*A1*
Loki Lounge, **4**	*A1*

ENTERTAINMENT

Wollman Rink, **22**	*C4*

Carousel, **20**	*D3*
Friends Cemetery, **21**	*B4*
Grand Army Plaza, **10**	*C2*
Leffert's Homestead, **19**	*D3*
Prospect Park Wildlife Center/Zoo, **18**	*C3*

SIGHTS

Bandshell, **17**	*B3*

MUSEUMS

Brooklyn Museum of Art, **12**	*D2*

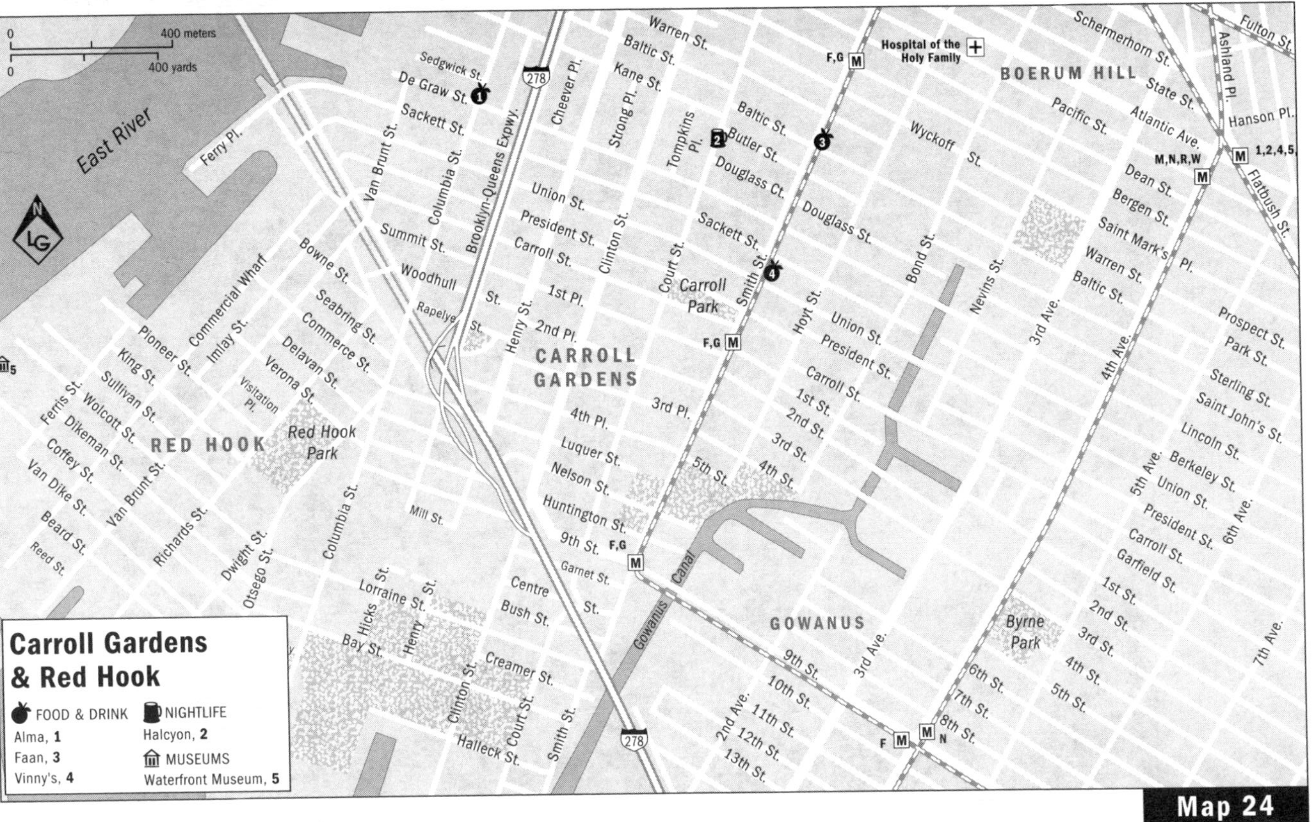
Map 24
Carroll Gardens & Red Hook
FOOD & DRINK
Alma, 1
Faan, 3
Vinny's, 4
NIGHTLIFE
Halcyon, 2
MUSEUMS
Waterfront Museum, 5
400 meters
400 yards
BOERUM HILL
CARROLL GARDENS
GOWANUS
RED HOOK
Carroll Park
Red Hook Park
Byrne Park
Hospital of the Holy Family
East River
Gowanus Canal
Brooklyn-Queens Expwy.
Fulton St.
Flatbush St.
Ashland Pl.
Hanson Pl.
Schermerhorn St.
State St.
Atlantic Ave.
Pacific St.
Dean St.
Bergen St.
Saint Mark's Pl.
Warren St.
Baltic St.
Butler St.
Douglass Ct.
Douglass St.
Sackett St.
Union St.
President St.
Carroll St.
1st St.
2nd St.
3rd St.
4th St.
5th St.
6th St.
7th St.
8th St.
9th St.
10th St.
11th St.
12th St.
13th St.
Prospect St.
Park St.
Sterling St.
Saint John's St.
Lincoln St.
Berkeley St.
Garfield St.
2nd Ave.
3rd Ave.
4th Ave.
5th Ave.
6th Ave.
7th Ave.
Nevins St.
Bond St.
Wyckoff St.
Hoyt St.
Smith St.
Court St.
Clinton St.
Tompkins Pl.
Kane St.
Strong Pl.
Cheever Pl.
1st Pl.
2nd Pl.
3rd Pl.
4th Pl.
Luquer St.
Nelson St.
Huntington St.
Garnet St.
Centre St.
Bush St.
Creamer St.
Halleck St.
Henry St.
Hicks St.
Columbia St.
Sedgwick St.
De Graw St.
Summit St.
Woodhull St.
Rapelye St.
Mill St.
Van Brunt St.
Bowne St.
Seabring St.
Commerce St.
Delavan St.
Verona St.
Visitation Pl.
Lorraine St.
Bay St.
Otsego St.
Dwight St.
Richards St.
Commercial Wharf
Imlay St.
Ferry Pl.
Pioneer St.
King St.
Sullivan St.
Wolcott St.
Dikeman St.
Coffey St.
Van Dike St.
Beard St.
Reed St.
Ferris St.
278
M
F,G
M,N,R,W
1,2,4,5
N
F

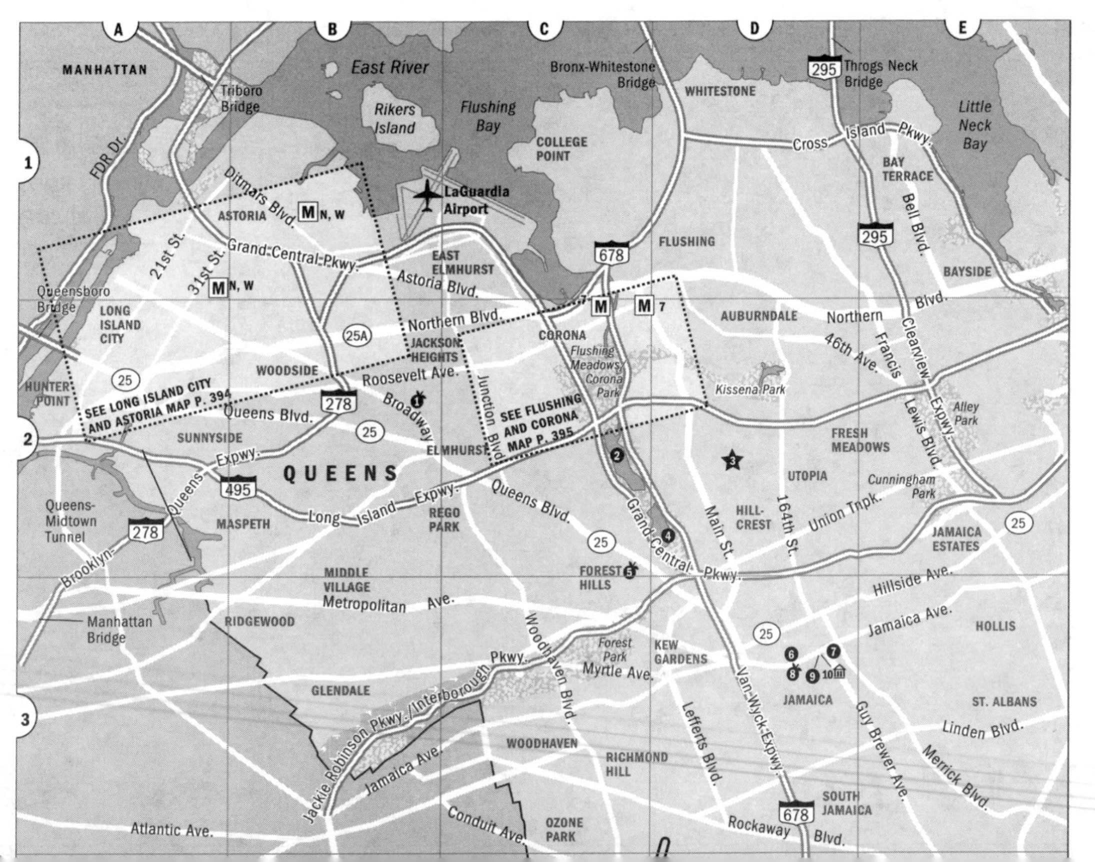

A
B
C
D
E
1
2
3
MANHATTAN
FDR Dr.
Triboro Bridge
Queensboro Bridge
East River
Rikers Island
Flushing Bay
LaGuardia Airport
Bronx-Whitestone Bridge
Throgs Neck Bridge
Little Neck Bay
COLLEGE POINT
WHITESTONE
FLUSHING
AUBURNDALE
BAY TERRACE
BAYSIDE
Bell Blvd.
Cross Island Pkwy.
Clearview Expwy.
Northern Blvd.
Francis Lewis Blvd.
46th Ave.
Alley Park
Cunningham Park
FRESH MEADOWS
UTOPIA
Union Tnpk.
164th St.
Kissena Park
HILL-CREST
Main St.
JAMAICA ESTATES
HOLLIS
ST. ALBANS
Linden Blvd.
Merrick Blvd.
Hillside Ave.
Jamaica Ave.
Guy Brewer Ave.
JAMAICA
SOUTH JAMAICA
Van Wyck Expwy.
Rockaway Blvd.
Lefferts Blvd.
KEW GARDENS
Grand Central Pkwy.
Flushing Meadows Corona Park
CORONA
SEE FLUSHING AND CORONA MAP P. 395
FOREST HILLS
Forest Park
Myrtle Ave.
RICHMOND HILL
Woodhaven Blvd.
WOODHAVEN
OZONE PARK
Conduit Ave.
EAST ELMHURST
Astoria Blvd.
Northern Blvd.
Junction Blvd.
JACKSON HEIGHTS
Roosevelt Ave.
Broadway
ELMHURST
Queens Blvd.
REGO PARK
Long Island Expwy.
QUEENS
MIDDLE VILLAGE
Metropolitan Ave.
GLENDALE
Interborough Pkwy.
Jackie Robinson Pkwy.
Jamaica Ave.
ASTORIA
Ditmars Blvd.
Grand Central Pkwy.
31st St.
21st St.
N, W
7
WOODSIDE
Queens Blvd.
SUNNYSIDE
MASPETH
RIDGEWOOD
Atlantic Ave.
SEE LONG ISLAND CITY AND ASTORIA MAP P. 394
LONG ISLAND CITY
HUNTER POINT
Queens-Midtown Tunnel
Brooklyn-Queens Expwy.
Manhattan Bridge
295
678
278
495
25
25A

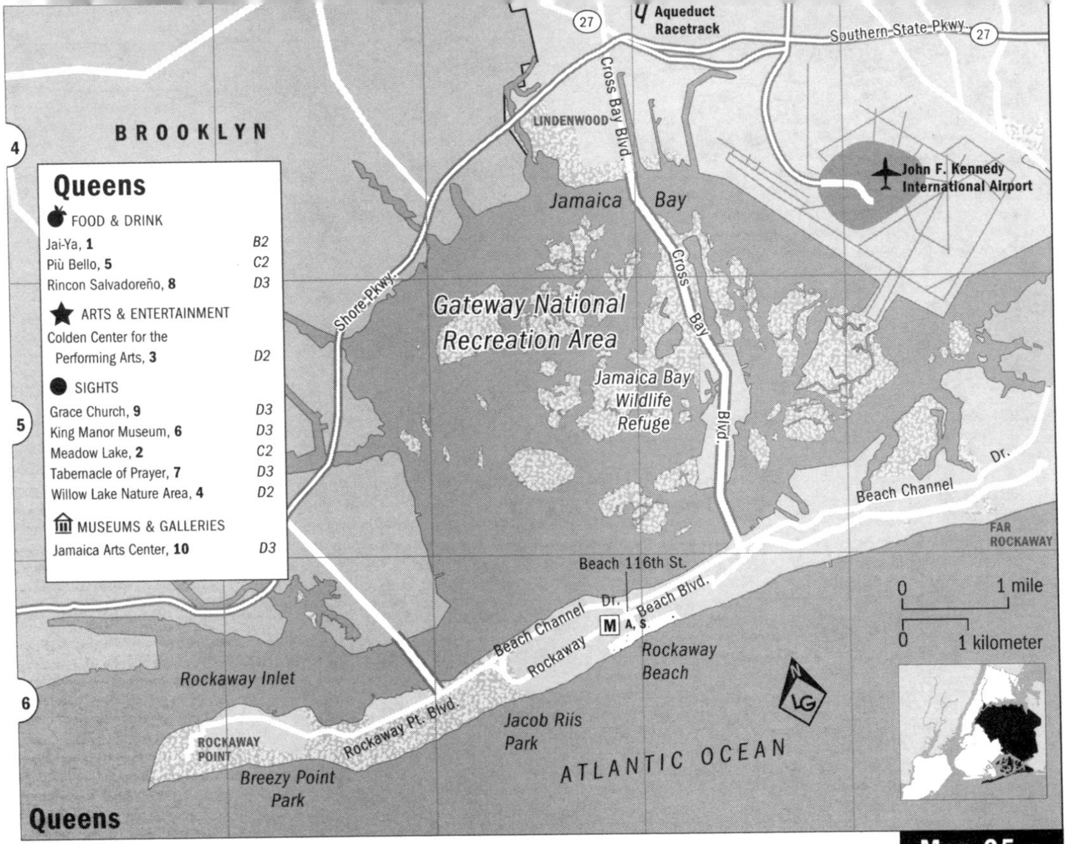

Queens
FOOD & DRINK
Jai-Ya, 1 B2
Più Bello, 5 C2
Rincon Salvadoreño, 8 D3
ARTS & ENTERTAINMENT
Colden Center for the Performing Arts, 3 D2
SIGHTS
Grace Church, 9 D3
King Manor Museum, 6 D3
Meadow Lake, 2 C2
Tabernacle of Prayer, 7 D3
Willow Lake Nature Area, 4 D2
MUSEUMS & GALLERIES
Jamaica Arts Center, 10 D3
BROOKLYN
Aqueduct Racetrack
27
Southern-State-Pkwy.
John F. Kennedy International Airport
LINDENWOOD
Cross Bay Blvd.
Jamaica Bay
Shore-Pkwy.
Gateway National Recreation Area
Jamaica Bay Wildlife Refuge
Beach Channel Dr.
FAR ROCKAWAY
Beach 116th St.
Rockaway Beach Blvd.
A, S
Rockaway Beach
Rockaway Inlet
Rockaway Pt. Blvd.
Jacob Riis Park
ROCKAWAY POINT
Breezy Point Park
ATLANTIC OCEAN
0 1 mile
0 1 kilometer
4
5
6
Queens

Map 25

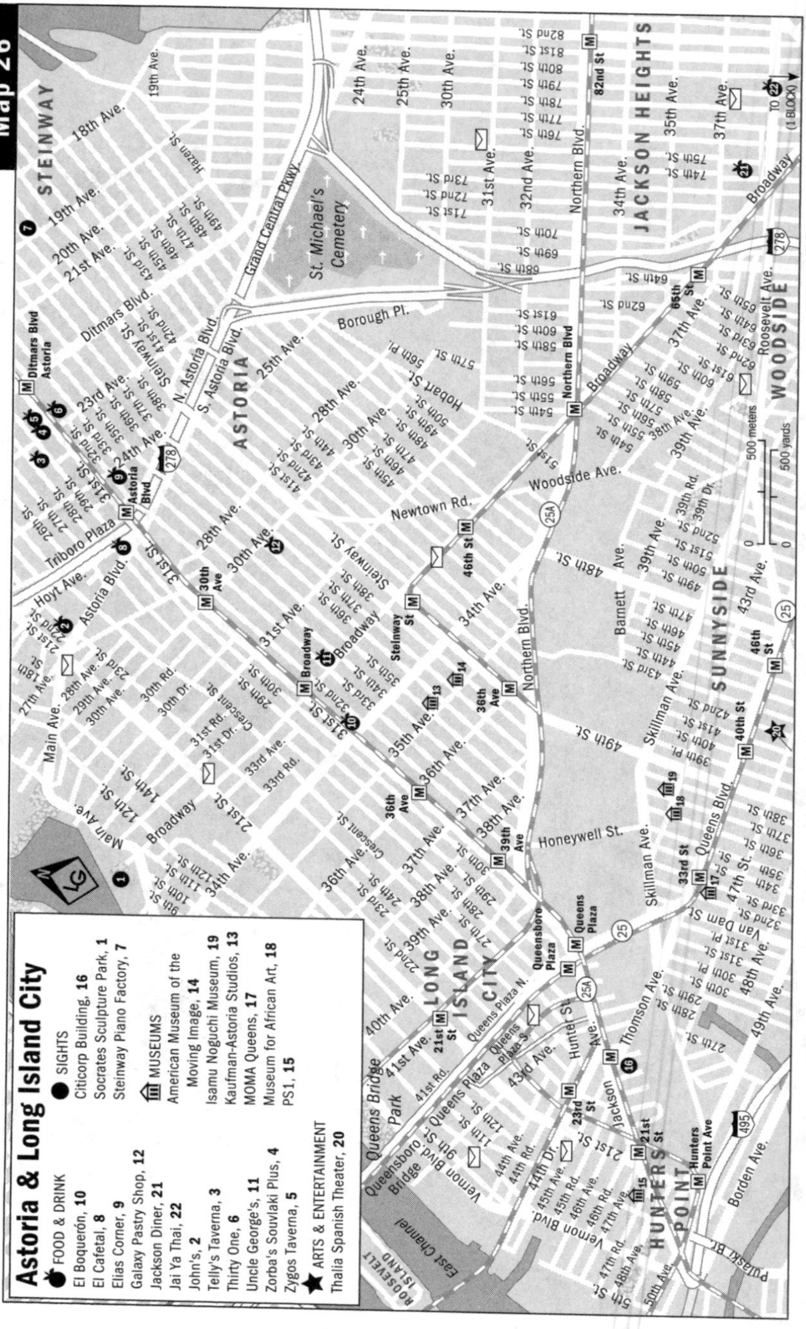
Map 26
Astoria & Long Island City
FOOD & DRINK
El Boquerón, 10
El Cafetal, 8
Elias Corner, 9
Galaxy Pastry Shop, 12
Jackson Diner, 21
Jai Ya Thai, 22
John's, 2
Telly's Taverna, 3
Thirty One, 6
Uncle George's, 11
Zorba's Souvlaki Plus, 4
Zygos Taverna, 5
SIGHTS
Citicorp Building, 16
Socrates Sculpture Park, 1
Steinway Piano Factory, 7
MUSEUMS
American Museum of the Moving Image, 14
Isamu Noguchi Museum, 19
Kaufman-Astoria Studios, 13
MOMA Queens, 17
Museum for African Art, 18
PS1, 15
ARTS & ENTERTAINMENT
Thalia Spanish Theater, 20
STEINWAY
ASTORIA
JACKSON HEIGHTS
WOODSIDE
SUNNYSIDE
LONG ISLAND CITY
HUNTERS POINT
St. Michael's Cemetery
ROOSEVELT ISLAND
East Channel
Queensboro Bridge
Queens Bridge Park
TO 22 (1 BLOCK)
500 meters
500 yards

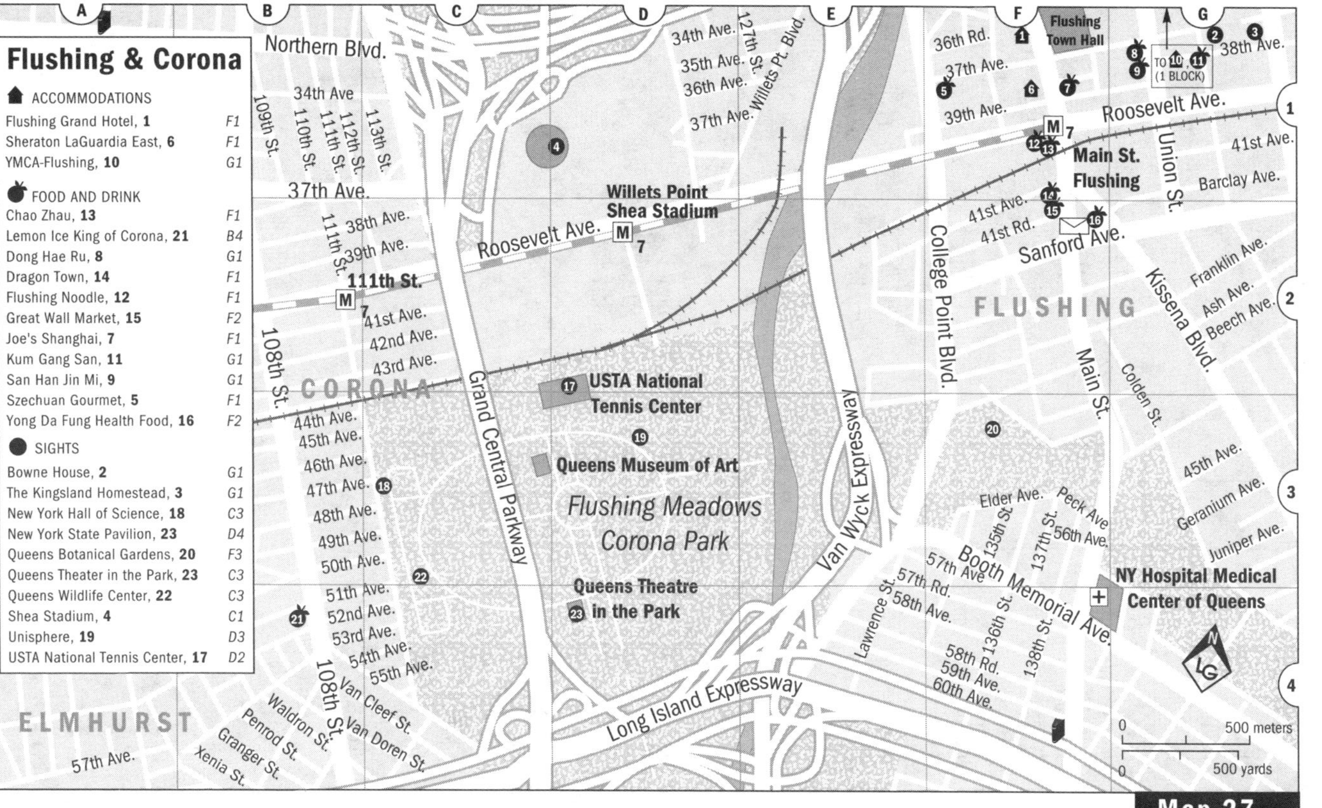
Flushing & Corona
ACCOMMODATIONS
Flushing Grand Hotel, 1 F1
Sheraton LaGuardia East, 6 F1
YMCA-Flushing, 10 G1
FOOD AND DRINK
Chao Zhau, 13 F1
Lemon Ice King of Corona, 21 B4
Dong Hae Ru, 8 G1
Dragon Town, 14 F1
Flushing Noodle, 12 F1
Great Wall Market, 15 F2
Joe's Shanghai, 7 F1
Kum Gang San, 11 G1
San Han Jin Mi, 9 G1
Szechuan Gourmet, 5 F1
Yong Da Fung Health Food, 16 F2
SIGHTS
Bowne House, 2 G1
The Kingsland Homestead, 3 G1
New York Hall of Science, 18 C3
New York State Pavilion, 23 D4
Queens Botanical Gardens, 20 F3
Queens Theater in the Park, 23 C3
Queens Wildlife Center, 22 C3
Shea Stadium, 4 C1
Unisphere, 19 D3
USTA National Tennis Center, 17 D2
Northern Blvd.
Flushing Town Hall
TO 10, 11 (1 BLOCK)
Roosevelt Ave.
Willets Point Shea Stadium
111th St.
Main St. Flushing
USTA National Tennis Center
Queens Museum of Art
Flushing Meadows Corona Park
Queens Theatre in the Park
NY Hospital Medical Center of Queens
FLUSHING
CORONA
ELMHURST
Grand Central Parkway
Van Wyck Expressway
Long Island Expressway
College Point Blvd.
Kissena Blvd.
Booth Memorial Ave.
Union St.
Main St.
Sanford Ave.
Willets Pt. Blvd.
108th St.
500 meters
500 yards
Map 27

Map 28

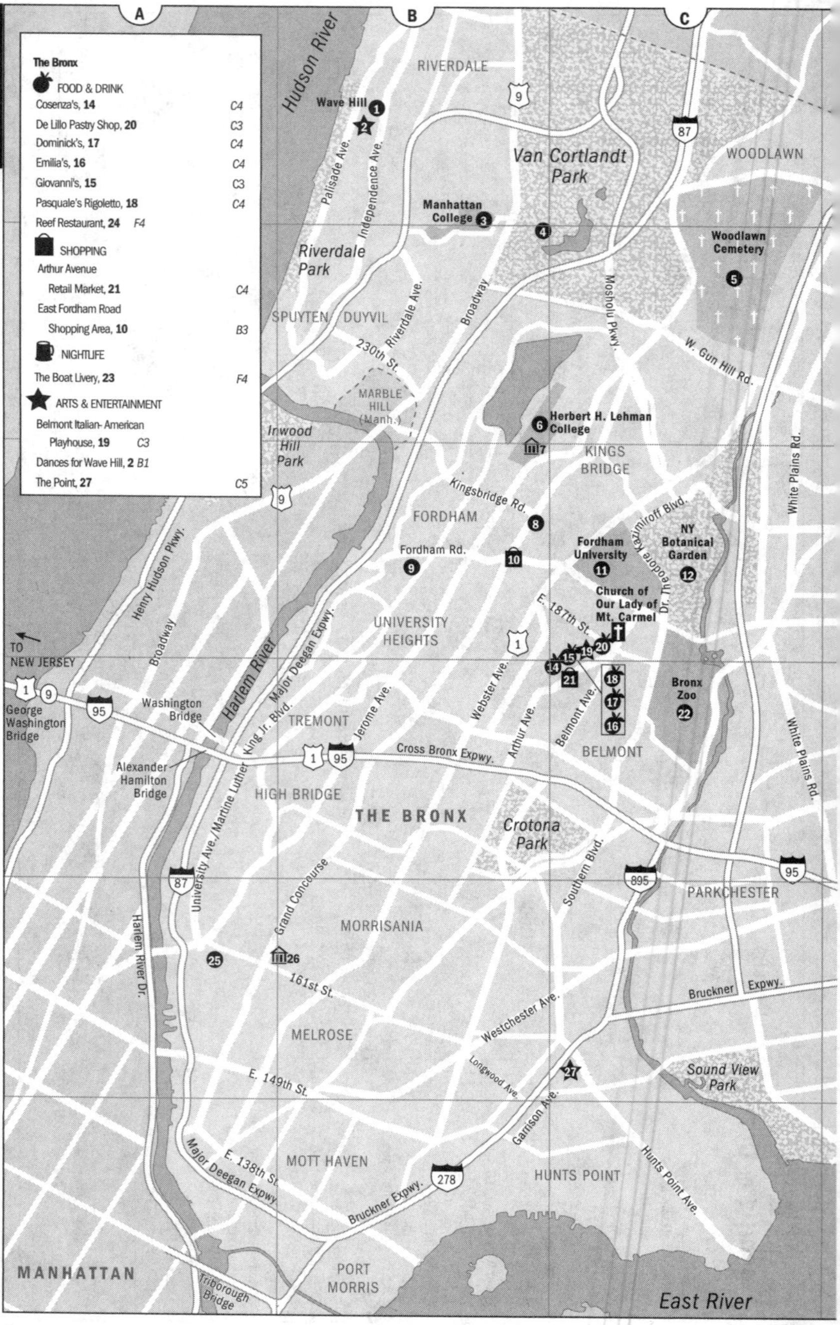

The Bronx

FOOD & DRINK

- Cosenza's, **14** C4
- De Lillo Pastry Shop, **20** C3
- Dominick's, **17** C4
- Emilia's, **16** C4
- Giovanni's, **15** C3
- Pasquale's Rigoletto, **18** C4
- Reef Restaurant, **24** F4

SHOPPING

- Arthur Avenue Retail Market, **21** C4
- East Fordham Road Shopping Area, **10** B3

NIGHTLIFE

- The Boat Livery, **23** F4

ARTS & ENTERTAINMENT

- Belmont Italian- American Playhouse, **19** C3
- Dances for Wave Hill, **2** B1
- The Point, **27** C5

A B C

Hudson River
Riverdale
Wave Hill 1
2
Palisade Ave.
Independence Ave.
9
87
Van Cortlandt Park
Woodlawn
Manhattan College 3
4
Riverdale Park
Woodlawn Cemetery
5
Riverdale Ave.
Broadway
Mosholu Pkwy.
Spuyten Duyvil
230th St.
W. Gun Hill Rd.
Marble Hill (Manh.)
Inwood Hill Park
6 Herbert H. Lehman College
7
Kings Bridge
9
Kingsbridge Rd.
Fordham
8
White Plains Rd.
Fordham Rd.
9
10
Fordham University 11
Dr. Theodore Kazimiroff Blvd.
NY Botanical Garden 12
Henry Hudson Pkwy.
Broadway
Major Deegan Expwy.
University Heights
Church of Our Lady of Mt. Carmel
E. 187th St.
1
20
19
15
14
21
To New Jersey
Harlem River
Webster Ave.
18
17
16
Bronx Zoo 22
1 9
George Washington Bridge
95
Washington Bridge
Martin Luther King Jr. Blvd.
Tremont
Jerome Ave.
Belmont Ave.
Arthur Ave.
Belmont
White Plains Rd.
Alexander Hamilton Bridge
1 95
Cross Bronx Expwy.
High Bridge
The Bronx
Crotona Park
University Ave./Martine Luther
Southern Blvd.
87
895
95
Parkchester
Grand Concourse
Harlem River Dr.
Morrisania
25
26
161st St.
Bruckner Expwy.
Westchester Ave.
Melrose
Longwood Ave.
27
E. 149th St.
Sound View Park
Garrison Ave.
Major Deegan Expwy
E. 138th St.
Mott Haven
278
Hunts Point
Hunts Point Ave.
Bruckner Expwy.
Manhattan
Port Morris
Triborough Bridge
East River

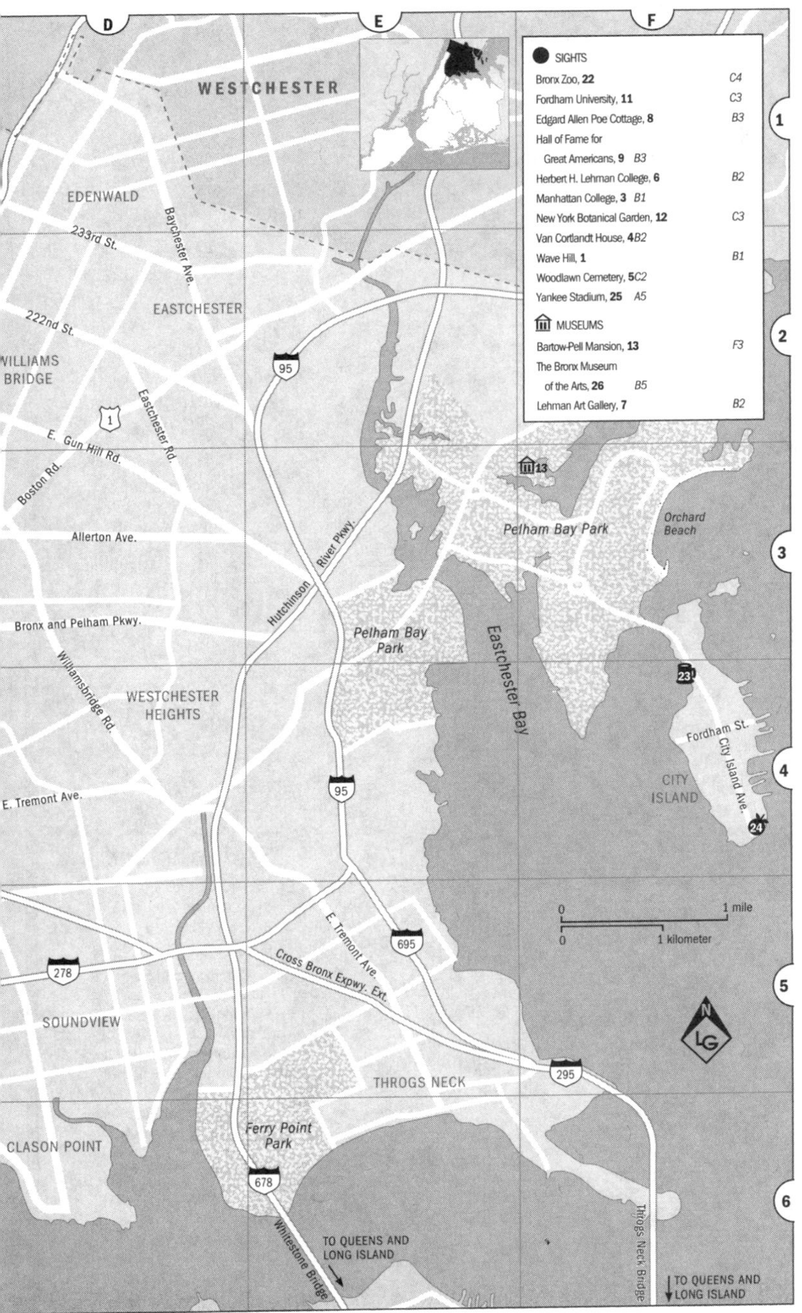

D
E
F
1
2
3
4
5
6
WESTCHESTER
EDENWALD
233rd St.
Baychester Ave.
EASTCHESTER
222nd St.
WILLIAMS
BRIDGE
Eastchester Rd.
E. Gun Hill Rd.
Boston Rd.
Allerton Ave.
Bronx and Pelham Pkwy.
Williamsbridge Rd.
WESTCHESTER
HEIGHTS
E. Tremont Ave.
Hutchinson River Pkwy.
Pelham Bay Park
Pelham Bay
Park
Eastchester Bay
Orchard
Beach
Fordham St.
City Island Ave.
CITY
ISLAND
E. Tremont Ave.
Cross Bronx Expwy. Ext.
SOUNDVIEW
THROGS NECK
Ferry Point
Park
CLASON POINT
Whitestone Bridge
Throgs Neck Bridge
TO QUEENS AND
LONG ISLAND
TO QUEENS AND
LONG ISLAND
95
95
1
695
278
295
678
13
23
24
0
1 mile
0
1 kilometer
N
LG
SIGHTS
Bronx Zoo, 22 C4
Fordham University, 11 C3
Edgard Allen Poe Cottage, 8 B3
Hall of Fame for
Great Americans, 9 B3
Herbert H. Lehman College, 6 B2
Manhattan College, 3 B1
New York Botanical Garden, 12 C3
Van Cortlandt House, 4B2
Wave Hill, 1 B1
Woodlawn Cemetery, 5C2
Yankee Stadium, 25 A5
MUSEUMS
Bartow-Pell Mansion, 13 F3
The Bronx Museum
of the Arts, 26 B5
Lehman Art Gallery, 7 B2

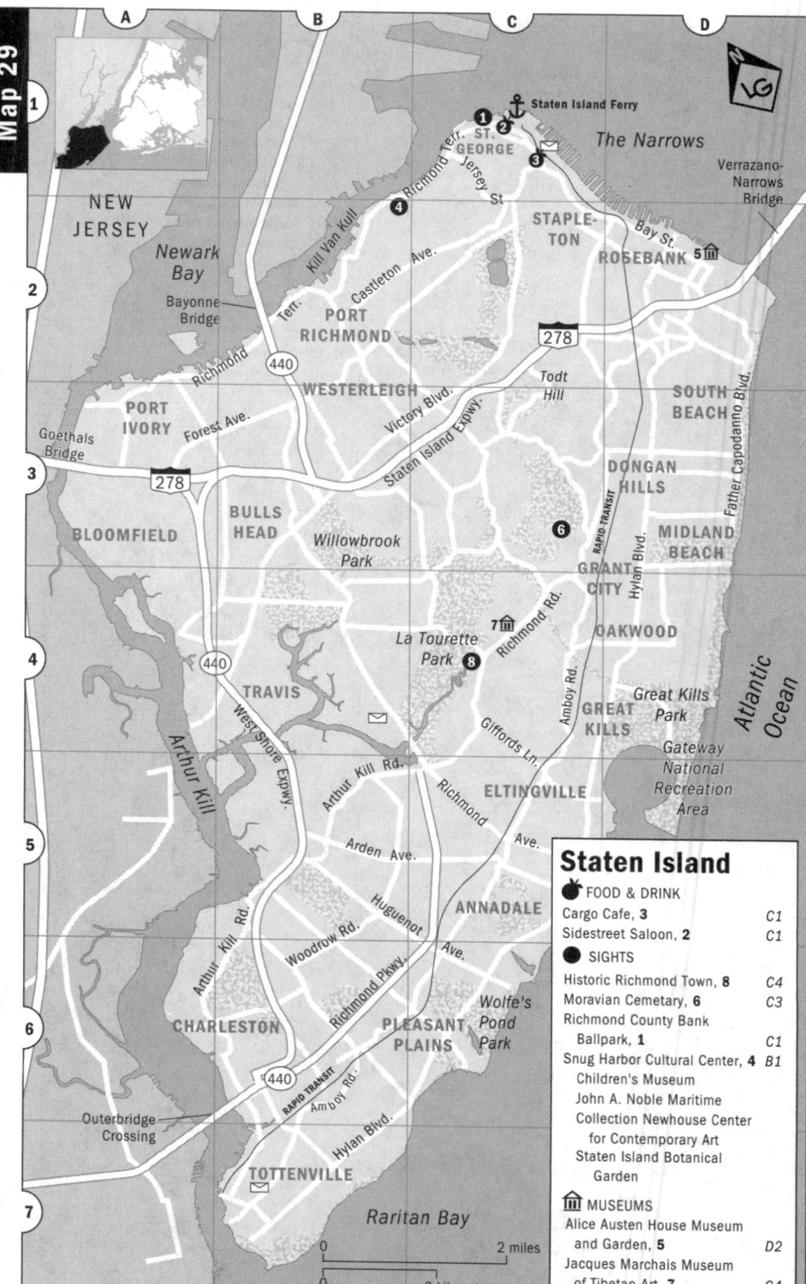

Staten Island

FOOD & DRINK

Cargo Cafe, **3**	*C1*
Sidestreet Saloon, **2**	*C1*

SIGHTS

Historic Richmond Town, **8**	*C4*
Moravian Cemetary, **6**	*C3*
Richmond County Bank Ballpark, **1**	*C1*
Snug Harbor Cultural Center, **4**	*B1*
Children's Museum	
John A. Noble Maritime Collection Newhouse Center for Contemporary Art	
Staten Island Botanical Garden	

MUSEUMS

Alice Austen House Museum and Garden, **5**	*D2*
Jacques Marchais Museum of Tibetan Art, **7**	*C4*

Map 30
CENTRAL PARK
Downtown Bus Routes
North-South routes
East-West routes
All numbers are Manhattan lines, which carry M-prefix on bus display.
"Q" are Queens lines;
"B" are Brooklyn lines
"X" are express lines
72 St
68 St
67 St
66 St
65 St
60 St
59 St
57 St
50 St
49 St
42 St
34 St
23 St
20 St
14 St
9 St
8 St
10 St.
Houston St
Canal St
Worth St
Chambers St
Columbus Av
Central Park West
Amsterdam Av
West End Av
Broadway
Madison Av
Lexington Av
Park Av S
5 Av
3 Av
2 Av
1 Av
York Av
12 Av
11 Av
10 Av
9 Av
8 Av
7 Av
6 Av
Greenwich St
Christopher St
West St
Hudson St
Varick St
Lafayette St
Bowery
Av A
Av B
Av C
Av D
E Broadway
Madison St
Manhattan Br
Trinity Pl

Map 31

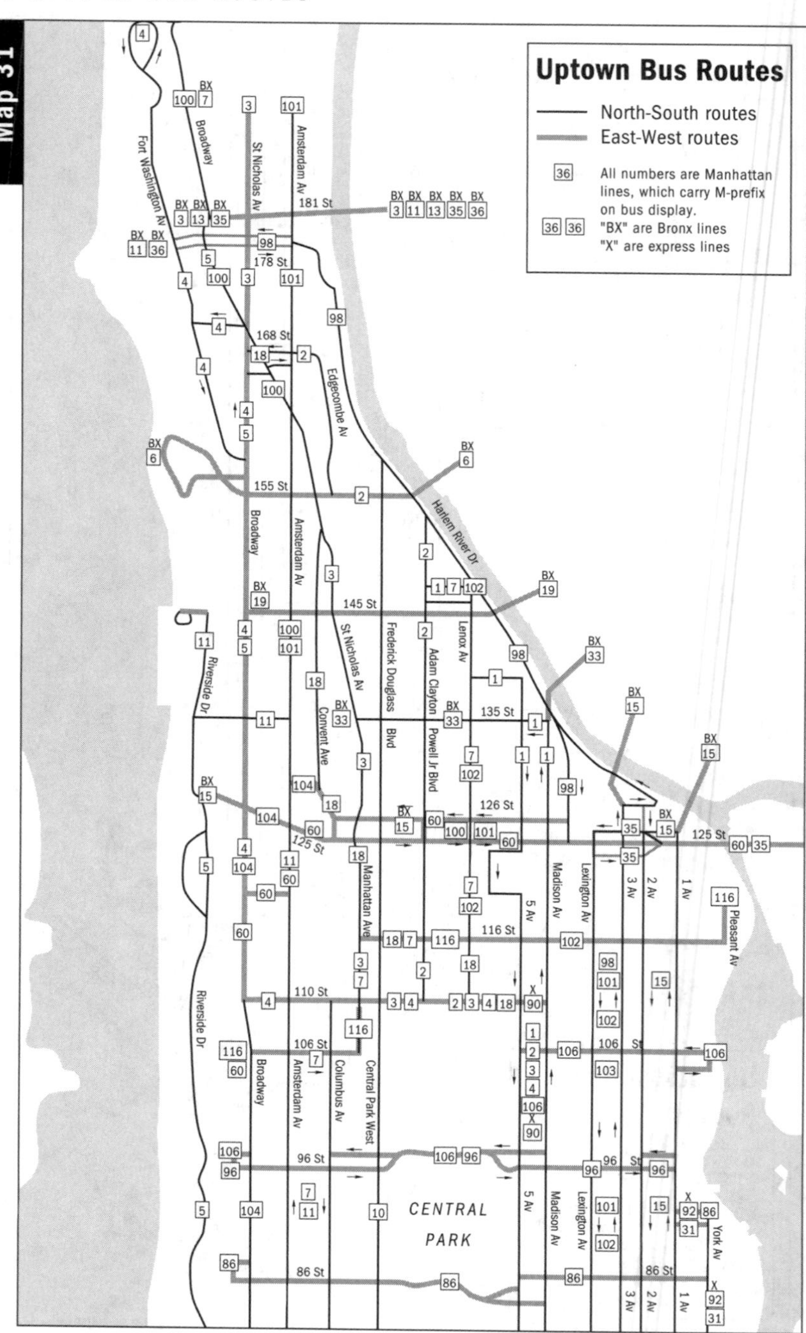
Uptown Bus Routes
North-South routes
East-West routes
All numbers are Manhattan lines, which carry M-prefix on bus display.
"BX" are Bronx lines
"X" are express lines
Broadway
Fort Washington Av
St Nicholas Av
Amsterdam Av
181 St
178 St
168 St
Edgecombe Av
155 St
Harlem River Dr
145 St
Frederick Douglass Blvd
Adam Clayton Powell Jr Blvd
Lenox Av
Riverside Dr
Convent Ave
135 St
126 St
125 St
Manhattan Ave
5 Av
Madison Av
Lexington Av
3 Av
2 Av
1 Av
Pleasant Av
116 St
110 St
106 St
Columbus Av
Central Park West
96 St
CENTRAL PARK
York Av
86 St

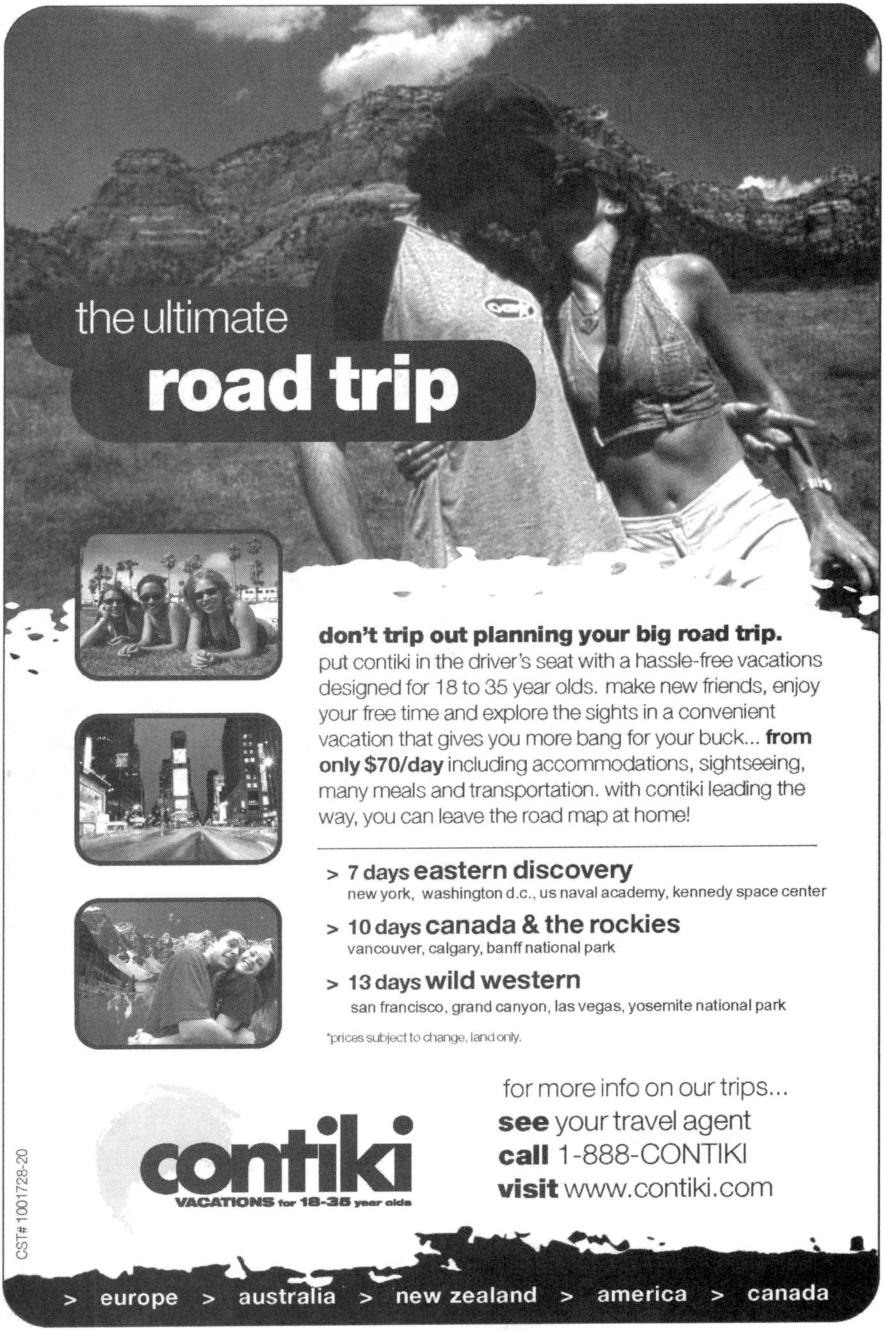
the ultimate
road trip
don't trip out planning your big road trip.
put contiki in the driver's seat with a hassle-free vacations designed for 18 to 35 year olds. make new friends, enjoy your free time and explore the sights in a convenient vacation that gives you more bang for your buck... from only $70/day including accommodations, sightseeing, many meals and transportation. with contiki leading the way, you can leave the road map at home!
> 7 days eastern discovery
new york, washington d.c., us naval academy, kennedy space center
> 10 days canada & the rockies
vancouver, calgary, banff national park
> 13 days wild western
san francisco, grand canyon, las vegas, yosemite national park
*prices subject to change, land only.
for more info on our trips...
see your travel agent
call 1-888-CONTIKI
visit www.contiki.com
contiki
VACATIONS for 18-35 year olds
CST# 1001728-20
> europe > australia > new zealand > america > canada

ABOUT LET'S GO

GUIDES FOR THE INDEPENDENT TRAVELER

Budget travel is more than a vacation. At *Let's Go*, we see every trip as the chance of a lifetime. If your dream is to grab a knapsack and a machete and forge through the jungles of Brazil, we can take you there. Or, if you'd rather enjoy the Riviera sun at a beachside cafe, we'll set you a table. If you know what you're doing, you can have any experience you want—whether it's camping among lions or sampling Tuscan desserts—without maxing out your credit card. We'll show you just how far your coins can go, and prove that the greatest limitation on your adventure is not your wallet, but your imagination. That said, we understand that you may want the occasional indulgence after a week of hostels and kebab stands, so we've added "Big Splurges" to let you know which establishments are worth those extra euros, as well as price ranges to help you quickly determine whether an accommodation or restaurant will break the bank. While we may have diversified, our emphasis will always be on finding the best values for your budget, giving you all the info you need to spend six days in London or six months in Tasmania.

BEYOND THE TOURIST EXPERIENCE

We write for travelers who know there's more to a vacation than riding double-deckers with tourists. Our researchers give you the heads-up on both world-renowned and lesser-known attractions, on the best local eats and the hottest nightclub beats. In our travels, we talk to everybody; we provide a snapshot of real life in the places you visit with our sidebars on topics like regional cuisine, local festivals, and hot political issues. We've opened our pages to respected writers and scholars to show you their take on a given destination, and turned to lifelong residents to learn the little things that make their city worth calling home. And we've even given you Alternatives to Tourism—ideas for how to give back to local communities through responsible travel and volunteering.

OVER FORTY YEARS OF WISDOM

When we started, way back in 1960, Let's Go consisted of a small group of well-traveled friends who compiled their budget travel tips into a 20-page packet for students on charter flights to Europe. Since then, we've expanded to suit all kinds of travelers, now publishing guides to six continents, including our newest guides: *Let's Go: Japan* and *Let's Go: Brazil.* Our guides are still annually researched and written entirely by students on shoe-string budgets, adventurous travelers who know that train strikes, stolen luggage, food poisoning, and marriage proposals are all part of a day's work. Even as you read this, work on next year's editions is well underway. Whether you're reading one of our new titles, like *Let's Go: Puerto Rico* or *Let's Go Adventure Guide: Alaska*, or our original best-seller, *Let's Go: Europe*, you'll find the same spirit of adventure that has made *Let's Go* the guide of choice for travelers the world over since 1960.

GETTING IN TOUCH

The best discoveries are often those you make yourself; on the road, when you find something worth sharing, please drop us a line. We're Let's Go Publications, 67 Mt. Auburn St., Cambridge, MA 02138, USA (feedback@letsgo.com).

For more info, visit our website: www.letsgo.com.